AFRICAN HISTORICAL DICTIONARIES
Edited by Jon Woronoff

HISTORICAL DICTIONARY OF UGANDA

by

M. LOUISE PIROUET

African Historical Dictionaries, No. 64

The Scarecrow Press, Inc.
Metuchen, N.J., & London
1995

British Library Cataloguing-in-Publication data available

Library of Congress Cataloging-in-Publication Data

Pirouet, M. Louise.
    Historical dictionary of Uganda / by M. Louise Pirouet.
       p.   cm.—(African historical dictionaries ; no. 64)
    Includes bibliographical references.
    ISBN 0-8108-2920-7 (alk. paper)
    1. Uganda—History—Dictionaries. I. Title. II. Series.
DT433.215.P57   1995
967.61'003—dc20   94-20483

Dedication
For Tom In Memory Of Hannah

CONTENTS

EDITOR'S FOREWORD

When Uganda attained independence in 1962 the future looked relatively bright. The population was well-educated and highly motivated, the economy was developing nicely and there was a degree of democracy in the political arena. But it did not take long for the situation to deteriorate in all respects, with the installation of a one-party system and then one-man rule, serious strife in different parts of the country, the collapse of the economy and the withering of everything that depended on it, from farms and factories to schools and hospitals. Not until recently could one cautiously feel that perhaps Uganda was finally taking a turn for the better.

Inevitably, this book contains much dismal material as it charts the often tense relations of pre-colonial days, the problems of the colonial era, the setbacks under Obote and the horror of Amin's rule and of Obote's second presidency. But it also shows how the Ugandans have repeatedly managed to adapt and rebuild. Both sides are dealt with in a very broad description of Uganda's recent and earlier past. Much of this information was hard to come by, and widely dispersed, until now. And those who want to know more about what has become of Uganda and what it may become in the future will be pleased to find so many useful entries on key persons, institutions and events. They will be further assisted by a handy chronology and extensive bibliography.

Given Uganda's travails, this book could only have been written by someone who not only approached the task objectively but also affectionately. Such a person is M. Louise Pirouet, who spent many years living there or nearby and has shown a keen interest even when further away. She was, among other things, a Research Assistant, Research Fellow and Lecturer in Religious Studies at Makerere University and a member of the Uganda Coordinating Group of Amnesty International. She has recently retired from a post as Senior Lecturer in Religious Studies,

Homerton College, University of Cambridge. Dr. Pirouet wrote her thesis on the expansion of the Church of Uganda and has since produced many articles and papers on church-related subjects. From this *Historical Dictionary of Uganda* it is obvious that she both knows and cares.

Jon Woronoff
Series Editor

ACKNOWLEDGMENTS

I am grateful to many people who have helped in one way or another with the production of this Historical Dictionary of Uganda. My particular thanks are due to Fr A. Anzioli, Heike Behrend, Winifred Brown, Jenny Cooper, Robin Cooper, Joan Cox, Hugh Dinwiddy, David Easterbrook, Oliver Furley, Michael Hutt, Christine Kyazze, Margaret Macpherson, Sarah Musisi, Joy Okello, John Rowe, Mary Rowe, Barbara Saben, Tshilemo Tshihiluka, Michael Tuck, Michael Twaddle, Kevin Ward, Sheelagh Warren, Fergus Wilson, Marcia Wright.

NOTE ON BANTU LANGUAGES

In Bantu languages the root of the word is modified by prefixes which modify the root meaning of the word. So the root 'Ganda' may be modified by the singular personal prefix 'mu-' to indicate one Ganda person; by the plural personal prefix 'ba-' to indicate more than one Ganda person; by the prefix indicating place 'bu-' to indicate the place where the Baganda live; by the language prefix 'Lu-' to indicate the language which the Baganda who live in Buganda speak. In some Bantu languages the language prefix is 'ki-', as in Kiswahili, or 'ru-' as in Runyankole and Runyoro. And the Batoro live in Toro and the Banyankole live in Ankole, though the Banyoro and the Bakedi live in Bunyoro and Bukedi respectively.

GLOSSARY

The following terms occur so frequently in the text that it would be tedious to underline them.

	Language	*Meaning*
bataka (s. mutaka)	Luganda	clan head
enganzi	Runyankole	chief minister
kabaka	Luganda	king
katikiro	Luganda	chief minister
kibuga	Luganda	royal capital of the Kabaka of Buganda
mailo	Luganda/English	mile; land allocated as freehold in units of square miles
lukiiko	Luganda	council of chiefs, local parliament
mugabe	Runyankole	king
mukama	Runyoro	king
rwot (pl. rwodi)	Acholi	chief, war leader
saza	Luganda	county

ABBREVIATIONS AND ACRONYMS

CMS	Church Missionary Society
DP	Democratic Party
FEDEMU/ FEDEMO	Federal Democratic Movement
FOBA	Force Obote Back Again
FUNA	Former Uganda National Army
IBEAC	Imperial British East Africa Company
ICRC	International Committee of the Red Cross
IMF	International Monetary Fund
KAR	King's African Rifles
KY	Kabaka Yekka
Legco	Legislative Council
NAAM	National Association for the Advancement of Muslims
NCC	National Consultative Council
NEC	National Executive Committee
NRA/M	National Resistance Army/Movement

OAU	Organization of African Unity
RC	Resistance Council
SAS	Special Air Services
UCW	Uganda Council of Women
UDC	Uganda Development Corporation
UDCA	United Democratic Christian Army
UFA/M	Uganda Freedom Army/Movement
UNC	Uganda National Congress
UNHCR	United Nations High Commissioner for Refugees
UNLA	Uganda National Liberation Army
UNLF	Uganda National Liberation Front
UNRF	Uganda National Rescue Front
UPC	Uganda People's Congress
UPDA/M	Uganda People's Democratic Army/Movement
UPDCA	Uganda People's Democratic Christian Army
UPF/A	Uganda People's Front/Army
USMC	Uganda Supreme Muslim Council
YWCA	Young Women's Christian Association

CHRONOLOGY

AD 500   Possible first movement of Bantu into Uganda.

1200–
1500   Establishment of the kingdoms of Buganda and Bunyoro Kitara.

1400   Possible beginnings of Lwoo settlement.

1500   Possible beginnings of Iteso/Ateker settlement.

1823   Ivory and slave traders from Egypt and Sudan reached northern Uganda.

1840s   First Muslim traders from the Swahili coast reached Buganda.

1850s   Swahili traders first settled at the court of the Kabaka (king) of Buganda.

1862   John Hanning Speke visited the court of Kabaka Mutesa I and recognized the Owen Falls as the source of the Nile.

1864   Samuel Baker reached Lake Albert.

1867   Ramadan was first observed at Kabaka Mutesa's court.

1872   Baker announced the annexation of Bunyoro to Egypt.

1875   Henry Morton Stanley visited Kabaka Mutesa's court and appealed to Britain for Christian missionaries.

1876   Some 200 Muslim converts were martyred.

1877   Missionaries of the [Anglican] Church Missionary Society (CMS) arrived in Buganda.

1879   Roman Catholic White Fathers arrived.

1881   Egypt's Equatoria Province by this time included most of modern Acholi and West Nile.

1884   Death of Mutesa I and accession of Mwanga.

1885   Death of the first three Christian martyrs following the murder of Bishop Hannington (CMS) on Mwanga's orders.

1886–
1887   Martyrdoms of 47 other Christian converts whose names are known, and from 100 to 200 others.

1888   The year of the three kings of Buganda: Mwanga, Kiwewa and Kalema. A Muslim coup forced Mwanga and the Christians to flee to Ankole and to the south of Lake Victoria.

1889   Mwanga reinstated as Kabaka by the Christian factions, but with his powers curtailed.

Stanley rescued Emin Pasha, Governor of Egypt's Equatoria Province who had been cut off by the Mahdist rising in Sudan, and took him back to Europe.

1890   Captain Frederick Lugard of the Imperial British East Africa Company (IBEAC) arrived in Buganda in December.

1891   Lugard marched through western Uganda to enlist Emin Pasha's abandoned Sudanese troops who had been settled there. En route he instated Kasagama as Mukama (king) of Toro.

1892   Battle of Mengo between Protestant and Catholic factions. Lugard ensured a Protestant victory by issuing them with extra arms.

1893   Gerald Portal of the IBEAC provisionally declared a British Protectorate over Uganda.

1894   Uganda formally declared a British Protectorate.

1895   The British and Dutch Mill Hill Fathers Mission invited to Uganda by the British administration to help defuse the antagonism between "French" Catholic converts and "English" Protestant converts.

        British influence extended to Toro.

1897   Mwanga and traditionalist chiefs rebelled against British rule, but were opposed by Christian factions.

        Sudanese troops mutinied.

        The first hospital founded at Mengo by the CMS.

1898   British administration established in Bunyoro after a prolonged armed campaign against Mukama Kabarega and his supporters. A British appointee became Mukama.

1899   Mwanga and Kabarega both captured and exiled to the Seychelles.

1900   [B]Uganda Agreement concluded. Astute chiefs were assisted by missionaries to obtain privileges unusual in colonial Africa.

        Toro Agreement concluded.

Taxation first imposed (hut tax).

The telegraph lines reached Kampala and a regular postal service was introduced.

1901   Ankole Agreement concluded.

The Uganda Railway inland from Mombasa reached its terminus at Port Florence (Kisumu) on Lake Victoria in what was then still part of eastern Uganda.

1902   Sleeping sickness identified.

Ugandan forces re-formed as the 4th and 5th Battalions of the King's African Rifles.

The eastern boundary of Uganda moved from the eastern edge of the eastern Rift Valley to its present position.

The Muganda general, Semei Kakungulu, removed from eastern Uganda which he had ruled, and direct British rule imposed.

Namilyango College founded.

1903   Coffee first exported.

The East African Standard, published in Nairobi, first began to circulate in Uganda.

1904   Cotton introduced.

1906   Evacuation of the shores of Lake Victoria begun because of sleeping sickness.

King's College, Budo, Gayaza High School and St Mary's College, Kisubi, founded.

Second, more liberal Toro agreement signed.

1907   Nyangire Rising in Bunyoro.

Ebifa, published by CMS bimonthly to begin with, became the first Ugandan-language newspaper.

1909   Sesse Islands evacuated because of sleeping sickness.

Hut tax abolished and replaced by a poll tax.

The Verona Fathers Mission started work in the north.

1910   Acholi placed under direct Protectorate rule.

1911   The Catholic Luganda newspaper, *Munno,* began publication.

Arabica coffee introduced.

1912   *The Uganda Herald* began publication.

Lamogi Rebellion in Acholi put down. Gulu became the seat of Protectorate administration for the area.

1913   The first government hospital founded at Mulago as a venereal diseases unit.

1914   The area north of Nimule on the Nile was ceded to Sudan, and the Lado Enclave given to Uganda.

Outbreak of World War I. Recruitment of Ugandans for military service began.

1917   Medical Assistant training began at Mengo Hospital.

1918   World War I ended.

Beginnings of the Bamalaki Sect.

1920   Legislative Council (Legco) established.

East African Currency Board established. The florin replaced the rupee.

1921   Bataka Association founded.

1922   Makerere College founded.

The shilling replaced the florin as the basic unit of currency.

1923   Forced labor ended. The British government's Devonshire White Paper decreed that in East Africa African interests were to be paramount.

1924   Mehta sugar refinery opened at Lugazi.

Ormsby-Gore Commission reported and raised fears among Africans of "closer union" with settler-dominated Kenya.

Phelps-Stokes Commission's report judged government contribution to education inadequate. Educational grants to missions were increased.

1925   E.R.J. Hussey was appointed as Uganda's first Director of Education.

1926   Sir Apollo Kagwa resigned as Katikiro (chief minister) of Buganda.

In a final adjustment of Uganda's borders the land between the Turkana Escarpment and Lake Rudolph was ceded to Kenya.

The Seventh Day Adventists started work.

1927   *Busulu* and *Envujo* Law on land-holding passed.

Tobacco first cultivated.

1929   Hilton-Young Commission reported on possible unified native policy in East Africa, again raising fears of closer union.

Tea first exported.

Reuben Spartas founded the African Greek Orthodox Church.

1931   Joint Parliamentary Select Committee heard evidence against "closer union."

The railway reached Kampala.

1933   Bunyoro Agreement concluded.

1936   Tribute labor for chiefs ended.

1937   Elliot Report on Unskilled Labour.

         De La Warr Commission on higher education in East
         Africa.

1939   Outbreak of World War II.

         Joseph Kiwanuka consecrated Catholic bishop of
         Masaka, the first black African bishop of modern
         times.

1944   Beginnings of African demands for greater representa-
         tion in the Legco.

1945   End of World War II in Europe.

         Martin Luther Nsibirwa, Katikiro of Buganda, mur-
         dered. Michael Kagwa appointed to succeed him.

1946   The first women completed courses at Makerere.

1947   East African High Commission established.

         Bataka Riots in Buganda.

         African Local Government Ordinance enacted.

         Legco Unofficial Members Organisation established.

         Kampala granted municipal status.

         Uganda Muslim Educational Association founded.

         The Legco approved a ten-year development plan to
         cost £15 million and to include a hydroelectric scheme.

1948   Uganda Electricity Board established.

1949   Further Bataka Riots led to the proscription of the
         Bataka Union.

1950   Makerere College established as a University College in special relationship with the University of London.

Cement industry established at Tororo and the Bell Brewery opened.

1951   New international airport opened at Entebbe.

1952   Uganda National Congress founded by I.K. Musazi in London.

Uganda Development Corporation established.

1953   Deportation crisis when Governor Sir Andrew Cohen deported Kabaka Mutesa II for refusing to cooperate with the Protectorate Government.

Roman Catholic hierarchy established.

1954   Owen Falls hydroelectric scheme opened.

Trade boycott of non-African businesses and shops.

New Bunyoro Agreement signed.

Hancock Commission heard evidence and reported on the constitutional crisis in Buganda arising from the Kabaka's non-cooperation and deportation.

1955   The Kabaka returned to Buganda.

Progressive Party founded by Eridadi Mulira.

Five Year Capital Development Plan announced. African Credit and Savings Bank founded. African Loan Fund established to help small farmers.

1956   Uganda Trade Union Congress inaugurated.

First direct elections to the Legco.

Democratic Party (DP) founded with Matayo Mugwanya as leader.

Lango District Council passed a resolution calling for self-government for the whole country.

The railway reached Kasese to help transport copper for export.

1958   Benedicto Kiwanuka replaced Mugwanya as leader of the DP. Uganda People's Union founded.

1959   Milton Obote founded the Uganda People's Congress (UPC) out of the Uganda National Congress and the Uganda People's Union.

A national census estimated the population at 6.5 million.

Wild Report suggested direct elections on a common roll and this recommendation was upheld by the British government.

1960   Buganda declared herself independent, fearing to lose the privileged status granted under the 1900 [B]Uganda Agreement if the country became independent as a unitary state. This was ignored by the Protectorate Government.

1961   National elections held in March were boycotted by most Baganda. This resulted in a DP victory.

Report of the Munster Commission on constitutional affairs.

17–23 July: first constitutional conference held in London.

30 October: new Buganda Agreement concluded.

The UPC and the Buganda government negotiated an understanding leading to Buganda's acceptance of moves to independence in a unitary state.

16 September–9 October: Lancaster House Constitutional Conference in London.

Beginnings of discontent among the Baamba and Bakonjo in the Ruwenzori Mountains out of which grew the Rwenzururu separatist movement.

1962 Direct elections to the Lukiiko (parliament of Buganda) won by Kabaka Yekka (KY, "the Kabaka only").

April: new national elections held. A UPC/KY alliance voted into power under the leadership of Milton Obote who became Prime Minister on 30 April.

June: Marlborough House constitutional conference held in London. A decision on the "Lost Counties" (areas lost by Bunyoro to Buganda in 1900) postponed for two years.

9 October: political independence granted.

1963 The UPC began to establish itself in Buganda in spite of an understanding that it would not compete with KY.

8 October: Kabaka Mutesa II became President of Uganda.

1964 23 January: the Uganda Army mutinied over continued British control. British troops called in. Most of the army's demands met. Idi Amin appointed Deputy Commander of the army.

June: Toro officials and the Uganda Army launched a major attack against the Bakonjo separatists, and many civilians were killed.

August: the UPC/KY alliance was ended as sufficient DP and KY MPs had crossed the floor of the National Assembly to give the UPC an overall majority.

18 October: 22 Catholic martyrs were canonized in St Peter's, Rome.

4 November: Bunyoro won a referendum on the Lost Counties.

10 November: massacre by security forces of at least six people at Nakulabye after a pub brawl.

Ugandan forces led by Idi Amin assisted Simba anti-Tshombe rebels in Congo (Zaire). Amin entrusted with gold and ivory to be used in payment for weapons. Uganda Army expanded.

1965   13 February: two West Nile villages reported bombed by Congolese planes. This provided an excuse for Ugandan intervention in Congo.

The army shot dead six Kisubi schoolboys after the bus in which they were traveling was in collision with an army lorry.

National Association for the Advancement of Muslims established.

24 May: Kenya intercepted Chinese weaponry bound for Congo via Uganda.

October: during the last quarter of the year there were rumors of assassination and coup attempts against Obote by the right wing of the UPC.

1966   Daudi Ocheng called for the suspension of Amin and for an enquiry into the receipt of Congolese gold and ivory by Amin, Obote and two government ministers.

22 February: five ministers detained without trial for allegedly plotting to overthrow the government. The President (Kabaka Mutesa) asked legal advice on how to dismiss Obote as Prime Minister, and approached the British High Commission for military assistance, which was refused.

24 February: 1962 Constitution suspended.

27 February: Minister of Internal Affairs Basil Bataringaya appointed a Commission under Judge de L'Estang to examine Ocheng's allegations. (The report was only released in 1971. It cleared Obote and his confederates of wrongdoing, but criticized Obote for trying to ride two horses at once.)

15 April: Obote ordered the National Assembly to pass unread a new constitution of which members would find copies later in their pigeonholes. Under it Obote became executive President, and Buganda lost her privileged position.

20 May: the Buganda Lukiiko refused to recognize the new constitution and ordered the central government out of Kampala and off Buganda soil by the end of the month.

24 May: during the second Battle of Mengo which ensued, the Kabaka escaped and fled to Britain where he died in exile five years later. The army officer responsible for the victory was Idi Amin.

June: a state of emergency was declared in Buganda and remained in force throughout the remainder of Obote's first presidency.

1967   17 September: the kingdoms and their privileges were abolished. Uganda became a republic with Obote its self-proclaimed President. Godfrey Binaisa QC resigned as Attorney-General in protest at the Public Security Act which allowed preventive detention without charge or trial.

A more equitable division of offices between Batoro, Baamba and Bakonjo ended many of the grievances which had led to the rise of the Rwenzururu movement.

1968   The Buganda parliament building was sold by the government to the Ministry of Defence.

The UPC determined on a move towards more socialist policies.

Restrictions placed on Asian trade.

1969   July: visit of Pope Paul VI to Uganda, the first visit of any Pope to Africa.

Uganda Immigration Act undermined the security of Asians still further.

Obote introduced the "Move to the Left." This was outlined in five documents:

1) October: "National Service Proposal"

2) December: "The Common Man's Charter"

19 December: attempted assassination of Obote at Lugogo Stadium. Amin temporarily fled. Responsibility for the attempt never firmly placed.

1970   25 January: murder of Brigadier Pierino Okoya, later believed to have been carried out on Amin's orders.

The "Brian Lea Affair." Lea, apparently attempting to investigate bribery in connection with Asian immigration to the UK on behalf of the British immigration authorities, was set up and disgraced.

3) April: "Communication from the Chair."

Obote aligned himself more closely with President Nimeiri of Sudan, and closed down the supply of Israeli arms to the secessionist Anya Nya movement in Southern Sudan.

4) May: "Nakivubo Pronouncement." Government to take a controlling share in all major businesses.

5) July and August: "One Plus Three" election proposal.

20 September: Idi Amin appointed overall military supremo.

November: 30,000 Kenyans ordered out of Uganda.

Britain and Uganda reached an agreement on immigration of British Asians. Uganda would process citizenship applications and Britain would speed up admissions. Both sides delayed its implementation.

1971   25 January: Idi Amin seized power in a coup while Obote was attending the Commonwealth Heads of Government Meeting in Singapore. Obote and his

companions were given sanctuary by President Nyerere of Tanzania.

Political prisoners of the previous regime released.

Many Acholi and Langi soldiers massacred in spite of
an amnesty being declared.

13 March: Amin declared himself President and Commander in Chief.

April: the favor of the Baganda was won when permission was granted for the body of Kabaka Mutesa to be
returned to Uganda for burial.

July: further massacres of Acholi and Langi troops in
barracks throughout the country.

The Organization of African Unity (OAU) Summit
Conference which was to have been held in Kampala,
was moved to Addis Ababa.

July: Amin visited Israel and London to seek aid for
buying arms.

October: a census of Asians was ordered. Baganda
requests for the restoration of the kingdom were rejected.

Massacre at Mutukula.

7 December: all Asian applications for citizenship
were cancelled.

1972   23 March: Amin broke with Israel after a visit to Libya.
All Israelis ordered out of Uganda. Libya offered to
take over training of the Uganda Army.

May: the Public Safety Unit was established.

Uganda Supreme Muslim Council was established.

4 August: expulsion of all British Asians ordered
within 90 days. All other non-citizen Asians were
quickly included, and then those Asians with Ugandan
citizenship.

August/September: visit of British minister Geoffrey

Rippon to assess the situation of Asians. Announcement made by him in Kampala that the British government would admit Asians with British citizenship.

17 September: invasion by pro-Obote exiles from Tanzania fails. Three days later Britain finally started airlift of Asians. Libya sent troop reinforcements.

31 September: murder of Chief Justice Benedicto Kiwanuka, apparently for issuing a writ of habeas corpus on behalf of a Briton detained illegally by the army.

7 October: the Mogadishu Agreement, a non-aggression pact between Tanzania and Uganda following the abortive invasion, was signed. Under it Tanzania closed the camps where Ugandan guerrillas opposed to Amin were training.

7 November: deadline for departure of Asians. The United Nations set up special centers as sanctuaries for remaining Asians until the airlift could be completed, declaring them to be UN territory.

The Uganda Supreme Muslim Council established which united previously quarreling factions.

1973   January: a promised government report into the disappearances of 85 prominent citizens revealed nothing at all.

12 February: a number of alleged guerrillas were publicly executed.

Fr Clement Kiggundu, editor of *Munno,* a Catholic Luganda-language newspaper, was murdered. Throughout Amin's presidency disappearances and killings continued, too numerous to list separately.

Yoweri Museveni launched his Front for National Salvation to oppose Amin.

30 June: all US aid to Uganda was discontinued.

October: Uganda expelled US Marines guarding the US Embassy. All US citizens advised to leave Uganda.

November: the United States broke off diplomatic relations with Uganda.

1974   January: visit of Colonel Gadafi of Libya. Amin became more militantly Muslim as a result of this visit.

23 March: the recent murder of Michael Ondoga, a Christian army officer, sparked a mutiny in the Malire Barracks. Brigadier Marella, whose extreme behavior was a cause of army grievances, was sent back to the Southern Sudan.

1975   Amin became Chairman of the OAU whose summit was held in Kampala.

10 July: British Prime Minister James Callaghan was forced to go to Uganda to rescue British subject Dennis Hills who was under a death threat for writing insultingly of Amin.

The USSR dissuaded Amin from erecting a statue to Hitler.

1976   February: the UN Human Rights Commission examined evidence given by the International Commission of Jurists, but failed to condemn Uganda for violating human rights.

13 February: Esther Chesire, a Makerere University student from western Kenya and a relative of Kenyan Vice-President Daniel arap Moi, disappeared at Entebbe Airport. Kenya made no announcement as yet.

15 February: Amin made claims to a "Greater Uganda," including the part of western Kenya which had been part of Uganda prior to 1902. Kenyan workers were encouraged to refuse to handle goods bound for Uganda.

6 March: a Makerere University student, Paul Serwanga, was shot dead by the security forces. The following day thousands of students marched to offer his family their condolences.

12 March: an official enquiry to look into this shooting was ordered, under the chairmanship of Professor Bryan Langlands.

27 March: Kenya announced the disappearance of Esther Chesire, now presumed dead. The Langlands Commission of Enquiry was ordered to add Chesire's disappearance to its remit.

Early June: Amin escaped an assassination attempt when hand grenades were thrown at Nsambya killing 20 people and injuring many others.

28 June: an Air France plane hijacked by Palestinians with many Israelis on board was landed at Entebbe. Amin was seen to be cooperating with the hijackers.

3–4 July: a spectacular raid by Israeli forces freed the hijack hostages, though with some casualties. Dora Bloch, a British subject, moved to Mulago Hospital because of illness, was murdered in her bed after the raid. Amin raged at Kenya for having permitted Israeli planes to land there. Kenya retaliated by claiming that Uganda had not paid bills relating to the transit of goods through Kenya, and refused to allow any more oil to be transported until the bills were paid. Kenya refused to admit that this amounted to an embargo. In late July Amin retaliated by cutting off electricity supplies from the Owen Falls Dam to Kenya. Talks followed on normalizing relations.

3–4 August: "invasion" of Makerere University by the army. Five students are believed to have died.

26 August: leaders of all the main religious groups met near Kampala under the chairmanship of Anglican Archbishop Janani Luwum to discuss the escalating violence in the country. When Amin learnt about the meeting, he demanded the minutes.

1977   The centenary year of the Church of Uganda.

10 February: the Bishops of the Church of Uganda wrote to Amin to complain of harassment of church

leaders by the security forces and of violence throughout the land.

17 February: Archbishop Luwum and two government ministers were murdered after allegations of involvement in an Acholi plot. The Chief Kadhi was seriously injured in a "car accident" after reproving Amin for Luwum's murder, and sent to Libya for treatment.

June: Amin was told he would not be welcome at the Commonwealth Heads of Government Meeting in London.

9 June: British businessman Robert Scanlon was arrested on spying charges, apparently in retaliation for Amin's humiliation over the Commonwealth Heads of Government Meeting. (In October it was reported, apparently correctly, that Scanlon had been hammered to death.)

14 June: the "whisky run," supplying comforts, including whisky, to Amin's troops from Stansted Airport, UK, was denounced.

July: the East African Community was finally dissolved.

September: 27 religious organizations were banned. Only Muslims, Roman Catholics, Church of Uganda (Anglicans), and the Orthodox Church were permitted to function.

9 September: 12 people publicly executed by firing squad although this was a Friday in Ramadan. Amin was allegedly ill and in the hospital and unavailable to answer questions on the matter.

1978   April and May: Amin carried out a purge of some of his closest associates including Vice-President Adrisi and Ali Towelli of the Public Safety Unit.

25 May: Bruce Mackenzie, former Kenya government Minister of Agriculture, was killed when the plane in which he was returning from Uganda with a group of

British businessmen was blown up by a bomb apparently placed on board at Entebbe Airport.

1 July: Tanzania warned Uganda against "repeated provocations" on the Tanzania/Uganda border. Uganda replied by accusing Tanzania of planning an invasion.

9 September: Uganda troops crossed the border into Tanzania.

13 September: Amin alleged that Uganda was being invaded by Tanzania.

28 September: Ugandan planes bombed two northwestern Tanzanian villages.

12 November: major Tanzanian offensive mounted against Ugandan troops who had invaded the Kagera Salient.

1979   The centenary year of the Roman Catholic Church in Uganda.

21 January: Tanzanian troops crossed the border into Uganda.

27 January: Tanzania announced that its troops, accompanied by about 1,000 Ugandan exiles, had crossed into Uganda.

24 February: Masaka and Mbarara were captured and sacked by the Tanzanians in retaliation for the destruction wrought in the Kagera Salient.

23–26 March: Moshi Unity Conference brought together 22 movements opposed to Amin and agreed to plans for the Uganda National Liberation Front under the chairmanship of Y.K. Lule to administer Uganda as it was freed from Amin's rule.

11 April: Kampala fell to the combined Tanzanian troops and Uganda National Liberation Army (UNLA). The city was looted. Y.K. Lule sworn in as President.

May: Tanzanian troops reached West Nile, Amin's home area. On Lule's orders they prevented the UNLA from crossing the Nile and taking vengeance on "Amin's people."

March–June: revenge massacres of Muslims in Ankole as the area was freed from Amin's forces.

20 June: the National Executive Committee (NEC) of the UNLF replaced Lule with Godfrey Binaisa, alleging that Lule was dominated by old guard Baganda.

9 July: religious leaders wrote jointly to Binaisa about continuing violence and human rights abuses by the UNLA.

October: the National Consultative Council was increased through elections among Council members.

1980   21 April: the UPC called a press conference and announced that Obote would be returning.

1 May: UNLA Chief David Oyite-Ojok carried out a search and impound operation in Kampala and detained 72 people illegally, for which Binaisa sacked him, bringing to a head a struggle for authority between the President and the military.

10 May: Paulo Muwanga ordered the UNLA to take control of Kampala and put Binaisa under house arrest.

27 May: Obote returned to Bushenyi where he had strong support, and received a hero's welcome.

June onwards: Uganda was effectively ruled by the Military Commission under Paulo Muwanga.

July: The Uganda Patriotic Movement was launched by Yoweri Museveni.

October: the Tanzanian army left West Nile and the UNLA took over. Amin supporters attacked the UNLA which then wreaked vengeance on the whole area. Thousands fled to Zaire and Sudan.

10/11 December: Obote returned to power through elections widely believed to have been rigged. The Commonwealth Observer Group report noted widespread malpractice, but concluded the elections were free and fair, and left. Muwanga then refused to allow the Electoral Commission to announce the results, delayed the announcement overnight, and then himself announced a UPC victory.

Paulo Muwanga appointed Vice President by Obote.

Yoweri Museveni, whose party won little support, refused to accept the results and took to the bush with an embryonic guerrilla force.

1981   Uganda National Rescue Front (Amin supporters) held most of West Nile.

April: several newspapers and periodicals banned.

Famine in Karamoja required international relief.

Six opposition MPs detained without trial.

June: last remaining Tanzanian troops withdrawn. In West Nile the UNLA wreaked vengeance on the population whom they accused of being Amin supporters. Civilians fled to missions for safety. Massacre of civilians at Ombachi Mission on 24 June.

July: Obote asked for British help in training the UNLA.

Human rights violations reported from all parts of the country. On 24 September religious leaders told Obote, ''The Uganda you lead is bleeding to death.''

December: massive UNLA offensive against rebels led to further flight of refugees: 250,000 sought refuge in Sudan, 60,000 in Zaire.

1982   First cases of AIDS recognized in Rakai District.

January: seven DP MPs from Busoga crossed the floor to join the UPC.

23 February: the Uganda Freedom Movement staged a rocket attack on the Lubiri Barracks in Kampala. The next day UNLA members broke into Rubaga Cathedral during an Ash Wednesday Service, claiming that they were searching for those responsible for the rocket attack. Cardinal Nsubuga refused to attend any public function until he received an apology. On 18 March Obote expressed "regret."

Museveni's National Resistance Movement/Army (NRM/A) gained control of most of the Luwero Triangle.

March: the International Committee of the Red Cross (ICRC) was asked to leave Uganda for reporting the Ombachi massacre. Last foreign correspondents ordered out of the country.

July: the UNLA launched a major attack against the NRA, rounding up civilians into camps.

July: Amnesty International reported on continuing human rights violations.

September: collapse of the Uganda Freedom Movement.

30 September: "Chasing of the Banyarwanda" refugees began; c. 80,000 refugees (and some Uganda citizens) were evicted from their homes, their lands and cattle stolen, and they themselves forced into Rwanda or into tiny enclaves. The latter were eventually resettled by the Office of the UN High Commissioner for Refugees (UNHCR).

December: UNLA campaign in the Luwero Triangle stepped up.

1983   January: civilians in Luwero rounded up and herded into camps. In March the Uganda Red Cross began relief operations in Luwero as civilians were without food, water, shelter or medical aid. By September the government had to call in the international agencies to assist in a relief operation for the 120,000 people believed to be in camps. In November people were ordered out of the camps, but no provision was made for them when they were returned to their devastated homesteads. Relief continued under increasing difficulties, and the ICRC returned to Uganda.

4 December: Armed Forces Commander-in-Chief David Oyite-Ojok killed in a helicopter crash.

1984   2 January: a British bank employee and two Swiss nationals killed. Level of violence highlighted when Archbishop of Canterbury visited hospitals, and Western journalists, allowed into the country to cover the Archbishop's visit, reported his comments.

ICRC team kidnapped by rebels and then released.

February: Britain agreed to continue military training after other Commonwealth countries pulled out because of the UNLA's human rights violations.

13 February: Cardinal Nsubuga protested publicly about UNLA violence against civilians.

March: UNLA operations in Karamoja forced 20,000 to flee from Namalu.

23 May: massacre of about 100 persons at Namugongo including the principal of the Church of Uganda Seminary by UNLA members. Yusuf Mollo of the nearby Kito Mosque was murdered by them at the same time, and a Catholic center was looted.

May: the ICRC cut back the level of relief work in the Luwero Triangle because of insecurity.

July: tripartite (Uganda, Sudan, UNHCR) plan for repatriation of refugees from Sudan was little taken up, and suffered a severe setback when al-Hajji Jabiri was murdered on his return.

August: Smith Opon-Acak, a Langi and fellow tribesman of Obote, appointed over the heads of two Acholi

(Tito Okello and Basilio Okello) as C.-in-C. of the armed forces.

9 August: Elliot Abrams of US State Department claimed in testimony given before a US Congressional Committee that up to 200,000 people had been killed in Luwero. Britain insisted this was an exaggeration and renewed the contract for training the UNLA.

18 August: aid agencies halted their Luwero operation after a Red Cross vehicle was fired on by the army.

October: North Korean troops arrived to train the UNLA.

December: the UNLA launched a new offensive against the NRA in Luwero.

1985   21 January: ex-President Lule died in London.

19 June: Amnesty International published a report: *Uganda, Six Years After Amin: Torture, Killings, Disappearances.* The British government was finally shocked into threatening to cut off aid unless human rights violations ceased.

7 July: clashes in Kampala between Langi and Acholi troops. The Acholi retreated northwards and re-grouped.

27 July: Obote fled the country when Acholi generals Tito Okello and Basilio Okello led a successful putsch against his regime. Kampala looted. Tito Okello sworn in as Head of State. Interim Military Council set up. "Warlordism" prevailed in Kampala and elsewhere, and the levels of violence were unabated.

Late August: peace talks opened in Nairobi between the Okello regime and the NRM/A under the chairmanship of Kenyan President Moi. A cease-fire was ordered. Within a fortnight this broke down. Talks frequently stalled and were resumed.

17 December: Nairobi Accords signed, but neither side attempted to keep to them. UNLA atrocities continued to be reported.

1986   25 January: 14 years to the day after Amin's seizure of power, the NRA fought its way into the western suburbs of Kampala.

29 January: Yoweri Museveni sworn in as President. His inaugural speech announced the NRM's "Ten Point Programme" for the rehabilitation of Uganda.

The NRM government signed the UN Convention Against Torture and the African Charter of Human and People's Rights.

The NRM government openly admitted the existence of AIDS in Uganda and solicited international aid.

April: the NRA completed its occupation of the main northern and eastern towns. In the east the Teso Militia, which had protected the people against Karamojong cattle raiders, was disbanded and the NRA failed to provide alternative protection. The UNLA and the Okellos took refuge in Sudan where they regrouped. Some returned to Uganda and surrendered, others returned to harass the NRA which was hastily reinforced with elements of former armies which had surrendered. The NRA's strict code of conduct broke down.

July: the Uganda People's Democratic Army/ Movement (UPDA/M) under Basilio Okello began operating from Sudan; "Force Obote Back Again" (FOBA) began operating in Busoga and Teso under two of Obote's former ministers, John Luwuliza-Kirunda and Peter Otai.

August: the NRM set up a Commission of Enquiry into Human Rights Violations between 1962 and 1985.

October: after reports of NRA atrocities in Acholi, the 35th Battalion, which had been posted there, was replaced.

Rebel movement led by prophetess Alice Lakwena began to gain support. Lakwena set out to cleanse the land and promised that bullets used against her followers would turn to water.

1987   January: Lakwena suffered a major defeat at Corner Kilak. Atrocities committed against civilians by her followers were reported. In March there were further NRA victories against Lakwena and 1,000 UPDA rebels in Acholi surrendered.

May: IMF Economic Recovery (structural adjustment) Program launched.

October: Lakwena met the Western press for the first time. In November she suffered a crushing defeat in Busoga. She herself escaped to Kenya.

December: clashes between Kenyan and Ugandan troops on the border. Two Ugandan diplomats ordered to leave Kenya. Kenyans reported to be angered by Ugandan plans to shift coffee exports by rail instead of road, so undercutting "exploitative" Kenyan road haulage businesses. On 29 December this dispute was officially ended.

1988   1 January: Lakwena was arrested and jailed by the Kenyan authorities.

The ICRC began to offer training to the NRA in the law and conduct of war.

January: three government ministers who tried to negotiate with Peter Otai's Uganda People's Front/ Army (UPF/A) were seized and held hostage. One managed to escape.

March: successor movements to Lakwena's emerged in Acholi. In April Lakwena was freed and asked for political asylum in Kenya.

14 April: insurgents in Teso took advantage of an amnesty and surrendered to the government.

June: a peace agreement was signed with a section of the UPDA in Acholi, and those who surrendered benefited from an amnesty.

July: the Uganda Law Society expressed disquiet about plans to allow summary trials in "areas of insurgency" (the government backed off from this proposal).

July: weapons alleged to have been sent through Nairobi for remaining UPDA rebels in Acholi.

4 August: one of the ministers taken hostage by the UPA was killed and the other wounded when the NRA attempted to rescue them by storming the stronghold where they were being held.

November: Ugandans who had fled to Sudan began to return because of an upsurge in the Sudan's civil war.

1989   January: Amin appeared in Zaire and offered his services to Uganda. He was deported from Kinshasa to Dakar, and after considerable hesitation Saudi Arabia, where he had been given asylum, agreed to have him back

11, 12, 18 February, 4 March: peaceful elections to National Resistance Councils marked a return to partial democracy. Ten cabinet ministers and four deputies lost their seats.

April: the "Holy Spirit" movement led by Joseph Kony in succession to Alice Lakwena gathered strength. The NRA rounded up civilians to create fire-free zones.

May: staff at Makerere University went on strike over pay.

July: 69 people, rounded up on suspicion of collaboration with rebels in Teso, but found not guilty, were locked into a railway wagon where they suffocated. The NRA admitted responsibility but no independent enquiry was held.

October: legislation was passed to establish a new science university at Mbarara to specialize in veterinary science.

10 October: a bill was passed to extend the rule of the NRA for five years from January 1990 to give time to produce a new constitution.

28 November: Major General Salim Saleh, Museveni's brother, was retired from his position as army commander. Major Generals Elly Tumwine and Fred Rwigyema were "sent on courses."

1990   Basilio Okello died in Khartoum.

February: in a major offensive against rebels in southern Teso thousands of civilians were rounded up into camps with insufficient food, water, sanitation or medical care. First the local churches and then the international aid agencies mounted emergency relief operations.

April: rail services to Gulu were restored for the first time in three years.

23 April: the Uganda Law Society urged Museveni to stop trying to solve "purely political issues through military means."

July: the currency was floated.

26 July: Uganda Human Rights Activists made a strongly worded statement on the deaths in Teso camps, and on detention without trial and the use of torture.

1 October: Major General Rwigyema invaded Rwanda with a force mainly of Rwandan exiles, many of whom had been recruited into the NRA. Teso was reported quieter with fewer soldiers there.

3 December: Makerere University students boycotted lectures over inadequate grants and study facilities. On 10 December police were called in and two students

were shot dead. Two commissions were set up to examine what had happened. A new Vice-Chancellor was appointed.

1991   30 March: in Acholi, which had been quieter, a new offensive was launched against rebels. Arrests made on suspicion included the mayor of Gulu and other community leaders. Joseph Kony renamed his "Holy Spirit" movement the Uganda People's Democratic Christian Army (UPDCA).

1 April: Paulo Muwanga died in Kampala.

20 April: Cardinal Emmanuel Nsubuga died at Rubaga.

8 May: 18 community leaders and elders in Acholi were arrested and charged with treason. When they appeared in court, some had been beaten up. They included Andrew Adimola, former High Commissioner in London. No proper charges were brought. Adimola was later released.

3 June: Report of the Visitation Committee to Makerere University issued which looked into staff and student grievances. It recommended depoliticizing the university's administration by appointing an eminent citizen as Chancellor instead of the President automatically filling this role.

9 August: atrocities by Joseph Kony's UPDCA were highlighted in the Uganda press.

December: the railway line to Port Bell on Lake Victoria was completed with the help of Danish aid.

1992   Rehabilitation was able to go ahead in both Acholi and Teso as peace was restored.

Throughout the year the Constitutional Commission heard submissions on what the people wanted to see in the new constitution. Some 20,000 submissions were received in writing and orally and were examined by the Commission. The most important issue was whether the old political parties were to be allowed to function.

January: several officials of the UPC and the DP were arrested. Some DP members who were refusing to cooperate with the government remained in custody for some weeks.

January: 3,000 Uganda refugees returned home from the Southern Sudan as security worsened in that country. A huge influx of Southern Sudanese fled to Uganda.

February–March: elections were held for local Resistance Councils. Many members of the old political parties won seats, though they had to campaign as individuals, not as representatives of their parties.

March: large numbers of Zaireans took refuge in Uganda as chaos in Zaire increased and the army ran out of control.

April: Museveni announced that the army would vacate the palace of the former Kabaka of Buganda and the former Buganda parliament building, and that they would be returned to the Baganda when alternative accommodation had been found.

May: a partial demobilization of the army was announced.

June: during the budget speech it was announced that the salaries of public servants would be raised to something nearer the amount needed to cover basic living expenses. Huge cuts in the number of civil servants employed were expected to continue. The collapse of coffee prices on the world market seriously affected Uganda's economy.

July: a massive rehabilitation program for Northern and Eastern Uganda was announced.

A cease-fire in the war in Rwanda was negotiated, easing the security situation in southwestern Uganda in spite of violations of the cease-fire.

1993   January: the draft Constitution was published.

31 July: Ronald Mutebi was crowned as Kabaka of Buganda, cultural head of his people but without any political powers.

Patrick Olimi returned to his kingdom of Toro, again as cultural head but without political powers.

July–August: a further huge influx of 30,000 Sudanese refugees crossed into Uganda.

November: Bunyoro decided to go ahead with the restoration of the monarchy, and after some dissension Solomon Iguru was nominated as the new Mukama, to be crowned in 1994.

1994   28 March: elections held for a Constituent Assembly called to legislate for a new Constitution.

UGANDA: Administrative Districts 1967

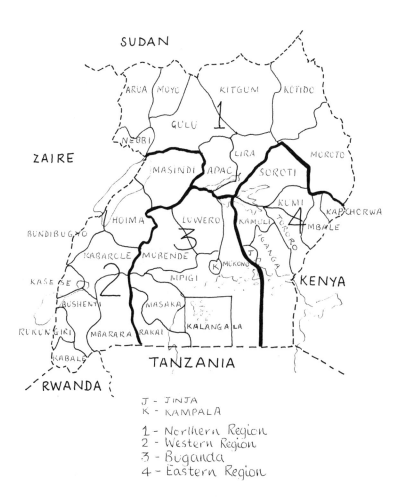

SUDAN

ZAIRE

ARUA MOYO KITGUM KOTIDO

GULU 1

NEBBI

MASINDI APAC LIRA MOROTO

SOROTI

HOIMA LUWERO KAMULI KUMI KAPCHORWA

BUNDIBUGYO 3 TORORO MBALE

KABAROLE MUBENDE IGANGA

KASESE K MUKONO KENYA

BUSHENYI MPIGI J

RUKUNGIRI MBARARA RAKAI MASAKA

KABALE KALANGALA

TANZANIA

RWANDA

J - JINJA
K - KAMPALA

1 - Northern Region
2 - Western Region
3 - Buganda
4 - Eastern Region

UGANDA: Administrative Districts & Regions
Boundaries 1974, Names 1979

INTRODUCTION

Geography

A landlocked country of 93,100 square miles (241,140 square kilometers), Uganda lies directly on the Equator in East Central Africa. Most of the country lies between 3,000 and 5,000 feet (500–900 meters) above sea level. In the west are the Ruwenzori Mountains whose highest point is Mount Stanley (16,760 feet; 5,109 meters), and in the extreme southwest the highlands of Kigezi and Kisoro rise towards the Bufumbira volcanoes on the Rwanda/Zaire border. In the east the Kenya/Uganda border runs through the Mount Elgon massif (14,176 feet; 4,321 meters). The lowest elevation above sea level is the Nile Valley north of Lake Albert where the river flows slowly towards the Sudan at an altitude of under 3,000 feet (900 meters). Uganda's high elevation moderates the tropical climate, and the variation in altitude is responsible for a very varied flora and fauna.

Some 17 percent of Uganda's land surface consists of fresh water lakes. The country lies on the northwest corner of Lake Victoria, whose waters are shared with Kenya and Tanzania. Lakes Albert, George and Edward are situated in the western arm of the Great Rift Valley which extends southwards as far as Lake Malawi and northwards to the Dead Sea and the Jordan Valley. The Nile flows northwards out of Lake Victoria at the site of the Owen Falls, now drowned under a hydroelectric dam. It continues northwards for some 80 miles before turning eastwards where downwarping spreads the river out into the slow-moving, shallow Lake Kyoga. From the eastern end of Lake Kyoga the Nile flows northwards again before turning east and plunging over the Kabarega (formerly Murchison) Falls towards Lake Albert. At Nimule it passes into Sudan. As well as rivers and open water, there are large areas of papyrus swamp, some parts of which have been drained to provide exceptionally fertile soil for market

1

gardening and agriculture. The number and extent of lakes and rivers means that fishing provides a substantial part of the diet in many parts of the country. Unfortunately the introduction of the huge and rapidly breeding Nile perch into Lake Victoria is endangering fish species native to that lake, including the valuable tilapia.

To the north and east of the Nile the land becomes progressively drier and hotter towards the western edge of the eastern arm of the Great Rift Valley. Semi-nomadic pastoralism is the traditional way of life of the Karamojong of northeastern Uganda. They traditionally lived largely on the milk and blood of their cattle. Karamoja and parts of Ankole in the southwest where cattle are ranched are the only regions of Uganda with less than 30 inches (750 millimeters) of annual rainfall. The Hima people of Ankole and Toro own large herds of long-horned cattle which traditionally grazed over wide areas. A mixture of pastoralism and agriculture is practiced by most other Ugandan peoples, and today even the Bahima and Karamojong practice some agriculture. In the drier north and east millet, cassava and specially-bred strains of fast-maturing maize are the staple crops, while in the wetter and more fertile areas south and west of the Nile the staples are maize and the *matooke* banana (a green banana which requires a long period of steaming before it can be eaten). Everywhere a wide range of vegetables and pulses is also grown, as well as sweet potatoes and groundnuts, to provide an interesting and varied diet. Cattle are kept for bridewealth as well as for the production of milk and meat, and ritual occasions may provide the main opportunities for meat-eating. Most families keep chickens, and sheep and goats are widely owned. Only in the extreme northeast are camels kept; elsewhere donkeys are sometimes used as beasts of burden. The vast majority of Ugandans live by farming.

The most important cash crop is coffee, both Arabica and Robusta being grown. It is also the country's most valuable export. Other important cash crops are tobacco, tea and cotton, though the importance of the last has declined, and its cultivation produces little profit. Copper is mined on a small scale in Kasese and Fort Portal in the west, and a cement industry is sited in the east at Tororo. Sugar is grown on plantations in Buganda and Busoga with an associated refining industry.

Uganda has a network of good, all-weather roads, many of them metalled in the early years of independence and recently rebuilt under the government of Yoweri Museveni after falling into disrepair. Main roads radiate out from Kampala, and a ring road connects the main northern and western district capitals. The Nile is bridged at Jinja where the road runs over the Owen Falls Dam, at Pakwach between West Nile and Acholi, and at the Karuma Falls on the road from Kampala to Gulu. Goods and people are transported around and across Lake Victoria by steamer and by smaller boats. A single-track railway connects Kampala with Nairobi and Mombasa, and is a main passenger and freight link. The railway extends westwards to the copper mines at Kasese, and from Tororo a northern loop goes to Soroti, Lira and Gulu, and an extension is planned to Arua. This northern line was closed for some years in the 1980s and 1990s because of insurgency in Acholi and Teso. The rail network became considerably run down as a result of the collapse of the modern sector under Amin and during Obote II, and problems arising when the East African Community collapsed. Kenya and Uganda then assumed responsibility for those parts of the railway which ran through their territories. International air connections are through Entebbe some 20 miles south of Kampala; most major towns are served by an airstrip.

Population

The 1969 census counted 9,584,847 people, including 74,000 Asians and 9,500 Europeans, and the population was growing at 3.8 percent per annum. By 1990 it had grown to some 17 million, in spite of a decline in the rate of increase as a result of the violence under Amin and Obote II. By the 1990s there was, therefore, beginning to be pressure on land for cultivation.

In spite of the small size of the country, the population is heterogeneous. The "Bantu Line," north of which Bantu languages are not spoken (though south of it enclaves of non-Bantu languages occur), passes through Uganda, running approximately along the Nile from Lake Albert to Lake Kyoga, through Lake Kyoga, and southeast to Tororo. North of that line are speakers of Sudanic, Nilotic and para-Nilotic languages who together make up about a third of the country's population. The remaining two thirds live to the south and west of that line and speak a variety of Bantu languages. Both English and Swahili are widely known, but there is no language which is fully acceptable as a lingua franca. Of all the languages indigenous to Uganda, Luganda is spoken as first language by the largest number. Swahili was originally the language of the coastal peoples of Kenya and Tanzania, and is now the lingua franca of both these countries as well as being spoken in parts of western Zaire, and it is, perhaps, the most likely language to become the lingua franca of Uganda. It is not possible to say with accuracy how many different languages and ethnic groups exist in Uganda because the count will depend on how a language and an ethnic group are defined, but on almost any count there are more than 20. There are cultural as well as linguistic differences between the Bantu and non-Bantu speakers, some of which result from the different means of livelihood practiced by different peoples, but the most obvious cultural differences are between the interlacustrine Bantu kingdoms which were traditionally strongly hierarchical, and the less centralized societies elsewhere.

The vast majority of Ugandans live in the countryside, with fewer than ten percent living in towns of more than 1,000 inhabitants. In the rural areas each family lives on its own land, perhaps cultivating only a few acres, though the pastoralists may graze cattle over vast tracts of country. The greatest concentrations of population are around Lake Victoria and in Kigezi where, since pre-colonial times a system of terracing the steep hillsides for cultivation has been practiced.

Immigrant groups include Banyarwanda who found employment with the Baganda and others as herdsmen, and who have immigrated into Uganda since pre-colonial days. Then there were Asians who entered as skilled workmen and entrepreneurs, and Kenyan Luo who sought any kind of employment and had a reputation for efficiency and hard work. Sudanese troops cut off from Khartoum by the Mahdist rising of the 1890s were enlisted by Captain Lugard of the Imperial British East Africa Company and have been a major constituent of the army ever since. Their descendants are the so-called Nubians. And finally there are various groups of refugees including Zaireans who fled the post-independence turbulence, Banyarwanda who fled ethnic massacres in the 1960s, and Southern Sudanese who fled civil war and persecution. The first wave of Sudanese refugees returned home from 1972 onwards. The 1990s have seen new influxes of both Sudanese and Zaireans. Although there has been little European settlement, missionaries, colonial officials, aid workers, businessmen and various categories of experts have from time to time been a significant and powerful presence.

As well as immigration, there have been major expulsions of population. Some 33,000 Kenyans were expelled by President Obote in 1970 (his first and second presidencies are usually referred to as Obote I and II); 50,000 Asians were expelled by President Amin in 1972; and 75,000 Rwandese in 1982–1983 by Obote after his return to power (Obote II). Amin's expulsion of the Asians was internationally censured; Obote's much larger expulsions passed largely unnoticed outside Africa.

Imbalances in the population have been brought about both by the violence which has characterized the country's history since 1971 and which has left many widows and orphans, and by the AIDS epidemic of the 1980s onwards which has decimated young adults in parts of the country.

Economy

At independence the Ugandan economy seemed set to develop well. By contrast with her two East African neighbors, Kenya and Tanzania, Uganda was blessed with fertile soil and good rainfall over much of the country. Coffee, tea, tobacco and cotton, which all fetched a good price, were grown by Ugandan farmers and were not a settler monopoly as in Kenya. Copper-mining was promising, though on a small scale. The manufacturing sector was very small, however, and largely directed at internal consumption.

Some of Uganda's problems since then have been common to most Third World countries: falling commodity prices, overproduction of primary products, and unfavorable terms of world trade. During Obote I great efforts were made to industrialize, and new export crops (including strawberries, flowers and other fruit and vegetables for the European market) were developed. The textile works at Jinja were expanded, and the manufacture of plastic goods and man-made fabrics was begun. Attempts were made to cut dependence on dairy and other processed food products from Kenya. Paper manufacture was started. The commercial and manufacturing sectors remained largely in Asian hands throughout Obote I, and Asian dominance of these sectors caused resentment. Import substitution often proved expensive because of the small size of the market.

Throughout Obote's first presidency the gross domestic product grew at 4.2 percent per annum. It continued to grow, but at the lesser rate of 3.1 percent during 1972. However, this year saw the expulsion of the Asians, and the loss of their creditworthiness as well as their expertise. In the period 1973 to 1980 the Ugandan economy declined more sharply than did the economies of other low-income countries of Sub-Saharan Africa and, at the same time, inflation, which had been running at between 5 and 6 percent during Obote I, rose to 45 percent per annum under Amin. In the 1980s the gross domestic product continued to fall, though less sharply by −2.4 percent per annum, but inflation rose to 92 percent per annum. As the modern sector of the Ugandan economy collapsed, agriculture's share of the economy rose from 52 percent in 1965 to 70 percent in the late 1980s. During Amin's presidency *magendo* (smuggling or black market trade carried on by *bayayi*—"wide boys"—whose activities were unregistered and uncontrolled and often verged on the criminal) became a way of life for many, and a new class of *mafuta mingi* (those who grew super rich on this type of trade) emerged. Barter replaced money transactions to some extent, and as the transport infrastructure declined, production and marketing patterns changed too: smallholders diversified and roadside markets sprang up every few miles. Foreign investment and aid slumped.

Aid has significantly increased since 1986, but inflation was still out of control at the end of the 1980s, and though the economy began to pick up under an International Monetary Fund recovery program, and there were significant improvements to the infrastructure, with roads and the railway being repaired and brought back into use, a large proportion of the budget still had to be spent on containing insurgency. Growth rates may appear impressive, but have to be set against the catastrophic decline earlier: much had to be done simply to regain lost ground.

One result of the collapse of the modern sector of the economy and the partial return to subsistence was that tax yields were too low for salaries paid to civil servants, teachers, health service personnel and other public employees to cover even the cost of food for a family. Most people, therefore, developed other sources of income, "lines," to enable them to survive, and much of their time had to be devoted to pursuing these. The public sector suffered as a result.

By 1993 the economy was showing strong signs of reviving. The virtual cessation of hostilities in the north and east had enabled the inhabitants there to return to their farms and start to rebuild. The repair of the country's infrastructure was continuing, and manufacture was beginning to revive. Inflation had been dramatically reduced, and it had been possible to increase public sector salaries to a more realistic level.

History

The pre-colonial histories of most of the peoples of modern Uganda have been studied in some depth. Archeological examination of the royal sites of western Uganda suggests an earlier date for these than do oral traditions, dating some of them back to the thirteenth century. It is less easy to check the migration histories of the peoples of the north and east, but there, too, events may have been telescoped. Oral traditions are concerned with explaining and legitimizing the present, not with providing precise chronologies, and must be evaluated accordingly. Where oral traditions concern more recent events, they can sometimes be checked against written sources, and are often found to be accurate.

By the mid-nineteenth century Buganda and Bunyoro were the most powerful of the interlacustrine Bantu kingdoms. Buganda was densely populated and efficiently administered, well-placed around the northwest corner of Lake Victoria to take advantage of Swahili trading initiatives, and powerful enough to curb these and use them to her own advantage. Bunyoro's sphere of influence was more far-flung: the Mukama (king) ruled through appointees who were kept loyal through family and clan ties, and by being required to return annually to the Mukama with their royal insignia. The rulers of Toro made a bid for "independence" in the early nineteenth century: other principalities to the south paid tribute but were only tenuously part of Bunyoro's hegemony.

Much the same could be said of the areas round Lake Kyoga where Bunyoro traded and wielded a greater or lesser degree of control. The British Protectorate administration was located in Buganda, and the Baganda were able to turn the British presence to their own advantage when the Protectorate authorities decided on a showdown with Mukama Kabarega in the late 1890s, and the land which was annexed to Buganda as a reward for their assistance against Kabarega was a major cause of contention between the two kingdoms up to and beyond independence. Several of the kingdoms and principalities of the southwest were tidied up under Protectorate rule into the kingdom of Ankole: Kigezi and Kisoro lay between Ankole and the powerful kingdom of Rwanda which came under Belgian colonial rule. The petty kingdoms of Busoga were likewise tidied up into an administrative district which was able to appoint a paramount ruler and claim kingdom status.

North and east of the Nile much less centralized societies had evolved. Over some four hundred years the Acholi had developed strong, clan-based chiefdoms and non-Acholi people among whom they had settled had been absorbed into these and Acholi-ized. Quarrels between different chiefdoms in the nineteenth century had given slave raiders from the Sudan and Egypt an entry into the area when one chief or another had asked for their help against a rival. In some parts of eastern Uganda people were still migrating southwards in the last quarter of the nineteenth century. Protectorate rule was established over these areas later than over the south and west, and further migration frozen.

European missionaries entered Uganda well before the colonial takeover, but not before the Kabaka of Buganda had become aware of external threats. He was particularly alarmed by Egyptian incursions to the north. The Swahili traders from the coast and the traveler, Henry Morton Stanley, both arrived with firearms, and it was in order to acquire this technology that the Kabaka welcomed a European presence provided he could keep it under his control. Like the Muslim Swahili, the missionaries talked about God and religion in a way that was unfamiliar, and he was interested. The missionaries proved little use to him over supplying firearms, though he was occasionally able to bully them into repairing those he already had. He kept them dancing attendance on his court, and this gave them access to the young men in training there for high office. Some of them had already become interested in Islam; now they were offered both the Protestant and Catholic forms of Christianity, and the literacy which went with the new creeds. In 1876, just before the missionaries' arrival, some 200 young men who had converted to Islam were executed for defying the Kabaka in the name of Islam. By the mid-1880s, under a new Kabaka still struggling to assert his authority, the same type of conflict arose with Christian converts at court, and between 100 and 200 perished, 50 of whose names are still known. The 22 Catholics among them were canonized in 1964.

In 1880–1890 conflict broke out between those who upheld the old ways and were loyal to the old sources of authority, and those who were experimenting with new faiths: Muslims, and Protestant and Catholic Christians. At first the followers of the new faiths made common cause in an attempt to win a measure of power for themselves from the old guard, but the alliance soon broke down. A Muslim coup drove the Christians into exile, but when the latter fought their way back and reinstated the Kabaka in order to legitimize their own position, they competed for power among themselves, as old and new fissures in society coincided.

In 1892 matters between the Christian factions came to a head in a battle precipitated by the presence of Captain F.D. Lugard of the Imperial British East Africa Company (IBEAC), whose instructions were to be absolutely impartial, but in the last resort to support the Protestant converts of the British missionaries rather than the Catholic converts of the French missionaries. The Battle of Mengo was won by the Protestant faction as a result, and the Catholics fled to Buddu in the south of Buganda, which has been a Catholic stronghold ever since. Under the agreement negotiated soon after this battle, political power in Buganda was allocated in the ratio of ten Protestant, eight Catholic and two Muslim senior chieftaincies. A somewhat similar apportionment of power was later applied elsewhere in the country, and religious factionalism persists into the present.

In 1894 a British Protectorate was formally declared over Uganda and administration was established, first over the central, western and southern areas of the country (in that order), and then more slowly over the north and east, and over Kisoro in the extreme south. Although armed force was used on several occasions between 1897 and 1912, notably against Bunyoro which suffered greatly as a result, in the main Ugandans followed a policy of "if you can't win, join in," and did so with apparent success up till independence. Under a policy of indirect rule the kingdoms succeeded in retaining something of their old institutions, though these were manipulated by the colonial overlords until their legitimacy was undermined. Not until independence did the weaknesses engendered by indirect rule, and in particular the privileged status granted to Buganda by the terms of the [B]Uganda Agreement of 1900 and the inequalities of development, become apparent.

Education and medicine were left to the missions to an almost unparalleled degree until after World War I. Because the missions had a near monopoly of education, Muslims were disadvantaged. Those Muslims who sought paid employment lacked the advantage of literacy and worked as taxi-drivers, and also, because they would eat only *halal* (ritually-slaughtered) meat, as butchers. Muslims were concentrated in Buganda, Bunyoro and West Nile. The Sudanese troops enlisted by Lugard remained largely unassimilated, and were either soldiers or traders.

The one other group of Muslims in Uganda were Asians. Unlike the African Muslims who were all Sunni, many of the Asian Muslims were Shia of the Ismaili, Ithna Asheri and Dawoodi Bohora sects. The first Asians (or Indians, as they were known before the partition of India and Pakistan) were brought into East Africa to build the railway, but most of these returned home when that was completed. Asian immigrant entrepreneurs and skilled workers were welcomed by the colonial authorities to provide amenities and do work for which Africans at first lacked the training and skills. During the colonial period, Africans demanded the type of education which would enable them to compete with their political masters rather than technical education, so the Asians had little competition. In any case the Protectorate government provided proportionately more money for Asian schools than for African, Asians were able to proceed to higher education sooner, and were employed by the administration in positions of responsibility. They dominated such manufacturing industry as there was as well as controlling much of Uganda's commerce, and many found their way into the professions after training abroad. Their wealth and success made them objects of resentment, and they found themselves caught between

Europeans and Africans in an uncomfortable vise. The poor Asians who eked out a living by running shops in small up-country townships were largely forgotten in this equation. When Amin decided to expel non-citizen Asians (and later citizens as well) in 1972, he made the most popular move of his presidency. Few Ugandans realized what the consequences would be. Ugandan Africans considered themselves fortunate by comparison with Kenyan Africans. They were not confined in reserves, they had a sufficiency of land, they retained more of their traditional institutions, and they had better educational opportunities: when it was decided to make provision for higher education in East Africa, it seemed natural to site it in Uganda. What really worried Ugandans was the possibility of "closer union" with the rest of British East Africa because they feared that this would bring about the dominance of Kenya and her settler-dominated politics. In 1924 and 1929 talk of "closer union" caused alarm; when the East African High Commission was established in 1947 to run the services (posts and telegraph, railways) which were common to the three territories, the new organization was viewed with great suspicion.

The growth of nationalism was late in Uganda. In the Bantu kingdoms, and most particularly in Buganda, attention was concentrated on retaining the traditions and privileges granted by their agreement status. The intensity of local feeling which was encouraged by indirect rule, the exceptional privileges enjoyed by Buganda and her arrogance towards the rest of the country, and the cultural differences between the north and the east on the one hand and the south and the west on the other made it difficult to achieve any real sense of nationalism. When political parties began to emerge in the latter half of the 1950s, they were differentiated primarily by religion rather than ethnicity or political policies, and were also as much concerned with retaining factional privileges as with achieving independence. In 1960 Buganda declared unilateral independence because she feared that, in a unitary independent state, she might lose the special status she enjoyed under the 1900 Agreement. This declaration was an empty gesture which was ignored by the colonial authorities, but Milton Obote, who became the first Prime Minister, nevertheless believed Buganda's cooperation was essential for his own political success, and made a deal with her in order to bring her back into the political process, even though after independence he quickly abandoned this.

Independence in 1962 came after prolonged constitutional maneuvering. Guy Hunter (in *The New Societies of Tropical Africa.* London: Oxford University Press, 1962, p. 295) was one of the few observers to recognize Uganda's potential instability. Prime Minister Milton Obote, though a wily politician, lacked charisma and suffered from the lack of a common language in which to communicate with the masses. He failed at the first hurdle: instead of dealing decisively with a mutiny in the army in 1964, he gave in to virtually all its demands. Faced with similar situations, both Nyerere in Tanzania and Jomo Kenyatta in Kenya acted far more decisively, and their more peaceful histories are partly the result of this. Uganda's slide into violence started at this time, even if at first it was not easy to detect. Arguably the 1900 [B]Uganda Agreement and the 1964 capitulation to the mutineers have been the two most important events in shaping Uganda's subsequent history.

At the end of that same year a section of the army, under Idi Amin, embarked on an adventure in Congo (Zaire) in support of the Simba rebels. Later Obote and Amin and two other ministers were accused of stealing a large amount of Congolese gold and ivory which had been entrusted to them for the purchase of arms for the Simba. They were later cleared of wrong-doing by an official enquiry, but no one will doubt that they were rewarded handsomely for their services. More seriously, the army rather than the politicians seems to have been calling the tune.

The accusations about the gold and ivory scandal were made early in 1966 and were followed by what appears to have been a coup attempt led by Grace Ibingira. Obote had Ibingira and the four other ministers involved arrested, and they remained in detention throughout the remainder of his first presidency. The showdown with Buganda occurred the same year when the Baganda, enraged by the prospect of a new constitution which would deprive them of all their former privileges, ordered the central government out of Kampala and off Buganda soil, and set up road blocks to try and immobilize the army. In the battle which followed the Baganda were heavily defeated and the Kabaka fled abroad. The new constitution was brought in in 1967, and Buganda remained under a state of emergency until Obote lost power, with the army on double pay as long as the emergency continued.

The next three years brought no policy initiatives, though there was steady development. It seemed as though, having defeated the Baganda, Obote was unsure of how to proceed. Not until October 1969 did he begin to publish the series of five policy documents which together outline the "Move to the Left." But this move came too late. In December 1969 Obote narrowly escaped an assassination attempt, the perpetrators of which were never apprehended, and the brief remainder of his presidency was tense. The remaining four documents were published, but were largely ineffective in rallying support for Obote and the Uganda People's Congress (UPC).

Factional infighting in the army surfaced occasionally. On 25 January 1970 Brigadier Pierino Okoya was murdered, apparently on Amin's orders because he was a rival for power. Obote took exception to overspending on the army by Amin, and had set up paramilitary units under his own control. The final showdown between Obote and that part of the army led by Amin came in January 1971 when Amin seized power in a coup, and proceeded to liquidate those sections of the army whom he could not trust to support him. Obote was attending a Commonwealth Heads of Government Meeting in Singapore at the time, where he enraged British Prime Minister Edward Heath on the subject of arms sales to South Africa. Britain was the first country to recognize Amin's government. Obote was given asylum in Tanzania by President Nyerere who had always been a friend and socialist ally.

Yet, in spite of all his boastful talk about being a military man, Amin was unable to control either the loyalty or the behavior of the army. The murders and disappearances for which his regime became notorious were frequently the work of soldiers acting on their own to enrich themselves or to remove personal enemies or rivals. Much of the slaughter was the result of anarchy as civil administration broke down. But there was also planned and systematic killing, especially by the members of the dreaded State Research Bureau whose personnel were supplied with sophisticated surveillance equipment purchased in Britain, and had elaborate hit lists of people who had been informed against, often as a result of torture.

During the eight years of Amin's misrule the modern sector of the economy collapsed, partly as a result of the expulsion of the Asians, partly as a result of mismanagement including greatly increased expenditure on the army, and partly because of insecurity. In some years no budget was even published. Growers were not paid for their coffee or cotton both of which had to be marketed through parastatal companies, and production declined. A black economy grew up as goods were smuggled in and out of the country. Manufacturing industry collapsed as expatriate and Asian expertise disappeared, plant was not maintained, credit-worthiness and business contacts disappeared, and the failure to train Ugandans took its toll. In spite of all this there were those who prospered, the so-called *mafuta mingi* ("very fat ones"), and they and the *bayayi* ("wide boys") engaged in *magendo* trade which flourished unregulated, non-taxpaying and sometimes violent alongside the formal economy. It was a survival tactic which could not be suppressed, and which the formal economy eventually had to adapt to. Perhaps partly because Uganda is so fertile that people were able to feed themselves whatever happened to the modern sector of the economy, and partly because enough people benefitted in some way from Amin's anarchy, no coherent opposition emerged. Among those who benefitted to begin with were the Baganda. They had rejoiced when Amin seized power and overthrew Obote. As a reward for their support, Amin allowed the body of Kabaka Mutesa to be brought back from London where he had died in exile, and be buried at Kasubi, the royal burial site.

1972 was a crucial year for Uganda under Amin. After visiting Libya in March, Amin broke with Israel and turned increasingly to the Arab world for support, invoking his allegiance to Islam. In August he ordered first the expulsion of British and other non-citizen Asians, and when he saw how popular this move was, he turned on Asians with Ugandan citizenship as well. British Asians were being admitted to Britain on a quota system, but the British were being dilatory over implementing a promise to speed up the process. It was some time before they took seriously Amin's deadline of 90 days for all to leave the country. The Asians were all got out on time with the aid of the United Nations and a massive airlift, and they went to a number of Western countries as well as to Britain and India.

In 1975 Amin became chairman of the Organization of African

Unity (OAU), and its summit meeting was held in Kampala. He deliberately snubbed Britain by making Prime Minister James Callaghan go to Kampala on behalf of Dennis Hills, a British subject resident in Uganda who had been condemned to death for describing Amin as a "village tyrant" in a book he had written. Early in 1976 Amin quarrelled with Kenya, claiming that western Kenya should once again belong to Uganda as it had done prior to 1902. This claim was clearly modelled on Somalia's claim to a "Greater Somalia," and was particularly galling to Kenya which was already threatened by Somali claims in the northeast. An oil blockade imposed by Kenya, allegedly because Uganda was behindhand with transport payments, brought Uganda almost to its knees. Amin's claims were hastily dropped.

Later in 1976 a hijacked Air France plane with a number of Israeli citizens on board was landed at Entebbe and Amin acted in league with the hijackers rather than trying to negotiate the release of the hostages. Israel mounted a spectacularly successful raid and rescued the hostages and at the same time wiped out most of Uganda's air force. When a month later Amin's army invaded the campus of Makerere University, the international media were prepared to believe almost anything and published stories claiming that hundreds of students had been killed. The true story—five students almost certainly died and there was massive disruption—was quite bad enough.

In late August Uganda's religious leaders met near Kampala under the chairmanship of Anglican Archbishop Janani Luwum to discuss what could be done about the ever-increasing violence in the country. Amin learnt of the meeting and demanded the minutes. He was incensed that the chief Muslim Kadhi had attended this meeting, and began to fear that the Muslims whom he believed to be his main supporters were turning against him as well as the Christians. He interpreted sermons about "fighting against evil" in a literal sense, and feared armed rebellion. In February 1977 his henchmen "found" a planted cache of arms at Archbishop Luwum's residence, and the Archbishop and two government ministers were murdered on 17 February after allegations that they were involved in an Acholi plot. It was quickly realized that Ugandan claims that they had died in a car accident were untrue. In June it was made clear to Amin that he would not be welcome at the Commonwealth Heads of Government meeting in London. A British businessman, Robert Scanlon paid the price for Amin's humiliation. He "disappeared," apparently murdered. Late in 1978 Amin sought to create a diversion for the army by claiming that Uganda was being invaded by Tanzania, and shortly afterwards Ugandan troops invaded and devastated the Kagera Salient in Tanzania. On 12 November the Tanzanian army mounted a major offensive to dislodge them. Finding the Uganda army far weaker than had been expected, the Tanzanians advanced over the border and, accompanied by a small contingent of Ugandans, fought their way slowly on foot to Kampala. The fiercest resistance was put up by a contingent of Libyan troops sent in by Gadafi. They suffered heavy casualties trying to defend Entebbe Airport. Kampala was freed on 11 April and looted by troops and civilians alike. Amin took refuge first in Libya and then in Saudi Arabia; some of the army surrendered, others fled to Sudan.

It is not possible to chronicle the long list of those who were murdered or who disappeared during these years. A hundred names of prominent people murdered by the regime are recorded by Henry Kyemba in *State of Blood: The Inside Story of Idi Amin's Reign of Fear* (London: Corgi, 1977) but as in most persecutions, the names of most are unrecorded and the reason for their killing unknown, which is part of the tragedy. The eight years of Amin's misrule did incalculable damage to Ugandan society, sowing distrust through an army of informers, creating chaos in the law—Amin ruled by decree—destroying the modern sector of the economy, and brutalizing a generation. The civil service was almost paralyzed. Violence became a way of life, and numbers of people who had been enlisted into the overblown army drifted back to their homes or into the towns, and were unable to settle down. Worse still, they enlisted in the new Uganda National Liberation Army (UNLA) and behaved exactly as they had behaved in Amin's army, pillaging and terrorizing the civilian population. About half the country's doctors had left, either fleeing into exile or being expelled because they were Asians, and the University lost many of its staff. It says much for the devotion of those who remained that medical and educational services survived at all.

The overthrow of Amin did little to improve the situation. No one had expected Amin's army to crumble as it did, and there was no coherent opposition. The exiles managed to put together some kind of a plan aimed in part at preventing Obote from returning, and Yusufu Lule, former Principal of Makerere University, was a compromise appointment as President. He was not a politician, lacked the skills to deal with a political crisis, and was ousted just 60 days later, accused of favoring the Baganda old guard. Already the UNLA, reinforced by elements of Amin's army, was out of control and behaving just as the army had done under Amin. When Godfrey Binaisa, a barrister and not a politician, was appointed President to succeed Lule, he fared little better, and the Military Council under Paulo Muwanga was determined to reinstate Obote. After disputed elections Obote and the UPC regained power in December, but having been reinstated by the wish of the Military Council, Obote could not hope to control the army.

Yoweri Museveni, whose party failed to make any impact in the elections, took to the bush with a small group of followers, and over the next few years built these into a highly disciplined force, trained to respect the civilian population on whose support they depended. In their attempts to counter this insurgency, and in taking their revenge on West Nile, whose population was accused of supporting Amin, the UNLA harassed the civilian population to the extent that some 300,000 took refuge in Sudan and Zaire, and perhaps 200,000 people in the Luwero Triangle, scene of major counter-insurgency operations, were thought to have died, their names and the circumstances of their deaths largely unknown and unrecorded. Obote blamed the situation on the need to put down the insurgency, but the UNLA was out of control well before the elections which gave rise to the insurgency: church leaders had complained to Binaisa when he was appointed President about the behavior of the army, and they protested again to Obote soon after his accession.

Thanks to International Monetary Fund (IMF) restructuring programs and the renewal of foreign aid, there was some improvement in the modern sector of the economy during Obote's second presidency. But the need for massive expenditure on the army and Obote's inability to carry out some of the most unpopular aspects of the structural adjustment program because of his need to retain the support of public service workers, meant that there were setbacks to the improvement and inflation got out of control.

In December 1983 the armed forces Chief-of-Staff David

Oyite-Ojok was killed in a helicopter crash. It was eight months before Obote replaced him by a fellow Langi. The delay was due to quarrelling over power in the army, and the appointment of Smith Opon-Acak did nothing to appease the aggrieved Acholi sections of the UNLA. In December 1984 a new offensive was launched against Museveni's guerrillas in the Luwero Triangle. It was alleged that the Acholi sections of the army were used disproportionately, and when they suffered severe setbacks, they were resentful. In mid-1985 two Acholi generals, Basilio Okello and Tito Okello, seized control of the army and of the capital in an army putsch. Human rights violations increased as army infighting continued. Peace talks were held in Nairobi under the chairmanship of Kenyan President Daniel arap Moi, but though an agreement was signed on 17 December, neither side implemented it. The Okello regime and the army was split several ways and could not deliver what it had agreed to, and the National Resistance Army (NRA) under Museveni was on the threshold of a military victory, and had no incentive to abide by the agreement which they had only signed under international pressure.

On January 25, 14 years to the day after Amin's coup, the NRA fought its way into the western suburbs of Kampala, and the following day Museveni was sworn in as President, pledged to restore respect for human rights and the rule of law, and put forward a Ten Point Programme for social and economic recovery. Hopes of being able to do so easily or rapidly were destroyed by three developments.

First there was renewed insurgency as the Okellos regrouped the remnants of their troops in Sudan and came back over the border to disturb the peace of Acholi. Secondly, in order to meet this threat the NRA recruited men who had surrendered from previous armies and put them into the field without adequate retraining. Probably no amount of retraining would have been effective. Discipline broke down as the NRA found itself having to act as a standing army against insurgents, a more difficult type of operation than initiating insurgency. As a result of the NRA's mistreatment of the civilian population, insurgency increased, and became an ongoing problem, tying up men and money and bringing the new government into disrepute because of human rights abuses which accompanied the counter-insurgency operations. Thirdly, the NRA made the mistake of disarming the Militia which the Teso people of eastern Uganda had been allowed to build up to defend themselves against their cattle-rustling neighbors, the Karamojong. The Teso now found themselves defenseless against raiders armed with modern weapons who rampaged through much of eastern and northern Uganda. The NRA were too preoccupied with rebellion in Acholi to contain them until relations between the Teso and the government had broken down, leaving room for insurgency to get a foothold in Teso as well as in the north.

The group of insurgents who hit the headlines in the late 1980s were the followers of Alice Lakwena, an Acholi prophetess who promised people immunity from bullets if they accepted her "medicine." She set out to free the country from evil, but seriously mistreated those who refused to join her movement. She was eventually defeated when her forces tried to operate outside their own area, but the strength of her following bears witness to despair: many of the Acholi were willing to follow anyone who seemed to offer the promise of a better future, no matter how unlikely the means proffered. Her father and Joseph Kony, who claimed to be her brother, continued to lead a "Holy Spirit" movement after Lakwena's defeat, but they and their followers proved little more than bandits, and the civilian population was, as always, caught between the rebel movement and the government forces, and suffered at the hands of both before both movements at last petered out.

Like his predecessors, then, Museveni had difficulty in controlling the army because he, like they, depended upon it to remain in power. His desire to restore respect for human rights was genuine enough, but once he became President and had to relinquish immediate control of the NRA to others, it was they, not he, who called the tune. Human rights violations were on a less massive scale; attempts were made to discipline the army, and except in zones of combat, these were fairly successful, but the test lay precisely in what happened in the zones of combat. However, a measure of law and order prevailed in non-combat areas such as had not been experienced for years; the modern sector of the economy began to recover; and for many Ugandans there seemed to be a real hope of a return to normal civilized standards. As for the insurgents, although the various groups claimed to be fighting to restore democracy and human rights, they were responsible for gross violations of human rights themselves. Moreover several of their leaders had played key roles in previous regimes which further discredited their claims to be on the side of right. But as long as the army fueled insurgency by its abuse of the civilian population, recovery could only be partial. By 1992 insurgency had been greatly reduced, and the government stepped up its attempts to bring about reconciliation. A London conference to which exile dissidents were invited was not successful, however: the bitterness of old divisions may even have been hardened. Within the country the government has had rather more success.

In 1988 there was a limited return to democracy by means of elections to "resistance councils" whose members then elected higher tiers of councils up to the National Resistance Council which formed the equivalent of a national assembly. These elections were conducted peacefully, old political parties being banned from electioneering. Voters had to queue behind the candidate of their choice: there was no secret ballot, partly because of the costs involved. A new constitution was promised, to be worked out after nationwide consultation, but the success of this depended on being able to secure the cooperation of people in areas disturbed by insurgency: unless they could participate in the process, a nationwide consultation could not be achieved.

By mid-1992 the east of the country was more peaceful, partly because a large section of the army had gone off to fight in Rwanda. The north was also more peaceful, and it proved possible to carry out a consultation in these areas. Some 20,000 memoranda were submitted to the Constitutional Commission from all levels of society in a variety of languages, and satisfaction was felt about the extent of popular participation. Elections for a Constituent Assembly to legislate on the new Constitution were scheduled for 28 March 1994. Baganda support for the Museveni government was assured by the decision to allow the Kabaka to be reinstated, though as a purely cultural figurehead without political powers, and Toro also restored its monarchy in this limited form, with Bunyoro to follow suit in 1994 and Ankole divided about doing so. This may prove to be a high-risk policy.

THE DICTIONARY

-A-

ABRAMS, ELLIOTT. Assistant Secretary of State, Bureau of Human Rights and Humanitarian Affairs, United States Government. In 1984 during the second presidency of Milton Obote (q.v.) he testified at a Joint Hearing of the Human Rights and African Affairs Subcommittees of the United States Congress on several African countries, including Uganda. He spoke of a serious deterioration in respect for human rights in Uganda, an army demoralized, underpaid and out of control, looting, raping and murdering in the Luwero Triangle (q.v.), and of disruption of relief efforts by insecurity. At the hearings he suggested a death toll of 200,000, a figure which was debated heatedly in the British press and vigorously disputed by the British government which was involved in training the Uganda National Liberation Army (q.v.). Abrams' estimate was later corroborated and even raised.

ACHOLI. The name of a major ethnic group, the language which they speak, and the area of northern Uganda which they inhabit. Lying north of Lake Kyoga and the Nile (q.v.), Acholi is drier and hotter than southern and central Uganda, and is more sparsely populated. The traditional staple was millet, but because of the area's proneness to drought, cassava has been welcomed as a foodstuff in spite of its poorer taste and nutritional value. Drought-resistant, fast-growing strains of maize are also grown. Cattle, sheep and goats are herded, and most households keep a few chickens. The Acholi hunt with dogs, and the meat caught supplements the diet.

The Acholi are Lwoo speakers (*see* Languages). Their oral history concerns their migration southwards from the original area of dispersal in the Sudan (q.v.). Ronald Atkinson suggests that in the late seventeenth century only a small scattering of Lwoo speakers inhabited the present Acholiland. He believes that the small kingdom states which characterized Acholi society in the eighteenth and nineteenth centuries were modelled on that evolved by the Palwo, a group of the earliest Lwoo to migrate into the area. They were tributary to the kingdom of Bunyoro-Kitara from which their rwot (pl. rwodi, chief) had received regalia, including a drum which was the symbol of authority. The Palwo rwodi were kings in miniature on the Banyoro (q.v.) model. Atkinson believes that the spread of ideas from Bunyoro via the Palwo rather than large-scale migration was responsible for remolding society. As the new type of rwotship spread, and more and more groups of people were drawn within its orbit, so the Lwoo language also spread, and former Sudanic and West Nilotic speakers became Lwoo-ized. Major droughts in the eighteenth century increased friction between different groups of Acholi, and between them and their neighbors, so that discontinuity and upheaval became a way of life.

By the mid-nineteenth century the Acholi began to be affected by Egyptian and Sudanese expansionism and trading. The slave and ivory traders from the north made easy inroads because of the feuds between the different groups, and the Acholi suffered severely during this period. At the same time this trade brought new means of acquiring wealth for some.

Christian missions (q.v.), Western education (q.v.), and colonial administration came to the Acholi relatively late, and by comparison with the more southerly areas of Uganda, Acholi is underdeveloped. The road to Gulu (q.v.), Acholi's administrative center, was only bituminized in the mid-1960s, and the railway was extended to Gulu from Tororo (q.v.) at the beginning of the same decade.

Under President Amin (q.v.) the Acholi fared badly. Many of those in the Uganda Army (q.v.) were massacred as it was feared they would not be loyal to Amin. When President Obote (q.v.) returned to power, Acholi were again recruited into the army and deployed in the Luwero Triangle (q.v.)

against the National Resistance Army (NRA) (q.v.). They suffered heavy casualties, and were accused of atrocities. In 1985 two Acholi generals, Basilio Okello (q.v.) and Tito Okello (q.v.), led an army putsch which overthrew Obote, but their brief period of rule was as brutal as that which had preceded it. When defeated by the NRA, they regrouped in Sudan and returned to raise a rebellion. The despair of the Acholi was demonstrated when a prophetess, Alice Lakwena (q.v.), who offered victory and magical protection from bullets, won a large following, and yet more Acholi suffered in her disastrous adventure. By the beginning of the 1990s little coherent resistance remained, and a start was made on rehabilitation under the guidance of Betty Bigombe (q.v.), though not all banditry had ended.

ACHTE, REVD FR AUGUSTE AMAND AIME (1861–1905). Pioneer Roman Catholic (q.v.) White Father (q.v.) missionary in Toro (q.v.). He arrived in Uganda in 1891 and worked in Kyagwe County, Buganda, and the Sesse Islands. After the Battle of Mengo 1892 (q.v.) he retreated with the defeated Catholic party to Buddu (q.v.). In 1894 he moved westward to found a new mission in Bugangaizi (*see* Lost Counties), and in November he arrived in Toro, the first European missionary to work and settle there. The following year he was recalled to Buganda as Superior of the mission's headquarters at Rubaga (q.v.). After various other postings Achte returned as Superior of the mission in Toro until his death in 1905. In the Toro mission diary Achte recorded what he could learn of the oral history of the Toro kingdom. His account agrees substantially with that given by Mrs Fisher in *Twilight Tales of the Black Baganda* in 1911.

ADOKO, AKENA (1931–). Cousin and close confidant of President Obote (q.v.), head of Obote's intelligence agency, the General Service Unit (q.v.), and President of the Uganda Law Society during Obote's first presidency. The son of Yakobo Adoko (q.v.), he was educated at Nyakasura School (*see* Education) in Toro, at University College, Khartoum, and at Calcutta University. He also studied law in Britain and Social Anthropology in the USA. He is the author of a number of books in verse, among them *Uganda Crisis,* (n.d.), an account of the 1966 Buganda (q.v.) Crisis; *From Obote to Obote,* (1983); *Gold Crisis in Uganda* (1985, a reissue of *Uganda Crisis*); and *The Lea Affair* (1985). He played a major role in the formulation of the Common Man's Charter (q.v.). After the coup of 1971 (q.v.), Adoko went into exile in Tanzania (q.v.), but returned during Obote's second presidency. By the early 1990s he had settled in Britain.

ADOKO, YAKOBO (c. 1897–1982). Rwot of Maruzi, Moroto and Oyam Counties, Lango. His father was Rwot Akaki, head of the Jo Oyima sub-clan, who ruled an area of South Lango prior to the establishment of British rule. Under the British he acted as Jago of Akokoro. In 1911 Adoko served under Daudi Odora (q.v.) and in 1916 was appointed to succeed his father as Jago of Akokoro because Akaki was becoming blind. By this time he had been baptized as a Protestant (q.v.) Christian. Part of his work was concerned with the introduction of cotton as a cash crop and the building of roads. He remained in this post until 1930 when he was appointed Rwot of Maruzi County. Later he was transferred to Moroto and Oyam counties in turn. In 1940 he became Chairman of the Local Native Council and in 1945 there was agitation for him to be given the title of Won Nyaci (literally "owner of the land") but the British insisted on the lesser title of Rwot Adwong (senior chief). Adoko was the first person to hold this title. In 1951 he became Chief Native Judge (Angol Kop) and spent three years in this job. It involved much safari work, and he considered it his most important public office. He retired in 1956. At the end of his life he had no doubt that great benefits had come to the Langi (q.v.) through education, but also that much that was valuable in traditional custom had been lost.

ADRISI, GENERAL MUSTAFA (?–   ). Vice-President of Uganda, 1977–1978. A Muslim Lugbara (q.v.) from West Nile (q.v.) who served for many years as a Sergeant in the King's African Rifles (q.v.) and was known as a strict disciplinarian. He spoke Kakwa, Lugbara and Swahili (*see*

Languages) but no English. In January 1967 when still a Lieutenant he was put in charge of the newly-formed Military Police. In 1974, after the removal from the army of Brigadier Hussain Marella (q.v.), he was made Commander-in-Chief and promoted to the rank of Brigadier General. In 1977 he informed Henry Kyemba (q.v.) that the Anglican Archbishop, Janani Luwum (q.v.), and the two ministers murdered with him, had died in a road traffic accident. In the same year he was removed from his post in command of the army and made Vice-President and Minister of Defence. By early 1978 Amin had fallen out with him. Adrisi then himself became the victim of a faked road traffic accident and was sent for medical treatment in Cairo. While he was there, Amin denounced him for inefficiency and relieved him of responsibility for prison administration. Later in the year a group of Lugbara soldiers is reported to have mutinied in support of him, but to no effect.

AFRICA INLAND MISSION (AIM). This conservative evangelical inter-denominational mission, which also works in Kenya (q.v.) and Tanzania (q.v.), was responsible for Protestant (q.v.) mission work in West Nile (q.v.). The mission began work there in 1918 and, by agreement with the Church Missionary Society (q.v.), only British Anglican missionaries were sent to Uganda (most AIM missionaries are American). The AIM is responsible for establishing the Church of Uganda (q.v.) in West Nile District. It works mainly among the Alur (q.v.) and Lugbara (q.v.). From 1923–1965 the Revd A.E. and Mrs Voller worked at Arua, and were largely responsible for developing Protestant schools in the area. A translation of the Bible into Alur was completed in 1955 and into Lugbara (*see* Languages) in 1964. Dr E. H. Williams began medical work in 1941 and a general and leper hospital was opened at Kuluva near Arua in 1951. By the time of independence this had 62 beds and was treating over 100,000 out-patients a year. The first two Ugandan priests from West Nile were ordained in 1941, and in 1969 the Church of Uganda (q.v.) in West Nile, previously part of the Diocese of Northern Uganda, became the Diocese of West Nile and

Madi. All AIM missionaries were forced to leave by President Amin (q.v.), but some were later able to return. The southern area of their work became the Diocese of Nebbi in 1993.

AFRICAN CHARTER OF HUMAN AND PEOPLE'S RIGHTS. When the Organization of African Unity (OAU) (q.v.) met in Monrovia in September 1979 it heard Godfrey Binaisa (q.v.), then President of Uganda, denounce violations of human rights in Equatorial Guinea and the Central African Republic and take the OAU to task for having done nothing about the presidents of these two states, Macias Ngouema and Jean Bedel Bokassa, and his own predecessor in Uganda, Idi Amin (q.v.). The Assembly responded positively to a motion calling upon it to "organize as soon as possible, in an African capital, a restricted meeting of highly qualified experts to prepare a preliminary draft of the African Charter of Human and People's Rights." The Charter which was the end product of this initiative came into force on 21 October 1986 when it had been signed by a majority of the member states of the OAU, Uganda among them.

There are two main streams of influence on the African Charter. One is the United Nations International Bill of Human Rights, which includes the Universal Declaration of Human Rights and the two Covenants which spell out in more detail first, civil and political rights, and secondly, economic, social and cultural rights. The second is the Universal Declaration on the Rights of Peoples drawn up in Algiers in 1976, an anti-imperialist and "revolutionary" document. Neither the Algiers Declaration nor the African Charter defines "people," and the most important sections of the African Charter are those which define individual human rights and freedoms. The African Charter is significantly weaker than the UN International Bill of Human Rights in that it grants rights "within the law" but without defining what would constitute just laws. It is, nevertheless, an important piece of international standard-setting legislation, and it includes a mechanism for monitoring human rights and examining complaints, and some attempts have been made to use this.

AGRICULTURE. The majority of Ugandans are still largely dependent on subsistence agriculture. Mixed farming is practiced over most of the country, with some livestock—cattle, sheep, goats and chickens—being kept. Most households grow at least a small surplus which they take to a local market or sell on to be taken to one of the towns; many also grow a cash crop. Bicycles and donkeys as well as lorries and vans are sometimes used to transport goods. Pastoralism is still a way of life for most of the Karamojong (q.v.), though their herds have suffered from drought, and there are incentives to settle. The main food crops are plantains (*matooke*) in Buganda (q.v.) and some adjacent areas, sorghum and other forms of millet in the north, cassava (which began by being grown as a famine crop in the drier areas of the north, but is now an accepted part of the diet there), maize, groundnuts, simsim (sesame), sweet potatoes, various kinds of peas and beans, and vegetables including onions, tomatoes, Irish potatoes, and cabbage. A wide range of local leaf vegetables is also eaten. Inter-planting of crops is widespread. Fishing provides a further source of food for those who live around Uganda's many lakes and rivers. A fish-freezing industry is based on Lake Victoria (q.v.). Bee-keeping is a minor industry though honey is still gathered informally from wild bees for household consumption.

Coffee is the country's most valuable cash crop although prices dropped on the world market in the 1980s and marketing and processing suffered as a result of the expulsion (q.v.) of the Asians (q.v.) by President Amin (q.v.). Production in the Luwero Triangle (q.v.), which had been a major coffee-growing area, suffered severely during the second presidency of Milton Obote (q.v.) when this area became the main arena of civil war. Throughout most of the 1970s and 1980s the parastatal organizations responsible for the marketing of cash crops were unable to pay the growers, and coffee bushes were sometimes uprooted or burnt because of this by angry growers. Robusta coffee is grown on small-holdings, and Arabica is cultivated on plantations in the higher and wetter regions near the Ruwenzori Mountains (q.v.) and Mount Elgon (q.v.). Tea is also grown in these two areas, but its production also declined seriously in the 1970s and 1980s. By the beginning of the 1990s efforts were under way to revive both the tea and the coffee processing industries.

Cotton production suffered even more severely. Cotton was uneconomic to grow even before the marketing and ginning system collapsed in the 1970s. Ugandan cotton is short staple, and the yield per acre is comparatively low. In spite of this there was a thriving textile industry at Jinja (q.v.) and cotton seed was used in soap-manufacture and was processed for animal feed. In the 1990s efforts were made to revive the industry.

Two other important cash crops are sugar, which was mainly grown on Asian-owned plantations, and tobacco, produced in the northwest and manufactured into cigarettes for local consumption. The sugar industry collapsed when its owners were expelled in 1972 by President Amin, and by the early 1990s full recovery was still a long way off, though major reinvestment had been made.

Like every other industry, dairying and cattle-ranching suffered during the insecurity of the 1970s and 1980s. Throughout the colonial period, most of Uganda's supplies of dairy products came from Kenya. In the 1960s great efforts were made to establish a dairy industry, and a good beginning had been made. Looting and disease wrought havoc on the dairy herds, and these were only starting to recover in the 1990s. A promising beginning had been made in reestablishing cattle-ranching which had flourished in eastern Ankole (q.v.) and in Bunyoro (q.v.). The Iteso (q.v.) lost most of their cattle to Karamojong (q.v.) raiders in the mid-1980s when the Teso militia, which had offered some protection against cattle raids, was disbanded by the incoming National Resistance Movement (q.v.) because of suspicions of Iteso loyalty. Restocking was a slow process.

The constant rainfall pattern over much of Uganda means that the country is seldom visited by serious famine that cannot be dealt with internally provided there is stability. The 1985 famine in Karamoja might have been contained without the need for foreign aid had it not been for the ravages of the previous decade and the prevailing insecurity.

AHMED BIN IBRAHIM. The first Muslim (*see* Islam) traders from the Swahili coast of what is now Kenya (q.v.) reached Buganda during the reign of Kabaka Suna (*see* Baganda). Ahmed bin Ibrahim is the first whose name is known with certainty. He reproved Suna for demonstrating his power by executing his subjects, and he taught Suna something of Islam, though the Kabaka did not become a Muslim. The date of Ahmed bin Ibrahim's arrival is not certain. He met Emin Pasha (q.v.) and told him he had first visited Buganda in 1260 A.H. (1844 A.D.). Most Baganda writers, e.g., James Miti (q.v.) and Apolo Kagwa (q.v.), put the first arrival of "Arabs" a little later, though they agree that their arrival was during the reign of Suna. Many of the names they record appear to be nicknames given by the Baganda. The arrival of Muslim traders from the coast was momentous: they introduced Islam, literacy, and new trade goods including fire-arms and Arab-style dress which was adopted by the Kabaka and his senior chiefs, and they brought Buganda into touch with the emerging world of the mid-nineteenth century on the eve of European colonial expansion into Africa.

AIDS (ACQUIRED IMMUNE DEFICIENCY SYNDROME). AIDs was first encountered in Uganda from a village on the shores of Lake Victoria (q.v.) near the border with Tanzania (q.v.) in 1982 when 17 deaths were reported in Rakai district. From there it spread rapidly into the area around Masaka (q.v.). It was quickly acknowledged by the government of President Museveni (q.v.) which came to power in 1986, perhaps the more readily because it was easily associated with the behavior of the Uganda National Liberation Army (q.v.) which had widely mistreated and raped the population. In fact its spread seems to be more closely associated with lorry trade routes. Uganda's openness about AIDS was met with large-scale international funding for research, and many theories have been advanced about the extent and nature of the spread of AIDS in Uganda. This has probably benefitted the researchers more than it has benefitted the AIDS sufferers. The disease is popularly known as "Slim" by Ugandans because of the emaciated condition of many sufferers. AIDS is largely an urban phenomenon, and the reports of the disease in rural areas of southwestern Uganda may have been exaggerated, though there are also fears that over the country as a whole it is underreported.

By mid-1990 17,400 cases of AIDS had been reported, and the number of actual AIDS cases was thought to be doubling every six months. Some 1.3 million people were estimated to be HIV positive, including 25,000 children under the age of 15. Some caution needs to be used in accepting these statistics: in a country whose administration and infrastructure was largely destroyed, exact statistics are impossible to come by, and often the tests used were impressionistic. The country's economic decline as a result of years of violence, the social disruption caused by insurgency and the measures taken to counter it, and the ravages suffered by the medical services have facilitated the spread of AIDS: AIDS, in its turn, now impedes economic reconstruction. Some researchers believe that the disease may already have peaked in some areas in certain age groups, but has still to attack others.

The government has mounted a vigorous education campaign to promote safe sex, a popular slogan being "graze carefully." The churches, whose influence is considerable, have preferred to use the slogans "love faithfully" and "zero grazing." In spite of these efforts, rich men (the elites have not escaped infection) are reported to have turned for sexual gratification to young girls whom they believe to be AIDS-free rather than to prostitutes, thus spreading the disease. There is widespread ignorance about AIDS and a sense of fatalism about it. The sale of quack remedies and a pseudo-religious cult supposed to offer a cure have been reported. The number of AIDS-related deaths and consequent requests for leave of absence from work for relatives to attend funerals has caused problems for employers.

ALI, MUSA (1939–   ). From West Nile (q.v.). Previously a teacher, he joined the Uganda Army (q.v.) in 1968 as an officer cadet. He trained in Israel (q.v.) as a paratroop instructor and tank commander, and was appointed to the staff of the Uganda Paratrooper School in 1969, and placed in charge of it in 1971, having been promoted to the rank of

Major. The following year he was made a Colonel. In 1973 he was appointed Minister for Provincial Administration by President Amin (q.v.), and in 1974 he was promoted Brigadier. From 1974–1977 Ali was a member of the shadowy Defence Council (q.v.) through which Amin claimed to rule, holding several different posts, including that of Minister of Finance from 1976–1978. When Amin was overthrown he left the country and joined the Uganda National Rescue Front (q.v.) which opposed President Obote (q.v.). President Museveni (q.v.) brought him into his widely-representative government, appointing him Minister of Youth, Culture and Sports.

ALLIMADI, OTEMA ERICA (1929–   ). Prime Minister of Uganda during the second presidency of Milton Obote (q.v.). An Acholi (q.v.) who was involved in the Uganda National Congress (q.v.) and the Uganda People's Congress (UPC) (q.v.) from the early 1950s when he was employed in a medical dispensary after serving in the army medical corps. After the Mutiny of 1964 (q.v.) Allimadi was appointed Chairman of a Censorship and Correction Board set up to scrutinize military matters and national security. Allimadi went into exile in Tanzania (q.v.) with Obote after the coup of 1971 (q.v.) which brought President Amin (q.v.) to power. He was one of the supporters of Obote who was only admitted to the Moshi Unity Conference (q.v.) in 1979 after an intervention by the Tanzanian Foreign Minister.

In the disputed Elections of 1980 (q.v.) which returned Obote to power, Allimadi stood as a UPC candidate and won, and he became Obote's Prime Minister. After Obote's overthrow Allimadi led an insurgent group in Acholi, the Uganda People's Democratic Movement (q.v.). In 1990, under the policy of national reconciliation instituted by President Museveni (q.v.), he signed a peace accord with the Uganda government. By early 1992 he was reported to be working together with Paul Ssemogerere (q.v.), leader of the Democratic Party (q.v.), to try and form the Uganda Democratic Congress, a broad-based movement which would seek to unite Ugandans and enable them to break loose from their old and bitter political alignments. The National Resistance

Army (NRA) (q.v.) was partially withdrawn from Acholi in order that Allimadi might have a chance of getting the people's support, and for the first time since 1986 Acholi was reported to be quiet apart from sporadic trouble from the rump of the followers of Joseph Kony (q.v.).

ALUR. A group of people speaking a Western Nilotic, Lwoo language closely related to Acholi and Lango (*see* Languages). Today they live north of Lake Albert and on the east bank of the Nile (q.v.) in the administrative district of Nebbi. They are also found in adjacent territory in Zaire (q.v.). Just to the south live the Jonam (q.v.), a closely related group. The Alur formerly lived further to the east, but their land was encroached on by the Acholi (q.v.) and by the creation of the Murchison, now Kabarega, National Park. They were traditionally organized into small chiefdoms, and by the late nineteenth century many of these owed allegiance to the Mukama of Bunyoro (q.v.).

AMIN, IDI, DADA (?–   ). President of Uganda, 1971–1979. The name "Dada" has given rise to much speculation and earned him the nickname of "Big Daddy" (but cf. Ould Daddah, President of Mauretania; Dada/Daddah is a Muslim name). Amin was probably born at Koboko in West Nile (q.v.) and was brought up in a Nubian (q.v.) army community. In 1946 he joined the King's African Rifles (q.v.) as an assistant cook, but his splendid physique made him a welcome recruit into the army proper, and he gained a reputation as a heavy-weight boxer and Rugby football player. He claimed to have fought in Burma during World War II, but downplayed his service in Kenya (q.v.) against the Mau Mau in the 1950s. In 1962 he was responsible for a massacre in northern Kenya. As he was one of only two Ugandan commissioned officers in the army, it was decided that action against him might be politically disastrous on the eve of independence. President Obote (q.v.) later admitted that he made a serious mistake in allowing him to be reprimanded rather than court-martialed. Amin was swiftly promoted. He was implicated in the Gold Scandal (q.v.) and led the army in the attack on the Kabaka's palace in the Battle of Mengo

1966 (q.v.). He initially fled in terror at the time of the attempted assassination (q.v.) of Obote in December 1969 instead of going to his aid.

In January 1971 he mounted a coup (q.v.) against Obote during the Commonwealth Heads of Government Meeting in Singapore, because he knew that he was about to be brought to book for overspending on the army, and for his involvement in the murder of Brigadier Pierino Okoya (q.v.) who had accused him of desertion at the time of the assassination attempt. He also knew that it was about to be revealed that at a time when Obote was moving to the left and allying himself with President Numeiri of Sudan (q.v.), he had assisted the Anya Nya (q.v.) rebels in Sudan. After the coup he moved quickly to eliminate his opponents in the army and then expanded the army with men from West Nile and later from Sudan who were likely to be loyal to him.

The coup was welcomed by the Conservative Government in Britain (q.v.) which was angered by Obote's denunciation of their decision to allow arms sales to South Africa, and when Amin visited Britain later in 1971 he received promises of a considerable amount of aid. He won over the Baganda (q.v.) by permitting the body of Kabaka Mutesa II (q.v.) to be returned from Britain for reburial. He appointed a cabinet of professionals rather than politicians, and lifted restrictions on travel. Other popular moves included the abandonment of Obote's socialist policies and the release of political prisoners. But his brutality quickly became apparent as his opponents, particularly those in the army, were massacred and people began to disappear. Early in 1972 he came under the influence of Col. Gadafi (q.v.), President of Libya (q.v.), and expelled the Israelis (q.v.) who had been giving him military assistance. The expulsion (q.v.) of the Asians (q.v.) later that year was welcomed by many Ugandans, and Amin's anti-imperialist rhetoric was acclaimed by numbers of Arab states and African nationalists who admired him for defying Western opinion. Besides, there were plenty of Ugandans who profited from his rule and took advantage of the anarchy which came to characterize it. Some exaggerated accounts of his brutalities were easily refuted, and made it more difficult to get the truth accepted. An attempted invasion (q.v.) in late

1972 by Obote supporters went off half-cocked and was easily defeated. This marked a high point in Amin's popularity among Ugandans, though the public executions of alleged guerrillas which followed revolted the more thoughtful section of the populace.

Amin promoted those who had helped him in the coup, and soon replaced civilians in government by soldiers, some of whom quickly fell out of favor. They were replaced by increasingly illiterate soldiers. Civil servants and professionals struggled to keep the country's institutions functioning while the modern sector of the economy crumbled as the so-called "economic war" (q.v.), in which the Asians were despoiled, proved an economic disaster. Pandering to the army consumed most of the budget.

Not all the violence of the Amin years was political or ordered by Amin himself, but it was his responsibility, arising out of his total failure to discipline the army. People with grudges soon learnt that informing on their enemies was an easy way of getting rid of them. There was also systematic state violence carried out by the Military Police, the Public Safety Unit (q.v.) and the dreaded State Research Bureau (q.v.). Meanwhile the army was steadily purged of non-Muslims and southerners as Amin tried to ensure its loyalty to himself.

In July 1975 Uganda hosted the Organization of African Unity (OAU) (q.v.) Summit Conference: in 1971 Kampala (q.v.) had been rejeced as its venue because of Amin's takeover. In line with normal OAU practice Amin, as President of the host government, became Chairman for that session and for the year ahead. His preoccupation with this post and with foreign policy took the heat off his own subjects for a while. He appointed himself a Field-Marshal, and in June 1976, Life-President. He also awarded himself a series of newly-invented military decorations. In February 1976 there was a major confrontation with Kenya (q.v.), a portion of which Amin claimed as part of "Greater Uganda" (q.v.). In July the Entebbe Raid (q.v.) left both him and his army totally discredited, and was particularly humiliating as it occurred during the 1976 OAU Summit. The Makerere Incident (q.v.) followed on 3–5 August. On 17 February

1977 Anglican Archbishop Janani Luwum (q.v.) was murdered together with two government ministers. In June 1977 it was clear to Amin that he would not be welcome at the Commonwealth Heads of Government Meeting to be held in London. The British-born Bob Scanlon, who was working in Uganda, was accused of spying and was killed, apparently in retaliation for this rebuff to Amin, and Britain cut its last diplomatic links with Uganda.

The beginning of the end came in October 1978 when Amin sent his army against Tanzania (q.v.), falsely claiming to have been attacked. After expelling Amin's troops, the Tanzanian army, accompanied by a small contingent of Ugandans, fought their way up the west of Lake Victoria (q.v.) and drove Amin's army out of Kampala (q.v.) in April, and then out of the rest of the country. Since his overthrow Amin has lived in Jeddah, Saudi Arabia, except for a brief period in January 1989 when he appeared in Zaire (q.v.), to that country's embarrassment, and Saudi Arabia readmitted him only with reluctance.

Amin had a kind of intelligence but he was undisciplined and uneducated, and appeared to lack any moral sense. Even his enemies said he possessed a commanding presence and could be charming, but he would fly into ungovernable rages. He did not understand either the process of government or the functioning of civil society. He made much play of being a Muslim (*see* Islam), but made little effort to practice the Muslim ethical code, and frequently offended against its norms, drinking to excess, for example, and ordering public executions on a Friday in Ramadan, as well as ruling through terror.

AMNESTY INTERNATIONAL. A London-based, international human rights organization, started in 1961 by a lawyer, Peter Benenson, who asked for an amnesty for all prisoners of conscience. By 1971, the year when President Amin (q.v.) came to power in a coup (q.v.), it had developed a capacity to monitor human rights abuses in many countries. Because of the nature of Amin's tyranny, Amnesty was not able to employ its usual tactic of getting groups of members to "adopt" prisoners of conscience because this would have endangered their families, but it reported on the general situation in the country, seldom mentioning names of people still alive but endangered.

When Tanzania (q.v.) allowed its troops not just to remove Ugandan troops from the Kagera Salient (q.v.) which they had invaded, but to go on and remove Amin from power, criticism of their action by other African countries was muted by reason of Amnesty's reports which were accepted as being impartial and accurate. In July 1979 Amnesty published a briefing paper for the British Parliament entitled *Tools of Repression for the Likes of Amin?* which raised questions about the export of repressive technology and material capable of military use to repressive regimes such as that of Idi Amin.

Because of Amnesty's work for Uganda during the Amin regime, President Obote (q.v.) permitted the organization to visit Uganda in January 1982. Amnesty followed up the visit by sending a memorandum to Obote detailing continued violations of human rights in Uganda including large-scale arrests of political opponents, the employment by the army of detention without charge or trial, systematic torture and ill-treatment of such prisoners, "disappearances" and deaths in prison, extrajudicial execution of civilians by the army, and widespread disregard of the rights of detainees. The Uganda High Commissioner in London, Shafiq Arain (q.v.), sent a long and rambling reply denying virtually everything. A further memorandum from Amnesty elicited no response, so in April 1983 Amnesty published the whole correspondence, as it had warned the Uganda government it would do. The documents showed that there had been little improvement in human rights since Amin's overthrow.

The most disturbing report on Uganda (and perhaps one of Amnesty's most shocking ever) was published in June 1985 and was entitled *Uganda Six Years After Amin: Torture . . . Killings . . . Disppearances . . . .* This at last had the effect of making the British government take seriously what was happening. Britain (q.v.) now warned the Uganda government that aid would be reconsidered unless there were real improvements in the human rights record.

President Museveni (q.v.) came to power with a pledge to

restore respect for human rights. When he found himself faced with insurgency and the army had to be hastily reinforced with men from former armies who had not been properly retrained, there was a breakdown of discipline in combat. Amnesty's report, *Uganda, the Human Rights Record 1986–1989,* was a substantial document, and disquieting, though it noted that important safeguards had been introduced, and that the army was more subject to the rule of law. It also showed that dialogue had become possible between Amnesty and the Uganda government, and a kind of working relationship embarked upon. Among the improvements resulting from Amnesty's work was the government's banning of the use of a method of torture known as *kandooya* (q.v.) or three-point-tying, when a person's arms were tied together behind the back at the wrists and elbows in such a way as to impede circulation in the arms. This sometimes led to permanent injury to the arms requiring amputation, and damage to the chest muscles.

Accurate reporting and impartiality have made it impossible for Uganda to ignore Amnesty International's reports. Greater freedom of the press under Museveni's government enabled Ugandan journalists to reproduce Amnesty material on Uganda and to investigate it and publish their findings. But by 1992 Museveni's attitude had apparently changed. In October 1992 a new report concentrated on the Uganda government's inability or unwillingness to bring to book those who had perpetrated human rights abuses. It listed incidents which the government had promised to enquire into, and stated that in hardly any cases had the findings of the enquiries been published or those responsible for wrongdoing been brought to justice. Human rights abuses had decreased, however, largely because much of the fighting in the north and east had died down.

ANGLICAN CHURCH. The Anglican Communion is a worldwide association of churches which have grown out of the mission work of the Church of England, and the need to provide pastoral care for Anglicans who emigrated to or worked in other parts of the world, particularly the British Empire/Commonwealth. The church in England broke away from the control of the Papacy during the reign of Henry VIII. It retained the episcopacy though it reformed its liturgy, and used the vernacular in worship, as well as having the scriptures translated into English. Its missionaries have followed this precedent and the liturgy and scriptures have been translated into local languages.

The full title of the autonomous Province of the Anglican Communion in Uganda is The Church of the Province of Uganda. It is commonly known as the Church of Uganda (q.v.), and its members in Uganda are frequently referred to simply as Protestants (q.v.) because between 1877, when the first Christian missionaries arrived, and 1926, Anglicans and Roman Catholics (q.v.) were the only two Christian denominations represented in the country. In 1926 the Seventh Day Adventists (q.v.) began a mission in Uganda, but it was not until after independence that other Protestant denominations entered Uganda.

There is considerable variety in Anglican worship. Those missionaries of the Church Missionary Society (CMS) (q.v.) who came to Uganda were of the evangelical, "low" church persuasion who set less store on sacrament, tradition and ritual than the "high" church mission which worked in parts of neighboring Tanzania (q.v.). The CMS emphasized the importance of preaching, of the Bible and of a personal conversion experience.

Two institutions help to keep the disparate Provinces of the Anglican Communion together: the Lambeth Conference, held every ten years in England, to which all bishops are invited, and the Anglican Consultative Council which has its headquarters in England, but exists to strengthen links between the different Provinces.

ANGLO-GERMAN TREATY (1890). Prior to this the dividing line between the British and German spheres of influence in East Africa had only been agreed as far as the eastern shore of Lake Victoria (q.v.), and there was doubt as to whether Britain would be able to maintain its claim to Uganda. Early in 1890 Carl Peters (q.v.) persuaded Kabaka Mwanga (q.v.) to sign a treaty which strengthened German claims to sovereignty. But by the time he was back in Europe the matter had been settled. It was agreed that from the point on the eastern shore of Lake Victoria the demarcation line would go westward across the lake to the Congo border along the line of latitude 1° south. Britain gave up any pretence to claims of land southwest of Lake Victoria, and ceded to Germany the North Sea island of Heligoland.

ANKOLE *see* BANYANKOLE

ANKOLE AGREEMENT (1901). This did not give Ankole (q.v.) the sort of privileges which Buganda had won the previous year. The Agreement defined the boundaries of Ankole, including within it several semi-independent chiefdoms. It acknowledged the rights of the Mugabe and senior chiefs to nominate their successors. However, because they lacked the education of the Baganda (q.v.) chiefs, Baganda agents were placed with them to assist them to comply with Protectorate requirements, and this was increasingly resented. If the Mugabe and his chiefs failed to abide by the terms of the Agreement, then the Protectorate government reserved the right to remove them from office. The land settlement was different from that in Buganda: all land was declared to be Crown Land, and the Mugabe and senior chiefs held their land directly from the Crown in freehold. No other freehold grants of land were made. Provision was made for introducing taxation. Finally, Ankole was to be subject "to the same laws and regulations as are generally in force throughout the Uganda Protectorate." When the Agreement was presented to the assembled chiefs for signature the only text was in English. The Ankole chiefs had to rely on an ex tempore translation by the Church Missionary Society (q.v.) missionary, J. J. Willis, whose knowledge of the language was still elementary, and two Baganda interpreters: some of the chiefs will have known some Luganda (*see* Languages). The Agreement was temporarily suspended after the murder of Galt (q.v.).

ANYA NYA. The name for Southern Sudanese resistance fighters during the first Civil War in Sudan (q.v.) from 1956–1972. From 1969 onwards they received increased supplies of arms from Israel (q.v.) via Uganda. General Amin (q.v.) was sympathetic towards them, and when President Obote (q.v.) aligned himself with President Nimeiri of Sudan in a leftist alliance, Amin continued to support the Anya Nya. After the coup (q.v.) in 1971 which brought Amin to power, he permitted aid for them to be sent more openly through Uganda. In March 1972 Col. Gadafi (q.v.) of Libya (q.v.) persuaded Amin to expel the Israelis, but by this time a peace had been concluded in Sudan. Amin increasingly recruited Southern Sudanese and ex-Anya Nya into the army (q.v.) where they acquired a reputation for particular brutality.

ARAIN, SHAFIQ (1938–). A wealthy Asian businessman who was active in nationalist politics before independence and a supporter of President Obote (q.v.). He helped to fund Obote's Uganda People's Congress (UPC) (q.v.) at the time of the disputed Elections of 1980 (q.v.) which brought Obote back to power. As a reward for his services, Shafiq Arain was made Uganda High Commissioner in London, and a member of the cabinet. He defended Obote and the UPC government with considerable diplomatic skill against the charges of massive human rights abuses documented by Amnesty International (q.v.). He successfully persuaded the British government that Obote was genuinely concerned to end human rights abuses and indiscipline in the army (q.v.), and that the situation was improving. He denied the allegations of horrific torture published by Amnesty International in 1985. When Obote fell from power and Amnesty's claims were vindicated, Arain was replaced. He was given a farewell party by the British Foreign and Commonwealth Office before retiring to a house he owned near London.

ARMY *see* UGANDA ARMY

ARUA. The district headquarters of West Nile (q.v.) District until 1974 when this was divided in two. Arua became headquarters of North and Central Nile, the district being renamed Arua in 1979. It is a center for marketing cotton and tobacco, the two main cash crops of the area. The Africa Inland Mission (q.v.) opened work in Arua in 1918, and started

Kuluva Hospital nearby. The Verona Fathers (q.v.) were responsible for starting Catholic missionary work in the town. During the second presidency of Milton Obote (q.v.) the town suffered severely in the fighting between the Ugandan National Liberation Army (q.v.) and various groups resisting Obote's rule.

ARUBE, CHARLES (?–1974). Brigadier and Army Chief of Staff. A Christian officer from the same tribe as President Amin (q.v.), the Kakwa (q.v.) of West Nile (q.v.). He attended a military training course in Moscow. In March 1974 the Mechanised Battalion of the Uganda Army (q.v.) under its commander, Lt Col. Elly Aseni (also a Christian Kakwa), and with the support of Charles Arube, attacked the headquarters of the Military Police at Makindye near Kampala (q.v.) which was under the command of the hated Hussain Marella (q.v.). The attack inflicted a good deal of damage on the barracks at Makindye and there was a number of casualties, but it failed in its immediate objective, which was to break the power of the Military Police. Arube himself was severely wounded and died on the operating table. The military report on his death said the gunshot wounds were self-inflicted: the medical report was ambigious. Marella was relieved of his post some time later. President Amin found he had to tread warily in dealing with the aftermath of this rebellion. Aseni was tried by a military tribunal which decided there was no case against him and freed him. He was later sent as Ambassador to Moscow.

ASIANS. The Asians in Uganda probably numbered around 77,500 at the time of independence in 1962, and increased slightly through the birth rate until the late 1960s. By 1972, when they were expelled, the number had dropped to probably around 50,000 as those with British passports emigrated, and others who were able to do so went abroad.

A few Indians were brought to Uganda in the 1890s as soldiers but the main immigration was of skilled workers and entrepreneurs who occupied an uncomfortable position between the British colonial masters and the indigenous African population. The story that the Indian workers brought in to build the railway (q.v.) stayed to form the nucleus of the later Asian community is not correct. Almost all the Asian immigrants were town dwellers, and they were well-represented in the import-export trade, manufacturing, engineering, and the construction industry. Because they had better access to education (q.v.) than the African population, they were also well-represented in the professions. They held important though not top level posts in the civil service. The nearest any of them came to being involved in agriculture (q.v.) was that Uganda's very important sugar estates and refineries were Asian-owned by the Mehta (q.v.) and Madhvani (q.v.) families.

The Asians were not in any way a homogeneous group. The only unifying factor was that most came from either the Punjab or Gujurat. Among them were Hindus (the largest group), Shi'a Muslims (mainly of the Ismaili sect whose leader is the Aga Khan, but also Dawoodi Bohoras and Ithna Asheris, these last being the same sect as the majority of Iranian Muslims) (*see* Islam), Sikhs, Roman Catholics from Goa whose ancestors were converted by St Francis Xavier, and a few other Indian Christians from the ancient churches which claim St Thomas as their founder, as well as a small number of Jains and Parsees (or Zoroastrians). The places of worship of all these diverse groups were well-known Kampala (q.v.) landmarks.

As is the case with all immigrant communities, their religious and cultural traditions were an important part of their identity, and they strove to retain them. Colonial society encouraged the formation of ghettoes, and fostered racial exclusiveness. Ugandan Africans were apt to blame the Asians for this, though there is little evidence that Africans really wished them to integrate. What was resented was their success in trade, commerce and the professions, and their resultant wealth. They were a target of envy in the way that successful immigrant communities always are, and it sometimes suited politicians, and particularly Idi Amin (q.v.), to play on this. Among the most successful Asian families were the Madhvanis and the Mehtas. A substantial proportion of the staff of Makerere University (q.v.) were Asians. Goans had a reputation for financial probity, and made a virtual corner for themselves as accountants and bookkeepers. Sikhs abounded in the building industry and associated trades. The most Westernized group after the Goans was the Ismaili community whose leader, the Aga Khan, is their living Imam and able to interpret the Qur'an for them, and who encouraged modernization and cooperation with others. He used his enormous wealth to fund the welfare initiatives of any group of Muslims on a shilling for shilling basis, a way of encouraging the Ismailis to make common cause with their fellow Muslims of whatever sect.

At independence the Asians had several possibilities with regard to nationality. The Indian government encouraged them to take out Ugandan citizenship, an option which was open to them during a specified period after independence. Others had the possibility of retaining or acquiring British or Indian citizenship. Many hesitated before making up their minds, and this was interpreted as a lack of confidence in Uganda. Some families tried to keep all their options open by different family members having different citizenships. The Asians did not have the possibility available to the British of taking Ugandan citizenship while retaining the right to revert to their British citizenship should the need arise. Nevertheless, some who took Ugandan citizenship failed to renounce their British citizenship as they were required to do, hoping to protect themselves thus, but instead they suddenly found themselves deprived of their Ugandan citizenship. Discussions about these potentially stateless people were underway at the time of the Amin coup (q.v.). After 1968, when new nationality legislation was enacted in Britain (q.v.), those with British passports were only very slowly admitted to settle, and this tardiness angered the Ugandan government. In 1970 an agreement was reached to speed up the acceptance of those Asians with a right to settle in Britain, but Britain then failed to implement this, which seems to have precipitated the eventual expulsion (q.v.) of the Asians by Amin.

The expulsion of the Asians should not have been entirely unexpected. Grumbling about the Asians had surfaced from time to time throughout the colonial period. By the time of their expulsion in 1972 a vigorous campaign for state assistance to and protection of African businessmen had been conducted for over a year, focusing on this long-standing grievance, and led by the Governor of the Bank of Uganda, Joseph Mubiru, businessman Sam Ssebagereka, and E.K.K. Ntende. They called for state protection against the ''monopoly and malicious competition practised by non-Africans,'' which referred, of course, to all foreign business ownership, not just Asian trade domination. This campaign was accompanied by calls for the Asians to become more fully integrated into Ugandan society. In response, Amin, still insecure, and wishing to consolidate his support, announced a review of Asian citizenship in August 1971, and a census in October.

Not until 4 August 1972 did Amin move against the Asians, in the first place setting a 90-day deadline for all British Asians to leave the country. When this proved popular, he ordered the expulsion of all other non-citizen Asians. Britain was eventually forced to accept all Asians who had British citizenship, whether they were heads of families or not. The Conservative Government of Prime Minister Edward Heath won undeserved praise for admitting just 27,000 of its own citizens whom it was in any case obliged to admit under international law.

Amin now claimed that he had won what he called the ''economic war'' (q.v.). The modern sector of the Ugandan economy has never recovered from the expulsion of the Asians.

ASTLES, BOB (1921–). A Briton who went to Uganda in 1949 at the time of the Bataka Riots (q.v.). He claims to have gone on British Foreign Office business. In 1952 he was posted to Uganda to the Special Branch of the Police. At independence the Uganda government took him on and he married a Ugandan. His Ugandan citizenship, which involved renouncing his British citizenship, was given him by President Amin (q.v.), as was his rank of ''major'': he denies ever having been a member of the Ugandan armed forces. Astles made himself useful to the independent government and was able to buy several houses. He holds a pilot's licence, and is credited by some sources with having flown the plane which brought the Congolese gold (*see* Gold Scandal) into Uganda in 1964. Under President Amin he rose to some prominence. According to the *New Scientist* of 10 May 1979 he helped to set up the notorious State Research Bureau (q.v.). He is said to have been involved in the publicity stunt during the meeting of the Organization of African Unity (q.v.) in 1975 when Amin was carried shoulder-high by four Europeans. On 18 February 1977, the morning after Archbishop Luwum (q.v.) had been shot, a newsman in Nairobi said he had been phoned by Astles who told him that important news was pending (the announcement of Luwum's death) and to reassure him that the Archbishop had been "gently treated." Towards the end of Amin's rule it was reported in the press that he had appointed Astles to run an anti-smuggling unit on Lake Victoria (q.v.). This group was accused by Captain Mzee Farouk of the State Research Bureau of killing many able young Ugandans. Reports in the Kenyan press linked Astles in some way with the bombing of a plane carrying British and Kenyan businessmen including the former Kenyan Agriculture Minister and advisor to President Jomo Kenyatta, Bruce Mackenzie, from Nairobi to Uganda in 1978. The pilot and three passengers were all killed.

When Amin was overthrown Astles fled to Kenya (q.v.) and was apparently astonished to find himself arrested and accused in the press of being associated with the murder of Bruce Mackenzie. He was extradited to Uganda after only minimal legal procedures, and was held in Luzira Prison and accused of various crimes including robbery and the murder of a fisherman, but the court hearing was delayed repeatedly. He was finally brought to court in October 1981 and acquitted on the murder charge but returned to prison for over five years. Other possible charges were threatened, and when these did not materialize, he was held under a detention order. In late 1985 after President Obote (q.v.) had been driven from power he was released from Luzira Prison after being forced to renounce his Ugandan citizenship and was deported to Britain. When he first came to Britain he defended Amin; later he changed his stance and denounced him; and finally he claimed that Amin was no worse than Obote during the latter's second presidency. He has only occasionally given interviews, and has revealed virtually nothing of what he must know. He has always protested his innocence of any crime. In 1992 he threatened to sue the BBC for libelling him by allowing him to be called a murderer in an interview. The case was settled out of court.

ATTEMPTED ASSASSINATION OF PRESIDENT OBOTE. In December 1969 an attempt was made on Obote's (q.v.) life at a Uganda People's Congress (q.v.) rally in Lugogo Stadium in Kampala (q.v.). Obote was shot in the mouth, but not seriously injured, and was rushed by the Uganda Army (q.v.) to Mulago Hospital. As many as 135 corpses were reported along the roads between Lugogo Stadium and Mulago Hospital, apparently the luckless victims of panicky soldiers. According to a journalist who was present, the shot came from a section of the stadium reserved for the military; others claimed that the Baganda (q.v.) were responsible for the attempt. No one was ever brought to book for the crime.

General Amin (q.v.) heard of the attempt at home, and after some hours when he could not be located, arrived at Mulago Hospital with cuts and abrasions for which he asked treatment. It was alleged that he received these when temporarily fleeing. In the immediate aftermath of the coup (q.v.), the state of emergency which had lasted since 1966 in Buganda was extended to the whole country, permission was necessary to travel any distance, and road-blocks manned by nervous soldiers sprang up at intervals along all the main roads outside the capital. Obote became increasingly anxious for his personal safety, and instead of crowds being called out to cheer him when he travelled, the roads were cleared.

AWICH, RWOT (CHIEF) IBURAHIM (c. 1860–1946). Head of the powerful Payira clan of Acholi (q.v.). He was the fourth son of Rwotcamo (q.v.) who claimed descent through 16 named generations from a man of the Shilluk of Sudan (q.v.) who left home with his people and settled on Kilak Hill in Acholi. Labongo, a member of this clan, was the common ancestor of both the Babito (q.v.), the ruling dynasty of Bunyoro (q.v.), and of Rwotcamo of Payira. Rwotcamo met Sir Samuel Baker (q.v.) and Emin Pasha (q.v.) and Awich was probably with him on both occasions. Rwotcamo was killed in 1887, and Awich was chosen to succeed his father in the year of the locusts, 1888. By this date his father's relations with Europeans had become embittered as a result of high-handed treatment he had experienced, and Awich's attitudes were informed by this. The Mukama Kabarega (q.v.) of Bunyoro sent him chiefly insignia in recognition of the bonds between the two clans.

In the year following his accession he joined forces with the Rwot of Labongo in a successful raid against the Padibe, and won a reputation as a warrior, but he failed to win back the royal drum which had been stolen. In 1899 he attacked the Paibona who were restless under his rule and made overtures to the British colonial officer, Major Delmé-Radcliffe, who arrived to find the villages of the Paibona destroyed, and Awich beyond his reach.

In 1893 the British had inflicted a defeat on Kabarega, some of whose followers had fled to Acholi. Kabarega himself had temporarily taken shelter with Awich. In 1899 Delmé-Radcliffe ordered Awich to hand over those who had taken sanctuary, but Awich refused to do so since to betray a person to whom one had given sanctuary would be a fundamental breach of honor. For two years he evaded capture. Eventually he was caught, tried, found guilty, and imprisoned for two years. However, in 1902 Awich was reinstated as Rwot of Payira. On his release he traveled to Acholi via Hoima in Bunyoro where he met the Revd A.B. Lloyd, a missionary of the Church Missionary Society (q.v.), and made his first contact with Christian teaching; on his return to Acholi he asked for Christian teachers to be sent. In 1904 Lloyd himself visited Acholi and founded a mission on Keyo Hill some miles west of the modern Gulu (q.v.). A government station was opened shortly afterwards, but neither mission nor government remained long. The people were hostile and the time did not seem ripe.

The next clash with the administration came in 1917 over a murdered Arab. Awich was accused of possessing a gun taken from the Arabs and was taken to court. He attacked one of the witnesses against him and the European official who went to the witness's aid. He was deprived of his chieftaincy, taken off to Kampala (q.v.) for trial, and served an eight-year prison sentence. Although he was allowed to return to Acholi, he was made to live at the administration headquarters at Kitgum in case his presence among the Payira caused them to rise up in his defense. Only in 1938 was he allowed to return to Laguti.

Awich was well-respected by the Acholi as a chief. He controlled a large area of Acholi through a network of small chieftainships over the Payira clan, and he exercised authority over a still wider area than Payira. He was trusted and popular. Although he was responsible for inviting Christian missionaries to Acholi, his clashes with the British made him reluctant to accept the new faith, and he was not baptized until 1943. He is remembered as a powerful chief who did not easily accept colonial restrictions on his power, and who operated according to traditional codes of honor.

-B-

BAAMBA. A Bantu-speaking ethnic group living in the administrative division of Bundibugyo on the border with Zaire (q.v.). The area they occupy is referred to as Bwamba. Much of Bwamba is low-lying, less than 3,000 feet (800 meters). In the north it runs down to the shores of Lake Albert, and in the southeast it rises into the foothills of the Ruwenzori Mountains (q.v.). Much of the area is forested, and divided into steep ridges by streams flowing down from the mountains into the Semliki River. Most of the people live on the somewhat flattened tops of the ridges. Rainfall is heavy and the soils are fertile, so agriculture prospers. The population is concentrated around the small town of Bundibugyo whose only link with the rest of Uganda is via a road round the northern end of the Ruwenzori which is so narrow as it winds its way around the contour line that traffic can only enter a single-track section from the east before midday, and from the west after two p.m.

Most Baamba speak either Kwamba (which is closely related to a Zairean language, Bira) or Lubwezi (closely related to Rutoro, the language of the Batoro [q.v.]) (*see* Languages). Until fairly recently the Baamba lived in compact villages of between 50 and a few hundred inhabitants whose men-folk were all members of the same patrilineage. The dwellings were neatly aligned along a wide street with an open-sided central meeting-place for the men. The Baamba were without chiefs, but each village was a political unit, and villages formed alliances with one another. After a stop had been put to the inter-village fighting which used to be characteristic of Bwamba, most of these villages have broken up, and extended family units now live scattered on the land they cultivate as is the pattern throughout most of rural Uganda.

In the past Bwamba was tributary first to Bunyoro (q.v.) and then to Toro (q.v.). It was reannexed to Bunyoro by Mukama Kabarega (q.v.) in the late nineteenth century. No attempt was made to administer the area until the turn of the century. Then it was reclaimed by Toro when that kingdom was revived under British rule. Petty chiefs were appointed, but not until after World War I was taxation collected from Bwamba. The construction of a road round the northern end of the Ruwenzori after World War II to the small town of Bundibugyo opened up Bwamba to the outside world, and Batoro moved in, purchased land from the Baamba, and established coffee plantations. Bundibugyo became a market town and district capital.

The Baamba came to resent the insensitive manner of Toro's rule, and they joined with their Bakonjo (q.v.) neighbors in demanding to be placed in a separate adminstrative district. Matters came to a head in 1962 when the representatives of both the Baamba and the Bakonjo walked out of the local Toro parliament in support of their claim. As disaffection grew, the parts of Toro inhabited by the Baamba and the Bakonjo were declared a disturbed area at the beginning of 1963, and the Uganda Army (q.v.) was sent in and drove many members of the secessionist Ruwenzururu (q.v.) movement across the border into Zaire. It was some time before a further enquiry and action by the central government to allow the Baamba and the Bakonjo a greater measure of control over their own affairs, more or less successfully defused the movement. The Bakonjo were identified to a greater extent with the emerging Ruwenzururu movement than were the Baamba, and its leader, Isaya Mukirane, was a Mutoro. In 1966 Baamba and Bundibugyo were at the epicenter of an earthquake which registered 6.5 on the Richter scale and which was felt as far away as Kampala (q.v.). The road round the north of the mountains was blocked for days by landslides, and aid was held up. Most casualties were among people whose houses were built of modern materials: traditional houses collapsed without causing too much injury. The death toll is unknown.

BABIIHA, JOHN (1913–). Vice-President of Uganda, 1967–1971. In 1954 he became the first elected member from Toro (q.v.) of the Legislative Council (q.v.) where he worked to protect Toro's interests. In 1957 he opposed the Uganda National Congress (q.v.) because it failed to take account of non-Baganda when calling for self-government. In 1960 he became National Chairman of the newly-established Uganda People's Congress (UPC) (q.v.) led by Milton Obote (q.v.), a party which aimed to be genuinely national, but which was rejected by the Baganda (q.v.). He submitted a memorandum to the Wild Committee which tried to set out a model for Uganda at independence which avoided both a unitary state in which the kingdoms lost their identity and privileges, and a federal state in which Buganda was unduly privileged. In 1961 he shared the deep dissatisfaction of Toro with the Local Administrations Bill which gave fewer powers to the kingdoms than had been expected. As a UPC member he found himself torn between loyalty to the Toro Kingdom Government and to the UPC which was working to ensure that an independent central government would have adequate powers over the regions, particularly over Buganda, but also over the other kingdoms with their pretensions to a semi-federal status.

In 1966 when Obote arrogated to himself the powers of Head of State and Kabaka Mutesa (q.v.), President of Uganda since independence, fled the country, John Babiiha became Vice-President, and hence party to Obote's dissolution of the kingdoms. In 1970 he narrowly escaped assassination when his car was mistaken for that of Obote, and he was shot at by gunmen who were never captured. Babiiha's political life ended with the seizure of power by Idi Amin (q.v.) in 1971.

BABITO. A dynasty of Bakama of Bunyoro (q.v.) which succeeded the legendary dynasties of the Batembuzi (q.v.) and the Bacwezi (q.v.). With the Babito we begin to reach the realms of history. According to the Bacwezi legends, the Babito came from the north and from beyond the Nile (q.v.), and most historians agree that they are of Nilotic origin, and had to be initiated into the cattle-culture of Bunyoro. They are said to have taken over the royal drums and other regalia of the Bacwezi. When first the traditions were written down in the early twentieth century, some 15 or 16 names of Babito rulers were given. In the middle of the century when the ruling Mukama, Sir Tito Winyi (q.v.), recorded the traditions, ten further names were added to the earlier part of the list, and this is now the standard version.

The European travelers Speke (q.v.), Grant and Baker (q.v.) all met Mukama Kamurasi, who died in 1869 and was succeeded by Kabarega (q.v.). When Kabarega was captured and exiled to the Seychelles by the British in 1899 he was temporarily succeeded by Kitehimbwa, but the British found him unsatisfactory, and replaced him with Andereya Duhaga (q.v.). He died in 1924 and was succeeded by Tito Winyi (q.v.). The kingdoms were abolished by President Obote (q.v.) in 1967, but in 1993 President Museveni (q.v.) allowed the restoration of the Mukama as a cultural, not political, head of the Banyoro. Solomon Iguru was to be installed as Mukama in 1994.

BACWEZI. The short dynasty of semi-mythical kings of Bunyoro (q.v.) linking the Batembuzi (q.v.), who are believed to be descended from the gods, with the Babito (q.v.), the present dynasty. Mukama Isimbwa, the first of the Bacwezi, is supposed to have been born in the underworld, and his son or grandson, Mukama Wamara, having named the Babito as his successors, is said to have disappeared into the lake which bears his name, whence the Bacwezi are still believed to influence people and events. They are the objects of a spirit-mediumship cult concerned with the well-being of Bunyoro, and the introduction of iron-working is linked with them.

BAGANDA. The inhabitants of Buganda and the most numerous of the Bantu-speaking peoples of Uganda. Their language is Luganda (*see* Languages). They inhabit the area of central Uganda lying in an arc round the northwest corner of Lake Victoria (q.v.). In 1967, when President Obote (q.v.) abolished the kingdoms, Uganda was divided into several administrative districts, none of which bore the name of Buganda at all, a move which seemed designed to humiliate them. In 1974 four major administrative divisions were created, one of which was Buganda. It in turn was divided into six administrative districts known as Kampala, Mukono, Luwero, Mubende, Masaka and Rakai Districts.

The pre-colonial kingdom of Buganda was roughly contained by two 40-mile arcs centered on Kampala (q.v.) and Masaka (q.v.). The southern area, Buddu (q.v.), was incorporated into Buganda only during the late eighteenth century. Buganda was very fertile and was densely populated, connected by a network of well-maintained roads and causeways through the swamps, intensively cultivated, and administered by an elaborate hierarchy of chiefs and of clan heads under its hereditary ruler, the Kabaka. Skilled craftsmen made canoes for fishing and for the Kabaka's warriors, others made the bark-cloth which was worn by the people, and there was a highly developed musical tradition: the Kabaka maintained a large and elaborate orchestra including strings, woodwinds and percussion, this last including both drums and the *amadinda* (xylophone).

The Baganda have a rich heritage of oral and clan histories, and genealogies of clan heads and of the Kabakas going back many generations have been recorded. The contributions of the Baganda historians Apolo Kagwa (q.v.) and James Miti (q.v.) are particularly important. There is a considerable literature in Luganda, only rivalled in East Africa by that in Swahili, the language of the Kenyan coast.

According to some widely-accepted theories, the initial migration into the area occurred between 1200 and 1400 AD. However, as has happened in the case of other areas of Uganda, oral histories may have been telescoped. Archeology has pushed back the dating of royal sites in some parts of Uganda much earlier than the oral traditions would suggest. By the second half of the nineteenth century Buganda was expanding at the expense of her rival to the north, Bunyoro (q.v.), and at the end of the century her leaders were able to turn an alliance with the British to their advantage.

Contact with traders from the East African coast began about the middle of the nineteenth century when Ahmed bin Ibrahim (q.v.) arrived at the court of Kabaka Suna. The first Europeans arrived in the 1860s in the reign of Kabaka Mutesa I (q.v.). Buganda was thus brought into contact with two world religions, Islam (q.v.) and Christianity, and the country was opened up to trade in ivory, slaves collected in border wars, firearms, and luxury goods. The first attempts at writing down Luganda were made in Arabic script.

Early European travelers such as Speke (q.v.) and Stanley (q.v.), and the missionaries of the Church Missionary Society (q.v.) and the White Fathers (q.v.) were impressed by the way in which the kingdom was organized and administered, by the wealth of the Kabaka's court, the intelligence of the young men in training there for future high office, and what they were able to recognize as the standard of civilization reached by the Baganda, albeit they deplored the cruelty which marked the Kabaka's autocratic rule.

Christian missions (q.v.) which arrived in the 1870s introduced literacy in Roman script, and established schools and hospitals (*see* Education and Medicine) in Buganda before anywhere else, so that the Baganda quickly gained an advantage in this respect over the rest of the country which has never been lost. The placing of the modern capital in Buganda has also been of great importance in giving the people a developmental lead.

During the colonial period Buganda achieved a special status within the Protectorate. The 1900 [B]Uganda Agreement (q.v.) introduced land freehold, not granted anywhere else, and gave the kingdom of Buganda quasi-federal status.

Baganda chiefs were appointed in other parts of the country, notably Bunyoro, and Baganda appointees were used as "sub-imperial" agents in many parts of the Protectorate. The most notable was the Muganda general, Semei Kakungulu (q.v.). Buganda's Lukiiko or assembly of chiefs had considerable powers, and the *Bulange* (meeting-place of the Buganda Lukiiko) faced the *Lubiri* (Kabaka's palace) down the length of *Kabaka Njagala* ("the Kabaka loves me") Avenue in the traditional capital, Mengo (q.v.), adjoining the modern capital of Kampala (q.v.). From 1900 onwards Buganda concentrated her energies on exploiting and retaining the privileges she had won under the 1900 Agreement. In 1953 Kabaka Mutesa II (q.v.) was exiled by Governor Sir Andrew Cohen for refusing to cooperate with the Protectorate Government, and there was unrest in Buganda until he returned. Fearful of losing its status, Buganda refused to send representatives to the national Legislative Council (Legco) (q.v.) in the runup to independence, and just before independence a political party, Kabaka Yekka ("the Kabaka only") (q.v.), was formed to protect the Kabakaship and Buganda's interests. Milton Obote (q.v.) won power by making an alliance with Kabaka Yekka and appointing the Kabaka as President of Uganda and himself as Prime Minister. Buganda again tried to secede from Uganda in 1966. She was defeated by the Uganda Army (q.v.) under Idi Amin (q.v.) in the Battle of Mengo 1966 (q.v.). The Kabaka fled to Britain where he died in exile. This confrontation led directly to the abolition of all the kingdoms, and to the Constitution (q.v.) of 1967. Buganda was further humiliated when the *Lubiri* and the *Bulange* were both taken over by the army.

At Amin's seizure of power and later when President Museveni (q.v.) came to power some Baganda hoped for the restoration of the kingdom, but these hopes were disappointed until July 1993 when Ronald Mutebi was installed as Kabaka Mutebi II, a cultural, not political leader.

BAGAYA, ELIZABETH (1940–) Elizabeth Nyabongo, Princess of Toro (q.v.), daughter of Mukama George Rukiidi III (q.v.). She was educated at Gayaza High School (*see* Education), Sherborne School for Girls, England, and Girton

College, Cambridge. She was called to the English Bar in 1965, becoming the first woman barrister in East Africa, but she never practiced. In 1966 after the death of Mukama George Rukiidi she became Batebe (Royal Sister) to her younger brother, Patrick Olimi, on his accession. The following year President Obote (q.v.) abolished the traditional kingdoms, and in 1968 Elizabeth Bagaya went into exile, following a career as a model. She returned to Uganda after Obote was overthrown by President Amin (q.v.) in 1971. In July of that year she was appointed Roving Ambassador for Uganda, and in 1974 was appointed Foreign Minister.

Before the end of the year she found herself in deep trouble for standing up to Amin. She was dismissed as Foreign Minister, and accused by Amin of having had sexual relations with a white man in a toilet at Orly Airport, an accusation which was repeated uncritically in a number of European newspapers, and for which she eventually successfully sued them. She had to escape over the border into Kenya (q.v.) and eventually made her way to Britain. There she married Wilbur Nyabongo in 1981 who was killed in a plane crash in 1986. She published an account of her life, *African Princess,* in 1983. After President Museveni (q.v.) came to power, she was sent as Ugandan Ambassador to the United States for two years.

BAGISU (or BAGISHU). A Bantu-speaking people living on the western slopes of Mount Elgon (q.v.) and around the town of Mbale (q.v.) in eastern Uganda. Their language is Lugisu (*see* Languages) and the area they inhabit is known as Bugisu. The adminstrative division called Bugisu until 1979 also included an area of the northern slopes of the mountain occupied by the Sebei (q.v.). It has historically been part of the migration corridor which runs between Lake Kyoga and the Nile (q.v.) to the east and Mount Elgon to the west, in which sections of several populations now live. The administrative district in which the Bagisu live is now known as Mbale District. According to their own traditions, they moved down onto their present lands from former homes higher up the mountain. It has been suggested that they originally came from further east, since their closest affinities seem to be with the Vugusu and other peoples who now live in western Kenya (q.v.). They may then have been forced up into the foothills of Mount Elgon by the warlike Nandi. Living now on the steep-sided ridges of the lower mountain slopes, they are a segmentary society with a strong, territorially-based clan system. There are also strong bonds between boys circumcised in the same year, and circumcision rituals play an important part in the annual and life cycles of the Bagisu.

In 1899 the Muganda (*see* Baganda) general, Semei Kakungulu (q.v.), was sent by the British administration to pacify the region. He was allotted a large estate near Mbale and his agents administered the district on behalf of the British. A small Baganda community still lives in this area. They once included many followers of the Bamalaki (q.v.) with which Kakungulu became involved, but which has since largely died out. From 1913 onwards Bagisu began to be appointed to junior chieftaincies, but the last Muganda agent did not retire until 1934, and only slowly did Bagisu take over more senior chieftaincies.

Bugisu is very well-watered and fertile with rich volcanic soils. Successful cooperatives grow Arabica coffee and high-quality tea, and the people cultivate plantains (cooking bananas), finger millet, and a wide variety of food crops. Their involvement in high-return cash crops has made the Bagisu relatively wealthy. The Bugisu Coffee Scheme was started in 1930 to buy up coffee from peasant growers and process it. In the lower and flatter areas of Bugisu true millet and sorghum are grown, with cotton as a cash crop. The Bagisu also trade in milk, hides and cattle. Since 1958 Bagisu farmers have been able to register their land as freehold under a successful Land Adjudication Scheme, and many have done so. The economic difficulties of the 1970s and 1980s led the Bagisu to withdraw from the state-controlled marketing of coffee and to prefer taking their crop over the border into Kenya, where it was indistinguishable from Kenyan-grown coffee, and fetched a far better price than in Uganda. Together with Kigezi (q.v.) in the southwest, Bugisu is one of the most densely populated areas of Uganda, and many Bagisu have been forced to migrate.

Mission activity began in 1899 when the Church Missionary Society (q.v.) opened a station at Nabumale, where there is now a long-established secondary school (*see* Education). The Mill Fathers (q.v.) began work shortly afterwards at Nyondo, and they too quickly established a network of schools. A community of Muslims (*see* Islam) has long lived near Mbale, and a new Muslim University was established at Mbale in the late 1980s.

BAHIMA. The pastoralists of western Uganda as distinct from the Bairu (q.v.) agriculturalists. They have traditionally been a dominant minority. The distinction between the two groups is more important in Ankole (q.v.) than elsewhere in western Uganda. The Bahima cattle are not the humped zebu cattle of most of Africa, but long-horned cattle similar to those shown in ancient Egyptian art, bred for the beauty and size of their horns. In the past the Bahima have ranged widely over the sparsely-inhabited grasslands of the west, though many in Ankole have now acquired ranches and have ceased to be semi-nomadic.

In his *Journal of the Discovery of the Source of the Nile,* J. H. Speke (q.v.) put forward the "Hamitic Myth" according to which the Bahima were "Hamites" who had migrated into East Africa from further north, imposing their rule on the indigenous agricultural Bairu population. They were believed to be racially different from and superior to the Bairu. It is now more generally held that the difference between the Bahima and the Bairu is one of occupation rather than race, pastoralism being the more prestigious occupation. It is occasionally possible to move from one group to another according as one acquires or loses cattle, the movement being almost always downwards. Inter-marriage between the two groups seems to be rare. They speak the same language, though with differences of pronunciation and vocabulary, and they have a common clan system, but with the Bairu and Bahima segments differently named. Bahima are often taller and slimmer than Bairu, possibly as a result of a high-protein milk- and blood-based diet over many years. A very strong-tasting soft cheese made with soured milk is a special delicacy. But by no means all Bahima fit the physical stereotype even in Ankole where the Bahima/Bairu division is most marked.

In Ankole the whole traditional culture of the Bahima is centered around their cattle. In many dances the women are seated, and with their arms and bodies mime the shape and movement of the horns of their cattle. Oral literature consists largely of praise poems of men and cattle, some of which were recorded by H. F. Morris (*see* Bibliography). Milk pots are carved from wood and their extremely finely-woven grass covers are worked with intricate patterns, as are the mats and baskets which adorn the small, beehive dwellings clustered around the cattle kraal in a traditional Bahima home.

In Toro (q.v.) and Bunyoro (q.v.) the Bahima are known as Bahuma, and the difference between them and the Bairu is largely one of status rather than occupation. These distinctions have been progressively eroded under colonial and post-colonial rule.

BAHINDA. A Bahima (q.v.) clan which was the royal and chiefly clan of Nkore (*see* Ankole) and of other neighboring pre-colonial states. The Bahinda are believed by their members to have an origin different from that of the Bahima (q.v.), but culturally they are indistinguishable from them. Throughout much of the nineteenth century the states ruled by the Bahinda gained in power while Bunyoro (q.v.) and its dependencies which were ruled by members of the Babito (q.v.) clan were weakened and broke away from dominance by Bunyoro. After the murder of Galt (q.v.) many of the Bahinda chiefs fled from Ankole, and their places were taken mostly by Bahima, but from then on it was also possible for Bairu (q.v.) to become senior chiefs as distinctions became blurred under colonial rule.

BAIRU. The majority agricultural people of western Uganda, as distinct from the dominant minority of pastoralist Bahima (q.v.), especially in Ankole (q.v.) where the occupational and social distinction is clearest. In some of the early anthropological literature, for example the writings of John Roscoe (q.v.), the Bairu are described as serfs, and there is a general lack of study of their customs and traditions.

Prior to the arrival of the British they formed the majority of the population in the principalities which lay to the west of Nkore and which were then brought within the colonial kingdom of Ankole. Their main grain crop was millet, and they also grew sweet potatoes, groundnuts, simsim and a variety of vegetables. Since the beginning of the century *matooke* bananas which are steamed slowly have been introduced from Buganda (q.v.) as a less labor-intensive, though also less nutritious staple, and millet is mainly used for beer. Under colonial rule it became increasingly possible for Bairu to become chiefs and to hold other offices under colonial and post-colonial rule as the old status-distinctions were eroded.

BAKER, SIR SAMUEL (1821–1893). A nineteenth century British traveler who was concerned with ascertaining the source and line of the Nile (q.v.). He twice reached Bunyoro (*see* Banyoro) from the north and stayed for some months on each occasion. In 1863 he reached Gondokoro in the southern Sudan (q.v.) where he learnt from Speke (q.v.) of the existence of the lake which he would later name Lake Albert, and which Speke believed to be the second source of the Nile, but had been unable to reach. Baker reached the Karuma Falls in January 1864 and sought to enter Bunyoro. Mukama Kamurasi was suspicious of him, and reluctant to let him travel freely. Baker for his part was impressed with the prosperity and order of Bunyoro, the people's skill in blacksmithing, and their decorative household articles. Baker reached Lake Albert near Kyangwali on 14 March 1864. He located the inflow of the Nile and was able to confirm its outflow at Pakwach. He then traveled up the Victoria Nile and reached the falls which he named the Murchison Falls (now the Kabarega Falls). For the first time Baker then met Mukama Kamurasi, from whom he learnt something of the history of Bunyoro Kitara. Baker's legacy to Bunyoro after this visit was a recipe for distilling *waragi* (the Ugandan name is derived from the Arabic *arak*) from sweet potatoes. His account of these travels is found in *The Albert N'yanza,* published in 1866.

Baker's second, and in many ways disastrous, visit to

Bunyoro took place in 1872 after he had been knighted and made Governor-General of Equatoria (q.v.). Kamurasi had died, and after much fighting, Kabarega (q.v.) had succeeded him. On 14 May Baker declared the annexation of Bunyoro to Egypt. There was serious trouble and fighting between Baker's men and the Banyoro, and Baker behaved with extreme highhandedness. His unfavorable accounts of Kabarega and the Banyoro in his *Ismailia,* published in 1874, prejudiced the British against them, with grievous consequences.

BAKIGA. The name of a Bantu-speaking agricultural people who live in the densely populated highlands of southwestern Uganda, and more loosely applied to all those who live in the former Kigezi (q.v.) District, now the administrative divisions of Kabale (q.v.) and Rukungiri. The language of the Bakiga, Rukiga, is closely related to the other Bantu languages of western Uganda, all of which are mutually intelligible (*see* Languages). In the southern part of Kabale many Kinyarwanda (*see* Rwanda) speakers are found. The precolonial history of the Bakiga is closely entwined with that of the kingdom states of Rwanda to the south, and of Mpororo and Ndorwa, the remnants of which are now absorbed as counties within Kabale and Rukungiri Districts, and with the kingdoms of western Zaire (q.v.).

Kiga society was segmentary and there was no overall political authority. Clan allegiances were of great importance in pre-colonial times, and are still important for family life. The continual formation of new clans suggests both population growth and the absorption of immigrant groups.

The Bakiga are industrious agriculturalists who developed a system of terracing which enables them to farm even steep hillsides. In more recent times they have drained some of the marshes in the fertile valley bottoms to grow vegetables and other food crops. By 1970 these were being marketed in Kampala (q.v.) and even exported, but these schemes suffered in the disruption of the 1970s and 1980s. Kabale (q.v.), an administrative center and market town, saw its trade severely reduced because of the war in Rwanda which started in 1990 and which almost wiped out the valuable cross-border trade between Uganda and Zaire.

BAKONJO. A Bantu-speaking people living on the eastern and southern slopes of the Ruwenzori Mountains (q.v.), who speak a dialect of Rutoro (*see* Languages). Traditionally they grew millet, peas and beans and kept sheep and goats. When preyed on by stronger neighbors, they found refuge by moving further into the mountains. In 1891, when Lugard (q.v.) installed Kasagama (q.v.) as Mukama of Toro (q.v.), the treaty which Kasagama had to sign ceded ultimate sovereignty of all the areas over which he ruled, including ''Bukonjo'' to the Imperial British East Africa Company (q.v.).

The Bakonjo and their neighbors, the Baamba (q.v.), came to resent Toro's harsh and insensitive rule, and sought to free themselves from it. This came to a head in 1962 when the Bakonjo and Baamba representatives to the local Toro parliament walked out to draw attention to their claim for a separate district. An investigation was ordered, which found the Toro government largely to blame for the discontent, though it rejected the demand for a separate district. By the beginning of 1963 trouble in the area became serious enough for the central government to intervene and declare Bukonjo and Bwamba disturbed areas. A Mukonjo teacher, Isaya Mukirane, emerged as leader of the Ruwenzururu Movement (q.v.), which then sought secession. The Uganda Army (q.v.) was called in and drove many of the Baamba and Bakonjo over the border into Zaire (q.v.), where they found little support for their aspirations. A further enquiry, and government action to see that the aggrieved peoples had greater control over their own affairs, defused the situation somewhat, though Ruwenzururu was not completely suppressed, and Mukirane did not give up his pretensions to rule over a separate state.

The Bakonjo were involved in further trouble in 1987 when the National Resistance Movement (q.v.) government of President Museveni (q.v.) acted to clamp down on cross-border coffee-smuggling into Zaire, and when both the

Zairean and the Ugandan governments clamped down on insurgents operating from each other's territory.

BALOKOLE *see* REVIVAL

BALYA, THE RT REVD ABERI KAKOMYA (1881–1979). The first East African to be consecrated to the Anglican (q.v.) episcopacy in Uganda. He was born at Matiri in Toro (q.v.) and as a child was taken to Bunyoro (q.v.) by the army of Mukama Kabarega (q.v.) and brought up at court because his aunt was one of Kabarega's wives. He returned to Toro in 1896 and served at the court of Mukama Kasagama (q.v.). Here he started to receive Christian teaching and was baptized in 1901. He married Ketura Byanga in 1907. Until 1910 he worked as a catechist in various places, including Mboga in the Congo, now Zaire (q.v.). In 1910–1911 Balya assisted with the translation of the Bible into Rutoro (*see* Languages) before being trained as a lay-reader at Bishop Tucker College, Mukono. In 1922 he returned there to train for ordination. In 1934 he was appointed Vicar of St John's Church, Kabarole, near Fort Portal (q.v.). In the same year he was made a Canon of Namirembe (q.v.) Cathedral in Mengo (q.v.) and a Life Governor of the Church Missionary Society (q.v.) four years later. In 1947 he was consecrated Bishop, and appointed Assistant to the Bishop of Namirembe, with responsibility for the Anglican Church in western Uganda. He was greatly respected, although he never joined the Revival movement (q.v.). Balya was awarded the OBE in 1952 and retired in 1960 though he remained active. When the Lost Counties (q.v.) were returned to Bunyoro he was invited to preach the sermon at the service of thanksgiving, and in 1966 he played an important role in the coronation of Patrick Olimi as Mukama of Toro. When he died, 60,000 people attended his funeral.

BAMALAKI (EKIBIINA KYA KATONDA OMU AYINZA BYONNA—SOCIETY OF THE ONE ALMIGHTY GOD). Its founder was Joswa Kate (q.v.), the Mugema (county chief of Busiro in Buganda). Ever since 1885 he had objected to the use of medicine, possibly because of a misunderstanding arising out of the translation into Luganda (*see* Languages) of the terms for "doctor" and "medicine" in the Bible. In 1914 a small group led by Kate separated from the church on this issue. Their chief agent was Malaki Musajjakawa, from whom the followers of the movement came to be called Bamalaki.

It is uncertain whether their main emphasis was on Kate's objection to the use of medicine or on Malaki's objection to the long periods of instruction and high standard of literacy required from candidates for baptism. Bamalaki offered baptism on far easier terms than the missions (q.v), and one nickname for the movement was *Dini ya Laisi,* "religion on the cheap." Their reading of the Bible suggested to the Bamalaki that Saturday rather than Sunday should be the day of rest. The eating of pork was banned, and up to four wives were allowed, perhaps under the influence of Islam (q.v.). At a time when the possession of a Christian name was a prerequisite for getting anywhere in Baganda (q.v.) society and monogamy was found burdensome, Malaki's terms were welcome. By 1921 the movement peaked with a membership of some 91,000 in Buganda.

The objection to medicine troubled the Protectorate administration when, in 1915, Bamalaki chiefs refused to allow vaccination against smallpox in their chieftaincies. In 1918 Kate instructed his chief cowherd not to report a case of rinderpest lest vaccination of the herds be ordered, and the following year he was deprived of his chieftaincy for his continued obduracy on this issue. By 1921 he was still unrepentant: he gave up all his cattle and was imprisoned rather than give in.

Under the influence of Semei Kakungulu (q.v.) the movement spread to the area around Mbale (q.v.) in eastern Uganda, and by 1930 it was estimated that it had 58,000 followers in Buganda and 11,300 elsewhere. But by then Malaki and Kate had been deported: in an outbreak of serious trouble over anti-plague regulations a European sanitary inspector had lost a hand, and punishment was meted out. The movement had already suffered a decline in numbers, and although it found a new leader in James Biriko who, in 1945, helped to found the Bataka Association (q.v.), its heyday was over. Tiny handfuls of mainly elderly followers survived into the post-colonial era, but the movement lost all influence.

BANNABIKIRA (DAUGHTERS OF THE VIRGIN). The oldest congregation of African religious sisters on the continent. In 1902 Mother Mechtilde of the White Sisters (q.v.) was appointed Superior of a newly-established community at Villa Maria (q.v.) in Buddu (q.v.). Almost immediately a few Baganda (q.v.) girls expressed a desire to follow the Sisters' way of life. In 1902 a first group of girls was trained, not as sisters, but as catechists. They took no vows, but they wore distinctive dress and worked especially among children, teaching reading and catechism. By 1907 their number had risen to 140, and some were asking to become nuns. In 1908 Mother Mechtilde was appointed to open a noviciate where 11 of the catechists might train as members of a sisterhood which would be bound by annual rather than permanent vows. No vow of poverty was taken. The first three were professed in 1910. The sisters kept their own names and the Sisterhood was named the Bannabikira. By 1913 more than 30 Bannabikira were working in nine communities. In 1919 a group began work in the eastern area of Uganda where the Mill Hill Fathers (q.v.) were at work, and they proved an inspiration to Catholic (q.v.) girls in that part of Uganda.

In 1921 a new headquarters was completed on land donated by the Catholic saza chief of Buddu (q.v.), and a new chapel was dedicated three years later when Mama Cecilia Nalube (later known as Mother Ursula) became the first Ugandan superior of the sisterhood.

At last in 1926 the Bannabikira was constituted as a full religious congregation whose members took the three vows of poverty, chastity and obedience, and who eventually bound themselves by vows taken for life. By 1957 the number of Bannabikira had risen to 256 and continued to rise steadily from then on. Their work became more varied, and by the 1960s an increasing number were becoming professionally qualified.

Outside Buganda, each Catholic diocese established an order of religious sisters who have proved indispensable to the church. The first congregation to be established after the Bannabikira was that of the Little Sisters of St Francis. Other congregations are the Bannyatereza in Fort Portal (q.v.) diocese (founded 1937), the Sisters of Mary Immaculate in Gulu (q.v.) diocese (1942), the African Sisters of Good Counsel in Mbarara (q.v.) diocese (1943), and the Sisters of the Immaculate Heart of Mary Reparatrix in Entebbe (q.v.) (1948). The Sisters of Perpetual Adoration in Arua (q.v.) diocese (1960) was the first entirely African order of contemplatives to be founded in Uganda. The Little Sisters of Jesus are an international order to which a number of Ugandans belong. By the late 1960s there were over 1,200 Ugandan sisters at work, and their numbers have continued to rise.

The Sisters have challenged a traditional way of life in which there was no place for women outside marriage. In the early years the vow of poverty proved as difficult as that of chastity. The Sisters have won a highly respected place for themselves in Ugandan society, and their presence has undoubtedly done much for the status of women (q.v.).

BANYANKOLE. The Bantu-speaking peoples who live within the boundaries of the kingdom of Ankole as it was delimited during the colonial era. Their language, Runyankole, is closely-related to the other Bantu languages of western Uganda (*see* Languages), most of which are mutually intelligible. The area traditionally known as Nkore was smaller than the kingdom of Ankole in southwestern Uganda recognized by the British. To the west lay smaller states which had previously been part of the empire of Bunyoro (q.v.), but with the weakening of Bunyoro's power in the nineteenth century they had been drawn into Nkore's sphere of influence. In 1967 President Obote (q.v.) abolished the kingdoms, and since 1974 the area has been divided into two administrative districts. Since 1979 these have been named after the towns of Mbarara (q.v.) and Bushenyi.

Two groups of people who are differentiated by their traditional way of life make up the Banyankole. The Bahima (q.v.) are pastoralists who graze their herds of long-horned cattle over wide tracts of countryside whilst the Bairu (q.v.) are agriculturalists who predominated in the western tributary states. Pastoralism was the more prestigious occupation and the Bahima exercised a measure of dominance over the Bairu. They speak the same language with slight dialectal differences.

The Mugabe was always a Muhima from the Bahinda (q.v.) clan, as were some other senior chiefs. The ritual symbol of his kingship was Bagyendanwa, the royal drum. In pre-colonial times the royal enclosure (the *orurembo*) moved from place to place, but under Protectorate rule Mbarara became the district headquarters of Ankole, and the Mugabe built himself a permanent brick-built palace. Mbarara is in the center of the part of Ankole occupied mainly by the Bahima. In a western arc around this area are higher lands mainly occupied by the Bairu, but these demarcations are not hard and fast, and modern Mbarara and other towns are inhabited by Ugandans from many parts of the country, and the educational institutions located there have a national clientele.

In 1899 the traveler H.M. Stanley (q.v.) passed through Ankole. Bucunku, a representative of the Mugabe Ntare V (q.v.) met him, and Stanley made a form of blood brotherhood with him. Stanley later claimed that Bucunku had ceded to him the territories of "Ankori and Mpororo." The document he produced did not bear even Bucunku's mark, however, and Bucunku would have had no right to make such a concession.

Two years later Captain Lugard (q.v.) passed through Ankole and an agreement was signed between Mugabe Ntare V (q.v.) and the Imperial British East Africa Company (q.v.) which promised Ntare British protection. During the 1890s Ankole was ravaged by rinderpest, which devastated the herds of cattle, and by smallpox which killed Ntare's only son and heir. Raids on neighboring states to capture cattle resulted in further disaster when Rwanda (q.v.) retaliated. By 1894 Ankole was, therefore, experiencing a major political and social crisis after a period in which she had extended her power. In 1894 Major Cunningham was instructed to enter into negotiations with Ntare V after a German troop column had passed through this area which Britain claimed was within her sphere. A new Agreement was signed, this time between the British government and Ntare, but the promise of protection meant little in practice. In 1895 Ntare V died, and the country was plunged into uncertainty over the succession. The Protectorate government became involved after receiving a call for assistance from the faction supporting Kahaya (q.v.), believed to be Ntare's son. A Protectorate was formally declared over Ankole, Toro (q.v.) and Bunyoro in 1896, but it was not until 1901 that Ankole was directly administered and a new Agreement signed.

The 1901 Agreement defined the limits of Ankole, including within it areas that had previously been within the sphere of influence of the Mugabe of Ankole, but not subject to him. These areas were mainly occupied by Bairu, and the proportion of Bairu to Bahima under the rule of the Mugabe was therefore greatly increased. Kahaya was recognized as rightful Mugabe, and it placed Mbaguta (q.v.), who claimed to be the most senior chief under the Mugabe, in a strong position. Mbaguta's claim was dubious, but he saw collaboration with the missions (q.v.) and the Protectorate government as a way to further his own aims and those of the royal Bashambo clan of Mpororo to which he belonged, and which was competing with the Bahinda for power and influence.

Literacy and Western education (q.v.) were introduced to Ankole in 1899 when the Church Missionary Society (CMS) (q.v.) arrived. The White Fathers (q.v.) arrived three years later. After considerable hestitation, Mugabe Kahaya and Mbaguta were baptized as Protestants (q.v.) in 1902, and others quickly followed their example. Since the CMS claimed the allegiance of many of the Bahima chiefs, the White Fathers went to the Bairu, and something of this denominational divide has survived into the present, and has political implications (*see* Democratic Party and Uganda People's Congress).

In 1904 a British official, H. St G. Galt (q.v.), was murdered. Disaffected Bahima chiefs were suspected of responsibility, but the motive was unclear. The murder created something of a crisis, and the Mugabe and his chiefs were heavily fined, and three chiefs were exiled. The Agreement was suspended and not restored until 1912.

Kahaya died in 1944 and was succeeded by a nephew,

Charles Godfrey Gasyonga (q.v.), later knighted by the British. Under Protectorate rule the traditional role of the Mugabe was steadily eroded as he was required to act as an agent of British rule. On the eve of independence Ankole shared some of the concern of Buganda (q.v.) and Toro to protect its privileges and retain a measure of independence from central government. It therefore welcomed the Western Kingdoms and Busoga Act of 1962 which had been incorporated into the independence constitution (q.v.), but which was watered down by the appointment of a Minister of Regional Affairs and by clauses which gave priority to central government legislation over local legislation in the event of any conflict. Gasyonga continued as Mugabe until President Obote (q.v.) dismantled the kingdoms in 1967, an act which was accepted remarkably quietly by the people of Ankole. In 1993 President Museveni (q.v.) allowed the former kingdoms to restore their monarchs as cultural, but not political, heads if they wished. The Banyankole were divided as to whether to do so or not.

BANYARWANDA. Immigrants from Rwanda (q.v.) entered Uganda during the nineteenth and twentieth centuries. By 1990 they comprised about 6 percent of the population of Uganda. They are Bantu-speakers (*see* Languages), and include Hutu agriculturalists, the majority of whom are ethnically related to the Bairu (q.v.) of Ankole (q.v.), and a cattle-keeping Tutsi minority who traditionally formed the ruling group and who are closely related to the Bahima (q.v.). Some of the immigrants were assimilated to their close ethnic relations in Ankole; others found work as herdsmen in Buganda (q.v.) and elsewhere; yet others worked on Asian-owned sugar plantations. Most of the migrants who sought work during the period of colonial rule were Hutu who found themselves increasingly oppressed by the ruling Tutsi minority.

In 1959, on the eve of independence, the Hutu of Rwanda rose against their Tutsi masters, massacring thousands, and causing some 80,000 more to become refugees (q.v.) in Uganda. They were settled in southern Ankole. In 1982–1983 these were evicted from the land they occupied; some were forced to flee back to Rwanda, others were resettled in sparsely occupied land in Toro (*see* Expulsions). Some joined the National Resistance Army (NRA) (q.v.), sections of which were operating in Ankole.

In October 1990 a group of Banyarwanda serving in the NRA under the command of General Rwigyema (q.v.) invaded Rwanda. They had been stationed in Teso where the population had been ground between the NRA and the guerrilla forces of the Uganda People's Democratic Army (q.v.). Their departure took the heat off the Iteso (q.v.) people, and a measure of peace began to return to that area. The Uganda government was ambivalent about the invasion and the President of Rwanda blamed President Museveni (q.v.) for it. Rwigyema was killed only two weeks later, apparently by one of his own supporters in an argument over strategy.

BANYORO. The Bantu-speaking people who inhabit Bunyoro in western Uganda. Their language is called Runyoro and is closely related to the other Bantu languages of western Uganda (*see* Languages), all of which are mutually intelligible. Under colonial rule Bunyoro included the low-lying land just to the south of Lake Albert occupied by the Jopalwo, a Lwoo (q.v.) group who were allied with the kingdom of Bunyoro-Kitara. The southern counties of Buyaga and Bugangaizi were allocated to Buganda (q.v.) in 1900 and the Banyoro campaigned for the return of these ''Lost Counties'' (q.v.) throughout the colonial era. President Obote (q.v.) abolished the kingdom of Bunyoro in 1967. In 1974 the area was divided into two administrative districts based on Hoima (q.v.) and Masindi (q.v.).

The Banyoro are agriculturalists who also keep some cattle, and for whom cattle-keeping is a prestigious occupation carried out by the aristocratic Bahima (q.v.) people. Until President Obote (q.v.) abolished the kingdoms in 1967 the Banyoro were ruled by a Mukama who always came from the ruling Babito (q.v.) clan. The oral traditions of Bunyoro-Kitara go back many centuries into a mythical past when the Batembuzi (q.v.) and the Bacwezi (q.v.) ruled the land. They were succeeded by the Babito, and with the later Babito rulers we enter the realms of legend and history rather than myth.

The heartland of the ancient empire of Bunyoro-Kitara lay to the southeast of Lake Albert in the modern counties of Buyaga, Bugangaizi (*see* Lost Counties) and Mwenge, now in Kabarole District. At the height of its power Bunyoro-Kitara's influence stretched from west of Lake Edward to the eastern end of Lake Kyoga, and from the northeastern fringes of Lake Kyoga to Rujumbura and Buhweju in what came to be colonial Ankole (q.v.). But this area was not all under the direct rule of the Mukama. He placed relatives and loyal servants to hold the more distant areas, binding them to him by gifts of drums and spears with which they had to return each year to renew their allegiance. The Mukama's own regalia and that of some of his most senior chiefs included a crown of feathers with a colobus monkey skin beard on a bead-embroidered, basket-work base, the Mukama's crown being marked by 18 long "needles" placed around the top. The ability of the Mukama to keep his hold over this vast area waxed and waned, and the center of rule shifted from time to time. Some royal burials were in Mwenge and others were in the Lost Counties. Royal burial sites were carefully tended by specially appointed guardians. In c. 1830 Toro (q.v.) broke away from Bunyoro, but in the 1870s the Mukama Kabarega (q.v.) restored much of what some of his predecessors had lost before he got caught up in resistance to the British and Baganda, and was finally captured and exiled.

In the first half of the twentieth century Bunyoro was at a very low ebb. War and disease had devastated the land, the British treated Bunyoro as a conquered territory, Bugangaizi and Buyaga and all lands south of the Kafu River had been given to Buganda as a reward for assisting the British in the campaign against Bunyoro, the people had lost their pride, and the benefits of education (q.v.) and medicine (q.v.) seemed slow in coming. Matters worsened considerably in 1907 when the Nyangire Rising (q.v.) against the Baganda chiefs who had been imposed on Bunyoro took place. Until the death of Mukama Kabarega in 1923, the British appointee, Andereya Duhaga, was not fully accepted by all Banyoro. He died the following year and was succeeded by Tito (later Sir Tito) Winyi (q.v.).

In 1927 J.R.P. Postlethwaite was appointed as District

Commissioner and proved far more understanding of Bunyoro and its rulers than his predecessors. He established good relations with the Mukama which his immediate successors maintained. Agriculture began to pick up and tobacco-growing to flourish. At last in 1933 the British concluded a Bunyoro Agreement (q.v.), thus placing the country on the same level as Toro and Ankole. By the outbreak of World War II Bunyoro had recovered considerably. The same year saw the death of Petero Bikunya (q.v.) who had been Chief Minister since 1917, and who was an exceptionally able and just man and had been greatly respected.

Bunyoro shared some of the concern of Buganda and Toro over the possibility that independence would bring a reduction of local sovereignty, and welcomed the Western Kingdoms and Busoga Act which was intended to guard the rights of the kingdoms. This was incorporated into the constitution (q.v.) of 1962, but watered down by the establishment of a Minister of Regional Affairs and clauses which ensured that the central government legislation would take precedence over local legislation in the event of any conflict of interest. Bunyoro's claim to the Lost Counties was a recurring theme in the runup to Uganda's independence, and a settlement was postponed till after independence was achieved, when under the constitution a referendum had to be called. The outcome of the referendum on the Lost Counties was an overwhelming vote for their return to Bunyoro. But having achieved this victory, the kingdom of Bunyoro had only a short time to run. Under the 1967 Constitution (q.v.), all the traditional kingdoms of Uganda were dismantled. Bunyoro accepted the new republican constitution with little fuss. In 1993 President Museveni (q.v.) allowed the restoration of the monarchs as cultural, not political, heads. Solomon Iguru was to be installed as Mukama in 1994.

BARUSURA. The army of Kabarega (q.v.), Mukama of Bunyoro in the late nineteenth century, which consisted of war bands each numbering from 3,000 to 5,000 men. Many of the *barusura* were not Banyoro (q.v.) but were recruited from neighboring areas which were in alliance with Bunyoro; others had been taken as captives in war. They were used to crush rebellions as well as in external wars, and their presence in an area might arouse fear because they lived off the land, and might raid a family's food stores and abduct women and children.

Membership of the *barusura* was also sometimes a route into the Mukama's administrative service for gifted individuals, and after Kabarega's capture and deportation, several *barusura* were among the first to take advantage of Western education (q.v.) offered by the missions (q.v.), and make their way in the new colonial society. An example of these was Mika Fataki (q.v.).

BASOGA. A Bantu-speaking people who live in the administrative districts of Jinja, Kamuli and Iganga, formerly Busoga. This area extends from the Nile (q.v.) which forms the western boundary to the Mpologoma swamp in the east, and from Lake Kyoga in the north to Lake Victoria (q.v.) in the south. Different dialects of Lusoga (*see* Languages) are spoken in the northeast, where Lupakoyo is related to Runyoro, and in the southwest, where Lutenga is closer to Luganda, the language spoken by the Baganda (q.v.). The southern part of Busoga is more fertile and has a higher rainfall than the northern part, and plantains (*matooke*) form the staple food. This is supplemented by finger millet in the northern part of Busoga. The north is more thinly populated and cattle are more widely kept. The shores of Lake Victoria are thickly forested, and this area was evacuated in 1907 in the epidemic of sleeping sickness (q.v.) which swept the country.

Jinja (q.v.), the administrative center of Busoga, lies on the Nile at the point where it is bridged by the Owen Falls dam (q.v.) which carries the road across the river. It became the capital of Busoga, a center of industrial development, and Uganda's second largest city. The Kyabazinga, the paramount ruler, built his palace just outside Jinja, and both the Church of Uganda (q.v.) and the Roman Catholic Church (q.v.) have cathedrals at Jinja. Many leading Basoga have been educated at Busoga College, Mwiri (*see* Education), a prestigious school established by the Church Missionary Society (q.v.) on a hilltop not far from Jinja. The Catholic

missions which worked in Busoga were the Mill Hill Fathers
(q.v.) and the associated Franciscan Missionary Sisters
(q.v.). Kamuli, Iganga and Namasagali are the other main
centers in Busoga.

At the end of the nineteenth century the Basoga lived in a
large number of small kingdoms or principalities, each with
all the paraphernalia of a court. The number has been
variously estimated at between 40 and 60. An even greater
number of clans existed, well over 200 by the end of the
nineteenth century. There was no paramount ruler, though
the area was a cultural unity. The north had been tributary to
the Mukama of Bunyoro (q.v.), but when Bunyoro collapsed
under the late nineteenth century onslaught by the British
and the Baganda (q.v.), this relationship came to an end. The
south was raided by the Baganda from the seventeenth
century onwards, but by the nineteenth century attempts at
conquest had been given up, though Busoga continued to be
subjected to occasional raids designed to extract tribute.
From time to time Baganda aid was also invited by one or
other warring Musoga prince. In 1885, when the newly
appointed Bishop James Hannington (q.v.) of the Church
Missionary Society (q.v.) attempted to approach Buganda
via Busoga, the Kabaka of Buganda, Mwanga (q.v.), was
able to order a Musoga chief, Luba, to assassinate him.

In 1892 Busoga came under the rule of the Imperial British
East Africa Company (q.v.). A British Protectorate was
declared in 1894, and in the following year Busoga became a
district within the Protectorate. Steps were taken to amalga-
mate the many small principalities into one administrative
unit, and in 1906 the Muganda General, Semei Kakungulu
(q.v.), was appointed as a paramount chief and President of
the Council of Chiefs which was modelled on the Lukiiko of
the Baganda. Baganda agents were sent to assist lesser
Basoga chiefs. Not until 1919 was a Musoga appointed to the
paramountcy. The paramount ruler took the title Isebantu
Kyabazinga ("the father of the people who unites them"),
generally shortened to Kyabazinga. He was elected every
three years by the Council of Chiefs. The chiefly family
which rose to prominence was that of Nadiope, of the
northern county of Gabula. Kyabazinga William Nadiope

(q.v.) was involved with the Uganda People's Congress (q.v.) under Milton Obote (q.v.) and was made Vice-President of Uganda at independence.

BATAKA (s. MUTAKA). The Luganda (*see* Languages) term for the heads of clans. All Baganda (q.v.) belong to one of 40 or so clans, all of which have traditional claims on lands which are the clan headquarters and of which the Bataka are the guardians, as well as on some lesser estates. The Bataka are not appointed by the Kabaka of Buganda, although they acknowledge the Kabaka as Ssabataka, head of the Bataka. Their authority is more ancient than that of other types of chiefs who are directly appointed by the Kabaka, but at the time of the 1900 [B]Uganda Agreement (q.v.) they lost out to the territorially-based saza chiefs. These latter were allocated mailo (q.v.) estates under the terms of the 1900 Agreement, some of which included clan lands. By the 1920s there was mounting dissatisfaction among the Bataka about their loss of land and power, and this eventually led to serious riots (*see* Bataka Riots).

BATAKA ASSOCIATION. In 1921 the Bataka (q.v.) of Buganda (q.v.) banded together to challenge the power of the landed saza chiefs who were directly appointed by the Kabaka. Their power had grown at the expense of the Bataka under colonial rule. The Bataka Association was led by James Miti (q.v.) and 16 clan heads. These included Joswa Kate (q.v.), the head of the Nkima (grey monkey) clan and saza chief of Busiro. They were particularly concerned at the way in which mailo land (q.v.) had been distributed as a result of the 1900 [B]Uganda Agreement (q.v.) when clan lands had been allocated to individuals and had therefore become alienable. The Bataka Association won the support of large numbers of peasants who not only all had clan loyalties but who also resented the rents charged by land-holding chiefs. It thus became a populist movement in Buganda. The Bataka took their case to the Lukiiko, and then on up to the Kabaka and to the Governor. In 1926 the Colonial Secretary ruled that it was not feasible to return to pre-Agreement land-holding, but in 1926 the Protectorate government passed the *Busulu* and

Envujo Law (q.v.) which restricted rents, encouraged peasant coffee production and protected small farmers, and so dealt with their most serious grievances. It thus undercut support for the Bataka Association.

BATAKA PARTY. Founded in 1946, this movement was led, as was its predecessor, the Bataka Association (q.v.), by James Miti (q.v.) and Joswa Kate (q.v.) among others, though it had few other links with its predecessor. It expanded rapidly in Buganda (q.v.) and in Busoga (q.v.) gaining wide popular support by appealing to clan loyalties and defining as a Mutaka (clan head) everyone who owned or leased some land. Its actual paid-up membership was probably not very great. In Buganda it campaigned with the slogan "Every Muganda is a Mutaka." It had the support of many small traders, and its main centers of activity in and around Kampala (q.v.) were Wandegaya, an area of African traders, and Namirembe (q.v.), then outside the city boundaries, and enjoying none of its modern amenities. The Bataka Party became a focus for grievances about cotton production. Its members demanded a better price, the right to gin their own cotton, and the right to market it overseas themselves instead of through the cotton marketing board. The party also deplored the unrepresentative nature of the Buganda kingdom government, and feared what were understood as moves towards "closer union" (q.v.). It was alarmed by plans to establish an East African High Commission (q.v.) to be responsible for common services (posts, railways, etc.) throughout British East Africa, and which was given the power to purchase land which particularly alarmed the Bataka Party. In many of their grievances the Bataka Party was supported by the Uganda African Farmers' Union.

BATAKA RIOTS OF 1949. In April 1949 the Bataka Party (q.v.) became involved in riots when it tried to present its grievances to the Kabaka. On 25 April a large crowd gathered outside the Kabaka's palace. A delegation of eight was allowed to present a petition, but the crowd outside grew restive, the police were called in, and arrests were made which provoked a violent response in which chiefs' houses were burnt. The unrest spread to a number of other areas, over 1,700 arrests were made, and it was several days before order was restored.

The Governor blamed the riots on a small number of people led on by communists, and the Protectorate government decided that the riots had amounted to a planned rebellion against the Kabaka and the Buganda (q.v.) kingdom government. However, reform of the Lukiiko to make it more representative was undertaken as a result of the riots.

BATARINGAYA, BASIL (1927–1972). From Ankole (q.v.), he was educated at Makerere College (q.v.). He was an elected member of the Legislative Council (q.v.), was Minister of Local Government in the Protectorate government, and attended the Constitutional Conference (q.v.) in 1961. He became Secretary-General of the Democratic Party (q.v.), but defected to the Uganda People's Congress (q.v.) in 1964, as did many others, saying that only in government could they achieve anything for Uganda. He was then appointed Minister of Internal Affairs and as such was Chairman of the Cabinet Committee on Internal Security which was charged with arresting General Amin (q.v.) before President Obote (q.v.) returned from the Commonwealth Heads of Government Meeting in Singapore in 1971. The committee failed to act so as to prevent the coup of 1971 (q.v.). Because of his very aged father and young children Bataringaya did not flee to Tanzania (q.v.) before the attempted invasion of late 1972 as Obote suggested he should do, but he fled to Fort Portal (q.v.) for a few days. On his return to Mbarara (q.v.) he was brutally murdered, and his wife was murdered in April 1977, apparently in reprisal for winning a court case to retain possession of her house against the wishes of an army officer.

BATEMBUZI. The mythical dynasty of gods and kings believed to be the founders and first rulers of Bunyoro (q.v.). Different versions of the traditions of Bunyoro begin with Ruhanga himself, the Creator, or with Kintu. The earliest published account of the Batembuzi was given to Ruth Fisher of the Church Missionary Society (q.v.) (*see* her misnamed *Twilight Tales of the Black Baganda*) and contains 11 names, beginning with Kintu. John Roscoe (q.v.) was given a list of 12 rather different names. The two Banyoro historians, John Nyakatura (q.v.) and Sir Tito Winyi (q.v.), who wrote under the initials "K.W.," both give longer and rather different lists. Creation myths and other etiological material of great importance in Banyoro thinking is attached to the Batembuzi. The name means "people from elsewhere who have moved and resettled," but what one is to deduce from this is unclear. Some efforts have been made, for instance by Fr Crazzolara (q.v.), to find a historical basis for the Batembuzi, but, in the absence of any archeological evidence to date, most historians are either disbelieving or agnostic on this score.

BATORO. A Bantu-speaking people who live in the former kingdom of Toro, in the modern administrative districts of Kabarole and Kasese. Their language, Rutoro, is closely-related to the other Bantu languages of western Uganda (*see* Languages), most of which are mutually intelligible.

According to tradition, Kaboyo, a son of Mukama Kyebambe III Nyakamatura of Bunyoro (q.v.) was sent to collect tribute from Toro in the early nineteenth century. Toro was then a small area just east of the Ruwenzori Mountains (q.v.). He grew to love the country and about 1830 he rebelled and sought independence, supported by Bakonjo (q.v.) and Batoro clans and the Bahima (q.v.) of Mwenge. Weakened by attacks from Buganda (q.v.), Nyakamatura accepted his son's action and sent him a drum and spear, thus granting him recognition in spite of his rebellion. During Kaboyo's reign, which probably lasted into the 1860s, he extended his rule southwards from the small enclave around the modern Fort Portal (q.v.), later referred to as "Toro Proper," into Busongora. From north to south the lands that Kaboyo ruled extended about 75 miles, and barely 20 from east to west. Kaboyo set up his court on the Bunyoro model, and ruled autocratically. The Bakonjo (q.v.) in particular came to resent this and withdrew into the Ruwenzori foothills. Kaboyo appears to have ruled a principality rather than a fully independent kingdom.

At Kaboyo's death three of his sons fought over the succession, Nyaika being eventually successful with help from the Banyankole (q.v.). By this date Kabarega (q.v.) had become Mukama of Bunyoro and he sent expeditions against Toro to subdue it to his rule. In all this fighting, the land and people suffered severely. When Nyaika died his sons were scattered. One, Kasagama (q.v.), was taken by his mother to Nkore where two of his brothers were killed by Mugabe Ntare V (q.v.) of Nkore on Kabarega's orders, and then on to Buganda where they were sheltered by Byakweyamba (q.v.), a fellow clansmen of the royal Babito (q.v.) clan who had been given a minor chieftaincy in Buddu (q.v.) after serving at the court of Buganda.

Kasagama was established as Mukama of Toro in 1891 by Lugard (q.v.) of the Imperial British East Africa Company (IBEAC) (q.v.) at the instigation of some leading Baganda (q.v.). Both Lugard and the Baganda shared an interest in seeing Kabarega's power reduced. Kasagama was established in "Toro Proper," and struggled to assert his rule. The most serious threats came from Byakweyamba and from the British who failed to understand the situation into which he had been precipitated. He was defended by the missionaries of the Church Missionary Society (CMS) (q.v.). He invited Christian teachers into his kingdom, favored the Protestants (q.v.), and urged his chiefs to propagate Christianity. The missionaries in turn mediated between him and the Protectorate authorities on more than one occasion. It was not until the Toro Agreement (q.v.) was signed in 1900 that the boundaries of Toro were extended from "Toro Proper" to include the eastern foothills of the Ruwenzori and a great arc of territory to the east stretching from Lake Albert to Lakes George and Katwe. This included Mwenge, once part of the heartland of the empire of Bunyoro-Kitara.

Mikaeri Rusoke, a senior chief and former chief minister, and one of Kasagama's closest confidants, retired in 1923. Mukama Kasagama ruled until 1929, his rule being marked by continuing episodes of friction with the Protectorate government. He was succeeded by his son, George Rukiidi (q.v.), whose long reign lasted until 1965 and was marked by more confident, cooperative relations with the colonial power.

During much of the colonial period before World War II Toro remained a little outside the mainstream of Ugandan life, cut off from the center by its remoteness and poor road links with Kampala (q.v.). The White Fathers (q.v.) and CMS established hospitals and teacher training colleges in the neighborhood of Fort Portal, and networks of schools throughout the area. World War II saw a significant increase in cash crops in response to higher prices, and brought an improvement in Toro living standards. Marko Kaboha, an energetic chief minister, unfortunately died in 1946, but his successor, Hosea Nkojo, continued with reforming policies. Expatriate-owned tea estates took advantage of the high rainfall generated by the Ruwenzoris, and the Kilembe copper mines were reopened in the 1950s which brought Toro closer to the mainstream of the economy. The railway (q.v.) was extended to Kasese in 1956 to enable the copper to be brought out. The newly-established Fish Marketing Board benefitted the fishermen of Lakes Edward and George.

Toro's first representative in the Legislative Assembly (Legco) (q.v.) was John Babiiha (q.v.) in 1954. Timothy Bazarrabuza (q.v.) joined him a little later by direct appointment of the Governor. In the runup to independence Toro sought to protect itself both against what it saw as Buganda's arrogance, and against being merged into a unitary state with no means of preserving its own institutions. When Governor Andrew Cohen planned to introduce direct elections to the Buganda Lukiiko in 1959 two years before the rest of the country, Toro joined in protesting. The memorandum which John Babiiha presented to the Wild Committee and which had the support of Mukama Rukiidi, suggested a future constitution for Uganda which was neither the federalism desired by Buganda nor a unitary state. In 1960 Rukiidi joined with other hereditary rulers in ''The Rulers' Proclamation'' which sought to protect the kingdoms and their traditions in the coming independent state of Uganda through a form of federalism. In 1961 Toro made a bid for a new Agreement with Britain (q.v.) to be negotiated before independence in an attempt to safeguard her position. The result was the Local Administrations Bill of 1962 which gave the kingdom governments only a little more power than the other local administrations. Babiiha protested on Toro's behalf, but threats of secession by Toro were not taken as seriously as in the case of Buganda. In the Elections of 1962 (q.v.) Toro voted Democratic Party (q.v.) out of distrust of the plans of the Uganda People's Congress (UPC) (q.v.) for a unitary state, but the UPC, in alliance with Buganda's Kabaka Yekka (q.v.) party, won in the country at large.

Rukiidi was present in London during the Constitutional Conference (q.v.) of June 1962. He and the other rulers of the Western Kingdoms negotiated temporary agreements with the British and succeeded in getting them enshrined in the Constitution (q.v.) of 1962. Each of the Western Kingdoms was granted a regional parliament and a public service commission free of central government control. Succession to the rulership was also to be determined locally if a dispute arose. The subsequent Western Kingdoms and Busoga Bill reduced the rights of the kingdoms through the establishment of a Minister of Regional Administrations, and by providing for central government legislation to take precedence over local legislation in the event of a conflict.

A conflict soon arose because the Baamba (q.v.) and the Bakonjo joined in expressing their discontent with their position in Toro by challenging Toro's right to rule them. The secessionists were led by Isaya Mukirane and called themselves the Rwenzururu (q.v.). The Uganda Army (q.v.) had to be called in. A Commission of Enquiry found that the Toro government was not entirely blameless, but ruled against the disaffected Bakonjo and Baamba being allowed to set up a district of their own. Central government then took over the administration of the disturbed areas of Toro, and refused to listen to the remonstrations of Toro's chief minister. The Uganda Army was unable to reduce the Rwenzururu quickly, and violence continued.

In 1965 Mukama Rukiidi died, and in May of the following year his son, Patrick Olimi, was crowned Mukama, the last coronation of a traditional ruler to be held in Uganda. The event was already doubly overshadowed, first by a severe earthquake which caused extensive damage in Fort Portal and in Bwamba to the west of the Ruwenzori whose people were cut off from aid for some time by rockfalls blocking the narrow road round the foothills of the mountain: many people saw in the earthquake a bad omen for the future.

Secondly the events in Buganda which led shortly afterwards to the Battle of Mengo of 1966 (q.v.) also boded ill for Toro. Within a few months the kingdoms of Uganda were dissolved and a new constitution (q.v.), that of 1967, restructured the country as a unitary republic. The people of Toro apparently accepted the loss of the monarchy with little regret, certainly with little fuss, although they had turned out in their thousands to celebrate the accession of a new Mukama and enjoy his lavish hospitality only a short time before. In 1993 President Museveni (q.v.) allowed Olimi to be reinstated as cultural, but not political, head of the Batoro.

BATTLE OF MENGO (1892). This was fought between the Ugandan adherents of the Protestant (q.v.) and Catholic (q.v.) missions, and resulted in a Protestant victory. The differences between the two groups had been exacerbated when Kabaka Mwanga (q.v.) of Buganda (q.v.) had attempted to win support by forming new chieftaincies. He had allocated two to Muslims (*see* Islam) and one each to Apolo Kagwa (q.v.), a leading Protestant, and Honorat Nyonyi-ntono (q.v.), a leading Catholic.

In December 1891 Lugard (q.v.) returned to the capital from western Uganda. During his absence the chiefs had kept the two Christian factions from battle, but Lugard's actions on his return led to a crisis. Mwanga was allied with the Catholics, but his identification with them, while lending their party some legitimacy, was also an embarrassment: he was not baptized, and his behavior was sometimes offensive to the Christians. Lugard did not understand the complexities of the situation, but plunged into it nevertheless. A Protestant was murdered in a quarrel over the theft of a gun, but the Kabaka found against the Protestants because it was they who had taken the law into their own hands and provoked the Catholics in the first place. Lugard refused to accept this decision and issued some 40 guns and gunpowder to the Protestants. The following morning Mwanga protested angrily, fearing that he would be attacked with these guns. On Sunday 24 January Mwanga became worried by the crowds of Catholics who could be seen milling about and sent to Lugard asking for protection. Lugard promised to protect him if the murderer were sent to him together with an apology for insults which he believed he had suffered. Lugard then issued some 450–500 guns together with ammunition to the Protestants, in the belief that battle was imminent and that the Protestants were the weaker force. The balance of power was significantly shifted by these two issues of arms, and it became impossible for the older and wiser chiefs to restrain the newly-armed men when the next in a series of traded insults occurred.

On 25 January the immediate casus belli seems to have been a deliberate insult in the shape of a theft of some sweet potatoes from the garden of a Protestant chief. Shots rang out, and Lugard demanded that the culprit be sent to him. But the prisoner who arrived was an innocent substitute. Lugard was just congratulating himself that the danger had been averted when a volley of shots rang out which signalled the beginning of the battle which raged for some two hours between 3:00 and 5:00 pm. The battle did not follow the course of events which Lugard eventually wrote up: it was a more muddled affair. The Protestant missionaries were sheltered in the fort built by the Imperial British East Africa Company (q.v.). Although the Catholic mission at Rubaga (q.v.) was set alight and the partly-built reed-and-thatch church destroyed, none of the missionaries (who were noncombatant observers of the battle) was killed, a matter of great relief to Lugard. Kagwa's enclosure was attacked, and he and his men retreated towards the Company fort, probably with the aim of bringing in Lugard's troops in their defense. Lugard's own decisive intervention with a Maxim gun occurred late on in the affray. The Sudanese troops were then sent to pursue the fleeing Catholics. Kabaka Mwanga fled with them, so lessening the extent of the Protestant victory.

A number of contentious and partisan reports of this battle and what led up to it appeared in the British and French presses and were put out by the missions (q.v.) in their own journals. Lugard sought to defend his own activities: J.R.L. Macdonald in his *Report on the Uganda Disturbances* of 1893 laid much of the blame on Lugard. Not until the late 1960s did J.A. Rowe use new evidence to elucidate what actually happened.

BATTLE OF MENGO (1966). The climax of the struggle between Prime Minister, later President, Milton Obote (q.v.) and the Baganda (q.v.). The crisis began with the Gold Scandal (q.v.), and deepened with the arrest of the five ministers (q.v.).

On 2 March Obote personally assumed all state powers with the support of the army and the police. In April he forced a new constitution (q.v.) on the country with himself as its Executive President, under whom there was to be "one country, one Parliament, one Government, one people." This brought to an end Buganda's privileged position under the 1962 Constitution which involved abolishing the other kingdom governments at the same time. A series of provisions undermined Buganda's privileges in detail. Unelected chiefs might no longer sit in local councils or legislatures; the Buganda Civil Service Commission was abolished: all civil servants would be apppointed by the central government in the future; the separate court system of the Buganda government was abolished; chiefs in Buganda might no longer own or benefit from official mailo land (*see* [B]Uganda Agreement); and finally local monarchs might no longer hold other official positions. It followed that Kabaka Mutesa II (q.v.) was no longer Head of State. Legal action taken on behalf of the Buganda government failed to prevent these changes.

The Buganda government reacted defiantly. The unelected chiefs refused to leave the Buganda Lukiiko (Parliament), and the Kabaka appealed to the United Nations and to the British Government, and ordered arms from a British firm. The Lukiiko ordered the central government out of Buganda by 30 May. This was an act of high risk defiance: Kampala (q.v.), the seat of central government, is within Buganda. Many of the Baganda rose in defense of their government and their privileges and barricaded the roads.

Obote did not wait for the ultimatum to expire. On 23 May three Baganda chiefs were arrested and a dusk-to-dawn curfew was ordered in Buganda. The following day the army under Idi Amin (q.v.) was ordered to investigate reports that arms were being secretly cached in the *Lubiri*, the Kabaka's palace. According to some accounts the resulting battle broke out because soldiers overstepped their orders. Other reports suggest that the army was ordered to take the palace. A fierce battle ensued, from which the Kabaka escaped by climbing over the back wall and finding a taxi which took him out of the country into Rwanda (q.v.), whence he fled to London. He told his side of the story in *Desecration of My Kingdom* (1967). Baganda claim that up to a thousand people were killed in the battle. Casualty figures were never published, but hospitals in Kampala said afterwards that they were called upon to treat many gunshot wounds, but were not allowed to log the casualties as such.

This second Battle of Mengo left the Baganda with an ineradicable sense of bitterness and hatred of Obote. Both the *Lubiri,* the palace, and the *Bulange,* the Buganda parliament building, were used by the military until in 1993 President Museveni (q.v.) promised that they would be returned to the Baganda when alternative accommodation could be found for the army and for the Ministry of Defence. This loss of the *Lubiri* and *Bulange* added greatly to Buganda's sense of bitterness.

BAZARRABUZA, TIMOTHY (1912–1966). Member of the Legislative Council (Legco) (q.v.) and Uganda's first High Commissioner in London. The son of a Mukonjo (*see* Bakonjo) Protestant church teacher, he was a school teacher and then school inspector until in 1954 he was appointed to the Legco. In 1958 he became one of the first directly elected members of the Legco, representing Toro (q.v.). He joined Milton Obote (q.v.) in criticizing the divisive part religion played in political party membership. In 1959 he became a member of the Wild Committee on constitutional development. At independence in 1963 he was appointed High Commissioner in London. A keen mountaineer, he was tragically killed in a climbing accident.

BELL, SIR HESKETH (1864–1952). Commissioner of Uganda, 1905–1907, Governor of Uganda, 1907–1909. Bell had previously been Administrator of Dominica in the West Indies. He arrived when the sleeping-sickness (q.v.) epidemic was at its height. Bell ordered the evacuation of the land along the shores of Lake Victoria (q.v.) in Buganda (q.v.) and Busoga (q.v.), in spite of Colonial Office hesitations because of the drastic nature of the scheme, and against some local medical opinion. The Sesse and Bavuma Islands in Lake Victoria were also evacuated. It is not clear that this was the life-saving operation that Bell believed: some people may have died as a result of the move. Some medical opinion believed that selective bush clearance would have been more effective, which seems to accord better with modern opinion.

Bell arrived at a time when major decisions about Uganda's economic future had to be made. He resisted calls for white settlement in Uganda and for Uganda to be federated with Kenya (q.v.), and believed that Uganda offered an opportunity for locally-based development towards a self-sustaining economy. In order to improve the quality of cotton, he banned the growing of any but the American Upland variety, the best-adapted for Uganda, and in spite of this arbitrary action, cotton-growing continued to expand, and he embarked on a program of road-building and encouraged the introduction of motor vehicles to transport cotton and other crops and goods.

BIBLE CHURCHMEN'S MISSIONARY SOCIETY (BCMS). A conservative evangelical missionary society of the Anglican Church (q.v.). It was formed in 1922 by some members of the Church Missionary Society (CMS) (q.v.) after a dispute between themselves and more liberal members of the Society. All BCMS members had to sign a declaration of faith which states that "the Canonical Books of the Old and New Testaments are wholly trustworthy, historically as well as in matters of faith and doctrine." Four further sections of this declaration of faith appear to be directed against Roman Catholic (q.v.) and high Anglican beliefs on the nature of the priesthood and the sacraments. After World War II the BCMS and the CMS developed a better understanding and in 1966 moved into a new shared headquarters building in London together with an Anglican mission working in Rwanda (q.v.).

In Uganda the BCMS works among the Karamojong (q.v.). The mission opened its first station in 1929 at Lotome, and a second in 1933 in Labwor. In the late 1950s a new emphasis was given to the work and the six Karamojong parishes were formed out of the Soroti (q.v.) Deanery, and placed under African leadership. In 1976 Karamoja was made a diocese of the Church of Uganda (q.v.). In 1986 the Rt Revd Peter Lomongin was appointed as its Bishop.

BIGO BYA MUGENYI. A large entrenched earthwork on the south bank of the Katonga River (0° 10′ N., 31°15′ E.), an iron-age site associated with the legendary Bacwezi (q.v.) kings, and the most important of the pre-historic earthworks in Uganda. Mugenyi appears in the legends as a cattle-keeper and a brother of one of the Bacwezi kings, Ndahura, a great warrior. A few miles to the east and west of Bigo there are smaller earthworks. When first discovered Bigo was thought to be a fortified enclosure. The Bigo complex was first described in 1909 and surveyed in 1921. More precise surveying and excavation was undertaken in the 1960s. Carbon datings placed its occupation somewhere between 1290 and 1575 AD. Its occupation by cattle-keepers and its design suggested assocations with the Bahima (q.v.) rulers of Ankole (q.v.) and Rwanda (q.v.) and its dating with the period of the Bacwezi, if oral traditions were taken at their face value. A bibliography of the main references to Bigo between 1909 and 1969 is found in M. Posnansky 1969. It appears to have been a defended site where large numbers of cattle could have been corralled in times of danger.

Bigo is one of a series of sites in western Uganda where similar types of pottery are found, and which therefore appear to belong together. Kibengo is near the southern end of Lake Albert, Munsa and Mubende lie between Kibengo and Bigo, and Ntusi just to the south of Bigo. Evidence from Ntusi which was excavated in the 1980s, including extensive pottery remains, suggests it was a town which flourished between the eleventh and sixteenth centuries. It did not have defensive earthworks. If it is correct that these sites were associated with the Bacwezi, then the carbon datings from Ntusi seem to push back the formation of centralized kingdoms in the interlacustrine area several hundred years, and suggest that the oral histories have been condensed. Mubende was, and still is, a ritual site. It is dominated by the so-called "witch tree" which may be as much as 400 years old. Munsa and Kibengo are both earthworks, though on a smaller scale than Bigo.

BIGOMBE, BETTY (1950–   ). Born in Gulu (q.v.), she was educated at Gayaza High School (*see* Education) and Makerere University (q.v.). She became a nominated member of the National Resistance Council (q.v.) in the government of President Museveni (q.v.), and in 1990 was appointed Minister of State in the Office of the Prime Minister with responsibility for the Pacification of the North. Her remit was the rehabilitation of those areas of northern Uganda which had suffered during the conflict between the National Resistance Army (q.v.) and resistance movements such as those led by Basilio Okello (q.v.) and Tito Okello (q.v.), Alice Lakwena (q.v.) and Joseph Kony (q.v.).

BIKUNYA, PETERO (?–1939). Katikiro (chief minister) of Bunyoro (q.v.) from 1917 to 1939. He was born at Bugoma. Before being appointed to a chieftaincy at Kyangwali in 1907 he was a Protestant (q.v.) church teacher. On the death of Paulo Byabacwezi (q.v.) Bikunya was appointed guardian of Zakayo Jawe, one of his two young sons. In 1927 the Sheldon Press, London, published his *Ky'Abakama ba Bunyoro* ("The Matters Concerning the Bakama of Bunyoro"), the earliest account in Runyoro (*see* Languages) of the history and customs of Bunyoro.

BINAISA, GODFREY LUKWONGA (1919–   ). President of Uganda from 22 June 1979–10 May 1980. He studied at Makerere College (q.v.) and King's College, London, where he graduated in law in 1955 and was called to the English Bar in 1956. In 1961 he was a founder member of the Buganda royalist party, Kabaka Yekka ("the Kabaka only") (q.v.). He was in private legal practice until 1962 when he became Attorney-General in the government of President Obote (q.v.) and President of the Uganda Law Society. He resigned in 1967 after the constitutional crisis of 1966–1967 and returned to private practice. In 1970 he was appointed Chairman of the Law Development Centre and a member of the Uganda Judicial Service Commission, and Chairman of the Commonwealth Lawyers' Conference in 1972. He was the first African to become a Queen's Counsel and an executive member of the Geneva-based International Commission of Jurists.

In 1973 his life was threatened by President Amin (q.v.) and he went into exile, first in Britain (q.v.), and from 1977 onwards in the USA where he practiced in New York. From there he returned to Uganda, becoming President after Y.K. Lule (q.v.) was ousted. He was largely dependent on the support of President Nyerere (q.v.) of Tanzania (q.v.). He clashed several times with the Military Commission (q.v.) and with Paulo Muwanga (q.v.), and was unable to bring the army under control and curb human rights abuses. He was ousted by the Military Commission, and placed under house arrest and there were fears for his safety, but he was released by Obote and allowed to leave the country.

BOUNDARIES. The modern boundaries of Uganda were not finally fixed until 1926. Between 1893 when a Protectorate was first provisionally declared and 1926 major adjustments were made to all Uganda's boundaries, the greatest changes being those made in the east with Kenya (q.v.).

In 1900 at the time of the [B]Uganda Agreement (q.v.) the northern and southern boundaries of Uganda were drawn along straight lines 5.2° N and 1° S. The eastern boundary ran down the western shore of Lake Rudolf and along the Laikipia Escarpment, including in Uganda the whole of what was later to be known as the Kavirondo Region of western Kenya. The western boundary was complicated, running northwards along the 30th parallel to Mboga, then turning northeast to include the western shore of Lake Albert, curving westwards round the southern portion of the Lado Enclave (q.v.) to Nimule, and then following the Nile (q.v.) northwards. The Lado Enclave was first leased to King Leopold of the Belgians and then administered by Sudan (q.v.), and did not become part of Uganda until 1914.

The southern half of the eastern boundary was redrawn in 1902 along its present line of demarcation through Mount

Elgon (q.v.) and south along the Lwakhakha and Sio Rivers to Lake Victoria (q.v.) when the area to the east, the former Eastern Province of Uganda, was reallocated to the East African Protectorate (later Kenya). The northern half of the boundary was redrawn further westward in 1926 when the former Rudolf Province of Uganda was ceded to Kenya.

The southern boundary with German East Africa was finally agreed in 1910 when an enclave south of 1° S was transferred to Uganda. The western boundary with the Congo (later known as Zaire [q.v.]) was drawn along its present line of demarcation in 1915 when a small area south of Lake Albert was added to Uganda and the western shore of Lake Albert was ceded to the Congo.

Until 1921 a large part of western Kenya remained part of the Anglican (q.v.) Diocese of Uganda although it had ceased to be part of the Uganda Protectorate. The Church Missionary Society (q.v.) was responsible for Anglican work in this area, but in settler-dominated Kenya the church had developed differently from the church in Uganda. Kenyan Anglicans were not at all pleased to find themselves part of the Diocese of Mombasa.

In 1976 President Amin (q.v.), during his term of office as Chairman of the Organization of African Unity (q.v.), announced claims to a ''Greater Uganda'' (q.v.) which would have included all the areas which at any time had belonged to Uganda. He seems to have been influenced by Somali claims to ''Greater Somalia.'' Kenya felt particularly threatened by this claim because it seemed to encourage Somalia's aspirations, and Kenya was concerned about instability from Somali *shifta* (bandits) on her northern border. Kenya therefore reacted furiously to Amin's claims, while Sudan treated them almost as a joke. There may have been a further reason for the strength of Kenya's reaction. Amin's claims were made on 15 February, just two days after a Kenyan student, Esther Chesire (q.v.), daughter of a prominent Kenyan banker, had ''disappeared'' at Entebbe Airport. Any claims to a ''Greater Uganda'' are specifically repudiated in *The Shaping of Modern Uganda* (1976) of which Amin claimed authorship.

BRITAIN AND UGANDA: THE COLONIAL PERIOD. Britain became somewhat reluctantly involved in Uganda in the 1890s. Missionaries of the Church Missionary Society (CMS) (q.v.) and the White Fathers (q.v.) had arrived in Buganda (q.v.) in 1877 and 1879 respectively and had quickly made converts. The Christian martyrdoms (q.v.) of 1885–1887 elicited widespread concern in Britain. At the same time Germany was making claims to the hinterland of the coastal strip of what is now Tanzania (q.v.) which endangered British interests in Zanzibar and the strip of the coast over which the Sultan of Zanzibar claimed sovereignty. In 1886 an agreement was reached by which the land behind the Tana River would become a British ''sphere of influence'' and that behind the Rovuma River would constitute a German sphere of influence. The line of demarcation extended to the shores of Lake Victoria (q.v.), leaving uncertainty about Uganda.

In 1890 the Anglo-German Treaty (q.v.) was signed under which Heligoland (an island in the North Sea) was ceded by Britain to Germany, and in return Uganda was recognized as being in the British sphere of influence. At the same time the British government granted a charter to the Imperial British East Africa Company (IBEAC) (q.v.), and Frederick Lugard (q.v.) was dispatched to Uganda as its emissary. He was to offer British protection to Kabaka Mwanga (q.v.), in return for allowing missionaries and traders free access to Buganda. By 1891 the IBEAC had run out of money, and Lugard was ordered to withdraw. This so alarmed the CMS missionaries that they raised a considerable sum in order to enable the Company to remain for a year, and in the meantime they lobbied vigorously for Britain to declare a protectorate.

The Battle of Mengo 1892 (q.v.) was felt to underline the dangers if Uganda were to be abandoned by the IBEAC and Britain, and ensured that Britain would intervene. This happened in 1893 when a provisional British Protectorate was declared which was made substantive the following year. The boundaries (q.v.), however, of what was to be Uganda were not settled for some time.

Early British administrators admired the kingdom states which they encountered in Uganda, and preserved aspects of traditional rule. Uganda became a showcase of the policy of indirect rule, the weaknesses of which did not become apparent until late in the colonial period and after independence. Uganda was less well-suited to European settlement than Kenya (q.v.), and a series of Governors (q.v.) made clear that Uganda would be developed by and for its African population, though under British tutelage. Its financial viability and its production of valuable commodity crops would be kept to the forefront of planning.

The Mau Mau uprising in Kenya (q.v.) and the expense of crushing it speeded up the decolonization process throughout East Africa. The semi-federal status of Buganda posed acute problems, and the Constitutional Conferences (q.v.) held at Marlborough House (q.v.) and Lancaster House (q.v.) patched together a constitution (q.v.) which quickly became unworkable. Independence was granted in 1963.

BRITAIN AND UGANDA: RELATIONS WITH PRESIDENT OBOTE 1963–1971. Britain continued to play an important role in Uganda after independence as the main provider of aid, and as the country referred to for policy guidance by the European Community and to a much lesser extent by the United States of America. The new Mulago Hospital (*see* Medicine) in Kampala (q.v.) and the National Assembly (q.v.) building were both gifts from Britain on the eve of independence designed to strengthen links between Britain and Uganda.

British policy towards Uganda since independence has been dominated by the cold war concern to counter communist influence. Any move towards socialism was viewed with alarm. It was thought important that Westminster-style democracy and capitalism should be seen to be successful. Britain was also anxious to preserve her commercial interests in Uganda, and aid was directed towards these two ends. The fragility of the new state and the seriousness of the legacy of unsolved problems which Uganda inherited at independence was not fully recognized. Britain's relations with South Africa and Rhodesia, where she was apparently more concerned with protecting white interests than black, vitiated her relations with Black Africa, including Uganda.

British policy on Uganda began to come seriously unstuck in the late 1960s. President Obote (q.v.) moved to nationalize banks and other commercial enterprises and announced a "Move to the Left" (q.v.). This alarmed the Conservative government in Britain. Prime Minister Heath was infuriated by Obote's attack on Britain for agreeing to sell arms to South Africa, and Britain therefore welcomed the news of the coup of 1971 (q.v.) which brought President Amin (q.v.) to power.

BRITAIN AND UGANDA: RELATIONS WITH PRESIDENT AMIN, 1971–1979. Britain was the first country to recognize the new government of President Amin (q.v.). There have been persistent allegations that Britain had some knowledge of what was pending, and was prepared to use the British troops which were exercising just across the border in Kenya (q.v.) to assist Amin if the need arose. The Conservative government in Britain was apparently unconcerned that a democratically elected government had been overthrown, and that as a result the elections which were pending would not take place.

Britain only woke up to the nature of the new regime when Amin moved to expel the Asians (q.v.). The British government then delayed the planned airlift of Asians as long as possible, apparently hoping that an invasion planned by Obote supporters would be successful. The processing of British Asians by the British High Commission in Kampala (q.v.) was done with extreme slowness, and at first Britain refused to take wives with British citizenship whose husbands had some other citizenship.

Relations with Uganda deteriorated steadily from this point onwards. Aid was stopped, and eventually diplomatic relations were broken off, yet trade was allowed to continue. The notorious "whisky run" from Stansted Airport transported spirits and other luxuries for Amin's henchmen; Amin's plane was serviced at Marshall's, Cambridge; and Pye Electronics provided sophisticated electronic surveillance equipment for the notorious State Research Bureau (q.v.). The British Parliament was told that it was being sent to detect TV license dodgers. Labour Prime Minister James

Callaghan was deeply humiliated in 1975 when he had to visit Uganda and plead for the life of Dennis Hills who had angered Amin by describing him in a book as a ''village tyrant.'' After the murder of Archbishop Janani Luwum (q.v.) it was made clear to Amin that he would not be welcome at the Commonwealth Heads of Government Meeting to be held in London.

BRITAIN AND UGANDA: RELATIONS WITH PRESIDENT OBOTE, 1980–1985. When Amin was overthrown in 1979 Britain quickly moved to support his successor, President Lule (q.v.). When he was removed after only 60 days, Britain delayed any recognition of his successor, President Binaisa (q.v.), but gave some minimal aid and some training for the depleted police force. Aid was halted when Binaisa too was ousted.

Considering Britain's previous attitude to Obote, it was astonishing that when he was returned to power after the disputed Elections of December 1980 (q.v.), Britain moved to support him in spite of mounting evidence of human rights violations. When a Commonwealth Military Training Programme ended because the participating states felt unable to continue in view of the nature of the regime, Britain kept the program going on her own with the controversial British Military Training Team (q.v.).

In 1983 Britain refused to join other European Community countries in condemning the expulsion of thousands of Banyarwanda refugees (q.v.). Nor would Britain accept the report by Elliot Abrams (q.v.) of the USA who claimed that between 100,000 and 200,000 people had been killed in the Luwero Triangle (q.v.) by 1984. Instead British Ministers quibbled about the numbers involved. In early 1985 the British High Commissioner in Kampala, Colin McLean, congratulated the Obote government for ''improving the security situation in the country since the last elections.'' The British Foreign Office and Ministry of Defence insisted that there had been ''a gradual improvement in the UNLA's standards and discipline.'' Undoubtedly the Ugandan High Commissioner in London, the plausible and urbane Shafiq Arain (q.v.), played a large part in misleading the British government. In early 1985 the British Home Office decided it was safe for refugees and asylum seekers to be returned to Uganda (this was stopped after an intervention by Amnesty International [q.v.] and the Office of the UN High Commissioner for Refugees).

Britain's complacency about conditions in Uganda was blown sky high by a horrific report on torture in Uganda published by Amnesty International in June 1985. The Foreign Office Minister, Malcolm Rifkind, commenting on the Amnesty Report, said that in spite of the information it contained, he believed the situation in Uganda was "a lot better today, and a lot more acceptable" [than during the Amin regime]. The British media read the Report and found the situation wholly unacceptable and lambasted Rifkind. The British government was forced to back down; High Commissioner Shafiq Arain was called to the Foreign Office, and was told that aid would be suspended unless human rights improved. However, within a few weeks Obote had been ousted by Tito Okello (q.v.) and Basilio Okello (q.v.).

BRITAIN AND UGANDA: RELATIONS WITH PRESIDENT MUSEVENI, 1986 ONWARDS. In February 1986, soon after President Museveni (q.v.) and the National Resistance Movement (NRM) (q.v.) came to power, it was revealed that private British firms which employed former members of Britain's crack squad, the Special Air Services (SAS), to work for the Obote regime in Uganda, continued operations throughout the period in which peace talks were going on in Nairobi. They serviced helicopter gunships and missiles for the army during the Okello interim, and only just got out of Kampala (q.v.) before it fell to the NRM. In spite of British government denials, it is impossible to believe that they had been able to operate unless they had been at least tacitly allowed to do so by the British Foreign Office.

When President Museveni and the National Resistance Movement came to power in 1986 there was, therefore, much fence-mending to be done by Britain. Many Ugandans were extremely bitter about what they saw as betrayal. A new Foreign Office Minister, Lynda Chalker, visited Uganda and was conciliatory and offered token aid. She seems to have persuaded the new government not to declare High Commissioner McLean persona non grata, promising instead to remove him quietly. Aid for reconstruction was promised. But Britain remained cautious at first, fearful that Museveni might be dangerously left-wing.

By the early 1990s, after the end of the cold war, relations between Uganda and Britain had greatly improved. Aid and assistance with training programs had been resumed. Britain once again began to be reluctant to believe any adverse criticisms of the Uganda government, apparently because she wanted an excuse to refuse Ugandan asylum seekers who were still entering Britain, though at a slower rate. Once again interventions had to be made to persuade the British government that, although the situation had greatly improved in Uganda, no country could recover in only a few years from such misrule as Uganda had experienced, and the army was still not totally under government control.

Because of the need for aid, the Uganda government has usually found it necessary to try to maintain good relations with Britain.

BRITISH MILITARY TRAINING TEAM. In 1982 the British Commonwealth responded to a request from President Obote (q.v.) to help train his Uganda National Liberation Army (UNLA) (q.v.). A 36-man, eight-nation team was sent to Jinja (q.v.) Barracks under the Briton, Colonel C.N. Clavering. Obote's government was facing insurgency led by Yoweri Museveni (q.v.) and his National Resistance Army (q.v.). The UNLA had been accused of gross human rights abuses. The training team is reported to have entered one barracks and discovered torture, but it was quickly evicted, and never allowed into any other barracks save the one where it was stationed.

In 1984 the Commonwealth countries which had shared the training with the British pulled out shortly after Elliot Abrams (q.v.) of the US State Department claimed that up to 200,000 people had been killed by the Uganda National Liberation Army in the Luwero Triangle (q.v.): the UNLA had proved impervious to training, and its human rights record was worse, if possible, than before. The British, however, refused to accept Abrams' estimate of killings and agreed to stay on, which was interpreted in the US as a snub to America. Because of the cold war Britain feared that if it did not retain a presence in Uganda, Obote would turn to the Eastern Bloc. Commercial considerations were also involved and may have been equally important. But continued training of the Uganda army proved embarrassingly controversial, and Britain was accused in sections of the media of condoning human rights abuses: even teaching the army to shoot straight endangered Ugandan civilians. The continued presence of the Military Training Team led to difficulties when Obote was overthrown. Fences were mended, however, at inter-governmental level, but the British officers involved were reported to be severely embarrassed by their assignment. They were apparently forbidden to speak to the media or to Amnesty International (q.v.) about their work.

BUDDU. A fertile area of southern Buganda (q.v.) separated from the rest of Buganda by the Lwera Swamp. Its headquarters are at Masaka (q.v.). It had been incorporated into Buganda only in the eighteenth century. In the Wars of Religion (q.v.) the Catholics (q.v.) fled to Buddu, and the area has remained predominantly Catholic up to the present. Its Catholic center is the parish of Villa Maria (q.v.), a few miles west of Masaka (q.v.), where there are schools, seminaries, a hospital, and the headquarters of the African Bannabikira (q.v.) Sisters (*Bannabikira* means "Daughters of the Virgin"), the oldest Catholic African religious congregation on the continent. Masaka suffered severely in the War of Liberation (q.v.) which ousted President Amin (q.v.): it was the first major town the Tanzanian army reached, and it was heavily shelled.

BUGANDA *see* BAGANDA.

[B]UGANDA AGREEMENT (1900). Among the many treaties made with Africans in the nineteenth century, the [B]Uganda Agreement holds a unique place. The regents and ruling chiefs of the Baganda (q.v.) were Christians and literate, understood the terms of the treaty very well, were well able to argue their case, and had the backing of missionaries who knew far more about the country than did the British officials, and were therefore indispensable as interpreters and mediators.

Harry Johnston (q.v.) arrived in Buganda just before Christmas 1899 and immediately started to negotiate with the chiefs, led by the three regents, Apolo Kagwa (q.v.), Stanislaus Mugwanya (q.v.) and Zakariya Kizito Kisingiri (q.v.). The three most important facets of the Agreement were (i) the fixing of Buganda's boundaries, (ii) the establishment of indirect rule through the Kabaka and the traditional hierarchy of chiefs, and (iii) the land settlement.

(i) Included in Buganda under the terms of the Agreement were two areas which had not previously been part of Buganda. The first was Kabula, a sparsely-inhabited area on the border with Ankole (q.v.) where many of the Christian faction had taken refuge during the Wars of Religion (q.v.). The second was Buyaga and Bugangaizi and all other land south of the Kafu River which had previously belonged to Bunyoro (q.v.) and which was now allocated to Buganda as a reward for fighting alongside the British against the Mukama Kabarega (q.v.) of Bunyoro. However, the Kabaka had to give up his very doubtful claims to tribute from Busoga (q.v.), Bunyoro, Toro (q.v.) and Ankole.

(ii) Buganda was made a province of the Protectorate equal in status to any other province, and subject to Protectorate laws, but provided that the Kabaka and his chiefs and people cooperated loyally with the Protectorate government, he was recognized as their ruler. His courts would try cases between Baganda, he and his chiefs would be salaried, and the land would be organized in 20 sazas (counties) each under a senior chief. There would be a lukiiko or council made up of the saza chiefs, three chief ministers, and 60 other members nominated by the Kabaka. This amounted to a considerable modification of traditional practice, while building on it and incorporating many traditional elements and values.

(iii) Most radical of all was the land settlement. This was a complete departure from tradition, and uniquely in East

Africa allowed land to be held in freehold. Just over half the land area of Buganda was declared to be forest or waste land, and was vested in the crown. The remainder was allocated to the Kabaka, certain royal personages, the regents and ministers, the saza chiefs, the missions (q.v.) and the government. The amounts of land to be granted to each were specified in square miles (hence the term mailo land [q.v.]), but the actual demarcation was left to the lukiiko. Mailo land-ownership radically changed the relations between chiefs and their clients, and led to greater movement of people as they searched about for good land to claim in the first instance, and later took to buying and selling land. No other area of Uganda was treated in the same way with regard to land.

The course of politics in Uganda before and after independence and up to 1966 was governed to a large degree by the efforts of the Baganda to retain and exploit the privileges which they believed were granted to them in the 1900 Agreement.

BUGISU *see* BAGISU.

BUKEDI. A small area (1,753 square miles; 4,500 square kilometers) of southeastern Uganda which was renamed the administrative district of Tororo (q.v.) in 1978. It is bounded in the west by the Mpologoma River which widens out into swamps, and in the east by Mbale (q.v.) and Mount Elgon (q.v.).

This area is part of an ancient migration corridor which contains the remnants of many groups which reached there, either ahead of the rest of their community, or who stayed behind when the rest of the community moved on. So within this area are found six ethnic groups. The Padhola are a Lwoo (q.v.) people; groups of Iteso (q.v.) live in Pallisa in the north; the remaining Banyuli, Badama, Samia-Bagwe and Bagwere are all Bantu-speaking peoples (*see* Languages). The *matooke* plantain is the staple food of the Bantu-speaking peoples; the other peoples use grains as their staple food, and this dietary difference is an important cultural marker.

There are serious ethnic and religious rivalries between these peoples. In 1960 riots broke out against the chiefs and the unpopular methods which they used to collect taxes. These were used to whip up ethnic and religious rivalries which were close to the surface; chiefs were attacked and two were killed; a Protestant (q.v.) chief proved totally unacceptable, and the Protectorate administration was forced to agree to the appointment of a Catholic (q.v.), P.C. Ofwono, who had local legitimacy. It was three weeks before order was restored. With independence fast approaching, religious tension took on a political coloring because of the identification of the Democratic Party (q.v.) with Catholicism and the rival Uganda People's Congress (q.v.) led by Milton Obote (q.v.) with the Church of Uganda (q.v.). Padhola became a stronghold of the Democratic Party.

BUNYORO *see* BANYORO

BUNYORO AGREEMENT. Not until 1933 was an Agreement entered into with Bunyoro (q.v.), thereby bringing her into line with Toro (q.v.) and Ankole (q.v.). Before then Bunyoro had been treated as a conquered country. The Agreement recognized the Mukama and his heirs as rightful rulers, and the Mukama was the greatest beneficiary. The Agreement was made between the Governor acting through the District Commissioner, and the Mukama. The Katikiro (chief minister) and other county- and sub-county chiefs were to be appointed by the Mukama subject to the Governor's approval, and appointments had to be made in consultation with the District Commissioner, who might recommend the dismissal of chiefs. All financial estimates had to be submitted to the District Commissioner. The Mukama might consult with the Rukurato (Bunyoro parliament), whose function was to discuss matters referred to it by the Mukama, and make recommendations. Not all the chiefs were happy to sign at first because so little recognition was given to their position. Although the Agreement set out the boundaries of Bunyoro, the Mukama made a formal claim to the "Lost Counties" (q.v.) at the ceremony when the Agreement was signed.

The Agreement gave few privileges in practice to Bunyoro, but gave Bunyoro a more dignified status, and was thus valued. It may also be seen as a milestone on the road to recovering the Lost Counties.

BURKITT, DR DENIS (1911–1993). A government surgeon who worked in Uganda from 1946 to 1964, and was then employed by the [British] Medical Research Council. He was the discoverer, while working in Uganda, of Burkitt's lymphoma, a form of cancer. It normally causes large, disfiguring and highly-malignant growths on the faces of young children, and Burkitt found that it occurred in a specific geographical area of Africa. He went on to discover that it responded easily to chemotherapy, and that it was caused by a virus. He published his first paper on the form of cancer which is named after him in 1958, but it was not until 1961 that the importance of his discovery was recognized. In the late 1960s his knowledge of African diets enabled him to recognize the importance of dietary fibre for avoiding conditions which were almost unknown in Uganda but common in the West where people ate over-refined foods. His work helped to put Mulago Hospital (*see* Medicine) on the international medical map. The staff of Makerere (q.v.) Medical School provided him with invaluable academic research backup without which he could not have achieved his breakthrough on Burkitt's lymphoma.

BUSHENYI MASSACRE (1979). Bushenyi lies in southwestern Uganda. There had been serious trouble in this area between Christians and Muslims before the fall of President Amin (q.v.), and this was one reason for the religious leaders' conference held in 1976 and chaired by Archbishop Janani Luwum (q.v.). In March 1979 after the fall of Mbarara (q.v.) to the advancing Tanzanian Army and the Uganda National Liberation Army (q.v.), Idd Tamukedde and three other Muslims (*see* Islam) were murdered by Protestants (q.v.) who prevented their bodies from being buried for two months. The killers were not brought to justice. In the aftermath of the capture of Kampala (q.v.) there was further harassment of Muslims, and several leading men were murdered. No official action was taken. Violence against Muslims increased during May and it was claimed that 27 mosques and 45 Muslim homes were burnt in the districts of Bushenyi and Mbarara.

On 25 June a Protestant was murdered and the Muslims were accused of the crime. The following day a group of Protestants rounded up over 60 people whose names are known, including men, women and children, and murdered them, throwing the bodies into the Rwizi River. The group included an old man of 85 and tiny children. Only 36 bodies were recovered, and these were buried in a mass grave at Nyamitanga Mosque. Many survivors fled the area. A school at Kakuuto catered for 96 children orphaned by the massacre. Eyewitnesses have been able to name the killers of nearly 40 of these, and to identify people who are illegally living on land stolen at this time. Only four of the murderers were jailed.

President Obote (q.v.) returned to Uganda in 1980 and landed in Bushenyi where he had wide support. Muslims claim that the anniversaries of his return became excuses for further harassment of Muslims.

The Bushenyi Massacre was brought to the attention of the Commission on Human Rights (q.v.) but those who did so were not satisfied that it was adequately dealt with. President Museveni (q.v.) was accused of being implicated: he gave his evidence in secret and was cleared by the Commission; Edward Rurangaranga, a Minister under Obote, also accused of being implicated, was not investigated.

BUSOGA *see* BASOGA

BUSULU AND *ENVUJO* LAW OF 1928. *Busulu* was the tribute due to a chief by the Baganda (q.v.) in pre-colonial times in return for his protection. *Envujo* was a gift of produce given to a chief as a pledge of loyalty. Traditionally it had been given in beer or the plantains (*matooke*) which are the staple food of the Baganda. Under the [B]Uganda Agreement of 1900 (q.v.), freehold mailo (q.v.) estates were allotted to chiefs. They could charge their tenants reasonable rents, but *busulu* and *envujo* payments were no longer strictly relevant. Some chiefs, however, increasingly demanded them. *Envujo* became in many cases, not a gift in the traditional manner, but the exaction of what was sometimes an unreasonably large portion of a tenant's cotton crop. *Busulu* became increasingly onerous.

By the late 1920s the exaction of *busulu* and *envujo* had reached a point where action had to be taken. The *Busulu* and *Envujo* Law came into force in January 1928 and provided protection for peasant tenant farmers on mailo land. The new law limited the amounts that might legally be charged, and protected tenants against unreasonable eviction. Eviction of tenants became illegal except when the land was required for public purposes (when compensation had to be paid), if the tenant defaulted on the payment of rent, or for other "good and sufficient cause."

BWAMBA *see* BAAMBA

BYABACWEZI, PAULO (?–1912). A hereditary Mujwarakondo (crown wearer), his chieftaincy of Bughaya being the foremost in Bunyoro (q.v.). When Mukama Kabarega (q.v.) fled to Lango (q.v.) in 1894 to evade capture by the British, he appointed Byabacwezi as his viceroy. The Banyoro were defeated twice by the British that year, and Byabacwezi therefore made what terms he could, so retaining his chieftaincy. The first Christian teachers of the Church Missionary Society (q.v.) operated from his headquarters in 1895, and he was baptized in 1899 after considerable hesitation. His primary commitment remained to the realization of his ambitions within the traditional social structures of Bunyoro, though he was prepared to make some accommodation with Christianity and colonialism if this would help him to achieve his goal. Soon after his baptism he married Damari Karujuka, a member of the royal Babito (q.v.) clan. Kabarega's defeat and capture in 1899 created a power vacuum. Yosiya Kitehimbwa, the British appointee as Mukama, was a minor and lacked legitimacy because Kabarega was still alive, though in exile, and for the next two years Byabacwezi and Rwabudongo vied for supremacy. Byabacwezi, as one of the regents, was accused of usurping powers which were the prerogative of the Mukama. Kitehimbwa was quickly replaced by the more able Andereya Duhaga (q.v.), but he too lacked legitimacy, and Byabacwezi's ambitions were not entirely quelled. In 1907, when the Nyangire Rising (q.v.) broke out, he called in question the Mukama's position, and sought high honor for himself. He died suddenly in 1912, his ambitions unfulfilled.

BYAKWEYAMBA, YAFETI (?–1912). Uncle of Mukama Daudi Kasagama (q.v.) of Toro (q.v.) and related to Mukama Kabarega (q.v.) of Bunyoro (q.v.). As a child he had been taken from Toro by the armies of Buganda (q.v.) and brought up as a page in the royal enclosure where he was made responsible for some of the royal wives. He was baptized in Buganda by the Church Missionary Society (q.v.) and in 1891 he and Kasagama were introduced by Zakariya Kizito Kisingiri (q.v.) to Captain Lugard (q.v.) as dispossessed Toro royalty. Lugard was on his way to the west to outflank Kabarega, and he decided that it would fit in well with his plans if the kingdom of Toro could be revived as a bulwark against Kabarega. At first Lugard seemed to think that Byakweyamba himself was the heir.

Once back in Toro, with Kasagama instated as Mukama, Byakweyamba challenged Kasagama by building himself a larger enclosure. He was sent away from the court to Mwenge on the borderland with Bunyoro, and which Bunyoro claimed, and was soon under attack from Kabarega. But when Kabarega was defeated in 1895, his tenure of Mwenge became secure enough for him to invite Christian teachers from Buganda to his headquarters. His increasing security also encouraged him to challenge Kasagama further by declaring himself independent of Toro overrule. He might have succeeded in this bid for power had it not been for colonial backing of Kasagama. In 1897, disappointed in his ambitions and suffering from a lame leg, he retreated to Buddu (q.v.) where he committed suicide in 1912.

-C-

CAMO, RWOT, OF ACHOLI *see* RWOTCAMO

CATHOLICS, ROMAN CATHOLIC CHURCH. The first Catholic missionaries to reach Uganda were the mainly French White Fathers (q.v.) who arrived in 1879, two years after the Church Missionary Society (CMS) (q.v.). At the time of the Wars of Religion (q.v.) their adherents were labelled Bafranza (French) whilst the adherents of the CMS were labelled Bangereza (English). The Protectorate government encouraged the Dutch and English Mill Hill Fathers (q.v.) to work in Uganda to help break down this stereotyping which was felt to be politically dangerous. The Italian Verona Fathers (q.v.) arrived later and worked in the north of Uganda. During World War II a number of Verona Fathers were interned, and this created difficulties for the church in the north.

After the hierarchy had been established in Uganda in 1953, what had been missionary areas under the ultimate direction of Propaganda Fide in Rome became fully established dioceses. An increasing number of Bishops were Ugandans, and members of other Catholic religious orders and congregations were invited to fulfill particular roles.

From the beginning Bishop Streicher (q.v.) laid great importance on the training of African priests, and these were required to reach the same educational standards as Catholic priests elsewhere in the world. Inevitably this meant that missionaries were only slowly able to hand over to Ugandans, but it also meant that Catholic priests were fully the counterparts of missionary priests and able to hold their own in ecumenical discussions after Vatican II, the council which opened up the Catholic Church to the modern world. Congregations of African sisters were founded, the Bannabikira (Daughters of the Virgin) (q.v.) centered on Villa Maria (q.v.) in Buddu (q.v.) and the Little Sisters of St Francis founded by Mother Kevin (q.v.) being two of the earliest and best known. Local congregations of sisters are found in each diocese. Congregations of Brothers are much smaller and fewer as boys with a vocation to the religious life usually become priests. There is also a large number of catechists, usually married men, without whom the parishes could not continue to provide for the faithful. Much effort has been put into the training of catechists and the laity since Vatican II. Each area of Uganda also has its Catholic schools for boys and girls, other educational establishments including teacher training, and a Catholic hospital.

When nationalist political parties were established in the 1950s and 1960s most Catholics joined the Democratic Party (q.v.) while the Uganda People's Congress (q.v.) became associated with the Protestants (q.v.). Religious bitterness, present ever since the Wars of Religion, was thus perpetuated into the present, and in spite of efforts by both church and political leaders, this religio-political cleavage persists.

Under President Amin (q.v.) both churches suffered severely, but the Catholics were probably slightly better able to ride out the storm because of their strong international and regional links. During the second presidency of Milton Obote (q.v.) the main opposition came from the Democratic Party and the Catholic Church: Obote divided the Christians by favoring the Protestants who found the advantages offered difficult to resist. The Justice and Peace Commission was established in Uganda in the 1980s, and is proving effective in training people at parish level in concepts of human rights and justice.

CHESIRE, ESTHER (d.1976). A Kenyan student at Makerere University (q.v.) who "disappeared" while attempting to fly home through Entebbe Airport on 13 February 1976. Her companion, Sally Githere, was set free and returned to Kenya (q.v.). It was reported that Chesire had been warned against going out with Ugandan security men, but that she had ignored warnings. She was the daughter of Robert Chesire, a prominent Kenyan banker, and a clan relative of Daniel arap Moi, then Kenyan Vice-President. Her "disappearance" was not made public until 27 March, presumably because the Kenyan authorities hoped she might be found unharmed as a result of diplomacy.

The Commission of Enquiry (q.v.) chaired by Professor

Langlands was ordered to add Chesire's "disappearance" to its remit, which, because it had international implications, endangered the Commission's work. No information was ever forthcoming about Chesire's fate.

CHRISTIAN MARTYRS. Between 1885 and 1887 one Briton and 50 Ugandans whose names are still known were martyred, half Catholics (q.v.) and half Protestants (q.v.), and perhaps another 150 whose names were not recorded may also have perished. The martyrdoms took place in the early years of the reign of Kabaka Mwanga (q.v.) against a background of insecurity and jostling for power among the religious and generational factions at his court. Part of Mwanga's insecurity arose from the perceived threat to Buganda (q.v.) from external imperial powers including Egypt, Britain and Germany.

The first three martydoms took place in January 1885. A.M. Mackay (q.v.) of the Church Missionary Society (q.v.) wanted to go south across Lake Victoria (q.v.) with letters. He refused the offer of an official legate to accompany him, not realizing that the presence of a legate was not an interference with his privacy, but a guarantee that he was traveling legitimately. He was accompanied down to the lakeshore by the Revd Robert Ashe and by several Ugandans including two young boys, Yusufu Lugalama and Marko Kakumba. Yusufu had been given to the mission by his master but without court permission, and Marko had deserted the royal service. The Kabaka was persuaded by his Katikiro (chief minister) that in accompanying the missionaries they were acting treasonably, and soldiers were sent to arrest them. Yusufu, Marko and an older boy, Nuwa Serwanga, who had been arrested later, were burnt to death at Mpimere-bera just west of the modern Kampala (q.v.).

The next to die was the British missionary, Bishop James Hannington (q.v.). The missionaries in Buganda tried to prevent him coming through Busoga (q.v.) because of the belief that anyone approaching from that direction would bring disaster on Buganda, but they failed. Hannington was murdered on Mwanga's orders probably on 29 October 1885 and this led directly to the martyrdom of Joseph Mukasa

Balikuddembe, a Catholic and a senior page at court. He had already pleaded the cause of the Protestant missionaries at some risk to himself, and he now reproved the Kabaka for the Bishop's death. Mwanga rounded on Balikuddembe, urged on by the Katikiro who saw in him a possible rival for power. The Katikiro saw to it that the execution was carried out quickly before the Kabaka could change his mind, which he did shortly afterwards, but it was too late.

In early 1886 the royal enclosure was twice burnt down, and Mwanga began to fear that the Christians were in some way responsible for this. Some of the Muslim (*see* Islam) faction encouraged him in this belief. In May a Christian princess married, which was contrary to custom, and then burnt her fetishes, actions which caused alarm at court lest divine retribution should come upon them for this sacrilege.

On 25 May there occurred the incident which sparked off the now inevitable confrontation. Mwanga returned unexpectedly early after an unsuccessful hippo hunt to find that a favorite page, Mwafu, was missing, learning to read (i.e., learning Christianity) with another page, Dennis Ssebuggwawo. Mwanga was given to the practice of sodomy, allegedly learnt from the Arabs, and the Christian pages often arranged to be missing when Mwanga wanted them, or else outright refused to gratify him. Mwafu's absence enraged the Kabaka because this page was still compliant: if he were now learning Christianity, Mwanga was likely to lose this partner. Denis Ssebuggwawo was arrested for deliberately inciting Mwafu to disobedience. Mwanga then raged through the court, beating up Apolo Kagwa (q.v.) and ordering Honorat Nyonyintono (q.v.) to be castrated. Both were known to be Christians, but were too valuable to be executed. Two others, Mudduwaguma and Eliya Mbwa, died as a result of castration. Many of the younger pages were able to flee, but there was no escape for the leaders and more senior Christian pages. Charles Lwanga, head page in the audience hall and leader of the Catholic pages, baptized five Catholic catechumens during the night in view of what might happen in the morning.

When morning came Mwanga castigated the chiefs for sending disobedient boys and the dregs of their clans to serve him at court. This was an accusation the chiefs were particularly sensitive about: they needed to demonstrate their own loyalty and did so by agreeing that the disobedient must be punished, and promising to provide more obedient substitutes. The executioners rounded up known Christians from among the pages at court and its surroundings. The Katikiro ensured that Andrew Kagwa, an increasingly influential page whose power he had begun to fear, was included among those to be executed, though the Kabaka was reluctant to order the death of a favorite. He was executed immediately, as Balikuddembe had been, before Mwanga could change his mind. The others were marched off to one of the official places of execution at Namugongo to the east of Kampala. Some were killed en route, but most were burnt to death at Namugongo itself. Those killed in the few days after 25 May were Athanasius Bazekuketta, Gonzaga Gonza, Mathias Kalemba, Luke Banabakintu, James Buzabaliawo, Gyavira, Alexander Kadoko, Ambrose Kibuka, Kifamunyanja, Anatole Kirigwajjo, Achilles Kiwanuka, Kiwanuka Giyaza, Kizito, Frederick Wigram Kizza, Kwabafu, Charles Lwanga, who was burnt separately before the others, Mbaga Tuzinde, Mugagga, Mukasa Kiriwawanvu, Adolphus Mukasa Ludigo, Robert Munyagabyanjo, Pontian Ngondwe, Muwanga Njigija, Bruno Serunkuma, Wasswa and Nuwa Walukaga. One other, David Muwanga, whose identity is uncertain, may also have perished at Namugongo. Besides these a group of Christians perished at Mityana among whom were Chief Omuwanga, Kayizzi Kibuka and Mayanja Kitogo. Two others from Mityana perished at Namugongo. Jean-Marie Muzeyi went into hiding knowing that the Katikiro had a special grudge against him, but he was a marked man and could not escape for ever. He gave himself up in January 1887 and then disappeared. There is some evidence that he was beheaded and his body thrown into a swamp.

Many Christians survived. They did so because even the non-Christian chiefs would not stand for the destruction of all the most promising of their sons and of the younger generation. They warned Mwanga that they could tolerate no more. Far from deterring people from becoming Christians, the numbers asking to learn and be baptized increased dramatically.

The 22 Catholic martyrs were canonized in 1964 and are commemorated annually on 3 June. The Protestants commemorate their martyrs on 25 October. Although all the martyrs were connected in one way or another with the court of Buganda, not all were Baganda (q.v.). They came from Ankole (q.v.), Busoga (q.v.), Bunyoro (q.v.) and Toro (q.v.) as well as Buganda, and are rightly called the Uganda Martyrs.

CHURCH MISSIONARY SOCIETY (CMS). The largest Anglican (q.v.) missionary society, the CMS represents the evangelical wing of the church. Founded in 1799 by a group of laymen, its main fields of work were in Africa and Asia. Its missionaries included lay people, especially medical and educational personnel. As the only non-Catholic mission in Uganda for many years, the CMS and its adherents were generally known in Uganda simply as Protestants (q.v.) as opposed to the Roman Catholics (q.v.). At the time of the Wars of Religion (q.v.) CMS converts were frequently called Bangereza (English) as opposed to the Bafranza (French) followers of the White Fathers (q.v.) mission.

The CMS was drawn to establish work in Uganda by the publication in Britain of a letter from the traveler H. M. Stanley (q.v.) who visited the court of Kabaka Mutesa I (q.v.) of Buganda (q.v.) in 1975, and who believed that Mutesa would welcome Christian missionaries. The first missionaries to arrive reached Uganda in 1877, and, like the Roman Catholic White Fathers (q.v.) who arrived in early 1879, were confined by Mutesa to the capital and drawn into confrontation with the Catholics by the Kabaka.

Among the outstanding missionaries of the early period was the Scot, Alexander Mackay (q.v.), a craftsman whose services were often called upon by the Kabaka, and whose ebullient personality proved attractive to many young men in training at court for future high office. George Pilkington was a brilliant linguist who was responsible for translating the Bible into Luganda. The literature produced by early

CMS missionaries includes a number of books which are important primary sources for the period. The Revd Robert Ashe wrote two of the most lively and valuable accounts of Uganda in the 1880s, *Two Kings of Uganda* (1889) and *Chronicles of Uganda* (1990). Ruth Fisher's *Twilight Tales of the Black Baganda* (1912), ineptly titled by her publisher, is a classic. The first Anglican Bishop to reach Uganda, A.R. Tucker (q.v.), wrote an account of his work in Uganda entitled *Eighteen Years in Uganda and East Africa* (1908). *Uganda Memories* by Sir Albert Cook (q.v.), founder of Protestant medical work in Uganda, was published by the Uganda Society in 1945. The Revd John Roscoe (q.v.) is known as an anthropologist rather than as a missionary, and the list of his works is extensive.

The CMS worked in most areas of Uganda, often sending European missionaries after African catechists had already pioneered the way. Protestant work in West Nile (q.v.), among the Karamojong (q.v.) and in Kigezi was carried out by other Christian missions (q.v.).

In the 1930s a Revival movement reached Uganda from Rwanda (q.v.) and became an important factor in the life of the mission and the church in Uganda.

CHURCH OF UGANDA. The name given to the Anglican Church (q.v.) in Uganda established as an autonomous Province of the Anglican Communion (q.v.) through the agency of the Church Missionary Society (CMS) (q.v.). Its full title is the Church of the Province of Uganda. Until the inauguration of the Province it was known as the Native Anglican Church. When the Province was inaugurated by the Archbishop of Canterbury on 16 April 1961 it also included the Anglican Church in Rwanda (q.v.), Burundi, and Mboga in western Zaire (q.v.), but these areas have since been hived off into separate provinces.

When the Province was inaugurated, there were five dioceses and three of its Bishops were expatriates, including the Most Revd Leslie Brown, a CMS missionary, who was elected as its first Archbishop. He resigned in 1965, and the first Ugandan Archbishop, the Most Revd Erica Sabiti (q.v.), was elected to succeed him. Within a few years the episcopate had been entirely Ugandanized. The best-known Archbishop of Uganda was the Most Revd Janani Luwum (q.v.), murdered in 1977 during the presidency of Idi Amin (q.v.). By 1993 the number of dioceses in Uganda had risen to 24, Nebbi being the most recently erected.

No accurate statistics of membership are available, but the best estimate is that some 28–30 percent of the total population identify themselves as members of the Church of Uganda. Not all are regular church attenders. The most vigorous section of the Church of Uganda is that influenced by the Revival movement (q.v.).

Theological training is centered at Bishop Tucker College, Mukono, established in 1917 in memory of Bishop Tucker (q.v.). The standard of theological education given there has been steadily raised. From 1965 onwards some students were entered for the external Diploma in Theology offered by Makerere (q.v.), and from 1982 onwards students have been able to study for the Bachelor of Divinity degree offered by the Association of Theological Institutions of East Africa. In 1963 the first course for women church workers was begun. A few women have taken the diploma and degree courses. Several dioceses have centers for less academic theological training.

The schools (*see* Education) which had been run by the Church Missionary Society (q.v.) and the Native Anglican Church (q.v.) were nationalized by the government shortly after independence, though church influence remains strong in many of them. Hospitals (*see* Medicine) remained in church hands, however. Mengo Hospital opened by Dr (later Sir) Albert Cook (q.v.) in 1897 is the oldest Church of Uganda hospital. There are also hospitals at Fort Portal (q.v.) in the west, Kuluva near Arua (q.v.), Ngora in Teso (q.v.), and Kangando and Kisiizi in the southwest.

CHWA, SIR DAUDI (1896–1939). Kabaka of Buganda (q.v.) 1897–1939. He was appointed Kabaka when his father, Kabaka Mwanga (q.v.), rebelled against British rule. As long as his father remained alive, many Baganda refused to recognize Chwa as Kabaka, and he remained without being invested with the regalia. His education was under the supervision of Mr (later Sir) John Sturrock, a colonial civil servant, and he later attended King's College, Budo (*see* Education). Daudi Chwa was concerned for the welfare of his old school throughout his life, and became chairman of its board of governors. In 1910 Kabaka Mwanga died and was buried at Kasubi. The following day Daudi Chwa was invested with the royal insignia outside the *Lubiri,* the royal palace of Buganda. In 1914, when he came of age in Buganda custom, he was crowned as Kabaka in the chapel of his school which had been built on the royal hill where the Kabakas were traditionally invested. The ceremonies were modified because, for the first time, Buganda had a Christian Kabaka. The chapel service included features borrowed from the English coronation service.

Until 1914 Daudi Chwa ruled through the regency of three of the leading chiefs of Buganda, the Katikiro (chief minister) Apolo Kagwa (q.v.), Zakariya Kizito Kisingiri (q.v.) and Stanislaus Mugwanya (q.v.), and Apolo Kagwa continued to dominate the Buganda government until he was forcibly retired in 1926. In 1924 when Closer Union (q.v.) between the three East African territories was under discussion, Chwa and the Buganda government made known their objections. This concern was reiterated in 1929 when the subject came once again under discussion. In 1926 Chwa set up a Commission to enquire into the finances of the Lukiiko (parliament of Buganda) after repeated allegations that they were being misused. The Commission found incompetence rather than dishonesty. Chwa's health declined from 1936 onwards and he was therefore unable to attend the coronation of King George VI. He died in 1939 just after the outbreak of World War II and was buried at Kasubi, the royal burial place on the outskirts of Kampala (q.v.). He was succeeded by his son, Kabaka Mutesa II (q.v.).

CLOSER UNION. Throughout much of the 1920s the closer union of the three British East African territories of Uganda, Kenya (q.v.) and Tanganyika (*see* Tanzania) was under consideration. As early as 1899 Sir Harry Johnston (q.v.) had been ordered to consider the possibility of bringing Uganda and what was then the East African Protectorate (now

Kenya) under one administration. Johnston became an enthusiastic advocate of the scheme, but the idea was dropped when the boundaries (q.v.) were altered in 1902 to bring the area between Tororo (q.v.) and the Laikipia Escarpment into Kenya, so placing the whole length of the newly-completed railway (q.v.) under one administration.

In 1923 the Devonshire White Paper stated clearly that the interests of Africans must be paramount in the East African territories. When Closer Union between Kenya and Uganda and the League of Nations mandated territory of Tanganyika was mooted from 1924 onwards, it was feared that African interests might be compromised in Uganda and Tanganyika if there were to be closer ties with Kenya. Kenyan settlers were demanding a majority of the seats in any Legislative Assembly as their price for joining such a federation, and it was their possible domination that Ugandan Africans so greatly feared.

Closer Union was the subject of the Ormsby-Gore Commission in 1925, specifically set up to examine reports of widespread African distrust of the Closer Union proposals. It concluded in its report (*The East Africa Commission Report*) that the proposals for Closer Union were premature, but it recommended the establishment of an East African Governors Conference, which was implemented in 1926 with Governor Edward Grigg of Kenya as its chairman. In 1927 the Hilton-Young Commission was sent to probe the situation further, and preferably to find evidence which would enable the British government to go ahead with Closer Union. In its *Report of the Commission on Closer Union in East Africa* published in 1929 it found that there was widespread African and Asian (q.v.) opposition, and that this was shared by many colonial civil servants. Eventually a Joint Select Committee on Closer Union in East Africa, which published its report in 1931, decided that each territory should retain its own identity.

Ugandan Africans, notably the government of Buganda (q.v.), and the Mukama of Bunyoro (q.v.), strongly opposed Closer Union. They did not wish the Uganda economy to go the same way as the Kenyan economy where Africans were encouraged to work on European farms. Kabaka Daudi Chwa (q.v.) and the Buganda government petitioned against Closer Union to each of these Commissions. The few European plantation owners in Uganda were equally opposed to being linked with Kenya where European farming needed constant government support to survive, whereas Ugandan farming was profitable.

Links between the three territories were strengthened during World War II to meet the wartime situation, and in 1943 Closer Union appeared on the agenda again when the Chambers of Commerce and Industry of Eastern Africa passed a resolution urging it. It met with fierce opposition from Ugandans. By this time European businessmen and planters in Uganda favored Closer Union, and in 1944 the British government began to think in terms of closer groupings of colonial territories, and European cotton growers supported stronger links, though not formal federation.

In 1948 an East Africa High Commission (q.v.) was established to coordinate posts, telecommunications, railways and harbors and this led to alarm among Africans. Its headquarters were almost inevitably in Nairobi, as were the headquarters of the common services it coordinated. Many banks and businesses had set up their headquarters in Nairobi, permitting Kenya to finance a trade deficit. Uganda on the other hand had to maintain a trade surplus sufficient to balance the payments she had to make to the Nairobi-based common services. The common currency also worked in Kenya's favor.

Fears of Closer Union greatly increased in 1953 when the ill-advised and short-lived Central African Federation of Northern and Southern Rhodesia and Nyasaland was established against the wishes of the African population by a Conservative government in Britain. The possibility of an East African Federation was voiced by Oliver Lyttleton, then Secretary of State for the Colonies. The local language press and the Buganda government were vociferous in their opposition, and the Governor Sir Andrew Cohen had to give public reassurances that Federation would not take place against the wishes of the people. The East Africa Common Services (q.v.), into which the East Africa High Commission developed, did not long outlast the independence of the three territories.

COMMISSION OF ENQUIRY. This was set up on 12 March 1976 to enquire into the events (*see* Makerere Incident) following the murder of a student, Paul Serwanga, by members of the Public Safety Unit (q.v.) just outside the campus of Makerere University (q.v.). The Commission was chaired by Professor Bryan Langlands, one of the few expatriate staff who still remained at Makerere. The Ugandan lawyer, Fred Mpanga, although terminally ill with cancer, appeared before the Commission on behalf of the University. The main witness to the murder fled to Kenya (q.v.) and refused to return, even when offered the promise of a safe-conduct. The disappearance of a Kenyan student, Esther Chesire (q.v.), in February was added to the enquiry's remit when that became known. On 24 June Mrs Theresa Nanziri Mukasa-Bukenya, Warden of the hall of residence where Chesire had lived, was due to give evidence. The previous day she disappeared, and two days later was found murdered, presumably to prevent her giving evidence. When the students returned from vacation on 8 July they wished to demonstrate about her murder, but were prevented. The Entebbe Raid (q.v.) had occurred on 3–4 July, and the situation in the country had become far more dangerous. Permission was refused for the Commission of Enquiry to add Mrs Mukasa-Bukenya's death to their remit, and on 29 July Professor Langlands was summarily expelled from the country. He was subsequently awarded an OBE by the British government for his long service to Makerere. Langlands tried to carry out a serious and impartial enquiry, and believed it could be done. The students and some other Ugandans were less hopeful. The Commission of Enquiry petered out after Langlands' departure.

COMMON MAN'S CHARTER. This was promulgated at a conference of the Uganda People's Congress (UPC) (q.v.) in December 1969 and was the first of the ideological statements which marked the attempt by President Obote (q.v.) to set out a socialist agenda for Uganda. It is subtitled "First Steps for Uganda to Move to the Left," and was to mark the beginning of "a new political culture and a new way of life, whereby the people of Uganda as a whole—their welfare and their voice in the National Government and in other local authorities—are paramount. It is therefore both anti-feudalism and anti-capitalism." It was a long document of over 6,000 words, obviously meant as the Ugandan counterpart to statements such as the Arusha Declaration produced by President Nyerere of Tanzania (q.v.). It was long on denunciation of tribalism, colonialism, capitalism and privilege and contained a fair amount of rhetoric, but it was short on specifics: these were to be contained in a series of other documents. This attempt to give the country a new direction and revive the UPC came too late: it was at this same conference that the attempted assassination (q.v.) of Obote took place, and the coup of 1971 (q.v.) which brought President Amin (q.v.) to power occurred only 13 months later.

COMMONWEALTH OBSERVER GROUP (COG). The Elections (q.v.) of December 1980 which returned Milton Obote (q.v.) and the Uganda People's Congress (UPC) (q.v.) to power were monitored by a group of nine observers from the Commonwealth: Ambassador E.M. Debrah (Ghana, Chairman), G. Christodoulou (Cyprus), The Hon. G.J. Danson, PC (Canada), G. Matenge (Botswana), K.R.P. Singh (India), R.J.C. Whalen (Australia), Senator John Wickham (Barbados), G.L.V. Williams (Sierra Leone), and Robin Wainwright CMG (Britain). All of them had great experience in public affairs. They each had an assistant, and four additional assistants from each of their countries for the period of the poll, besides a 22-person secretariat.

The COG produced an *Interim Report* on 11 December while counting was still under way and before final results had been declared. In it were noted the difficulties created by the legacy of the Amin (q.v.) years, the intense and dangerous political bitterness between the parties, and the speed with which registration of voters had been carried out. In particular it noted that only one party (which it did not name) had experienced no difficulties in registering nominations, and it noted its own failure to get redress for candidates in Kasese who had been wrongly disqualified. It also noted grave concerns about irregularities in West Nile (q.v.) which led to one party's candidates being declared unopposed. Again the party was not named. It was, in both cases, the UPC. About the elections in Kampala (q.v.) it was far more critical: they were "marred by inordinate and inexcusable delays." Polling stations had not opened until evening in some cases, and the COG found it difficult to believe that this was due to mere incompetence. A sudden announcement that polling would be extended until 2:00 pm the following day caused great anxiety. In spite of these imperfections the COG said it believed the elections had been a valid electoral exercise and reflected the expressed choice of the people of Uganda.

This *Interim Report* was completed before the final results had been declared. At 8:00 pm on 11 December Paulo Muwanga (q.v.), Chairman of the Military Commission (q.v.), issued a proclamation changing the electoral law retrospectively, after results had already begun to be announced. The decree stated that when the result of the poll in a constituency had been ascertained, the returning officer was not to declare it but submit it to the Chairman of the Military Commission, Muwanga himself, who would either declare the candidate with the majority of votes to have been elected, or declare the election null and void (which declaration would not be open to challenge in any court of law) and order a new election. This proclamation was deemed to have come into effect on the previous day, 10 December. The results of the election were announced throughout 12 December, but the COG left the country before that day was out. A number of results were seriously disputed, but challenges at law were unsuccessful. The whole result of the election was called into question in the minds of many of the people of Uganda.

The *Final Report* of the COG dealt with the shortcomings and irregularities of the election in far more detail. The Electoral Commission had been moribund for many years and had had to be revived. Only the Chairman, K. M. S.

Kikira, had any experience at all of running elections, and the Commissioners were hampered by a severely weakened district administration. The COG noted grave concerns about the compilation of the electoral registers. It had received complaints about wrongful inclusions and exclusions. Turbulence in much of West Nile District prevented registers being compiled. In 17 constituencies there and elsewhere UPC candidates had been unopposed as a result of these and other failings of the system for registration of voters and candidates. The COG received reports that 14 District Commissioners had been dismissed and replaced by UPC supporters. The Chief Justice was also replaced just days before the election, which engendered further suspicion. The irregularities over nominations were particularly great, and the report contains evidence of malpractice by the Electoral Commission which the Commission refused to rectify in spite of representations by the COG. Democratic Party (DP) candidates were ruled out by this malpractice. The COG noted that the only English-language, nationally-available newspaper supported the UPC and on occasions "distorted news to advance the cause of that party." The radio gave a disproportionate amount of time to UPC election broadcasts. Experience elsewhere led the COG to express surprise that there was not more actual intimidation.

There was great difficulty in holding the Military Commission to its undertaking that counting would take place, not centrally, but at each polling station. This was considered essential if the exercise was to have any public credibility. On 6 December the COG learnt that the Electoral Commission had persuaded the Military Commission not to honor this undertaking. The COG made it known that it might withdraw unless the undertaking was honored, and the Electoral Commission then announced that counting would be done at polling stations. The late opening of polls in Kampala (q.v.), Mbarara (q.v.) and some other places was noted, and the fears generated by a late-afternoon announcement on polling day that polling would continue into the following day. At stake was the security of polling officers and ballot boxes, but in the event little untoward occurred. In

Nebbi there were insufficient ballot papers at a number of polling stations. In Ndeeba, Kampala West, a presiding officer was arrested because of complaints that he had entered the polling booths with people and instructed them on how to place their votes. The COG praised the conduct of the Police. The COG considered that the actual count had gone off peacefully. It noted its dismay at the retrospective proclamation concerning the announcement of election results, and dismissed what it considered to have been premature claims by the DP that it had won the election. The COG concluded that in spite of a great many shortcomings which it believed could have been overcome, "surmounting all obstacles, the people of Uganda, like some great tidal wave, carried the electoral process to a worthy and valid conclusion."

The UPC claimed an overwhelming victory, and insisted that the COG Report proved that it had won this victory fairly. The defeated parties used the detail of the report, and the retrospective proclamation, whose importance may have been underestimated by the COG, to claim that the elections had not been free or fair. The Uganda Patriotic Movement (q.v.) refused to accept the results at all and, under its leader, Yoweri Museveni (q.v.), took to the bush as the National Resistance Movement (q.v.). The failings and irregularities of the electoral process which the COG report noted, and the action taken by Paulo Muwanga to channel all the results through himself before they were announced, meant that the elections failed to provide the UPC government under Obote with the unassailable mandate they had hoped for.

A number of impartial outsiders have had difficulty in reconciling the long list of malpractices contained in the COG Final Report with the Group's conclusion that the elections were brought to a "worthy and valid conclusion." What, in fact, the COG seems to suggest in the final paragraphs of its Report is that the outcome would still in all probability have been a UPC victory even if the elections had been fully free and fair, and that it was therefore prepared to accept the result. Such a conclusion, while it may have been correct, was obviously unacceptable to the defeated opposition parties.

CONSERVATIVE PARTY. This small party was founded in 1966 in the aftermath of the Battle of Mengo 1966 (q.v.) by Joshua Mayanja-Nkangi, then Katikiro (chief minister) of Buganda. He had previously been leader of the Buganda nationalist party, Kabaka Yekka (''the Kabaka only'') (q.v.). The Conservative Party campaigns for a return to the 1962 Constitution (q.v.) which means a return to a federal form of government and the restoration of the monarchies. In the Elections of 1980 (q.v.) it failed to win any seats at all. Mayanja-Nkangi was given a seat in President Museveni's (q.v.) first cabinet which was broadly-based to try to ensure national acceptance of the new government. A number of Conservative Party supporters have chosen to remain in exile in London.

CONSTITUTIONAL CONFERENCES. Two constitutional conferences were held in London in the runup to Ugandan independence, at Lancaster House (q.v.) and Marlborough House (q.v.). The agenda for the 1961 conference was the Report of the Munster Commission (q.v.) which dealt with the relationships between the central government and the kingdoms. Outstanding matters were dealt with at a further conference at Marlborough House in 1962. At both conferences the main point of contention was the relationship between Buganda (q.v.) and the central government. The privileged position accorded to Buganda by the [B]Uganda Agreement (q.v.) of 1900, and Buganda's reluctance to be part of a unitary state left a legacy of problems which had to be resolved after independence. Among them was the status of the ''Lost Counties'' (q.v.). The fragility of the independence constitutional arrangements was demonstrated in 1966 when Buganda defied the central government and was defeated in the Battle of Mengo 1966 (q.v.).

CONSTITUTIONS. The 1962 independence constitution was worked out at the Lancaster House (q.v.) Conference held the previous year and at the Marlborough House (q.v.) Conference held earlier in 1962. It came into force in March 1962 when Uganda was granted internal self-government, and elections were held. It established Westminster-style democracy, provided for multi-party rule, made provision for a prime minister and non-executive president, and gave semi-federal status to Buganda (q.v.) within a unitary state. Certain privileges were also granted to the Western Kingdoms of Ankole (q.v.), Toro (q.v.) and Bunyoro (q.v.), and to Busoga (q.v.). A referendum was to be held on the thorny issue of the "Lost Counties" (q.v.) within two years.

In 1966, after accusations against President Obote (q.v.) and others had been made in what became known as the Gold Scandal (q.v.), Obote announced the suspension of the 1962 Constitution, and the members of the National Assembly (q.v.) were required to pass, without having read it, an interim constitution which they were told would be found in their pigeon-holes. It came to be known as the "Pigeon-Hole Constitution." Seven MPs who represented constituencies in Buganda refused to accept it.

In 1967 after much discussion a new republican constitution was introduced. Under this constitution the traditional rulers and the kingdom states were abolished. Obote became Executive President. The administrative districts were redefined and renamed with the name of Buganda removed from the map following her attempted secession and her defeat the previous year at the Battle of Mengo 1966 (q.v.). At its conference in 1969 the Uganda People's Congress (UPC) (q.v.) urged President Obote to introduce a one-party state. The attempted assassination (q.v.) of Obote provided an opportunity to do this without amending the constitution: in the panic which followed, all parties other than the UPC were banned. Elections to the National Assembly were postponed until 1971, and seven Buganda constituencies were left unrepresented. When Obote returned to power in 1980 the 1967 Constitution once again operated.

President Museveni (q.v.) and the National Resistance Movement (q.v.) undertook to introduce a new constitution after national consultation. This took longer than expected, in part because no consultation could take place in the disturbed north and east of the country until insurgency there had been brought under control. By mid-1992 this had been more or less achieved. A Constitutional Commission worked full time and received many thousands of submissions, both written and oral, from both groups and individuals. In early 1993 a draft constitution was produced.

In some quarters a high degree of expectancy prevailed. What would happen if groups and individuals found that their suggestions had not been accepted was not clear: would they be willing to accept the inevitable give and take? In February 1993 the Chairman of the Constitutional Commission, Professor Dan Mudoola, was killed by a hand-grenade which killed one other man and injured several more. There were allegations that grants made to the Commission by the Danish, Swedish and British governments had been misappropriated. Some Ugandans accused Museveni of being a Rwandan and the work of the Commission a Rwandan plot (*see* Rwanda). In fact Museveni is a Muhinda (q.v.) from Mpororo in Kigezi (q.v.). If the National Resistance Movement government is unable to deliver a constitution which is broadly acceptable, the consequences may be serious.

COOK, SIR ALBERT RUSKIN, M.D. (1870–1951). Member of the Church Missionary Society (q.v.). He arrived in Uganda in 1897 and Mengo (q.v.) Hospital was opened in May of that year. The mission's initiative in starting formal hospital work was vindicated immediately when it was called on to treat casualties of Kabaka Mwanga's (q.v.) rebellion against the British, and the Sudanese Mutiny (q.v.). Cook kept careful medical records from the first which are today lodged in the Medical Library at Mulago Hospital. He made several long safaris, often accompanying Bishop Tucker (q.v.), assessing locations for further mission work, and treating patients at the various stopping places. They visited Koki in 1897, Toro (q.v.) and Mboga beyond the Semliki River in 1898, Ankole (q.v.) and Toro in 1899, Toro again in 1901, Mount Elgon (q.v.) in 1903, the Sudan (q.v.) in 1905, Teso (q.v.) and the eastern regions of Uganda in 1909 and 1914, and Rwanda (q.v.) in 1921. In 1918 he was awarded the Croix de Chevalier de l'Ordre de Léopold and the OBE for his services during World War I when Mengo Hospital played an important part in treating war casualties.

After the war he became concerned with measures to

combat venereal disease which was reaching serious propor-
tions (though his estimate of how widespread it was was
probably exaggerated). Mengo Hospital also pioneered nurse
and medical assistant training under Cook and his wife who
was for many years Matron. He received further honors for
his medical work, and a knighthood in 1932. The following
year he became first President of the Uganda Society (q.v.)
which published the *Uganda Journal* and did much to
encourage the study of Uganda. His *Uganda Memories* was
published by the Uganda Society in 1945. In 1934 he retired
to land given to him by the Buganda Government on
Makindye Hill where he lived until his death.

COUP OF 1971. The coup in which Idi Amin (q.v.) and a section
of the Uganda Army (q.v.) seized power took place in the
early hours of 25 January 1971. Hostility between President
Obote (q.v.) and Amin had been building up since the
attempted assassination (q.v.) of Obote in December 1969
when Amin had fled rather than going to Obote's aid, for
which he had been charged with cowardice by his rival,
Brigadier Okoya (q.v.). Ever since the Battle of Mengo 1966
(q.v.), when Amin had led the attack which defeated
Buganda, Amin's power had increased. As a too-powerful
General he threatened the civilian President. Amin had
further personal reasons for leading a coup: he was in
disagreement with Obote over the Southern Sudan (q.v.)
resistance movement, the Anya Nya (q.v.). He had continued
to assist them at a time when Obote was allying himself with
the Sudanese President Nimeiri who had socialist leanings at
this juncture that chimed in with Obote's own projected
"Move to the Left" (q.v.). A white mercenary assisting the
Southern Sudanese, Rolf Steiner, was openly friendly with
Amin. Steiner was captured in Uganda and returned to Sudan
on 11 December 1970, having refused to give evidence
against Amin. Uganda seems to have been expecting a
considerable payoff for this which Amin may have hoped to
benefit from. The immediate cause of the coup seems to have
been an attempt by Obote to curb overexpenditure on the
military, and to bring Amin to book for this. During Obote's

absence in Singapore at a meeting of the Commonwealth Heads of Government, Amin preempted a strike against himself by seizing power.

His move was particularly welcomed by Baganda (q.v.) who were angry and resentful at the suppression of their kingdom in 1966 and the state of emergency under which they had been governed ever since. Some Baganda leaders knew of the impending coup 36 hours beforehand. Amin was able to assure himself that there would be no opposition from them. Its results were most dreaded by the Acholi (q.v.), many of whom were in the army and were opposed to Amin, and by the people of Lango (q.v.) who were of the same tribe as Obote. Although there was shooting during the night, casualties at this stage seem to have been few. The success of the coup was announced at 4:00 pm over Uganda Radio when an 18-point statement was read out by a soldier. Elections were promised within a short time and an undertaking was given that the military would stand down in favor of a civilian government very shortly. There was wild rejoicing among the Baganda in particular which led some foreign journalists to believe that this rejoicing was typical of the country as a whole. Although some Baganda succeeded in profiting from the coup, Baganda were not exempt from the violence and lawlessness of the Amin years.

In the immediate aftermath of the coup roadblocks were removed, and political prisoners were released. Human rights and civil liberties had been seriously eroded under Obote, and there was a brief period in which the new regime was open to popular demands. But the main demand made by royalist Baganda was that the body of Kabaka Mutesa II (q.v.), who had died in Britain, should be returned for burial. This Amin permitted, though he did not permit the restoration of the kingdom.

Amin quickly embarked on the elimination of rival elements in the army, especially the Acholi who had not forgiven the murder of Brigadier Okoya (q.v.) the previous year, almost certainly at Amin's instigation. The army itself, which already had a reputation for indiscipline, quickly got further out of hand, and took advantage of Amin's dependence on it to loot and plunder without let or hindrance.

CRAWFORD, SIR FREDERICK (1906–1978). Governor of Uganda, 1957–1962. Crawford held power during Uganda's troubled runup to independence. In 1958 he had to deal with elections on a restricted franchise to some of the seats to be held by Ugandan Africans in the Legislative Council (q.v.). At the time of the Deportation Crisis (q.v.) it had been agreed that if the Kabaka of Buganda (q.v.) were permitted to return, the government of Buganda would agree to representatives elected by an electoral college taking their seats in the Legislative Council. At the same time Buganda accepted membership in a unitary state, but in a semi-federal relationship with it. Other areas of Uganda campaigned vigorously against this and urged direct elections, and Crawford was pressured into accepting these in any area whose District Council wished. Some other areas as well as Buganda refused to participate in these direct elections because of local ethnic and religious rivalries, and Buganda moved towards attempted secession. Crawford has been criticized for giving in to these pressures and undermining the agreement which had been made with Buganda. Buganda's most-favored status was, however, unacceptable to the country as a whole.

In 1960 Crawford announced that a commission would be set up to enquire into the form which the direct Elections of 1961 (q.v.) should take. This was the Wild Committee whose findings were important for the Constitutional Conferences (q.v.) held at Lancaster House (q.v.) and Marlborough House (q.v.) in London in 1961 and 1962. However, on its publication, Crawford announced that it would not be accepted in full. In particular the government would retain the right to nominate some members to protect non-African groups, and internal self-government would not be granted immediately. A further commission was set up to enquire into the relationships of the kingdoms and districts of Uganda with the central government because the other kingdoms were pressing their case for special treatment. The Report of the Munster Commission (q.v.) resulted in the Western Kingdoms and Busoga Act which defined their much more limited privileges and proposed a referendum on the Lost Counties (q.v.). Crawford took part in both constitutional conferences. At the time of internal self-government Crawford officially handed over his executive powers to Benedicto Kiwanuka (q.v.), Uganda's first Prime Minister, and on 9 March 1962 he officially dissolved the Legislative Council prior to the independence Elections of 1962 (q.v.) due to be held in April.

CRAZZOLARA, FR PASQUALE (1884–1976). A member of the Verona Fathers' (q.v.) Mission, and a noted linguist and anthropologist who studied in the universities of Vienna and London. In 1910 after working for two years in the Sudan (q.v.) he went to Uganda where the Verona Fathers were starting work. He was posted first to Omach in West Nile (q.v.) and then to Gulu (q.v.) in Acholi (q.v.). There he was responsible for composing the first Catholic catechism and school texts in the Acholi language (*see* Languages) and was called on to help relieve the tensions which led to the Lamogi Rebellion (q.v.) of 1911–1912. He then worked mainly in the Sudan until 1928 when he returned to Uganda permanently. Aside from his work as a pastoral and educational missionary, he became a leading authority on the languages and ethnology of several of the peoples of Sudan and Uganda, especially the Acholi. Besides publishing grammars of Nuer, Lugbara, Pokot and Acholi (*see* Languages), he is the author of *The Lwoo,* written in English and published in Italy in three volumes (1950–1954), a definitive work of scholarship, the results of his lifelong study of the people to whose welfare he devoted himself. He was awarded the medal of the Royal African Society and recognition by both the British and Italian governments for his work.

-D-

DE BUNSEN, SIR BERNARD (1907–1990). Principal of Makerere University College (q.v.), 1950–1963; Vice-Chancellor of the University of East Africa, 1963–1965. Educated at Leighton Park School and Balliol College, Oxford, he had a varied career in teaching and educational administration before being appointed Professor of Education at Makerere in 1948. His Principalship covered the difficult years leading up to independence. Under him, Makerere embarked on large-scale expansion and achieved an international reputation in a number of fields. As well as being a highly competent administrator, he was exceptionally approachable by all grades of staff, and good staff-student relations were given a high priority. After his retirement to London he worked for the African Educational Trust, and on behalf of Ugandans who were exiled during the time of President Amin (q.v.) and the second presidency of Obote (q.v.).

DEFENCE COUNCIL. The shadowy group through whom President Amin (q.v.) claimed to rule. Its constitution was never clear, and Amin increasingly ruled without any formal consultation.

DEMOCRATIC PARTY (DP). This was founded as a national political party in 1954 by eight Baganda (q.v.), all of whom were Catholics (q.v.), and led by Matayo Mugwanya. In 1958 the leadership passed to Benedicto Kiwanuka (q.v.). The DP was originally a focus for Catholic discontent at the way in which the Protestants (q.v.) dominated the state and appointments to chieftaincies under colonial rule. It has remained a predominantly though not exclusively Catholic party. It was strongly anti-communist and opposed to the nationalization of church-run schools and hospitals which it feared might follow independence.

The DP came to power in 1961 with Benedicto Kiwanuka as Prime Minister. It was able to win these elections because the government of Buganda called for them to be boycotted. The DP alone of the political parties ignored the boycott, and as a result won 20 out of 21 Buganda seats in the National Assembly (q.v.) but with only a 2 percent turnout of voters. Although this meant it won the elections, the DP demonstrated the weakness of its support in Buganda. Kiwanuka was accused of arrogance in his dealings with the Baganda and with the Kabaka in particular. In the following year the DP lost power because of an alliance between the UPC and Kabaka Yekka (KY) (q.v.). KY claimed that a vote for any other party indicated disloyalty to the Kabaka. Consequently it won almost every seat in the Lukiiko, the local parliament of Buganda, and the Lukiiko in turn appointed KY members to the National Assembly, enabling Milton Obote (q.v.) to come to power as Prime Minister (the DP had vigorously opposed indirect elections by the Lukiiko to the National Assembly).

Within the next three years a number of DP members of the National Assembly crossed the floor and joined the UPC, giving it an overall majority and enabling it to dispense with its alliance with KY. Among the DP defectors was Basil Bataringaya (q.v.), the DP's Secretary-General. At the time of the Gold Scandal (q.v.) the few remaining DP members aligned themselves with Grace Ibingira (q.v.) and others in a vote of censure of Obote. In late 1969 after the attempted asssassination (q.v.) of Obote, all political parties other than the UPC were banned, and Uganda briefly became a de facto one-party state.

President Amin (q.v.) ruled by decree and without reference to the constitution. The Democratic Party was unable to function, but it emerged again when he was overthrown. All the signs were that the Elections of 1980 (q.v.) would be very close-run, though the Commonwealth Observer Group (q.v.) gathered much evidence of malpractice by those who supported Obote's return to power, with a number of DP candidates being prevented from presenting their nomination papers, or wrongly disqualified. Even so the DP was sure enough of victory to claim it even before all the results had been declared. However, after a highly controversial intervention by Paulo Muwanga (q.v.), head of the Military Commission (q.v.) which was ruling Uganda prior to the election, it was announced that the UPC was the winner. The DP, under its new leader, Dr Paul Ssemogerere (q.v.), found itself in an increasingly helpless opposition in spite of the strong backing of the Catholic Church. It has never accepted the validity of the 1980 election results. Its members were criticized in some quarters for taking up their seats in the National Assembly and lending legitimacy to Obote's second presidency as Uganda plunged into further bloodshed.

The DP newspaper, *Munnansi* (Fellow Citizens), won respect for its fearless reporting of the repression which marked Obote's second presidency. But it was starved of paper and was reduced to being little more than a cyclostyled weekly. Coupled with the DP's acceptance of seats in the National Assembly, the existence of *Munnansi* enabled Obote's government to claim that there was a legal opposition and freedom of the press, and so to safeguard the continuance of Western aid. Ssemogerere also made a controversial decision to accept office during the short-lived regime of Tito Okello (q.v.) and Basilio Okello (q.v.).

When President Museveni (q.v.) and his National Resistance Movement (NRM) (q.v.) seized power in 1986 the former political parties were forbidden to operate. They were blamed for many of Uganda's troubles by fostering ethnic and religious strife. However, the NRM did not command widespread political allegiance, and the old party loyalties remained strong, though the NRM saw them as part of the outdated divisive structures which it wanted to do away with. In order to govern, the NRM adopted a policy of national reconciliation and tried to incorporate as many groups as possible in its administration. In the first handout of cabinet positions, the DP adherents did very well. Even if they had not supported Museveni, they had opposed the Obote government against which the NRM had fought. In the 1989 elections candidates had to stand as individuals, not as representatives of political parties, though the UPC and DP were allowed to keep their party headquarters and to issue general statements. At this time the ban on party political activity was extended for a further seven years, the NRM apparently hoping that the political parties will wither away.

DEPORTATION CRISIS. Under the terms of the [B]Uganda Agreement (q.v.), as long as the Kabaka of Buganda cooperated with the Protectorate government, he was recognized as rightful ruler of Buganda, and Buganda retained a privileged, semi-federal status within Uganda.

A speech by Oliver Lyttleton, British Colonial Secretary, on 30 June 1953 led to a crisis between the Kabaka and the newly-arrived Governor, Sir Andrew Cohen. Lyttleton referred to the possibility ''of still larger measures of unification and possibly still larger measures of federation of the whole East African territories.'' There had been a long history of Ugandan resistance to "closer union" (q.v.) of the East African territories because of fears that settler-dominated Kenya (q.v.) would gain an undue influence. The Baganda (q.v.) were particularly fearful. Moreover there was an acute awareness of how African opinion was being ridden over roughshod in the formation of the Central African Federation. Neither the Buganda government nor the Kabaka was satisfied with assurances that the British government had no plans "at present" to make any changes in policy. No doubt the Colonial Office could not go further than this without directly contradicting the Colonial Secretary, but more strongly-worded assurances on this issue had been given in the past, so that the Kabaka and his government felt they could detect a change in British attitudes.

These objections were set out in a long and cogently-argued letter, and the Kabaka went on to demand that the affairs of Buganda should in the future be handled by the Foreign Office rather than the Colonial Office, and that a timetable should be agreed for progress towards Buganda's independence without regard for the rest of Uganda. This demand amounted to a request to secede. Changes introduced in the Legislative Council (q.v.) had already aroused Baganda suspicions (the existence in all three territories of similar unrepresentative Legislative Councils had been used to legitimize federation in Central Africa), and the Baganda felt they had good reason to distrust British intentions. Their distrust may well have been justified, but their demands were unrealistic and did not represent any public demand. In a series of meetings between the Governor and the Kabaka stalemate was reached. A showdown became inevitable.

On 30 November 1953 the Governor summoned the Kabaka and required him to give three undertakings: (i) that he would not in any way oppose the decisions of Her Majesty's Government or encourage others to oppose them, and that he would instruct the Lukiiko publicly that they must be obeyed; (ii) that he would positively cooperate in the progress of Buganda within a unified Uganda, would submit names for appointment to the Legislative Council, and would inform the Lukiiko publicly that he had done so; and (iii) that he would loyally cooperate with Her Majesty's Government and the Protectorate government in accordance with the 1900 Agreement. He refused to give any of these assurances, and recognition was therefore withdrawn from him, and he was deported to Britain. Emergency laws were put into force and regents sworn in.

Almost overnight a Kabaka who had become somewhat unpopular began to be referred to by extravagant traditional praise names, and the whole of Buganda went into something like mourning (the rest of the country was largely unmoved). There was a revival of traditional customs and even religion, although the Kabaka had been brought up in Western ways and had repudiated much of the pre-Christian past. Baganda opinion steadily hardened in favor of the Kabaka and against Britain and the Protectorate government, and increasingly extravagant claims were made about the Kabaka's position. Baganda delegations were sent to the British Government in Whitehall and the Archbishop of Canterbury.

In February 1954 a constitutional committee was set up under the chairmanship of Professor Sir Keith Hancock, Director of the Institute of Commonwealth Studies, University of London. The Lukiiko wisely nominated some of the best educated Baganda available, and avoided political extremists and reactionaries. Among those who eventually agreed to serve were Apolo Kironde (q.v.), E.M.K. Mulira (q.v.), Y.K. Lule (q.v.), S.W. Kulubya (q.v.) and Bishop Joseph Kiwanuka (q.v.). The committee met, first alone, and then with the Governor from the end of June to mid-September. Its recommendations provided for Buganda to move towards a democratic form of government. Ministers would be responsible to the Lukiiko, not to the Kabaka; the Governor's plans for health, education and some other services in Buganda to be transferred from the central government to the Buganda government would go ahead; a civil service board would control local administration; the judiciary would gain in independence; the Kabaka would become the symbol of the unity of the Baganda and of their historical continuity, and, it was hoped, be above political controversy; most importantly the Kabaka would sign a new agreement which would set out far more clearly his relationship with the Protectorate government, and he would pledge himself to abide by the new constitutional arrangements. The Protectorate government would no longer appoint chiefs: that would be done by an appointments board; the Protectorate government would retain a final authority, but would deal with the Buganda government as a government, not at individual level. The committee hoped that these new arrangements would satisfy the colonial authorities and enable the Kabaka to return to Buganda.

In September 1954 some Lukiiko members brought a court case to test the legality of the deportation. The Chief Justice, Kenneth Diplock QC, ruled that the Kabaka had indeed broken the terms of the 1900 Agreement, but that he had been deported under the wrong article of the Agreement. Not wishing to set aside the entire Agreement, the Governor had invoked Article 6 (which provided for withdrawal of recognition from the Kabaka if he failed to cooperate with the Protectorate government) rather than Article 20 (which would have involved setting the whole Agreement aside, which the Governor did not wish to do). When news of the judgment broke, the waiting crowd burst into shouts of triumph (*"Gavana talina buyinza!"* "The Governor has no power over us!") without even waiting to hear the second part of the judgment. Although the people's claim was based on a profound misunderstanding, the decision nevertheless weakened the Protectorate government's case, and both the Protectorate government and the British Colonial Office were by now looking for some way in which they could back down on their former irreversible decision and allow the Kabaka to return: deporting him had created rather than avoided difficulties. This court decision provided the opportunity they were looking for. On 16 November an announcement was made that within nine months of the Lukiiko accepting the Hancock Committee's recommendations in toto, they might either elect a new Kabaka, or call for Mutesa to return.

This did not end the crisis. The Lukiiko refused to accept the conditions; the Baganda were angry that they were expected to accept the package in its entirety without any opportunity for discussion; the members of the Hancock

Committee became divided; the Uganda National Congress (q.v.) was jealous that it had played no part in the deal. The situation was saved by a Lukiiko committee which sat with Justice Diplock and which persuaded the Lukiiko to accept the Hancock Committee recommendations with only minor amendments. Despite some last minute hitches, the Baganda were persuaded to send members to the Legislative Council, and the Lukiiko agreed to accept the Hancock recommendations formally prior to the Kabaka's return. The Protectorate government, for its part, agreed to allow the Kabaka to return just six weeks after the Lukiiko's acceptance instead of nine months after. The frenzy of excitement about the Kabaka's return probably persuaded it that it would be wise to bring matters to a conclusion as soon as possible. In the celebrations which accompanied the return all sections of Baganda society vied in showing loyalty and enthusiasm. Those who were branded as having been ''disloyal'' to the Kabaka were humiliated and sometimes physically assaulted.

Perhaps the longest-lasting effect of the Deportation Crisis was to enhance the office of the Kabaka in the eyes of the Baganda, and to surround Kabaka Mutesa with a popularity which was in striking contrast to that accorded him before his deportation. Although the Protectorate government temporarily succeeded in bending the Buganda government at least in part to its will, the deportation probably hardened Baganda attitudes on their relations with the rest of the country, and this created grave problems on the eve of independence (*see* Kabaka Yekka).

DIPLOCK, KENNETH *see* DEPORTATION CRISIS

DONGO, REVD CANON SIRA (c. 1880–1938). An Alur (q.v.) who was born near Ang'uzzi in what is now Zaire (q.v.). He and his sisters were captured in childhood by the *barusura* (q.v.) of Mukama Kabarega (q.v.) of Bunyoro (q.v.), one of whom took Dongo as a gun-bearer. This man sold him to a Muganda (*see* Baganda) in payment of a debt, and Dongo began to receive Christian instruction while in his new master's service. The Muganda took him to Bunyoro where he eventually gained his freedom and was baptized in 1903.

From there he went with a CMS (q.v.) missionary to Acholi (q.v.), having married Lucira Farwenyo. Because he spoke Alur, a language closely related to Acholi (*see* Languages), he was able to help with translation. His ability and his dedication to his new faith were quickly recognized, and Dongo started up the slow ladder which eventually led to his ordination as a priest in 1919. Together with an Acholi colleague, Muca Ali, he worked throughout Acholi and Lango (q.v.) which has a cognate language, helping to start the first mission at Boroboro near Lira (q.v.). He became an immensely respected Christian leader, and in 1936 his tireless work was recognized when he was made a Canon of the Anglican Diocese of the Upper Nile. He died two years later.

DUHAGA, ANDEREYA BISEREKO (c. 1880–1924). Mukama of Bunyoro (q.v.) 1902–1924. He was appointed Mukama by the British administration to replace Yosiya Kitehimbwa who had proved incapable as a ruler. He was a loyal adherent of the Native Anglican Church (q.v.) and a star pupil of the Church Missionary Society (q.v.) in Bunyoro. Duhaga found difficulty in gaining the loyalty of the people so long as the deposed Mukama Kabarega (q.v.) was still alive, but he eventually gained their respect and worked wholeheartedly on behalf of his people. In 1907 during the Nyangire Rebellion (q.v.) he was accused of weakness by the British authorities, but he finally come out against the rebellion, persuaded the lukiiko (local parliament) to submit to the Protectorate authorities, and was thus instrumental in bringing Nyangire to an end.

By 1908 Duhaga felt sufficiently secure to revive the *empango* celebrations. Traditionally an *empango* was a coronation anniversary ceremony. He used the occasion to affirm the new strength of his position. In fact Duhaga had not undergone the full traditional investiture because Kabarega was still alive, so some other suitable day had to be chosen. He selected the anniversary of his baptism, and the traditional rituals were considerably curtailed, but Duhaga's authority was further enhanced by the occasion. He had as yet no Katikiro (chief minister), so occupied an executive as well as a ceremonial position. A few years later in 1912 the administration moved its headquarters from Hoima (q.v.) to Masindi (q.v.), and the Bunyoro government followed. A new palace was built for Duhaga. In the same year the senior chief Paulo Byabacwezi (q.v.) died, and his death left Duhaga in an unrivalled position.

In 1917 a Katikiro was at last appointed. Petero Bikunya (q.v.), first holder of that office, was able to take over some of the work done by the Mukama. Duhaga's health was beginning to fail, and World War I and the need to substitute local for imported supplies had considerably increased his responsibilities. In 1923 Duhaga was able to persuade the authorities to allow Kabarega to return from exile, though not to Bunyoro. Kabarega died only a few weeks after settling at Jinja (q.v.). Duhaga was then able at last to undergo the full coronation ceremony, but he himself died suddenly in March of the following year, and was succeeded by Tito Winyi (q.v.).

-E-

EAST AFRICA COMMON SERVICES. The common currency, postal services, telecommunications, tax provisions, customs, and common transport network administered by the East Africa High Commission (q.v.) which came into being in 1948. These were taken over by the East African Community (q.v.) soon after the three countries had achieved independence.

EAST AFRICA HIGH COMMISSION. In 1945 the post-World War II Labour government in Britain put forward a proposal for Closer Union (q.v.) between the three East African territories. Many Ugandan Africans, especially the Baganda (q.v.), opposed it because they feared the domination of Kenya (q.v.) where white settlers wielded undue influence. Kenya settlers opposed the original proposals because they had been proposed by a Labour government which had little sympathy with their claims. Revised proposals reduced the number of unofficials, and reassured the Kenya settlers but alarmed Africans. The proposals were accepted, however, by Britain, and the High Commission came into being in January 1948. It administered the East Africa Common Services (q.v.) and African fears were not realized.

EAST AFRICAN COMMUNITY (EAC). After independence President Nyerere of Tanzania (q.v.) urged the creation of an East African Federation, and prophesied correctly that if a federation were not entered into at that stage, it never would be. In 1967, however, the non-federal East African Community was created. The previous year the East African Currency Board had been dismantled, and the three countries had set up their own central banks and currencies. However, the three currencies were held at par, and the other East Africa Common Services (q.v.) previously administered by the East Africa High Commission (q.v.) remained in place. By the end of the decade the real value of the currencies were beginning to diverge and a black market between Kenya and Uganda burgeoned as the Ugandan economy plummeted as a result of the "economic war" (q.v.) waged by President Amin (q.v.). By the mid-1970s the black market had extended to dealings in postage stamps and airline tickets purchased in Uganda, with Uganda shillings bought at less than a tenth of the official rate, and then sold in Kenya at enormous profit. The breakup of the EAC became inevitable.

Uganda's bad relations with Tanzania, which had given refuge to the overthrown President Obote (q.v.), also helped towards the breakup of the EAC. Trouble began as early as 1971 when Tanzania accused Amin of breaching the Treaty provisions for the appointment of officials, and each country excluded persons appointed by the other from taking office. Uganda closed its borders with Tanzania and East African Airways flights between Uganda and Tanzania were suspended. Tanzania had refused to recognize the Amin regime, and Amin demanded virtual recognition in return for signing the financial appropriations bill without which the EAC could not continue to function. Relations with Kenya (q.v.) deteriorated following the Entebbe Raid (q.v.) in 1976 and Uganda's claims to a "Greater Uganda" (q.v.). It was, however, the disparity between the three currencies and the divergencies in their economic policies which made the demise of the East African Community inevitable. The Court of Appeal of Eastern Africa was dismantled at the same time as the EAC. The replacement of these services involved Uganda in huge costs.

ECONOMIC WAR. The name given by President Amin (q.v.) to the expropriation and redistribution of Asian assets after the owners had been expelled in 1972 (*see* Asians and Expulsions). Among the assets annexed were a large part of the retail trade, many import-export companies, and most of the country's manufacturing and construction industry. A Board was set up to oversee the allocation of Asian businesses to Ugandan Africans, but much of the property fell into the hands of Nubians (q.v.) and others with little or no entrepreneurial experience and with no access to credit or import facilities, with the result that many businesses were mismanaged and went bankrupt. The ''economic war'' amounted to pillage, and those who lost the ''economic war'' were not only the Asians but Ugandans in general. Amin, however, remained sure the war had been won, and his actions were supported by many Ugandan Africans.

EDUCATION. Traditional education was informal and given either within the family or, in the case of Baganda (q.v.) chiefly families, by a family to whom a boy was sent to be trained for future responsibility. The household of the Kabaka of Buganda had hundreds of such ''pages'' who served in the royal enclosure and expected to be appointed to high office.

Swahili written in Arabic characters was introduced to the court of Buganda during the reign of Kabaka Mutesa I (q.v.). When Christian missions (q.v.) arrived in the later 1870s they introduced the Roman script and required literacy of baptism candidates. By the beginning of the twentieth century hundreds of Ugandan Christian catechists were teaching literacy while embryonic schools at mission stations offered some general education. During the next decade both Catholic (q.v.) and Protestant (q.v.) missions established boarding schools to train future Christian elites: Mengo High School and King's College, Budo (Protestant), and Namilyango College and St Mary's College, Kisubi (Catholic), admitted boys from all over the country. In 1905 the Church Missionary Society (q.v.) opened Gayaza School for girls, but it was not until much later that girls were offered education of a comparable academic standard to that of the boys' schools. The missions opened normal schools to train teachers.

Not until the 1920s did government take any direct responsibility for education. A technical school was then opened at Makerere (q.v.) and the missions received grants-in-aid for their schools. In 1924 the Phelps-Stokes Commission investigating education in tropical Africa visited Uganda. It was critical of the low standards of the "bush" schools, and considered much education over-academic, though it recognized the high quality of the leading schools. It criticized government for leaving education to the missions. In 1926 a Department of Education was set up and expenditure increased steadily, though for many years most of the funding went into mission schools.

By 1936 about a quarter of a million children were in school, the vast majority (228,000) in unaided "bush" schools run by untrained mission teachers, and only a little over 2,000 in middle and junior secondary schools. The latter were all mission run: Budo, Nyakasura in western Uganda and Mwiri in the east were CMS schools, while Kisubi and Namilyango, both near Kampala (q.v.), were run by the White Fathers (q.v,) and the Mill Hill Fathers (q.v.) respectively. In 1936 the first few Ugandans sat for the Cambridge Overseas School Certificate. The Department of Education ran Makerere College (q.v.) and two schools for Asians (q.v.). King's College, Budo was the most prestigious and academically ambitious school and admitted a few girls, but there were instances of serious indiscipline from time to time. Education stagnated during World War II, but from 1953 onwards expenditure on education greatly increased in response to a Nuffield Foundation report. Teacher training and secondary education were reorganized and primary education became a local responsibility.

By 1960 there were 19 senior secondary schools for Africans and six for Asians. Gayaza High School (Protestant), Mount St Mary's, Namagunga and Trinity College, Nabbingo (both Catholic), were among the most prestigious for girls. Junior secondary and primary education had likewise greatly expanded, and several schools and a teacher training college could now be found in most district headquarters. Makerere College was preparing students from throughout East Africa for external degrees of London University as well as offering diplomas for teachers. There were eight technical schools at various levels and 33 teacher training institutions.

In 1964 after independence all education was taken over by government although in practice the missions and churches retained a measure of responsibility for many schools. Schools were no longer allowed to be denominationally exclusive, and Muslim (see Islam) education, which had been handicapped by mission domination of the educational scene, now began to expand (it was, however, two ex-missionaries who began the first secondary school for Muslim girls, without attempting to convert the pupils). The 1960s saw an unprecedented expansion of education. As always, educational institutions tended to be clustered around the capital, though by the time of independence, secondary schools had been established in all regions of the country.

The purpose of education came increasingly under scrutiny after independence. Government found it difficult to exercise ideological control because of its dependence on expatriates at senior levels. It pushed ahead with programs of Africanization, diversification of expatriate appointees to include some from socialist countries, and control of appointments to administrative positions, particularly in further and higher education. Vocational education was increased, with the country's economic needs in mind.

Under President Amin (q.v.) and during Obote's (q.v.) second presidency, the education system, starved of resources, and against a background of violence and civil strife, struggled on under intense difficulties. Most expatriates and all the Asians (q.v.) had been driven out of the country. The state of the country's economy has allowed little improvement since. Surprisingly high standards have been maintained in the leading schools.

Attendance at government-recognized and aided schools has never been the only way of attaining literacy in Uganda. Studies in the early 1970s showed that at least as many people gained basic literacy by attending church classes, the successors to the "bush" schools. As with those children whose parents could not afford more than two or three years of schooling, it is likely that many of these subsequently lost their literacy, though if they continued to attend church, their literacy might be reinforced. Mosques ran Qur'anic schools in which some children achieved literacy in Arabic, though again, sometimes of a very limited type. Independent secondary schools also proliferated in Uganda, and in the 1940s and 1950s these attracted African pupils from Kenya (q.v.) who were frustrated by the lack of opportunity there. These schools are seldom as well resourced as government-aided schools, and often take less able pupils who have failed to gain entrance to a government-run school.

The Roman Catholic Church has run junior and senior seminaries for boys wishing to enter the priesthood. Only a few of those who join them proceed to ordination, but many boys have received a good education in the seminaries, and proceeded to higher and further education. Many junior seminaries were closed after Vatican II.

By the beginning of the 1990s there were five universities in Uganda: Makerere University, Kampala; a science university at Mbarara (q.v.) in the west concentrating on veterinary science; a Muslim university with external funding at Mbale (q.v.); and two Christian foundations, the Catholic Martyrs' University at Nkozi and a Protestant university at Ndejje.

ELECTIONS. Since 1960 there have only been three full-scale general elections in Uganda, and each of these has been eventful and contentious.

Elections of 1961. In June 1960 the Protectorate government announced that direct elections would be held in March 1961 as a prelude to the granting of self-government. These were opposed by Buganda (q.v.) which feared that she would lose the privileged status she had acquired under the [B]Uganda Agreement (q.v.) of 1900 unless this was specially guaranteed. Kabaka Mutesa II (q.v.) pressed for elections to be delayed until Buganda had been granted federal status within a self-governing state, a move which angered the rest of the country, and which the British government rejected. The Buganda government therefore decided to boycott the elections, and announced that she would become independent regardless of the rest of Uganda on 31 December 1960, a move which was ignored by the Protectorate government and rendered ineffective. The Kabaka and his government mounted so vigorous a campaign against the elections that the Elections 1961 (Prevention of Intimidation) Act was passed granting powers to detain anyone who transgressed it during the registration of voters and polling. It failed to prevent intimidation because those responsible for law and order in the rural areas were the chiefs who were involved in the boycott campaign. As a result only some three to four percent of the electorate of Buganda registered themselves as voters.

Two parties contended these elections, the Uganda People's Congress (UPC) (q.v.) led by Milton Obote (q.v.) and the Democratic Party (DP) (q.v.) led by Benedicto Kiwanuka (q.v.). Religious allegiance frequently determined party political allegiance: UPC supporters were mainly Protestant (q.v.) and the party was nicknamed ''United Protestants of Canterbury,'' while DP supporters tended to be Catholics (q.v.), the party nickname being *Dini ya Papa*—''religion of the Pope.'' The party divide was not solely along denominational lines, but there was a very marked concurrence between religious and political affiliation. Most of those who registered to vote in Buganda were supporters of the DP; the UPC was unable to organize itself in Buganda partly because Protestant Baganda supported the boycott.

The 19 seats which the DP won in Buganda as a result of the boycott enabled it to win the elections nationally. The DP won 43 seats with only 407,816 votes because so few Baganda voted; the UPC won 35 seats with 488,332 votes. As a prelude to independence this was plainly an unsatisfactory outcome. It suggested that unless a party could win the support of Buganda, it could not win overall power in Uganda. And although the Baganda had achieved a boycott of the elections, the result dismayed them: a government in which the ruling party was overwhelmingly Catholic was unwelcome because the ruling oligarchy in Buganda was predominantly Protestant.

Elections of 1962. Prior to these elections, which were held on the eve of full independence, Milton Obote (q.v.) reached an understanding with Buganda in order to persuade her to take part in the processes leading up to the independence of Uganda as a unitary state. The Baganda (q.v.) were to be allowed indirect elections to the National Assembly (q.v.). A directly-elected Lukiiko (local parliament) would be constituted as an electoral college which would then elect members to the National Assembly. The police would remain under the control of the Governor rather than the Prime Minister in the runup to the elections, an expression of distrust in the self-governing status granted to Uganda. Buganda would be allowed to control her own civil service of chiefs and officials free of supervision from the central government. These chiefs were hardly impartial and many accusations of intimidation were made against them. In Buganda the main political party was Kabaka Yekka, "the Kabaka only" (KY) (q.v.), and it and the Uganda People's Congress (UPC) (q.v.) acted in alliance and successfully excluded the Democratic Party (DP) (q.v.) in Buganda. Voting for the DP was declared to be an act of disloyalty to the Kabaka. The Catholic Church (q.v.) protested strongly but ineffectively. Kabaka Yekka won 65 out of the 68 seats in the Lukiiko amid many reports of malpractice. The Lukiiko acting as an electoral college then sent 21 KY members to the new National Assembly. The outcome of the elections was a clear victory for the UPC/Kabaka Yekka alliance which won 37 seats with 537,598 votes to the DP's 24 seats with 474,256 votes. In accordance with the provisions of the constitution, nine specially elected members were chosen, six being UPC and three KY. The alliance between KY and the UPC thus gave Obote an overwhelming majority.

No further elections took place between 1962 and 1980. Elections should have been held in 1967 but the sudden introduction of the 1967 Constitution (q.v.) allowed President Obote to postpone this. He planned to hold elections in

1971. In order to try to overcome ethnic factionalism, a complicated procedure was worked out under which each candidate would have to stand in four different areas of the country. However, Obote was overthrown by the coup of 1971 (q.v.) which brought President Amin (q.v.) to power before he could do so. Amin made no attempt to hold elections.

Elections of 1980. The 1980 elections were the most controversial of all Uganda's elections. A Commonwealth Observer Group (COG) (q.v.) monitored these elections and produced a comprehensive report. The elections were held in very difficult circumstances. Uganda had little experience of elections; the years of Amin's (q.v.) presidency had wrought mayhem and parts of the country, notably West Nile (q.v.), were still disturbed. The civil service was seriously depleted. The elections were held in haste, and there was inadequate time for the registration of voters and the publication of lists of registered voters. Aspects of the electoral procedures remained unsettled until the last minute. The ruling Military Commission (q.v.) had no legitimacy and its leaders were desperate to ensure their retention of power. They could only be certain of doing so if the presidency of Milton Obote (q.v.) could be restored.

The Uganda People's Congress (UPC) (q.v.) was the best organized party during the campaign leading up to these elections. It was funded by a group of Asians including Shafiq Arain (q.v.), all of whom stood to benefit from a UPC victory. The Democratic Party (q.v.) led by Dr Paul Ssemogerere (q.v.) was the chief rival to the UPC and had the support of the Catholic Church (q.v.). The newly-formed Uganda Patriotic Movement (UPM) (q.v.), led by Yoweri Museveni (q.v.), was a newcomer to the political scene. Its manifesto was felt by many non-Ugandan observers to be the most thoughtful, while the newspaper *Topic* which supported it was described by the Commonwealth Observers as "the most intellectually stimulating publication in the country." But the UPM attracted few voters. All the old allegiances resurfaced, and the country was divided ethnically as well as religiously. The Baganda (q.v.) in particular hated Obote for their defeat in the Battle of Mengo 1966 (q.v.) and because he had abolished the kingdoms. The Langi (q.v.) were Obote's natural supporters since he came from their area. Other northerners tended to support Obote rather than parties whose leadership was in southern hands as in the case of the DP and the UPM.

The Commonwealth Observer Group compiled a report which detailed irregularities and malpractices, yet concluded that, given the situation in the country, the outcome fairly represented public opinion. But the results were unacceptable to many Ugandans not just because of the extensive malpractices recorded by the COG, but because, when the results were already being announced, Paulo Muwanga (q.v.), head of the Military Commission, stepped in and issued a proclamation, applied retrospectively to the day before, by which no result was to be announced until he had approved it. Since all the malpractices benefited the UPC and disadvantaged the other parties, it was not unnaturally assumed that Muwanga had acted thus so as to ensure that the UPC won, whether by fair means or foul. The Democratic Party was left with genuine grievances. Museveni, leader of the UPM, refused altogether to accept the election result and took to the bush and waged a guerrilla campaign which finally brought him to power as leader of the National Resistance Movement (NRM) (q.v.) five years later.

Elections of 1989. These elections were called at short notice in February 1989. The government of the National Resistance Movement (NRM) (q.v.) under President Museveni (q.v.) had promised elections, and was determined that this promise should be honored. Voting took place in almost every part of the country but the elections were not fully democratic, They were, however, accepted by most people as the first free and fair elections ever to be held in Uganda.

These elections did not offer the possibility of replacing the NRM government. What people were asked to do was to elect representatives to the lowest tier of the National Resistance Councils (q.v.). There were five tiers of these, the highest tier acting as the national parliament. Each tier was then responsible for electing representatives to the tier immediately above. The NRM reserved the right to appoint a number of people at national level so as to guarantee in advance that it would not lose control of the assembly. The general public therefore played a strictly limited role and was represented at national level only remotely. But at local level very widespread involvement in government was made possible.

There was no time to print ballot papers or compile lists of voters: the electors queued up behind the candidates of their choice. Campaigning along party lines was not permitted; candidates were to be elected as individuals, not as party members; they were unable to campaign through leaflets or in the press in the usual way: there was no time to organize such campaigns. Intimidation was not used, in spite of the queuing method of voting.

Once the rules were laid, the government did not interfere in the electoral process. The people were offered a measure of genuine choice, even if this was limited. A number of ministers lost their jobs, and even people who were recognized as being opponents of the NRM were able to stand and some such were elected. Opposition groups based outside Uganda, some of them involved in supporting insurgency in the north and east of the country, denounced these elections as a charade, but a comparison with Uganda's previous experience of elections raises the question whether fully democratic elections are feasible as yet.

ELGON, MOUNT. An extinct volcano which reaches a height of 14,178 feet (4,332 meters), just below the permanent snow line. The border between Uganda and Kenya (q.v.) runs through its summit. The massif is some 50 miles (80 kilometers) in diameter; the crater is 5 miles (8 kilometers) in diameter and 2,000 feet (610 meters) deep. Dense forests clothe the mountain's lower slopes running up to mountain bamboo and heath, which in turn give way at about 8,000 feet (2,400 meters) to giant groundsels and lobelias and other plants of the unique East African high montane flora. In places the lower slopes have been cleared for cultivation by the Sebei (q.v.) and the Bagisu (q.v.). The fertile soils, which are deep and friable and not subject to erosion, and the high rainfall make the area suitable for Arabica coffee and good quality tea, both produced by Bagisu cooperatives.

ELLIOT REPORT. In 1935 Governor Sir Philip Mitchell (q.v.) became concerned about poor working conditions for unskilled labor and reported shortages of unskilled workers in Uganda. He appointed a colonial civil servant, J. R. MacD. Elliot, to report on this. Elliot was only able to spend three months on this assignment and his report was somewhat delayed, but in 1937 he reported that there would be no shortages if employers offered better working conditions, and urged a further investigation. This was undertaken by H.B. Thomas (q.v.) who supported Elliot's findings, suggested that opportunities for wage labor should be gradually increased, and went on to urge that the remuneration for clerks and other educated workers should be raised to a more realistic level.

EMIN PASHA (DR EDUARD SCHNITZER) 1840–1893. A German-Jewish doctor with a keen interest in natural history. He practiced medicine in the Middle East, learnt Arabic, claimed to be a Turk, and converted to Islam. In Khartoum he met General Gordon who was seeking to extend Anglo-Egyptian rule as far south as Lake Victoria (q.v.). In 1876 Gordon appointed Emin as his emissary to Kabaka Mutesa I (q.v.) of Buganda. He was also authorized to treat with Mukama Kabarega (q.v.) of Bunyoro (q.v.). He visited both rulers in 1876. He established good relations with Kabarega, with whom he was able to converse in Arabic, the one European to recognize the Mukama's good qualities and win his trust. Mutesa also received him well, and both rulers were persuaded to send emissaries to Khartoum, but nothing was to come of this as Egypt lacked the resources to extend its influence so far south. Emin was appointed Governor of Equatoria (q.v.), but from 1881 onwards he was cut off from his base in the north by the Mahdist uprising in the Sudan (q.v.). Emin moved southwards and established himself at Wadelai just to the north of Lake Albert. Here he was found and ''rescued'' by the explorer H. M. Stanley (q.v.) in 1887. Reluctantly he agreed to accompany Stanley to the coast, but his Sudanese troops remained behind. They were recruited by Lugard (q.v.) in 1893 and formed the nucleus of the "Nubians" (q.v.) of Uganda. Emin insisted on returning to the interior and was murdered by Arab slave traders near Stanley Falls in the Congo in 1892.

ENTEBBE. A town on the shore of Lake Victoria (q.v.), 22 miles (35 kilometers) south of Kampala (q.v.), the site of the Protectorate government prior to independence, and of State House, formerly the Governor's residence, and after independence the official residence of the President. A small zoo and fine botanic garden border the lake shore. Since independence only the existence of Uganda's international airport and of a large hotel of international standard have preserved Entebbe's importance. The airport was enlarged and modernized in the early 1970s with Israeli (q.v.) aid and expertise. A memorial stone marks the place where the first White Fathers (q.v.) landed in 1879. The name Entebbe is a corruption of the Swahili *ntebe* (chair) and was given to the place when it was made the seat of government.

ENTEBBE RAID. On 28 June 1976 an Air France plane was hijacked by members of the Popular Front for the Liberation of Palestine with German accomplices. Its passengers included 103 Israelis and Jews. It was landed at Entebbe (q.v.) where the Israelis and Jews were separated from the other passengers and taken into the airport buildings: the other passengers were released. It quickly became clear that President Amin (q.v.) was siding with and assisting the hijackers.

On 3 July Israel (q.v.) mounted a dramatic rescue. The Israelis had designed and built the new airport buildings, so they were thoroughly familiar with the layout. Long-haul Hercules planes flew down the Red Sea, across Ethiopia and Kenya (q.v.), and landed at Entebbe at midnight taking the Uganda Army (q.v.), which was guarding the hijacked plane, by complete surprise. In a brilliantly swift operation the Israeli commandoes succeeded in destroying most of Uganda's air force which was standing on the tarmac, and rescuing the hostages. Three hostages and one Israeli soldier were killed in the attack as well as the five Palestinians and two Germans who had carried out the hijacking. One hostage, Mrs Dora Bloch, a 75-year-old woman with joint British and Israeli nationality, had been taken to a hospital in Kampala (q.v.), and had to be left behind. She was taken from her bed and murdered.

The raid took place while the Organization of African Unity (OAU) (q.v.) was holding its summit in Mauritius. Amin, who had just completed his year as President of the OAU, had returned to Uganda early. He was totally unaware of the raid until some hours later, and few things could have shamed him more than this humiliating defeat which caught the world's attention by its daring.

On their return flight the Israeli planes landed at Nairobi airport in Kenya, where they refueled with the connivance of the Kenya government. A storm of indignation from the OAU, which felt that Africa, not just Uganda, had been humiliated by the raid, and which supported the Palestinian cause, made the Kenya government draw back and try to distance itself from what had happened. The episode gave rise to two best-selling paperbacks (*see* Bibliography) and a successful film.

EQUATORIA. A large and ill-defined area of the present southern Sudan (q.v.) and northern Uganda which was annexed to Egypt by the Khedive Isma'il in 1869. Egyptian rule was steadily extended southwards towards the great lakes, and by 1874 reached the northern end of Lake Albert and included large parts of Acholi (q.v.). Its governors included [General] Charles Gordon, Sir Samuel Baker (q.v.) and Emin Pasha (q.v.). Egyptian rule was brought to an end in 1889 by the Mahdist uprising.

EXPULSIONS. Three major expulsions of non-Ugandans have taken place since the country became independent.

Expulsion of Kenyans. This took place during the first presidency of Milton Obote (q.v.). Unemployment had become a politically sensitive issue, and Obote moved against Kenyans working in Uganda. Some 33,000 were expelled on the grounds that they did not have work permits. Many had worked in Uganda since well before work permits were required. Not all Kenyans were expelled: some were skilled workers who could not easily be replaced; others had become assimilated and were not noticed. After a relatively short time a number began filtering back again. The episode soured relations between the two countries for some time.

Expulsion of the Asians. In 1972 the expulsion by President Amin (q.v.) of the Asians (q.v.) drew international attention. Some 27,000 were British citizens, and it was against these that Amin moved to begin with. When this proved popular, Amin went on to expel all the Asians, including those with Ugandan nationality, which drew a massed protest from the students of Makerere University (q.v.). A deadline of 90 days was set for the Asians to leave. The registration of those due to go to Britain was delayed until tension ran dangerously high. The British blamed Amin, but appear to have been responsible for the delay themselves. They seem to have gotten wind of an impending invasion from Tanzania (q.v.), to have believed that this would be successful, and that the Asians would not, after all, be expelled. In the event the invasion failed dismally. The small invading land force was easily defeated, and a plane bound for Entebbe (q.v.) did not get off the ground.

The Office of the UN High Commissioner for Refugees (UNHCR) was involved in organizing an air lift, and succeeded in moving almost all the 50,000 people involved by the deadline. The few who still remained were moved into two temples in Kampala (q.v.) which were declared to be United Nations territory, and were cared for by hastily recruited UN staff who wore blue UN armbands. This ruse worked, and all the Asians were safely evacuated. They were allowed to take only a few possessions and the equivalent of £UK50 with them. Many were despoiled even of personal jewelry at the airport or at road blocks on the way there. Amin named the despoiling of the Asians and the reallocation of their businesses to Africans his "economic war" (q.v,) and declared that by this means he had won a great victory for the African population. In fact the modern sector of the economy was ruined and has never recovered, and inflation soared out of control. Businesses were handed to inexperienced people who did not have the skills or credit-worthiness required to conduct a commercial enterprise. The expulsions also persuaded the West that Amin was a brute: so long as he struck only at the African population he was not taken seriously by the West.

Expulsion of Banyarwanda Refugees. A still greater num-ber of people was expelled in 1982/3 during the second presidency of Milton Obote (q.v.) when some 71,000 Ba-nyarwanda (q.v.) UN-registered refugees (q.v.) and other Banyarwanda were expelled from the area in Ankole (q.v.) where they had settled. Immigrants from Rwanda (q.v.) had moved into Uganda since the end of the nineteenth century. In the colonial era those Banyarwanda who migrated into Uganda were mainly Hutu who were increasingly harassed by the Tutsi ruling majority. In Uganda they found work as herdsmen and as laborers on sugar plantations. In 1959 on the eve of independence the Hutu in Rwanda turned on their Tutsi overlords and massacred thousands. Refugees poured over the border into Uganda. There they were placed in settlements in Ankole, and gradually built up their herds of cattle.

By the 1980s the refugees had become vulnerable for several reasons. They had welcomed the coup of 1971 (q.v.) which had brought Amin to power because they had felt threatened by Obote's attitude towards them, and they were accused of supporting Amin. There is no evidence that they did so to any greater extent than any other ethnic group. Secondly they were Tutsi, ethnically related to the cattle-keeping Bahima (q.v.) of Ankole, and so to Yoweri Mu-seveni (q.v.) who was leading a guerrilla movement against the government of President Obote and his ruling Uganda People's Congress (UPC) (q.v.), and they were suspected by some of aiding and abetting this movement. In fact Obote's treatment of them drove some into the arms of Museveni's National Resistance Army (q.v.). Thirdly most of them were Catholics (q.v.) whereas Obote's UPC was predominantly Protestant (q.v.), which provided yet another reason why they could be viewed as suspect. The most important reason for their vulnerability was their ownership of cattle and occupancy of land, both of which were coveted by their neighbors. Suspicion of disloyalty to the regime was probably largely an excuse.

In late 1982 the Youth Wing of the UPC, urged on by local party officials and encouraged by Chris Rwakasisi, a Minister of State in the President's Office, drove the Banyarwanda from their settlements. They seized their cattle and possessions, and forced many of them to the Rwandan border. Some of the immigrants were readmitted to Rwanda, but many refugees were afraid to return. Rwanda could not cope with the influx and closed the border, leaving several thousand people stranded for months in a no man's land. The Office of the UN High Commissioner for Refugees moved the remaining refugees to new camps in a remote and sparsely occupied area of Toro (q.v.) where they had to start life again from scratch. In spite of the large numbers of people involved and the fact that the expulsion of refugees is a violation of the UN Convention on Refugees, these expulsions went largely unnoticed. President Obote denied all responsibility.

-F-

FATAKI, MIKA (1854–1934). A leading chief in Bunyoro (q.v.) in the early twentieth century. The son of a chief in Busoga (q.v.), his original name was Lubaale. During the reign of Kabaka Mwanga (q.v.) he took service at the royal court of Buganda as an *askari* (paid soldier). In 1888 (*see* Wars of Religion) he fled to Ankole (q.v.) with the Christians, though not yet one himself. He then went to Bunyoro (q.v.) and joined the *barusura* (q.v.), where he earned his nickname, Fataki (the Swahili word for a gun-cap), because of his good marksmanship. He was eventually instrumental in getting Protestant (q.v.) teachers of the Church Missionary Society (q.v.) to Bunyoro in spite of opposition from other leading chiefs. In 1901 he became senior chief of Chope, the area which included the town of Masindi (q.v.). He retired to Kigaya in 1915. In 1931 he wrote an account in Runyoro (*see* Languages) of the coming of Christianity to Bunyoro and his own share in it which was published in the *Bunyoro Church*

Magazine. Throughout his life Fataki was as active on behalf of the church as in his chieftaincy. He is an example of many Ugandans who after an unsettled youth were open to new ideas.

FEDEMU (sometimes FEDEMO) *see* UGANDA FEDERAL DEMOCRATIC MOVEMENT

FIVE MINISTERS. These were all ministers in the government of President Obote (q.v.) during the first years after independence. They were Grace Ibingira (q.v.), Minister of State and Secretary-General of the Uganda People's Congress (UPC) (q.v.); Dr E.B.S. Lumu, Minister of Health and Chairman of the UPC in Buganda; B. K. Kirya, Minister for Mineral and Water Resources; Mathias Ngobe, Minister of Agriculture and Cooperatives; and George Magezi, Minister of Housing and Labour. They were detained by President Obote in 1966 and remained in detention until released by President Amin (q.v.) after the coup of 1971 (q.v.) in which he seized power. They represented the right wing of the UPC which did not approve of Obote's support for the Simba rebels in the Congo (later Zaire [q.v.]) on whose behalf Obote and Amin had secretly intervened. When the Gold Scandal (q.v.) broke, they supported the motion of censure passed on Obote, Amin and others in the National Assembly (q.v.) during Obote's absence. On Obote's return to the capital there were rumors of troop movements, and Obote feared the five ministers were plotting to overthrow him. He therefore ordered their arrest which took place at a Cabinet Meeting on 22 February 1966.

FORCE OBOTE BACK AGAIN (FOBA). A group based in Teso (q.v.) dedicated to ousting President Museveni (q.v.) by force and reinstating President Obote (q.v.). It was led by two of Obote's former ministers, Peter Otai (q.v.), former Minister of Defence, and John Luwuliza-Kirunda (q.v.), former Minister of Internal Affairs. The movement changed its name to the Uganda People's Front/Army (q.v.).

FORMER UGANDA NATIONAL ARMY (FUNA). A group of members of the army of President Amin (q.v.) which was defeated by the Tanzanians in 1979. They regrouped under Major General Lumago and operated spasmodically against the government of President Obote (q.v.) in the northwest of Uganda. They were coopted by President Museveni (q.v.) and incorporated into the National Resistance Army (q.v.).

FORT PORTAL. During the colonial era Fort Portal, which lies some 200 miles (320 kilometers) west of Kampala (q.v.), was the administrative headquarters of Toro (q.v.), and the capital of the Kingdom of Toro. Since 1974 it has been the administrative headquarters of the smaller Kabarole District.

It originated in a small stockaded fort built in 1893. The Imperial British East Africa Company (q.v.) had been forced by lack of funds to withdraw from Uganda, and Sir Gerald Portal, sent to review the situation, recommended that Britain should declare a Protectorate only over Buganda. The Mukama Kasagama (q.v.), whom Lugard (q.v.) had recently installed as ruler of Toro, was therefore advised to move away from an area in which he could no longer be given British protection. This he was extremely reluctant to do. Major Roderick Owen therefore authorized the building of Fort Jerry (named after Sir Gerald Portal) close to Kasagama's headquarters to protect him. Later it was renamed Fort Portal when Sir Gerald Portal was appointed Commissioner (as the first Governors [q.v.] of Uganda were entitled). As well as being an administrative headquarters it is a center of both the Catholic Church (q.v.) and the Church of Uganda (q.v.), with several schools and hospitals.

FRANCISCAN MISSIONARY SISTERS. The order of religious sisters who work with the Mill Hill Fathers (q.v.) in southeastern and eastern Uganda and in Kenya (q.v,). The best known member of the order was Mother Kevin (q.v.), a Franciscan who was given permission in 1929 to establish special noviciates to train Franciscan Sisters for mission work in Africa. In 1952 the Franciscan Missionary Sisters were established as a separate congregation. They work not only in East Africa but in other African countries and elsewhere in the world. The first six sisters arrived in Uganda in 1903, and their numbers rose rapidly after 1930.

FRONT FOR NATIONAL SALVATION (FRONASA). The only movement to attempt armed resistance against President Amin (q.v.) inside Uganda. It was led by Yoweri Museveni (q.v.) and was involved in the failed invasion from Tanzania (q.v.) in late 1972. Its tiny band of fighters regrouped, but they were unable to achieve anything significant against Amin's regime though they carried out occasional acts of sabotage.

-G-

GADAFI, COLONEL MUAMAR. President of Libya (q.v.). Colonel Gadafi became personally involved in Ugandan affairs when President Amin (q.v.) visited Libya in February 1972 and when he paid a return visit to Uganda in 1974. He persuaded Amin to take a more militantly Islamic stand both in foreign affairs and in Uganda. Libyans were sent to assist Amin when Kampala (q.v.) was about to fall in the War of Liberation (q.v.) of 1979. They took large numbers of casualties in the battle for Entebbe (q.v.), and others were captured and taken back to Tanzania (q.v.). Their release was eventually negotiated by Algeria in return for a payment to Tanzania of several million pounds.

GALT, HARRY ST GEORGE (d. 19 May 1905). Acting Sub-Commissioner of what was then the Western Province of Uganda, he was murdered by a lone spearman at the rest house near Ibanda in northern Ankole (q.v.). Enquiries into the murder were frustrated but eventually a peasant named Rutaraka was alleged to have carried out the crime. He was found hanged, and it was unclear whether his death was suicide or murder. It was generally assumed that he had carried out the murder of Galt, though not instigated it, but no evidence to show this was ever forthcoming. The colonial authorities looked into a variety of possible political motives for the murder, and suspicion was cast on a number of different people, with two men eventually being found guilty. However, the Appeal Court ordered an acquittal because of the unsatisfactory nature of the evidence. Colonial officials suspected that the Mugabe Kahaya (q.v.) and other chiefs knew more than they would reveal, and many of the Bahinda (q.v.) chiefs left Ankole and did not return. The kingdom was fined heavily in cattle, and the Ankole Agreement (q.v.) was suspended until 1912. Galt's murder long remained a mystery. All researchers could discover was a general insistence among those whom they interviewed that the murder was intended to damage Mbaguta (q.v.), the chief minister and collaborator with the British and Baganda (q.v.), though in fact he had benefitted.

The archives of the White Fathers (q.v.) were opened to researchers in the 1960s and contain an account of events written by Fr (later Bishop) Gorju. This suggests that the intention of those who planned the murder, who included the Mugabe, was to kill Mbaguta because of the threat he constituted to Bahinda power. Mbaguta was expected to pass through Ibanda in the company of a British official, but arrived there earlier than expected, and the hired assassin, whoever he may have been, knowing that the arrival of a white man was the signal for action, murdered the next one who came along who happened to be Galt. According to this interpretation, Galt was simply a chance victim of a plot that went wrong. The Mugabe and chiefs then conspired to confuse the enquiry, and were greatly relieved to get off with a communal fine. The documents seem to suggest that Mbaguta's murder may have been intended as the prelude to an uprising against the Baganda and colonial rule for which spears were already being amassed, though there was disagreement about the wisdom of such a course. In the event Mbaguta benefitted as the colonial authorities felt he was one of the few people they could trust, and his power was enhanced.

GASYONGA, CHARLES GODFREY (1910–1982). Mugabe of Ankole (q.v.), 1944–1967. The son of Rwakatogoro, one of the rejected claimants to the position of Mugabe on the death of Ntare V (q.v.). Gasyonga's predecessor, Mugabe Kahaya (q.v.), had no sons and there was some difficulty in finding a suitable successor following the withdrawal of many Bahima (q.v.) from central Ankole after the murder of the colonial officer, Galt (q.v.). The Bairu (q.v.) showed no particular attachment to the office of the Mugabe, and Gasyonga's powers were steadily eroded during the colonial era. He did not wield the authority that his fellow monarchs did in Toro (q.v.) or Bunyoro (q.v.). However, his symbolic and ceremonial role increased as his real powers were diminished. He took an interest in education (q.v.), encouraging the raising of standards in Ankole, and he initiated the translation of the Bible into Runyankole/Rukiga (*see* Languages).

In 1962 he joined with the other kings of Uganda to bid for the retention of the royal prerogatives and the privileges of the kingdoms when Uganda became independent. A new Ankole Agreement was entered into in 1962 and incorporated into the independence constitution (q.v.). In 1967, when President Obote (q.v.) abolished the monarchies, the royal drum, Bagyendanwa, the symbol of royal power, was loaded onto a lorry and carried away without protest. Gasyonga received a pension and went into retirement as a private person. Early in his presidency Idi Amin (q.v.) consulted with selected elders in various parts of the country about the possible revival of the kingdoms, and Gasyonga was among those who signed a memorandum on behalf of the elders of Ankole supporting their abolition. In 1993 President Museveni (q.v.) allowed the kingdoms to reinstate their rulers as cultural figureheads without political power. Ankole was uncertain whether to take advantage of this or not.

GENERAL SERVICE UNIT. A paramilitary unit set up by President Obote (q.v.) soon after the Mutiny of 1964 (q.v.), and intended as a counterweight to the Uganda Army (q.v.). It was placed under the control of Akena Adoko (q.v.), a clan relative of Obote's. Its strength quickly rose to 800 men, and they were placed at strategic locations around the country. They received some training in Israel (q.v.). They were used to deal with any perceived danger to the state, and their ruthlessness made them generally feared and hated by the civilian population. The Uganda Army viewed them as a threat to its monopoly of armed power.

GOLD SCANDAL. In 1965 Prime Minister Moise Tshombe of the Congo (now Zaire [q.v.]), faced a major uprising by rebels calling themselves the Simba. President Obote (q.v.)

aided the Simba on the grounds that Tshombe was a puppet of Western capitalist interests. General Idi Amin (q.v.) led the Ugandan forces involved. This was kept secret even from the Cabinet, the right wing of which supported Tshombe. Amin was entrusted by the Simba with gold and ivory to be sold and the proceeds used for purchasing arms. Amin deposited Uganda Shillings 480,000 (£UK24,000) in his bank account from the sale of the gold. This became known and Daudi Ocheng (q.v.), a member of the National Assembly (q.v,) and Secretary-General of Kabaka Yekka ("the Kabaka only") (q.v.), agreed to take action. He was dying of cancer, and felt secure against victimization. He accused Amin in the National Assembly (q.v.) of embezzling the money and of plotting to overthrow the constitution. He brought a motion calling for an enquiry into the actions of Obote, Amin and two government ministers, Felix Onama and Adoko Nekyon, which the Assembly accepted.

Obote was away from Kampala (q.v.) at the time. Immediately on his return he acted to detain five ministers (q.v.) on the right of the party whom he suspected of being behind the allegations, and of plotting a coup against him. He suspended the 1962 Constitution (q.v.) and set up an enquiry under Judge Sir Clement Nageon De L'Estang, Vice-President of the Court of Appeal of Eastern Africa. The full text of the enquiry was not published until after the coup of 1971 (q.v.) in which Amin seized power from Obote. The transcript of the evidence suggests that very few witnesses told the whole truth. De L'Estang cleared Obote and the ministers alleged to have been involved with him of any actual wrongdoing, though he reproved Obote for unwisely "trying to ride two horses at once." The Report accepted little of Amin's evidence as being truthful, but could nevertheless find no firm evidence against him. It concluded that Amin had certainly obtained "one gold bar weighing 20 lbs and probably ten more," and concluded that the money paid into Amin's account was probably the result of the sale of gold.

This series of events altered the course of Ugandan history. It broke apart the ruling Uganda People's Congress (q.v.), led directly to Obote's assumption of presidential powers, to the Battle of Mengo 1966 (q.v.), and to the 1967

Constitution (q.v.). It strengthened Amin's position, and so contributed to the 1971 coup (q.v.).

GOVERNORS OF UGANDA DURING THE TIME OF THE BRITISH PROTECTORATE.

Until 1907 the highest ranking British administrator was entitled "Commissioner."

1893	Sir Gerald Portal
1895	Mr Ernest Berkeley
1899	Sir Harry Johnston (q.v.)
1902	Sir James Hayes-Sadler
1905	Sir Hesketh Bell (q.v.)
1911	Sir Frederick Jackson (q.v.)
1917	Sir Robert Coryndon
1922	Sir Geoffrey Archer
1925	Sir William Gowers
1932	Sir Bernard Bourdillon
1935	Sir Philip Mitchell (q.v.)
1940	Sir Charles Dundas
1944	Sir John Hall
1952	Sir Andrew Cohen
1957	Sir Frederick Crawford

GRAY, SIR JOHN MILNER (1889–1970). Colonial civil servant, Chief Justice of Zanzibar and pioneer historian of Uganda and East Africa. He first arrived in Uganda in 1920 as an Assistant District Officer. *The Uganda Journal* was founded in 1934, and Gray became a regular contributor, with over 50 articles and notes to his credit. He collected books, papers and vernacular material on East African history and made or commissioned translations as necessary, often quoting them in extenso in his writings. *The Uganda Journal,* 35, 2, 1971 published a 14-page bibliography of his extensive published and unpublished works. Gray's papers are held in the University Library, Cambridge, UK. His articles in the *Uganda Journal,* "Mutesa of Uganda," which appeared in two parts in 1934, and "The Year of the Three Kings of Buganda: Mwanga—Kiwewa—Kalema; 1888–1889," were some of the earliest attempts at writing pre-colonial history based in part on Ugandan language sources, and much of what he wrote still stands today.

"GREATER UGANDA." On 25 January 1976, the fifth anniversary of the coup of 1971 (q.v.) which brought President Amin (q.v.) to power, he made claims to a "Greater Uganda" which he amplified in a speech on 16 February. In doing so he seems to have been influenced by Somalia's claims to parts of all the neighboring territories where Somali people lived, claims which greatly angered those neighbors. Amin's claims were not based on ethnic links, but on the fact that the boundaries (q.v.) of Uganda had only slowly been finalized during the colonial period. He made his claim with regard to Kenya (q.v.) the day after the government of Kenya had begun to make enquiries about a Kenyan student, Esther Chesire (q.v.), who had "disappeared." The Kenyan government was extremely angry about Amin's claims, and Amin was forced to back down, and claim that his speech on the subject had been misinterpreted. President Nimeiri of Sudan (q.v.) was reported to have pointed out that the area from which Amin came had once formed part of Sudan, so perhaps Amin was Sudanese rather than Ugandan.

Later in 1976 a book appeared entitled *The Shaping of Modern Uganda* which purported to be written by Amin. It reprinted documents relating to the demarcation of Uganda's boundaries and some old maps, and had almost certainly been put together by the Professor of Geography at Makerere University (q.v.) on Amin's instructions. It reproduced some photographs of historical interest as well as photographs intended to glorify Amin. At the end it contained the text of the Decree issued in 1975 by which all land in Uganda was nationalized, and the text of a speech given by Amin on Habitat Day, 29 February 1976. The publication of the book, and particularly the Introduction, amounted to a climbdown by Amin on his claims to a "Greater Uganda." He had merely been instructing his subjects on a matter of historical geography, he declared.

GULU. The administrative center of the present district of that name and the chief urban center of the area occupied by the

Acholi (q.v.). It is a church center with both Roman Catholic (q.v.) and Church of Uganda (q.v.) cathedrals in or near the town, church schools, and a Catholic hospital and seminary close by. A large contingent of the National Resistance Army (q.v.) was quartered there from 1986 onwards when Basilio Okello (q.v.) and Tito Okello (q.v.) led an insurrection among the Acholi against the government of President Museveni (q.v.). There was further trouble in the area in connection with the Holy Spirit Movement led by Alice Lakwena (q.v.). By mid-1992 the security situation had improved, but Gulu remained heavily garrisoned.

-H-

HANCOCK COMMITTEE. The committee chaired by Professor Sir Keith Hancock and set up to examine the relations between the Kabaka of Buganda (q.v.) and his government on the one hand and the Protectorate government on the other at the time of the Deportation Crisis (q.v.). Their work led to the return of the Kabaka in 1954.

HANLON, BISHOP HENRY (1862–1937). The leader of first group of priests from the Mill Hill Fathers (q.v.) to work in Uganda. In 1894 he was consecrated Bishop and made Vicar Apostolic of the newly-created Vicariate of the Upper Nile, the area of eastern Uganda for which the mission was given responsibility. In 1897 he was present when Daudi Chwa (q.v.) was proclaimed Kabaka in place of Kabaka Mwanga (q.v.) who had rebelled against British rule. He steered the mission through the difficult days of the Sudanese Mutiny (q.v.) and the Rebellion of 1897 (q.v.), and in 1900 was a witness to the [B]Uganda Agreement (q.v.). Hanlon was responsible for recruiting Franciscan sisters to work in Uganda (*see* Franciscan Missionary Sisters and Mother Kevin). Ill-health forced him to retire in 1912 and he traveled back to England via the Holy Land, Rome and Paris taking Stanislaus Mugwanya (q.v.) with him, and presenting him to King George V. On his retirement he was appointed Rector of St Alban's, Blackburn.

HANNINGTON, BISHOP JAMES (1847–1885). A missionary of the Church Missionary Society (CMS) (q.v.) who first went to East Africa in 1882. In 1883 he returned to England and in January 1884 was consecrated the first Church of England (q.v.) Bishop of Eastern Equatorial Africa, an area which included the modern Kenya (q.v.) and Tanzania (q.v.). In July 1885 he left the coast to travel to Uganda via Masai country, intending to enter Buganda (q.v.) via Busoga (q.v.). This was dangerous because of a belief in Buganda that anyone approaching by that "back door" route would bring trouble, and would try to "eat" (i.e., conquer) Buganda. Warnings sent to the Bishop about the danger of this route seem not to have reached him in time. News of German annexations on the coast had reached Kabaka Mwanga (q.v.) in Buganda, the first three Christian martyrs (q.v.) had already been executed, and the situation was extremely tense. A boat was sent to intercept Hannington, and the missionaries assured Mwanga that he would not arrive by this route, and had no intention of "eating" Buganda. But the Bishop did not travel by the mission boat, which missed him altogether. He went on through Busoga, stopping at the village of Chief Luba towards the end of October, where he was held as a prisoner for eight days before being murdered on the orders of Kabaka Mwanga on 29 October 1885 along with Pinto, his Goan cook, and many of the porters traveling with him. His diary was rescued by a survivor and delivered to the mission in Buganda. It was reported that his last words were "Tell the king that I die for Buganda. I have bought this road with my life." There is no evidence that Hannington understood that by traveling this route he was endangering himself.

After the Bishop's death the people of that area of Busoga became very troubled about a series of misfortunes that befell them. They decided these might be the result of the murder. They therefore gathered together Hannington's few remains and sent them out of their country to Mumias, now in western Kenya, so that his spirit might trouble them no more. In 1892 Bishop Tucker (q.v.) was shown where they were buried, and had them disinterred and brought to Uganda where they were reburied at a great memorial service at Namirembe (q.v.)

HARRISON, CHARLES (1921–). A distinguished journalist who joined the Nairobi-based *East African Standard* in 1953, and two years later launched the *Uganda Argus* and became its editor. The *Argus* was Uganda's leading English-language newspaper until 1972. Harrison acted as an agent for Reuter's News Agency and also wrote for the London *Times* and for the BBC. Soon after President Amin (q.v.) came to power Harrison moved to Nairobi where he continued to be an authority on events in Uganda.

HEALTH *see* MEDICINE

HILTON YOUNG COMMISSION *see* CLOSER UNION

HOIMA. For much of the colonial era Hoima was the capital of the Bunyoro (q.v.) kingdom, and the administrative headquarters in Bunyoro of the Protectorate government. Since 1974 Bunyoro has been divided in two, and Hoima is the administrative headquarters of the district of that name which comprises the southern part of the former Bunyoro. For a time early in the colonial period Masindi (q.v.) was the district headquarters, and for a short time the Mukama of Bunyoro transferred his capital there.

    The town of Hoima is largely a colonial creation. It grew up around the administration and the churches, schools and hospital established by the missions (q.v.).

HUMAN RIGHTS COMMISSION. This was established in 1986 by President Museveni (q.v.) to enquire into human rights violations between the achievement of independence and the assumption of power by the National Resistance Movement (q.v.). Its Chairman was a lawyer, Judge Oder, but its members included laymen and women. Its hearings were held in a variety of locations to enable people to attend easily. If it found evidence warranting prosecution, then the material had to be handed over to the police to prosecute. Considering the extent of human rights abuses, there have been relatively few prosecutions, largely because of the difficulty of finding surviving witnesses, and witnesses willing to expose themselves. At least as important as its prosecutory role have been its educational and cathartic effects.

-I-

IBINGIRA, GRACE STUART (1932–   ). Lawyer and politician from Ankole (q.v.). A practicing advocate since 1959, Ibingira first won a seat in the Legislative Council (q.v.) in 1960 as a member of the Uganda People's Congress (UPC) (q.v.), one of only a few influential Bahima (q.v.) to do so. He was one of those who helped establish the alliance between the UPC and the Baganda (q.v.) royalist party, Kabaka Yekka (KY) (q.v.), which enabled Prime Minister Milton Obote (q.v.) to win the Elections of 1962 (q.v.). In those elections Ibingira won a seat in the National Assembly (q.v.) and was appointed Minister of Justice. In 1964 he was made Minister of State in the Prime Minister's Office and Secretary-General of the UPC in succession to John Kakonge who failed to carry the party with him when advocating a more radical form of socialism than Obote was prepared to accept at that time. He antagonized many of the Youth Wing of the UPC by getting some of the more militant youth expelled from the party, and by his opposition to socialism.

Ibingira began to build a personal following among the more conservative members of the UPC and KY supporters. Within a year a split between two factions of the UPC opened up, one led by Obote, the other by Ibingira. In the same year the alliance between KY and the UPC which had enabled Obote to gain power was dissolved, and the leaders of Buganda began to ally themselves with Ibingira in opposition to Obote. KY broke up and its members were encouraged to join the UPC in order to strengthen Ibingira's faction.

In late 1965 accusations were made in the National Assembly against Obote and three others of embezzling gold and ivory paid them by the Congo rebels (see Gold Scandal). Early in February 1966 the National Assembly voted almost unanimously for an enquiry to be set up to examine these allegations. In order to preempt a coup against himself, Obote ordered the detention of the five ministers (q.v.) who were the ringleaders. Ibingira remained in detention until all Obote's political detainees were released by President Amin (q.v.) after his seizure of power in 1971.

Amin appointed Ibingira Permanent Representative to the United Nations, and he remained in this post until 1973, when he defected. From 1975–1985 he was a senior legal consultant with the UN Development Program. From 1975–1977 he held a fellowship at the Smithsonian Institute. He returned to Uganda after the National Resistance Movement (q.v.) won power in 1986 but did not return to politics. From 1988–1989 he was a member of the African Commission on Human Rights. Ibingira is the author of *The Forging of an African Nation* (1973), *Bitter Harvest* (1980) and *African Upheavals Since Independence* (1980).

IGUMIRA (?–1925), A nephew of Mugabe Ntare V (q.v.) of Ankole (q.v.). After Ntare's death he supported the candidature of Kahaya (q.v.) whom he claimed was a son of Ntare and his rightful heir, though today it is widely believed that he was actually Igumira's son. Kahaya was recognized as Mugabe, and at first Igumira virtually ruled through him. In 1897 the Protectorate was extended to Ankole and Igumira found his power being curbed. He and other Bahima (q.v.) particularly resented the rising power of the collaborationist Mbaguta (q.v.). When Igumira tried to seize a neighboring chieftaincy in 1900 he was arrested, fined 150 cattle, and exiled from Ankole. His former chieftaincies were handed over to his rival, Mbaguta. Igumira's treatment was suspected of being one of the motives for the murder of the British colonial official, Galt (q.v.), in 1905, and he was exiled for the second time. For the last 20 years of his life he lived in obscurity in Buganda (q.v.).

IMPERIAL BRITISH EAST AFRICA COMPANY (IBEAC). In 1886 Sir William MacKinnon, Chairman of the British India Steamship Company, founded the British East Africa Company to exploit the trading opportunities offered by the declaration of a British sphere of influence in East Africa and to protect its interests in Zanzibar against the threat of German encroachments. He then offered to administer these territories on behalf of the British government, which did not wish to be directly involved, and as a result his company was granted a Charter and renamed the Imperial British East Africa Company.

The first of its agents to reach Uganda was F. J. Jackson (q.v.) in 1890. Kabaka Mwanga (q.v.) of Buganda (q.v.) had been persuaded to sign a treaty by the German, Karl Peters (q.v.), and Jackson failed to persuade him to set this aside and sign a treaty with the Company. He therefore left Ernest Gedge behind in Uganda with an armed force, and returned to the coast for further instructions. However, by the Anglo-German Agreement of 1890 (q.v.), Uganda fell within the British sphere of influence, so this no longer mattered.

The second agent of the IBEAC to reach Uganda, Frederick Lugard (q.v.), did so later that year. He was instructed to take Mwanga under the protection of the Company and try to persuade him not to sign treaties with representatives of other powers. Lugard then marched to the west where the IBEAC had interests in the ivory trade. On the way to the west he made blood brotherhood with the Mugabe Ntare V (q.v.) of Ankole (q.v.) and obtained a treaty between him and the Company. He also installed Kasagama (q.v.) as Mukama of Toro (q.v,), and placed the Sudanese troops left behind by Emin Pasha along the border between Toro and Bunyoro (q.v.) to protect the former.

When he returned to Buganda in December 1891 he found orders to return to Britain because the IBEAC could no longer afford to keep a representative in Uganda. There was acute tension between the Protestant (q.v.) and Catholic (q.v.) factions in the capital and the British missionaries in particular feared what might happen if the company withdrew and left them and their converts unprotected. The Church Missionary Society (q.v.) raised sufficient monies to keep the IBEAC in Uganda for a further year because of the dangers they feared. One aspect of the danger was illustrated when, early in January 1892, fighting between the Ugandan members of the two factions broke out, and the Protestants were victorious in the 1892 Battle of Mengo (q.v.). There followed a campaign by Lugard and the Protestant missionaries to persuade the British government to declare a Protectorate over Uganda since the Company was unable to continue offering protection. The Company's mandate was extended until the end of March 1893, and in November 1892 Sir Gerald Portal was sent to report on the situation in Uganda. As a result of Portal's mission, a provisional protectorate was declared on 29 May 1893, and the IBEAC's role came to an end. A full Protectorate was declared in June of the following year.

INSPECTOR GENERAL OF GOVERNMENT. In 1986 the National Resistance Movement (q.v.) led by President Museveni (q.v.) appointed an Inspector General of Government (an ombudsman) with wide-ranging powers and directly responsible to the President. The person appointed to the post was Augustine Ruzindana. The Inspector General of Government can deal with allegations of human rights abuses as well as corruption, maladministration and abuse of bureaucratic power. He has had considerable success in dealing with corruption, but has lacked the resources to act as decisively in the human rights field as was hoped.

INTERNATIONAL COMMITTEE OF THE RED CROSS (ICRC). The ICRC bases its work on the Geneva Conventions of 1949 relating to the protection of the sick and wounded in war, of prisoners of war, and of civilians in time of war. Since 1977 it has been able to extend its work to armed conflicts not of an international character and to situations of internal disturbances and tensions if it is permitted to do so by the government of the country in question. It has had a presence in Uganda since the overthrow of President Amin (q.v.).

In 1981 it was alleged that a massacre by the Uganda National Liberation Army (q.v.) at Ombachi Catholic Mission in West Nile (q.v.) was publicized by the ICRC. This led to demands by the government of President Obote (q.v.) that it should leave the country. It was forced to do so briefly, but there was international pressure on the Obote government for it to be allowed to return. During Obote's second presidency the ICRC was not permitted to visit barracks where many civilians were illegally held and where torture was endemic.

When the National Resistance Movement (q.v.) led by President Museveni (q.v.) took power the ICRC was given greater access to prisoners. The ICRC was permitted to visit detainees in civil prisons and some barracks and police stations. This has undoubtedly helped to reduce the incidence of torture, though torture has not been totally eliminated. The ICRC was also given permission to train army officers in the Law of War and the Geneva Conventions.

INVASION OF 1972. In September 1972 groups of exiled supporters of President Obote (q.v.) in Tanzania (q.v.) attempted to invade Uganda and seize power back from President Amin (q.v.). One group crossed the Tanzania/ Uganda land border; a second group attempted to fly in from Arusha airport to Entebbe (q.v.), but their plane was unable to get off the ground. The invaders hoped that Ugandans would rise to support them as they advanced, but on the contrary this marked the height of Amin's popularity, coming, as it did, shortly after he had announced the expulsion (q.v.) of the Asians (q.v.). The land forces would have had to fight their way through Buganda, and the Baganda (q.v.) were bitterly opposed to Obote since the Battle of Mengo 1966 (q.v.) and the dissolution of their kingdom. When the invasion had been defeated, a number of alleged guerrillas were publicly executed, the first public executions in Uganda since 1893. Among the guerrillas who survived and escaped back to Tanzania was Yoweri (later President) Museveni (q.v.).

ISLAM. Islam was first brought to Uganda by Swahili and Arab traders from the East African coast who arrived in the reigns of Kabaka Suna and Kabaka Mutesa I (q.v.) of Buganda (*see* Baganda). The first whose name is known was Ahmed bin Ibrahim (q.v.). They came as traders, not religious teachers, but a number of pages at the court converted to Islam, and Luganda (*see* Languages) was first written down in Arabic characters. From the court some knowledge of Islam spread into the countryside. The Islam the traders brought was Sunni Islam and they followed the Shafi school of law. Kabaka Mutesa I began to keep the Ramadan fast, and ordered his people to use Muslim greetings and follow Islam. Knowing that ablutions were important for Muslims, people put stones on which to stand when washing one's feet outside their doors, hoping thus to be safe from prying officials sent round to see the Kabaka's orders were obeyed. The Kabaka knew little of Islam's moral code, and when his pages refused to obey an order for what they claimed were religious reasons, he had 200 of them executed in 1876 (*see* Muslim Martyrs). Christian missions (q.v.) arrived the following year, and many at court started to learn with the missions.

Twelve years later it again seemed that Islam might become the national religion of Buganda. In 1888 Kabaka Mwanga (q.v.) was ousted by an alliance of Christians and Muslims. Traditionalist Baganda and Muslims then made common cause against the Christians, and a Muslim Kabaka, Nuhu Kalema, was installed, but was removed by a Christian coalition in the Wars of Religion (q.v.).

After the introduction of Christianity and the Wars of Religion, Muslims fell into third place behind the two Christian groups. They were educationally disadvantaged because Muslim parents feared to send their children to Christian schools and Qur'anic schools did not offer a comparable education (q.v.). Among those who were concerned about Muslim education was Prince Badru Kakungulu (q.v.).

Islam also reached Uganda from Egypt and Sudan (q.v.), and a Muslim community grew up in West Nile (q.v.). These Muslims belonged to the Malakite school of Islamic law. The Sudanese troops, whose descendants are the Nubians (q.v.), who were left behind by Emin Pasha (q.v,) and brought into Uganda by Lugard (q.v.), formed a third Muslim group, also adherents of the Malakite law school. Indians (*see* Asians) who arrived from the early 1900s onwards included some Shi'ite Muslims of the Ithna Asheri, Ismaili (q.v.), and Dawoodi Bohora sects. Each group built its own mosques. The first two Asian Muslims went on *Hajj* (pilgrimage) to Mecca in 1910, and the first two Africans in 1920, and from then on the number going on *Hajj* grew. *Mawlid* celebrations (celebrations of the birthday of a venerated person, especially the Prophet Muhammad) came to play an increasingly important part in Ugandan Islam, not just as religious feasts but as community gatherings.

From 1920 onwards serious doctrinal splits, compounded by personal rivalries, developed among Muslims over the number of prayers to be said at Friday (*Juma*) prayers. The Zukhuli sect, based on the Kibuli mosque and under the patronage of Prince Badru, insisted on the need to say an extra *al-Zuhur* (noonday prayer) on Fridays; the Juma sect which thought this unnecessary flourished among Muslims in the Buganda county of Butambala. Every effort to heal this division exacerbated it further. In 1947 a great assembly at Kibuli, which intended to bring unity, resulted in further schism. The majority New Juma group, based on Kibuli, agreed to give up the extra *al-Zuhur* prayer, and a great new Friday mosque was built at Kibuli. However, one section of this sect refused to give up the extra prayer, and an Old Juma group not only refused to accept Kakungulu's leadership and kept the extra prayer, but also insisted on the use of published calendars to determine the events of the Muslim lunar year rather than on sightings of the moon. They also banned the use of drums at religious meetings. These divisions resulted in disputes over schools, the appointment of Registrars of Marriage, and land, and some of these disputes ended up in the courts.

Certain Sheikhs are remembered as great religious teachers, including Sheikh Abdul Kadir Mayanja who was converted during the reign of Kabaka Mutesa I and who taught Sheikhs Nsambu of Nateete and Abdalla Ssekimwanyi; Sheikh Haji Mohammed Abdullah, a Nigerian; and Sheikh Swaibu Ssemakula (q.v.) who trained a whole generation of Muslim teachers.

Before the 1950s Islam spread only slowly. In 1945 the Aga Khan, spiritual leader of the wealthy Ismailis, founded the East African Muslim Welfare Society to help all Muslims, not only his own followers. He gave towards African Muslim projects on a shilling for shilling basis and by 1956 the society had donated over six million shillings. Help for African Muslims had come from other sections of the Asian community, and Muslim schooling began to improve. Muslims who had entered trade because they did not have the educational qualifications for professional careers began to do well and become relatively well off.

The increasing numbers and influence of Muslims meant that they became political targets after independence. President Obote (q.v.) tried to unite and control them through the National Association for the Advancement of Muslims (NAAM) (q.v.). President Amin (q.v.) tried to do the same through the Uganda Muslim Supreme Council (q.v.). This received enormous amounts of Arab money, but much of it went astray. Large numbers of conversions were claimed by Amin but on the other hand the expulsion (q.v.) of the Asians included Muslims, and his reign of terror claimed Muslim victims. Amin's overthrow left Muslims afraid of vengeance being wreaked on them. In the main this did not happen, though the Bushenyi Massacre (q.v.) of 1979 was a shocking example of what Muslims feared.

ISMAILIS. A group of Shi'a Muslims (*see* Islam) who follow the Aga Khan, their living Imam who is able to interpret the Qur'an for them. They came from India to East Africa and in Uganda were the most Westernized Muslim group, encouraged to become so by the Aga Khan.

ISRAEL. Diplomatic relations with Israel were established in 1962, and the following year an agreement on aid and assistance was signed. Israel was involved in road building, the construction of a new airport at Entebbe (q.v.) and military and air force training under General Bar-Lev who established a friendly relationship with General (later President) Idi Amin (q.v.). This relationship enabled Israel to channel arms through Uganda to the Anya Nya (q.v.) who were waging a civil war in Sudan (q.v.) against Northern oppression. This war tied down Arab forces which might otherwise have been used in the growing Arab-Israeli confrontation in the Middle East. In 1969 General Nimeiri seized power in Sudan and established a socialist government. President Obote (q.v.) was in the process of leading Uganda into a "Move to the Left" (q.v.), and their shared leftist policies brought the two governments into a closer alliance. As a result Obote moved to prevent arms reaching

Sudan through Uganda, and arrested and planned to hand over to Sudan the mercenary, Rolf Steiner, who had been assisting the Anya Nya. Before this could happen, Amin seized power in the coup of 1971 (q.v.).

Amin had close ties with Southern Sudan and restored the supply of arms to the Anya Nya (he had covertly continued to facilitate the supply in spite of Obote's ruling). For his first year in power he continued a close alliance with the Israelis, They may have been involved in the coup which brought him to power. However, Amin was a Muslim and was therefore open to the influence of Muslim Arab states. In February 1972 he visited Libya (q.v.), and it was apparently mainly as a result of pressure from Colonel Gadafi (q.v.) that he reversed his stance on Israel, and made a number of accusations against Israel to justify the expulsion. The war in Sudan had just ended so Israel's usefulness in supporting the Anya Nya had ceased, and preventing further aid to the Anya Nya helped to ensure that the Addis Ababa Agreement setting out the peace terms was ratified. Israel imposed an immediate trade embargo.

In 1976 a plane carrying a large number of Jewish passengers was hijacked and landed at Entebbe airport. Amin openly supported the hijackers and their lives were thought to be in immediate peril. Israel therefore mounted the successful Entebbe Raid (q.v.) to rescue them. No subsequent Ugandan government has restored diplomatic relations with Israel.

ITESO. The area in which the Iteso live lies around Lake Salisbury and the eastern end of Lake Kyoga. This whole area was known as Teso District until 1974 when it was divided into two districts, now called Soroti and Kumi after the towns which are their administrative headquarters. Except in the sparsely-populated northeast where it borders on Karamoja, Teso is fairly evenly populated. The Iteso belong to the same language group as the Karamojong (q.v.), speaking an Eastern Nilotic language (*see* Languages) called Ateso. Migration into this area from less fertile lands to the northeast appears to have taken place over perhaps three centuries before the colonial era (people were still moving into the eastern parts of Amuria and Serere counties in the earlier part of the twentieth century). When the Karamojong overran the Woropom state to the east in about 1830, a major influx occurred. The new arrivals seem to have been assimilated quickly. Some Iteso, in turn, were pushed westward into Busoga where they lost their language and became assimilated to the Basoga (q.v.), though they kept their Teso clan names.

As they moved into the well-watered and increasingly densely-populated lands around Lakes Salisbury and Kyoga the new arrivals adopted the agricultural practices of the people they settled amongst in addition to cattle-keeping, and became settled instead of semi-nomadic. They acquired iron hoes from Bunyoro (q.v.) and the refugees from Woropom brought a knowledge of blacksmithing. Friction grew up between the Iteso and the Karamojong, and the latter took to raiding for cattle, to all of which they claimed a God-given right. In 1894–1896 an exceptionally severe famine occurred which was named after Okadaro, an *emuron* (foreteller) who fell from power after he had repeatedly performed the rain-making ceremonies without success. The desperation of the Iteso led to worsened relations with their neighbors and war broke out over the possession of water-holes. This provided the opportunity for the British through their Baganda (q.v.) allies to bring Teso under colonial rule using the Muganda general, Semei Kakungulu (q.v.), and his men as their agents for several years.

Colonial officials found great difficulty in locating the traditional authorities because the whole social structure of the Iteso was in a state of flux. The age-sets which had been their most important social institutions had been weakened by migration, and when Kakungulu banned the holding of initiation ceremonies in the part of Teso over which he ruled, the system collapsed. The clans may originally have been territorially based, but migration brought together in one area people from many different clans, and no system of territorial authority had evolved by the end of the nineteenth century.

The missions (q.v.) arrived at Ngora in Teso in 1908 and cotton was introduced in the same year, rapidly becoming an important cash crop. Ngora High School (*see* Education) was opened in 1909, and in spite of the need to charge fees the number of pupils had risen to 150 by 1913. Many of those who were later appointed to chieftaincies had been educated at this school. Pupils were introduced to the use of the plough and instructed in cotton cultivation.

Development progressed, even if slowly, throughout the colonial period and during the 1960s. During the presidency of Idi Amin (q.v.) Teso was relatively unmolested. When Amin's troops fled north in 1979 they sold their guns to the Karamojong who also helped themselves to ammunition. Their periodic raids on their neighbors became more dangerous, but the Iteso were permitted to raise a militia and by this means the Karamojong were kept in check. In 1985 the Karamojong again gained arms when the junta led by Basilio Okello (q.v.) and Tito Okello (q.v.) collapsed.

The incoming National Resistance Movement (q.v.) government seriously misjudged the situation in Teso. It was unnecessarily wary of the Teso militia and disarmed it at a time when the National Resistance Army (NRA) (q.v.) was unable or unwilling or both to protect the Iteso from the Karamojong, and the country was devastated in raids in which people as well as cattle were attacked. The Iteso were therefore easily recruited by the insurgent movements headed by Peter Otai (q.v.) and John Luwuliza-Kirunda (q.v.). The people found themselves caught between the NRA and insurgent bands, and were mistreated by both sides. In February 1990 they were herded into camps while the NRA swept through the area looking for guerrillas, and the international aid agencies had to be called in to help feed and rehabilitate the people. In October 1990 the area became much quieter when many of the NRA soldiers who had served in Teso went off to join the invasion of Rwanda (q.v.) led by Fred Rwigyema (q.v.), a former army commander in Teso. Since then major efforts at rehabilitation have been under way.

-J-

JACKSON, SIR FREDERICK (1860–1929). Governor of Uganda, 1911–1917. Before becoming Governor, Jackson had been an employee of the Imperial British East Africa Company (IBEAC) (q.v.) and then served in the Protectorate administration. In 1889 he had led an IBEAC expedition to western Kenya (q.v.), then known as Kavirondo, where he had been contacted by Kabaka Mwanga (q.v.) asking for his help. In reply he urged Mwanga to accept Company protection. Mwanga's full acceptance of Jackson's terms arrived after Jackson had moved on northwards, and in the meantime the German, Karl Peters (q.v.), intercepted the letter written on Mwanga's behalf by Fr Lourdel (q.v.) and traveled to Buganda where he persuaded Mwanga to sign a form of treaty. Jackson in turn arrived in Buganda and offered to take Baganda (q.v.) envoys to the coast to find out whether Buganda was to be in the British or the German sphere. In 1897 Jackson was wounded in the Sudanese Mutiny (q.v.). In 1894, 1897 and 1901 Jackson acted as Commissioner (the title used for the most senior British official prior to 1905, after which he was called the Governor). In April 1901 Mugabe Kahaya (q.v.) of Ankole visited Kampala (q.v.) and asked for an Agreement such as Toro (q.v.) already had. Jackson thought this would be premature as Kahaya was not fully accepted as paramount (this difficulty was overcome before the year was out).

Prior to his appointment as Governor of Uganda, Jackson had served as Deputy Commissioner in Kenya, responsible for the former Eastern Province which had been transferred from Uganda to the East African Protectorate (*see* Boundaries) in order to bring the whole line of the newly-completed railway (q.v.) under one administration.

Jackson is better known for his writings than for his activities as Governor of Uganda. His *Notes on the Game Birds of Kenya and Uganda* published in 1926 and his *Early Days in East Africa* (1930) are both works of major importance.

JINJA. Uganda's second most important town, situated on the east bank of the Nile (q.v.) close to the Owen Falls dam (q.v.) and the road and rail bridges across the Nile. It is the administrative headquarters of the district named after it, and was formerly the administrative center of Busoga (*see* Basoga) which was divided in three in 1974. Jinja formerly had a large Asian (q.v.) population and is an industrial center with a brewery, textile works and a cigarette factory, all powered with electricity generated by the hydroelectric dam. In the colonial period the Jinja Barracks was the headquarters of the Uganda Army (q.v.). The Kyabazinga (paramount ruler) of the Basoga had his headquarters at Jinja until the kingdoms were abolished in 1967 by President Obote (q.v.). Like all Uganda's major towns it was a center of mission (q.v.) activity and for education (q.v.).

JOHNSTON, SIR HARRY HAMILTON (1858–1927). Special Commissioner of Uganda, 1899–1902 (prior to 1907 the highest ranking colonial administrator was entitled Commissioner, not Governor). A gifted naturalist, artist and linguist who had already had wide experience in Africa before arriving in Uganda. The years immediately preceding his arrival had seen the Sudanese Mutiny (q.v.), the rebellion by Kabaka Mwanga (q.v.) and some of the Baganda (q.v.) chiefs against British rule, and the closing stages of the war against Mukama Kabarega (q.v.) of Bunyoro (q.v.). He and Mwanga were both captured and exiled to the Seychelles in 1899. Johnston was given a wide-ranging remit to look into the whole question of the future development of Uganda, its boundaries (q.v.), its economic development and the organization of its administration. He recommended the amalgamation of Uganda with the East African Protectorate, but this was not accepted. This was the first foreshadowing of what became the contentious issue of "closer union" (q.v.), resisted by Ugandan Africans. Johnston's first task on arrival was to negotiate the [B]Uganda Agreement (q.v.) and to set the Protectorate on a peaceful course, and the Agreement bears witness to his commitment to indirect rule. Both this and his decision to allocate freehold "mailo" (q.v.) land were momentous. Johnston also served in Kenya. His *Uganda Protectorate* (1902) is an important work.

JONAM. A small group of Lwoo (q.v.) speakers living at the northern tip of Lake Albert sandwiched between the Alur (q.v.) to the west and the Acholi (q.v.) to the east. Their name means "people of the lake." They occupy part of the administrative district of Nebbi. Many of them are engaged in fishing.

-K-

KABAKA YEKKA (KY) ("the Kabaka only"). A political party which emerged in Buganda in 1961 with the sole aim of preserving Buganda's privileges at independence. The Baganda (q.v.) had boycotted the Elections of 1961 (q.v.) because the Kabaka's government argued that elections should not take place until Buganda had been granted federal status in an independent Uganda. The government had gone ahead and held the elections in spite of Buganda, and as a result of the boycott the Democratic Party (DP) (q.v.) won. This was not the outcome the Baganda wished for: the DP was mainly a Catholic (q.v.) Party and the Kabaka and most of the ruling oligarchy were Protestants (q.v.). The DP opposed Buganda's claims to federal status and resisted demands for indirect elections to the National Assembly (q.v.).

In June 1961 a trial meeting of a royalist party was held and drew huge crowds. The new party soon won wide support by tapping into Baganda royalist loyalties. To vote for KY was "to vote for the Kabaka" and a vote against KY was alleged to be a vote against the Kabaka and therefore disloyalty. Few Baganda were willing to run the risk of being charged with such disloyalty. Among KY's founder members were Prince Badru Kakungulu (q.v.), Abu Mayanja (q.v.), E.M.K. Mulira (q.v.), Apolo Kironde (q.v.), and Godfrey Binaisa (q.v.). Some of these were left-wing radicals, and their real reasons for joining such a party are not clear. A number of small Baganda loyalist movements merged into KY.

Milton Obote (q.v,), leader of the Uganda People's Congress (UPC) (q.v.), realized that he would be unlikely to win an election without Baganda support, and he reached an agreement with KY by which he would support their demands for indirect elections to the National Assembly in return for KY support. As a result of this alliance between

KY and the UPC, the latter won a clear victory in the 1962 elections (q.v.). Only four years later Obote was able to dispense with Baganda support; the Kabaka fled the country after the Battle of Mengo of 1966 (q.v.), and all the traditional kingdoms were dismantled with the support of several of the founder members of KY.

KABALE. A town in southwestern Uganda formerly the administrative center of Kigezi (q.v.) District which was divided into three districts in 1974. Kabale District is the southernmost of these. It lies at an altitude of c. 6,200 feet (c. 2,000 meters) above sea level, and is cool and often misty. Before the misrule of President Amin (q.v.) it was a center of tourism (q.v.). Since the outbreak of war in Rwanda (q.v.) it has suffered from the disruption of trade between the two countries. The missions (q.v.) did not reach Kabale until after World War I, though catechists, notably Johana Kitagana (q.v.), had pioneered the way before Europeans arrived. Kabale is now a diocesan headquarters for both the Roman Catholics (q.v.) and the Church of Uganda (q.v.).

KABAREGA, CHWA II (c. 1845–1923). Mukama of Bunyoro (q.v.), 1870–1899. A son of Mukama Kamurasi (*see* Babito) and remembered with admiration as the Ugandan ruler who put up the most strenuous resistance against the British. Kamurasi died in 1869, having expressed the wish that Kabarega should succeed him, but there were rivals, and Kabarega won power only in 1870 with the help of Mutesa I (q.v.) of Buganda (q.v.). He then had to deal with threats from Arab slave-traders, and from attempts by General Gordon, Samuel Baker (q.v.) and Emin Pasha (q.v.) to annex Bunyoro to Egypt. Kabarega acquired arms from the Arab traders and built up a standing army of between 3,000 and 5,000 *barusura* (q.v.) to consolidate his hold over his domains. Eventually he was able to reach a proper understanding with Emin, the only European with whom he came into contact who knew Arabic and could therefore communicate directly with him, and the only European to have a good opinion of him.

By 1890 Kabarega was at the height of his powers. His

suzerainty stretched from beyond the Semliki River to the Nile (q.v.), and key chieftaincies around Lake Kyoga held allegiance to him. To the south the kingdom of Toro (q.v.) had been reconquered, and Bunyoro's influence stretched still further south to Buhweju in the modern Ankole (q.v.). His arch-rival was Buganda (in spite of Mutesa's earlier intervention on his behalf), and this rivalry further poisoned his relations with the British, who accepted Buganda's and Baker's estimates of him.

From 1890 onwards the British in Buganda were edged by the Baganda towards aggression against Bunyoro. When Lugard (q.v.) marched through Kabarega's domains to enlist Emin's abandoned troops, he inevitably came into conflict with outposts of Bunyoro. When Lugard, prompted by the Baganda chiefs Apolo Kagwa (q.v.) and Zakariya Kizito Kisingiri (q.v.), installed Kasagama (q.v.) as Mukama of Toro, Kabarega was enraged by this hostile act. The Baganda frustrated Kabarega's attempts to meet Lugard and reach an understanding with him. Emin's troops, left by Lugard to guard Kasagama in Toro, took to looting in Bunyoro. When they were transferred nearer to Buganda, Kabarega moved to try to reassert his control in Toro. In 1893 the British officer, Macdonald, ordered a full-scale offensive against Kabarega who for the next seven years fought a skillful and often successful guerrilla campaign against the British and Baganda. Even after a Protectorate was declared over Bunyoro in 1896, Kabarega evaded capture and tied down a considerable force who were engaged in hunting him down. The British appointed Kitehimbwa as Mukama in his place in 1898, and quickly replaced this unsatisfactory puppet with the abler Andereya Duhaga (q.v.). For the majority of the Banyoro, Kabarega remained the rightful Mukama.

Kabarega and Kabaka Mwanga (q.v.) of Buganda, who rebelled against the British in 1897 and joined forces with Kabarega, were eventually captured in their hiding place in the swamps of south Lango (q.v.), and both were exiled to the Seychelles. Kabarega was wounded in the course of capture and tried to tear the bandages from his arm in order to bleed to death. Eventually the limb had to be amputated. Mwanga died in 1904, but Kabarega lived on until, in 1923, the British relented to the extent of allowing him to return to Uganda, where he died in Jinja (q.v.) just two months later. He was buried at Mparo, his favorite residence, with Christian rites, having been baptized in exile.

Kabarega's resistance to the British cost Bunyoro dear. The wars brought devastation, and Bunyoro was treated as a subject country until the 1930s. But in later years the Banyoro recovered their pride, and with independence Kabarega won recognition as a hero, and the stubborn valor of his attempts to keep his country free of alien rule were ⋅ increasingly admired.

KABOHA, LEO (c. 1860–1937). A leading Catholic chief in Bunyoro (q.v.) in the early twentieth century. He was born in Mwenge on the borderland between Toro (q.v.) and Bunyoro. His father died when he was very young and when the country was ravaged by smallpox and cattle-disease, so the family moved to Bunyoro. As a young man he stayed around the court and joined in some of Kabarega's (q.v.) campaigns, making himself a name for reliance and leadership. In 1905 Kaboha was promoted from a sub-chieftaincy to a saza (senior) chieftaincy. By this time he had been baptized as a Catholic (q.v.). Because of his involvement in the Nyangire (q.v.) rising he was deprived of his chieftaincy and sent back to Mwenge, now part of Toro. There he was quickly given a saza chieftaincy. Throughout Kabarega's lifetime he remained loyal to him and insisted that the members of his household refer to Kabarega as the Mukama of Bunyoro. His son, Marko Kaboha, became chief minister of Toro.

KAGERA SALIENT. A triangle of land immediately south of the Uganda border with Tanzania (q.v.) lying between 1° South and the Kagera River. The boundary (*see* Boundaries) had been fixed along the parallel rather than along the Kagera River by the Anglo-German Treaty (q.v.) of 1890. In late October 1978 President Amin (q.v.) moved troops across the border, devastated the Kagera Salient, and crossed the Kagera. It took the Tanzanians until 14 November to recross the Kagera and not until 21 January did they finally drive the Ugandan army back across the border. They then successfully prosecuted the War of Liberation (q.v.).

KAGWA, SIR APOLO (c. 1869–1926). Kagwa was a page at the court of Kabaka Mutesa I (q.v.) of Buganda. Before the arrival of Christian missions (q.v.) he had started to learn about Islam (q.v.) and was for a time in charge of the mosque at the court of Kabaka Mutesa I. Later he turned to Christianity and was baptized by the Church Missionary Society (q.v.) sometime before 1885. During the persecutions under Kabaka Mwanga (q.v.) he escaped with a severe beating. Kagwa was quickly restored to favor and made leader of one of the newly-formed companies of royal guards. In 1888 he held a senior chieftaincy for a short time under Kabaka Kiwewa, but when the Muslim faction seized power during the Wars of Religion (q.v.) he took refuge in Ankole (q.v.), becoming leader of the Christian forces there after the death of the Catholic, Honorat Nyonyintono (q.v.). In 1891 he was leader of the Baganda (q.v.) forces which fought their way back to power, and in 1892 became Katikiro (chief minister) of Buganda. In 1894 he led the Baganda forces which together with the British attacked Bunyoro.

By this time Kagwa was leader of the Protestant (q.v.) faction and influential on the Mengo (q.v.) Church Council, then a important body. Over the next few years he was instrumental in getting Protestant Baganda teachers sent to Koki, Toro, Bunyoro, and Ankole, being as much concerned to increase the influence of Buganda as to spread the Christian gospel.

When Kabaka Mwanga rebelled against the British in 1897, Kagwa and the leading Catholic chief, Stanislaus Mugwanya (q.v.), sided with the British, judging that their future lay in collaboration, not in rebellion, and when Mwanga was deposed by the British and succeeded by the infant Daudi Chwa (q.v.), Kagwa was appointed one of the three regents. He was a major signatory to the 1900 [B]Uganda Agreement (q.v.), and he received one of the largest allocations of mailo land (q.v.): 30 square miles.

Throughout his years as Katikiro, Kagwa worked for the

advancement of his people through education (q.v.) and through coming to terms, at least for the time being, with the British administration. But he was also fiercely proud of Buganda, and of his own rights and powers, and when Daudi Chwa came of age in 1914 he was reluctant to let go of the powers he had wielded as regent. In the postwar years the British found him increasingly difficult and reactionary. He was forced to resign in 1925, and died the following year.

Kagwa was a prolific writer, and his first book, *Bassekabaka be Buganda* (The Kings of Buganda) was published in Luganda in 1901, as a result of the work he did with John Roscoe (q.v.), the missionary anthropologist. This has been translated into English by M.S.M. Kiwanuka. In 1902 Kagwa visited Britain for the coronation of King Edward VII, and his visit is described by his secretary, Ham Mukasa (q.v.), in *Uganda's Katikiro in England.* During this visit he received his knighthood. Kagwa's own further writings, several of which have been reprinted many times, include *Engero za Baganda* (Folktales of the Baganda) (1902); *Ekitabo Kye Kika Kya Nsenene* (The Book of the Grasshopper Clan) (1904); *Ekitabo Kye Empisa Za Buganda* (The Book of the Traditions and Customs of the Baganda) (1905); *Amanya Agabami Abakakano Abomu Buganda* (Names of the Present Chiefs in Buganda) (1907); *Ekitabo Ky'Ebika byа Baganda* (The Book of the Clans of the Baganda) (1908); as well as some 50 boxes of personal papers held in the Makerere University Library Archives, a truly astonishing achievement.

KAHAYA, EDWARD SULEIMAN (?–1944). Mugabe of Ankole (q.v.), 1895–1944. He was helped to the succession by Igumira (q.v.) whose son he almost certainly was, though Igumira claimed that he was the son of Mugabe Ntare V (q.v.). The support of Mbaguta (q.v.), his chief minister and the foremost collaborator with the British in Ankole, was also important. The Ankole Agreement (q.v.) was signed in 1901. He was a very young man in 1895, and first Igumira and then Mbaguta wielded more power than he did. In 1899 he somewhat reluctantly agreed to catechists of the Church Missionary Society (q.v.) beginning work at the *rurembo* (royal kraal), and was baptized in 1902. He broke with tradition, and established a permanent headqarters at Mbarara (q.v.) instead of moving the *rurembo* as the royal herds were moved. The extent to which Kahaya was involved in the events leading to the murder of the British official, Galt (q.v.), in 1905 is unclear, but he shared the immense relief of his chiefs when two people only were charged and a communal fine was exacted. Aside from this his reign was largely uneventful. He survived Mbaguta by only two months, and it was Mbaguta rather than he who dominated Ankole.

KAKUNGULU, PRINCE BADRU WASSAJJA, AL-HAJJI (1907–1991). Son of Prince Nuhu Mbogo and an uncle of Kabaka Mutesa II (q.v.). In 1921 he succeeded his father as the senior Muslim (*see* Islam) member of the royal family of Buganda (*see* Baganda) and leader of the Ugandan Muslim community. He began his education in a Qur'an school, but the government became concerned that it did not offer an education of comparable standard to that being given to Christian chiefs and princes. Two Muslim schools offering Western-type education as well as Islamic teaching were opened in direct response to this problem, one at Kibuli and the other at Butambala. Kakungulu later attended King's College, Budo (*see* Education). His concern for the education of Muslims arose from his own experience, and he gave 80 acres of land at Kibuli for the building of schools, a teacher training college and a health center. He was President of the Uganda Muslim Educational Association which had been funded by the government since the 1940s. He opposed those Sheikhs who resisted any modification of Qur'an schools to introduce secular subjects.

Kakungulu's succession as secular leader of the Muslims caused a split: Abdalla Ssekimwanyi was bitter at not being appointed chief Mu'allim (religous teacher) and therefore led a faction against Kakungulu whom he had previously supported. He and the county chief of Butambala, Taibu Magatto, headed the Butambala faction which had the ear of Apolo Kagwa (q.v.); Kakungulu had the ear of Kabaka Daudi Chwa (q.v.). The two groups became differentiated on abstruse points of religious law concerning prayers on Friday. Kakungulu's group became known as the Zukhuli sect because they insisted on saying an extra noonday prayer (*al-Zuhur*) after the *Juma* (Friday) prayers. Attempts to resolve the quarrel only complicated matters further.

In 1965 the National Association for the Advancement of Muslims (NAAM) (q.v.) was formed with connections with the Uganda People's Congress (UPC) (q.v.) led by President Obote (q.v.). It was widely seen as an attempt to undermine the influence of Kakungulu and his Uganda Muslim Community which was dominated by Baganda. The NAAM was dominated by non-Baganda Muslims, mainly from the north, who were not only ethnically different, but also followed a different school of Islamic Law. Constant confrontation between the NAAM and Muslims loyal to Kakungulu eventually led to Kakungulu's detention in October 1970. He had become a focus of attention for many Baganda who wished to see the Buganda kingdom restored.

Kakungulu gave up any claim to be leader of all Ugandan Muslims when he was released by President Amin (q.v.). He supported, but did not become actively involved in the Uganda Muslim Supreme Council (q.v.) which was established in a further attempt to unite all Muslims. When Amin was overthrown, Kakungulu stepped forward again to help prevent the massacre of Muslims which he feared might follow.

KAKUNGULU, SEMEI LWAKIRENZI (1868–1928). Muganda (*see* Baganda) general and administrator, under the British, of Bukedi (q.v.) and then Busoga (q.v.). He was a gifted and ambitious individualist for whom there was no place in colonial Buganda. He came from Kooki on the southwest fringe of Buganda, and was appointed by Kabaka Mutesa I (q.v.) to be his elephant hunter in Buddu (q.v.). Kakungulu was therefore able to read only intermittently with the Protestant (q.v.) missionaries, and was not baptized until much later. He was saved from execution in 1886 (*see* Christian Martyrs) by a pagan chief whose life he had saved in battle. In the Wars of Religion (q.v.) he was among the Christians who took refuge in Ankole (q.v.). When the

Christians fought their way back to power, he distinguished himself in battle. Because of his success and popularity as a general, Kakungulu was appointed by Kabaka Mwanga (q.v.) to lead the campaign to retake the capital in preference to Apolo Kagwa (q.v.), but once the war was over, Kagwa was the natural peacetime leader. During the Muslim revolt of 1893 Kakungulu again emerged as a successful general, and was active from 1897 to 1899 in the campaign against Mwanga and Mukama Kabarega (q.v.) of Bunyoro (q.v.), though here his loyalty may have been somewhat strained by his friendship with Mwanga.

In peacetime Kakungulu found his ambitions thwarted. From 1889 to 1892 he held a minor chieftaincy in Bugerere and in 1898 he was briefly-appointed Chief Judge in Busoga, but such positions did not satisfy him. He first turned to the area around Lake Kyoga and tried to build up a power base for himself in those areas whose chiefs had been in alliance with Kabarega of Bunyoro. Then from 1899 he was encouraged by the British to "pacify" Teso, Bukedi and Bugisu on their behalf. He established his headquarters successively at Nabumali, Budaka and Mbale (q.v.), set up an administration based on the Buganda model, and claimed that he had been given the title of Kabaka wa Bukedi (king of Bukedi) by the British.

In 1906 Kakungulu was moved to Busoga and made President of the Busoga lukiiko (assembly of chiefs) by the British. The followers he brought with him included Muslims as well as Christians. In 1913 he had to be retired from this position because he became too autocratic. He retained land and cattle in North Bugerere where his headquarters were named Galiraya (Galilee), and he was appointed to a senior chieftaincy near Mbale, but he strongly resented this demotion. He was in close touch with Joswa Kate (q.v.) and in 1914 joined the Bamalaki (q.v.) and encouraged the spread of this teaching throughout the areas of eastern Uganda where he had influence. Not long afterwards he started up his own offshoot of the Bamalaki, the Bayudaya (Jews), believing that it was the Jews who had the true knowledge of God. He and his close followers began to wear what they believed to be Jewish robes and to practice circumcision.

The British administration found Kakungulu uncooperative, particularly over his refusal to have his cattle vaccinated
because of the Bamalaki objection to medicine, and over the
compulsory purchase of some of his land for Makerere
College (q.v.). In 1923 he was retired from his chieftaincy,
and he died five years later. The Bayudaya continued for a
while, but by the time Ugandan independence was achieved
they had virtually died out. As well as a number of unpublished Luganda lives of Kakungulu, there are pioneer studies
of him by H.B. Thomas and Sir John Gray in the *Uganda
Journal* and a political biography by Michael Twaddle, 1993.

KAKWA. Living in the extreme northwest of Uganda and
stretching across into Zaire (q.v.) and Sudan (q.v.), the
Kakwa speak a language previously known as Eastern
Nilotic, though the preferred term is now Sudanic (*see*
Languages). They claim to have reached their present lands
from the east through what is now the Southern Sudan, and
have intermingled with the Madi (q.v.), Bari and Lotuke
peoples. From 1864 to 1878 Kakwa territory became part of
Equatoria (q.v.) under the temporary rule of governors
appointed by Egypt. A number of Kakwa are Muslims (*see*
Islam) as a result of these contacts. Their chief traditional
religious functionaries are rainmakers who are accorded
great respect. The rainmakers were responsible for producing
Yakan Water (q.v.) which the people believed was able to
protect them from death and disease and when they transgressed colonial laws. Christian missions (q.v.), education
(q.v.) and Western medicine (q.v.) came late to the area. The
Kakwa practice both agriculture and cattle-keeping, and
those who live by the Nile (q.v.) fish.

In the sleeping sickness (q.v.) epidemic the Kakwa were
moved away from the Nile, and many were pushed over the
border into the Sudan. As a result they were unable to visit
their ancestral graves and an important shrine near Koboko
where many of the rainmakers lived, and they looked to the
Yakan Water Cult to protect them when they disobeyed
colonial regulations.

President Amin (q.v.) was sympathetic to the Anya Nya
(q.v.), which included Sudanese Kakwa in its forces, and

supplies were routed to them via Koboko. When President Obote (q.v.) attempted to clamp down on the supply of arms from Israel (q.v.) to the Anya Nya, Amin arranged for the supply to continue. Kakwa from Uganda and Sudan gave Amin support both during and after the 1971 coup (q.v.) which brought him to power. In 1974 a group of Christian Kakwa army officers led by Brigadier Charles Arube (q.v.) led a coup attempt against Amin, apparently in a move to wrest control from the non-Ugandans who had been recruited into the army, and especially the notorious Brigadier Marella (q.v.) from Sudan, and Isaac Maliyamungu (a Zairean) (q.v.), However, the coup attempt failed.

The Kakwa sprang into unfortunate prominence during the Presidency of Idi Amin (q.v.) because he was of part-Kakwa parentage. They suffered badly when Amin was overthrown and the Uganda National Liberation Army (q.v.) took revenge on the people of West Nile (q.v.) for Amin's brutalities. Many became refugees (q.v.) in Sudan, and others joined the Uganda National Rescue Front (q.v.). President Museveni (q.v.) won the cooperation of this group and its leader was coopted into the new government.

KALEMA, RHODA NSIBIRWA (1929–   ). A prominent public servant in the field of community development. After attending King's College, Budo (*see* Education), she took a Diploma in Social Science at Edinburgh University in 1956–1958. She then worked as a Community Development Officer from 1958–1966. She was also a member of the Uganda Council of Women (q.v.), and was Chairman of the Status of Women Sub-Committee, a member of the Management Committee of Save the Children Fund (Uganda), and of the Tourist Advisory Board (*see* Tourism). During the presidency of Idi Amin (q.v.) her husband, William Kalema, was murdered, and at one stage she too was held under arrest. In 1979–1980 Rhoda Kalema was a member of the National Consultative Council, the body which served as a national forum after the overthrow of President Amin and before the Elections of 1980 (q.v.), and was Minister of Culture and Community Development. When President Museveni (q.v,) came to power in 1986 she became a member of the National

Resistance Council (q.v.) and of its National Executive Committee (q.v.), and Deputy Minister of Public Service and Cabinet Affairs, a post from which she retired in 1992.

KAMPALA. Originally the name of the hill on which Captain Lugard (q.v.) built a fort and flew the flag of the Imperial British East Africa Company (q.v.). A fort was later erected on this hill which then gave its name to the British-controlled town which grew up alongside the capital of the Kabaka of Buganda.

Kampala is now the modern capital of Uganda with a population in excess of 500,000, about half the total urban population of the country. It is the hub of road and rail communications throughout the country. During the colonial period Entebbe (q.v.) was the capital, but Kampala was always a far larger city and the country's commercial center. Government departments had begun to be located in Kampala before independence and the Legislative Council (q.v.) met in Kampala. Much of the cost of its town hall was donated by Mahendrakumar Nanjibhai Mehta (q.v.). Among those who have been Mayors of Kampala are Sir Amir Nath Maini (q.v.), Barbara Saben who was important in the Women's movement (q.v.), Serwano Kulubya (q.v.) and Paulo Kavuma (q.v.).

Adjacent to Kampala lay the *kibuga,* the capital of the Kabaka of Buganda (*see* Baganda). This lacked the modern facilities of Kampala and after the kingdoms were abolished in 1967 by President Obote (q.v.) it became part of Kampala and was brought under the Kampala City Council. The numerous low hills over which Kampala spreads are dominated by the Roman Catholic (q.v.) cathedrals at Rubaga (q.v.) and Nsambya (q.v.), the Church of Uganda (q.v.) cathedral at Namirembe (q.v.), the Sunni mosque at Kibuli (*see* Islam), the fort built by Lugard (q.v.), the Kabaka's palace which became a barracks after the Battle of Mengo 1966 (q.v.), Mulago Hospital, Makerere University (q.v.), and some of the smarter residential areas. Special legislation was required to bring Makerere within the boundaries of what was then the municipality of Kampala in order that it might benefit from the municipality's services. There are densely-packed poor areas of non-permanent housing and shanties, often situated in the valleys. In the *kibuga* and on the edges of Kampala are semi-urban areas where small houses are surrounded by an acre or half an acre of land on which the owners grow food crops. A study by A. W. Southall and P.C.W. Gutkind, *Townsmen in the Making: Kampala and its Suburbs* (1957), is now out of date but of historical interest.

KAMUGUNGUNU, LAZARO (c. 1886–1976). Chief Minister of Ankole (*see* Banyankole) and a greatly respected repository of Ankole tradition and history. Probably born in the late 1880s, he was baptized in 1903 as one of the first Protestant (q.v.) converts, and attended Mengo High School (*see* Education). He returned to Ankole in 1908 to be clerk to the Enganzi (chief minister) Nuwa Mbaguta (q.v.) who became his father-in-law, and he then progressed to various minor posts. Kamugungunu first became a county chief in 1918, and in 1926 was appointed Kihimba (head of the Ankole civil service). From 1938 until his retirement in 1947 he was Enganzi. On his retirement he went back to cattle-keeping and purchased land on the Ankole Ranching Scheme where he owned one of the finest herds of Ankole cattle. He was the author, with A. G. Katate, of *Abagabe b'Ankole* (the Kings of Ankole) (1955)

KANDOOYA. Sometimes referred to as "three-piece tying." A method of torture used by some members of the National Resistance Army (q.v.) in 1986–1987, primarily in the fighting in Acholi (q.v.), on people they captured and suspected of being insurgents. The person's arms were fastened together behind the back by being tied at the wrists and elbows. This imposed great strains on the chest, and could damage the nerves in the arm, sometimes so severely that amputation was required. Its use was brought to international attention by Amnesty International (q.v.). In 1987 *kandooya* was forbidden, but it was some time before the order to desist was obeyed, and the practice was never entirely eradicated.

KANYEIHAMBA, GEORGE (1940–   ). A highly qualified barrister and academic lawyer, he was educated at Kigezi High School (*see* Education), Makerere University (q.v.) and in Britain. Kanyeihamba was called to the Bar in London in 1966. He was an advocate of the Uganda High Court and a Senior Lecturer at Makerere University. During the presidency of Idi Amin (q.v.) he lived in exile in Britain, where he set up and acted as Chairman of the Uganda Human Rights UK movement. On returning to Uganda after Amin's overthrow he was appointed Minister of Justice and Attorney General, but he found himself unable to work for President Obote (q.v.) during his second presidency and he returned to his lecturing job in Cardiff. In 1986 Kanyeihamba again returned to Uganda and served as Minister of Commerce from 1986–1988 when he was appointed to the position of Minister of Justice and Attorney-General. He has written *Urban Planning in East Africa* (1973) and *Constitutional Law and Government in Uganda* (1975).

KARAMOJA *see* KARAMOJONG

KARAMOJONG. A pastoral nomadic people living in northeastern Uganda, in the southern half of what was, until 1974, known as Karamoja. Their oral traditions tell of their forced migration into their present homeland from further north. They speak an eastern Nilotic language (*see* Languages) related to that of other groups living in the former Karamoja District, to Ateso (*see* Iteso), and to neighboring peoples in Kenya (q.v.). The area in which they live is dry and arid and lies at a slightly lower altitude than most of Uganda though it rises to Mounts Moroto and Debasien in the east. Karamojong social organization is based on clans and age-sets and daily life is centered on their cattle. In the dry season the men take the cattle to seasonal cattle-camps. A herd is usually owned by a group of brothers. Meat, milk and blood from the cattle are important in the people's diet, but the women also cultivate and engage in food-gathering. They have resisted change, few of them have settled, and this is the least developed region of Uganda. The missions (q.v.)

arrived only in the 1930s when the Verona Fathers (q.v.) and the Bible Churchmen's Missionary Society (q.v.) began work.

Karamojong traditions claim that in the beginning God gave all the cattle to them. Cattle belonging to others are therefore alleged to have been stolen from the Karamojong, and this has provided them with an excuse for raiding their neighbors and stealing their cattle. They have frequently raided across the border into Kenya, and raids on the Iteso have also been a regular feature. Under colonial rule and throughout the first presidency of Milton Obote (q.v.) these raids were held within bounds and were to some extent ritualized. When the armies of President Amin (q.v.) fled in 1979, fleeing soldiers sold sophisticated weapons to the Karamojong, and they seized large amounts of ammunition. The Iteso had been allowed to raise a militia to protect themselves against raids, but this was disbanded by the National Resistance Movement (NRM) (q.v.) in 1986. The Karamojong promptly raided not only the Iteso, but a swathe of northern Uganda as far west as Nebbi, some of the raiding being led by ex-army officers. In this unprecedented raiding the Iteso lost almost all their cattle and many lives, and became disaffected from the NRM government which was unable or unwilling to help them. As a result insurgency gained a foothold in Teso. At the same time the Karamojong were suffering from a severe famine and one reason for raiding was the poor state of their own cattle.

KASAGAMA, DAUDI (c. 1865–1928). Mukama of Toro, 1891–1928. The kingdom of Toro (q.v.), founded by secession from Bunyoro (q.v.) about 1830, was reconquered by Mukama Kabarega (q.v.) about 1870 when the Mukama Nyaika was defeated, and his sons were killed or fled. One, Kasagama, was taken by his mother first to Ankole (q.v.), and then to Buganda (q.v.), where they found shelter with Byakweyamba (q.v.), a member of the royal clan. He had been captured in war, served as a page at the court of Kabaka Mutesa (q.v.) of Buganda, and been rewarded with a chieftaincy in Buddu (q.v.). He had been converted to Christianity and baptized as a Protestant (q.v.) in 1886. Kasagama also began to receive Christian instruction while living in his household.

In 1890 the newly-arrived representative of the Imperial British East Africa Company (q.v.), Frederick Lugard (q.v.), traveled to Western Uganda to collect the Sudanese troops (*see* King's African Rifles) left there by Emin Pasha (q.v.). On the way two Baganda chiefs, Apolo Kagwa (q.v.) and Zakariya Kizito Kisingiri (q.v.), introduced Byakweyamba and Kasagama to Lugard as claimants to the throne of Toro. It would be advantageous to Buganda to have a pliant ruler in Toro rather than have the area under the rule of their archrival, Kabarega of Bunyoro. This also suited Lugard's plans, and he therefore took them with him and proclaimed Kasagama as Mukama. A treaty was drawn up and signed placing Toro and all its dependencies (in fact a rather small area) under the IBEAC, and granting Kasagama the Company's protection.

The early years of Kasagama's reign were troubled. The Sudanese troops sent to guard Toro from Bunyoro preyed on Toro as well as on Bunyoro; Kasagama was accused of illicit arms dealing; and British officials in Toro found him uncooperative. Fortunately for him he was supported by Bishop Tucker (q.v.) who found him a promising convert and pleaded his cause. He was baptized in Namirembe (q.v.) Cathedral in the presence of the Commissioner, Mr Ernest Berkeley, in 1896. Mission sponsorship coupled with a softer government line gave Kasagama a chance to consolidate his position and enlarge the area over which his rule ran.

A British Protectorate was declared over Toro in 1896, and in 1900 Commissioner Harry Johnston (q.v.) arrived and peremptorily imposed the Toro Agreement (q.v.). A hierarchy of chiefs on the Buganda model was imposed, and Toro's boundaries settled. Taxation and a land settlement were included in the agreement. Amendments had to be made to accommodate structural arrangements already in place which Johnston had not understood, but on the whole the Agreement pleased Kasagama since it extended and defined the boundaries of Toro and confirmed him as Mukama, in spite of certain restrictions on his powers and problems about the Rukurato (Council of Chiefs which evolved into a local parliament) which had to be worked out later. He remained anxious about his position vis-à-vis his neighbors, and defended Toro's position vigorously whenever he met their rulers.

In 1908 an *empango* ceremony was held for the first time. This was a traditional ceremony held to mark the anniversary of a Mukama's coronation. In fact when Kasagama had been proclaimed the situation was too uncertain for the traditional ceremonies to be carried out. The *empango* therefore marked a milestone in the consolidation of Kasagama's power, and was innovatory in that it contained both Christian and traditional elements.

From 1912 onwards Kasagama had a number of clashes with the administration when he tried to protect chiefs whom the administration found incompetent or corrupt. However, during World War I he won credit in the eyes of the Protectorate government by actively recruiting men for the forces, and he was rewarded with an MBE.

But the administration continued to find Kasagama's rule unsatisfactory: there was trouble over land allocations and rights to levy taxes which technically Kasagama had no right to make, and he appeared unconcerned about the mass of the peasant population who were driven to petition against him in 1926. The administration recognized that the Agreements were unsatisfactory with regard to land tenure and the rights to salt revenues and changes were made, but Kasagama died on the last day of 1928 before new measures had had much effect. He was not greatly mourned by either his chiefs or his people, yet he had succeeded in establishing himself as ruler of an independent Toro, and ensured that his successor would be his son, George Rukiidi (q.v.).

KATE, JOSWA DAMULIRA (1850–1942). He held the position of Mugema (county chief of Busiro in Buganda [q.v.]), was head of the Nkima (Grey Monkey) clan, and founder of the Bamalaki (q.v.). He was attracted to Islam (q.v.), but then became a follower of Alexander Mackay (q.v.) of the Church Missionary Society (q.v.). He was baptized at the time of the martyrdoms (*see* Christian Martyrs), and became an ardent evangelist and was licensed as a lay-reader by Bishop Tucker (q.v.). He is remembered as an excellent chief and a generous man who was concerned for the welfare of his people.

One of Kate's numerous curious but strongly-held beliefs was that the use of medicine of any kind was wrong. This led to clashes with the Protectorate administration and to the establishment of the Society of the One Almighty God whose members were called Bamalaki (q.v.) after Malaki Musajjakawa who became the sect's chief activist. In 1929 Bamalaki refused to carry out anti-plague measures ordered by the government. A European official was wounded, and Kate and Musajjakawa were both exiled. Kate was allowed home from Arua (q.v.) in 1942 to die.

KATEGAYA, ERIYA (1945–   ). A graduate in law, Kategaya was a part-time lecturer at the Institute of Public Administration in 1970–1971, and was appointed a State Attorney, Civil Section, in the Attorney General's Chambers in 1971, but the following year went into private practice. During the presidency of Amin (q.v.) he left Uganda, as did many lawyers, and took refuge in Zambia where from 1975–1979 he was a State Attorney in the Zambian Attorney General's Chambers. He returned to Uganda when Amin was overthrown and was first District Commissioner of Bushenyi for a few months and then a member of the National Consultative Council (q.v.) in the period before President Obote (q.v.) came to power for the second time. In 1980 Kategaya joined Yoweri Museveni (q.v.) as a founder member of the National Resistance Movement (q.v.) and a member of its High Command until it seized power in January 1986. He was then appointed Minister of State in the President's Office, and one of three Deputy Prime Ministers, the others being Paul Ssemogerere (q.v.) and Abubaker Mayanja (q.v.).

KAVUMA, PAULO, (1900–1989). Katikiro (chief minister) of Buganda (q.v.), 1950–1955, regent during the Deportation Crisis (q.v.) and member of the Hancock Committee (q.v.). The son of a minor chief, his parents were Protestant (q.v.) Christians who sent him to work for a missionary in order to earn his fees at Mengo High School and in 1917 he won a scholarship to King's College, Budo (*see* Education). He entered the Buganda administration as a clerk in 1920. Here his abilities were noticed, and in 1930 Kavuma was appointed African Assistant to the Provincial Commissioner. In 1938 he was one of the founder members of a proto-political party, the Sons of Kintu, a populist association of capitalist farmers, traders, chiefs and clan heads. In 1943 he was appointed saza (county) chief of Buruli, moving two years later to the more important chieftaincy of Kyagwe. In 1950 he was appointed Katikiro of Buganda with the approval of the Protectorate government. In this office Kavuma was scrupulously fair over appointments.

Although deeply loyal to Buganda, he saw it as his duty to act as regent during the deportation of the Kabaka, at considerable personal risk from angry Baganda who could not accept his action. In this position he had to cooperate with the Governor, Sir Andrew Cohen, while at the same time working for the Kabaka's return. Kavuma served on the Hancock Committee which reported on the constitutional situation created by the deportation, retiring from government service after the Kabaka's return. From 1963–1965 he served as Mayor of Kampala (q.v.), and from 1964 until his death he was President of the Uganda Red Cross. His *Crisis in Buganda, 1953–55* (1979) is redolent of his loyalty and integrity, and is a valuable historical document. Although he more than once had to visit London for medical treatment in the 1970s, he played an active part in Buganda public life up to shortly before his death.

KENYA. During the colonial period Ugandans were very wary of plans for "closer union" (q.v.) between the three East African territories because of the extent to which Kenya was dominated by European settlers. Close ties grew up between the African peoples of Kenya and Uganda, however. They worked together in the East Africa Common Services (q.v.) run jointly for the three countries, and many Kenyans were educated in Uganda, as Makerere College (q.v.) was the sole institution of higher education for all three for many years.

After independence Kenya and Uganda drifted apart in spite of the creation of the East African Community (q.v.). Border controls and separate currencies were introduced.

Kenya pursued a capitalist path and was nervous of Uganda's increasing socialism, especially towards the end of the first presidency of Milton Obote (q.v.). Nairobi, the Kenyan capital, was already something of a regional capital even before independence: the headquarters of the East Africa Common Services were situated there, and after independence foreign investors often preferred to invest in Kenya than in either of the other two East African territories because both had socialist governments. However, longstanding personal ties between educated Kenyans and Ugandans in government, the professions and the Common Services remained strong, and many Kenyan students preferred to study at Makerere University College rather than in Nairobi.

During the presidency of Idi Amin (q.v.) relations between the two countries became increasingly strained. Amin's claims to a "Greater Uganda" (q.v.), attacks on Kenyan lorry drivers, the "disappearance" of Kenyan student Esther Chesire (q.v.), and from 1977 onwards an increasing number of refugees (q.v.) crossing the border, soured relations. The collapse of the Ugandan currency resulting from Amin's "economic war" (q.v.) led to the dissolution of the East African Community and of the Common Services. Assets had to be disentangled, and each country had to set up its own transport system. Uganda was furious that Kenya allowed the Israeli planes which carried out the Entebbe Raid (q.v.) to refuel in Kenya.

During his second presidency Obote dropped his previous socialist stance. He urgently needed aid from the West, and he was careful to maintain amicable relations with Western-oriented Kenya. Uganda's main export route lay through Kenya, and when Amin had fallen foul of Kenya, this had been put at risk.

In late 1985 Kenya hosted peace talks between the different Ugandan factions: the junta led by Basilio Okello (q.v.) and Tito Okello (q.v.), the National Resistance Movement (q.v.) and some smaller organizations. President Daniel arap Moi of Kenya chaired these talks and invested a great deal of his prestige in bringing them to a successful conclusion. He was angered when, having signed the Nairobi Accords (q.v.), Yoweri Museveni (q.v.) and his army ignored the agreement and successfully fought their way to power six weeks later, and he resented what he perceived as Museveni's lack of respect towards himself, now the senior East African President.

Museveni had previously shown leanings towards socialism and Marxism, and his strictly pragmatic goal of a mixed economy and encouragement of foreign investment by the West was distrusted by Kenya. This was followed by a trade war which escalated into a serious crisis. Museveni decided to shift the transport of coffee to rail in order to save costs. This infuriated Kenyan trucking firms and the Kenya government retaliated: telephone services and imports were disrupted, and on several occasions the border was closed. In 1987 Uganda retaliated by cutting off electricity supplied to Kenya from the Owen Falls (q.v.) hydroelectric scheme. Kenya then accused the Ugandan army of violating its border, and for several days there were armed clashes before this dangerous situation was calmed in face-to-face talks between the two Presidents. A further outbreak of hostilities occurred two years later when Kenya again accused Ugandan troops of violating the border and attacking Kenyan villages. The Kenyan government was extremely nervous of a shadowy dissident movement called Mwakenya, and it blamed Uganda for encouraging this. Uganda claimed that the alleged border violation was nothing but an instance of the longstanding cattle-raiding carried out by both Kenyan and Ugandan groups such as the Karamojong (q.v.), and went on to accuse the Kenyans of helping to arm Ugandan dissidents in the north and east. Once more it required a high-level meeting between the two Presidents to sort this out and restore relations to normal.

KEVIN, MOTHER (1875–1957). Pioneer Catholic (q.v.) woman missionary in eastern Uganda. Founder of the Franciscan Missionary Sisters of Africa (q.v.) and of the Little Sisters of St Francis. Born in Ireland, she was professed as a Franciscan nun in 1898 at St Mary's Abbey, Mill Hill, which was closely associated with the Mill Hill Fathers (q.v.). Mother Kevin arrived in Uganda in 1903 with the first party of Franciscan

Sisters having traveled on the first through train to Kisumu after the building of the railway (q.v.). In 1906 she and two other sisters founded a second convent at Nagalama 30 miles from the mission headquarters at Nsambya (q.v.) on the outskirts of Kampala (q.v.). In 1908 she returned to Nsambya as Superior, and remained in charge of her order for many years, being the moving spirit behind the expansion of their work. In 1921, with the help of Dr Evelyn Connolly, she was able to open the first Catholic training school for Ugandan midwives (nuns were not permitted to practice midwifery until 1936). Dr Connolly eventually became a Franciscan Sister. Two years later the African congregation of the Little Sisters of St Francis was founded at the request of a number of young Ugandan women. The Bannabikira (q.v.) had been at work in the area for some years and had provided part of the inspiration. The new congregation moved to Nkokonjeru in 1927. All the sisters were given three years of secondary education, and Mother Kevin planned a teacher training course to succeed this.

Mother Kevin constantly felt frustrated at the fewness of the sisters her order was able to send her to work in Uganda, and in 1929 she launched noviciates specifically to provide sisters to meet the need of the missions. From then on she was able to open convents throughout eastern Uganda which she visited and encouraged regularly. In 1952 these sisters became the Franciscan Missionary Sisters for Africa. In 1931 the leprosarium at Nyenga was opened by her sisters to be followed by that at Buluba where Dr Wanda Blenska became the leading authority on leprosy in Uganda. Mother Kevin's determination to provide a good education for Ugandan girls was crowned by the establishment of Mount St Mary's School, Namagunga, in 1940 (*see* Education). During World War II her sisters extended their work to Kenya (q.v.). She resigned after a brief period as Superior General of the Franciscan Missionary Sisters for Africa in 1955, and traveled in Europe and America to promote the work of the order. She died in America in 1957 and her body was eventually brought back to Nkokonjeru for burial. There is a biography of her (*Love Is the Answer*) by Sr Mary Louis (1964).

KIBUBURA, JULIYA (c. 1866–1951). The only woman in Uganda to be a gombolola (sub-county) chief during the colonial period. In 1903 Kibubura inherited from her sister the chieftaincy of Ibanda in the saza (county) of Mitooma in northern Ankole (q.v.). Her sister was a descendant of one known only as Murogo, diviner, who guarded the northern marches of the pre-colonial kingdom of Nkore. Her function was to give warning of the approach of any enemies, and to provide supernatural protection for the Mugabe on raids he might conduct. It is said that she and her descendants controlled an intelligence network acting in the Mugabe's interests. The incumbent at the time when the missions (q.v.) and the colonial administration reached Ankole was Ki-shokye. Realizing that if the Mugabe Kahaya (q.v.) was receiving Christian instruction it would mean the end of her traditional role, she decided it would be politic to follow his example and in late 1901 she sent to Mbarara (q.v.) saying she was willing to receive Christian teachers. However, she died in 1903 before she had been baptized.

She was succeeded by Kibubura who was recognized by the colonial administration as gombolola chief of Ibanda with the title of Mutuba Muto. She was baptized by the Church Missionary Society (q.v.) the following year taking the name of Juliya. She became a devoted Christian and made the church at Ibanda her special care throughout her life, and she carried out her chiefly duties in an exemplary fashion. When the British official, Galt (q.v.), was murdered at Ibanda the following year she is said to have tried to find the offender, and she was quickly cleared of any suspicion, though her saza chief, Gabrieli Rwakaikara, came under suspicion and was replaced by the hated Muganda, Abdul Aziz Bulwadde. In 1921 Kibubura was rewarded for her work as a chief by the gift for life of a square mile of land. She retired in 1926 and received a government pension. She continued to live at Ibanda, took an interest in all who stayed in the government rest house, and concerned herself with the church, presenting it with a pulpit. In 1949 she was present in Mbarara at the celebrations marking the Jubilee of the first founding of the church in Ankole. When she died the

Mugabe and the Mukama of Toro (q.v.) sent representatives to her funeral.

KIBUKA, KATOLINI ESITA NDAGIRE, "KATIE" (1922–1985). Leading member of women's movements (q.v.) and founder, headmistress and chairperson of the Nangabo Self-help Centre, near Kampala (q.v.). She was a devout church-woman, renowned for her cheerfulness and generosity, and her Christian faith provided the inspiration for her work. Her father was headmaster of Kasaka Central School, Gomba, and then a schools inspector, and Katie was educated at Kira, Uganda's first nursery school, and then at Gayaza High School (*see* Education). She stayed on to teach Home Economics at Gayaza before marrying Kupulyiano Kibuka, then teaching at Bishop Tucker Theological College, Mukono.

Katie was also a founding member of the Uganda YWCA (q.v.) and one of the first two Ugandan women to go to the USA in 1952 for a one-year training program in connection with the YWCA. She was a prominent member of the Mothers' Union and the Uganda Council of Women (q.v.). With small children of her own she founded a nursery school at Makerere (q.v.), taught at Mengo Girls' School and helped at the Mwana Mugimu ("healthy child") Clinic at Mulago Hospital. This treated seriously malnourished children and taught good nutritional practices to the parents. She contributed to research projects on children's education at the East African Institute of Social Research of Makerere College (q.v.).

In 1969, when her husband retired from government service, they moved to Nangabo ten miles north of Kampala. The Nangabo Centre was started a year later as a project to help girls whose education ended when they left primary school, to provide a play-center for the small children of Nangabo, and to provide a community center for the adults. It also developed courses for "0" level school leavers, and offers them training in handicrafts, dressmaking, childcare and nutrition, agriculture and other skills, and has expanded to include a nursery school, and a boys' project which provides a pottery course and training in basic mechanical and electrical engineering. Outdoor games and a library are made available to the wider community. A farm and gardens contribute towards the Centre's costs, and fees are also supplemented by donations. The Centre was a beacon of light throughout the troubles of the 1970s and early 1980s. Sadly Katie did not live to see a measure of peace restored to Uganda, but the Centre she started continues to thrive.

KIGEZI. This southernmost area of Uganda is mainly occupied by the Bakiga (q.v.). The former Kigezi District was divided in two in 1974, Kabale District to the south and Rukungiri District to the north. The town of Kabale (q.v.) is the main town in the area. The area is high and mountainous and still densely forested in large parts. In the north of Rukungiri District the land falls away sharply to the grasslands around Lake Edward. In the south, where Kisoro borders on Rwanda (q.v.) and Zaire (q.v.), the northern slopes of the Bufumbiro volcanoes, Mounts Muhavura, Mgahinga and Sabinio, lie within Uganda and reach heights of 13,547, 11,960 and 11,400 feet (4,129, 3,645 and 3,474 meters). In the diminishing forests which clothe their slopes a gorilla sanctuary is situated, threatened by a growing population needing to clear land for crops, as well as by war in Rwanda in the late 1980s and early 1990s.

KING'S AFRICAN RIFLES (KAR). The name given to the combined forces of the British East African territories during the colonial period. Until 1914 it formed a regiment. Initially made up of small existing forces of Indians and Sudanese (q.v.) in 1902, Africans began to be recruited from 1903 onwards. The Indian troops were disbanded in 1913, and Acholi (q.v.) and other northern Ugandans became the main source of Ugandan recruits. Until 1914 Uganda provided one battalion. Then forces raised in Uganda to meet the needs of World War I were given regimental status and six battalions had been formed by the end of the war. They fought in Tanganyika (now Tanzania [q.v.]) in the long-running campaign against the German General Von Lettow-Vorbek who fought a brilliant series of rearguard guerrilla actions which kept British-led forces tied down until the end of the war, and inflicted heavy casualties on them. When the war was over the KAR was reduced in size. The 4th KAR (Uganda) and the 3rd KAR (Kenya) Battalions were brought together to form the Northern Brigade commanded from Nairobi and used mainly in Kenya (q.v.).

During World War II some 77,000 Africans were recruited into the KAR from Uganda. Large numbers fought in Burma, and they also fought in the Middle East and in the Abyssinian campaign. After the war they were quickly demobilized and assisted back into civilian life by various resettlement and training schemes, by tax relief and by grants. In the postwar years the Ugandan Battalion was used mainly in Kenya, and was deployed against the Mau Mau uprising of 1952–1956 when Corporal (later President) Idi Amin (q.v.) distinguished himself.

In 1957 the armed forces of the three East African territories were briefly brought under the central control of the Defence Council of the East Africa High Commission (q.v.), but within a year control passed back to the three separate administrations. The Uganda Rifles were used to put down the Bukedi Riots (q.v.) in 1960, the same year in which Africans first became eligible for commissions. Idi Amin was one of the first two to be commissioned. Among other Ugandans commissioned on the eve of independence were Tito Lutwa Okello (q.v.) and Pierino Okoya (q.v.). The delay in commissioning Ugandan officers, and a failure to recruit educated men into the officer corps, proved disastrous. The former was one cause of the Mutiny of 1964 (q.v.). (For further developments, *see* Uganda Army.)

KIRONDE, APOLO (1915–). A grandson of Apolo Kagwa (q.v.), a teacher, lawyer and politician. He was educated at King's College, Budo (*see* Education), and Makerere College (q.v.) and then went back to Budo on the staff. He and 18 other members of the staff of Budo resigned in 1941 after disturbances at the school when they disagreed with the way in which the trouble had been dealt with. He went to Britain to study law and was called to the Bar in 1950. In 1952 Kironde became a founder member of the Uganda National

Congress (UNC) (q.v.). At the time of the Deportation Crisis (q.v.) he was one of those chosen to form a delegation to Britain, and on his return he was invited to join the Hancock Committee (q.v.). He helped to bring an action to test the legality of the British government's withdrawal of recognition from the Kabaka. In 1955 he was one of five members of the UNC appointed as members of the Legislative Council (q.v.). He was appointed by the Governor as Assistant Minister for Social Services with a seat on the Executive Committee of the Legislative Council. Kironde was also one of those eminent Baganda (q.v.) chosen to form the Electoral College which appointed Buganda's representatives to the Legislative Council. In 1960 in the runup to independence he left the UNC and helped to found Kabaka Yekka ("the Kabaka only") (q.v.) together with Abu Mayanja (q.v.) and Y.K. Lule (q.v.). After independence he was appointed Ugandan Ambassador to the United Nations from 1962–1967. From 1970–1971 he was Minister for Foreign Affairs. When President Amin (q.v.) seized power he appointed Kironde Minister for Planning and Economic Development and in 1972 transferred him to be Minister for Tourism, a post he held until later that year. Subsequently he became an exile in Britain where he remains involved in exile politics as leader of the Conservative Party (q.v.) which wants the restoration of the 1962 Constitution (q.v.): in other words, the restoration of the kingdoms, and that of Buganda in particular, in a federal state.

KIRONDE, ERISA (c. 1920–1986). Politician and administrator. Educated at King's College, Budo (*see* Education), Makerere College (q.v.) and Cambridge, he spent some years teaching at his old school before being appointed a lecturer at Makerere in 1959. A few years later he was appointed to be the first Ugandan Chairman of the Uganda Electricity Board. He was one of the younger educated Baganda (q.v.) who, though loyal to Buganda, was first and foremost a Ugandan. He was for a time Acting General Secretary of the Uganda National Congress (q.v.), which, in 1960, formed the nucleus of the Uganda People's Congress (UPC) (q.v.). In 1961 Kironde was a coopted member of the Constitutional Committee which set the agenda for the next stage in the moves towards independence. After the 1966 Battle of Mengo (q.v.), when the UPC drew back from holding elections, and was considering scrapping the kingdom governments, he wrote a long article which appeared in *The People* newspaper calling for elections to be held, warning Buganda against unrealistic expectations, and calling for the Buganda government and the office of the Kabaka to be redefined, not scrapped. At the time of the expulsion (q.v.) of the Asians (q.v.) in 1972 by President Amin (q.v.) he was Chairman of the Uganda Red Cross and one of the few Ugandans to protest at the expulsions. As a result of the stand he took, Kironde went into exile and worked for UNICEF for a time, returning after the War of Liberation (q.v.). Among his interests was drama: he wrote several plays and was closely involved with the National Theatre.

KISEKKA, SAMSON BABI MULULU (1912–   ). Prime Minister and Vice-President in the government of President Museveni (q.v.), he is married to Mary Nanfuka. A medical doctor (*see* Medicine), in 1945 he was appointed African District Medical Officer in the Ministry of Health. From 1954–1966 Kisekka was an elected member of the Lukiiko, the parliament of Buganda, and Minister of Health and Minister of Works in the Buganda Kingdom Government. He has been associated with several private hospitals and is a member of the Seventh Day Adventist Church (q.v.) and President of its Welfare Assocation. He runs the Kisekka Foundation for the education of young Ugandans. From 1985–1986 he was External Coordinator of the National Resistance Movement (NRM) (q.v.) in succession to Yusufu Lule (q.v.). When the NRM came to power, he was appointed Prime Minister and in 1991 was appointed Vice-President. A collection of his speeches (ed. Syed A.H. Abidi) was published by the Kisekka Foundation in 1992 as *Challenge to Leadership.*

KISINGIRI, ZAKARIYA KIZITO (1854–1917). Kangao (county chief) of Bulemezi and regent during the minority of Kabaka Daudi Chwa (q.v.). As a young man he served as a Mutongole (official directly responsible to the Kabaka) under Mutesa I (q.v.). He was baptized by the Church Missionary Society (q.v.) in 1883, and in 1888 became one of the leaders of the Christian faction which took refuge in Ankole (q.v.) during the Wars of Religion (q.v.). Kisingiri was rewarded with a chieftaincy in Buddu (q.v.). In 1891 he introduced Daudi Kasagama (q.v.) and Yafeti Byakweyamba (q.v.) to Lugard (q.v.), and accompanied Lugard on his journey through western Uganda during which Kasagama was instated as Mukama of Toro (q.v.). In 1892 he was appointed to the saza (county) chieftaincy of Bulemezi. British officials gained a high opinion of his integrity, and in 1893 when Kabaka Mwanga (q.v.) rose in arms and was on the run and deposed, and the infant Daudi Chwa (q.v.) was appointed Kabaka in his place, Kisingiri was appointed one of the three regents, the others being Stanislaus Mugwanya (q.v.) and Apolo Kagwa (q.v.). In 1900 he was one of the signatories to the [B]Uganda Agreement (q.v.).

Kisingiri was a devout Christian, was ordained Deacon by Bishop Tucker (q.v.) in 1891, stood as godfather to Mukama Kasagama at his baptism, and was instrumental in persuading the ruler of Ankole to accept Christian missionaries. After his appointment as Kangao of Bulemezi he had little time to act as a clergyman, but remained an influential member of the church.

KISOSONKOLE, PUMLA ELLEN (1911–). Born in South Africa, she was educated at Fort Hare and the Institute of Education, London. She married Christopher M.S. Kisosonkole, county chief of Kyagwe in Buganda. In 1957 she was President of the Uganda Council of Women (q.v.) and from 1959–1962 she was President of the International Council of Women. Pumla Kisosonkole represented Uganda at a number of important international fora: she was a Uganda representative at the Seminar for African Women held in 1960; she was a member of the Economic Commission for Africa's Standing Committee on Social Welfare and Community Development in 1961–1962; she was a representative of Uganda at the United Nations General Assembly in the year 1963–1964; she was a member of the UNESCO Committee of Experts on the Eradication of World Illiteracy, and a Vice-President of this Committee in 1964. During the International Year for Human Rights she was President of the United Nations Association in Uganda, and a delegate to the Council on World Tensions in 1964–1965.

Pumla Kisosonkole was also an active churchwoman. She was a delegate to the Christian Education Conference in 1962, a member of the Executive Committee of the All Africa Conference of Churches from 1963–1964, and a member of the Ecumenical Programme for Emergency Action. In 1963 she attended a conference held at Makerere College (q.v.) by the All Africa Conference of Churches on "Christian Women in Africa: Share in Responsibility" and was one of the main speakers.

KITAGANA, YOHANA (c. 1858–1938). A Catholic (q.v.) catechist, born and converted in Buganda (*see* Baganda). He was baptized by the White Fathers (q.v.) in 1896 and in 1901 offered to go as a catechist to any remote place where the mission might send him. He was first sent, with others, to Hoima (q.v.) to start Catholic mission work among the Banyoro (q.v.). He set out with only a sleeping-mat, stick and drinking gourd after giving away all his possessions (originally a polygamist, he had already decided to become celibate). In 1902 he was sent to help start work among the Banyankole (q.v.). He worked first at Mbarara (q.v.), but in 1906 went to Sheema in the west where he won the confidence of the people by simple medical treatment and by caring for orphans and destitute persons. In 1924 he and one other catechist pioneered Catholic work in the south of Kigezi (q.v.) where he again won the confidence of the people by caring for the sick, by patient visiting and by his transparent charity. His work paved the way for the permanent mission work which started four years later. In 1930 old age forced him to retire from full-time work, but he continued to care for orphans and others in need. His devoted service and humble life made him honored by Catholics in somewhat the same way that Apolo Kivebulaya (q.v.) was honored by Protestants (q.v.). He was awarded the MBE in recognition of his work for the people of Kigezi by the Protectorate government.

KIVEBULAYA, REVD APOLO (1864–1933). Born in Ssingo in Buganda (q.v.), he was one of twins. He seems to have gone to the Kabaka's court because his brother was one of the bodyguards of Kabaka Mwanga (q.v.), and he was attracted by what his brother told him of the reading taught by the missionaries. He attended some of the reading classes held by Alexander Mackay (q.v.) of the Church Missionary Society (CMS) (q.v.), but found it hard to learn. During the Wars of Religion (q.v.) Apolo joined the Christian exiles in Ankole (q.v.), returning with them when they fought their way back to power, and beginning to attend classes at the mission more seriously. In 1891, however, he joined the force which Lugard (q.v.) took to western Uganda to bring in the soldiers left behind by Emin Pasha (q.v.), and in 1893 he joined the Baganda army led by the British officer, Colville, in a campaign against Mukama Kabarega (q.v.) of Bunyoro (q.v.), and then went with the forces which reinstated Mukama Kasagama (q.v.) in Toro (q.v.) after he had been driven out by Kabarega. In 1895 he was back at the capital and was baptized, and was sent back to Toro, this time as a Christian teacher.

Kivebulaya was not very successful in Toro, and the following year he crossed the Semliki River and went to Mboga which was then under British rule. In 1899 this area was taken over by the Belgians and missionary work became impossible. He returned to Toro and worked as a rural dean until 1915, travelling tirelessly round the churches in his care. In 1915 he was able to return to Mboga; the tiny Christian community he had founded was revitalized and spread, and in 1921 he moved into the Ituri Forest and began to teach the pygmies, work which made his name famous. He established that they did indeed have their own language (this had been doubted) by reducing it to writing, and translating some parts of the Bible into it.

In 1933 Kivebulaya became ill and went to Kampala (q.v.) for medical examination. Dr Cook (q.v.) diagnosed heart trouble, and told him to rest, but he knew he was dying and insisted on returning to Mboga to die among his people. He left his two cows, virtually his only possessions, to the church at Mboga. His exceptional sweetness of character, his almost Franciscan poverty and his joyousness were noted and admired by all who met him. He was married but had no children. There are three small hagiographical books by A.B. Lloyd on Kivebulaya and a modern biography by Anne Luck, *African Saint: The Story of Apolo Kivebulaya* (1963). His brief diaries are in Makerere University (q.v.) Library and the CMS Archives.

KIVENGERE, BISHOP FESTO (c. 1919–1988). An Anglican (q.v.) Bishop with an international reputation for his charismatic preaching, breadth of vision, and stand on human rights. A chief's son from Kigezi (q.v.) who became a teacher after only two years' secondary education, he was deeply influenced by the Revival (q.v.), and witnessed to its message even though this cost him his teaching job in Tanzania (q.v.) in 1949. He became associated with American evangelist Billy Graham in the 1950s. Kivengere completed a course at the London University Institute of Education in 1959, but felt called to the priesthood. Rejected for this in Uganda, he was ordained Deacon at the Reformed Seminary in Chicago and priest in Uganda in 1967 after further studies at Pittsburgh Seminary. In the years that followed, his reputation as a preacher grew and he launched African Evangelistic Enterprise in East Africa.

Kivengere was consecrated Bishop in late 1972, soon after President Amin (q.v.) had expelled the Asians (q.v.), and at a time of great tension. On several occasions he faced Amin, telling him, for instance, that because Uganda was a deeply Christian country, public executions were unacceptable. After a particularly outspoken sermon against violence in late 1976, and the murder of Archbishop Luwum (q.v.) in February 1977, he had to flee the country. During the second presidency of Obote (q.v.) Bishop Kivengere again spoke out in defense of human rights, most notably when the government ordered the expulsion (q.v.) of thousands of Banyarwanda (q.v.) refugees (q.v.) in 1982. He organized relief aid for them at a time when it was very risky to do so. Late in 1983 he went ahead in the face of opposition and ordained three women to the priesthood in his diocese, a move which was widely acclaimed among his own flock. Throughout the years of his episcopate he continued to travel internationally, drawing large and appreciative crowds in the USA, Australia, Britain and elsewhere. He died of leukemia in May 1988.

KIWANUKA, BENEDICTO (c. 1930–1972). First Prime Minister of Uganda, 1961; Chief Justice, 1971–1972. He was called to the Bar in Gray's Inn, London in 1956. He became President of the Democratic Party (q.v.) in 1958 and Chief Minister after the Elections of 1961 (q.v.) with the possibility of becoming Prime Minister after independence. He was a Muganda (*see* Baganda) but non-royal, and a Catholic (q.v.), whereas the Baganda ruling oligarchy was Protestant (q.v.). The possibility of his ranking above their Kabaka was anathema to Baganda and he inflamed the situation by a lack of tact and finesse. President Obote (q.v.) and the Uganda People's Congress (q.v.) came to power in the Elections of 1962 (q.v.) by making an alliance with the royalist Kabaka Yekka (q.v.) party. Kiwanuka lost his seat and Basil Batari-ngaya (q.v.) succeeded him as Democratic Party leader in the National Assembly (q.v.). Kiwanuka was detained by Obote under security legislation following the declaration of an emergency in Buganda in 1966. In 1971 he was released by President Amin (q.v.) in January and made Chief Justice in June. In September of the following year he was dragged in broad daylight from his chambers and murdered by Amin's henchmen, apparently because he had made several rulings against the government and earlier in September had granted a writ of habeas corpus on behalf of a British businessman, Donald Stewart, stating that the military "had no power of arrest of any kind at all."

KIWANUKA, ARCHBISHOP JOSEPH (1899–1966). Roman Catholic (q.v.) Bishop of Masaka (q.v.), 1939–1953, Archbishop of Rubaga (q.v.) from 1960–1966. His parents were Christians, and four of his relatives had been among the Christian martyrs (q.v.). His mother taught him to read and write, and in 1914 he entered the seminary, persevering through the long course until his ordination as priest in 1929. In 1932 be obtained a doctorate in canon law from Rome, and then joined the White Fathers (q.v.), returning to Uganda in 1933 to serve at Bikira and Bujuni in Buddu (q.v.).

In spite of warnings that the action might be premature, the Catholic Church went ahead with its plan to establish a diocese which would be fully under African control, and in 1939 Kiwanuka was consecrated Bishop and put in charge of the diocese of Masaka which was coterminous with Buddu. Here he made the training of African clergy and their ongoing care his top priority, sending many of his priests for further study overseas. He also encouraged the growth of the church press, the preparation of lay Christian leaders, the improvement of schools, the raising of the status of women, and community development, including the formation of cooperatives. During the 20 years of his episcopate the numbers of Catholic Christians and of priests in his diocese doubled. In 1953 he helped to preserve calm during the Deportation Crisis (q.v.) and was a member of the Hancock Commission (q.v.).

In 1960 Kiwanuka was appointed Archbishop of Rubaga (q.v.), his diocese covering western Buganda (*see* Baganda) aside from Buddu. He was at the center of a storm at the time of the Elections of 1962 (q.v.) because of a pastoral letter in which he criticized the Kabaka's involvement in politics, and the tactics of Kabaka Yekka (q.v.), the party dedicated to preserving Buganda's special privileges, which maintained that a vote for any other party was a vote against the Kabaka. Catholics who wished to vote for the Democratic Party (q.v.) were accused of not being proper Baganda, and some changed their allegiance as a result of constant taunting. Archbishop Kiwanuka had just left the country when this letter was read aloud in all the Catholic churches in Rubaga Diocese. In his absence the Kabaka arrested his assistant, Monsignor Joseph Sebayigga.

On the occasion of independence Archbishop Kiwanuka issued a statement together with the Anglican (q.v.) Archbishop, Leslie Brown, which helped to usher in a new spirit of ecumenism. In 1964, during his time as Archbishop of

Rubaga, the Catholics among the Christian martyrs were canonized amid great celebrations. Archbishop Kiwanuka attended the Second Vatican Council called by Pope John XXIII in Rome, and died shortly after his return to Uganda.

KONY, JOSEPH. An Acholi (q.v.) who claimed to be a brother or cousin of Alice Lakwena (q.v) and who continued to lead a "Holy Spirit" movement after her defeat. At first he was able to attract quite large numbers of followers and they constituted a serious threat in Acholi. By 1992 his movement was reduced to a very small group of perhaps 40 men. Part of this decline may have been due to their mistreatment of the civilian population and their war-weariness.

KULUBYA, SERWANO WOFUNIRA (1892–1969). Educated at King's College, Budo (*see* Education), and Makerere College (q.v.). In 1928 he was appointed Omuwanika (treasurer) of the Buganda Kingdom Government, one of a group of younger, better educated senior chiefs who came to the fore after the resignation of Apolo Kagwa (q.v.). Kulubya brought in much-needed financial reforms and tightened up the administration in a way which inevitably brought him into conflict with some who resented being made more accountable. In 1931 he led the delegates from Buganda (q.v.) who opposed Closer Union (q.v.) with Kenya (q.v.) and Tanzania (q.v.), and presented Buganda's case in a long and cogently-argued submission, becoming the first African to address the British Parliament. In the 1940s an ultra-conservative element in Buganda formed the Bataka Movement (q.v.) led by the clan heads who had lost out under colonial rule to the saza (county) chiefs. In the Riots of 1945 (q.v.) some Baganda clan heads and saza chiefs demanded Kulubya's resignation. He gave in to these demands when threats were made against the lives of others if he did not resign. He was defended at this time by E.M.K. Mulira (q.v.) who described him as one of the most able and progressive men in Buganda.

In 1950 he was appointed as one of Buganda's representatives in the Legislative Council (q.v.), and rose to become its Deputy Speaker, an office he retained when the Legco became the National Assembly (q.v.) at independence.

Kulubya was also active in local government and in 1959 he became the first Ugandan Mayor of Kampala (q.v.). In 1952 he was a member of the de Bunsen (q.v.) Commission which examined Uganda's educational needs.

In 1953 Buganda was concerned that a speech by the British Minister, Oliver Lyttleton, seemed to suggest that Closer Union was again being considered, and Buganda refused to be reassured by statements that it would not be pursued "for the time being." This led directly to the Deportation Crisis (q.v.). Kulubya was one of the two members of the Executive Committee of the Legislative Council who joined the Hancock Committee (q.v.) set up to look into the relation between Buganda and the Protectorate government. He stood by the Committee's recommendations when some other members of the Committee later went back on them.

In the year 1941–1942 Kulubya was the first African President of the Uganda Society (q.v.) and an Honorary Trustee from 1959 until his death. He was active in the church, in sports, in the Scouts, and with St John's Ambulance Brigade.

KYEMBA, HENRY (1939–   ). Born into a chiefly family in Busoga (q.v.), Kyemba was educated at Busoga College (*see* Education), and Makerere College (q.v.). From 1966–1971 he was Private Secretary to President Obote (q.v.). He was then appointed Principal Private Secretary to President Amin (q.v.), and later that year Permanent Secretary in the Ministry of Culture and Community Development. In November 1972 he was made Minister of Culture and Community Development, and early in 1974 was moved to become Minister of Health. In connection with this appointment, he was Chairman of the African Health Ministers, and was made a Vice-President of the World Health Organization at the meeting in Geneva which provided him with a means of escape from Uganda. Warned that he was "next on the list," he decided to flee soon after the murder of Archbishop Janani Luwum (q.v.) in February 1977, and took refuge in Britain. His *State of Blood: The Inside Story of Idi Amin* was published later that same year. This is the most detailed account by an insider of events during Amin's presidency.

-L-

LADO ENCLAVE. This was a large area of the Southern Sudan (q.v.) and what later became the West Nile (q.v.) District of Uganda. It was leased by Britain to King Leopold of the Belgians between 1894 and 1909 and administered by the Belgians during this period. In 1910 it reverted to British control but was administered as part of Sudan. The southern part became part of Uganda in 1914.

LAKE VICTORIA. The second largest fresh-water lake in the world, Lake Victoria covers an area of 26,828 sq. miles (69,485 sq. kilometers), but it is relatively shallow, its greatest depth being c. 280 feet (85 meters). The building of the hydroelectric Owen Falls dam (q.v.) at Jinja (q.v.) raised the lake level by some 10 to 12 feet. Most of the northern half of the lake and its islands are within the borders of Uganda. There is a thriving fishing industry around the lake shores, but the introduction of Nile perch, which can grow to an immense size, is said to be threatening the stocks of smaller fish.

Arab traders from the East African coast introduced clinker-built boats in the mid-nineteenth century: until then dugout canoes had been used, some with outriggers and of a great size. The Kabaka of Buganda possessed a fleet of war canoes. When the railway (q.v.) reached the lake at Kisumu in Kenya, steamers were introduced. Uganda's main lake port is Port Bell near Kampala (q.v.).

LAKWENA, ALICE. Alice Auma, later known as Alice Lakwena after the "holy spirit" which she believed possessed her, was a young Acholi (q.v.) woman who claimed that on 6 August 1986 she was ordered by this spirit to build up an army to fight against evil. She invented rituals which claimed to cleanse her followers from witchcraft and evil, and she promised her followers that if they obeyed her orders and anointed themselves with "medicine," bullets aimed against them would turn to water. She was known as *laor* (messenger) by her followers, sometimes by others as *nebbi* (prophet), and as *ajwaka* (pagan spirit medium) by those opposed to her teaching.

She was able to recruit a large following from among the Acholi people who were in a state of near-despair. The Acholi had suffered severely under President Amin (q.v.) who had massacred large numbers of Acholi soldiers. Acholi sections of the Uganda National Liberation Army (q.v.) had been used extensively in the campaign against Yoweri Museveni's (q.v.) National Resistance Army (NRA) (q.v.) in the Luwero Triangle (q.v.) where they had suffered a series of humiliating defeats, and had been blamed for the atrocities committed there. Many had joined Tito Okello (q.v.) and Basilio Okello (q.v.) after the army putsch against President Obote (q.v.) in 1985, and they had again been severely beaten. Some fled across the border into Sudan (q.v.) to regroup and return to fight the victorious NRA, with little success. Those who did not remain in the army found it difficult to settle back into civilian life, not least because of the insurgency in Acholi. The civilian population was harassed by both the insurgents and the army and their situation was desperate. Lakwena's "divine" message seemed to offer hope of cleansing the land of evil and getting rid of their enemies, and she was able to recruit many former soldiers. Reports that force was used to recruit people in Acholi are disputed. Later, when she and her followers reached Busoga (q.v.), they did use force.

In spite of some defeats, notably at Corner Kilak in January 1987, Alice Lakwena retained the loyalty and faith of the "Holy Spirit Movement," and the army was unable to win a decisive victory until Lakwena led her people out of Acholi and northern Uganda into Busoga where they were in unfamiliar territory and got no support from the population. In October 1987 they were utterly defeated, and a month later Lakwena, who had somehow evaded capture, fled to Kenya (q.v.), where she was imprisoned. Her father Severino Lukoya, and Joseph Kony (q.v.) who claimed kinship with her to legitimize his position, took up her mantle. Lukoya was captured and imprisoned, but Joseph Kony remained at large and by 1992 was still able to terrorize parts of Acholi and evade capture, though he and his followers, calling themselves the Uganda People's Democratic Christian Army, had disintegrated into little more than a band of brigands.

Alice Lakwena and her movement stand in a succession of such movements which have erupted in Africa in the nineteenth and twentieth centuries, usually arising out of situations of despair. The best known are the Xhosa cattle-killing movement of 1856–1857 led by the young woman Nongqawuse, and the Maji Maji Rising in Tanzania (q.v.) in the early years of the twentieth century. In a larger context one might compare the "Holy Spirit Movement" of Alice Lakwena with the millennial cults of the European Middle Ages which also promised salvation by divine intervention to people driven to despair.

LAMOGI REBELLION (1911–1912). Since the days of slave-raiders from Egypt, firearms had proliferated in Acholi (q.v.). In 1911 and 1912 efforts were made to register all firearms in that part of Acholi which was under British administration, and then to disarm the people. The Lamogi clan who lived in west Acholi refused, first to provide labor to build a rest house for traveling colonial officers, and then to register their firearms, fearing that registration would be the prelude to confiscation. When an official accompanied by the chief of the Patiko clan went to try and persuade them to comply, the Lamogi feared a plot between the British and the Patiko, and prepared to fight if need be. Their defiance began to spread to other clans but action against them was delayed while a large enough force was mustered. By early 1912 people from other clans had arrived to swell the numbers of the Lamogi, gathering in the caves in the Guruguru Hills. Here they took refuge when a force of 130 officers and men were brought against them. Some Lamogi escaped from the caves, but others were besieged there, suffering from lack of food and good water. At the end of February 1912 the besieged men gave in and were taken prisoner, the ringleaders were taken to Kampala (q.v.), several people were given two-year prison sentences, and a communal fine of 200 cattle was imposed.

The Lamogi were then moved to Gulu (q.v.). They were

harassed by rival clans on the way there and when they arrived, and for years after, they remained embittered as a result of their treatment. In 1916 they were allowed to settle at Keyo, about halfway between Gulu and their original home. In 1937 they were permitted to settle in Olwal, part of their ancient clan land, but they were not permitted to return to Guruguru itself.

LANCASTER HOUSE. One of two elegant London venues (*see* also Marlborough House) used for constitutional conferences in preparation for the independence of British colonies and protectorates in Africa. The Uganda Constitutional Conference (q.v.) of July 1961 met there.

LANGI. A people of northern Uganda whose language and social organization are very closely related to Acholi (q.v.) but who do not accept the designation Lwoo (q.v.). Unlike the Acholi, but like the Iteso (q.v.) and Karamojong (q.v.), they claim to have reached their present homeland from the northeast. According to some oral traditions, the Langi are related to the Karamojong, from whom they broke away some four or five hundred years ago. When they settled in their present lands they then adopted the Acholi language with dialectal modifications. It seems most likely that they are an amalgam of para-Nilotic and Lwoo peoples, and that secondary migration within Lango continued until nearly the end of the nineteenth century. The Kumam live on the borders of Lango and Teso with close connections with both their neighbors, though they speak a Lwoo language with Ateso elements.

The area in which the Langi live, formerly known as Lango District, was divided in two in 1974 and the two districts are now named Lira (q.v.) and Apac. It is a relatively flat, dry area north of Lake Kyoga whose landscape is varied by granite inselbergs and borassus palms. Settlement patterns were determined by soil fertility, and early settlements were along the swampy lakeshores of Lake Kwania. The main staple food crops are millets, though fast-maturing maize and cassava are also grown. Sheep, goats and cattle are raised, and game meat is also eaten, though this was far more important in the past when game was more plentiful than it is today. The chief cash crop is cotton, which suffered severe setbacks in the 1970s but began to recover in the late 1980s.

The Langi suffered from Arab slave- and ivory-raiding expeditions from the north in the nineteenth century. Between 1894 and 1899 several British-led expeditions passed through Lango in pursuit of the Sudanese Mutineers (q.v.) and Mukama Kabarega (q.v.) who made his headquarters in Lango after being driven out of Bunyoro (q.v.). A number of Langi groups supported Kabarega, and they suffered considerably from looting by Baganda (q.v.) troops employed in operations against Kabarega. However, the foreign presence in Lango appeared transitory at this juncture. In the early years of the century Daudi Odora (q.v.) rose to prominence and a county chieftaincy by means of a judicious association with British officials. The first colonial government post was opened at Bululu in 1908 and it was not for two more years that the administration was established in central Lango. Throughout the colonial period Lango remained underdeveloped, and was not served by a tarmac road until the early 1970s. The first President of Uganda, Milton Obote (q.v.), came from Lango as did some of his closest political associates. President Amin (q.v.) accused Obote of favoring his own area and of pouring money into its development unfairly to the detriment of other parts of Uganda, though there was little real evidence of this. However, these accusations served as a justification for the severe reprisals suffered by the Langi in which many of the Okokoro, Obote's clan, as well as others, were massacred.

LANGO *see* LANGI

LANGUAGES OF UGANDA. The "Bantu Line," north of which no Bantu languages are spoken, though some non-Bantu languages are spoken to the south of it, cuts through Uganda diagonally, roughly from the northern end of Lake Albert in the west, following the line of the Nile (q.v.) and Lake Kyoga, and then continuing in an easterly direction to the northern slopes of Mount Elgon (q.v.). Some two-thirds of Ugandans live south of this line and speak Bantu languages. These include Rukiga, Runyankole, Rutoro, Runyoro, Luganda, Lusoga, Lugisu, and the languages of other small Bantu-speaking groups in the extreme west and east of the country, as well as Kinyarwanda (*see* Rwanda) and Lingala (a language of Zaire [q.v.]), spoken by immigrant and refugee groups who are long-term residents of Uganda. North of the Bantu Line live speakers of Central Sudanic languages (Lugbara, Madi [qq.v.]), East Nilotic languages (Karamojong [q.v.], Jie, Dodoth, Tepeth, Itesiot, Kakwa), and West Nilotic languages (Acholi, Langi, Alur [qq.v.]). Between 20 and 40 different languages are spoken, the count depending on how a language is defined. Sometimes the correspondences between two or three members of each group are so close that the languages are quite easily mutually intelligible, but local pride insists that there are different languages.

Language surveys have shown that the most widely known languages are Luganda (*see* Baganda) and Swahili, the Bantu language which is the lingua franca of most of East Africa and the national language of Kenya (q.v.) and Tanzania (q.v.). It is less well-known in Uganda than elsewhere, and is not altogether acceptable to many Ugandans because of its associations with white settlers in Kenya and with the Uganda Army (q.v.) which has used Swahili as its common language. Besides Kinyarwanda and Lingala, "immigrant" languages include a form of Arabic ("KiNubi") spoken by the so-called Nubians (q.v.), and, until the expulsion of the Asians (q.v.) by President Amin (q.v.) in 1972, Gujurati, Urdu, Punjabi, Konkani and some other languages of the Indian subcontinent. Uganda's "language problem" has dogged successive governments, since neither Luganda nor Swahili is fully acceptable as a national language, and the national language, English, is known only to the educated, or to those who have picked it up in the workplace. Radio broadcasts are made in six key languages as well as English.

LAVIGERIE, CARDINAL CHARLES MARTIAL ALLE-MAND (1825–1892). Founder of the Société des Missionaires d'Afrique, the White Fathers (q.v.). From 1879 until his death he kept in close contact with the missionaries in Uganda, sending them long and careful instructions throughout this critical period of the mission's development. A selection of these may be found in his *Instructions aux Missionaires* (1950).

LEGISLATIVE COUNCIL (LEGCO). In 1920 an Executive and a Legislative Council were set up. The Executive Council consisted of Protectorate civil servants responsible for the main departments of administration and was chaired by the Governor (q.v.). The Legislative Council, Legco, had a wider membership and was intended to advise the Governor and the Executive Council. Representatives of the European and Asian (q.v.) communities were quickly appointed. Ugandan Africans did not sit on the Legco until after World War II. An Unofficial Members Organization was established in 1947, but not until 1956 were any of the Legco's members directly elected. At independence the Legco was dissolved and superseded by a National Assembly (q.v.) which could, for the first time, initiate legislation. Because the Legco was not fully democratic, and because no members at all were directly elected until 1956, it failed to be an adequate democratic training ground though its members claimed that it had trained them in tolerant and good-natured debate.

LIBERATION WAR (1979). In late October 1978 President Amin (q.v.) invaded the Kagera Salient (q.v.). The Uganda Army (q.v.) was cleared out of Tanzania (q.v.) by the end of January 1979, and the Tanzanian forces retaliated by crossing into Uganda and destroying the town of Masaka (q.v.). Reinforced by about a thousand Ugandans who had lived in exile in Tanzania, and finding the Ugandan defense much weaker than they had expected, they then pressed on until they were able to take Kampala (q.v.) in April 1979.

The Tanzanian forces were not fully mechanized: they advanced on foot. They had much better command and control procedures than Amin's forces and were better disciplined, and although in places they met stiff resistance, as for instance, round Mbarara (q.v.), the promised "last stand" by Amin's men did not occur. One of the stiffest battles of the war was against the forces sent by Colonel Gadafi (q.v.) of Libya (q.v.) who fought desperately in an attempt to defend the airport at Entebbe (q.v.), their one means of safe exit from Uganda. Freeing the rest of the country from Amin's retreating troops took until June. Casualties among the Tanzanian forces and the Ugandans who had fought with them were relatively slight: 373 Tanzanians were killed and c. 150 Ugandans. Much heavier casualties were suffered by the Libyans and Amin's troops, perhaps 600 and 1,000, but the numbers of dead among these is unknown, as is the number of civilian casualties. The last Tanzanian troops left Uganda in June 1981, having stayed on to help keep peace because Uganda had no properly trained army. When they left they handed over to the Uganda National Liberation Army (q.v.). This had already conducted itself so badly (*see* Ombachi Massacre) that Tanzania was glad to be rid of its Ugandan obligations.

LIBYA. Libya began to play a role in Ugandan affairs when President Amin (q.v.) visited Libya in February 1972. Colonel Gadafi (q.v.), the Libyan President, appealed to Amin as a Muslim (*see* Islam), pointing out that a number of the policies Uganda had been pursuing were anti-Islamic, and persuaded Amin to break with Israel (q.v.) and adopt a pro-Palestinian stand. In 1972 Libya gave Uganda some military aid at the time of the abortive invasion (q.v.) and offered help in training the Uganda Army (q.v.). Gadafi visited Uganda in 1974 and encouraged Amin to dispense with Christians in the army and government. Gadafi apparently believed that 70 percent of Ugandans were Muslims and that Uganda's population statistics had been falsified under colonial rule. Gadafi again sent Libyan troops to aid Amin in 1979, but they arrived too late and many were either killed or captured defending the airport at Entebbe (q.v.). The return of Libyan prisoners of war who were held in Tanzania (q.v.) was brokered by Algeria which had given Tanzania some military assistance during the War of Liberation (q.v.). Libya had to pay Tanzania $10 million towards the cost of the war.

When President Museveni (q.v.) came to power in 1986 some Western governments became alarmed because of a barter deal for oil between Libya and Uganda. There was no evidence that this was of political significance.

LIRA. The chief town and administrative headquarters of Lango District (the area inhabited by the Langi [q.v.]) during the colonial period. In 1974 the District was divided, and its eastern half named Lira District. A tarmac road only reached Lira in the 1970s. The missions (q.v.) arrived only shortly before World War I, and it is therefore less well-developed as an educational and medical center than most other older district headquarters.

LOST COUNTIES. The lands lost by Bunyoro (q.v.) to Buganda as a result of the war fought against Bunyoro by the British and Baganda (q.v.) in the 1890s. The 1900 [B]Uganda Agreement (q.v.) formalized the allocation to Buganda of all lands south of the Kafu River which had previously belonged to Bunyoro. Bunyoro felt most keenly the loss of Buyaga and Bugangaizi, two counties mainly inhabited by Banyoro. The county of Mwenge had been lost by Bunyoro to Toro (q.v.) earlier, and Mubende to Buganda. Both of these had previously been part of the heartland of Bunyoro.

The agreement signed between Bunyoro and the British in 1933 did not return these counties to Bunyoro. From then onwards the Banyoro campaigned unceasingly for the return of their lands, but the British authorities stone-walled, insisting that their allocation to Buganda was enshrined in the [B]Uganda Agreement, and that Buganda would have to consent to any changes to that Agreement. After his retirement from government service, John Nyakatura (q.v.) led the Lost Counties Campaign. Not until the Munster Commission reported on the eve of independence did the colonial authorities concede that the allocation of these lands to Buganda was a genuine grievance, and that some action had to be taken. However, the British balked at taking any decisive action which would anger the Baganda with whom there were already major difficulties. It was left to the post-independence government to hold a referendum in Buyaga and Bugangaizi not earlier than two years after independence.

The Baganda and the Buganda Kingdom Government remained bitterly opposed to any suggestion that the Lost Counties should be returned. Baganda ex-servicemen were settled in Buyaga and Bugangaizi to swell the numbers of those who would vote to remain part of Buganda, but in the event newcomers were disqualified from voting. Nevertheless many Baganda, misled by their government, were stunned when there was an overwhelming majority for reincorporation in Bunyoro, and there were near-riots. In Bugangaizi the vote was 5,275 for reincorporation and 2,253 against; in Buyaga 8,327 voted for reincorporation, and only 1,289 were against. A tiny minority voted for the two counties to become a separate district.

Buganda contested the results in the Uganda High Court, but lost. An attempt to appeal further to the Privy Council also failed. Kabaka Mutesa II (q.v.) of Buganda, who was also President of Uganda, refused to sign the instruments legalizing the return of the two counties to Bunyoro, but from 1 January 1965 they were transferred de facto.

LOURDEL, REVD FATHER SIMEON (1853–1890). Known to the Baganda (q.v.) as ''Mapera'' (from the French ''Mon Père''). He was a pioneer Catholic (q.v.) missionary, and member of the White Fathers (q.v.). He and Br Amans were the first two Catholic missionaries to settle in Uganda. Lourdel was quickly drawn into controversy with Mackay (q.v.) of the Church Missionary Society (q.v.) in the presence of the Kabaka, Mutesa I (q.v.), but despite Protestant (q.v.) denunciations, Mutesa permitted the new missionaries to stay. Canoes were sent to convey the rest of the party and their belongings to Uganda. Before the end of the year the Kabaka had allocated them land, they had built a house and chapel, and were beginning to teach the first few enquirers. They were unable to obey the instructions given by Lavigerie (q.v.) to put a substantial distance between themselves and any Protestant missions they might encounter in order to avoid strife: Mutesa kept both missions close by the court and encouraged them to debate their differences until Cardinal Lavigerie ordered the White Fathers not to be drawn into such arguments. The White Fathers were called to the court almost every day, and Lourdel was chosen to respond to these calls. Relations between the mission and Mutesa improved greatly when Lourdel successfully treated the

Kabaka during an illness. Lourdel's warm and passionate character and qualities of leadership helped to draw an increasing number of people to the mission to learn the new faith.

In 1882 the White Fathers temporarily withdrew to Bukumbi, south of Lake Victoria (q.v.) after hearing exaggerated stories of the misconduct of some of their adherents, and rumors that Mutesa was planning to have them killed. Lourdel was the first to realize that their fears had been exaggerated. They returned in 1885 after Mutesa's death, with Lourdel as head of the mission in the absence of Bishop Livinhac. They returned to a more dangerous situation than the one they had fled in 1882. During the next three years numbers of Christians were martyred (*see* Christian Martyrs) and the missionaries themselves were not safe. Lourdel kept up daily visits to the court in a vain effort to protect the Christian converts, and instructed and encouraged those who braved danger to attend the mission.

The Wars of Religion (q.v.) again drove the missionaries into exile. Lourdel established a Catholic mission at Nyegezi at the southern end of the lake which was dedicated to "Our Lady of the Exiles." It provided pastoral care for the Catholic converts who had accompanied the missionaries as well as establishing the Catholic church locally. In 1890 Lourdel and the other missionaries were able to return to Uganda and establish the mission at Rubaga (q.v.), but in May he was taken ill and died. There is a biography by A. Nicq, *Le Père Siméon Lourdel* (1922).

LUBEGA, FLORENCE ALICE (1925–). The daughter of Katikiro Samwiri Wamala, she was educated at Gayaza High School (*see* Education), Buloba Teacher Training College, and Makerere University College (q.v.) when she was one of the first women to be admitted to a diploma course in 1945–1946. Florence Lubega subsequently went to St Hugh's College, Oxford and London University in 1950–1951. She taught at Gayaza and Makerere College School and was Assistant Warden of Women, Mary Stuart Hall, Makerere from 1951–1953. She was Vice-President of the Uganda Council of Women (q.v.), and in 1958 became a nominated Member of the Legislative Council (q.v.). At independence she was elected to the National Assembly (q.v.) and appointed Parliamentary Secretary in the Ministry of Community Development and Labour in the government of Prime Minister, later President, Obote (q.v.). In 1963 her article ''Women in Uganda'' appeared in the *Journal of the Ministry of Community Development.* Florence Lubega eventually retired to family land at Mityana where she hoped to set up a village cooperative.

LUGARD, FREDERICK DEALTRY (1858–1945). British official and soldier, created Baron in 1928. As Captain Lugard, an official of the Imperial British East Africa Company (IBEAC) (q.v.), he served in Uganda from 1890–1892, a brief period which left a disproportionately large legacy. He was educated at Rossall and at Sandhurst and saw service in Afghanistan, Burma and the Lake Nyasa area before arriving in Uganda in December 1890.

Lugard arrived with only 50 troops and found a tense situation. Refusing to camp where Kabaka Mwanga (q.v.) had allocated him a site, he seized Kampala (q.v.) hill and established himself where the brick-built fort still stands. In the standoff between Catholics (q.v.) and Protestants (q.v.), war was narrowly averted on several occasions by the wiser and more moderate of the chiefs who successfully calmed their underlings. The missionaries of the Church Missionary Society (q.v.) and the White Fathers (q.v.) supported their own adherents, but were powerless to control them. The Protestant faction had pinned its hopes on the arrival of the IBEAC and had already raised the company flag. The Catholics agreed reluctantly to sign the treaty which Lugard extracted from an unwilling Mwanga within a week of arrival, although he had to accept Mwanga's refusal to fly the company flag. The treaty technically gave the Company the right to rule, but Lugard had little effective power: that was in the hands of the chiefs.

In May 1891 Lugard decided to march via western Uganda to Equatoria (q.v.) to enlist the Sudanese troops (*see* Nubians) which Emin Pasha (q.v.) had left behind in order to strengthen his position. On the way there he made a treaty with an emissary of Mugabe Ntare V (q.v.) of Ankole (q.v.) promising protection, he installed Kasagama (q.v.) as Mukama of Toro (q.v.), set up a line of forts manned by some of the Sudanese to defend Toro and Buganda from Mukama Kabarega (q.v.), and was able to add 100 troops to the garrison in Kampala on his return in December 1891.

During his absence the chiefs had continued to hold their followers in check, but tensions had not lessened. Lugard's attempts to hold the ring and administer justice added to the tensions since he was not fully aware of the complexities of the cases in which he tried to intervene. His orders were to be impartial in the Protestant/Catholic conflict, but in the last resort to support the Protestants. On 24 January he issued nearly 500 guns to the Protestants, believing them to be in imminent danger, and this helped to precipitate the Battle of Mengo of 1892 (q.v.). The Protestants won thanks to Lugard's arms and his use of his Maxim gun. In the battle the Catholic mission at Rubaga (q.v.) was burnt, and although none of the missionaries was killed or injured, no aspect of the affair caused Lugard more concern. His actions and the course of the battle had international repercussions. Lugard's own accounts, those of the two missions, and that given by J.R.L. Macdonald who was sent to investigate, all gave different versions of events, and there was vigorous debate in the British and French press of the time.

The Catholics fled to Bulingugwe Island and thence to Buddu (q.v.), and Mwanga fled south of the lake. Lugard ordered Mwanga to return, treated with leading Catholics as well as Protestants, and imposed a settlement in spite of the intrigues and objections of some Protestant chiefs. Buddu and some of the Sesse Islands were allocated to the Catholics; the rest of Buganda went to the Protestants except for a small buffer zone between the two which was allocated to the Muslims (*see* Islam) under the leadership of Prince Nuhu Mbogo. At this point Mwanga decided to identify himself with the Protestant party who were plainly the winning side.

In June Lugard set out for England, concerned that the IBEAC was planning to withdraw from Uganda. The campaign he and others waged, the Church Missionary Society in particular, together with reports from Uganda, persuaded the

British government that they had a responsibility to retain control of Uganda: if they did not step in and take over from the Company, the missions, and particularly the Protestants with their British connections, would be endangered.

Lugard's actions in Uganda, and the Battle of Mengo in particular, gave rise to much discussion at the time, and historians continue to disagree about his role.

LUGBARA. The Lugbara live in the northern part of what was known during colonial rule as West Nile (q.v.) along the Nile-Congo watershed and along the border with Zaire (q.v.). They speak a Central Sudanic language (*see* Languages). Linguistically and culturally they are closely related to and intermixed with the Madi (q.v.) who live just to the east of them in the lower-lying country by the Nile (q.v.). They inhabit a high, fertile plateau and their main staples are millet and sorghum. Cattle, sheep, goats and chickens are kept, and their principal cash crop is tobacco which has been very successfully grown and marketed. They did not develop a centralized state structure, but live in large family groupings, and are organized in lineages and clans. The highest authority among the Lugbara were the rainmakers whose position was hereditary. There was much feuding between clans.

Towards the end of the nineteenth century Sudanese (q.v.) slave traders failed to penetrate the highlands where the Lugbara live, though societies around them were seriously disrupted. They were able to repulse the Mahdists who had risen against Egyptian rule in the Sudan (q.v.) with the help of the Yakan Water Cult (q.v.), and when Emin Pasha (q.v.) left Wadelai in 1889, the Lugbara wiped out a company of his troops as well as an avenging patrol after they had drunk the Yakan Water. In the 1890s the Lugbara suffered from epidemics of smallpox and plague, and lost many cattle from rinderpest. Lugbara country was in the Lado Enclave (q.v.) and in 1900 the Belgians set up a first administrative post at Ofude and in 1905 a second post was set up. The Belgians commandeered food from the people to feed the troops at Ofude but otherwise had little contact with them aside from skirmishing with them because they resisted Belgian rule. The Belgians appointed some Yakan leaders as administrative chiefs who then became unpopular because they had to raise taxes. The area was transferred to Sudan in 1909 and administered from Kajo Kaji. The chiefs whom the Belgians appointed lost much of their power, though they retained the wealth they had gained. Finally in 1914 this part of the Lado Enclave became part of Uganda. An administrative post was set up at Arua (q.v.) which became the chief town in the area from then on. A.E. Weatherhead, a vigorous colonial official, worked to eliminate ivory poaching and clan feuding, and most of the former chiefs were reappointed. The Verona Fathers (q.v.), the first mission to reach this part of Uganda, did not arrive until 1913. The Africa Inland Mission (q.v.) which arrived in 1918 concentrated its work around Arua.

The Lugbara suffered severely, as did all the peoples of West Nile, when they were collectively blamed for the oppression of President Idi Amin (q.v.) who came from this area. Between 1980 and 1986 many of them lived as refugees (q.v.) in Zaire (q.v.) or Sudan.

LULE, YUSUFU KIRONDE (1912–1985). Principal of Makerere University College (q.v.) and briefly President of Uganda in 1979. Born in Buganda into a Muslim (*see* Islam) family, Lule got his first education at King's College, Budo (*see* Education), when he accompanied the Muslim Prince Badru Kakungulu (q.v.) in the role of a servant. His academic ability soon became evident, and in 1934 he entered Makerere College. In 1936 he won a scholarship to Fort Hare in South Africa, where he graduated with a B.Sc. in 1939. From then until 1948 he taught science at his old school.

After World War II Britain began to train Africans for eventual, though remote, independence, and Lule was sent to Bristol and Edinburgh Universities. From 1951–1955 he lectured in education at Makerere. At the time of the Deportation Crisis (q.v.) Lule was appointed a member of the Hancock Committee (q.v.). In 1955 he became Minister of Rural Development and then of Education and Social Development in the colonial administration, in 1962 moving to become Deputy Chairman and then Chairman of the Public Service Commission. Two years later he was appointed the first Ugandan Principal of Makerere University College, where he remained until 1970, a distinguished and respected, if cautious, administrator. In that year Lule was removed by President Obote (q.v.) and went to London to become Assistant Secretary-General of the Commonwealth Secretariat. In 1972 he moved to Ghana as Joint Vice-President of the Association of African Universities.

Lule retired to London in 1977, but in 1979 was chosen, a compromise candidate, to become President of Uganda after the fall of President Amin (q.v.), a position he held for just 68 days. He lacked the political skill to deal with an extremely complex and fraught situation, and refused to compromise over appointments. After a brief period of virtual house arrest in Tanzania (q.v.), he once more went to London where he became the leader there of the National Resistance Movement (q.v.) which, under the future President Museveni (q.v.), seized power in 1986, but Lule did not live to see this.

LUWERO TRIANGLE. An area of land lying northeast of Kampala (q.v.) roughly bounded by the roads leading from Kampala to Masindi (q.v.) and Fort Portal (q.v.). It was not truly triangular in shape and also took in Mpigi to the south. During the second presidency of Milton Obote (q.v.) the anti-government forces of the National Resistance Movement (NRM) (q.v.) led by Yoweri Museveni (q.v.) took control of much of the Luwero Triangle. Counter-insurgency operations by the Uganda National Liberation Army (q.v.) were carried out without mercy for the civilian population. The area was devastated between 1981 and 1985. The international aid agencies, which were called in by Obote's government to give aid to the civilians who had been moved into ''peace'' camps, were appalled at the ferocity and indiscipline of the army. They feared to publicize it lest they be forbidden to continue to operate, but news gradually leaked out about conditions. In 1984 Elliott Abrams (q.v.) testified to the US Congress that some 200,000 people had probably lost their lives in these counter-insurgency operations.

After the NRM came to power in 1986 much of the Luwero Triangle was found to be depopulated, buildings had been destroyed, farms had fallen into disrepair and become overgrown, a major coffee growing area needed to be rehabilitated, and hundreds of skulls and human remains were exhumed from mass graves and put on display.

Some politicians who continued to support Obote such as Peter Otai (q.v.) and some surviving soldiers who had been employed in the counter-insurgency operations in the Luwero Triangle refused to accept the evidence of destruction. They claimed that the skeletons found were of soldiers killed by the NRM, not of civilians. The depopulation and destruction in the area and the vast numbers of skulls cast doubt on their claims.

LUWULIZA-KIRUNDA, JOHN MIKLOTH MAGOOLA (1940–). Educated at Busoga College (*see* Education), Makerere University College (q.v.), Birmingham and Liverpool Universities where he qualified in medicine. He was a lecturer and professor in Makerere University Medical School from 1972–1977 when he became an exile from the regime of President Amin (q.v.). In the Elections of 1980 (q.v.) he joined the Uganda People's Congress (q.v.) and stood for Iganga North East in Busoga. He was appointed first Minister of Labour and then Minister of Internal Affairs in the government of President Obote (q.v.). When President Museveni (q.v.) came to power in 1986, Luwuliza-Kirunda left the country and joined with Peter Otai (q.v.) to raise armed resistance against the new government. FOBA, "Force Obote Back Again" (q.v.), which Luwuliza-Kirunda and Otai ran from exile, was later renamed the Uganda People's Front/Army (q.v.).

LUWUM, ARCHBISHOP JANANI (1922–1977). Anglican (q.v.) Archbishop of Uganda, 1974–1977, murdered by the Amin regime. Born in Mucwini, Acholi (q.v.), of Christian parents, he was educated at Gulu High School, Boroboro Teacher Training College at Lira, Lango (*see* Langi), Buwalasi Theological College in eastern Uganda, St Augustine's College, Canterbury and the London Bible College. He was ordained in 1955, and after working in a parish and spending some time as Principal of Buwalasi, he moved to Kampala (q.v.) in 1966 to be Provincial Secretary to the Anglican Province of Uganda, Rwanda (q.v.) and Burundi. On 25 January 1969 he was consecrated Bishop of Northern Uganda centred on Gulu. The coup (q.v.) which brought President Amin (q.v.) to power occurred two years to the day after his consecration, and brought mourning and trouble to Luwum's diocese. Luwum and other Bishops met with President Amin to plead with him to curb the violence, but Amin was unmoved. In 1972 when attending a meeting of the World Council of Churches he helped draft a motion deploring the expulsion of the Asians (q.v.). His involvement in this must have been known to the Uganda government.

On 7 May 1974 Luwum was elected Archbishop of Uganda in succession to Archbishop Erica Sabiti (q.v.). People regularly turned to him for help in those troubled times, and on several occasions he drove to the State Research Bureau (q.v.) to try to find information about someone who had been arrested and taken away by soldiers. At the time of the Makerere Incident (q.v.) he and Cardinal Nsubuga (q.v.) went to the university to find out what was happening and offer help. The two church leaders developed a close working relationship.

In 1976 church leaders became concerned at growing antagonism between Christians and Muslims (*see* Islam), particularly in Ankole (q.v.). In late August the Bishops of the Anglican and Catholic (q.v.) churches met in conference together with the head of the Muslim community, the Sheikh Mufti, at Lweza near Kampala, and Luwum chaired the meeting. The minutes noted that they had discussed the violence in the country, the indiscipline of the army, and people's fear that there were "black lists" in existence. The church leaders noted that people were accused and beaten up and detained without proper trials being held, they expressed concern about the State Research Bureau, deplored the use of the Military Police for civilian arrests, and pledged themselves to fight against the evil that was plaguing the land. After the conference they requested an interview with the

President. Amin was furious that they had met without his knowledge and demanded the minutes of the conference. He took literally the phrases about "fighting evil" and was afraid that the Muslims as well as the Christians had turned against him. Luwum was a marked man because he had chaired the conference.

On 28 January Luwum consecrated a new Bishop in Ankole. Government representatives were present, and heard Bishop Festo Kivengere (q.v.) preach a sermon in which he challenged those present who were misusing authority and "crushing men's faces into the dust." A week later on 5 February armed men raided Luwum's house in the early hours and claimed to have discovered a cache of arms (Acholi exiles in Nairobi were involved in plotting at this time, but Luwum was not involved). The Anglican Bishops were summoned to Kampala to a meeting to coincide with that of the Catholic Bishops. A memorandum was drawn up which confronted head-on what was happening in the country, and both Catholics and Anglicans agreed to sign it. An interview with the President was requested, but there was no response from him. At the last moment a hitch occurred, and only the Anglicans signed the document.

The memorandum was delivered to members of the government and church leaders on 14 February. On 16 February Luwum was summoned to the International Conference Centre, and six of his Bishops went with him. Here he was accused of being involved in a plot to overthrow Amin by force, and thousands of soldiers called for him to be shot. The crowds were sent away, and Luwum was separated from the other Bishops and taken to Amin. He was never seen alive again. The following morning Radio Uganda announced that Luwum and two government ministers had been killed in a fatal car accident, a story which no one believed, and whose untruth was quickly demonstrated. The church was refused permission to hold his funeral at its Namirembe (q.v.) headquarters in Kampala, and his body was taken to Acholi and buried hurriedly by soldiers, but not before people had seen the gunshot wounds. On the following Sunday huge crowds of Protestant and Catholic Christians were joined by Muslims at Namirembe, and whether the government liked it or no, the normal services turned into a huge memorial-service-cum-political-demonstration against the government. Another memorial service was held the same day in Nairobi Cathedral in Kenya (q.v.) at which representatives of the World Council of Churches and the Anglican Communion were present, having been refused permission to enter Uganda. Six Anglican Bishops who felt particularly endangered, including Bishop Kivengere, went into exile. Luwum's murder led directly to Amin being told he would not be welcome at the Commonwealth Heads of Government meeting in London later that year.

Luwum was quickly acclaimed as a martyr. After the overthrow of Amin his body was reburied at Namirembe. There is a memorial window to him in Canterbury Cathedral, the mother church of the Anglican Communion.

LWOO. The name given to a group of Nilotic peoples inhabiting parts of the Southern Sudan (q.v.), northern and eastern Uganda and northwestern Kenya (q.v.), and spilling over into a corner of northern Tanzania (q.v.), and also to the languages they speak, which are to some extent mutually intelligible. The language of the Langi (q.v.) is closely related, but the Langi do not include themselves in the Lwoo grouping. In Uganda the Lwoo comprise the Acholi (q.v.), the Alur (q.v.) and the Jopadhola. They all share a history of migration from what is now the Southern Sudan. The Kenya Luo historian, Professor Bethwell Ogot, believes that the Lwoo dispersal began from an area northwest of Lake Rudolph (Turkana). The Alur moved southeast to Bunyoro (q.v.), and fanned out from there, intermingling with the Acholi and Bunyoro, and settling as Alur just to the north of Lake Albert in what became the West Nile District of Uganda (but cf. Ronald Atkinson's views on Acholi). The main dispersal took a more complicated route, circling round to the north, and then moving southwards, with groups settling and becoming known as Acholi, as Jopadhola in the neighborhood of the modern Ugandan town of Tororo (q.v.), and further southwards still, where the settlers became the Luo of western Kenya and northern Tanzania.

-M-

MACKAY, ALEXANDER MOREHEAD (1849–1890). Pioneer missionary of the Church Missionary Society (CMS) (q.v.). He was born in Rhynie, Scotland, and brought up in the Calvinistic Free Church. He was educated at Aberdeen Grammar School and Edinburgh University and Berlin where he studied engineering. He went to East Africa with the first Uganda-bound party, but remained at the coast to engineer a road to Mpwapwa partway inland, only reaching Uganda in December 1878. His engineering skills were quickly put to use, in setting up a printing press, cutting type for it and printing thousands of reading sheets and portions of the Bible; in erecting a giant flagstaff for Kabaka Mutesa I (q.v.); in reluctantly mending guns when importuned to do so by the Kabaka; in boat-building and maintaining the boat's engine; in making lead coffins for the queen mother and eventually for the Kabaka himself.

Mackay was constantly surrounded by Baganda (q.v.) chiefs and young men from the royal household learning to read, and he visited the Kabaka's palace almost daily to lead prayers and teach Christianity when he was often extremely forthright with the Kabaka but won his respect. When the first White Fathers (q.v.) arrived, Fr Lourdel (q.v.) asked Mackay to act as interpreter for him in an interview with the Kabaka. Mackay had received courteous help from Catholic (q.v.) missionaries at the coast, so this seemed a reasonable request. However, Mackay's Calvinism got the upper hand of him, and he used the opportunity to denounce Catholicism. Other CMS missionaries were apologetic about Mackay's outburst. Further debates were encouraged by the Kabaka, as were debates about Islam (q.v.). In these latter, the Muslims increasingly saw him as a dangerous adversary, both because he challenged their religion, and also because his engineering skills far surpassed theirs and gave him the technological advantage which had formerly been theirs and which impressed the Baganda.

Mackay's very impetuosity and enthusiasm helped him to win a loyal following among the Baganda and the loyalty and admiration of both missionaries and travelers such as H.M.

Stanley (q.v.), though it also sometimes got him into trouble with the mission authorities. He did not lack courage either. After the executions of the Christian martyrs (q.v.), his fellow-missionary R.P. Ashe, a chronicler of events whose writings are an important historical source (*see* Bibliography), left because of illness. For the next dangerous year Mackay was the only CMS missionary in Buganda. Without his determination the mission might well have foundered. In July 1887 the traditionalist chiefs and Muslims persuaded Kabaka Mwanga (q.v.) to expel Mackay, and he therefore went across Lake Victoria (q.v.) to Usambiro where he worked on translations of parts of the New Testament into Luganda (*see* Languages), completing St Matthew's Gospel, which was published by the British and Foreign Bible Society the same year. Both Swahili and Luganda had first been written down in Arabic script; Mackay was largely responsible for reducing it to writing in Roman script. In 1888 during the Wars of Religion (q.v.) he was joined by Christians forced to flee. He died there suddenly in 1890 and was buried in Usambiro. In 1927, the Jubilee of CMS work in Uganda, Mackay's remains were brought to Namirembe (q.v.) and reinterred outside the Anglican Cathedral, and Canon Apolo Kivebulaya (q.v.), who had first begun to learn Christianity with Mackay, read the lesson.

A year after his death his sister published a life of Mackay made up in large part of extracts from his lively letters (*see* [Mackay's Sister] in the Bibliography). There is no modern biography.

MADHVANI, JAYANT MULJIBHAI (1922–1971). Businessman and son of Muljibhai Madhvani, the founder of the family business empire built around their sugar plantation and processing plant at Kakira near Jinja (q.v.). By 1970 the firm's business assets in Uganda were worth 640 million shillings. J.M. Madhvani was educated at Bombay University from 1937–1944, graduating in science and law. Among his other business interests were textiles, steel, breweries and glass manufacture in both Uganda and Kenya (q.v.). He was a founder and President of the Lions Club of Uganda. He became a member of the Legislative Council (q.v.) and in

1960 of the first Constitutional Council which worked on the agenda for the Constitutional Conference (q.v.) held at Lancaster House (q.v.) prior to independence in 1962. His son, Manubhai Muljibhai Madhvani carried on the business. As well as his involvement in the family sugar industry, M.M. Madhvani had a number of other business interests including the Uganda Cement Industry. He became a Chairman of the Lions Club of Uganda, and served on numerous committees of educational, social and welfare organizations, and was a Councillor of Jinja Municipal Council. When President Amin (q.v.) expelled the Asians (q.v.), M.M. Madhvani left the country. Since Amin's fall some attempt has been made to reconstruct the sugar and cement industries, and several members of the Madhvani family, including M.M. Madhvani, have been involved in restarting the family businesses.

MADI. A Sudanic speaking people (*see* Languages) who live in the extreme northwest of Uganda and in adjacent areas in Zaire (q.v.) and Sudan (q.v.). In the second half of the nineteenth century they were seriously affected by Sudanese and Egyptian slave raiders. There was much displacement, and the area became ethnically confused. The Madi are predominantly agriculturalists, their staple crop being finger millet. Fish from the Nile (q.v.) and game also figure prominently in their diet. The main cash crop is tobacco.

The Madi are an acephalous society who traditionally lived in large joint family homesteads, and were organized in lineages. The colonial government picked clan heads to act as administrative chiefs. Sub-chiefs were known as *jaogi,* a term borrowed from Acholi, and county chiefs were known as *wakil,* an Arabic term. Rainmakers, *opi ei dri,* were also of great importance in traditional society, at least one being found in each clan-section. Madi country was part of the Lado Enclave (q.v.) and between 1900 and 1914 they were admininstered by the Belgians (1900–1909) and then briefly became part of Sudan (q.v.). The area was finally incorporated into Uganda in 1914. The Madi were at first resistant to the third government to administer them in so few years, and were forcibly subjugated. The Verona Fathers (q.v.) are the main mission among the Madi, many of whom are Muslims (*see* Islam). The Verona Fathers began work at Palaro in 1912, but moved to Moyo in 1917. Protestant (q.v.) Christianity arrived much later still: modern education and medicine were therefore late in developing in this area.

Since the overthrow of President Amin (q.v.) in 1979 the Madi, in common with the other people of West Nile (q.v.), have suffered severely as all were held guilty by association with Amin who came from West Nile. The Uganda National Liberation Army (q.v.) took its revenge on the whole area, and there was strong resistance to the rule of President Obote (q.v.) from the Uganda National Resistance Front (q.v.). As a result many Madi and others fled across the border to either Zaire or Sudan, not returning until after Obote in his turn had been overthrown.

MAFTAA, DALLINGTON SCOPION (?1859–?). A slave from Nyasaland who was freed in Zanzibar and educated by the Universities' Mission to Central Africa and baptized. H.M. Stanley (q.v.) engaged him as a servant on his journey to Lake Victoria (q.v.) and the court of Kabaka Mutesa I (q.v.) which he reached in 1875. When Stanley left, Mutesa asked Maftaa to remain and instruct him in Christianity, probably because he saw the new religion as a counterweight to Islam (q.v.). Dallington conducted prayers at court, and transliterated portions of the Swahili Bible into Arabic script which the Kabaka and a number of courtiers could read. When the first missionaries of the Church Missionary Society (q.v.) arrived, he translated for them. However, within a year or two he accepted a minor chieftaincy in Buddu (q.v.) and gave up practicing Christianity.

MAILO LAND. Square miles of land allocated to Baganda (q.v.) chiefs and to the missions (q.v.) under the terms of the [B]Uganda Agreement (q.v.) and held in freehold. Mailo land could therefore be bought and sold. This system was alien to traditional land-holding practice in Buganda, and caused serious difficulties over clan headquarters lands which now passed into the hands of individuals and became alienable. This became a grievance of the Bataka (q.v.), the clan heads. The mailo system was not extended to any other part of Uganda.

MAINI, SIR AMIR NATH (1911–   ). Educated at the London School of Economics, Maini became a barrister. He gave up his legal practice and moved from Kenya (q.v.) to Uganda in 1939, settling in Kampala (q.v.) and becoming involved in the family business ventures. From 1944 to 1961 he was a member of the Legislative Council (q.v.). He became a member of Kampala Municipal Council, and served as Mayor of Kampala from 1950–1955. From 1955–1958 he was Minister of Corporations and Regional Communications. He was concerned at the plight of impoverished Indians and was involved with reviving welfare associations (the Indian Assocation and the Central Council of Indian Associations) to assist them. He believed that limiting further immigration and recruiting Africans into Asian businesses might reduce tensions between Asians and Africans. This proved not to be the case. He was forced to leave the country in 1972 when President Amin (q.v.) expelled the Asians (q.v.).

MAKERERE COLLEGE, MAKERERE UNIVERSITY COLLEGE, MAKERERE UNIVERSITY, KAMPALA. Makerere as an institution of higher learning had its origins in 1922 when the Uganda Technical College on Makerere Hill was opened. Its name was changed to Makerere College, and it was quickly seen as a future university. Courses in engineering, agriculture, veterinary science and for the training of teachers and medical assistants (*see* Medicine) were started, for both day and residential students from the three East African territories. By 1949 the range of studies offered by Makerere had been greatly extended and the courses upgraded so that Makerere was able to enter into a special relationship with London University. It now offered both academic and professional courses leading to London degrees. Those who graduated in this period were proud of the international standing of their qualifications. Makerere was already well-known for its medical training and was beginning to be known for its Art Department, later the Margaret Trowell School of Fine Art.

In 1963 the University of East Africa was established, and Makerere became one of its three constituent colleges (the others were Nairobi and Dar es Salaam), and changed its name to Makerere University College. The following year Yusufu K. Lule (q.v.) was appointed as its first Ugandan Principal in succession to Sir Bernard de Bunsen (q.v.). Since its foundation Makerere had expanded steadily, and the pace of expansion accelerated with Uganda's achievement of independence. Its student numbers grew from some 1,500 in 1963 to 3,500 by the end of the decade and new halls of residence and extensions to existing ones as well as extra staff housing were required. Independence from London University gave it the opportunity to make its teaching program more Afro-centric, exciting new fields of research opened up, and it began to acquire an international reputation in a variety of disciplines.

In 1946 a social research program was begun which developed into the East African Institute of Social Research, later the Makerere Institute of Social Research, closely linked with the Faculty of Social Science. As well as resident fellows, it catered for post-graduate students, often from overseas, doing fieldwork for higher degrees. Its Library houses a great many research papers written by fellows and associates, often of prime importance in the fields of economics, education, geography, history, political science, religious studies, sociology and social psychology.

In 1945 women students were admitted to Makerere for the first time. The six women selected for a special course were Yemima Ntungwerisho, Marjorie Kabuzi, Florence Lubega (q.v.), Mary Senkatuka, Catherine Senkatuka and Margaret Mulyanti, several of whom became prominent public servants. A small wooden house next to their first hall of residence (now the University Guest House) was constructed for the Warden. Men students had to apply to the Warden for permission to take the women out, collecting them from the "box," and the name "boxer" has stuck to women students ever since. When teaching for the University of London intermediate examination started in 1950, one of those admitted was Josephine Namboze who had taken her school certificate examination at Trinity College, Nabbingo (*see* Education). She made history by becoming the first Ugandan African woman to qualify in medicine, and she received her qualification from Queen Elizabeth the Queen Mother in 1959. Mary Stuart Hall for women was opened in 1953, and was filled far sooner than had been expected, with women quickly showing themselves able to compete on equal terms with the men students. Numbers grew so rapidly that a large extension was added during the 1960s, and a second hall of residence for women, Africa Hall, followed in 1973.

In 1970 the three constituent colleges of the University of East Africa became full universities independent of each other. A new Vice-Chancellor, Frank Kalimuzo, was appointed by President Obote (q.v.), and greater political control was exercised over the university. At this stage Makerere added commerce, forestry, law, and technology to the list of disciplines which it offered (Ugandan students wishing to study in these fields had previously had to go to one of the other university colleges of the University of East Africa); veterinary medicine returned to Makerere, music, dance and drama became degree subjects, and the Extra-Mural Department was greatly enlarged. A School of Librarianship had already been added, and extensions to the fine Library, which includes a valuable collection of Africana and important archives, and, in the Medical School, the Albert Cook (q.v.) Medical Library. Makerere also trained statisticians for a wide region of Africa. An extensive building program which included a gallery for the School of Fine Art, was needed to cope with these developments.

Until 1970 almost all students were residential, living in halls of residence which developed their own cherished traditions and characters. Since 1970 rapid increases in numbers have meant that more students live off campus or share overcrowded rooms, with a resulting lack of space and quiet for study.

The seizure of power by President Amin (q.v.) in 1971, the collapse of the modern sector of the economy which resulted from the expulsion (q.v.) of the Asians (q.v.) in 1972, and growing insecurity had a seriously deleterious effect on Makerere. Vice-Chancellor Kalimuzo "disappeared" just before the Golden Jubilee Celebrations of 1972. The expulsion of the Asians had already started by the time of the Jubilee, and Makerere lost its Asian academic and technical staff as well as a number of students. By the end of 1972 most British staff had also been forced to leave, and several academic staff had been killed or had "disappeared," including Professor V. Emiru, an ophthalmologist. Makerere nevertheless struggled to maintain standards. There was an exodus of Ugandan doctors threatened by the regime from Mulago Hospital and the Medical School. It was a great blow when lack of drugs and other treatment facilities in the teaching hospital at Mulago led to the withdrawal of British recognition of Makerere medical degrees. The building program came to a halt and book purchase became increasingly difficult because of the lack of foreign exchange.

Five students were probably killed in the "Makerere Incident" (q.v.) in 1976. In the War of Liberation (q.v.) of 1979 several buildings were damaged by shellfire. During the first half of the 1980s insecurity continued to hamper progress, and continuing high inflation and the erosion of salaries discouraged staff from returning from exile even when security in southern Uganda improved after the accession of President Museveni (q.v.). In 1990 staff were driven to take action over the erosion of their pay and two students were killed when police opened fire during a demonstration about grants, and the Vice-Chancellor had to be replaced. A Visitation Report recommended loosening the ties between the government and the university, and depoliticizing the Vice-Chancellorship by appointing a prominent and respected citizen rather than the national president as Chancellor.

In 1990–1991 a much-needed refurbishment of buildings was carried out with the help of overseas aid. The School of Education, which had fallen into serious structural disrepair, was renovated with European Community aid, and a new science building was donated by the Japanese. Distance Learning courses are run from Makerere, a Bachelor of

Theology degree course has been introduced, and an MA in Women's Studies under Dr Victoria Mwaka assisted by Deborah Kasente who was a visiting lecturer at Sussex University before her appointment. She had previously been a Warden of Mary Stuart Hall.

Principals of Makerere:
Douglas Tomblings: 1923–1938
George Turner: 1938–1946
William D. Lamont: 1946–1949
Bernard de Bunsen: 1949–1964
Yusufu Lule: 1964–1970

Vice-Chancellors of Makerere:
Frank K. Kalimuzo: 1970–1972
Asavia Wandira: 1972–1974
Joseph Lutwama: 1974–1978
William Senteza-Kajubi: 1978–1981
Asavia Wandira: 1981–1985
George Kirya: 1985–1990
William Senteza-Kajubi: 1990–1993

By the 1990s Makerere University had become one of five institutions of higher education in Uganda. Mbarara University of Science and Technology is government sponsored. There are also three privately sponsored universities: Mbale Muslim University, the Catholic Martyrs' Memorial University at Nkozi, and the Protestant Christian University of East Africa at Ndejje.

MAKERERE INCIDENT (1976). This took place on the 3–4 August 1976. Tension was high after the murder by President Amin's (q.v.) Public Safety Unit (q.v.) of a student, Paul Serwanga, the disappearance of a Kenyan student, Esther Chesire (q.v.), and the murder of Mrs Mukasa-Bukenya, Warden of the hall of residence at Makerere University (q.v.) where Chesire had lived. The Langlands Commission (q.v.) had been given the task of enquiring into these events. On a number of occasions the students had acted to express their disgust with the government, including marching through the town to sympathize with Paul Serwanga's family, and had escaped punishment. Amin was alleged to be anxious not to upset the university because he was just about to receive an honorary doctorate in law (a move which had up till then been successfully resisted by the university).

By the time the new term opened on 5 July 1976 the situation was entirely different. The Entebbe Raid (q.v.) had taken place on 3–4 July and Uganda and Amin had been deeply humiliated by the Israeli (q.v.) success in rescuing the hijack hostages. Kenya (q.v.) had imposed an oil embargo on Uganda as a result of Amin's insults following the Entebbe Raid and his claims to a "Greater Uganda" including much of western Kenya. Amin and his government were in an embattled and nervous state, and the students were prevented from staging a protest at the murder of Mrs Mukasa-Bukenya. Two expatriate members of staff wrote a public request for an enquiry into her death, and the instigator, Fr John O'Donoghue, was lucky to escape from Uganda with his life. Precisely what finally sparked the student protests which erupted on 3 August is not clear, but they had a very long list of grievances including the murders of Serwanga and Mukasa-Bukenya, the poor living and studying conditions in the university, and the presence in the university of Taban, Amin's son, who was resident in Mitchell Hall trying to improve his English: it was apparently hoped that he might go to Britain to train with the Royal Air Force.

On 3 August the students massed in front of the main building of the university on what had become known as Freedom Square because they had there previously confronted the Minister of Education, Brigadier Kili. It seems likely that they had not realized the enormity of the international humiliation suffered as a result of the Entebbe Raid, and had consequently misjudged the mood of the government. The Vice-Chancellor apparently panicked and called the Minister of Education. At about 10:30 am the Uganda Army (q.v.) arrived and quietly surrounded the students. At a given signal they charged, beating up those whom they caught. Others were rounded up from the halls of residence which were looted, and one woman student suffered multiple rape. Throughout the day batches of students including some women were taken in lorries to Makindye Barracks where they were further roughed up until Colonel Mustapha ordered the soldiers to desist and they were eventually allowed to go late in the evening. There was further violence on the campus in the afternoon when some soldiers returned, apparently against orders.

That afternoon Cardinal Nsubuga (q.v.) and the Anglican Archbishop Janani Luwum (q.v.) heard reports of trouble at Makerere and drove up to invesitgate. The Vice-Chancellor assured them that all was calm.

There was further serious trouble at about 2:00 am when Lumumba Hall was invaded by soldiers. On this occasion students were thrown out of windows, others were raped, and some serious injuries occurred. Some people were forced to lie out on the grass all night. Mitchell Hall, where Taban had been lodged, was viciously attacked. The following day Colonel Mustapha came to the University with several injured students who had been detained at Makindye Barracks overnight. He told the students that next time they caused any trouble, they would be shot.

Were there any deaths? The first reports, received in Nairobi the day after the invasion, claimed that five students had died. According to many British newspaper reports hundreds of students died. This quickly became 800 in the London Sunday paper, *The Observer.* Investigators found just one firm report of deaths. A Catholic missionary traveling south from Kampala (q.v.) just after the incident found a crowd of people staring at four bodies in the water at the first river bridge south of the Equator on the Masaka road. They were clothed in the distinctive red Makerere undergraduate gowns (which is puzzling, since the students had not worn gowns to demonstrate). He was able to state that two of them had been buried in a nearby Catholic parish. It is now generally accepted that no general massacre took place, but the whole affair was yet one more blot on the violent record of Amin's government.

MALIYAMUNGU, ISAAC. A junior non-commissioned officer who swiftly rose to the rank of Brigadier General under President Amin (q.v.), and is remembered as one of his most vicious killers. Before joining the army he had been employed as a gatekeeper at the textile factory in Jinja (q.v.). He was a "Christian" Kakwa (q.v.), whose original home was across the border in Zaire (q.v.). He drove a tank in the 1971 coup (q.v.) which brought President Amin to power and he became a member of Amin's Defence Council (q.v.). When the Asians (q.v.) were expelled, he was put in charge of "abandoned shops" in Masaka (q.v.) to ensure they were fairly distributed. He was responsible for the exceptionally brutal murder of Mayor Francis Walugembe of Masaka. As Commander of the 2nd Infantry Brigade, he was also put in charge of the Magamaga Ordnance Depot and later became Chief of Operations in the Uganda Army (q.v.). It was he who was in charge of the proceedings when Archbishop Janani Luwum (q.v.) was accused by Amin and subsequently murdered. During the War of Liberation (q.v.) he was in command at the Masaka Barracks. He apparently fled to Sudan (q.v.).

MARELLA, HUSSAIN (also spelled as MARELA or MALERA). A Southern Sudanese (q.v.) lieutenant who was promoted Brigadier and Chief of Staff of the Uganda Army (q.v.) soon after the coup of 1971 (q.v.) which brought President Amin (q.v.) to power. He was one of those soldiers specially recruited by Amin prior to the coup and placed in a unit whose loyalties were to Amin alone. President Obote (q.v.) tried to disband this unit, but failed to do so. In late 1971 when still a colonel Marella was put in charge of the Military Police and of Makindye Prison. The Military Police were notorious for their brutality and were attacked by Brigadier Charles Arube (q.v.) in 1974 in a coup attempt which failed. Some time later Marella was relieved of his post. He left Uganda before Amin was overthrown taking with him a huge convoy of lorries carrying loot, and set up as a businessman in Yei in Southern Sudan.

MARLBOROUGH HOUSE. One of two elegant London venues (*see* also Lancaster House) used for constitutional conferences in preparation for the independence of British colonies and protectorates in Africa. The final Constitutional Conference (q.v.) for Uganda was held there in June 1962.

MARTYRS, MARTYRDOMS *see* CHRISTIAN MARTYRS; MUSLIM MARTYRS

MASAKA. The chief town of Buddu (q.v.), and an important road junction. To the west the road leads through to Mbarara (q.v.), Kabale (q.v.) and Rwanda (q.v.); to the south it leads to Tanzania (q.v.). It is the administrative headquarters of the present Masaka District. Unusually it was not a main mission center. Villa Maria (q.v.), the Catholic (q.v.) center, is some miles to the north, and the Church of Uganda (q.v.) center is at Kako to the northeast, though both churches also have town parishes.

MASINDI. One of two towns in the colonial-era district of Bunyoro (q.v.). The administrative headquarters of the district was moved from Hoima (q.v.) to Masindi and back again, and the Mukama of Bunyoro moved his court when the administration moved. In 1921 it was finally decided to locate the administration at Hoima. It was feared that Masindi would decline, but its port facilities ensured its continuance. The missions (q.v.) moved their main station in Bunyoro in line with the Protectorate administration, and Masindi therefore became a less important educational and medical center than Hoima. In 1974 the former Bunyoro District was divided, and Masindi became headquarters of the northern half which was named after it.

MAYANJA, ABUBAKER KAKYAMA, AL-HAJJI (1929–   ). Educated at Makerere University College (q.v.) and Cambridge, he graduated in law and was called to the English Bar at Lincoln's Inn, London. In 1952 he was co-founder with I.K. Musazi (q.v.) of the Uganda National Congress (UNC) (q.v.). In 1959, when the UNC split, he supported Milton Obote (q.v.) in the section of the UNC which became the Uganda People's Congress (UPC) (q.v.). In 1960, when he was Minister of Education in the Kabaka's government in Buganda (q.v.), Mayanja was the one minister who refused to sign the decree by which Buganda tried to secede, fearing that she would lose her special status if Uganda became independent as a unitary state. The same year he was

Chairman of the Elections Committee when the Democratic Party (DP) (q.v.) was virtually excluded from the Lukiiko, the Buganda parliament. He and Daudi Ocheng (q.v.) arranged the coalition between Buganda's Kabaka Yekka (q.v.) party and Obote's UPC. This alliance enabled Obote to become Prime Minister at independence with KY support. In July 1964 he led four other KY members in crossing the floor of the National Assembly (q.v.) to join the UPC.

Abu Mayanja did not give Obote his unqualified support. In 1968 he dissented from the opinions expressed by Picho Ali, Obote's spokesman, in an article in the journal *Transition.* Mayanja suggested that tribalism was preventing the Africanization of the judiciary, the implication being that Obote did not want to appoint Baganda, who accounted for most of the trained African lawyers. Mayanja and the Editor of *Transition,* Rajat Neogy, were both charged with sedition, acquitted, and then detained without trial, becoming Uganda's first post-independence political detainees. Mayanja was only released after the 1971 coup (q.v.) which brought Idi Amin (q.v.) to power, and, presumably because he was a Muslim (*see* Islam), he was the one person who had served as a minister under Obote to be given a post in Amin's first cabinet. But this did not last long.

Abu Mayanja was elected as a Member of Parliament again in the disputed Elections of 1980 (q.v.) when he represented Mubende South East. However, he later went into exile in Kenya (q.v.), having once again fallen out with Obote. When President Museveni (q.v.) came to power, Abu Mayanja was appointed as one of the three Deputy Prime Ministers, the other two then being Eriya Kategaya (q.v.) and Paul Ssemogerere (q.v.).

MBAGUTA, NUWA (c. 1867–1944). Enganzi (chief minister) of Ankole (q.v.) from 1901 to 1938 and saza (county) chief of Kashari, Shema and Ngarama, 1901–1924. He was of the Bashambo clan, the royal clan of the neigboring kingdom of Mpororo, parts of which were incorporated into Ankole by the British. There was a measure of strife between the Bahinda (q.v.) rulers of Ankole and the Bashambo, but it was not unusual for an Enganzi to be non-Hinda.

When aged about 12 he went to the court of the Mugabe of Ankole, Ntare V (q.v.), where he eventually attracted the Mugabe's attention and was taken into his service. When the Christian exiles fled from Buganda (q.v.) to Ankole during the Wars of Religion (q.v.), Mbaguta was put in charge of them. In the succession struggle which followed Ntare's death in 1895, Mbaguta supported Kahaya (q.v.), the contender who eventually gained power, and in 1897 he was sent to Buganda to ask for troops to support Kahaya. His relations with Kahaya once British rule was established were, however, often fraught. From his contacts with Buganda, Mbaguta knew what had happened to Bunyoro (q.v.) which had resisted British rule, and how the leaders of Buganda had prospered as a result of aligning themselves with the British, and he realized that Ankole had more to gain from collaboration than from resistance. In particular, when Johnston (q.v.) appointed him Enganzi he seems to have been aware of the successful career of Apolo Kagwa (q.v.), Katikiro (chief minister) of Buganda, although traditionally the Enganzi had fulfilled a different function in Ankole from the Katikiro of Buganda. His collaboration angered the conservative Bahima (q.v.) chiefs of Ankole, and made him enemies.

There is general agreement that the murder in 1905 of the British colonial official, H. St G. Galt (q.v.), was intended in some way to harm Mbaguta. The intention may, in fact, have been to murder Mbaguta himself. The plot misfired and strengthened his position vis-à-vis the British.

Mbaguta was a determined modernizer. He had actively supported the Protestant (q.v.) mission when first it tried to gain access to Ankole in 1899, and in 1902 he persuaded the Mugabe to join him in applying to join baptism classes. They were both baptized at Christmas of that year. Before schools were properly established in Ankole, he encouraged boys to go to school in Buganda. Over the years he personally paid the school fees of many school pupils as well as donating generously to the schools of both the Protestant and Catholic (q.v.) missions. He encouraged the growing of *matooke* bananas (the type which, steamed, are the staple food of Buganda) as a precaution against famine. Because the Mugabe Kahaya was retiring and hesitant, it was Mbaguta who wielded authority in Ankole, and that generally meant that it was he through whom the British exercised indirect rule.

By 1938 the British decided it was time for him to retire, in part because relations between him and Kahaya were so poor that it was creating administrative problems. Kahaya died just two months after Mbaguta in 1944.

MBALE. The administrative headquarters of Bugisu (q.v.) District during the colonial period. This was renamed Mbale District in 1974. The town stands on land given to Semei Kakungulu (q.v.) in 1902 and chosen because of the supply of *matooke* (plantain) available in the vicinity. Here his men built a sizable settlement centered on the large house Kakungulu built for himself, and roads radiated out from the settlement. This was big enough to attract a considerable trade, and Swahili ivory traders were among those who visited it as well as Asian (q.v.) and Baganda (q.v.) traders. In 1904 the Protectorate administration moved its headquarters in the area from Budaka to Mbale where it found a more stimulating community. Some of the descendants of Kakungulu's followers still live in the area. There is also a long-established Muslim (*see* Islam) community in Mbale, and in the 1980s a Muslim University was established there with external funding.

MBARARA. The administrative headquarters of Ankole (q.v.) District and seat of the Ankole Kingdom Government during the colonial era. The post-1974 District of Mbarara consists of the eastern half of the former Ankole District. The town was a colonial creation, the administration and the missions (q.v.) positioning themselves near the royal enclosure of the Mugabe of Ankole. The town suffered severely during the War of Liberation (q.v.). Uganda's second university specializing in veterinary science is located at Mbarara.

MEDICINE. Traditional healers included diviners, bone-setters and herbalists, some of whose work was genuinely therapeutic. Until recently Westerners dismissed all traditional healing practices as superstitious because they were interwoven with traditional religious practices, and they were seen as unscientific and dangerous. Some doctors trained in Western medicine now have a better understanding of the beneficial aspects of traditional methods.

Even before the arrival of qualified medical practitioners, both A.M. Mackay (q.v.) and Fr Lourdel (q.v.) treated Ugandan patients with medicaments they had brought with them, and also attempted to treat Kabaka Mutesa I (q.v.) who probably suffered from gonorrhoea. Most missionaries gave what help they could, and qualified medical doctors visited occasionally or spent time in government service, but the beginnings of a proper medical service had to wait until 1897. That year saw a budget for a government Medical Department for the first time and the arrival of Dr (later Sir) Albert Cook (q.v.) of the Church Missionary Society (CMS) (q.v.). He established Mengo (q.v.) Hospital at Namirembe (q.v.), and a network of dispensaries and maternity centers was established around it. Mengo Hospital set up the first medical school in 1917 to train medical orderlies and dispensers. Women had been trained as nursing aides at Mengo from 1902 onwards, and in 1921 the formal training of midwives was begun. These helped to staff Mengo Hospital and maternity centers in the surrounding countryside. Kabarole Hospital at Fort Portal in Toro (q.v.) was begun under Dr Ashton Bond in 1903 and Ngora Hospital in Teso (q.v.) in 1922. Hospitals were also sited at Kuluva near Arua (q.v.) in 1951 by the Africa Inland Mission (q.v.) and at Amudat in Karamoja (q.v.) by the Bible Churchmen's Missionary Society (q.v.).

Although the Catholics (q.v.) started medical work a little later, they eventually established a more comprehensive network of hospitals with one at each major colonial-era district headquarters. Under the leadership of Mother Kevin (q.v.) a hospital was established at Nsambya (q.v.) where midwifery training was started in 1921. In 1955 the Medical Missionaries of Mary and in 1962 the Medical Mission Sisters came to supplement the medical work of the existing Catholic missions (q.v.). All the mission hospitals trained nurses to high standards.

The Government Medical Department's services for the general public stemmed from the work of three army doctors who were sent to Uganda in 1908. They established medical centers in Kampala (q.v.), Masaka (q.v.) and near Mityana. Mulago Hospital, which developed into the country's leading hospital and medical school (*see* Makerere University), was first opened in 1913 as a venereal diseases hospital. It was closed between 1914 and 1920 because of a shortage of medical staff. However, during World War I about 1,000 Ugandans were recruited into the African Native Medical Corps and received some medical training. Some of these men formed the core staff of Mulago when it was reopened. The first buildings had been of mud and wattle, but by 1960 bungalow wards in permanent building materials housed 650 beds. In 1962 New Mulago Hospital and Medical School was opened in fine buildings with 900 beds paid for with British aid as an independence gift. The old buildings continued to be used as well, and both hospitals frequently treated more in-patients than there were beds for.

As well as Mulago, the Protectorate government developed and ran hospitals throughout the country. During the 1960s President Obote (q.v.) planned the building of 22 further district and regional hospitals. Smaller units, health centers and dispensaries, were situated throughout the country, and few people were further than ten miles from one or another of these services. Uganda had a health service that was as good as any in tropical Africa.

Makerere Medical School has developed alongside Mulago Hospital. In 1936 a Certificate of Proficiency in Medicine was introduced for those who qualified in the Medical School. This was later superseded by the East African Diploma in Medicine and then in 1951 by the Licentiateship in Medicine and Surgery which was recognized by the General Medical Council of Great Britain in 1956. The first Ugandan woman doctor was Josephine Namboze who had been educated at Trinity College, Nabbingo (*see* Education), and who qualified in medicine in 1959, to be followed by many others. Among these is Dr Catherine Nyapidi Omaswa, an anesthetist of international repute. In 1963 the University of East Africa introduced its own medical degrees, and those who had qualified as Licentiates were able to convert their qualifications to the

MB ChB of the University of East Africa. Specialist post-graduate degrees were introduced in 1967. It was at Mulago that Dr Denis Burkitt (q.v.) recognized the viral cause of the lymphoma that was named after him. Nursing training is also carried on at Mulago, and nurses may qualify as Uganda Registered Nurses.

The insecurity of the 1970s and 1980s destroyed much of this. The expulsion (q.v.) of the Asians (q.v.) resulted in a huge loss of doctors, though the percentage of nurses to population continued to improve. Many Asian doctors worked in upcountry hospitals, so these suffered particularly badly. Ugandan doctors and support staff also fled the country in large numbers. Between 1960 and 1980 the ratio of doctors to population fell from 1:15,050 to 1:26,810 in spite of a huge increase in the number completing their training at Makerere Medical School during the 1960s, and in contrast to almost every other country in Africa. The crisis which resulted from the "economic war" (q.v.) waged by President Amin (q.v.) meant that supplies of drugs could not be maintained. The missions (q.v.) imported drugs through the joint Catholic-Protestant Medical Bureau when they were no longer able to get supplies through government sources. Apparatus broke down and was not repaired. In Kampala the water supply frequently failed and electricity became unreliable, with serious results for hygiene and hospitals. With the severe decline in medical services during the 1970s, recognition by the British General Medical Council of doctors trained at Makerere was withdrawn. When Amin was overthrown the country suffered an outbreak of looting in which some hospitals were stripped of everything movable. The situation did not improve during the first half of the 1980s. On top of this came the outbreak of the AIDS (q.v.) epidemic. By the 1990s the health services have picked up in spite of being near-swamped by the AIDS epidemic, and medical training at Makerere is believed to be better than that in a number of other African countries.

Sleeping sickness (q.v.) in the early years of the twentieth century and leprosy have both required special medical provision. The long-term care of leprosy patients and the pioneering of special services for deaf, blind and disabled people have all been carried out by the missions.

MEHTA, MAHENDRAKUMAR NANJIBHAI (1932–). Businessman, son of Nanji Kalidas Mehta, whose business empire was built around sugar estates at Lugazi started in 1922. The Mehta conglomerate had become the third largest business empire in Uganda by 1970, and in the 1940s the Mehta family donated £10,000 towards the cost of new buildings for Kampala (q.v.) municipal authority. M.N. Mehta was educated in Uganda, India and Britain. As well as his involvement in the family sugar businesses at Lugazi, the Uganda Sugar Factory, East African Sugar Industries Ltd and Mehta Sons Africa Ltd, he was a director of Uganda Tea Estates. He was forced to leave Uganda in 1972 when President Amin (q.v.) expelled the Asians (q.v.). Since Amin's overthrow work has been in progress to revive the sugar industry, and M.N. Mehta has been involved in this.

MENGO. The name of the capital (in Luganda, *kibuga*) of the Kabaka of Buganda (q.v.). In pre-colonial times the capital was moved from time to time. Kabaka Mutesa I (q.v.) had his capital at Rubaga (q.v.). Kabaka Mwanga (q.v.) moved it to Mengo where it twice caught fire, but was rebuilt, and it has remained there ever since. In the colonial era the municipality of Mengo was a large area to the west of Kampala (q.v.) including Namirembe (q.v.) where Mengo Hospital founded by Sir Albert Cook (q.v.) is situated, and Rubaga (q.v.), the Catholic (q.v.) mission headquarters. In 1967 Mengo became part of the city of Kampala.

MENGO, BATTLE OF *see* BATTLE OF MENGO

MILITARY COMMISSION. This was set up after the overthrow of President Amin (q.v.) in 1979. Neither Presidents Lule (q.v.) nor Binaisa (q.v.) was able to establish control over it. It ruled as a military junta under the Chairmanship of Paulo Muwanga (q.v.) between the ousting of President Binaisa (q.v.) and the return to power of President Obote (q.v.).

MILL HILL FATHERS. Formally called St Joseph's Foreign Missionary Society, this Roman Catholic (q.v.) mission was founded in 1886 by Cardinal Vaughan. Its mother house is at Mill Hill, London. Its members are a community of priests and lay brothers who are pledged to serve the missions entrusted to them by the Holy See. Work in Africa is only a small part of their work worldwide.

In the 1890s during the Wars of Religion (q.v.) Protestants (q.v.) were labeled Bangereza (English) and Catholics Bafransa (French). The Mill Hill Fathers were invited to Uganda to try and break this association. They arrived in 1895 under the leadership of Bishop Henry Hanlon (q.v.) and set up their headquarters at Nsambya (q.v.), in eastern Kampala (q.v.). They were made responsible for work to the east of Uganda and from there spread into Kenya (q.v.) as well. Their work has been shared by the Franciscan Sisters (*see* Franciscan Missionary Sisters and Mother Kevin). In Uganda the Mill Hill Fathers work in Eastern Buganda (q.v.), Busoga (q.v.), Bukedi (q.v.) and Teso (q.v.). Although the Sudanese Mutiny (q.v.) and the Rebellion of 1897 (q.v.) occurred soon after their arrival, by the time the Mill Hill Fathers arrived in Uganda the worst of the turbulence was past and they were able to build up their work in the relative quiet of the colonial period.

Bishop Hanlon was succeeded in 1912 by Bishop John Biermans as Vicar Apostolic of the Upper Nile, as the Mill Hill Mission's area was called. He had arrived in Uganda in 1897 and served in Uganda until 1924 when he was appointed Superior General of the mission.

Namilyango College and Mount St Mary's School, Namagunga (*see* Education), were founded by the Mill Hill Fathers and Franciscan Sisters, and a network of other schools and teacher training institutions was established in the area for which they were responsible. Nsambya Hospital, Kampala, and the leprosarium at Buluba have particularly fine reputations.

MISSIONS, CHRISTIAN. Uganda is unusual in Africa in that throughout the colonial period only two main churches, the Roman Catholic (q.v.) and the Anglican (q.v.), worked in the country. The (British) Church Missionary Society (CMS, Anglican) (q.v.) arrived first, in 1877. The mainly French Roman Catholic White Fathers (Société des Missionaires d'Afrique) (q.v.) founded by Cardinal Lavigerie (q.v.) arrived just under two years later in February 1879. The adherents of the two missions became identified as Bangereza (English) and Bafranza (French). In 1895 after the Wars of Religion (q.v.) the British encouraged the Dutch and English Mill Hill Fathers (q.v.) to begin work in an attempt to break down this stereotyping which was felt to be politically undesirable. In 1904 the Italian Catholic mission, the Verona Fathers (q.v.), started work in northern Uganda. They had been trying to work their way down the Nile (q.v.) towards the Great Lakes since the mid-nineteenth century. The three Catholic missions occupied different areas of Uganda: the White Fathers worked from the Kampala (q.v.) area at Rubaga (q.v.) out to the west and south; the Mill Hill Mission also had its headquarters in the Kampala area at Nsambya (q.v.), but worked outwards to the east; and the Verona Fathers confined their work to West Nile (q.v.), Acholi (q.v.) and Lango (q.v.) in northern Uganda. Two other conservative evangelical Anglican missions worked in Uganda: the Ruanda Mission, associated with the CMS, began work in Kabale (q.v.) in 1921 and the Bible Churchmen's Missionary Society (q.v.) began work in Karamoja (q.v.) in the 1930s. The Africa Inland Mission (q.v.), an inter-denominational, conservative evangelical society, agreed to send only Anglican missionaries to work in West Nile.

In 1926 one other denomination began work in Uganda, moving in from Kenya (q.v.): the Seventh Day Adventists (q.v.). Their work has always remained very small, but they make great demands on their adherents, who have a good name for living blameless lives, and they have a well-run hospital at Bushenyi in Ankole (q.v.). Since independence the Seventh Day Adventists have moved towards more contacts with other Christian denominations, and become more accepted by them.

A number of American missions, mostly of a fundamentalist persuasion, have begun work in Uganda. Most of these are small and are either Baptist or Pentecostalist.

The Orthodox Church is also found in Uganda. This was founded by Reuben Spartas (q.v.). Kenyan workers introduced a variety of independent churches, mainly into the Kampala area. In the late 1980s and 1990s missions have been run by individual German and American preachers who have often claimed to possess healing powers, but these have been one-shot affairs which have not sought to establish churches, though they have been critical of existing Christian institutions.

MITCHELL, SIR PHILIP EUEN (1890–1964). Governor of Uganda, 1935–1940. Before coming to Uganda, Mitchell had served in Nyasaland and Tanganyika (*see* Tanzania) and, during World War I, in the King's African Rifles (q.v.). He was fluent in three African languages and had been selected to implement indirect rule in Tanganyika.

On his arrival in Uganda he sought to revitalize and modernize the administration which he found old-fashioned. In Buganda (q.v.) he sought to widen the basis of representation, fearing that the Buganda government was insufficiently responsive to the people it was to serve. He was particularly concerned to develop the quality of African leadership, and believed in the need to build up an elite. To this end he set up a Commission under Earl de la Warr to enquire into Makerere College (q.v.). When this reported it recommended that Makerere should begin to work towards becoming a university for East Africa in buildings worthy of such an institution. This could not be accomplished without concomitant improvements in primary and secondary education (q.v.), and better prospects for educated Africans. Within two years funds had been found to set Makerere on its way.

Mitchell also believed that large-scale capital expenditure on development was needed if Uganda was to make real progress. A large loan was raised to improve the infrastructure, to provide better housing for African civil servants, and to improve cotton production and processing. The outbreak of World War II curtailed what could be done. Mitchell steered Uganda into becoming increasingly reliant upon her own resources rather than relying on imports. In 1940 Mitchell resigned to take up a special wartime appointment of Deputy Chairman of the Conference of East African Governors, and in 1945 he became Governor of Kenya (q.v.). Mitchell's *African Afterthoughts* (1945) reflects on his experiences in Uganda and elsewhere in East Africa.

MITI, JAMES (?–1949). Senior chief in Buganda (q.v.) and Bunyoro (q.v.), leader of the Bataka movements, and historian of Buganda. He first studied Islam (q.v.) before turning to Christianity. He narrowly escaped execution in the persecution of 1885–1887, the time of the Christian Martyrs (q.v.). In 1890 he became Mutaka (head, *see* Bataka) of the Genet clan in Mawokota county, but when this land passed to the Catholics (q.v.) in 1893 after the Wars of Religion (q.v.), he lost this land to a Catholic, though as a chief he held land elsewhere. When he tried to reclaim it through a court case some years later, he lost. In 1902 he was appointed to be saza (county) chief of Bujenje in Bunyoro, one of two Baganda (q.v.) senior chiefs sent to help administer Bunyoro where few people had had the educational opportunities open to the Baganda. Their presence, together with that of many other Baganda agents and minor chiefs, bred resentment which erupted in the Nyangire Rebellion (q.v.) of 1907. Although no more Baganda were appointed after this, Miti and others kept their positions. In 1912 the British administration was severely critical of him, finding him capable but autocratic and unreliable. By 1921 colonial district records show they had a better opinion of him than of most other saza chiefs.

On his return to Buganda he became a member of the Bataka Association (q.v.) and later of the Bataka Party (q.v.). This was involved in the Bataka Riots (q.v.) of 1949, the year in which Miti died.

MOSHI UNITY CONFERENCE. Soon after President Amin (q.v.) invaded the Kagera Salient (q.v.) in northern Tanzania (q.v.), ex-President Obote (q.v.) summoned leading exiled politicians to try to form a unified front which might be able to take over if and when Amin was toppled. The next few months demonstrated the lack of unity among the Ugandan exiles, and the reservations many of them had about supporting any move which might result in Obote resuming power.

President Nyerere of Tanzania, who had supported Obote, became increasingly aware that the ex-President was widely distrusted by Ugandans, and that Kenya (q.v.) would deplore any attempt to reinstate him as President. Meanwhile leaders of exile groups in Zambia and Kenya also prepared to meet to discuss future plans, and divisions among exiled Ugandans threatened to destroy any moves to decide on a post-Amin strategy. In March, after much lobbying and horse-trading, Tanzania agreed that a major conference of exiled politicians representing all shades of opinion should be held at Moshi under Tanzanian government sponsorship.

Far more people turned up at the conference than were allowed to be seated. No clear criteria for admission were laid down, but those who were excluded tended to be Obote-supporters and left-wingers. Otema Allimadi (q.v.), Paulo Muwanga (q.v.) and Godfrey Binaisa (q.v.) were among those who were at first excluded.

When the Moshi Unity Conference finally met on 23 March, Obote did not attend. Nyerere successfully persuaded him that he should send a delegation, but should stay out of the conference itself. Yusufu Lule (q.v.), a former Chairman of the Public Service Commission and Principal of Makerere University College (q.v.), emerged at the conference as the compromise candidate for the presidency.

On the first day the conference decided to form the Uganda National Liberation Front (UNLF) (q.v.) and reached agreement that there should be a National Consultative Council (NCC) with 30 members who would include representatives of all the groups which had come together at Moshi, and a National Executive Committee (NEC) which would supervise three commissions handling finance and administration, political and diplomatic affairs, and military affairs. Two groups of Obote's supporters boycotted day one of the conference, and there was great relief when they were persuaded, with the help of Tanzanian officials, to return on the second day, Obote himself agreeing that they should do so.

On day two agreement was reached over checks and balances. The UNLF Chairman's powers were to be carefully limited, and multi-party elections were to be held within two years. Edward Rugumayo was elected Chairman of the NCC. But there was an impasse over the Chairmanship of the NEC, the conference being equally and bitterly divided between those who supported Lule and those who supported Paulo Muwanga. In the end Lule was declared elected to the Chairmanship of the NEC and Paulo Muwanga was appointed Chairman of the Military Commission. This post was intended to be equal in importance to the Chairmanship of the NEC and Muwanga's appointment was to have disastrous consequences as he and the military arrogated to themselves undue power. President Julius Nyerere went to Moshi to congratulate the participants in the conference on its achievements.

But already the War of Liberation (q.v.) was drawing to a climax far sooner than had been expected. The participants did not have sufficient time to work through their plans and deal with the substantial differences which emerged, and the working misunderstandings which had enabled them to reach a show of unity, before they had to take over the government.

MOVE TO THE LEFT. In 1969 President Obote (q.v.) announced that Uganda would move in a more socialist direction. His new policies were outlined in five documents.

(1) *The National Service Proposal* (October 1969) proposed a two-year period of national service for every able-bodied person, which might be served for a continuous period of two years, or in annual three-month blocks. The proposal paid no regard to agricultural realities.

(2) *The Common Man's Charter* (December 1969) called for a program of nationalization which might even include the nationalization of mailo (q.v.) land and some privately-owned businesses. The document was long on rhetoric but somewhat short on practical proposals.

(3) *The Comunication from the Chair* (April 1970) proposed unified pay scales for state employees and sought to end some of their privileges.

(4) *The Nakivubo Pronouncement* (May 1970) refined aspects of the Common Man's Charter (q.v.). It proposed that the state should take 60 percent of the shares of some

84 firms. There were some surprising omissions and inclusions. It was also proposed that the right to strike should be abolished. Both proposals were bitterly opposed by those who would be adversely affected.

(5) *The "Three Plus One" proposal* concerned elections. Each member of the National Assembly (q.v.) would be required to seek election in three constituencies in addition to his home constituency in order to try and break down "tribal" politicking.

As with all five documents, this issue does not seem to have been fully thought through, and the attempt to form a coherent ideology came too late. Few of the proposals were carried out, and there was no time left to Obote for their effects to be tested. In the short term their economic impact was adverse as foreign investors took fright. The coup of 1971 (q.v.) put an end to this experiment in socialism.

MPANGA, JOYCE R. (1934–). Educationist and worker for women. Joyce Mpanga was educated at Gayaza High School (*see* Education) (where she was one of the first four girls to sit the Cambridge School Certificate), Makerere University College (q.v.) and the University of Indiana, USA. From 1958–1961 she taught at Gayaza High School and was then for a year a member of the Legislative Council (q.v.) before that ceased to exist at independence. She then returned to Gayaza as Deputy Headmistress. During the 1970s she worked for the newly-established Uganda Examinations Council. Under the government of President Museveni (q.v.) Joyce Mpanga became a member of the National Resistance Council (q.v.) for Mubende District and from 1987–1989 was Minister of State for Women's Affairs, when she was moved to be Minister of State for Primary Education until 1991. She has been Vice-President of the Uganda Teachers' Association and a member of the Executive Council of the Uganda Council of Women (q.v.), and is Chairman of Uganda Women's Effort to Save Orphans, an organization founded by Mrs Janet Museveni, wife of President Museveni.

MUGWANYA, STANISLAUS (1849–1938). Senior Roman Catholic (q.v.) chief among the Baganda (q.v.) and one of the regents during the minority of Kabaka Daudi Chwa (q.v.). Mugwanya was born at Bukeerere and in 1858 became a page at the court of Kabaka Mutesa I (q.v.) where his fine appearance and musical ability won him Mutesa's favor. He was appointed to be the Kabaka's elephant hunter in Kyagwe. He read Islam (q.v.) at court before the arrival of Christian missions (q.v.) and he was one of the first people to learn to read and write Arabic, but he did not become a Muslim, and by 1884 he had secretly begun to learn with the White Fathers (q.v.). At the time of the Christian martyrs (q.v.) Mugwanya was saved by his brother who held an important position. During the Wars of Religion (q.v.) he was a prominent Christian leader among the exiles in Kabula, and he won a reputation for bravery in the ensuing war. When the Christians won back power, he was rewarded by being appointed Kimbugwe, one of the most important chieftainships. After the Battle of Mengo 1892 (q.v.) he was one of the Catholic leaders in the negotiations leading to a settlement with the Protestants (q.v.). He and Apolo Kagwa (q.v.) were appointed Catholic and Protestant Katikiro respectively. When Kabaka Mwanga (q.v.) rebelled in 1897 and was deposed by the British, Mugwanya was appointed to one of the three regencies during the minority of Kabaka Daudi Chwa, and he also played a leading role in the negotiations leading up to the signing of the 1900 [B]Uganda Agreement (q.v.). He was then appointed Omulamuzi, Chief Justice of Buganda.

As leader of the Baganda Catholics Mugwanya was particularly interested in education (q.v.), in Namilyango College (which later moved to Kisubi), and St Peter's, Nsambya (q.v.). He paid the school fees for many boys, some of whom boarded in his home while they attended school. Kagwa, the senior Protestant chief, had received a knighthood and had traveled to England for the coronation of King Edward VII: the Catholics were not to be outdone. In 1912 Mugwanya was made a Papal Knight of the Order of St Sylvester for his services to the Catholic Church. In 1914

Bishop Hanlon (q.v.) took him to the Holy Land, Algeria (where the White Fathers [q.v.] had their headquarters), Rome, Paris and England, where he was received in audience by King George V. He wrote up his experiences in a book which he called *Ekitabo eky'Olugendo lwa Stanislaus Mugwanya, KGCSS, Omulamuzi we Buganda, mu Bulaya* (The Book of the Journey of Stanislaus Mugwanya, KGCSS, Chief Justice of Buganda, to England), published in 1914.

In 1915, when he was 65, Mugwanya asked to be allowed to retire, but both the Kabaka and the Governor urged him to stay on and he did not finally retire until 1921. Ten years later, when Kabaka Daudi Chwa inaugurated the Order of the Shield and the Spear, he was the first person to receive the award and in 1937 he was awarded the OBE by King George VI for his services to the Protectorate.

On his retirement he went back to Bukerere and acted as Muluka (parish) chief and guardian of his clan lands. Edward Frederick Mutesa (q.v.), son and heir of Kabaka Daudi Chwa, spent his school holidays at his home. He died on 28 November 1938 and was given a magnificent burial. His body was placed in a brass coffin, and the grave was half filled with ginned cotton as a mark of respect.

There is a substantial biography of Mugwanya in Luganda by Joseph Kasirye: *Obulamu bwa Stanislaus Mugwanya* (1963). A translation into English is held by the History Department, Makerere University.

MUHINDA *see* BAHINDA

MUHUMUZA. In c. 1895 Muhumuza, a wife of the Mwami (king) of Rwanda (q.v.), fled to Ndorwa when, after the death of the Mwami, her son failed to win backing in a war of succession. Ndorwa was largely occupied by agriculturalists reluctant to submit themselves to the Mwami and the ruling Tutsi pastoralist elite, and to the Germans who were the Mwami's patrons. Muhumuza built up a power base for herself by declaring herself to be possessed by Nyabingi (q.v.), and became a focus for resistance to the new Mwami's rule. She was arrested by the Germans in 1908, and imprisoned in Bukoba for two years. On her release Muhumuza made a bid to place her son on the throne of Rwanda. Because the Germans had recognized the incumbent Mwami, they considered Muhumuza to be a threat to their rule, and she failed in her attempt. Thwarted, she then tried to carve out a kingdom in Ndorwa for her son, promising people great wealth in cattle if they followed her, and immunity from harm: bullets fired against them would, she said, turn to water (cf. Alice Lakwena [q.v.]). But the British cooperated with the Germans and captured her near Kabale (q.v.). She was removed to Kampala (q.v.) in 1911, where she ended her days. A detailed and lively account of these events is given by Paul Ngologoza (q.v.) in *Kigezi and its People*. Attracted by Muhumuza's promises, Ngologoza was only prevented from joining the uprising by his mother's pleas.

MUKASA, HAM (1871–1956). Mukasa was brought up as a page at the court of Kabaka Mutesa I (q.v.) where he first studied Islam (q.v.). During the reign of Kabaka Mwanga (q.v.) he went to live with Nuwa Walukaga, the court blacksmith, where he learnt to read from a member of Nuwa's household. He narrowly escaped persecution at the time of the Christian martyrs (q.v.) by being hidden by a Christian chief on his country estate. After the martyrdoms he was pardoned by Mwanga and put in charge of the pages at the court, and was baptized in 1887. In the Wars of Religion (q.v.) he acquitted himself well by seizing two boats which were carrying arms for the Muslim (*see* Islam) faction, and he was wounded in the knee. In 1900 a commentary he had written in Luganda (*see* Languages) on St Matthew's Gospel was published. In 1902 he went as secretary to Katikiro Apolo Kagwa (q.v.) when he visited Britain to attend the coronation of King Edward VII, and wrote an account of the visit. This was translated into English and edited by the Revd Ernest Millar of the Church Missionary Society (q.v.) and published under the title *Uganda's Katikiro in England,* published in 1904. It has been re-edited by Taban lo Liyong and a shortened version published in 1975 as *Sir Apolo Kagwa Discovers Britain.*

In 1905 he was appointed to the important saza chieftaincy of Kyagwe with the title of Sekibobo with his headquarters at

Mukono fourteen miles east of Kampala (q.v.), and he gave to the church the land on which Bishop Tucker Theological College now stands. Here he continued to write. He visited England again in 1913 with Kabaka Daudi Chwa (q.v.), and made a record of that visit as well as a visit to Bukedi in 1917 and to Nairobi in 1927. These accounts remain in manuscript. His most important work was *Simuda Nyuma* (Don't Turn Back). This is a history in three volumes. The first deals with the reign of Kabaka Mutesa I (q.v.) and was published in 1938. The second volume covering the reign of Kabaka Mwanga was published in 1942. It deals extensively with the Christian martyrs. Volume III dealing with the Wars of Religion (q.v.) was lost, but a carbon copy of the manuscript original was found after his death, and is placed in the Archives at Makerere University (q.v.) together with large quantities of others of his papers. Some idea of his detailed and lively style can be deduced from the one work translated into English. He was an avid reader on many subjects, and liked to read several newspapers a day.

Although a noted preacher, he did not become ordained, but throughout his life he led morning and evening prayers for his household, and encouraged everyone to attend church on Sundays. He was also fascinated by timekeeping, and kept about 20 clocks. His first wife, Hanna Wawemuka, daughter of Mukasa, Katikiro of Kabaka Mutesa I, died in 1919. In the following year he married Sarah Nakibolo who outlived him.

MUKASA, MARJORIE NAJUMA (1905–   ). Leading churchwoman and worker on behalf of women and girls. She was educated at Gayaza High School (*see* Education). In 1957 she spent a year in Britain on a course on women's organizations and farming. From 1927–1935 she was Secretary of the Uganda Mothers' Union and its Vice-President from 1957–1960. She was a founder member of the Uganda Council of Women (q.v.), and for two years a member of its Executive Committee. She served on the Board of Directors of the Young Women's Christian Association (YWCA) (q.v.) and in 1961 became a member of its Membership Committee. She opened branches of the YWCA at Kakiri, Sentama, Nansansa and Kitagobwa. Among the other committees on which she served were the Kampala Girl Guides Committee, Gayaza Farm Committee and Discharged Prisoners' Aid Committee, and she was a trustee of this last organization.

MUKASA, SARAH (c. 1900–1989). Leading churchwoman and eminent worker on behalf of women. She was educated at Gayaza High School (*see* Education) and at Iganga Boarding School, and she then taught for a year before marrying Ham Mukasa (q.v.). From 1920–1935 she was Secretary of the Mothers' Union, Vice-President from 1938–1943, and President from 1943–1953. In 1938 she was made a Life-Governor of the Church Missionary Society (q.v.). From 1935–1942 she was a member of the Board of Governors of Gayaza High School, and she also served on the Boards of Governors of Bishop Tucker Theological College at Mukono and Mengo Hospital. In 1953 she became a life member of the Young Women's Christian Association (YWCA) (q.v.) and its Chairman in 1959. In 1947 she became a member of the Uganda Council of Women (q.v.) and served the organization for many years. From 1962–1966 she served on the Kyagwe [County] Council.

MUKIRANE, ISAYA. Leader of the Rwenzururu Movement (q.v.).

MULIRA, ERIDADI MEDADI KASIRYE (c. 1917–). Educated at King's College, Budo (*see* Education), Makerere College (q.v.), Achimota and London University. He worked for a short time in the 1940s as editor of the Luganda (*see* Languages) newspaper *Ebifa,* and from 1953–1961 was proprietor and for a while editor of *Uganda Empya,* another Luganda paper. In 1948 he was an East African representative to the first meeting of the World Council of Churches. He played a key role during the Deportation Crisis (q.v.) when, as a member of the Lukiiko (Buganda parliament) he was involved in negotiating the Kabaka's return. He was both a member of the delegation to London and a member of the Namirembe Conference. He also had business interests.

In 1955 Mulira founded the Progressive Party (q.v.), a mainly Baganda (q.v.) party, and was its President from

1955–1959. He was critical of the chiefs, whom he accused of ignoring the plight of the poor, and tried to work out what genuinely representative and democratic government might mean in Uganda. When the Lukiiko tried to arrange the distribution of 196 square miles of mailo (q.v.) which had still not been allocated from the time of the [B]Uganda Agreement (q.v.), he declared that such land should belong to all, not be the personal property of individuals, and this point of view eventually won the day. Mulira was expelled from the Lukiiko in a complex row arising out of this issue, though his expulsion was later reversed. When the Progressive Party ceased to exist, Mulira moved to the Uganda National Movement and was temporarily exiled to northern Uganda after this was proscribed because of the violence which accompanied the Trade Boycott of 1959 (q.v.) which it had organized. Mulira then became publicity secretary of Kabaka Yekka (q.v.). With the collapse of Kabaka Yekka, he dropped out of politics, a highly principled man who failed to find a following. He was the author of a number of publications in English and Luganda, including *No Constitution Without the Sovereignty of the People* (n.d.), *Thoughts of a Young African* (1945), *Troubled Uganda* (1950), and *The Vernacular in African Education* (1951). He also contributed to *A Luganda Grammar* (1954), the standard grammar of the language and considered to be one of the best grammars of any Bantu language published up till then.

MULIRA, REBECCA MUKASA ALLEN (c. 1920–). A churchwoman who has been active in local government, public service and work for women. She was educated at Gayaza High School (*see* Education) and briefly in London. From 1947–1962 she was President of the Busoga Diocese Young Wives' Group and Treasurer of the Mothers' Union at national level from 1957–1959. She was a Director of the Young Women's Christian Association (YWCA) (q.v.) for many years from 1953, and in 1964 was made Chairman of its Public Relations Committee. In 1958 she attended the inaugural meeting of the All Africa Conference of Churches in Nigeria.

Her interest in working for women was not confined to the

Mungonya, Zakariya C. K. / 265

church. She was Leader of the Uganda African Women's League from 1953–1959, became National President of the Uganda Council of Women (q.v.) in 1963, and was made an honorary Life President in 1964. In that year she attended the Jerusalem Conference on the Role of Women in the Struggle for Peace and Development. In 1967 she attended the Executive Committee Meeting of the International Council of Women in London and also the International Seminar on Population Growth and Development.

In 1962 she became a member of the Mengo (q.v.) Municipal Council and of the West Mengo Regional Council in 1967. From 1962–1965 she served on the Kampala (q.v.) City Council. Among her public service appointments have been membership of the Board of Governors of Gayaza High School 1953–1964, Uganda Broadcasting Advisory Board, 1954–1960, and General Hospital Advisory Board from 1956–.

MUNGONYA, ZAKARIYA C. K. (1900–1981). Educated at Mbarara High School (*see* Education) and Makerere College (q.v.), he became a teacher. From 1937–1942 he was Treasurer and from 1948–1955 he was Enganzi (chief minister) of the Ankole (q.v.) Kingdom Government. In 1955 he entered the Legislative Council (q.v.) and was the first Ugandan to be appointed to a ministry: he was Minister of Land and Tenure from 1955 until his retirement in 1961. He had wide interests and continued to play a leading role in Ankole public life in retirement.

MUNSTER COMMISSION (RELATIONSHIPS COMMISSION). This Commission, headed by the Earl of Munster, was set up in 1960 to advise on the relationship between central government and the regions of Uganda after independence. With regard to Buganda (q.v.) it recommended that there should be direct elections to the Lukiiko (local parliament of Buganda); a division of powers between the Lukiiko and the National Assembly (q.v.) on matters relating to Buganda; and that Buganda should be constitutionally required to provide representatives to the National Assembly, but that it should be left to the Lukiiko to decide whether these should be directly elected or nominated by the Lukiiko. The Commission also recommended that a referendum should be held in the "Lost Counties" (q.v.) and in one other county transferred to Buganda from Bunyoro (q.v.) under the 1900 [B]Uganda Agreement (q.v.), to determine whether the inhabitants wanted to remain within Buganda or be reincorporated into Bunyoro (however, the question of the Lost Counties was deferred until after independence). For Toro (q.v.), Bunyoro, Ankole (q.v.) and Busoga (q.v.), the Commission recommended a semi-federal relationship which preserved the status of their rulers and protected local customs, but otherwise placed them in the same relationship to central government as the non-agreement districts. These recommendations formed the basis for the Constitutional Conference (q.v.) held in September 1961.

MUSAZI, IGNATIUS KANGAYE (1905–). Politician and trade unionist. The son of a middle-ranking chief in Bulemezi county, Musazi was educated at Mengo High School (*see* Education) and St Augustine's, Canterbury. He taught at King's College, Budo, and then worked in the Education Inspectorate before turning to politics. He was chief organizer and first Secretary of the Bana ba Kintu (Sons of Kintu), an early Baganda (q.v.) political association founded in 1938, another of whose leading spirits was Reuben Spartas (q.v.). Its aim was to voice the complaints of ordinary people such as farmers and traders, and it campaigned against the acquisition by the state of mailo (q.v.) land for Makerere College (q.v.). It sought to oust members of the Buganda government such as Katikiro Martin Luther Nsibirwa (q.v.) who were seen to be over-subservient to the Protectorate authorities, and it succeeded in rousing people at the parish level. Resentment against the Buganda government festered throughout World War II. In 1940–1941 Musazi spent a year in jail for forgery. When faced with the Riots of 1945 (q.v.) which were precipitated by low wages and economic recession, the Protectorate government saw in them a subversive conspiracy, and Musazi was one of a group of political leaders who were sent into internal exile.

Earlier in 1938 Musazi had helped to found the Uganda

Motor Drivers' Association, the first trade union (q.v.) in Uganda. In 1946 he was released from deportation and was back in politics organizing farmers' groups. These later developed into the Uganda African Farmers' Union which overlapped with the Bataka Party (q.v.), and campaigned against the low price paid to growers for cotton and for African participation in cotton ginning. After the Bataka Riots (q.v.) the Bataka Party and the Uganda African Farmers' Union were banned. Musazi then founded the Federation of Partnerships which went bankrupt in 1950, but out of which developed the neo-traditional and largely Baganda Uganda National Congress (q.v.) which Musazi founded in London two years later with Abu Mayanja (q.v.), becoming a member of its Central Committee. When visiting London on the issue of cotton marketing he had gotten to know George Padmore and the British socialist Fenner Brockway who helped in founding the new party. Musazi was also a member of the Legislative Council (q.v.). By 1959 his alleged high-handedness and the issues of Pan-Africanism and nationalism tore the party apart. Musazi, who was not radical enough for many, was expelled. In 1959 he, E.M.K. Mulira (q.v.) and Augustine Kamya formed the Uganda National Movement which organized the Trade Boycott (q.v.) of non-African businesses in Buganda. Musazi and Mulira were deported to northern Uganda and the Uganda National Movement was proscribed. Finally in 1961 Musazi joined the Baganda royalist Kabaka Yekka (q.v.) movement.

MUSEVENI, YOWERI KAGUTA (1944–). President of Uganda, 1986– . His family is from Mpororo, once an independent principality, now a part of Kigezi (q.v.). Museveni was educated at Mbarara High School, Ntare V School, Mbarara (*see* Education), and Dar es Salaam University in Tanzania (q.v.). He married Janet Kataha in 1972. In 1969 he was in Mozambique with FRELIMO which was fighting for independence, a formative experience. In 1970–1971 he was a Research Assistant in President Obote's (q.v.) Office in Uganda. He became an exile in Tanzania after the coup which brought President Amin (q.v.) to power, and from 1972 onwards he organized the Front for National

Salvation (FRONASA) (q.v.), but this achieved little. However, a group of Ugandan exiles, including FRONASA, accompanied the Tanzanian army which overthrew Amin in 1979. He held a variety of positions under Presidents Lule (q.v.) and Binaisa (q.v.) including the Vice-Presidency of the Military Commission (q.v.) which deposed Binaisa.

In the disputed Elections of 1980 (q.v.) he founded the Uganda Patriotic Movement (q.v.) and stood for Mbarara North, but both he and his movement were heavily defeated in spite of a thoughtful manifesto. Asserting that the election results had been rigged, he took to the bush with a handful of men, determined to resist Obote. In 1981 he became Vice-Chairman of the National Resistance Movement (NRM) (q.v.), and then its Chairman after the death of ex-President Lule (q.v.). The NRM was strictly disciplined and won the trust of the people in the areas where fighting took place, and went on to fight its way to power in spite of the attempts of President Moi of Kenya (q.v.) to work out a peace agreement.

The NRM entered Kampala (q.v.) 14 years to the day after the Amin coup, and Museveni was sworn in as President on 29 January 1986. His Ten Point Programme (q.v.) outlined his political objectives for Uganda's return to good government, respect for human rights, and economic development. In spite of his earlier socialism, his politics, once in office, have been essentially pragmatic, and the Ten Point Programme promised a mixed economy.

Within a few months of coming to power, Museveni found himself faced by armed insurrection in the north and east of the country. Despite his own commitment to disciplining the army (*see* Uganda National Liberation Army) and restoring respect for human rights, it has proved difficult to control the activities of an army that had to be rapidly expanded. Like his predecessors in the presidency, Museveni has found himself hampered by being dependent on the army for power. Insurrection was reduced by military victories and by amnesties, but both it and banditry proved difficult to eradicate. In 1993 a scheme for buying in weapons looked promising.

Under Museveni there was a return to a form of limited democracy, with elections in 1989 (q.v.) to the National Resistance Councils (q.v.), the highest level of which functions as the National Assembly (q.v.). The old political parties, the Uganda People's Congress (q.v.) and the Democratic Party (q.v.), which had divided the country along largely sectarian lines, were forbidden to campaign in an effort to avoid the bitterness and violence of the Elections of 1980 (q.v.), although their members were permitted to stand for election as individuals. In 1993 a new draft constitution (q.v.) was published and elections scheduled for April 1994.

MUSLIM MARTYRS. Although variously dated by early European and Baganda (q.v.) writers, the consensus among historians now is that the Muslim martyrdoms took place in 1876 soon after the departure of H.M. Stanley (q.v.) from the court of Kabaka Mutesa I (q.v.). A variety of reasons emerge which led Mutesa to turn against the Muslim converts at his court. In 1876 Muslim teachers arrived from Egypt who were stricter in their observance of Islam (q.v.) than those from the East African coast. They insisted that the mosques were wrongly aligned and must be rebuilt, that meat not killed by Muslims must be avoided, that the Kabaka had disobeyed Islamic law by eating pork, and that he should not lead prayers because he was uncircumcised. Many Muslim courtiers absented themselves from prayers led by Mutesa and attended those led by a circumcised imam. All this gave great offense at court.

This insult to the Kabaka may have been the last straw. Traditionalist chiefs encouraged the Kabaka's suspicions of young men who seemed to be slipping out of his control. Stanley's visit, and the presence of Dallington Scopion Maftaa (q.v.), a Christian from Zanzibar, offered the Kabaka a religious alternative. The Kabaka turned on the Muslims, a purge was ordered, and the executioners slaughtered 70 courtiers and perhaps a thousand other people. Some Baganda (q.v.) Muslims were able to escape with Arab caravans to the coast. Ham Mukasa (q.v.) recognized that they suffered for their faith in much the same way that the Christian martyrs (q.v.) did ten years later. There is a mosque-shrine where the Muslim martyrs are commemorated close to the Christian shrines at Namugongo (q.v.), the official place of execution.

MUTESA I, MUKAABYA WALUGEMBE (1838–1884). Kabaka of Buganda (*see* Baganda), 1857–1884. Mutesa succeeded Kabaka Suna after a succession struggle, taking the name Mutesa only when he came to the throne. He learnt Arabic from the Muslim Swahili and Arab traders (*see* Islam) from the coast who had traded with Buganda since the middle of the nineteenth century, and partially adopted Islam: the horror of the Baganda for bodily mutilation, as well as a belief that anyone who caused the Kabaka physical harm was worthy of death, prevented him, and many other Baganda, from being circumcised. Although respected by Baganda for ruling wisely, particularly during the latter half of his reign when he had to deal with external forces, Mutesa was ruthless in repressing his enemies, and executions were common at this court.

In 1862 the European travelers Speke (q.v.) and Grant arrived at Mutesa's capital, both of whom were impressed by its sophistication and wealth. By the mid-1860s the court was becoming Islamized, and Ramadan was observed in 1865–1867, though Islam made little real progress outside the capital. In 1869 there was an exchange of embassies between Buganda and the Sultan of Zanzibar. Trade goods reached the Kabaka's court in greater quantities and Arab dress was worn at court. Islam reached its zenith in 1875 when Kabaka Mutesa ordered all his subjects to follow Islam on pain of death. Knowing little of what Islam meant, but aware that ablutions before prayers were important, many Baganda, as a token of their obedience to the Kabaka's decree, put large stones outside their doors on which people could stand when washing their feet, but this was not always enough to save them from overzealous officials.

The 1870s were dominated by the threat of Egyptian expansion, particularly after Baker (q.v.) had clashed with Kabarega (q.v.), Mukama of Bunyoro (q.v.). In 1874 Gordon sent the American Chaillé Long to visit Mutesa. Mutesa appealed to Charles Gordon (General Gordon of Khartoum) on Kabarega's behalf, fearing that he would be the next victim of Egyptian expansion, and not realizing that Gordon was also employed by the Khedive. However, Gordon was deterred from pressing further southwards for a variety of reasons. In 1875 Stanley (q.v.) visited Mutesa on his circumnavigation of Lake Victoria (q.v.), and was as impressed by him and his court as Speke and Grant had been. Stanley sent word to England that Mutesa would welcome Christian missionaries. Although genuinely interested in religion, Mutesa's real concern was to secure his position against Egyptian encroachment: an alliance with Europeans might be advantageous because of their superior firearms. He replaced a Turkish by an English flag given him by Stanley. It was probably in 1876 that he executed a large number of Baganda Muslims (*see* Muslim Martyrs) who had refused to eat meat killed by the Kabaka's butcher on the grounds that it had not been ritually slaughtered. In the tense political situation, Mutesa construed this as a challenge to his absolute power, and therefore dangerous.

In 1877 missionaries sent by the Church Missionary Society (CMS) (q.v.) arrived in Uganda. Death and illness prevented any real work until 1879 when the first White Fathers (q.v.) also arrived. Mutesa insisted that both groups should stay close to the court, listened to both, and made them defend their different versions of the Christian faith. He himself kept aloof from Christianity, though he did not prevent his subjects from learning with the missions (q.v.). Mutesa accepted the British missionaries' urgings to send an embassy to England in 1879, and received gifts from Queen Victoria.

By this time Mutesa was seriously ill, probably with gonorrhea, and when his own priests and medicine men failed to relieve him, he was glad to avail himself of the missionaries' remedies, though these were only palliative, no cure being available. In his final illness he accepted Arab medicine: those who administered it set it about with so many conditions that if he failed to recover, they could not be blamed. Inevitably it failed to work, and Mutesa I died in 1884, having committed himself to none of the new faiths which were now claiming adherents among his subjects, but having succeeded in keeping his kingdom intact and strong in spite of external threats.

MUTESA II, SIR EDWARD FREDERICK WILLIAM WALUGEMBE (1924–1969). Kabaka of Buganda (*see* Baganda), 1939–1966; President of Uganda, 1962–1966. He was educated at King's College, Budo (*see* Education). He also spent a year at Makerere College (q.v.) and attended a course of specially arranged study at Cambridge before being commissioned in the Grenadier Guards. His father, Kabaka Daudi Chwa (q.v.), died in 1939 while Mutesa was still at Budo. Mutesa was acclaimed as his successor and was ceremonially installed as Kabaka, but since he was still a minor, regents were appointed. When he came of age in 1942 he was crowned in ceremonies in Namirembe (q.v.) Cathedral and on Budo Hill, the traditional place for coronations in Buganda.

Only after his return to Uganda from Cambridge and his marriage in 1948 to Damali Kisosonkole did he take up his duties as Kabaka. He found himself caught between the demands of his traditional role as Kabaka of Buganda and the demands of the Protectorate authorities. He was the head of a state-within-a-state which was trying to retain privileges the extent of which were sometimes overstated, and which were resented by other Ugandans. Many Baganda wanted progress towards greater democracy and modernized institutions at the same time as keeping ancient privileges. The difficulties of the situation were illustrated by the riots of 1945 (q.v.) when Mutesa supported the modernizing Kulubya (q.v.) whose financial reforms were resented. The Bataka Party (q.v.) attacked Mutesa for being a tool of the British, though the British were slow to defend him at the time of the Bataka Riots of 1949 (q.v.).

Mutesa offended much Christian opinion by his affair with the wife of E.M.K. Mulira (q.v.), who filed a case against him in the High Court for seducing her, and by what they considered his riotous lifestyle. By the beginning of the 1950s Mutesa had become somewhat unpopular.

The Deportation Crisis (q.v.) changed all that. A suggestion by the British Colonial Secretary that "closer union" (q.v.) between the three East African territories was on some future agenda, sparked this off. The Kabaka and the Buganda government refused to accept the assurances they were given, and when Mutesa refused to cooperate with demands of Governor Sir Andrew Cohen, he was deemed to have broken the [B]Uganda Agreement (q.v.) and was exiled to London. The quarrel leading to the deportation occurred on an issue over which he had widespread support from his people, and the likely Baganda response to the deportation seems to have been underestimated by Cohen. When Mutesa was allowed to return to Uganda less than two years later, both he personally and the office he held were venerated as never before by the Baganda who turned out in their thousands to greet him.

In 1960 to 1962 Buganda's semi-federal status within Uganda caused great difficulties in the runup to independence, and a political party emerged in Buganda, Kabaka Yekka ("the Kabaka only") (q.v.) to defend Buganda's privileges. Its leaders were able to draw on the greatly enhanced respect for the Kabaka and his office which had resulted from the Deportation Crisis (q.v.). Milton Obote (q.v.) realized that the only way he could win an election was through forging an alliance between his Uganda People's Congress (UPC) (q.v.) and Kabaka Yekka, which he successfully did. As a result he came to power in 1962 as Prime Minister, and Kabaka Mutesa was Uganda's first President.

Mutesa was then required to fill two conflicting roles. As Kabaka of Buganda he was pledged to preserve Buganda's and his own privileged status; as President he should have worked for the good of Uganda as a unitary state. He failed to fulfill this second role. This failure was apparent in 1964 over the Lost Counties (q.v.). When they voted to return to Bunyoro (q.v.), Mutesa refused to sign the Acts formalizing this.

The final showdown between Mutesa and the Baganda on the one hand, and Obote and the central government on the other, came in 1964. Obote preempted a possible coup by arresting five ministers (q.v.), suspending the 1962 Constitution (q.v.) and assuming all state powers himself, thus usurping the President's powers. By this time Obote no longer needed the support of the Baganda. When the Buganda government ordered the central government off the soil of Buganda and barricaded the roads, Obote retaliated by sending the army under Amin (q.v.) against the *Lubiri* (the Kabaka's palace) on 24 May (*see* Battle of Mengo 1966). The Kabaka escaped over the back wall and made his way to Britain with one or two companions.

Mutesa died in London of alcohol poisoning three years later on 21 November 1969 aged 45. In Buganda local newspapers announced his death by poisoning, omitting the reference to alcohol, and many people came to believe that he had been deliberately poisoned. Others refused to believe that he was dead, and yet others came to believe that he would rise from the dead to rule his people once again. After the coup of 1971 (q.v.) when Amin seized power, the Baganda demanded the return of his body, and many hoped for the restoration of the kingdom. One reason why Amin allowed the return of his body may have been to scotch the myths that had come to surround him. His son, Ronald Mutebi, was allowed to return to Buganda and was installed as head of the clans, but not as Kabaka, and then returned to exile in Britain until 1993 when President Museveni (q.v.) allowed the restoration of the kings as cultural, not political, heads.

Mutesa's autobiography, *Desecration of My Kingdom* (1967), is partisan, but is nevertheless a useful document. It reveals Mutesa as somewhat self-indulgent, overconscious of his rank, and with a narrowly Buganda-centered outlook, a slightly tragic figure, unable to rise to the demands of the situation in which he found himself.

MUTINY OF 1897 *see* SUDANESE MUTINY

MUTINY OF 23 JANUARY 1964. In 1964, just after the three East African countries, Kenya (q.v.), Uganda and Tanzania (q.v.), had achieved independence, the armies of all three mutinied. Precisely why all three armies mutinied and how much coordination there was between them has never been fully explained. The Presidents of all three countries called in British troops who put down the mutinies with embarrassing ease. The three governments then dealt quite differently with the aftermath. In Tanzania the army was disbanded and a People's Defence Force created which would assist in social development as well as being trained in defense; Kenya rejected outright any negotiation with the mutinous troops, retained a British military presence, kept the size of the army small until the 1980s, and built up a highly professional and disciplined force. The Uganda government gave in to most of the mutineers' demands.

The Minister of Defence, Felix Onama, sent by President Obote (q.v.) to deal with the mutineers, was held captive by them, and gave the mutineers much of what they wanted before British troops arrived. A major cause of disaffection was the extent of British control still remaining in the army, and the number of British personnel was progressively reduced. The evidence suggests that soldiers were promoted from the ranks far too fast.

Three hundred of the mutineers were dismissed, but were later reinstated, and several were imprisoned at Luzira, but otherwise they went unpunished. Huge pay rises had already been agreed on, and were back-dated to 1 January 1964. By February the number of African commissioned officers had risen from 18 to 55. Among them was Idi Amin (q.v.) who was promoted from temporary Major to Lieutenant Colonel in command of signals at Army Headquarters in a matter of months.

The government put in hand some measures designed to control the army (*see* Uganda Army) better. The General Service Unit (q.v.) was created under the command of Akena Adoko (q.v.), a paramilitary unit which acted as something of a counter-weight to the army, and Army Headquarters were moved from Jinja (q.v.) to Mbuya on the outskirts of Kampala (q.v.). But later events demonstrated all too clearly that the army was never brought under adequate control.

MUWANGA, PAULO (1924–1991). Vice-President of Uganda, 1980–1985. Born in Nyondo, in Mpigi District of Buganda. After completing primary school he became a post office clerk, and in the 1950s moved into politics. He was a founder member of the Uganda People's Congress (UPC) (q.v.) and played a leading role in it in the runup to independence. In the 1960s he became Ambassador to Egypt and from 1969–1971 was Chief of Protocol for the Uganda government.

Under President Amin (q.v.) he was Ambassador to France from 1971–1973, where he allegedly sold the contents of the embassy before fleeing to Tanzania (q.v.) to join the exiled President Obote (q.v.) for two years before making his way to London where he ran a fish and chips shop. In 1977 he rejoined Obote in Tanzania and returned to Uganda when Amin was overthrown to become Chairman of the Military Commission (q.v.).

At the time of the Elections of 1980 (q.v.) he intervened during the count and ordered that no results be announced except through himself as the Chairman of the Military Commission, a move which ensured that the elections were believed to have been rigged in Obote's favor (*see* also Commonwealth Observer Group). During Obote's second presidency he was Minister of Defence and Vice-President. As the former, he must bear a share of the responsibility for the atrocities perpetrated against the civilian population. His own home area, Mpigi, suffered severely in those years. In 1985 he changed his allegiance and joined Basilio Okello (q.v.) and Tito Okello (q.v.) when they overthrew Obote in a putsch, becoming Prime Minister briefly. When President Museveni (q.v.) came to power in 1986, Muwanga appeared before the Human Rights Commission (q.v.) charged first with treason and then with murder, and brazened it out during his interrogation. He was imprisoned, but it proved impossible to make charges stick against him, and he was released in October 1990 because he was terminally ill with diabetes. He died, a rich man, on 1 April 1991. An obituary in the London *Times* spoke of his "reign of terror," and the *Guardian* described him as "one of Africa's most ruthless politicians."

MWANGA, DANIERI (c. 1865–1904). Kabaka of Buganda (*see* Baganda), 1884–1899. As a ruler his lack of judgement and inability to cope with the complex situation created by the arrival of new influences and the factionalism which these exacerbated plunged Buganda into crisis and permanently altered the course of its history.

He was the eventual winner in the disputed succession to Kabaka Mutesa I (q.v.). The early years of his reign were marked by a series of catastrophic fires and epidemics, and he failed to gain the unquestioning allegiance of all of the various factions at court. These included older men who had achieved power under Mutesa, and the younger followers of the new faiths, Islam (q.v.) and both Protestant (q.v.) and Catholic (q.v.) Christianity. These all jockeyed for influence and promotion. Mwanga's insecurity was increased when he heard that a European (Bishop Hannington [q.v.]) was approaching Buganda through the "back door" of Busoga (q.v.): local superstition held that anyone who used that route would bring trouble to Buganda. There followed the martyr-doms (*see* Christian Martyrs) of Hannington and of some 50 Christians whose names are still known and up to 150 others, until in 1887 even those traditionalist chiefs who opposed Christianity warned Mwanga that this slaughter could not continue: he was cutting down the flower of young manhood.

Mwanga then turned to the younger men and adherents of the new faiths, and tried to build out of them a group whose whole loyalty would be to him, but his mishandling of the situation led straight to the Wars of Religion (q.v.) in which the three politico-religious parties first combined to seize power from him and then fought among themselves until the Christians were driven out, and he was forced into exile with the White Fathers (q.v.) at the southern end of Lake Victoria (q.v.). When they finally fought their way back to power they found that they needed Mwanga to legitimize their rule. Because at that juncture Mwanga seemed to be leaning towards Catholicism, the Catholics found themselves at a slight advantage. Finally the fragile truce between Protes-tants and Catholics broke down at a time when Captain Lugard (q.v.) of the Imperial British East Africa Cmpany (q.v.) had arrived in the country. Assisted by firearms given out by Lugard the Protestants were victorious in the Battle of Mengo 1892 (q.v.). A British Protectorate was declared shortly afterwards. In the new order of things imposed by the victorious Protestants and by the British, Mwanga's powers were limited.

Mwanga did not follow the example of his leading sub-jects and convert to any of the new faiths, but fretted under the new restraints and inclined to the traditionalists. In 1897 he and the traditionalist chiefs rebelled against the British. The Christian chiefs supported the British authorities in resisting the rebellion of 1897 (q.v.). The Christian chiefs supported the British to suppress the rebellion, and Mwanga took refuge with Mukama Kabarega (q.v.) of Bunyoro (q.v.). They were on the run for two years and were finally captured in south Lango (q.v.) hiding in the marshes on the edge of Lake Kyoga, from where both were taken into captivity and exiled to the Seychelles. They were accompanied into exile by Christian teachers, and Mwanga was baptized with the name Daniel, the Old Testament prophet who was flung into the den of lions. Meanwhile his infant son, Daudi Chwa (q.v.), succeeded him under a regency of three leading chiefs. Mwanga was allowed to return to Uganda in 1903 but died only a few months after his return home. As he had been baptized, he was given a Christian burial.

-N-

NADIOPE, SIR WILLIAM WILBERFORCE KADHUMBULA (1910–). Kyabazinga (constitutional head and quasi-king) of Busoga (*see* Basoga), 1949–1955, 1962–1967; Vice-President of Uganda, 1963–1966. He was born into a princely family and was educated at Busoga College (*see* Education) and Trent College in Britain. He did military service during World War II. From 1958 he became a member of the Legislative Council (q.v.) and helped to form the Uganda People's Union, a grouping of unofficial Legco members. Nadiope became a member of the Uganda People's Congress (UPC) (q.v.) led by Milton Obote (q.v.) and an influential member of its Executive Committee. However, in 1966 when there was a showdown between Buganda (q.v.) and the central government, Nadiope was accused by Obote of having colluded with Kabaka Mutesa II (q.v.) in approaching Britain for help against the unconstitutional action of Obote's government. In 1967, when the kingdoms were abolished, Nadiope lost his position and retired as a private person.

NAIROBI ACCORDS. The agreement signed on 17 December 1985 between the National Resistance Movement (NRM) (q.v.), Tito Okello (q.v.) and Basilio Okello (q.v.) and a number of other Ugandan groups. Talks had been held under the chairmanship of President Daniel arap Moi of Kenya (q.v.) in an attempt to bring to an end the guerrilla war waged by the NRM under the leadership of Yoweri Museveni (q.v.). Museveni only signed the Accords under great international pressure. They would have given the NRM a say in a broadly-based government, but not a sufficiently command-ing position to be sure of carrying through its program of reform. The goverment of national unity outlined in the Accords brought together many bitterly-opposed factions and it is doubtful that it could have worked. In the event the NRM was so close to victory that the Accords were ignored. President Moi was angered by this and afraid of Museveni's past socialism. Relations between Kenya and Uganda were bad for more than two years. A small group composed mostly of exiles refused to accept the NRM victory and continues to call for the implementation of the Nairobi Accords.

NAKULABYE MASSACRE. On 10 November 1964 the police were called to a nightclub brawl at Nakulabye in Kampala (q.v.). The incident was grossly mishandled. The police eventually admitted to shooting dead six people; it was generally believed that the number was at least three times that. It was the first of the violent incidents which have marred Uganda's history since independence.

NAMIREMBE. The headquarters of the Church Missionary Society (q.v.) and the Church of Uganda (q.v.). The mission was early established on this site which lies close to the palace of the Kabaka of Buganda (q.v.). Mengo High School (*see* Education), which grew out of an existing central school, was opened in 1905, and Mengo Hospital (*see* Medicine) in 1897 by Dr Albert Cook (q.v.). A series of cathedrals has stood on the top of the hill: the first was made of reeds, palm trees and thatch and blew down in a storm in 1894 two years after it was built. The second similarly constructed cathedral was taken down in 1901 to make way for a more permanent building with brick walls and a thatched roof. This was consecrated in 1904 but destroyed by fire after being struck by lightning in 1910. The present one of brick with a tiled roof was consecrated in 1919. The Archbishop of Uganda has his residence on the hill and the Church of Uganda's Provincial Secretariat is situated there. Bishop Hannington (q.v.), Alexander Mackay (q.v.) and Archbishop Janani Luwum (q.v.) are buried in the cathedral churchyard among other pioneer missionaries and Ugandan dignitaries.

NAMUGONGO MASSACRE. Namugongo is the Buganda (q.v.) execution site where the Muslim martyrs (q.v.) were executed in 1876 and some of the Christian martyrs (q.v.) ten years later. On 23 May 1984 during the second presidency of Milton Obote (q.v.) the Uganda National Liberation Army (UNLA) (q.v.) massacred some one hundred students at a Church of Uganda (q.v.) theological college at Namugongo and villagers living in the neighborhood. The dead included the Principal, the Revd Godfrey Bazira, whose mutilated body was found nearby. Several other people were arrested, held in military custody and tortured before being released without charge. The UNLA soldiers said they suspected the seminary of harboring guerrillas. They left slogans signed ''UNLA Boys'' scrawled on the walls threatening death to all Christians, whom they accused of assisting guerrillas. The UNLA also murdered Sheikh Yusuf Mollo, Imam of the nearby Kito Mosque, and the Catholic Center was attacked and looted. Unusually the Uganda government admitted the outrage, and one soldier was said to have been arrested, but no proper enquiry was held into a massacre which was clearly the work of more than one person.

NATIONAL ASSEMBLY. The chief legislature of Uganda, successor to the Legislative Council (q.v.) which was dissolved when Uganda achieved internal self-government in 1962. The impressive building erected on a commanding site in central Kampala (q.v.) contains offices for members of the Assembly as well as the debating chamber. Both the design of the debating chamber and the procedures of the Assembly were on the Westminster model. The Westminster pattern of a loyal opposition failed to take root, however. During the first presidency of Milton Obote (q.v.) many of the opposition Democratic Party (q.v.) members "crossed the floor" to join the government, as did members of Kabaka Yekka (q.v.). Proper procedures were overridden in 1966 when Obote forced through an interim constitution (q.v.) sight unseen. After the attempted assassination (q.v.) of Obote, the opposition was outlawed. The National Assembly ceased to function under President Amin (q.v.). It was revived during Obote's second presidency, but the Democratic Party (q.v.) members came in for criticism for taking up their seats after the disputed Elections of 1980 (q.v.), thus lending credence to Obote's claim to have reintroduced democracy. The Assembly was, in any case, ineffective during this period. By 1993 party politics had not been revived, though the building is in use as the venue for the meetings of the National Resistance Council (q.v.).

NATIONAL ASSOCIATION FOR THE ADVANCEMENT OF MUSLIMS (NAAM). This movement was created in 1965 to try to recruit Muslims (*see* Islam) to support the policies of the Uganda People's Congress (q.v.) government of President Obote (q.v.), and to reduce the influence of Prince Badru Kakungulu (q.v.) which was particularly strong among Baganda (q.v.) Muslims. Factionalism and ethnicity among Muslims was exploited in order to do this. Most of the leaders of the NAAM were non-Baganda, and although a number of Baganda Sheikhs supported the NAAM, most of the opposition to it came from Baganda Muslims loyal to Prince Badru, including Abu Mayanja (q.v.). From 1968 onwards the NAAM was recognized by the government as being the representative body for all Muslims in Uganda. From its ranks Sheikh Swaibu Ssemakula (q.v.) was elected Sheikh Mufti and national spokesman for the Muslim community. Muslims who accepted the NAAM were rewarded: seven Muslims were appointed to saza (county) chieftaincies in Buganda and others to lesser chieftaincies. Mosques whose leaders did not endorse the NAAM were forcibly taken over, and NAAM supporters were recruited into the much-feared General Service Unit (q.v.). Prince Badru and others were arrested and detained towards the end of 1970.

After the coup of 1971 (q.v.) which brought President Amin (q.v.) to power, the tables were turned. Some of the leaders of the NAAM had their homes destroyed and the association was abruptly ended.

NATIONAL EXECUTIVE COMMITTEE (NEC). The "cabinet" of the National Resistance Movement (q.v.) government of President Museveni (q.v.). It is formed from members of the National Resistance Council (NRC) (q.v.), and has a mixture of elected and nominated members including ten presidential nominees from among the members of the NRC. The bodies which elect members to the NEC are the District Resistance Councils (RC5s), the top tier of the five-tier pyramid of Resistance Councils (q.v.) through which the National Resistance Movement governs.

NATIONAL RESISTANCE ARMY (NRA), NATIONAL RESISTANCE MOVEMENT (NRM). These were founded by Yoweri Museveni (q.v.), later President of Uganda, immediately after the disputed Elections of 1980 (q.v.) in which his party, the Uganda Patriotic Movement (q.v.), was defeated. Museveni took to the bush with a handful of soldiers and over the next five years built up a well-disciplined guerrilla army of 5,000 to 6,000 men. The Luwero Triangle (q.v.) was the main scene of operations. The *Uganda Resistance News* began to be published in 1981 and the Ten Point Programme (q.v.) worked out. Although under international pressure Museveni and the NRA signed the Nairobi Accords (q.v.) in late 1985, the NRA was by then so near victory that by the time of signing the situation had already moved beyond the provisions that had been worked out. On 25 January 1986 the NRA moved into the western suburbs of Kampala (q.v.), and the new government took power the next day.

The NRM government was well-accepted in the south and west of Uganda, but resisted in Acholi (q.v.) and Teso (q.v.). The NRA had to be hurriedly reinforced with men from the Uganda National Liberation Army (q.v.) who had surrendered themselves, and the inclusion of troops who had not received the strict training and discipline of the NRA had a serious effect on the character of the NRA, lowering its disciplinary standards and its behavior to the civilian population. Not until 1993 was peace restored.

The NRM has refused to allow the old political parties to contest elections, and is trying to build democracy from the grassroots upwards through a five-tier structure of Resistance Councils (q.v.) topped by the National Executive Committee (q.v.). A draft constitution (q.v.) had been worked out by 1993 which was in process of discussion. Elections for a Constituent Assembly to enact a new constitution were held in March 1994.

NATIONAL RESISTANCE COUNCIL (NRC). The national level council below which are the five tiers of Resistance Councils (q.v.) through which the government of President Yoweri Museveni (q.v.) has governed since he and the National Resistance Movement (q.v.) came to power in 1986. It has a guaranteed percentage of women among its members.

NATIONAL RESISTANCE MOVEMENT see NATIONAL RESISTANCE ARMY

NGOLOGOZA, PAUL (c. 1897–?). Senior chief and administrator in Kigezi (q.v.) and local historian. He received only minimal education through learning to read in baptism classes, but he worked his way up through minor chieftaincies until in 1936 he was appointed to a senior chieftaincy. Ten years later he was appointed Secretary-General of Kigezi District, and in 1956 Chief Judge. He became Chairman of the Kigezi Appointments Board in 1959, and after his retirement just a year later he was elected Deputy Chairman of Kigezi District Council. His history of Kigezi, *Kigezi n'Abantu Baamwo* (Kigezi and its People), was published in 1967, and an English translation by B.J. Turyahikayo-Rugyema appeared two years later. In the Introduction he recounts how he traveled round the district to collect information, and the care he took to assess this correctly.

NILE. The nineteenth century search by European explorers and geographers for the source of the Nile drew travelers such as J.H. Speke (q.v.), Samuel Baker (q.v.) and H.M. Stanley (q.v.) to Uganda. Desire to control the Nile and its sources and also the trade in slaves and ivory which followed the course of the river southwards ensured the interest of Egypt and Sudan (q.v.) and led to the annexation of Equatoria (q.v.). In twentieth-century Uganda the Nile is still only bridged at three places: Jinja (q.v.) where the road bridge is carried by the Owen Falls hydroelectric dam (q.v.) with a rail bridge slightly further upstream, the Karuma Falls, and Pakwach where the Nile flows out of Lake Albert. The last two were both built after independence. The possibility of utilizing the Kabarega Falls (formerly the Murchison Falls) for generating electricity has been discussed. R.O. Collins' comprehensive *The Waters of the Nile* (1990) includes discussion of the uses of the Nile in Uganda.

NSAMBYA. The Kampala (q.v.) hill on which stands the head-quarters of the Mill Hill Mission (q.v.). Three quarters of a square mile was given to Bishop Hanlon (q.v.) in 1895 by Kabaka Mwanga (q.v.). Nsambya Cathedral Church and Nsambya Hospital (*see* Mother Kevin and Medicine) are sited on the hill.

NSIBIRWA, MARTIN LUTHER (?–1945). Katikiro (chief minister) of Buganda (q.v.) from 1930–1941, 1945. He was promoted to this position in middle age as one of the more successful of an older generation of senior chiefs, many of whom were removed at this time by the Protectorate government to be replaced by more progressive men. He was criticized by the Bataka (q.v.) movement and the Sons of Kintu (*see* Musazi) for being autocratic and out of touch with popular opinion and for flouting custom in supporting the remarriage of the widow of Kabaka Daudi Chwa (q.v.). His resignation was forced in 1941 on this issue, but he was reinstated by the Protectorate government at the time of the Riots of 1945 (q.v.). He became extremely unpopular for supporting compulsory land purchase of mailo (q.v.) land to extend Makerere College (q.v.) and a Cotton Research establishment at Nakasongole. The Baganda saw this as a plot to acquire land for European settlement. The day after the measure was forced through a reluctant Lukiiko he was murdered on the steps of Namirembe (q.v.) Cathedral.

NSUBUGA, CARDINAL EMMANUEL (c. 1920–1991). Leader of the Roman Catholic Church (q.v.) in Uganda for 25 years. He entered Katigondo Seminary to train for the priesthood in 1937 and was ordained priest at Rubaga (q.v.) on 15 December 1946. He served in various parishes until in 1961 he was appointed Vicar General of Rubaga. After the death of Archbishop Joseph Kiwanuka (q.v.) in 1966 he was nominated Vicar Capitular. He was consecrated Bishop by Cardinal Rugambwa of Tanzania (q.v.) in Nakivubo Stadium, Kampala (q.v.), on 30 October 1966 and was appointed to the newly-created Archdiocese of Kampala not long after the Battle of Mengo 1966 (q.v.). He steered his diocese and the Ugandan Catholic Church through more than two decades of great insecurity and difficulty. In 1967 when attending a synod in Rome he invited Pope Paul V to visit Uganda. The visit took place in July and August 1969.

In 1974 Archbishop Nsubuga traveled to Europe to visit the birthplaces and relatives of the first Catholic missionaries to Uganda, and decided that the remains of the five proto-missionaries should be brought back to Uganda to rest among the Christians who were the fruit of their work. This was accomplished in 1975 at a very difficult period for the church because of the suspicions of President Amin (q.v.). Amin was unable to prevent an outpouring of joy and loyalty to the Catholic Church by its members. On 24 May 1976 Archbishop Nsubuga was invested as a Cardinal. Although Amin tried to prevent a public demonstration when Nsubuga returned to Uganda, word went round and he was given a tremendous welcome. After the fall of Amin and the return to power of President Obote (q.v.) the Catholic Church continued to find itself in opposition to the abuses of human rights perpetrated by the regime. In February 1984 the Cardinal protested publicly about violence against civilians by the Uganda National Liberation Army (q.v.). From 1989 onwards his health began to fail, and he died on 20 April 1991.

NTARE V (?–1895). Mugabe of Nkore (*see* Banyankole), c. 1877–1895. Ntare became Mukama as a result of a prolonged succession war following the death of Mukama Mutambuka in c. 1875. He is remembered as a great warrior during whose rule Nkore's power was extended westward.

However, during the last years of his reign he also had to contend with the rising power of Buganda (*see* Baganda), and with epidemics of smallpox and of the cattle disease, rinderpest, in 1891–1892 which decimated the herds on which the Bahima (q.v.) depended. Raids to replenish the herds were carried out and were spectacularly successful, but retaliation followed, and Ntare's reign ended with Nkore under threat from the kingdom of Rwanda (q.v.) to the south which invaded Nkore in 1894 in revenge. Ntare had no clear successor (his only son had died of smallpox), and only after a period of great uncertainty was Kahaya (q.v.) recognized as the new Mugabe. Ntare V Secondary School in Mbarara (q.v.), one of Uganda's leading secondary schools (*see* Education), is named after him.

It was also during Ntare's reign that the first European contacts occurred. Stanley (q.v.) passed through in 1889 and met the Mugabe's emissary, Bucunku, with whom he made a form of blood brotherhood and claimed to have made a treaty by which Bucunku allegedly ceded sovereignty. In 1891 Lugard (q.v.) passed through and a treaty was made between Ntare's envoys and the Imperial British East Africa Company (q.v.) offering Ntare the Company's protection. Yet another treaty was made in 1894 when Ntare was faced with rival German claims. Colonial rule was not effectively extended to the enlarged kingdom of Ankole until 1901.

NTOKIIBIRI. The years 1916 to 1917 saw a major resurgence of the Nyabingi (q.v.) cult in Kigezi (q.v.) led by Ntokiibiri ("the two-fingered one": he had only two fingers on one hand). A Hunde from the Belgian Congo (now Zaire [q.v.]), he declared himself to be a Nyabingi medium. He was accompanied by a woman medium, Kaigirwa. He and his followers attacked both Belgian and German posts. He was driven off repeatedly, but retreated each time and evaded capture. In 1917 he master-minded an attack by some 1,400 men from a number of different chieftaincies on a particularly hated agent, Abdulla, and his Baganda (q.v.) followers. Although Abdulla survived, many others were killed. The British were alarmed by the extent of support for the attack and the secrecy which had shrouded its planning. They quickly blamed Nyabingi for being the inspiration behind it, and strengthened the Witchcraft Ordinance enacted in 1912 to counter Nyabingi. Ntokiibiri and Kaigirwa, however, both escaped, though a number of other mediums were imprisoned. Their ability to escape capture seemed to be proof of the power of Nyabingi.

In 1919 they led a further and potentially more serious revolt and the Bakiga (q.v.) flocked to join them. Luganda (*see* Languages) was made the official language in Kigezi, and the Baganda agents' powers were increased. Their exploitation of the local population also increased. The government post and the mission station at Kabale (q.v.) were directly threatened. On this occasion the Belgian authorities cooperated with the British in a hunt to track down and apprehend Ntokiibiri and the other Nyabingi mediums. Ntokiibiri was finally surprised in a forest hideout and killed together with a second medium, Luhemba, but Kaigirwa remained at large. The British displayed Ntokiibiri's body to dispel any doubt about his death, and his sacred white sheep was publicly burnt. A series of unexplained accidents to the District Commissioner's house and to his sheep must have seemed to the Bakiga proof that Nyabingi's power had not been completely overcome, despite the setback it had received. Kaigirwa made one more bid for power, but was forced to retreat, and according to one account was later killed. At any rate, no more was heard of her.

NUBIANS. Descendants of the Sudanese (q.v.) troops left behind by Emin Pasha (q.v.) and brought into Uganda by Lugard (q.v.) to strengthen his forces. In spite of their name they are not from the Nuba Mountains of Sudan. They were mostly Southern Sudanese of the Bari and Kakwa (q.v.) peoples who had been converted to Islam (q.v.). Because of their army connections, they settled around Bombo, 20 miles north of Kampala (q.v.) and in Gulu (q.v.) in Acholi (q.v.). They developed a separate identity and stood aloof from Ugandans, retained their adherence to Islam, and spoke "Kinubi" (a bastard Arabic) and Swahili (*see* Languages). The women wore distinctive, brightly colored cloths and nose- and ear-rings, and often sold baskets they had made. Those who married into the community adopted its culture.

During the presidency of Idi Amin (q.v.) they benefitted from their employment in the army and their profession of Islam. They were allocated many of the businesses seized from the departing Asians (q.v.) in 1972, though not all had the entrepreneurial skills to run these successfully.

NYABINGI. The name of a spirit cult in Kigezi (q.v.). The word means one who possesses, or who distributes, great riches. In some traditions Nyabingi was originally a ruler in an area bordering on Rwanda (q.v.) whose spirit returned from time to time and was incarnated in priest-mediums who were usually women, like the original Nyabingi herself. The origins of the cult and its history before 1900 are unclear, and a variety of different histories and analyses are given in the literature. At times the cult functioned in much the same way as other spirit cults, but in the 1890s matters took a different turn. It was then associated with Ndorwa, an area in the extreme south of the modern Uganda, and on the northern border of Rwanda.

In c. 1895 Muhumuza (q.v.), a widow of the Mwami (king) of Rwanda, fled to Ndorwa—now in Kabale (q.v.) District—after her son had failed in a bid for the Rwandan throne. She declared herself to be an incarnation of Nyabingi, won a following, and challenged the Mwami's rule on her son's behalf. In 1908 the Germans saw her as a danger to stability in Rwanda, and imprisoned her for two years. When released she made a further bid to place her son on the throne of Rwanda. When this also failed she built up a power base in Ndorwa by promising wealth and immunity in war to those who followed her: bullets would turn to water when used against them. Muhumuza was captured by the British and removed to Kampala (q.v.) in 1911.

The fate of Ndungutsi, her son, is disputed. The Germans claimed to have killed him in 1912, but the area continued to be disturbed by someone who claimed to be Ndungutsi and who became a focus of resistance to colonial rule. He was captured in 1913 in Ankole (q.v.) and exiled to Busoga (q.v.), and a number of local chiefs felt it wise to submit to the British in the wake of his defeat. His resistance was again linked with a resurgence of Nyabingi.

In 1912 British rule was extended to Kigezi (q.v.). As in other areas of Uganda, they used Baganda (q.v.) agents who exploited the people and became intensely resented. In 1914 taxation was imposed on the Bakiga (q.v.) and collected by the agents. From 1914 to 1928 there were repeated outbreaks of violence against Baganda agents and British officials. These outbursts do not seem to have been inspired by Nyabingi mediums, but they supported it and became rallying points for it. The outbreak of World War I and the proximity of German territory gave urgency to the matter of controlling Kigezi. Resisters who found themselves threatened when British columns were sent against them could easily slip across the border into Rwanda, and German-inspired raids into British territory by Tutsi threatened the stability of the whole area. The Mwami of Rwanda saw in the raids an opportunity of extending his rule. Late in 1914 there was a major confrontation between the British and Bakiga who refused to provide food and porters and who murdered one of the Baganda agents. A recurrence of Nyabingi in 1915 was dealt with summarily, but as soon as one medium was suppressed by the British, another appeared.

There were further resurgences of Nyabingi in 1916 and 1917 led by Ntokiibiri (q.v.) and a woman medium, Kaigirwa. They led attacks on both Belgian and German posts and were repeatedly driven off, but succeeded in escaping each time. In order to counter Nyabingi the British authorities strengthened the Witchcraft Ordinance enacted in 1912 to counter the cult. Those who professed to be mediums (or, as the British put it, "to practice witchcraft") or who possessed ritual objects could be apprehended. All cult activity was outlawed, including that which was benevolent and curative. A number of other mediums were imprisoned, but Ntokiibiri and Kaigirwa escaped, and thus enhanced their reputation for possessing spiritual power. There was further serious trouble in 1919 when Kabale was threatened, but British and Belgian cooperation eventually led to the discovery of Ntokiibiri's hideout. He and his sacred sheep were killed and his body displayed lest anyone should doubt reports of his death. Kaigirwa was routed later that year.

For the next few years an uneasy peace prevailed. Nyabingi mediums were still known to be active, but were thought to be politically harmless. Mission work was not begun by the Church Missionary Society (q.v.) until 1921, and by the White Fathers (q.v.) until 1923, though in both cases Ugandan catechists had arrived some years earlier and prepared the ground for more formal mission activity. For the first time British rule in Kigezi brought some benefits (education [q.v.] and medicine [q.v.]) to the Bakiga. In the south, however, Tutsi chiefs were hostile to the missions (q.v.), though they admitted that education might be beneficial. Resistance to taxation and to the chiefs who were imposed on Kigezi grew, and the Nyabingi cult throve. "Witchcraft" cases dealt with by the courts multiplied. Events climaxed in 1928 when Nyabingi mediums successfully persuaded cult followers to refrain from cultivation on Mondays and Tuesdays, which days were to be set apart for Nyabingi. This interrupted labor exacted by the chiefs for public works. Again the people were promised that bullets used against them would turn to water. A further attack was planned against the government headquarters and mission station at Kabale, but this was preempted, and the leaders fled to Rwanda.

This further defeat brought to an end overt practice, not only of the Nyabingi cult but of other cults as well, though they continued in secret. Perhaps disillusioned by the failure of Nyabingi to fulfill its promises, perhaps seeking a safe haven, people flocked to the missions and denied all involvement in "witchcraft." For years they refused to speak about it to outsiders and researchers. M.M. Edel (see Bibliography) in the 1930s was unable to gather any significant information, and not until after colonial control had ended did people feel free to discuss Nyabingi.

The local historian, Paul Ngologoza (q.v.), does not mention Nyabingi in connection with events after the defeat of Muhumuza, though he tells of the rebellions discussed here. The British authorities seem to have believed that behind all the rebellion in Kigezi lay a sinister and mysterious heathen cult. The truth seems to be that after 1912 the cause of rebellion was secular—resistance against oppressive alien rule and the imposition of taxes and foreign Baganda chiefs on a society which had never had chiefs. However, not surprisingly, the dominant religious cult became involved and provided support for resistance.

NYABONGO, AKIIKI (c. 1906–1976). The eldest son of Mukama Daudi Kasagama (q.v.) of Toro (q.v.), he was educated at King's College, Budo (*see* Education), Harvard and Queen's College, Oxford, where he obtained a D. Phil. An eccentric who rebelled against his royal background and against colonial rule, he is best known for his novel *Africa Answers Back* (1936) which was banned by the Protectorate government of the time which feared it would incite rebellion or at least raise questions which they preferred to have unasked. He dropped his royal title and became a member of the Uganda People's Congress (q.v.). In 1963 he was appointed Chairman of the Town and Country Planning Board, an appointment which he took very seriously, and worked to Africanize the Board's membership and thinking, sometimes pushing through against all the odds his own understanding of what Africans wanted.

NYAKATURA, JOHN (1895–   ). Chief in Bunyoro (q.v.) and local historian. Nyakatura was born in Buyaga, one of the "Lost Counties" (q.v.) annexed to Buganda at he end of the nineteenth century. Between 1911 when he finished his education and 1928 he was employed first as a clerk and then as a salt inspector at Katwe. He then held a number of minor chieftaincies before being appointed to a senior chieftaincy in 1940. In 1951 he became Omulamuzi (chief justice) in the Bunyoro (q.v.) government. He retired in 1953, and spent much of his time from then on working for the restoration to Bunyoro of the "Lost Counties." His *Abakama be Bunyoro*

(The Kings of Bunyoro), whose title in translation is *Anatomy of an African Kingdom,* was written in the 1950s and follows the outline given by Mukama Tito Winyi (q.v.) who learnt the traditions from his father, Mukama Kabarega (q.v.), and is his great contribution to Ugandan historical writing. It is the Bunyoro parallel to *Basekabaka be Buganda* (The Kings of Buganda) by Apolo Kagwa (q.v.). Nyakatura's own father served both Kabarega and his predecessor, Mukama Kamurasi, and had passed on to his son his knowledge of Bunyoro tradition. Nyakatura's second volume, translated into English by Zebiya Rigby, *Aspects of Bunyoro Customs,* appeared in 1970, and is a valuable supplement to his earlier work.

NYANGIRE RISING. An uprising in Bunyoro (q.v.) against the Baganda (q.v.) agents of British rule. The word means "I have refused." At the beginning of 1907 the Banyoro sub-chiefs began to refuse the Baganda chiefs and agents who had been imposed on them after the subjugation of the kingdom, the defeat of Mukama Kabarega (q.v.), and the loss of territory to Buganda (*see* Lost Counties). The most powerful of these chiefs were James Miti (q.v.) and Mika Fataki (q.v.), the latter a Musoga but brought up in Buganda. By March 1907 the Baganda had to be withdrawn to the district headquarters at Hoima (q.v.) for their own safety, and the Banyoro chiefs were ordered to reinstate the Baganda.

A series of grievances lay behind the Nyangire Rising. First was the fact of conquest by the British and the Baganda. Secondly the Banyoro bitterly resented the allocation of large tracts of Bunyoro territory to Buganda. Many Banyoro had fled across the Kafu River from the two counties of Buyaga and Bugangaizi because of the harsh rule of the Baganda over them in the Lost Counties. Thirdly they resented being ruled over by their conquerors who treated them as inferiors both because of the conquest, and also because Western education had come much later to Bunyoro. With the Baganda chiefs and agents had come a multitude of Baganda hangers-on, and their presence too was unwelcome. Then there was the natural grievance at the imposition of taxation by the British and at the Baganda agents and chiefs who were responsible for its collection. Even the Mukama Andereya Duhaga (q.v.) came in for criticism by the supporters of Nyangire. His position was in any case precarious because the previous Mukama, Kabarega (q.v.), was still alive, exiled to the Seychelles by the British. Some Banyoro saw Duhaga as an usurper because of this. He was also blamed for permitting the Baganda to come into the kingdom and for collaborating with them.

The outbreak of Nyangire was precipitated by the discovery by Banyoro adherents of the Church Missionary Society (CMS) (q.v.) of a mission recommendation that Luganda (*see* Languages) should be used in teaching and by the church because its use was spreading, and Bunyoro was coming increasingly under the influence of Buganda: there was therefore no need for a translation of the Bible into Runyoro (*see* Languages). These opinions had been voiced to the Revd H. Maddox in Toro (q.v.) by the Revd A.B. Fisher, senior CMS missionary in Bunyoro, who was usually more sensitive to the Banyoro. Maddox had read the letter out to the Toro Church Council which included among its members several senior Toro chiefs. They promptly informed their Banyoro counterparts of what had been said. It was the last straw for many Banyoro. The rebellion actually began when the powerful James Miti was away. It won the support of the senior Banyoro chiefs, Paulo Byabacwezi (q.v.) and Leo Kaboha (q.v.). Emissaries were sent to Toro and Ankole (q.v.) in the hope of widening the rebellion— Baganda chiefs and agents were employed in both—but without success.

The lack of violence and the determination of the Banyoro persuaded the British that the protest was well-organized and controlled, and needed diplomatic handling. A series of meetings was held between British officials and the Banyoro chiefs. The District Officer was twice replaced in the hope that a new approach might result in the Banyoro capitulating. Some of the senior Banyoro chiefs including Byabacwezi wavered, but the sub-chiefs did not and the Banyoro continued to refuse to comply with the order to reinstate the Baganda. On 16 May 54 Banyoro chiefs of all ranks were arrested. Various punishments were meted out, Leo Kaboha, the leading Catholic chief, and 11 sub-chiefs who were believed to be the ringleaders, being exiled to Toro. The Roman Catholics (q.v.), including the missionaries themselves, came under undeserved suspicion from the authorities, and made great efforts to rebut this.

Although the Baganda chiefs were reinstated, no further Baganda were appointed, and they soon began to be replaced by Banyoro. The Banyoro were therefore able to see Nyangire as something of a victory.

NYONYINTONO, HONORAT (?–1889). A leading Catholic (q.v.) who was a page at the court of Kabaka Mwanga (q.v.). On 6 December 1885 he was made head of the pages in Twekobe, the Kabaka's personal residence. In May 1886 he announced publicly that he was a Christian, a courageous act, for Mwanga had turned against the Christians and they were in great danger. Nyonyintono was arrested and mutilated. While he was in prison he was confirmed by Fr Lourdel (q.v.). Later in the year he was restored to the Kabaka's favor, and urged to become a Muslim (*see* Islam), but he refused. After the uprising of the Christians and Muslims in 1888 (*see* Wars of Religion) he was briefly Katikiro to Kabaka Kiwewa, but when Kiwewa was overthrown by the Muslims, he fled to Ankole (q.v.) with the Christians. He there became leader of the Catholic party, and in 1889 he led the joint Catholic and Protestent (q.v.) forces back into Buddu (q.v.), but he was killed in the Battle of Kawuki. His death was a serious loss, for he was one of the few people who was trusted by both Catholics and Protestants, and who might have been able to prevent the enmity which grew up between them and eventually flared into the Battle of Mengo 1892 (q.v.).

-O-

OBOTE, APOLO MILTON (1925–). Prime Minister of Uganda, 1962–1966; President of Uganda, 1966–1971, 1981–1985. Born in Lango (q.v.) in 1925 and educated at

Lira Secondary School, Gulu High School, Busoga College, Mwiri (*see* Education), and Makerere College (q.v.) which he left after only two years in 1950. He then went to Kenya (q.v.) until 1957 where he was active with the Kenya African Union, the organization alleged to have been the brains behind the Mau Mau movement. Only a year after his return he got himself nominated to the Legislative Council (q.v.) as Member for Lango. He was outspoken in attacking the Protectorate government, demanding independence. He joined the Uganda National Congress (UNC) (q.v.) founded in 1952 by I.K. Musazi (q.v.) and Abu Mayanja (q.v.), and took over the leadership from them. His faction of the UNC became the Uganda People's Congress (UPC) (q.v.), the ruling party at independence. He was able to wrest electoral success from the Democratic Party (q.v.) by making an alliance with Kabaka Yekka (q.v.), the Baganda (q.v.) royalist party. He then worked to render this alliance unnecessary and to establish a one-party state.

Obote's first presidency was marked by a series of crises. The first major crisis was the Mutiny of 1964 (q.v.) when he was forced to call in British troops, and made the mistake of granting the Uganda Army (q.v.) virtually all it demanded. An action which had far-reaching consequences and precipitated major crises was his use of Ugandan troops under the command of Idi Amin (q.v.) to assist the Simba rebels in the Congo (now Zaire [q.v.]). The army was enlarged and Amin's power enhanced, but the extent of Uganda's role was kept secret even from the cabinet, not all of whom would have supported this action. In 1965 there was a major crisis in relations with Kenya when the Kenyan authorities seized 75 tons of Chinese weaponry being transported from Tanzania to Uganda through western Kenya, and presumably bound for the Congo rebels. The arms and the Ugandan troops guarding them were held by the Kenyans until Obote travelled to Nairobi and apologized in person to President Kenyatta, a public humiliation. Early the following year the Gold Scandal (q.v.) was a further repercussion of the Congolese adventure which came within an ace of bringing down Obote's government. Accused by Daudi Ocheng (q.v.) of misappropriating a large quantity of gold and ivory, Obote outsmarted his opponents by detaining the five ministers (q.v.) whom he suspected of intending a coup against him, introducing a new constitution (q.v.) which he made the National Assembly (q.v.) accept sight unseen, and taking upon himself full Presidential powers.

This in turn created a further crisis with Buganda which refused to accept the usurpation of presidential powers from Kabaka Mutesa II (q.v.). The Battle of Mengo 1966 (q.v.) in which the army, under Idi Amin, defeated the Baganda (q.v.) followed, leaving lasting hatred for Obote among the Baganda. In 1967 a new constitution (q.v.) was passed which abolished the kingdoms of Bunyoro (q.v.), Toro (q.v.) and Ankole (q.v.) and the special status of Busoga (q.v.).

Not until 1969 did Obote attempt to set out an ideology and goals for the future development of the country. He then introduced the "Move to the Left" (q.v.), but it came too late. His own cabinet was divided over the proposed socialist measures. In December 1969 there occurred the attempted assassination (q.v.), which made Obote increasingly fearful and his rule increasingly oppressive. Further steps towards socialism were announced in April and May 1970, and foreign businesses investing in Uganda took fright when the second of these moves involved the nationalization of many companies. This helped to precipitate an economic crisis. In November 1970 Obote expelled 30,000 Kenyan workers (*see* Expulsions), mainly Luo from western Kenya.

The coup (q.v.) in which he was ousted took place in January 1971 during his absence at a Commonwealth Heads of Government Meeting. It could be said of his first presidency that Obote lacked the charisma of his contemporaries, President Julius Nyerere of Tanzania (q.v.) and President Jomo Kenyatta of Kenya. Uganda has no common language (*see* Languages) in which he could address the nation, and Obote was, in any case, not a great orator. He was unable to inspire a country deeply divided along ethnic and religious lines to work for a common aim. His skill lay in manipulation, but this left deep resentments among those whom he worsted.

It could also be argued that it was largely the Uganda

Army that was Obote's undoing. Just prior to independence it was discovered that Idi Amin was responsible for a massacre in operations against the Turkana in Kenya. Obote and the Protectorate authorities agreed that it would be impolitic to court-martial one of the army's only two Ugandan commissioned officers at this juncture, and instead Amin was promoted, in retrospect a disastrous mistake. The Mutiny of 1964 was ominous for the future. Virtually all the demands of the Uganda Army were granted, and Obote was unable to establish full control over the army. Obote's sanctioning of assistance to the Simba in the Congo proved disastrous, and matters were made worse by his need to use the army against the Baganda in 1966. A state of emergency was declared in Buganda and was never lifted: the army remained on double pay throughout an emergency and therefore resisted its being ended. Obote was unable to control defense expenditure, and a major reason for the 1971 coup which brought Amin to power was that Amin decided to preempt enquiries into his overspending.

During Amin's presidency, Obote was given sanctuary in Tanzania by his friend President Nyerere who shared his socialist outlook. He returned to Uganda in 1980 to campaign for reelection. His return was engineered by Paulo Muwanga (q.v.) and a faction in Uganda who presumably thought they could secure their own positions and sources of wealth if he were President. The Elections of 1980 (q.v.) which returned him to power were fatally flawed and were not accepted by a large section of the population. The Uganda National Liberation Army (q.v.) was already hopelessly out of control and senior religious leaders drew the world's attention to this in a public statement in 1981 in which they told Obote, ''The Uganda you lead is bleeding to death.'' Obote failed to take any effective steps to control the army.

Obote won Western approval and aid by dropping his socialism and accepting World Bank and IMF advisors in a bid to halt the disastrous economic decline. Britain (q.v.) in particular supported him and refused to accept the reports of barbarities which marked this period of his rule.

From almost the beginning of his second presidency Obote was faced with insurgency as the National Resistance Army/Movement (q.v.) led by Yoweri Museveni (q.v.) took to the bush and mounted an increasingly successful guerrilla campaign against him. Once again the army was his undoing. News of the Ombachi Massacre (q.v.) and atrocities in the Luwero Triangle (q.v.) became known, although the figures given by the US Assistant Secretary of State Elliot Abrams (q.v.) were disputed by Britain. More importantly the atrocities alienated the population from his government and made them welcome the well-disciplined guerrillas. Internal disputes divided the army, especially after the death in a helicopter accident of Army Chief-of-Staff David Oyite-Ojok (q.v.), and the appointment over the heads of Generals Basilio Okello (q.v.) and Tito Okello (q.v.) of the inexperienced Smith Opon-Acak (q.v.), a clan relative of Obote's. These quarrels weakened the army against Museveni's guerrillas, and erupted in the putsch of 1985 which drove Obote from power for the second time. He was refused asylum in any neighboring country and went to live in semi-isolation in Zambia.

OCHENG, DAUDI (1925–1967). Educated at King's College, Budo (*see* Education), Makerere College (q.v.) and the University of Wales. After graduating he moved to Buganda (q.v.) and became a member of Kabaka Yekka (q.v.). In 1964 he was elected member of the National Assembly (q.v.) for Mityana and the following year he was appointed Opposition Chief Whip. In 1965 he first made allegations against Idi Amin (q.v.) and other members of the government including President Obote (q.v.) in connection with gold and ivory from the Simba rebels in the Congo the proceeds of which he suggested had been misappropriated (*see* Gold Scandal). It is said that he was chosen to do so because he was known to be dying of cancer and was therefore likely to be safe from retaliation.

ODORA, DAUDI (c. 1880–?). Clan leader and county chief in Lango (q.v.). About the turn of the century the clan section, the Jo Oyakori, led by Odora's putative father, suffered a major defeat at the hands of the Jo Ocukuru when seeking out new land, and took refuge in Kungu, an unhealthy spot in south Lango, but protected on three sides by a bend in the Nile (q.v.). There they came into contact with the Banyoro (q.v.). At about this time Odora emerged as leader of the Jo Oyakori because of his military prowess and his skill in dealing with the Banyoro. Because of continued harassment by the Jo Ocukuru, he built up contacts with the court of Mukama Andereya Duhaga (q.v.) and with the Revd A.B. Lloyd of the Church Missionary Society (q.v.). He pledged allegiance to the Mukama and in 1905 accepted mission catechists. The Protestant (q.v.) church in Aduku knew a biblicized version of this story in which Odora was guided by a dream to seek for help in Bunyoro, and salvation came when the catechists arrived to teach Christianity. The church drums there are said to have been given by Mukama Duhaga.

When British officials took action to round up Banyoro supporters of the deposed Mukama Kabarega (q.v.) who had taken refuge in Lango, Odora assisted them. As a reward he was given guns and ammunition and allowed to occupy the defensive earthworks built during the campaign against Kabarega and the Sudanese mutineers (q.v.). This greatly enhanced his standing. People flocked to serve him, enabling him to mount successful raids and reward his followers with booty. He built up a household on the pattern of chiefly households in Bunyoro, encouraging his followers to learn literacy and Christianity from the catechists who formed part of his household. Even the Jo Ocukuru were impressed by his Protectorate patronage and agreed to elect him as senior chief. He exploited this patronage further when he moved his headquarters to Ibuje which was to become a government post. In 1913 he became county chief of Kwania and remained in this office until his retirement in 1927. His adopted son was the first boy from Lango to attend Gulu High School, and many literate chiefs and clerks emerged from among the members of his household.

OGWANGGUJI, ISAYA (c. 1893–?). Rwot of Erute County, Lango (q.v.), and Rwot Adwong (senior chief) of Lango,

1951–1952. He was the son of Olet Apar who ruled a small area around Ngeta Rock, just north of Lira (q.v.), and who was the last rainmaker among the Langi (q.v.) of any widespread influence. When British officials arrived in 1911 they built on his power. Olet got into difficulties with the administration when a Muganda was killed and he failed to take action, but in spite of a brief period of imprisonment he was allowed to continue as a chief. By 1913 Ogwangguji, then aged about 20, was beginning to take the old man's place. He was one of a new generation in Lango who decided that it would be most advantageous to himself and to Lango District to cooperate with the Protectorate administration, and he was well rewarded for this choice. He became Jago (sub-chief) of Lira in 1916 when his father died of plague, and a year later the Muganda (*see* Baganda) Agent, appointed until the authorities thought the Langi were able to administer themselves, was withdrawn. In 1918 Ogwangguji was baptized as a Protestant (q.v.) and in the same year he was elected Rwot of Erute County in succession to his father and in deference to his father's expressed wishes.

In the year of his appointment there was trouble north of the Moroto River, the area of Lango most recently brought under direct rule by the British. A Jago was fined for non-cooperation, and when the Muganda Agent and another Jago went to collect the fine, the area rose in rebellion, and several Baganda were killed. It fell to Ogwangguji to deal with the affair, which he did with speed and efficiency, and stopped the trouble from spreading. Shortly after this he was forced to act when there was trouble over demands for labor for public works. Aside from one short period, when he found the British official J.E.T. Philipps difficult to work with, his abilities were appreciated by the colonial authorities.

He was extremely popular, and the people of Erute County refused to allow him to be transferred to another area. In 1951 he was elected Rwot Adwong, senior chief of Lango, for a one-year term, after which he returned to Erute. He was rewarded by the British with the award of an MBE in 1956, and the following year he retired.

OKELLO, LT.-GEN. BASILIO OLARA (?–1990). Okello joined the King's African Rifles (q.v.) in 1949 and received his commission in 1966. He was appointed to a senior position after the War of Liberation (q.v.), and was responsible for brutalities when he was army commander in Kampala (q.v.) at the time of the overthrow of President Binaisa (q.v.). In 1982 he was put in charge of operations in the Luwero Triangle (q.v.) which involved massive abuse of the civilian population. He was so ineffective that he was later moved back to his home area, Acholi (q.v.). He was one of the Acholi senior army officers passed over by President Obote (q.v.) in 1983 when Army Chief-of-Staff David Oyite-Ojok (q.v.) was killed in a plane crash. He did not have the full confidence of the President, and together with Tito Okello (q.v.), was alleged to have been involved in plots against Obote. In July 1985 Basilio Okello led the attack in the army putsch which met little resistance and which brought him and General Tito Okello to brief power. He was among the signatories of the Nairobi Accords (q.v.) which attempted to bring peace to Uganda through power-sharing, but quarrelling in the Okello faction led to its breakup and resistance to the National Resistance Army (q.v.) was collapsing.

When the National Resistance Movement (q.v.) took power under President Museveni (q.v.) in 1986, the Okellos fled across the border into Sudan (q.v.) with the remnants of the army which remained loyal to them. There they regrouped, and crossed back into Uganda to mount resistance to President Museveni's government, although Basilio Okello himself remained in Khartoum. Calling themselves the Uganda People's Democratic Movement (q.v.) they met with only limited success, and in 1989 were weakened further by infighting amongst themselves. Otema Erica Allimadi (q.v.) was expelled from the Movement by Basilio Okello and blamed for large-scale defections to the Uganda government, when he and about 1,000 rebels surrendered and made peace. Okello died in exile in Khartoum in January 1990.

OKELLO, GEN. TITO LUTWA (1914–   ). Head of state for six months in 1985. An older man than Basilio Okello (q.v.),

Tito Okello joined the King's African Rifles (q.v.) in 1940 and was among the first few Ugandans to become commissioned officers. In 1979 he was commander of the small contingent of Ugandans who marched with the Tanzanians in the War of Liberation (q.v.) with David Oyite-Ojok (q.v.) as his deputy, and as such he attended the Moshi Unity Conference (q.v.). After the fall of Kampala (q.v.) to the Uganda National Liberation Army (UNLA) (q.v.) he was promoted from Colonel to be Major-General and Commander of the UNLA. President Yusufu Lule (q.v.) claimed that when he and David Oyite-Ojok, who was his Chief of Staff, asked permission to go and wreak vengeance on West Nile (q.v.), the homeland of ex-President Amin (q.v.), Lule asked the Tanzanian General who had led the War of Liberation to prevent them from entering the area. Okello was promoted to full General soon after the return to power of President Obote (q.v.), though he did not have the full confidence of the President and was even suspected of being involved in plots against him together with Basilio Okello.

After the army putsch in July 1985, Tito Okello became head of state briefly. He commanded slightly more respect than Basilio Okello though he was relatively uneducated and spoke no English, and under his command the indiscipline in the army led to atrocities against the civilian population. The latter part of 1985 was one of the most violent periods in Uganda's history, with faction-fighting within the army. Tito Okello was one of the signatories of the Nairobi Accords (q.v.) signed in December 1985, but never implemented since resistance to the National Resistance Army (q.v.) collapsed. When the National Resistance Movement (q.v.) seized power in 1986 he fled north into Sudan (q.v.) with Basilio Okello to mount resistance from there. After this collapsed, Tito Okello returned briefly to Uganda under an amnesty.

OKOT P'BITEK (1931–1982). Uganda's best-known poet was born in Acholi (q.v.) to devout Protestant (q.v.) Christian parents: his father was a church teacher. He was educated at

Gulu High School and King's College, Budo (*see* Education), before doing a teacher's course in 1952–1953. In the 1960s he studied at Bristol, Aberystwyth and Oxford Universities, presenting a thesis on Acholi oral literature for a Master's degree. In 1964 he returned to Uganda to teach at Makerere University College (q.v.), and two years later was appointed Director of the Uganda Cultural Centre. In 1968 he went to Kenya (q.v.) because of the political pressures which were building up in Uganda, and remained there teaching at Nairobi University until the overthrow of President Amin (q.v.).

His writings include *Lak Tar* (1953), a novel in Acholi (*see* Languages); *Song of Lawino* (1966), his best-known work, a moving and satirical book-length poem on themes connected with his native Acholi culture; *Song of Ocol* (1970); *Song of Prisoner* and *Song of Malaya* (1970) which probed these themes further and mused on Uganda's sufferings; *Religion of the Central Luo* (1971) which criticized what Okot saw as a tendency among African Religious Studies writers to Hellenize African thought; *Africa's Cultural Revolution* (1973), a collection of writings regretting the bastardization of African culture for the benefit of the tourist trade; and *Horn of My Love* (1974), a collection of poems in both Acholi and English.

OKOYA, BRIGADIER PIERINO YERE (d. 1970). An Acholi (q.v.) army officer murdered on 25 January 1970, almost certainly by Amin (q.v.) or at his instigation. Okoya was one of those non-commissioned officers of the Uganda Rifles (*see* Uganda Army) who was promoted on the eve of independence. In 1964, when he had achieved the rank of Major in little more than two years, he became Acting Commanding Officer of the newly-formed Third Battalion stationed at Mubende. By 1968 Okoya, then a Brigadier General, was beginning to be seen by Amin as a rival for power. At the time of the attempted assassination (q.v.) of President Obote (q.v.) in December 1969, Okoya took charge in the absence of Amin who had temporarily fled, and he openly challenged Amin over his behavior, accusing him of cowardice. Okoya then went north to his home five miles outside Gulu (q.v.). He was found murdered, shot at point-blank range, together with his wife, the day before he was due back in Kampala (q.v.) for a meeting when charges against Amin would have been pressed further. The enquiry into his death was headed by Brigadier Hussain, another of Amin's rivals. All police enquiries led to the army, where Amin was able to frustrate them. Okoya was the highest-ranking Acholi army officer, and the Acholi were very angry that no progress was made in these enquiries. Acholi soldiers did not support Amin's seizure of power in the coup (q.v.) of 25 January 1971, and suffered severely for this.

OMBACHI MASSACRE. After the overthrow of President Binaisa (q.v.) in May 1980, Langi (q.v.) and Acholi (q.v.) soldiers of the Uganda National Liberation Army (UNLA) (q.v.) replaced the Tanzanian troops which had garrisoned West Nile (q.v.) since the end of the Liberation War (q.v.). Ambushes and trouble from some former soldiers who had served under ex-President Amin (q.v.) gave the UNLA an excuse to take revenge on the people of Amin's home region. Atrocities occurred on a number of occasions in various parts of West Nile and thousands of civilians fled across the border into Sudan (q.v.) and Zaire (q.v.). During the fighting a group of wounded soldiers opposed to the UNLA was brought to Ombachi Catholic Mission where aid officials and refugees in large numbers were sheltering. The International Committee of the Red Cross (ICRC) (q.v.) allowed the wounded to be taken in and treated provided the mission and the refugees were unmolested. In the morning the guerrillas left quietly. The mission was then invaded by UNLA soldiers who accused the staff of aiding the guerrillas, and attacked the people sheltering there indiscriminately. It was some time before another unit of the UNLA arrived and restored order. At least 60 people were killed and many more were wounded. The government insisted that the mission had been harboring guerrillas. The ICRC believed the incident to be so serious that, contrary to its usual practice, it issued a communiqué to counter false information. In retaliation for this, it was told to leave the country, and it was some time before the ICRC was able to return.

ONAMA, FELIX (c. 1925–   ). A Madi (q.v.) from West Nile (q.v.) who was Minister of Works and Labour from 1962–1963, Minister of Internal Affairs from 1963–1965 and then Minister of State for Defence in the first government of President Obote (q.v.). He was educated at St Mary's College, Kisubi (*see* Education), and Makerere University College (q.v.). In 1964 he was sent to Jinja (q.v.) to deal with the Mutiny of 1964 (q.v.), was taken captive by the mutineers, and gave in to most of the demands of the Uganda Army (q.v.). He was a strong believer in the special role of the peoples of northern Uganda in the armed forces. In 1965 he was accused by Daudi Ocheng (q.v.) of being involved in the Gold Scandal (q.v.). In 1968 he was elected Secretary-General of the Uganda People's Congress (UPC) (q.v.) for a seven-year term. In the early years of Obote's government he had been one of the centrists who, like Obote himself, supported middle class interests. However, by 1970 when the Common Man's Charter (q.v.) was launched, he had shifted his ground as his business interests had grown: not only had he become a large-scale landowner, but he was a director of a transport company and general manager of the West Nile Cooperative Union and had little sympathy with the Move to the Left (q.v.). He was pushed aside within the UPC and Basil Bataringaya (q.v.) was appointed to organize the next meeting of the Congress. Rumor began to associate his name with that of General Idi Amin (q.v.) and with the possibility of a coup. He was associated with Amin in gross overspending by the army and in permitting aid to be channelled to the Anya Nya (q.v.), in spite of Obote's order that this should end. However, he played no part in the regime of President Amin, who did not trust him and placed him under house arrest for a while in 1972.

ONDOGA, LT.-COL. MICHAEL, (d. 1974). A Christian Lugbara (q.v.) from West Nile (q.v.). Ondoga was promoted to Lieutenant-Colonel in September 1970. After the coup (q.v.)

which brought President Amin (q.v.) to power, he was appointed Ambassador to the USSR (q.v.). He was recalled in mid-1973 when Foreign Minister Wanume Kibedi defected, and appointed in his place.

Towards the end of 1973 Ondoga helped himself to a vacant Asian (q.v.) house on Kololo Hill near Amin's house. Although acquiring property in this way was accepted practice, Amin was extremely angry when he heard about it, and ordered the Military Police to eject him. At a graduation ceremony at Makerere University (q.v.) in February 1974 Amin announced that he had fired Ondoga as Foreign Minister, and replaced him with Elizabeth Bagaya (q.v.). Shortly afterwards Ondoga was seized by men of the State Research Bureau (q.v.) and his body, with gunshot and stab wounds, was taken out of the Nile. The USSR found Amin unreliable and wanted to replace him with someone they trusted, and Amin, knowing this, was wary of those with Soviet contacts. Little more than a month later Charles Arube (q.v.), who had undergone some military training in Moscow, led an attack on the Military Police headquarters.

OPON-ACAK, GEN. SMITH (?–   ). A Langi (q.v.), he joined the Uganda Army in 1968, and, as one of the better-educated recruits, spent two years in Greece receiving officer-training. He was commissioned in 1972, served under President Amin (q.v.) and received further training in the USSR (q.v.). He was one of those who, after the War of Liberation (q.v.), was integrated into the Uganda National Liberation Army (q.v.), and in 1982 was sent to the Command and Staff College in the USA. In August 1984 he was promoted from Lieutenant-Colonel to Brigadier-General and made Chief-of-Staff of the armed forces. President Obote (q.v.) may have had reason to distrust more senior officers such as Basilio Okello (q.v.) and Tito Okello (q.v.), but the appointment of a clan relative and one with relatively little proven experience was a recipe for disaster. It led to an even greater collapse of discipline in the already seriously out-of-hand army, and the resentment of the Okellos led to the putsch of July 1985 in which Obote was overthrown: in June 1985 Opon-Acak ordered a contingent of Acholi (q.v.) troops to be sent to the front line against the National Resistance Army (q.v.). This precipitated a shoot-out between Langi and Acholi soldiers and this enmity escalated into the July 1985 putsch.

ORGANIZATION OF AFRICAN UNITY (OAU). With its secretariat in the Ethiopian capital, Addis Ababa, the OAU is the council of independent nations of the African continent. A summit meeting of heads of government is held annually, and the head of state of the country in which it meets normally acts as Chairman for the year following. The 1971 summit had been scheduled to be held in Kampala (q.v.) in June, and US$10 million had been allocated to the construction of a prestigious conference center built by the Yugoslavs. However, because of the coup of 1971 (q.v.) which brought Idi Amin (q.v.) to power, the meeting was transferred to Addis Ababa when it became clear that a significant number of heads of state, including Kenneth Kaunda of Zambia, the current Chairman of the OAU, and Julius Nyerere of Tanzania (q.v.) would not attend if it were to be held in Kampala. They had supported the ousted President Obote (q.v.) in his stand against Britain's policies on arms to South Africa, and did not wish to do anything which might seem to condone the Uganda military coup. By 1975 Amin succeeded in overcoming the OAU's reluctance: the summit meeting that year was held in Kampala in the International Conference Centre, and Amin became Chairman. It was during the 1976 summit held in Mauritius that the Entebbe Raid (q.v.) was successfully carried out by Israel (q.v.) to rescue hostages taken in a hijacking and held at Entebbe (q.v.). The timing was particularly humiliating to Amin. The meeting condemned the raid which revealed Africa's vulnerability, but Amin's cooperation with the hijackers was an embarrassment to the OAU.

Although the OAU summit of 1979 made ritual denunciations of Tanzania for invading Uganda during the War of Liberation (q.v.), it permitted President Binaisa (q.v.) to be seated and responded positively to his strictures on their failure to act against the human rights violations perpetrated by Amin and other dictators (*see* African Charter of Human and People's Rights). The evidence suggests that the OAU had been severely embarrassed by Amin, by Ngouema of Equatorial Guinea and by "Emperor" Bokassa of the Central African Republic in particular, all of whom had become bywords for brutality, and all of whom fell from power in 1979.

The OAU has a more generous definition of refugees (q.v.) than that in the 1951 UN Convention Relating to the Status of Refugees. The OAU Convention on Refugees drawn up in 1969, which came into force in 1974, states that the term refugee should also cover those forced to flee because of "external aggression, occupation, foreign domination or events seriously disturbing public order in either part or the whole of his country of origin or nationality," a definition which has enabled the Office of the UN High Commissioner for Refugees to assist many who would otherwise have fallen outside its remit.

ORMSBY-GORE COMMISSION *see* CLOSER UNION

OTAI, PETER (?–   ). Otai studied political science in Reading and London. In 1981 he was appointed Minister of State for Defence in the Vice-President's Office after the return to power of President Obote (q.v.). During his tenure of this office a Commonwealth Team helped to train the Uganda National Liberation Army (UNLA) (q.v.), but withdrew in 1984, apparently because the UNLA failed to respond, and indiscipline was endemic. The British Military Training Team (q.v.) then took on the task. Otai regularly insisted that discipline in the army was improving, in spite of the Luwero Triangle (q.v.) atrocities, which he denied. He also denied reports of torture even after the 1985 report by Amnesty International (q.v.) which documented horrific instances. When President Museveni (q.v.) took power in 1986 Otai went to Kenya (q.v.) and has lived there and in Britain since.

He and Dr John Luwuliza-Kirunda (q.v.) were behind the movement at first known as Force Obote Back Again (FOBA) (q.v.) and later renamed the Uganda People's Front/Army (UPF/A) (q.v.) which has operated mainly in Teso (q.v.). Otai is responsible for publishing a sometimes vituperative newsletter or series of documents under the name of the UPF/A. Most are datelined "Headquarters, Kampala" but they are in fact sent out from an accommodation address in Sutton, Surrey, UK. By 1992 the rebellion he had fostered had petered out, many of the rebels having surrendered earlier.

OWEN FALLS DAM. In 1947 the Uganda Electricity Survey was produced which recommended the building of a hydroelectric dam at the Owen Falls site, just below where the Nile (q.v.) flows out of Lake Victoria (q.v.). The Ripon Falls close to where the Nile exits from the lake were to be submerged by the rising waters (both these falls were rapids rather than waterfalls). Action was taken quickly and the Uganda Electricity Board came into being in January 1948. Agreement was reached with Egypt after some considerable difficulty over details of the flow of water out of Lake Victoria, and Lake Victoria became part of Egypt's "century storage" plan. Labor lines were built so that when the contract was awarded to a consortium of British, Danish, Dutch and Italian firms in 1949, work was able to begin at once. The railway (q.v.) bridge was realigned, and a new road bridge passed over the dam. Cement works at Tororo (q.v.) were developed to meet the needs of the dam construction, but they came on stream later than expected, and much cement had to be imported. Power began to be generated in 1954, and was sold under a long-term contract to Kenya (q.v.) as well as in Uganda.

The cost of the dam was £13 million, three times the original estimate, and at first the demand for electricity was less than had been expected, though by the 1980s sites for a second scheme were being considered. The dam and hydroelectric turbines were inadequately maintained during the 1970s, and since then major repairs costing some £10 million have had to be undertaken. The structure of the dam itself has also had to be strengthened as the type of cement used had deteriorated.

The building of the dam meant an overall rise in the level of Lake Victoria by some six feet. In 1961 exceptionally heavy rains raised the water of Lake Victoria significantly higher than had been anticipated, and a decision to build the dam higher than was strictly necessary for the generation of electricity proved fortuitous when the water rose to within 18 inches of the roadway.

OYITE-OJOK, MAJ. GEN. DAVID (?–1983). He joined the Uganda Army (q.v.) in 1963, and after the 1966 Battle of Mengo (q.v.) he was transferred to Army Headquarters as Deputy Assistant Adjutant and Quartermaster-General in recognition of his loyal support of President Obote (q.v.). In 1970 Major Ojok, as he then was, became Assistant Military Secretary in the Ministry of Defence, a newly-created post which included the Secretaryship of the Planning Committee. When Obote left for the Commonwealth Heads of Government Meeting in 1971, Ojok was one of the small group of Obote-loyalists charged with arresting Amin (q.v.), but Amin struck first and seized power in the coup of 1971 (q.v.). Ojok joined Obote in exile in Tanzania (q.v.) and in 1979 was Deputy Commander under Tito Okello (q.v.) of the small group of exiles who accompanied the Tanzanian Army when it invaded Uganda and overthrew Amin. Ojok was then promoted Brigadier and later Major General, and appointed Chief of Staff of the armed forces in April of that year. Under his command the army lacked discipline, and human rights abuses against the civilian population were widespread. People were illegally detained in barracks, and torture and extra-judicial execution were frequent. In December 1983 he was killed in a helicopter crash in which all aboard perished. Despite rumors, the crash seems to have been an accident, not the result of sabotage. His death led to yet further disintegration in the army as Acholi (q.v.) officers such as Basilio Okello (q.v.) and Tito Okello (q.v.) were passed over for promotion.

-P-

PETERS, DR CARL (1856–1918). The founder of the Society for German Colonization in 1884. In 1887 he went to East Africa for a second time with a German expedition whose ostensible aim was the relief of Emin Pasha (q.v.). In fact Peters sought to repeat his previous achievement in persuading African chiefs to sign "treaties" ceding sovereignty to Germany. In early 1890 he reached Uganda. It was still unclear whether Uganda was to fall in the British or German sphere of influence: a demarcation line between the two spheres had been agreed as far as Lake Victoria (q.v.), but no further (*see* Boundaries). The British Protestant (q.v.) missionaries of the Church Missionary Society (q.v.) were disturbed by his approach, hoping for British rule; the Catholic (q.v.) French White Fathers (q.v.) would have preferred German rule. Also present in East Africa was F.J. Jackson (q.v.) of the Imperial British East Africa Company (q.v.) who was under orders not to become involved in Uganda because of the Company's limited resources.

In Uganda Kabaka Mwanga (q.v.) was fighting his way back to power in the Wars of Religion (q.v.), and he sent a letter to Jackson from the Sesse Islands where he was encamped asking for his help. Jackson replied cautiously, making the granting of a treaty a condition of his help. Mwanga gave no firm promise of a treaty, so Jackson continued on his way. Mwanga then wrote again, telling of a victory over Kalema and repeating a request for help. This letter was intercepted by Peters, who allowed the messengers to take the letter on to Jackson, but who himself went as fast as possible to Buganda (q.v.). Although Mwanga had defeated Kalema by this time, the Muslims (*see* Islam) were grouped in Bunyoro (q.v.) and Mwanga still felt in need of support. The Catholic missionaries persuaded him to sign the treaty, to the chagrin of the Protestant faction. Jackson arrived very shortly after this, and tried to persuade him to sign a treaty with the Company, but Mwanga refused as its terms were less favorable to him than the one he had already signed with Peters. In the event the Peters' treaty was nullified by the Anglo-German Agreement (q.v.) of 1890. Peters later served in German East Africa.

PHELPS-STOKES COMMISSION *see* EDUCATION

PROGRESSIVE PARTY. This small Baganda (q.v.) party was founded in 1955 by E.M.K. Mulira (q.v.) who was its President until 1959 when the party ceased to exist. Its main support came from educated professionals and businessmen. It won 12 seats in the Lukiiko (Buganda local parliament) where it campaigned against the carve-up of unallocated mailo (q.v.) land, arguing that it should be used for the benefit of all, not just parcelled out among a fortunate few. The Progressive Party eventually won its case, but also earned the dislike of the chiefs and others who had hoped to benefit from the land deal. The party failed to win widespread popular support.

PROTESTANTS. The name given to all non-Catholics, but primarily to Anglican (q.v.) Christians converted through the work of the Church Missionary Society (CMS) (q.v.) and the three other Anglican Christian missions (q.v.) which worked in conjunction with the CMS in Uganda. All were from the evangelical wing of the Anglican Church rather than from the "high" ritualistic Anglo-Catholic wing of the church which was represented by the Universities Mission to Central Africa which worked in eastern Tanzania (q.v.).

During the Wars of Religion (q.v.) the Protestants were frequently referred to as Bangereza (English) and the adherents of the Roman Catholic (q.v.) White Fathers (q.v.) were called Bafranza (French). The English and Dutch Mill Hill Fathers (q.v.) were encouraged to work in Uganda in order to break this stereotyping which the Protectorate government found politically undesirable. In the 1950s and 1960s, when nationalist political parties were being formed to work for independence, the Uganda People's Congress (q.v.) led by Milton Obote (q.v.) became a predominantly Protestant party and the Democratic Party (q.v.) predominantly Catholic. Both churches suffered severely under President Amin (q.v.): the Protestants having fewer and weaker international links than the Catholics were at somewhat of a disadvantage. Archbishop Janani Luwum (q.v.) was murdered and six other Bishops fled into exile. Obote (q.v.) drove a wedge between the two churches by favoring the Protestants. Both churches expressed concern at the continuing violence which marked his return to power in 1980. The Catholics and the opposition Democratic Party took the stronger stand against the barbarities of Obote's second presidency.

President Museveni (q.v.) refused to allow the old political parties to campaign in the Elections of 1989 (q.v.), but this coincidence of religious and political allegiance continues to bedevil national life in spite of efforts by both secular and religious leaders to overcome it.

Since independence a number of mainly American Baptist and Pentecostalist missions have entered Uganda. Their work is mainly confined to the towns.

PUBLIC SAFETY UNIT. This misnamed group was an armed group with wide powers set up by President Amin (q.v.) to protect the military regime from the general public. Among the killings attributed to it was the murder of a student outside Makerere University (q.v.) in March 1976 which led to the establishment of the Commission of Enquiry (q.v.) chaired by Professor Bryan Langlands.

-R-

RAILWAY. The Uganda Railway was begun in 1896 and reached Port Florence (Kisumu), then part of the Uganda Protectorate (*see* Boundaries), in 1902. Its construction was a great engineering feat and adventure saga as engineers and plate-layers faced waterless thorn scrub, the man-eating lions of Tsavo, and the engineering problems of negotiating the Rift Valley and the descent from the highlands to Lake Victoria (q.v.) which inspired a number of published accounts.

The idea for a railway inland was first floated in the mid-1880s but was only seriously taken up in 1892 after the Brussels Convention which sought ways of ending the slave trade, opening up the interior of Africa, and ending the use of head portering which had cost hundreds of lives. Sir William McKinnon of the Imperial British East Africa Company (q.v.) received a small grant from the British government to build the first part of the Central Africa Railway. He succeeded in getting seven miles of very narrow gauge track laid which was later pulled up and used as tram-track in Mombasa.

After a Protectorate had been declared over Uganda in 1893, the British government began to think seriously of a railway to be used for troop movements, though in public only its contribution to ending the slave trade was mentioned. A survey had already been carried out by Captain J.R.L. MacDonald to find a route which would avoid tunnelling and as many deep cuttings, viaducts and bridges as possible because of the impossibility of getting heavy machinery inland. Britain was jolted into action by French colonial ambitions, especially the railway they were preparing to build inland from Djibouti which it was feared would threaten British claims on the Sudan (q.v.). Work actually began in May 1986 in spite of fears summarized by the writer of the famous jingle which ended with the words, "It is clearly naught but a lunatic line." Thereafter East Africa prided itself on its "lunatic line" which actually negotiates a spiral on its ascent out of Mombasa. Several thousand Indians were brought in as workers, most of whom returned home afterwards. Entrepreneurs also arrived, one of whom was the famous supplier, Allidina Visram (q.v.), who laid the foundations for future Asian (q.v.) trade expansion in inland East Africa.

The railway reached Nairobi in 1899 and Lake Victoria in December 1901 though it was some time before regular services were established along the length of the line. The railway traversed 580 miles (930 kilometers) and reached a maximum altitude of 8,379 feet (2,553 meters) above sea level. Between Mau Summit and Lake Victoria the track descended 4,600 feet (1,420 meters) in 90 miles (145 kilometers). From Port Florence a steamer service was put into operation from there to Port Bell and the journey time between Uganda and the coast was reduced from three months to the inside of a week. In 1902 the boundary (q.v.)

was moved westward so that the entire length of rail was within one administration. The line was nevertheless called the Uganda Railway, and railway furniture and cutlery inscribed accordingly are occasionally found in use 90 years later.

In 1931 the railway finally reached Kampala (q.v.). From Nakuru in Kenya onwards it took a more northerly route than the original line to Kisumu, crossing Timboroa Summit at an altitude of 9,136 feet (2,784 meters), the highest point of any railway in the former British Empire. It passed through Eldoret before descending to Tororo (q.v.) and crossing the Nile (q.v.) at Jinja (q.v.). In 1956 it was extended westwards to the copper mines at Kasese. A northern branch line from Tororo reached Soroti (q.v.) by 1929, but was only extended to Gulu (q.v.) in 1963, and to Pakwach on the Nile the following year. Plans to take it across the Nile to Arua (q.v.) had not materialized by the early 1990s.

The railway is Uganda's main export route. It was run by the East African Railways and Harbours Board until the breakup of the East African Community (q.v.) in 1977. The Uganda economy was in bad shape then, and the railway deteriorated seriously, much Ugandan coffee being taken by road until the mid-1980s when refurbishment began.

REBELLION OF 1897. In July 1897 Kabaka Mwanga (q.v.) fled across Lake Victoria (q.v.) to Buddu (q.v.) to join a growing army of malcontents and raise a rebellion. Mwanga had been humiliated both by the British and by their Baganda (q.v.) collaborators, and he and those who supported him believed that not only he, but also Buganda, had suffered humiliation. Among the rebels were many Catholics (q.v.) including Gabrieli Kintu, the Catholic commander of the army who had been deposed for disloyalty, and a number of Catholic pages, as well as Muslims, traditionalists and a few Protestants (q.v.). The Catholic missionaries and most great Catholic chiefs would have nothing to do with the rebellion, and warned their followers against it. The British were by this time so well entrenched that it was, in any case, a hopeless cause. Mwanga suffered a heavy defeat from a force of 500 Sudanese (q.v.) troops and a large army of Baganda (q.v.).

He fled to German territory and was sent to Mwanza, but escaped and took refuge with Mukama Kabarega (q.v.) in Bunyoro (q.v.). The British deposed Mwanga and installed Daudi Chwa (q.v.) his infant son in his place under the regency of Apolo Kagwa (q.v.), Zakariya Kizito Kisingiri (q.v.) and Stanislaus Mugwanya (q.v.). Gabrieli Kintu held out against the British in Kabula on the border of Ankole (q.v.) for nearly two years, and Mwanga and Kabarega evaded capture for as long. Eventually they were both cornered in the swamps of south Lango (q.v.) in April 1899, and deported to the Seychelles. The position of the chiefs who supported the British was greatly strengthened and Buganda gained territorially after the war against Mwanga and against Bunyoro by having the county of Kabula and the "Lost Counties" (q.v.) and land south of the Kafu River ceded to her.

REFUGEES. Uganda has both received and generated large numbers of refugees since 1960, the "year of independence" for many African countries. By the time Uganda became independent in 1963 there were already over 33,000 refugees from the Congo, now Zaire (q.v.), 80,000 from Rwanda (q.v.) and a few thousand from Sudan (q.v.) being cared for in Uganda. This last group grew steadily until by 1972, when the Addis Ababa Agreement ended the first Sudanese Civil War, over 75,000 Southern Sudanese refugees had been registered and the true total was believed to be well over 100,000. It is unclear how many of these returned to Sudan: at least 6,000 remained in Uganda, probably more. Although there was occasional trouble and dissatisfaction among the refugees, Uganda operated a generous policy towards them until 1982. Schools were enlarged with international money to take refugee pupils, and the churches were closely involved with assistance programs.

In 1982, during the second period in office of President Obote (q.v.), the Uganda People's Congress (UPC) (q.v.) turned on the Banyarwanda (q.v.) refugees in Ankole (q.v.) expelling many, and forcing the Office of the UN High Commissioner for Refugees (UNHCR) to relocate many others (*see* Expulsions). The Zairean refugees were more scattered among the population and were left unmolested. In 1992–1993 a deterioration in the Southern Sudan led to many thousands of Sudanese again moving southwards into areas of Acholi (q.v.) and West Nile (q.v.), and there was a new influx of Zaireans fleeing ethnic cleansing in Kivu Province.

Ugandans first became refugees in 1966 after the Battle of Mengo 1966 (q.v.). A number of royalist Baganda (q.v.) have lived in Britain ever since. During the presidency of Idi Amin (q.v.) Uganda generated thousands of refugees. About 10,000 went to Kenya (q.v.) and several thousand more to Tanzania (q.v.), Britain and North America. The expulsion of the Asians (q.v.) turned them into refugees in 1972. The main exodus of Ugandans during Amin's presidency occurred in 1977 when the Acholi found themselves marked out for harassment. The violence of the Amin regime was unpredictable and random, so fewer people fled than during Obote's second presidency when whole groups found themselves targeted and when a very different type of oppression coupled with insurgency was experienced.

In 1980 30,000 people took refuge in Sudan and over 100,000 in Haut-Zaire because of the violence perpetrated by the Uganda National Liberation Army (UNLA) (q.v.) during electioneering prior to the Elections of 1980 (q.v.). After the elections the violence continued as the UNLA took revenge on West Nile (q.v.) whose population it identified with Amin's oppression. The Ombachi Massacre (q.v.) was one incident in a series which drove 100,000 into Zaire and up to 50,000 into Sudan. An even larger exodus to Sudan occurred in 1982–1983 when 200,000 Ugandans were in UNHCR camps in Sudan, and perhaps a further 100,000 were self-settled. Those in Zaire gradually returned over the next few years but by 1984 some 63,000 still remained, the majority of them in UNHCR settlements. Very few returned from Sudan into northern West Nile because of continuing insurgency there. So indiscriminate had been the military violence against the civilian population that there were officials of the ruling Uganda People's Congress (q.v.) among the refugees in Sudan. During the early 1980s there was also massive internal displacement both within and from the Luwero Triangle (q.v.).

Since the National Resistance Movement (q.v.) led by President Museveni (q.v.) came to power in 1986 many refugees have returned to Uganda, but others have fled, though in far smaller numbers. Most of the new refugees have been from Acholi and Teso (q.v.), both of which have been disturbed by insurgency, and in both of which the army got out of control. By mid-1992 most of the fighting had died down, but in spite of amnesties it was not always safe for refugees and displaced people to return: if they had witnessed atrocities by the National Resistance Army (q.v.) they might well be turned on if recognized by soldiers who knew they could give evidence about the atrocities they had observed. A trickle of people seeking asylum was still leaving Uganda in early 1994, though the numbers were tiny compared with previous flows.

RELIGION *see* ANGLICANS; CATHOLICS; CHRISTIAN MARTYRS; CHURCH MISSIONARY SOCIETY; ISLAM; ISMAILIS; MISSIONS; MUSLIM MARTYRS; PROTESTANTS; REVIVAL; SEVENTH DAY ADVENTISTS; VERONA FATHERS; WARS OF RELIGION; WHITE FATHERS; WHITE SISTERS

RESISTANCE COUNCILS (RCs). The National Resistance Movement (q.v.) governs through a five-tier pyramid of Resistance Councils. Above the top tier (RC5) is the National Resistance Council (q.v.) which functions as the country's Parliament. Elections to the lowest tier, the Village Resistance Councils (RC1s), are open to everyone over the age of 18. Membership of each higher level is elected by the members of the Executive Committee (EC) of the RC one rung below it. So the EC of RC1s elect the members of RC2s and so on. Provision has been made to ensure that a percentage of women is elected. RC1s are responsible for law and order in their localities, and the control they exercise is generally benign and a welcome relief from the previous state of lawlessness under Presidents Amin (q.v.) and Obote (q.v.). In some cases representatives of the old political parties, the Uganda People's Congress (q.v.) and the Democratic Party (q.v.), wield power in the RCs.

REVIVAL *(BALOKOLE)* MOVEMENT. *Balokole* is a Luganda *(see* Languages) word meaning "the saved ones," and is the name usually given to those members of the Church of Uganda (q.v.) who have been influenced by the Revival movement which began in the 1930s, reaching Uganda from Rwanda (q.v.). After the Wars of Religion (q.v.) it became fashionable for Ugandans to become Christians, and the allegiance of many was minimal. The years between the two world wars saw a hardening of colonial attitudes and a withdrawal of responsibility from African churchmen and women. The economic depression of the 1930s led missions (q.v.) to concentrate on educational and medical work for which government subsidies were available, and the nominal membership of the church was increased by pupils baptized almost routinely during their schooldays. The need for spiritual rekindling and for new relationships between black and white Christians was therefore great.

The Revival began in Rwanda where a Ugandan, Blazio Kigozi, and a friend underwent a profound spiritual experience resulting in a joyful sense of forgiveness which proved infectious among both missionaries and African Christians. The intensity of the experience led to some excesses and hysteria in the early days, and it was a while before these excesses were controlled, and the essential truth of the Revival message could be seen. Evangelistic teams of Africans and Europeans working together in a new way spread the message widely, and strong fellowships were formed, welcoming Christians into a new community. Kigozi died in 1936, but the movement continued to spread, and with such force that only the patience and tact of Bishop Stuart of Uganda kept the Church of Uganda together. Like all such movements, the Revival has sometimes tended to become stereotyped, introverted and, at its worst, self-righteous and judgmental, but leaders like Bishop Festo Kivengere (q.v.) and Archbishop Janani Luwum (q.v.) have been aware of this danger. Much of the strength of the Church of Uganda lies in the Revival movement, most of its clergy are drawn from among its members, and *Balokole* have a high reputation for honesty, hard work, and high ethical standards. It fulfills some of the functions of a clan, and this genuinely indigenous aspect of it has made it hard for some non-African Christians to feel at home within it. The movement has spread widely in Kenya (q.v.) and Tanzania (q.v.) among Protestant (q.v.) Christians.

RIOTS OF 1945. In January riots and strikes broke out in a number of towns taking the authorities completely by surprise. In Masaka (q.v.), Entebbe (q.v.) and Kampala (q.v.) workers returned to work when wage increases were offered. In the second week of January strikes became much more widespread and involved workers throughout the public services and in private sector employment in many parts of the country. Violence occurred during this phase of the strikes and reinforcements from Kenya (q.v.) were called in when the Uganda Police were overwhelmed. On 20 January Kabaka Mutesa II (q.v.) of Buganda (q.v.) met representatives of those on strike in Kampala. They demanded better prices for their crops, increased rates of pay for workers, and certain changes in the Kabaka's government. The following week a crowd outside the Kabaka's palace demanded the resignation of Serwano Kulubya (q.v.), the reforming Treasurer of the Buganda government. Because of threats against others than himself, he gave in to their demands to avoid bloodshed. Further strikes occurred later that week in Masaka, Jinja (q.v.), Lira (q.v.) and Gulu (q.v.). Nine people in all were killed during these strikes and riots, and 14 more were injured. This was one of the most serious breakdowns of law and order ever in colonial Uganda after 1900.

Because of the demands for Kulubya's resignation, the Protectorate government concluded that a sinister and well-planned and coordinated plot against the Buganda Kingdom Government lay behind the strikes. Most historians have accepted this view. However, the cost of living had increased greatly as a result of World War II, and consumer goods were in very short supply, imports having been virtually stopped. The cost of cotton cloth, hoes, lamps and bicycles, for instance, rose steeply, and these were all goods on which even people on low wages had come to depend. A number of strikes were quickly settled when wages were raised, and many of the strikes occurred outside Buganda. An expected wage-rise had not materialized (it was announced soon after the riots ended). The real reason for the disturbances may well have been economic, with political grievances riding on the back of the strikes in Buganda alone.

ROMAN CATHOLICS *see* CATHOLICS

ROSCOE, REVD JOHN (1862–1932). Missionary and pioneer anthropologist. Roscoe was trained as an engineer, and first went to East Africa with the Church Missionary Society (q.v.) in 1884 aged 22. He was ordained in 1893 by Bishop Tucker (q.v.) and for ten years from 1899–1909 was Principal of the Church of Uganda (q.v.) theological school at Mengo (q.v.). He retired from Uganda the following year and was awarded an MA by Cambridge University for his anthropological work. He had worked closely with Apolo Kagwa (q.v.) who actually got into print before Roscoe. On his return to England he became Rector of Ovington in Norfolk where he continued to write up his anthropological material which was published over a number of years. At the invitation of the Royal Society he led the Mackie Ethnological Expedition to Africa. His best work is that on the Baganda (q.v.) but he also wrote valuable studies of several other Bantu peoples of Uganda (*see* Bibliography for a full list of these).

RUBAGA. In the 1880s this was the location of the royal enclosure of Kabaka Mwanga (q.v.). The land was given to the White Fathers (q.v.) by Mwanga in 1890 after the Wars of Religion (q.v.), and it is now the hill on which the Catholic (q.v.) Cathedral church of St Mary stands, together with the residence of the Archbishop of Kampala (q.v.) and the headquarters of the Catholic Church in Uganda. Rubaga Hospital is sited on the hill as well as schools, convents and the headquarters of the Grail, a lay missionary movement. The first church to be built here was destroyed in the Battle of Mengo 1892 (q.v.). A series of temporary buildings was erected, and in 1901 a large church of sun-dried brick was built which remained for 24 years, though preparations for a permanent building began as early as 1910. The new cathedral was completed in 1924 and consecrated in 1925 by Bishop Streicher (q.v.), construction having been interrupted by World War I.

On Ash Wednesday 1982 the Cathedral was violated during Mass by soldiers of the Uganda National Liberation Army (q.v.), the priests and congregation were forced out at gun point, and offices searched without a search warrant. The soldiers said they believed guerrillas were hidden there after an attack made from the vicinity earlier in the week, but none was found. Cardinal Nsubuga (q.v.) sent a very strongly worded complaint to President Obote (q.v.) and refused to attend any public civil ceremonies until he had received a proper apology for the sacrilege. An apology was eventually forthcoming.

RUKIIDI III, GEORGE DAVID MATTHEW KAMURASI (c. 1895–1966). Mukama of Toro (*see* Batoro), 1929–1965. He had served in the King's African Rifles (q.v.) and had spent a year in England before succeeding his father, Daudi Kasagama (q.v.). Kasagama had always had a difficult relationship with the Protectorate authorities who did not understand the insecurity of his authority over areas not previously subject to the Mukama of Toro but included within its boundaries by the British. Rukiidi inherited some of these problems. In particular he had to defend his position under the Toro Agreement (q.v.) against an administration which saw him as little more than a local chief. However, in 1932 he was able to replace two Baganda (q.v.) senior chiefs with Batoro, one of whom was Mikaeri Rusoke who had been dismissed by the Protectorate government from the position of Katikiro (chief minister) some years previously. Rusoke was appointed to Mwenge, the most important county chieftaincy. In 1936 the new Governor, Sir Philip Mitchell (q.v.), who had little use for indirect rule, proposed a revision of the Toro Agreement (q.v.) and made it clear that he did not see Rukiidi's position as in any way parallel to that of the Kabaka of Buganda: the Toro Agreement could be interpreted as the British thought fit. Rukiidi procrastinated, and the Governor apparently decided against what might have been a major showdown, and the suggestion was dropped.

By the end of World War II the position had changed: Rukiidi had become an elder statesman, well-liked by his subjects and his chiefs, and he was able to cooperate with the Protectorate government in development. 1950 was the fiftieth anniversary of the signing of the Toro Agreement, and this was the occasion for great celebrations in Toro. On the eve of independence Rukiidi again had to defend the Toro Agreement. In 1960 the Kabaka of Buganda, the Mugabe of Ankole (q.v.) and the Mukama of Toro, supported by the Mukama of Bunyoro (q.v.) published "The Rulers' Proclamation" calling for a meeting of the chief ministers of the kingdoms to meet to discuss ways of protecting the rights of the kingdoms. A threat to secede unless these were safeguarded was not taken seriously by the British. The most Rukiidi was able to achieve for Toro was that the prerogatives of the Mukama were protected in the 1962 Constitution (q.v.), and in particular the succession was protected against outside interference. Rukiidi died in December 1965 just before President Obote (q.v.) abolished the traditional kingdoms.

RUWENZORI MOUNTAINS. These fabled "Mountains of the Moon" lie on Uganda's border with Zaire (q.v.), the highest peaks rising to a height of almost 17,000 feet (5,100 meters), well above the snow line. They are frequently cloud-covered and invisible for days on end, and some early European travelers passed close by them without being aware of their presence. They stretch for some 75 miles from north to south. The massif was formed by volcanic activity, and rises out of the Western Rift Valley. The Ruwenzori are much wetter than the other high mountains of East Africa and hence more dangerous for climbers. The mountain slopes are densely forested, trees giving way first to bamboo, and then to the unique high altitude flora of East Africa: giant heaths, giant lobelia and giant groundsel. The lower slopes on the eastern side have been cleared for tea plantations and for Arabica coffee.

The Baamba (q.v.) and the Bakonjo (q.v.) live on the mountain slopes. The Rwenzururu Movement (q.v.), in which both these peoples were involved, operated from hideouts in the mountains.

RWANDA. Since before the colonial era people have migrated northwards from Rwanda into Uganda to escape turbulence and were integrated into the borderlands of Kigezi (q.v.). During the colonial period labor migration continued, Banyarwanda (q.v.) being employed as herdsmen and servants by the Baganda (q.v.) in particular. Relations between Uganda and Rwanda were soured in the 1960s by an influx of 80,000 refugees (q.v.) from massacres perpetrated by the Hutu majority on the Tutsi minority who had been the traditional rulers of the country. In 1982–1983 during the second presidency of Milton Obote (q.v.) these were displaced and many forced back over the border (*see* Expulsions). In October 1990 General Fred Rwigyema (q.v.) led a group of officers and soldiers of Rwandan origin who had joined the National Resistance Army (q.v.) in an invasion of Rwanda. This caused immense disruption in Rwanda and brought trade between the two countries to a temporary halt.

RWENZURURU MOVEMENT. A secessionist movement which emerged among the Bakonjo (q.v.) of Toro (q.v.) in the early 1960s under the leadership of a teacher, Isaya Mukirane. The Baamba (q.v.) also became involved. The Bakonjo live in the foothills of the Ruwenzori Mountains (q.v.) and the Baamba on the northwest lower slopes of the mountains. Both peoples were discontented with their lot as part of Toro. They were taxed but neglected, particularly as regarded education (q.v.), and they were inadequately represented in the local Toro Parliament.

In 1962 when work was in progress on the Administration (Western Kingdoms) Act, which would determine the position of the traditional kingdoms at independence, Bakonjo and Baamba discontent boiled over and they demanded secession from Toro. There were serious disturbances which the Uganda Army (q.v.) was brought in to deal with. A full enquiry was carried out under the aegis of central government which found that the Toro Kingdom Government was to blame for neglecting the Bakonjo and Baamba. It was decided that educational provision must be improved in their areas, and they must be more fully represented on all local government committees. Secession was ruled out. When the

Toro government failed to respond adequately to these recommendations, central government moved in to administer the troubled areas. However, trouble spread, and the areas in which the Bakonjo and Baamba live were declared to be disturbed areas. The Uganda Army drove many of the followers of the Rwenzururu movement over the Ruwenzori into Zaire (q.v.). There they found little sympathy for their cause.

Isaya Mukirane evaded capture, and continued to encourage discontent, but the movement was eventually more or less contained. However, in the 1980s it resurfaced in a small way. In 1987 the Parti de Libération Congolaise (PLC), dedicated to the overthrow of Zairean President Mobutu Sese Seko, mounted attacks on his regime from hideouts in the Ruwenzori mountains on Ugandan soil, and established a liaison with the remnants of the Rwenzururu movement. Mobutu accused the National Resistance Movement (NRM) (q.v.) government of Uganda of supporting the rebels. But the PLC's links with Rwenzururu in fact ensured that the NRM opposed both movements. Nevertheless Mobutu retaliated against Uganda by aiding Ugandan rebel supporters of the deposed President Obote (q.v.) who were trying to win their way back to power. The NRM moved in to deal with the Ruwenzururu and also mounted attacks against Bakonjo coffee smugglers who were transporting Ugandan coffee over the mountains to sell in Zaire. The area remained unsettled until the end of the decade.

RWIGYEMA, MAJ.-GEN. FRED (?–1990). Of Rwandan origin, Rwigyema was recruited into the National Resistance Army (NRA) (q.v.). He was one of those in charge of counterinsurgency operations in Teso (q.v.) in the late 1980s which resulted in massive dislocation and oppression of the civilian population and some well-documented instances of atrocities. In November 1989 the army commander, Salim Saleh, was removed from his command, and Major Generals Elly Tumwine and Rwigyema were "sent on courses." At the beginning of October 1990 Rwigyema led an invasion of Rwanda (q.v.) by many officers and men of the NRA of Rwandan origin. Rwigyema was killed very shortly afterwards in a quarrel over leadership. Teso was reported to be much quieter after so many of the army had left the area, but Rwanda suffered years of warfare and massacre and Kabale (q.v.) District of Uganda suffered from a loss of trade resulting from the closure of the border.

RWOTCAMO (RWOT LABWOR OCHAMO) (?–1887). He became Rwot of Payira in western Acholi (q.v.) and ruled over a wide area. He became chief shortly before 1862 when the first Egyptian ivory and slave traders, known to the Acholi as the Kuturia, established posts at Paloro and at Patiko north of the modern Gulu (q.v.). From these posts they raided into the countryside, and their depredations are recorded by J.H. Speke (q.v.) and J.A. Grant. In 1872 Samuel Baker (q.v.) was welcomed to Patiko by Rwotcamo whose people were suffering severely from the slave raids. Baker attacked the garrison at Patiko, drove out the Kuturia, recovered over 300 head of cattle and released 130 slaves. He promised Rwotcamo protection and left a small garrison while he went to Bunyoro (q.v.). They were unable to beat off attacks from the raiders, and Rwotcamo begged Baker to return. He and Baker got on well, but when Baker left, the Kuturia grossly insulted Rwotcamo by putting him in chains and beating him, treatment which so disgraced him in the eyes of his people that special ceremonies had to be performed before he could be "brought back to life" again.

By the time Emin Pasha (q.v.) arrived on the scene in 1878 Rwotcamo kept his distance. He refused to go to Patiko but invited Emin to visit him. The first visit was a great success, the second, a year later, less so, and on that occasion Emin described his people's apparent lack of respect for the old chief. During the next few years Acholi was administered by Emin's lieutenants who generally behaved badly. Rwotcamo became increasingly uncooperative, and in 1887 there was a battle in which the people of Padibe used Emin's troops against the Payira to settle old scores. Rwotcamo was killed in the battle and the Padibe were accused of stealing the royal drum of Payira and placing Rwotcamo's skull inside it. There was long-lasting enmity between the Padibe and the Payira after this. In 1923 the drum is said to have come into the possession of Awich (q.v.), a son of Rwotcamo and Rwot of Payira in succession to him, but what became of it or Rwotcamo's skull, if indeed it was inside the drum, is unknown. Rwotcamo's name is variously spelled in the contemporary European accounts. He is described by Baker as King of Shuli (Acholi), a misunderstanding of his position.

-S-

SABITI, ARCHBISHOP ERICA (1903–1985). The first Ugandan Archbishop of the Anglican (q.v.) Province of Uganda, Rwanda (q.v.) and Burundi. He was educated at Mbarara High School, King's College, Budo (*see* Education), and Makerere College (q.v.) where he was one of the first to gain a Teacher's Certificate. He was ordained in 1934 and consecrated Bishop and appointed to the newly-created see of Ruwenzori in 1960 with his seat at Fort Portal (q.v.). This was not his home area, and that fact, coupled with his sometimes uncompromising Christian stand, made him some enemies. When in 1966 he was elected Archbishop he met considerable opposition from the Baganda (q.v.) who had been sure that one of them would be appointed to this position, and for a time until the Diocese of Kampala (q.v.) had been carved out of the Diocese of Namirembe (q.v.) to give the Archbishop a base, he had to continue to live in Fort Portal, far from the capital. In 1969 he welcomed Pope Paul VI to the Anglican martyrs' shrine (*see* Christian Martyrs) at Namugongo. In 1971–1972 he played an important role in providing assistance to the beleaguered Christians of the Southern Sudan during the last stages of the first Sudan Civil War (*see* Sudan), and assisting the processes which led to a peace agreement being signed in Addis Ababa. He remained as Archbishop during the first three difficult years under President Amin (q.v.), retiring in 1974. In 1977 when the life of his successor Archbishop Janani Luwum (q.v.) was threatened, he prayed with him on the morning of 17 February: Luwum was murdered later that day. The church was not allowed to hold a memorial service for Luwum, but the Sunday morning service became a memorial service, and Sabiti preached the sermon. He spent his retirement in his own home area, Ankole (q.v.).

SEBEI. The Sebei are Kalenjin speakers, their language (*see* Languages) related to several spoken by Rift Valley peoples of Kenya (q.v.). Their society is based on clan allegiance and age-sets. They were originally nomadic pastoralists who lived on the southwestern slopes of Mount Elgon (q.v.), but who now live on the densely populated northern slopes. They were driven out of their previous home by the encroaching Bagisu (q.v.), and now cultivate sorghum, millet and maize, having lost their grazing lands. They have constantly had to defend themselves against raids from the Karamojong (q.v.) and from their Kenyan neighbors. The first European visited the area in 1890, and in 1898 it became a supply base for Sudan (q.v.). In the early years of the century colonial administration was introduced by Baganda (q.v.) agents under Semei Kakungulu (q.v.). A military post was established in Sebei country in 1914, and raiding was much reduced. The British banned witchcraft and oathing and the prophets who were the guardians of community rituals. These died out, and something of a power-vacuum resulted. Sebei became a separate district on the eve of independence. Not until 1972 did electricity reach Kapchorwa, the township which is the administrative center of the district. President Amin (q.v.) removed Aloni Muzungyu, the Sebei chief who had been appointed District Commissioner, and replaced him by an army officer. Tension between the Bagisu and the Sebei increased and fighting broke out after the fall of President Amin when guns became widely available, taken from or sold by his fleeing troops. It was some time before the area was quiet again.

SEVENTH DAY ADVENTISTS. Members of this denomination share with other Christians the beliefs formulated in the historic creeds. They differ from other Christians in attaching great importance to keeping the seventh day of the week rather than Sunday as their day for rest and worship, and in laying great emphasis on special interpretations of Scripture regarding the second coming of Christ and the end of the world. They practice abstinence from tobacco and alcohol, and recommend abstinence from meat and stimulants such as tea and coffee. Their presence in Uganda dates from 1927 when Pastor Maxwell and two Africans from Kenya (q.v.) opened a mission near Mubende. Their work in Uganda is now centered on Kireka near Kampala (q.v.). They also work around Mbale (q.v.) and have a hospital at Ishaka in Bushenyi and small networks of schools which do not receive government grants. They have never won a large following, but those who have joined the church have a reputation for high ethical standards. Church membership stood at c. 6,000 in 1970.

SLEEPING SICKNESS (TRYPANOSOMIASIS). An epidemic of sleeping sickness affected Uganda between 1900 and 1920. It is likely that between 250,000 and 300,000 people died, up to a third of the population in the worst affected areas such as the shores of Lake Victoria (q.v.) in Buganda (q.v.) and Busoga (q.v.). It probably occurred in a non-immune population, and although the source of the infection is not known, it may perhaps have been introduced by the Sudanese (q.v.) brought into Uganda by Lugard (q.v.), having previously reached the area of the Nile-Congo watershed as a result of the expedition of H.M. Stanley (q.v.). The epidemic in Uganda began in Busoga and was first diagnosed by Dr Albert Cook (q.v.) in 1900, by which time it was well-established. The epidemic peaked in 1902–1903, just at the same time as its cause, the bite of the tsetse fly (glossina morsitans), was discovered by Colonel David Bruce who had been sent to Uganda by the Royal Society in London to investigate the disease. In 1906 Governor Sir Hesketh Bell (q.v.) decided to evacuate the lakeshore in order to save the remaining population, and this was undertaken without trouble the following year in spite of British government hesitation in London about such a drastic measure. The Busoga lakeshore was evacuated in 1908 and the Sesse Islands in 1909. Other foci of the disease were around Lakes Edward and George, around Lake Albert, along the Nile (q.v.) as it flowed northward from Lake Albert towards the

Sudan (q.v.), and along the shores of Lake Victoria in Bukedi (q.v.). The epidemic in these areas was far smaller than that on the Buganda and Busoga shores of Lake Victoria.

SOROTI. The administrative center of Soroti District, formerly the headquarters of Teso (q.v.) which also included Kumi District. The railway (q.v.) reached Soroti in 1929 but a tarmac road had to wait many years. The town is an ecclesiastical center for both the Catholic Church (q.v.) and the Church of Uganda (q.v.). Soroti suffered both when troops of President Amin (q.v.) fled through after his over-throw, and again when Basilio Okello (q.v.) and Tito Okello (q.v.) fled northwards after their overthrow in 1986. The whole Teso area was disrupted by insurgency inspired by John Luwuliza-Kirunda (q.v.) and Peter Otai (q.v.) between 1986 and 1990, when the fighting died down.

SPARTAS, REUBEN SEBBANJA SSEDIMBA MUKASA (1899–1988). He was born to Christian parents and started school at what was then the early age of eight. He was taken into the household of Archdeacon Daniel at Bishop Tucker College, Mukono, to continue his schooling. Praised by a teacher for showing the spirit of the ancient Greek city of Sparta, he took that as his name, later adding an ''s'' when told this was the masculine form. He won a scholarship to King's College, Budo (*see* Education), and then joined the African Native Medical Corps in 1914, completing his schooling after World War I in 1920. He considered being ordained in the Anglican Church (q.v.) but his reading in the library at Mukono persuaded him that ''Anglicanism was a mere branch of the true church.'' He joined the King's African Rifles (q.v.) where he met Obadiah Basajjakitale, another critic of the Anglican Church. In 1926 they founded a private school and tried without success to found the African Progressive Association and the Christian Army for the Salvation of Africa. In 1929 they announced that they had broken with the Anglican Church and were setting up the African Orthodox Church. In 1934 this became the African Greek Orthodox Church. Spartas joined with I.K. Musazi (q.v.) in founding the Sons of Kintu, and in 1945 he was active in the Bataka Party (q.v.). After the Bataka Riots of 1949 (q.v.) he was imprisoned with James Miti (q.v.) and ten others for "rebelling against His Highness the Kabaka—thereby contravening native custom." After he was released four years later he continued to be active in politics, and in 1955 became a founder member of the Progressive Party (q.v.). The following year he became a member of the Buganda Lukiiko (local parliament), being nominated by the Kabaka.

Meanwhile Spartas had also continued his religious activity. In 1932 he and Basajjakitale were ordained priest by Archbishop Alexander of the African Orthodox Church of South Africa. Their orders were recognized by the Orthodox Patriarch of Alexandria in 1946 who seems not to have realized that Alexander was not regularly ordained. When Spartas' wife died in 1946 he did not marry again in obedience to the rules of the Orthodox Church. In the 1960s the Greek Orthodox Church realized that the Orthodox Church in Uganda was in fact somewhat irregular, and decided to offer it assistance including clergy training in Greece. Spartas was passed over as Bishop. The Orthodox Church became fully accepted by the Catholics (q.v.) and the Church of Uganda (q.v.) and its new leader, Bishop Ireneo Nankyama, signed memoranda to the government alongside the Cardinal, the Church of Uganda Archbishop and the Chief Kadhi, leader of the Muslims, on several occasions.

Spartas was unhappy at being sidelined and for a time he separated himself from the church he had founded and formed a small splinter group. However, as he grew older the animosity faded, and he became accepted as an elder statesman, though without real authority. He died in 1988 aged around 90.

SPEKE, JOHN HANNING (1827–1864). A British traveler who recognized Lake Victoria (q.v.) at the Ripon Falls as the source of the Nile (q.v.). In 1855 he was commissioned by the Royal Geographical Society to explore Lake Nyasa (now Lake Malawi) and the surrounding country. It was in 1858, after visiting Lake Tanganyika, that he sighted Lake Victoria and guessed this to be the source of the Nile. In 1860 the

Royal Geographical Society commissioned Speke and Grant to test this in a further journey to central Africa. In 1862 Speke sighted the Nile and a week later reached the falls at its outflow from Lake Victoria, naming these the Ripon Falls. He was prevented from following the course of the Nile through Uganda, but he sighted the Karuma Falls and learnt of the existence of Lake Albert (known to the Banyoro [q.v.] as Luta Nzige), and that the Nile flowed into and out of this lake. He then traveled northward on his way back to Europe. In England some sceptics refused to accept his assumption that he had found the source of the Nile.

SSEMAKULA, SHEIKH SWAIBU (?–1973). He was the son of Christian parents but converted to Islam (q.v.) when he went with a group of Muslim porters to Kenya (q.v.) and was well-cared for by them when he fell ill. He studied Islam under various Baganda (q.v.) teachers and was made a Sheikh in 1911. His fame as a teacher grew steadily. He became one of the best-known Muslim teachers and was responsible for teaching a whole generation of Muslim Sheikhs. In 1962 he was chosen by Prince Badru Kakungulu (q.v.) to lead the Muslim prayers at Uganda's independence ceremony. In 1965 he joined the National Association of African Muslims (NAAM) (q.v.) and was appointed Sheikh Mufti in 1968, and the only government-recognized Muslim spokesman. This earned him the dislike of many Baganda Muslims. After the fall of President Obote (q.v.) in 1971 he found himself out of favor and ignored, and he died in obscurity.

SSEMOGERERE, PAUL KAWANGA (1932–). President of the Democratic Party (DP) (q.v.) and Leader of the Opposition, 1981–1985; appointed Deputy Prime Minister in 1986. He was educated at Makerere College (q.v.) and Syracuse University, USA, where he gained a Ph.D. In 1961, already active in politics, he became secretary to Benedicto Kiwanuka (q.v.) who was then Chief Minister of Uganda. During Obote's (q.v.) second presidency his role as Leader of the Opposition was a controversial one as the existence of an opposition party, however, emasculated, helped to give credence to Obote's dubious claim to be running a parliamentary democracy, and helped to disarm international criticism of his regime. However, under Ssemogerere the DP took a brave stand against Obote's excesses, especially through its official newspaper, *Munnansi*. He also laid himself open to criticism for taking office as Minister of Internal Affairs under President Tito Okello (q.v.), but he was quickly confirmed in this post when President Museveni (q.v.) came to power, and remained in it until 1988. He has shown a consistent regard for parliamentary democracy and human rights. He is married to Dr Germina Nnamatovu.

STANLEY, HENRY MORTON (1841–1904). Explorer and writer. The man who found Dr David Livingstone ("Dr Livingstone I presume") and the first European to travel right across Africa. Stanley visited Uganda twice, on his journey of 1874–1877 when he circumnavigated Lake Victoria (q.v.) and met Kabaka Mutesa I (q.v.) of Buganda (q.v.), and again when he traversed Africa from west to east in 1887–1889 and passed through Ankole (q.v.).

Like many nineteenth century European travelers he was greatly impressed by the sophistication of the court of Buganda (q.v.), and by Mutesa in particular with whom he got on very well, Mutesa being impressed in his turn by Stanley. They first met on 5 April 1875, a momentous meeting in its consequences for Uganda. This was not long after Stanley had parted from Livingstone for whom he cherished a great admiration. Livingstone had already formed the impression from what he had read and heard of Buganda that the preaching of Christianity to Mutesa could be of great importance. Stanley for his part realized that to gain an entrance for Christianity in Buganda would be a publicity coup, and he therefore found himself in the unusual role of a promoter of the Christian faith. Mutesa was a willing listener because he was worried about Egyptian expansionism, and saw the possibility of getting access to European firearms, which were superior to those possessed by his Muslim (*see* Islam) allies, and the chance to forge an alliance which might help to stave off the threat from the north.

Stanley sent off a letter, published in the *Daily Telegraph,* inviting Christian missionaries to Buganda in Mutesa's name without, apparently, realizing what was in Mutesa's mind. This call received an enthusiastic response from the Church Missionary Society (q.v.), the first of whose missionaries arrived in Buganda in 1877, and thereby set the history of the area off in a quite new direction.

Stanley's second visit to Uganda was in 1889 after he had persuaded Emin Pasha (q.v.) to accompany him to the coast. He left Lake Edward on 4 July having decided to avoid Buganda, which was in the throes of the Wars of Religion (q.v.), and travel back to the East African coast via a more southerly route.

Mugabe Ntare V (q.v.) of Ankole (q.v.) was very wary of Stanley and would not meet him. The people of Ankole treated Stanley with great courtesy, however, and food was provided free for his caravan. Some of the Baganda Christian exiles asked for Stanley's help against the Muslim faction which had taken power, but Stanley refused. Near Mbarara (q.v.) Stanley was met by Bucunku, Ntare's first cousin, and he and Stanley went through a form of blood brotherhood. The treaty which was made between Stanley and Bucunku apparently ceded all rights of government over Ankole to Stanley who in turn passed them on to the Imperial British East Africa Company (IBEAC) (q.v.). The Germans in East Africa refused to recognize it, and it was never tested as a new agreement was entered into between the IBEAC and Ntare himself. Whereas Stanley's intervention in Buganda was of great importance, his visit to Ankole was of no lasting significance.

STATE RESEARCH BUREAU. President Amin's (q.v.) most feared and hated institution of coercion, located at Nakasero, Kampala (q.v.), and headed first by Major L.M.P. Ozi, then by Lt Col. Francis Itabuka until 1977, and from 1978 until Amin's overthrow, by Lt Col. Farouk Minawa. The State Research Bureau had almost unlimited powers to collect information, harass, torture and kill people. Its members operated in cars with the registration letters UVS (so were often referred to as ''UVS boys'') and even entered Kenya (q.v.) in these vehicles from time to time, and the thousands of Ugandan refugees (q.v.) in Kenya feared abduction. UVS cars were seen in Nairobi on the day when a memorial service was held in Nairobi Cathedral for the murdered Archbishop Janani Luwum (q.v.). Among the many incidents for which they were responsible was the disappearance of a Kenyan student of Makerere University (q.v.), Esther Chesire (q.v.). When Amin was overthrown there was a horrified reaction to the conditions found in the State Research Bureau buildings. As well as corpses, bloodstains and evidence of torture, files showed that a more systematic operation had been carried out than had been realized, and that British-manufactured electronic equipment had continued to be supplied, in spite of the death of Bob Scanlon, representative of a British electronics firm. Amnesty International (q.v.) asked for tighter export controls on such equipment, and in 1981 published *The Repression Trade,* which included evidence about the trade between Britain (q.v.) and Uganda. British Prime Minister Margaret Thatcher wrote to Amnesty refusing to consider tighter controls.

STREICHER, ARCHBISHOP HENRI (1863–1952). Streicher was accepted by Cardinal Lavigerie (q.v.), founder of the Catholic (q.v.) White Fathers (q.v.), in 1884, ordained priest in 1887, and arrived in Uganda in February 1891. He went straight to Buddu (q.v.) where he opened a new mission, but during the Wars of Religion (q.v.) he and his colleagues had to flee to German territory south of Lake Victoria (q.v.). After the Battle of Mengo of 1892 (q.v.), Buddu was allocated to the Catholics and Streicher reopened the mission at Villa Maria (q.v.). In 1896 he was appointed to succeed Bishop Hirth as Vicar Apostolic of Nyanza.

During the next few years when there were frequent misunderstandings between the British colonial administration and French Catholic missionaries, Streicher did much to reduce the tension, and during the uprising of Mwanga (q.v.) against the British in 1897 he played a conspicuous part in maintaining the loyalty of Ugandan Catholics to the British administration.

In 1893 Streicher was put in charge of the seminary

founded by Hirth, and throughout his episcopate he continued to work for the establishment of an indigenous clergy, refusing to be discouraged by those who said the time had not yet come. The first two African priests were ordained in 1913, Uganda taking the lead in this respect for the whole African continent. His episcopate also saw the growth and deepening of the work of the White Fathers' Mission throughout western and central Uganda, and the establishment of schools (*see* Education) and medical work (*see* Medicine).

In 1913 he retired to the Catholic Mission at Ibanda, was made titular Archbishop of Brisi and a Papal Count, and awarded the CBE by the British government.

SUDAN. The boundary (q.v.) between Uganda and Sudan was not finally agreed until 1926, and like most colonial boundaries it makes little demographic sense in that it divides ethnic groups all along its line. During the colonial period there were no border controls, and milestones in northern Uganda showed the distance to Juba in Southern Sudan. After Sudan gained its independence in 1956 rebellion developed in the south against the colonialism and religious aggression of the Khartoum government, and this erupted into full-scale civil war in 1964. Even before this the first wave of Southern Sudanese refugees (q.v.) had reached Uganda. Relations between Uganda and the Sudanese government in Khartoum were strained in the early years of independence, but in 1969 when Gaafer Nimeiri came to power in Sudan at the head of a socialist government, they improved, and President Obote (q.v.) tried to stop aid to the Anya Nya (q.v.) guerrillas in the Sudan. General (later President) Idi Amin (q.v.) favored the Anya Nya, and relations with Sudan seem to have been a contributory factor in the coup of 1971 (q.v.) which brought Amin to power. During Obote's second presidency up to 350,000 Ugandans took refuge in Sudan, but from 1992 onwards Sudanese again fled to Uganda in large numbers.

SUDANESE. The inhabitants of Sudan (q.v.). The troops left behind in Equatoria (q.v.) by Emin Pasha (q.v.) and brought into Uganda by Lugard (q.v.) in 1891 were generally referred to, quite correctly, as Sudanese. Their descendants, however, are usually referred to as Nubians (q.v.).

SUDANESE MUTINY (1897). The Sudanese (q.v.) troops brought by Lugard (q.v.) into Uganda in 1891 were used to break the Rebellion of 1897 (q.v.). When Kabaka Mwanga (q.v.) had been defeated and fled, a detachment of Sudanese was ordered to march to the northeast to intercept French expeditions believed to be converging on the Nile (q.v.). From there they would possibly be taken north to reinforce Khartoum. In late September they reached Ngare Nyuki overlooking the eastern Rift Valley in what is now Kenya (q.v.). They were poorly clothed, force-marched, underpaid and with pay often in arrears, and aggrieved at the prospect of an expedition of unknown length. To add to their grievances they were forbidden to take with them their women who normally cooked for them. They made their complaints known to F. J. Jackson (q.v.) and to J.R.L. Macdonald who was to lead the expedition, and whom they had served under in the past and disliked. They asked to be allowed to return to Uganda where their families were, and when this was refused, they mutinied. They made their way back, passing through Nandi where they were joined by the garrison there, and they helped themselves to arms and ammunition, and reached Busoga (q.v.). There they seized the fort at Luba's, killing three European officers. This made negotiations impossible, and a force commanded by Macdonald was sent to surround the fort. Reinforcements from India were expected, but not immediately, and the mutiny posed a serious threat. In a major battle on 11 December 1897 George Pilkington of the Church Missionary Society (q.v.), who was acting as an interpreter, was among those killed.

At this point Mwanga reappeared in Buddu (q.v.) with a considerable force. Macdonald was forced to take a section of his army south to deal with this new threat, and the Sudanese thereupon succeeded in breaking out of Luba's and made off northwards to try and join up with the other Sudanese garrisons to spread the mutiny. Macdonald, returning from Buddu where Mwanga had been defeated for a second time, caught up with them, and with a small contingent of newly-arrived Indian troops stormed their encampment. Some escaped northwards, but further Indian reinforcements were expected, and the real threat which the mutiny had at first presented was now past. Twelve of the mutineers were hanged and between 400 and 500 died; there were 280 deaths among those who put down the mutiny and another 555 men were wounded. Immediately afterwards army pay was greatly increased, and the army was reinforced with Indian and Swahili troops employed on permanent terms.

-T-

TANZANIA. After World War I German East Africa was administered by Britain (q.v.) under a League of Nations mandate and known as Tanganyika. Ties between the three British-ruled East African territories were close. Tanganyika became independent in 1962. In 1964 there was a rebellion on Zanzibar and following this Zanzibar united with Tanganyika and the joint republic was renamed Tanzania. Relations with Uganda were good during the first decade of independence as both President Nyerere of Tanzania and President Obote (q.v.) of Uganda pursued socialist policies. The 1971 coup (q.v.) when President Amin (q.v.) seized power changed that. Obote was given refuge in Tanzania, and Nyerere refused to recognize Amin's government. In October 1972 an unsuccessful invasion was organized by Obote from Tanzania. In late 1978 Amin's troops invaded the Kagera Salient (q.v.). The counter-measures taken by Tanzania did not end with expelling the invading Ugandans: the War of Liberation (q.v.), in which a small contingent of Ugandans fought alongside the Tanzanian People's Defence Force, ended up by overthrowing Amin. Because Uganda had no proper army or police force, Tanzanian troops remained in the country until the Elections of 1980 (q.v.). During Obote's second presidency relations between the two countries remained cool, and when he was overthrown a second time he was not welcomed back to Tanzania, but went to Zambia where he was less able to interfere in

Uganda's affairs. Relations between the government of President Museveni (q.v.) and Tanzania have been untroubled by contrast with relations between Uganda and Kenya (q.v.).

TEN POINT PROGRAMME. The political program of the National Resistance Movement/Army (NRM/A) (q.v.) led by President Museveni (q.v.). It was drawn up during the period when the NRA was fighting in the bush, and it was the basis of the speech made by Museveni in 1986 when he was sworn in as President. It stems from his analysis of the way in which former post-independence administrations had governed by exploiting already-existing ethnic and religious cleavages, and failing to correct severe economic imbalances. First, democracy was to be restored from the grassroots upwards. Local Resistance Councils (q.v.) accessible to all were to be the basis for this. Secondly, the public had to be given personal security. The police and army had to be disciplined and politicized so that they understood what they were doing and why. Thirdly, all forms of sectarianism had to be rooted out, both ethnic and religious. Fourthly, genuine independence had to be achieved. Uganda had to think out its own policies and become genuinely non-aligned. The Fifth point is closely related: an independent, integrated and self-sustaining national economy had to be built. Sixthly came a policy of improving social services and rehabilitating the war-ravaged areas. People needed to be mobilized to protect their own health, and illiteracy could be wiped out if all those who could read taught others. Seventh on the list came the need to end corruption and the misuse of power. Point Eight is a kind of catch-all which lists some of the major injustices needing to be put right, in particular major problems left by ill-conceived development projects, the plight of the Karamojong (q.v.), and the plight of salaried staffs who had seen their earnings eroded by hyperinflation until they were forced to neglect their jobs in order to supplement their salaries. Ninthly was placed the need to cooperate with other African countries in defending human and democratic rights, and finally came the need for pragmatism and for a mixed economy.

Progress towards the implementation of these policies has been slow and uneven, impeded by insecurity in Acholi (q.v.) and Teso (q.v.) in particular, and by the legacy of the previous 14 years of violence, but the Ten Point Programme remains the guide to government policy-making, and by 1993 progress with regard to many of its aims was evident.

TESO *see* ITESO

THOMAS, HAROLD BEKEN ("H.B.") (1888–1971). An officer of the Uganda Lands and Surveys Department from 1911–1940, rising to be its Director. Thomas was a regular contributor to the *Uganda Journal.* He became fluent in Luganda (*see* Languages), and his *Uganda,* published by Oxford University Press in 1935, which he wrote in collaboration with Robert Scott, is a tribute both to his knowledge of the country and to his painstaking scholarship. H.B. Thomas was responsible for building up the Entebbe Secretariat Library, a catalog of which he published in 1940. He continued to support the Uganda Society (q.v.) and the *Uganda Journal* long after he had retired to Britain. From 1947–1961 he saw most issues of the *Uganda Journal* through the press, acting as the editor's London representative. After retirement he also acted as buyer for the Uganda Society's Library, and many volumes in that Library were purchased by H.B. who scoured second-hand booksellers for them, and he was generous in sharing his knowledge and experience with scholars working on Uganda. He was for many years a supporter of the Church Missionary Society (q.v.) and a member of its Committee in London.

TORO *see* BATORO

TORO AGREEMENT. This was signed in 1900 without any of the negotiation which characterized the [B]Uganda Agreement (q.v.). It was drawn up without a proper understanding of practice and custom in Toro or of what had occurred since Kasagama (q.v.) had been instated as Mukama in 1891. The result was a series of disagreements which dogged relations between the Mukama of Toro and the British administration for many years.

In 1900 Sir Harry Johnston (q.v.) called Mukama Kasagama and the chiefs together, and then the English text was orally translated first into Swahili and then into Luganda (*see* Languages). Although not all of the chiefs understood either of these languages, they were required to sign the treaty or lose their chieftaincies. The treaty defined the boundaries of Toro, adding areas to the east and south, including Mwenge which had previously belonged to Bunyoro (q.v.) and was prime grazing land, and Bwamba to the west of the Ruwenzori Mountains (q.v.) which was to be administered by a Protectorate official until the boundary (*see* Boundaries) with the Congo was defined. Mukama Kasagama was to act as a saza (County) chief in Toro proper, and to have authority over the saza chiefs of the other five sazas. Grants of both official and private land were made to the chiefs, the private land being inheritable. Kasagama was to receive ten percent of the taxes raised in Toro proper as well as ten percent of those raised throughout the rest of Toro. The other saza chiefs were to receive ten percent of the taxes raised in their own sazas. Hut and gun taxes were imposed on all adult males, and all forms of tribute were abolished. Saza chiefs would administer justice, with appeals going to the Rukurato (local assembly of chiefs) and finally to a European colonial official. If the terms of the Agreement were broken it might be annulled and the administration might install any form of government it thought fit. Not until Kasagama took the text to a missionary and got it fully translated did it emerge that no note had been taken of the fact that the Mukama had already divided Toro proper into five sazas and appointed chiefs to them. The only change Johnston would agree to was to give each of these chiefs an allowance of private land.

Kasagama was pleased to have his authority acknowledged by treaty, but there was much in the Agreement that was unworkable. In the first place the removal of tribute rights undermined the powers of the chiefs, and Kasagama's own authority was undermined because the Agreement did not give him power to appoint chiefs or to make grants of land throughout Toro, which he had, in any case, already been doing. He was deprived of income from the salt deposits, though he was later allowed to lease these temporarily from the Protectorate. Parts of the Agreement were simply ignored as Kasagama continued to exercise his traditional rights to grant land and appoint chiefs. Since the composition of the Rukurato had not been laid down, Kasagama included in it the saza chiefs he had appointed within Toro proper, and though there were arguments with British officials over this, Kasagama got his way.

In 1905 the Agreement was amended to make Kasagama's position as Mukama clear, to allow three, though not five, sazas in Toro Proper, and to put all saza chiefs on the same level. In 1927 the Agreement was further modified to meet Batoro objections. The lease of the salt lakes had been terminated in 1922 and Kasagama deprived of income. He was now compensated with an annual payment of £100 per annum. His authority over Bwamba was strengthened, as were some other powers.

TORORO. A town on the border with Kenya (q.v.) at the main crossing point between the two countries. The Jopadhola, a Lwoo (q.v.) people, live around Tororo. A cement works was sited there to provide cement for the Owen Falls dam (q.v.). Tororo is also a railway (q.v.) junction, the main line going on to Kampala (q.v.), and a secondary line branching northwards to Soroti (q.v.), Gulu (q.v.) and Pakwach on the Nile (q.v.). The Trypanosomiasis Research Establishment is situated near Tororo (*see* Sleeping Sickness). Tororo Rock, the core of an extinct volcano, is a landmark visible for miles around.

TOURISM. Uganda's scenic variety and excellent game parks made the country attractive to tourists until the end of the 1960s. A chain of hotels offering a high standard of service was established in the main towns, Kampala (q.v.) boasted three major hotels of international standard, and lodges were built in the Murchison Falls, Queen Elizabeth II and Kidepo Game Parks, all of which abounded in a wide variety of wild game and birds. Some 85,000 foreign tourists visited Uganda in 1971, and tourism was the third largest foreign currency earner (after coffee and cotton) in that year. A relatively small number of tourists climbed Mount Elgon (q.v.), an easy climb requiring no mountaineering experience; and fewer still the Ruwenzoris (q.v.), whose greater height, remoteness, exceptionally high rainfall, and lack of any mountain rescue services meant that the inexperienced sometimes got into difficulties, occasionally with tragic results. Huts were provided by the Uganda Alpine Club on both mountains. The forests of Bunyoro and of the extreme southwest on the Rwanda (q.v.) border were also popular with tourists, especially bird-watchers. The sale of craftwork accounted for a growing proportion of the income from the tourist trade, and various schemes trained Ugandans to refine and diversify their skills and products.

Tourism collapsed as a result of the insecurity of the Amin (q.v.) regime, and herds of elephant and other wild animals were decimated by soldiers who hunted with automatic weapons. Tourism did not begin to recover until the National Resistance Movement (q.v.) takeover in 1986. Roads, game parks and hotels have all had to be rehabilitated since then. The Murchison Falls Game Park remained out of bounds for some time after this as it was affected by insurgency in Acholi (q.v.). Since 1986 large new hotels have been built at Fort Portal (q.v.), Jinja (q.v.), Masaka (q.v.) where the hotel was destroyed in the War of Liberation (q.v.), and Mbale. The airport, damaged in the Entebbe Raid (q.v.) and fought over in the War of Liberation, has had to be extensively repaired. Thanks to these efforts, by the end of the 1980s the number of tourists had grown to about 50,000, and the annual income from tourism was approaching US$ 5 million.

TRADE BOYCOTT OF 1959. In 1959 the Baganda (q.v.) in particular grew fearful about unrestricted Asian (q.v.) immigration and the incursion into what had been African areas of trade outside the main towns. Their fears led to a boycott of Asian traders in Buganda organized by the Uganda National Movement, a grouping of Baganda belonging to the Uganda National Congress (q.v.) among whose leaders were I.K. Musazi (q.v.) and E.M.K. Mulira (q.v.). The boycott was initially supported by all Baganda, and many Asian traders were driven out of rural areas. When the movement turned violent the Protectorate administration ordered Kabaka Mutesa II (q.v.) to denounce it. It eventually petered out because African retailers depended for supplies on Asian wholesalers. The Uganda National Movement was proscribed by the Protectorate government and Musazi and Mulira were temporarily deported to northern Uganda.

TRADE UNIONS. The trade union movement in Uganda developed relatively late and never achieved great strength. Widespread reliance on subsistence farming and slow urbanization and industrialization discouraged its growth. The Riots of 1945 (q.v.) were seen by the Protectorate administration as politically motivated and potentially seditious, but were in fact a demand for better wages after the depressed conditions resulting from World War II. The Motor Drivers' Association led by I.K. Musazi (q.v.) was involved in these though it did not lead the strikes, and it was not a true trade union. When released in 1946, Musazi again involved himself in organizing trade unions which were in part vehicles for his own political ambitions. Both the Transport and General Workers' Union, registered in 1949, and the Uganda African Farmers' Union were involved in the Bataka Riots of 1949 (q.v.) after which the Unions were banned and the leaders temporarily exiled from Kampala (q.v.).

The first genuine trade union in Uganda was a branch of the Kenya-based Railway Union in 1946. Further development took place in the 1950s during the governorship of Sir Andrew Cohen who introduced legislation in 1952 to prevent trade unions from becoming merely covers for political action, and only one or two unions registered under the new provisions. In 1955 there was a rash of strikes among unestablished and ununionized workers in public service, and in particular in the Public Works Department. These were precipitated by wage rises given to established workers. A conciliation committee was set up, and Kenneth Ingham, Professor of History at Makerere College (q.v.), was reluctantly accepted by the government as chairman. It feared that anyone from Makerere would be ''pro-African.'' The workers for their part wanted at all costs to avoid politicization, and won considerable advantages including compensation for groups which had been underpaid in the past.

By 1957 trade unions began to seem more attractive to Ugandans as recession and unemployment developed. The presence of Kenyan workers, whose home country was far more unionized than Uganda, assisted in the development of unions: employers were willing to employ Kenyans in spite of unemployment among Ugandans because the former were often experienced in factory working. The British Trades Union Congress was willing to assist Ugandan unions, and in 1958 the International Confederation of Free Trade Unions established a college in Kampala (q.v.) for training union officials from English-speaking Africa. The number of Ugandan trade unionists grew remarkably in the period immediately preceding independence from 259 to 39,862, and the number of unions grew from three to 34. Employers' organizations at first operated in secret lest they give encouragement to workers to join unions. Only in 1960 was the Society of Employers registered, quickly changing its name to the Federation of Uganda Employers.

When Uganda became independent the new government realized that expectations of greatly improved living standards could not be met. Uganda experienced a wave of strikes, the blame for which was placed on Kenyans, and the Uganda Trade Union Congress was accused of setting itself up as a rival to government. The Uganda government therefore moved to ensure that the unions did not pose a political or economic threat, and the politicians set about coopting and taming the unions. In 1964 unions and employers came to an agreement on the terms of a Charter, but government stood aside from signing this and soon afterwards introduced legislation which prevented the Public Employees' Union from joining in collective bargaining and forced a split between higher and lower grades. Established civil servants were deprived of effective union representation. Trade unions were not able to function at all under President Amin (q.v.) and with the collapse of industry they have played little part in Ugandan life since the mid-1960s.

TUCKER, BISHOP ALFRED ROBERT (1849–1914). Member of the Church Missionary Society (CMS) (q.v.). On 25 April 1890 he was consecrated third Bishop of Eastern Equatorial Africa after the deaths of Bishop Hannington (q.v.), who was murdered in Busoga in 1885, and Bishop Parker, who died south of Lake Victoria (q.v.) before reaching Uganda. Tucker visited Uganda in 1891 and again in 1893 when he ordained the first Ugandans. In the same year he returned to England at the request of the CMS in connection with the expected report by Sir Gerald Portal on the future of Uganda. The CMS was anxious that Uganda should become a British Protectorate, fearing the consequences for the mission and for Ugandan Christians should Britain withdraw. In 1897 Tucker's huge diocese was divided, Tucker becoming Bishop of Uganda which then included a large slice of what is now western Kenya (q.v.), and with responsibility for Nassa at the southern end of Lake Victoria (q.v.) which was a staging post for missionaries traveling inland through Tanganyika (now Tanzania [q.v.]).

The years of Tucker's episcopate covered the period of major expansion of Protestant (q.v.) Christianity from Mengo (q.v.) to the outlying areas of Buganda (q.v.), and from there throughout most of Uganda and into Kavirondo to the east, and to Mboga beyond the Semliki River in the west, Ugandan catechists leading the way. Besides walking up from the coast before the Uganda Railway (q.v.) was built, Tucker visited almost all these areas on foot. He had immense faith in the Ugandan Church, and in 1897 proposed a church constitution so far in advance of its time that the missionaries would not accept it—under it they would have become merged into a self-governing Native Anglican Church (q.v.). Not until 1909 was the mission willing to accept a much modified constitution under which the mission continued to operate outside the jurisdiction of the church.

During Tucker's episcopate an indigenous ministry and corps of catechists were established, schools were founded to educate the future elite as well as to give education (q.v.) more widely, and medical work based on Mengo Hospital was established.

Tucker was a considerable watercolor artist, and some of his paintings are reproduced in half-tone in his *Visits to Ruwenzori* (1899) and his *Eighteen Years in Uganda and East Africa* (1908). He retired on health grounds in 1911 and was made a Canon of Durham Cathedral. He died suddenly in 1914.

-U-

UGANDA ARMY. During the colonial period the Ugandan armed forces consisted of one battalion of 700 men who formed part of the King's African Rifles (q.v.). At independence the battalion was renamed the Uganda Rifles. Almost all the commissioned officers were still British: one of the first few Ugandans to be made a commissioned officer was Idi Amin (q.v.). Dissatisfaction with pay and promotion prospects were among the issues which led to the Mutiny of 1964 (q.v.). The size of the army was quickly doubled and continued to grow and promotions were overfast. It speedily won a reputation for indiscipline: in early 1965 an accident on the Entebbe road involved an army lorry and a bus carrying a group of schoolboys from Kisubi School. The army shot dead six of the schoolboys and for some time prevented ambulances and medical workers approaching. The army was deployed in the Congo (later Zaire [q.v.]) to assist the Simba rebels (*see* Gold Scandal) and against the Baganda (q.v.) in the Battle of Mengo 1966 (q.v.). President Obote (q.v.) tried to buy the loyalty of the army with favors, and defense expenditure grew unduly large. In 1967 the Military Police was created to try to curb the army. It was disproportionately northern in composition, only four out of its 36 officers being of Bantu origin, as was the officer corps in the army. In spite of Obote's efforts to win the loyalty of the army, the attempted assassination (q.v.) when he was shot at during a rally of the Uganda People's Congress (q.v.) in 1969 was almost certainly the work of a faction of the army.

After the coup of 1971 (q.v.) which brought Amin to power as President, the army's size was increased yet further in spite of purges and massacres of Acholi (q.v.) and Langi (q.v.) men and officers, and indiscipline grew until the Uganda Army became an international byword for brutality. Amin increased the army's ethnic imbalance by recruiting men from West Nile (q.v.) in large numbers. The invasion of the Kagera Salient (q.v.) left that area devastated, but also spelt the end for Amin's army which, for all its size and armaments, was defeated by the less well-equipped but far better disciplined Tanzanian People's Defence Force in the War of Liberation (q.v.). The new army in Uganda was known as the Uganda National Liberation Army (q.v.) which quickly showed itself to be no less brutal and ill-disciplined than the army from whom it took over.

UGANDA COUNCIL OF WOMEN (UCW). This was established in 1946 with multi-racial and multi-religious membership to campaign on women's issues and press for government recognition of their importance. The founder members included Rhoda Kalema (q.v.), Mary Stuart, wife of the Anglican (q.v.) Bishop of Uganda (the first hall of residence for women at Makerere College [q.v.] was named after her), Barbara Saben, sometime Mayor of Kampala (q.v.), Rebecca Mulira (q.v.), Katie Kibuka (q.v.), Pumla Kisosonkole (q.v.) and Florence Lubega (q.v.). Representatives of various women's religious groups and of community development groups throughout the country were brought together. In 1953 Mary Stuart was succeeded by Winifred Brown, author of *Marriage, Divorce and Inheritance: The Uganda Council of Women's Movement for Legislative Reform* (1988), which gives an account of an important aspect of the Council's work.

A conference held by the UCW in 1960 passed a series of resolutions which received wide press publicity on bride wealth, women's property rights, the right of women to work and the marriage laws. They urged that information on laws dealing with marriage, divorce, inheritance and succession should be made widely available and that all marriages should be registered. More generally they asked that government should codify and amend laws on marriage, inheritance and succession. Much of what they had to say met with male resistance. In 1961 the UCW issued a booklet entitled *Laws about Marriage in Uganda* which was published in English and four Ugandan languages, and which was in great demand. These matters continued to be pressed during the first decade of independence.

Government response to these demands was piecemeal and slow. A Hindu Marriage Ordinance was passed in the Legislative Council (q.v.) in 1961. In 1964 the government of President Obote (q.v.) established a Commission on the Laws of Marriage in Uganda whose Report was published the following year and caused intense debate. In 1966 the Succession Act was made applicable to Ugandan Africans enabling them to make wills instead of being bound by traditional customs on inheritance. Not until 1973 did the demand for all marriages to be registered meet with success. By Decree 16 of 1973 not only civil and religious marriages but all customary marriages had to be registered, giving women married under customary law better property and custodial rights. Regrettably, little has been done to implement this legislation, but women have continued to campaign for improvements and safeguards in all these fields.

UGANDA DEVELOPMENT CORPORATION (UDC). The UDC was set up in 1952 with an initial capital of £5 million with the aim of modernizing the economy, investigating and developing its industrial and mineral potential, and diversifying away from an overdependence on cotton, tea and coffee exports. It was hoped that foreign capital would also be attracted. However, some of its schemes fell through, and the establishment of a cement industry involved a financial loss, but the copper deposits at Kilembe were exploited and proved financially profitable. Asians (q.v.) rather than Africans took advantage of most of the capital available, and UDC money helped start industry at Jinja (q.v.). The UDC's importance increased after independence, but it was brought to the verge of bankruptcy when its funds were used unwisely in non-viable projects by politicians seeking to benefit their own home areas.

UGANDA FEDERAL DEMOCRATIC MOVEMENT (FEDEMU, sometimes FEDEMO). A small resistance movement based in Buganda (q.v.) directed against Milton Obote (q.v.) during his second presidency. Its leader, Laurence Ssemakula, became an exile in Kenya (q.v.) and was abducted from there by Uganda security forces, allegedly with the connivance of the Kenyan authorities. During the brief rule of the junta led by Tito Okello (q.v.) and Basilio Okello (q.v.), the remnants of FEDEMU joined forces with the Uganda National Liberation Army (q.v.) and fought the National Resistance Army (NRA) (q.v.) until the very end. Under their new leader, David Lwanga, their alliance with the Okellos earned them a place at the peace talks held in late 1985 in Nairobi, Kenya, and the Nairobi Accords (q.v.) would have given them two places on the Military Council and permitted the incorporation of their soldiers into a new army. However, the NRA victory meant that the Nairobi Accords were bypassed.

UGANDA FREEDOM ARMY/MOVEMENT (UFA/M). This guerrilla movement, led by Andrew Kayiira, emerged during the second presidency of Milton Obote (q.v.). The group was active to begin with, but was able to achieve rather little, and its leaders fled abroad. In 1985 during the time of the military junta led by Basilio Okello (q.v.) and Tito Okello (q.v.) the UFA/M accepted a seat on the Military Commission, and they took part in the negotiations which led to the Nairobi Accords (q.v.). Kayiira returned from the USA and recruited into the UFA's depleted ranks many people who were released from prison by the Okellos. They thus inflated their numbers so that, by the terms of the Accords, they would have a right to be represented in a newly constituted army: a total of 1,200 soldiers was to be shared among the four smallest movements, the UFA/M, FEDEMU (q.v.), FUNA (q.v.), and the Uganda National Rescue Front (q.v.). In the event nothing came of this because of the victory of the National Resistance Army/Movement (q.v.).

UGANDA MUSEUM. The original impetus for a museum came from Governor Sir Hesketh Bell (q.v.) in 1907 when he urged

District Commissioners to send in examples of "articles of historical, ethnological and industrial interest." A tiny building was erected on Old Kampala (q.v.) Hill near the fort built by Lugard (q.v.), and here the collection moldered until Governor Sir Philip Mitchell (q.v.) decided to set up a museum in 1939, and Margaret Trowell, Head of the Art Department at Makerere College (q.v.), became part-time curator. Classifying the random collection on Old Kampala took six years, and Margaret Trowell continually added to it, trying to ensure that each part of Uganda was adequately represented. At the end of this time the work was taken over by Dr K.P. Wachsmann, a musicologist and an authority on African crafts. In 1965 a new and worthy building was completed for this collection and this was shared by the Uganda Society (q.v.).

UGANDA NATIONAL CONGRESS (UNC). This was founded in 1952 under the leadership of Erisa Kironde (q.v.), Apolo Kironde (q.v.), Abu Mayanja (q.v.), E.M.K. Mulira (q.v.), I.K. Musazi (q.v.), and Milton Obote (q.v.). It fragmented during the 1950s: breakaway groups included the Uganda People's Union, one of whose leaders was William Nadiope (q.v.), and the Progressive Party (q.v.). In 1959 the UNC itself split, and the section led by Obote joined up with the Uganda People's Union to form the Uganda People's Congress (q.v.) which came to power at independence.

UGANDA NATIONAL LIBERATION ARMY (UNLA). A small contingent of Ugandans fought with the Tanzanian People's Defence Force during the War of Liberation (q.v.), and called themselves the UNLA. They were reinforced by men who had deserted from the former army of President Amin (q.v.). The size of the UNLA was increased very fast, and it quickly became apparent that it was no less brutal than Amin's army had been. In July 1979 Uganda's religious leaders wrote to President Binaisa (q.v.) accusing the UNLA of being no better than the soldiers of the previous regime, and demanding that they be returned to barracks. In July the following year the religious leaders wrote again along the same lines. After President Obote (q.v.) was returned to power, he claimed that the UNLA was merely responding to the insurgency of the National Resistance Army/Movement (q.v.), but as the religious leaders' letters show, the UNLA was out of hand long before this started. Both the Military Commission (q.v.) and Obote were virtually powerless to discipline the army even had they been inclined to do so because they were dependent upon it. The UNLA's behavior came to international attention when the religious leaders published an appeal to Obote and used the phrase "the Uganda you lead is bleeding to death" which caught the attention of foreign journalists. The conduct of the UNLA in the Luwero Triangle (q.v.) and its mistreatment of civilians became internationally notorious.

In 1982 a Commonwealth team agreed to provide training for the UNLA. This role was taken on by the British Military Training Team (q.v.) in 1984 when the Commonwealth pulled out. The training team failed to bring about any improvement in the conduct of the UNLA. Ethnic tensions in the UNLA became particularly serious after the death of Chief-of-Staff David Oyite-Ojok (q.v.). In the last stages of the war with the NRA/M the UNLA broke up, parts of it refusing to continue the fight. Some UNLA soldiers who surrendered were recruited into the NRA in the second half of 1986 when the NRA needed to be reinforced to deal with rebellion led by Basilio Okello (q.v.) and Tito Okello (q.v.) in Acholi (q.v.). They were given only minimal retraining, and their recruitment helped to lower the disciplinary standards of the NRA.

UGANDA NATIONAL RESCUE FRONT (UNRF). One of the armed groups which opposed Milton Obote (q.v.) during his second presidency. The UNRF was led by Brigadier Musa Ali (q.v.) and was based in West Nile (q.v.). It was one of the groups which took part in the negotiations leading to the Nairobi Accords (q.v.), and one of its leaders, Major Amin Onzi, became a member of the Military Commission (q.v.). When President Museveni (q.v.) took power he won over the remnants of the group and Musa Ali became his Minister of Youth, Sports and Culture.

UGANDA PATRIOTIC MOVEMENT (UPM). The party formed by Yoweri Museveni (q.v.) to fight the Elections of 1980 (q.v.) when he broke away from the Military Commission (q.v.). It had a coherent political program which brought new thinking into the political scene, but was unable to contest all constituencies, and won only one seat. Museveni quickly took to the bush and formed the National Resistance Army/Movement (q.v.) which won power in 1986.

UGANDA PEOPLE'S CONGRESS (UPC). The UPC was formed in 1960 under the leadership of Milton Obote (q.v.), and had its roots in the Uganda National Congress (q.v.). It won the Elections of 1962 (q.v.) through an alliance with the Baganda (q.v.) party, Kabaka Yekka (q.v.), and therefore became the ruling party at independence. Until 1965 Obote's chief political aim was to persuade as many as possible of the opposition Democratic Party (q.v.) and of Kabaka Yekka to "cross the floor" and join the UPC in the interests of national unity, and in order to end his dependence on the ethnically-bound Kabaka Yekka. While Obote himself was a socialist, he was not always able to carry his party with him, joined as it had been by people of other parties who did not support his attitude towards capitalism and private property. Consequently a fully socialist program had to wait intil 1970 when the "Move to the Left" (q.v.) was announced, and this proved to be too late. The move finally alienated the West which welcomed the regime's overthrow a year later in the coup of 1971 (q.v.). Obote's Eastern bloc allies, if they existed, were unable to support him. In any case party membership depended less for many people on political programs than on religious ties: the UPC was identified with the Protestants (q.v.) and the Democratic Party with the Catholics (q.v.), although each party made much of the fact that it had some members of the opposite religious persuasion. The Baganda, who had supported Kabaka Yekka and the initial alliance with the UPC, were fatally alienated in 1966 when they were defeated at the Battle of Mengo 1966 (q.v.) and when Kabaka Mutesa II (q.v.) fled to the United Kingdom. By 1970 party enthusiasm had dimmed considerably: rallies were poorly attended, and cooercion was increasingly used. Many Baganda initially welcomed the 1971 coup (q.v.) which brought Idi Amin (q.v.) to power.

When Obote returned to power in 1980 the UPC abandoned its socialism in the interests of obtaining Western aid needed to rebuild the shattered economy. Religious factionalism was intensified as Obote favored the Church of Uganda (q.v.) in order to divide what he understood as opposition to his regime from religious leaders: leaders of both churches had protested jointly at abuses of human rights by the army which he was unable or unwilling to control. Obote also came to depend increasingly on northerners and on members of his own ethnic group, the Langi (q.v.). The Youth Wing of the UPC was instrumental in the expulsion of Banyarwanda (q.v.) in 1982–1983. Since President Museveni (q.v.) came to power political parties have been forbidden to campaign in elections though persons with known party allegiances, including members of the UPC, have been allowed to campaign as individuals and have been elected to the National Resistance Councils (q.v.) at various levels.

UGANDA PEOPLE'S DEMOCRATIC ARMY/MOVEMENT (UPDA/M). An insurgent group in Acholi (q.v.) opposed to the rule of the National Resistance Movement (q.v.) and President Museveni (q.v.), originally directed by Basilio Okello (q.v.) and Tito Okello (q.v.). In June 1988 its leader in Uganda, Colonel John Okello, concluded a peace agreement with the government, and many of his men surrendered. A dwindling remnant fought on until mid-1992, by which time the UPDA/M had virtually ceased to exist. A number of its members who surrendered were absorbed into the National Resistance Army.

UGANDA PEOPLE'S FRONT/ARMY (UPF/A). An insurgent group in Teso (q.v.) opposed to the rule of the National Resistance Movement (q.v.) and President Museveni (q.v.). Its leaders were J. Luwuliza-Kirunda (q.v.) and Peter Otai (q.v.) who directed the movement from Kenya (q.v.) and Britain. In April 1988 soldiers of the UPA/F were among 3,000 members of various insurgent movements who surren-

dered under a government amnesty. Remnants of the movement fought on but by 1991 Teso was largely free from
insurgency and peaceful, and any funding which the group
may have had earlier from Kenya had ceased.

UGANDA SOCIETY. In 1923 a Uganda Literary and Scientific
Society was formed with its headquarters in Entebbe (q.v.),
but by 1928 it had become moribund and almost entirely
restricted to residents of Entebbe. In 1933 it was reconsti-
tuted as the Uganda Society. Its headquarters were moved to
Kampala (q.v.), a quarterly publication, the *Uganda Journal,*
was produced, and membership soared. Sir Albert Cook
(q.v.) was its first President, and in 1945 the Society
published his *Uganda Memories.* Another of its Presidents
was Serwano Kulubya (q.v.). The *Uganda Journal,* published twice a year from 1946 onwards, contains a wealth of
scholarly work on many aspects of Uganda. From the early
1960s it contained an extensive bibliography of published
work on Uganda each year until it ceased regular publication in
1971. The Uganda Society collected together a considerable
library, many of the books for which were purchased for the
Society by H.B. Thomas (q.v.) in Britain after his retirement.
The annual lecture, given by the Society's President, was
published in the *Journal.* The hyper-inflation and insecurity
which has marked much of Uganda's history since the coup of
1971 (q.v.) has resulted in the *Uganda Journal* being published
only at long and irregular intervals. *Mawazo,* originally the
Makerere Journal, seems to some extent to have taken its place
as a publishing outlet for Ugandan scholars.

UGANDA SUPREME MUSLIM COUNCIL (USMC). This was
established in 1972 by President Idi Amin (q.v.) in order to
unite all Muslims. It received huge sums of money from
Arab governments, and some schemes were put in hand, but
much of the money disappeared and the planned central
mosque was never built. The constitution of the USMC
caused problems because voting was based on political units
regardless of how many Muslims there were in the population of those units, and areas where Islam (q.v.) was strong
felt cheated at having no more say than areas where there

were scarcely any Muslims. Further problems arose because Amin interfered in the affairs of the Council, particularly over appointments. Two Chief Kadhis (senior judicial authorities) were dismissed by Amin, for instance, and soldiers were appointed to Council positions. It therefore failed to become the unifying force that it was intended to be.

UNION OF SOVIET SOCIALIST REPUBLICS (USSR). During the 1960s the USSR attempted to build up links with Uganda, and an embassy was established in 1965, but relations were never close. After the coup of 1971 (q.v.), the Israelis persuaded Amin to expel most of the Soviet military advisors, but after he broke with Israel (q.v.) in 1972, Soviet influence increased. The USSR supplied Uganda with arms, and made what use it could of Amin's anti-imperialist rhetoric, but found him an unreliable ally. When Amin threatened the Briton, Denis Hills, with the death penalty for describing him as a "village tyrant" in a book about Uganda, the Soviet Ambassador drew Amin's attention to Mikhail Bulgakov's play, *The Black Snow,* which was critical of Stalin's rule, but which Stalin had seen many times. The inference was obvious. At about the same time the Soviet Ambassador persuaded Amin not to erect a statue to Hitler, and was responsible for a broadcast in which Amin thanked the Ambassador for making him realize that Hitler was extremely evil. After this the USSR cooled its relations with Amin, and refused to assist the Ugandan army in the War of Liberation (q.v.). The National Resistance Movement (q.v.) government of President Museveni (q.v.) restored friendly relations with the USSR and received some non-military aid.

UNITED DEMOCRATIC CHRISTIAN ARMY (UDCA). The name given by Joseph Kony (q.v.) to his "Holy Spirit" movement which emerged after the defeat of Alice Lakwena (q.v.). In August 1991 photographs of civilians maimed and mutilated by his forces were published, and this helped to discredit him and his movement. At the same time a massive military operation was carried out when the civilian population of Acholi (q.v.) was combed through for guerrillas. The UDCA was reduced to small bands of men operating on the southern edges of Acholi and to the west of Kitgum. The civilian population suffered severely both from the UDCA and from government operations, but in the end the government was better able to provide security.

-V-

VERONA FATHERS. A missionary society, based in Verona, Italy, which has responsibility for Catholic (q.v.) mission work in northern Uganda. The precursors of the Verona Fathers were a few priests who set out for Khartoum in 1847 when it first became possible for foreigners to enter the country. They and succeeding groups were dogged by sickness and death. Among those who went to Sudan (q.v.) in 1861 was Daniel Comboni who became convinced that Africans themselves must play a major role if Africa was to be evangelized. He kept the work alive in spite of immense difficulties and established the Verona Sisters in 1874. He was made a Bishop and entrusted with extending the work up the Nile (q.v.) towards the Great Lakes, but he died in 1881 before the mission could reach its goal. Not until 1910 did it reach any part of modern Uganda. In that year its first mission station was established at Omach among the Alur (q.v.) in West Nile (q.v.). Another was opened at Gulu (q.v.) two years later. The Verona Fathers reached Karamoja (q.v.) later still in 1929, but by the time of independence they had established a network of missions with churches, schools, teacher training institutions, hospitals and seminaries across the whole of northern Uganda. In Kampala (q.v.) they have a parish at Mbuya on the east of the city. Fr Crazzolara (q.v.) became one of their best-known missionaries because of his scholarly work in anthropology and linguistics. From the 1960s onwards refugees (q.v.) from Sudan, where the Verona Fathers had founded the Catholic Church, have taken refuge in northern Uganda and have become a special responsibility of the mission in Uganda. Some Verona Fathers and Sisters were able to remain at their posts throughout the period from 1980–1986 when West Nile suffered extreme disturbance (*see* Ombachi Massacre and Refugees), and from 1986–1991 when Acholi (q.v.) was rent by strife (*see* Alice Lakwena, Uganda People's Democratic Movement, and United Democratic Christian Movement). Their presence was of great importance to Ugandans in these troubled areas.

VILLA MARIA. The main Catholic (q.v.) mission in Buddu (q.v.) opened by the White Fathers (q.v.) in 1891. It was first located at Kiwala, but this station was destroyed at the time of the Battle of Mengo of 1892 (q.v.), and was refounded a few miles north of Masaka (q.v.). A minor seminary was opened in 1893, but this was moved to Rubaga (q.v.) later that year because of epidemics and famine in Buddu. Although the mission was destroyed again during the rebellion of Kabaka Mwanga (q.v.) in 1897, it was quickly rebuilt and became the main hub of Catholic activity outside the environs of Kampala (q.v.), and the heart of the strongly Catholic Province of Buddu. The seminary finally settled at Bukalasa, just a mile from Villa Maria, in 1906, and when a major seminary was needed, it was placed close by at Katigondo. Meanwhile a White Sisters' convent, schools, and the headquarters of the Bannabikira (q.v.) were all established around the mission house and large church at Villa Maria. Land was given by the leading Catholic chief, Alexis Ssebowa. The area remains a stronghold of Catholicism.

VISRAM, ALLIDINA (1863–1916). A member of the Ismaili Muslim (see Islam) community and a pioneer Asian (q.v.) trader and businessman with interests throughout East Africa and in the Congo (now Zaire [q.v.]). He arrived in Uganda soon after the establishment of the Protectorate and opened stores wherever government posts were established, trading in local and imported goods. He owned a small fleet of vessels on Lake Victoria (q.v.) as part of his transport business, and pioneered cart-transport in Uganda in the days before the advent of the automobile. In 1912 he invested a considerable sum in a cotton ginnery in Kampala (q.v.), and helped to establish other manufacturing in Uganda. He contributed to the rebuilding of Namirembe (q.v.) Cathedral, to the Red Cross and to a hospital in Kampala (q.v.) as well as being generous to African Muslims. The businesses

Allidina Visram had built up collapsed some years after his death. In Kampala, as in other East African towns, a street was named after him in the business district.

-W-

WAR OF LIBERATION. The name given to the war of 1978–1979 which liberated Uganda from the rule of President Amin (q.v.). In late October 1978, after several months of provocations and troop movements, Amin's troops invaded the Kagera Salient (q.v.), claiming that Uganda was being attacked by Tanzania (q.v.). The Tanzanian People's Defence Force (TPDF) was below strength in the area and unable to counter the invasion immediately. Not until 9 November was it able to move back north across the Kagera River and retake the Salient. The Tanzanians then decided that the border could not be made safe unless the high ground around the Ugandan border town of Mutukula was captured. On 21 January 1979 the TPDF moved across the border and sacked the town with a newly reinforced army which now included a battalion of Ugandan exiles.

The decision to do more than this was made in spite of the possibility of hostile international opinion, and the part played by Ugandan exiles was exaggerated to provide cover for what was happening. A conference of exiled groups was hastily convened at Moshi, and the Moshi Unity Conference (q.v.) tried to work out a strategy for liberation. The TPDF planned to take the southern towns of Masaka (q.v.) and Mbarara (q.v.) in retaliation for the invasion and destruction of the Kagera Salient. Meanwhile it was hoped that Ugandans elsewhere would rise against Amin and topple him while most of his army was involved in the south. Masaka was defended by the Suicide Battalion (*see* Uganda Army) under the command of Isaac Maliyamungu (q.v.), and a major attack had to be mounted before the town fell on 24 February. Mbarara fell the following day and both towns were systematically destroyed. The expected Ugandan uprising did not materialize, and an attempt by Ugandans to open a second front in the east failed. But the Tanzanian forces were now so deeply involved that they could not withdraw without leaving southern Uganda open to the possibility of ferocious retaliation by Amin. In spite of a peace initiative by the Organization of African Unity (q.v.) and the expected international outcry, Tanzania pursued the war against Amin to its conclusion. By the time the invading force had moved north of Masaka, Amin's army had been reinforced by contingents of Palestinians who had been training in Uganda and of Libyans (*see* Libya), and their presence gave Tanzania the excuse it needed for continuing its advance. The TPDF claimed large numbers of Libyans killed and imprisoned on the journey northward from Masaka and in the battle for Entebbe (q.v.). Kampala (q.v.) was entered and taken on 10 April 1979, and the victory was announced by Colonel Oyite-Ojok (q.v.) in the name of the Uganda National Liberation Front (q.v.). For three days the city was looted. Yusufu Lule (q.v.) was sworn in as President on 14 April.

Meanwhile Amin and the remnants of his army fled eastwards along the corridor deliberately left by the Tanzanians so that diplomats and other expatriates could escape. Amin had threatened to make his final stand at Jinja (q.v.), and there were fears for the safety of the hydroelectric station and the Owen Falls dam (q.v.), but the town had been deserted by Amin and his troops by the time the Tanzanians arrived. From Jinja they moved on eastwards to Tororo (q.v.) and the Kenya (q.v.) border before turning northwards. Meanwhile other battalions of the TPDF moved up through central Uganda and northwards through western Uganda into Acholi (q.v.) and West Nile (q.v.). Aside from some harassment from fleeing troops, they met no real resistance except in West Nile. Amin's armies fled before them into Sudan (q.v.) and Zaire (q.v.). By 3 June the whole country had been liberated.

The TPDF remained for over a year in a peace-keeping role, though its soldiers also took to looting on occasion. The Uganda National Liberation Army (q.v.) quickly proved to be as undisciplined as Amin's army, and in West Nile, the area from which Amin came, it took revenge. Much of the population temporarily became refugees (q.v.).

Casualties in the war have been estimated at 373 Tanzanians, c. 150 members of the Ugandan contingent who had accompanied the Tanzanians, c. 600 Libyans and 500 Ugandan civilians (this last would seem to be a conservative estimate). No estimate is available for casualties suffered by Amin's army.

WARS OF RELIGION. In 1888 after the execution of the Christian martyrs (q.v.), armed conflict broke out between those leaders in Buganda (q.v.) who remained true to traditional beliefs and customs and the adherents of the two new faiths which had reached Buganda, Islam (q.v.) and Christianity, the latter represented by both Catholics (q.v.) and Protestants (q.v.).

The Christians became convinced that Kabaka Mwanga (q.v.) had determined to massacre them, and they joined forces with the Muslims to rebel against the Kabaka against the advice of the missionaries. On 10 September they attacked Mwanga and installed one of the princes, Kiwewa, as Kabaka in his place. Mwanga fled south across Lake Victoria (q.v.). The Muslims then turned against the Christians, Kiwewa was ousted, and Kalema, newly-circumcised as a Muslim, was installed as Kabaka in his place. The missionaries had already gone to the south of the lake; their Uganda converts now followed them into exile either south of the lake or on the borders of Ankole (q.v.). The Muslims then succeeded in antagonizing the uncommitted, who began to drift off to join the Christians.

Under the leadership of Honorat Nyonyintono (q.v.) and Apolo Kagwa (q.v.), the Christians regrouped. Nyonyintono was killed in battle and Semei Kakungulu (q.v.) emerged as the most notable general. The Christians succeeded in fighting their way back to power, stopping for some time on Bulingugwe Island to regroup before the final attack on the capital. By October they had routed the Muslims and driven them towards Bunyoro (q.v.). However, in order to legitimize their seizure of power, they reinstated Mwanga as Kabaka once the Muslims, who had adopted Kiwewa as their leader, had been finally defeated in February 1990. Kiwewa was killed shortly afterwards. The Christian coalition did not last long: the Battle of Mengo 1892 (q.v.) was to follow.

WEST NILE. The area north of Lake Albert and west of the Nile
(q.v.). This area has not always been part of Uganda (*see*
Boundaries and Lado Enclave). Southern West Nile is
demographically linked with Uganda: the Alur (q.v.) are
related to the Acholi (q.v.) and the Jonam, and all these
groups are Lwoo speakers (*see* Languages). In the north the
Kakwa (q.v.), Madi (q.v.) and Lugbara (q.v.) are related to
the peoples of Sudan (q.v.) and Zaire (q.v.) and are Sudanic
speakers. West Nile was reached by the missions (q.v.) later
than most of the rest of Uganda, so that education and
medical services came late to the area. The missions which
work in the area are the Africa Inland Mission (q.v.) and the
Verona Fathers (q.v.). Since 1974 West Nile has been
divided into the administrative districts of Arua and Nebbi.
West Nile suffered greatly during the second presidency of
Obote (q.v.) when the UNLA (q.v.) wreaked vengeance on it
because it was the home area of President Amin (q.v.), and
thousands of people became refugees (q.v.) in Zaire and
Sudan.

WHITE FATHERS. The formal name of this Catholic missionary
society is Société des Missionaires de Nôtre Dame d'Afrique. It was founded by Cardinal Lavigerie (q.v.), Archbishop
of Algiers; its early members were mainly French. The
Fathers got their popular name from the white, Arab-style
burnous which they wore.

Lavigerie insisted that the White Fathers give a high
priority to language study and study of the countries they
worked in, their peoples and their customs. Within three
years of reaching Uganda the first grammar and dictionary of
Luganda (*see* Languages) had been prepared. The White
Fathers Archives in Rome are a repository of ethnographic
and historical material of great interest.

The first group of White Fathers traveled to Uganda in
1879, and on 17 February Fr Siméon Lourdel (q.v.) and
Brother Amans landed at Entebbe (q.v.). Their landing is
marked by a pillar, now out in the water because the lake
level has risen. Lourdel was a warm-hearted, determined
man who attracted many young Baganda (q.v.) to the
Catholic faith, and is sometimes referred to as the apostle of

Uganda. In June they were joined by the rest of the party, which included Fr Livinhac, later to be appointed Superior General of the White Fathers.

The White Fathers usually required a four-year catechumenate for those wishing to be baptized. After the Wars of Religion (q.v.) they were able to expand their work beyond the capital into the south and west of Uganda. In the environs of the capital they established their headquarters at Rubaga (q.v.), and Villa Maria (q.v.) near Masaka (q.v.) in Buddu (q.v.) became the second Catholic stronghold. Here Bishop Streicher (q.v.) of the White Fathers pioneered the training of African priests. By the 1960s, Africa's decade of independence, most of the African priests on the continent had been trained in areas where the White Fathers were working, and the first African Bishop of modern times, Joseph Kiwanuka (q.v.), was a Ugandan trained by this mission. In Uganda they went on to establish stations in Toro (q.v.), Bunyoro (q.v.), Ankole (q.v.) and Kigezi (q.v.).

WHITE SISTERS. The White Sisters were founded by Cardinal Lavigerie (q.v.) in 1869 and first reached Uganda in 1899 to engage in teaching, in caring for the sick and in parish work among women. They were responsible for founding the oldest Catholic sisterhood for African women, the Bannabikira (Daughters of the Virgin) (q.v.), which grew out of a group of women catechists whom they had trained in Uganda.

WINYI, SIR TITO GAFABUSA (c. 1890–1972). Mukama of Bunyoro (*see* Banyoro), 1924–1967. Winyi was a son of Mukama Kabarega (q.v.). He was brought up at Ibanda in Ankole (q.v.) and attended Mengo High School and King's College, Budo (*see* Education). From 1910 to 1920 he was with his exiled father in the Seychelles acting as his private secretary. In 1924 Winyi was chosen by the Rukurato (assembly of chiefs) as successor to Mukama Andereya Duhaga (q.v.) who had died suddenly of a heart attack. Winyi found Bunyoro still suffering from the wars waged against Mukama Kabarega by the British and by the Baganda (q.v.) at the end of the nineteenth century. At last in 1933 the

Bunyoro Agreement (q.v.) was signed, bringing Bunyoro into line with the other kingdoms of Uganda. Two years previously Winyi had made an important intervention against proposals that there should be Closer Union (q.v.) between the three East African territories under British rule, something Uganda resisted strongly for many years fearing subjection to settler-dominated Kenya (q.v.).

During the time Winyi spent with Kabarega in the Seychelles he learnt from his father the Bunyoro traditions which he wrote up and published in three articles in 1935–1937 in the *Uganda Journal* entitled "The Kings of Bunyoro-Kitara." They are signed "K.W." for Kabarega and Winyi, and are an important contribution to historical writing on Bunyoro. When John Nyakatura (q.v.) came to write his history of Bunyoro he drew on these articles. By the 1950s the younger and better-educated Banyoro had become increasingly resentful of Winyi's personal and authoritarian manner of rule. In 1955 he eventually agreed to a new Agreement by which he became a constitutional monarch, and appointment to chieftaincies became the responsibility of an Appointments Committee. However, he still wielded considerable personal influence.

Throughout his reign he repeatedly raised the issue of the Lost Counties (q.v.) with the Protectorate government and with the British government, but not until 1961 was the matter taken seriously. In 1967 his rule ended when President Obote (q.v.) abolished the traditional kingdoms, and he went into retirement living as a private person. In 1993 President Museveni (q.v.) gave permission for the kingdoms to restore their monarchs as cultural, not political heads, and Solomon Iguru was chosen as the new Mukama.

WOMEN'S MOVEMENTS. The oldest women's movements in Uganda are church movements, the Mothers' Union, of which Rebecca Mulira (q.v.) was a prominent member, and the Young Wives' Fellowship (both Church of Uganda [q.v.]). There were also strong women's movements in the Catholic Church (q.v.), and the women's religious orders have played a big part in raising the status of women. The Bannabikira (q.v.) is the oldest African religious order on the continent. When the Uganda Council of Women (q.v.) was formed in 1946, some of its first members came from the church women's groups. In the same year, 1946, a Women's Section was established in the Department of Social Welfare, later the Ministry of Community Development, in which Rhoda Kalema (q.v.) worked. The Young Women's Christian Association (q.v.) came to Uganda at the invitation of the Uganda Council of Women, and Rebecca Mulira (q.v.) was its Director for a number of years. Women's organizations proliferated in the next decade, and UNICEF agreed to provide training for 3,500 women who would work as leaders of women's clubs and societies. In 1966 these were brought together in the Association of Women's Organizations.

In 1963, the year of Ugandan independence, the All Africa Conference of Churches held a conference at Makerere College (q.v.) entitled ''The Responsibility of Christian Women in Africa Today'' at which Ugandan women were strongly represented, and two of them, Marjorie Kabuzi and Pumla Kisosonkole (q.v.), were among the main conference speakers.

During the time of President Amin (q.v.) women lawyers banded together as the Uganda Association of Women Lawyers, an active group. Amin set up a National Council of Women in 1977, but this proved to be a retrograde step, for the decree setting it up effectively banned all other women's organizations from operating. The Ministry of Culture deliberately refrained from bringing that section of the decree into operation, but what had happened alienated women from the Ministry and from the government. They continued to send delegates to conferences in order to avoid an outright clash with the government, but in all other respects they withdrew their support from the Ministry, and the National Council of Women ceased to function meaningfully.

During the second presidency of Milton Obote (q.v.) the National Council of Women was infiltrated by members of the women's wing of the Uganda People's Congress (q.v.) who attempted to manipulate the Council for political ends, and succeeded in temporarily destroying its credibility.

The National Resistance Movement (q.v.) led by President

Museveni (q.v.) has increased the number of women in government and has established structures which ensure that they are included in Resistance Councils (q.v.) at all levels. In the Elections of 1989 (q.v.) to the National Resistance Council (q.v.), 34 women won seats reserved for them, and two others defeated male contenders. Women have been appointed to important responsibilities and to ministries. Among these have been Joyce Mpanga (q.v.) in 1987 as Minister for Women's Development, succeeded by Gertrude Lubega Byekwaso, and Betty Bigombe (q.v.) in 1988 as Minister of State in the Office of the Prime Minister with responsibility for Pacification of the North. Rhoda Kalema (q.v.) was made Deputy Minister of Public Service and Cabinet Affairs. Joan Kakwenzire was appointed to the Human Rights Commission (q.v.), and Sarah Ntiro has served in the Vice-President's Office.

A number of other initiatives must be mentioned. The Uganda Association of Women Lawyers has been active under the NRM government in setting up a legal aid clinic to help widowed and divorced women to protect their rights, and it campaigns for improvements in the legal status of women. ACFODE (Action for Development) campaigns on women's issues in its well-produced periodical, *Arise*. Mrs Janet Museveni, wife of the President, is founder of Uganda Women's Effort to Save Orphans. A further important development is the inauguration of a masters' course in women's studies at Makerere University (q.v.) under Dr Victoria Mwaka assisted by Deborah Kasente.

-Y-

YAKAN WATER CULT. Also known as the Allah Water Cult. This cult emerged among a group of peoples living in the borderlands of Uganda, Zaire (q.v.) and Sudan (q.v.) at the end of the nineteenth century in response to the dislocation of society caused by slave-traders and the Mahdist rising in the Sudan in the 1880s. Further disruption was caused by epidemics of smallpox, cerebro-spinal meningitis, plague, and rinderpest in cattle. The cult appears to have started among the Dinka in the Sudan who in 1883 rose against a Mahdist garrison and wiped it out, attributing their victory to the drinking of protective medicine which became known as Yakan or Allah Water.

Like the "medicine" used in Maji Maji against the Germans in East Africa a few years later, Yakan Water was believed to protect those who drank it by turning to water bullets fired against them. When the cult first appeared in response to what were felt as unprecedented external threats, it offered a way of overcoming clan and tribal divisions and enabling a more widespread resistance to these threats than would otherwise have been possible. In this respect too it can be compared to Maji Maji.

Other groups in Sudan obtained the water and were also successful against the Mahdists. In the late 1880s it reached the Kakwa (q.v.), Madi (q.v.) and Lugbara (q.v.) of northern Uganda who all obtained it through the agency of a man called Rembe. In 1889, when Emin Pasha (q.v.) left, a company of his troops who had remained were wiped out by the Lugbara, as also was a party sent to avenge them. The cult is then said to have taken hold among Emin Pasha's troops themselves. This area of Uganda was part of the Lado Enclave (q.v.) and came under Belgian rule from 1894 to 1909. The Belgians began to administer the area in 1900, and little was heard of the cult among the Lugbara until 1912 when Rembe himself came to the area and distributed the water. In 1910 the area passed under the jurisdiction of Sudan and in 1914 was finally incorporated into Uganda. The British officer, Weatherby, who was sent to administer West Nile (q.v.), found the southern Lugbara around Arua (q.v.) very uncooperative. It took him until 1918 to "pacify" the area and considerable force had to be used on occasion.

A year later the British officials were surprised to be faced with possible widespread rebellion. Many chiefs were found to be implicated in Yakan and were believed to be involved in plotting against the government. The movement's emphasis had by now changed and much time was spent on organizing and drilling people in an apparent attempt to lay hold on the source of the Europeans' power. This phase of the cult may have been influenced by former members of the

King's African Rifles (q.v.) who were discharged at the end of World War I and returned home. At this stage the cult appeared to pose a real danger and measures were taken against it. Several chiefs were exiled to Ankole (q.v.) until 1925, and Rembe himself was caught and hanged. In 1920 the cult changed emphasis and direction and appeared as a disease-prevention cult among the southern Lugbara who were again threatened by an epidemic. In 1924 it reemerged in its anti-European form among the Alur (q.v.) and Jonam, but there was no actual fighting.

Through Emin Pasha's troops, who were brought into Uganda in 1892 by Lugard (q.v.), the Yakan Water Cult is said to have been passed to the King's African Rifles. Those who mutinied in 1897 (*see* Sudanese Mutiny) are all alleged to have drunk the Allah Water.

YOUNG WOMEN'S CHRISTIAN ASSOCIATION (YWCA). The YWCA of Uganda was founded in 1952, but its origins go back to 1948 when Mary Stuart, wife of the Anglican (q.v.) Bishop of Uganda, and Mrs Lamont, the wife of the then Principal of Makerere College (q.v.), decided a YWCA was needed, and started to raise funds. World YWCA arrived from Geneva to assess the situation the following year, a program was drawn up for Uganda, and in 1952 Rebecca Mulira (q.v.) and Katie Kibuka (q.v.) attended an International Leadership Project in New York. The Uganda Council of Women (q.v.) provided office space when Sue Stille of the USA YWCA arrived in 1953 to help get the Uganda project off the ground, and UCW members were prominent on the first YWCA committee. The first YWCA and Y-Teen groups were formed and a plot of land for a hostel located on George Street in Kampala (q.v.) near the Central Police Station. In 1957 Governor Sir Andrew Cohen was able to lay the foundation stone of the first hostel which provided 54 places. It was funded by a Barclay's Bank loan obtained through the Ministry of Community Development, and additional funding from the World YWCA. In 1960 an educational program was begun with classes in sewing, cookery, child care, English, and health care for girls who had had to leave school early.

By the mid-1960s the YWCA was entirely in Ugandan hands, and among those who served as office bearers were Pumla Kisosonkole (q.v.) and Sarah Ntiro. Mary Kasozi-Kaya steered the YWCA through the difficult years in the 1970s under President Amin (q.v.). By the time the YWCA celebrated 30 years in Uganda its membership was about 100,000 spread throughout the country, and by 1987 its membership had trebled and 35 clubs had been established as peace returned to large parts of Uganda. By 1993 its membership was reported to be the fastest growing in the world. Its educational program had been greatly widened, and a new headquarters and modernized hostel had been opened. A program for rural areas runs agricultural clubs and livestock programs. Although the YWCA caters primarily for young women, it also organizes groups for elderly women to help them towards greater independence, and the YWCA is in the forefront of work with and for women on women's issues under its General Secretary, Joyce Mungherera. Annual events include a national conference in April, leadership training courses, refresher courses for nursery school teachers, baby competitions, garden competitions, and sponsorship of the Women's World Day of Prayer in February and the World YM/YWCA Week of Prayer in November.

-Z-

ZAIRE. Formerly the Belgian Congo. The border between Uganda and the Congo was not finally demarcated in all sectors until 1915 (*see* Boundaries). The Congo was given independence in 1960 without adequate preparation, and quickly descended into violence which resulted in 33,000 Congolese becoming refugees (q.v.) in Uganda. There was further trouble in the Congo at the time of the Simba rebellion against the pro-Western Prime Minister Moise Tshombe. Prime Minister Obote (q.v.) did not inform his cabinet that the Uganda Army (q.v.) was giving assistance to the Simba. The Gold Scandal (q.v.), which nearly brought down Obote's government, grew out of this intervention. Relations between President Amin (q.v.) and President

Mobutu Sese Seko of Zaire were extremely cordial, and Lake Albert was temporarily renamed after the Zairean president. Between 1980 and 1986 during Obote's second presidency thousands of people from West Nile (q.v.) became refugees in Zaire as a result of insurgency and the barbarities of the Uganda National Liberation Army (q.v.). From 1990 onwards Zaireans have again sought refuge in Uganda from the breakdown of law and order in their own country, and from "ethnic cleansing" of people of Banyarwanda (q.v.) origin in Kivu Province.

SELECT BIBLIOGRAPHY

Introduction

This select bibliography is largely limited to works in English. There is a very extensive literature in Luganda, the language of the Baganda who live in the central area of Uganda, which includes history, biography and political comment of great value. There is also a thriving Luganda language press. A little published literature exists in other Ugandan languages, and some unpublished manuscripts in various Ugandan languages have been collected and deposited in Makerere University Library. Partial guides to writing in Luganda may be found in J.A. Rowe's "Myth, Memoir and Moral Admonition: Luganda Historical Writing" (*Uganda Journal,* 33, 1, 1969, 17–40) and in M.C. Fallers' *The Eastern Lacustrine Bantu (Ganda and Soga)* (Ethnographic Survey of Africa: East Central Africa, Part 11, London: International African Institute, 1960).

As well as the bibliographies listed at 1.2, certain books contain particularly useful bibliographical sections. H.B. Thomas's and R. Scott's scholarly *Uganda* (London: Oxford University Press, 1935) has a bibliography of remarkable length for a book published at this date. The three volumes of the *Oxford History of East Africa* (Oxford: Clarendon Press, 1963, 1965 and 1976) are useful in listing British and Uganda Protectorate Government reports and papers for the colonial period. These and other British government papers dealing with the colonial period are available in the Public Record Office, Chancery Lane, London, WC2. The book review and bibliographical sections of the *Uganda Journal* are invaluable.

Dr Cherry Gertzel's *Uganda: An Annotated Bibliography* (Sevenoaks, UK: Hans Zell Publishers, 1991) gives some indication of the amount and scope of post-1970 official Uganda Government material which can be located by the researcher who goes to Uganda. The Entebbe Secretariat Archives (the archives of the protectorate administration) have deteriorated through lack of conservation, but are of prime importance for the colonial period. Unpublished seminar papers which are not generally available outside Uganda are not usually listed in this bibliography. Such papers are collected both in Makerere University Library and also in the Library of the Makerere Institute of Social Research. The Faculties of Arts and Social and Political Sciences have produced mimeographed material of considerable value. Valuable archive collections can be found at Makerere University and in the Albert Cook Memorial Library at the Medical School, Mulago Hospital. The Centre for Basic Research, P.O. Box 9863, Kampala also publishes papers by Ugandan researchers and from time to time issues a complete list of these.

Mission and church archives and publications are of great importance for the history of Uganda. The archives of the Church Missionary Society, now located at Birmingham University, UK; of the White Fathers located at Via Aurelia 269, Rome 00165; of the Mill Hill Fathers at St Joseph's College, Lawrence Street, Mill Hill, London; and the Verona Fathers (Missionari Comboniani), in Verona, Italy, are all important. Mission headquarters at many of the older-established parishes in Uganda also house archival material of great interest, much of which at parish level is still unexplored. Most Roman Catholic Missions kept mission diaries which have been little used in spite of their value as source material. Mission periodical publications of particular importance include the *Annual Reports* of the Church Missionary Society, the *Church Missionary Intelligencer* (before 1906), the *Church Missionary Review* (1906 onwards), *Mengo Notes* (published in Uganda 1900–1902) and *Uganda Notes* (also published in Uganda 1902–1913), the *Chroniques Trimestrielles* and the *Rapports Annuels* of the White Fathers, the *Annalen van het Missiehus to Rozendaal* (from 1895–1914) of the Mill Hill Fathers and the *Daystar in Africa* published by the Franciscan Missionary Sisters which were associated with the Mill Hill Fathers, are all valuable. Christopher Smith, *Index 1912–1990 International Review of Missions,* Geneva: World Council of Churches, 1993, is a guide to the contents of the leading journal of missions and missiology in English. Some material from the Muslim community has been housed in Makerere University Library.

Novels, plays, poetry and other literary works in English are not covered by the bibliography, though the Dictionary includes entries on some prominent writers and artists. Dictionaries and grammars of Ugandan languages, some of them of great erudition, have also had to be omitted. Geography is also largely omitted, as is scientific literature, including scientific aspects of medicine. Section 9 deals with the history of medical provision and with such events as the sleeping sickness and AIDS epidemics.

Uganda has often been international "news" during the post-independence years, and the British and Kenyan presses and specialist Africa publications contain frequent and sometimes substantial articles on Uganda. Valuable though much of this material is, it has not proved practicable to include reference to it in this bibliography, and except in one or two instances articles of no more than three or four pages have been omitted. The following (non-Ugandan) publications, published in London unless otherwise stated, all contain important references to Uganda from time to time: *Africa, Africa Analysis, Africa Confidential, Africa Contemporary Record, Africa Defence Journal* (Paris), *Africa Economic Digest, Africa News, Africa Now, Africa Events, Africa Report, Africa Research Bulletin* (Oxford), *BBC Monitoring Service Reports* (Reading, UK), *The Economist, Indian Ocean Newsletter* (Paris), *Keesing's Contemporary Archives, New African, South, Translations on Sub-Saharan Africa (Joint Publications Research Service* (Washington), *The Weekly Review* (Nairobi).

Some repetition will be found in this bibliography, and books and articles may appear in two different sections for convenience of reference.

ARRANGEMENT OF THE BIBLIOGRAPHY

1 General Works and Bibliographies

1.1 AFRICA AND EAST AFRICA: BIBLIOGRAPHIES AND GENERAL WORKS

Africa South of the Sahara, Index to Periodical Literature 1900–1970. Boston, MA: G.K. Hall, Vol. 4, 1971, 424–522.

————. First Supplement, 1973, 361–368.

————. Second Supplement, 1982, 388–412.

African Affairs. London: Royal African Society, 1901– . Contains regular listings of material received, and select lists of articles on Africa appearing in non-Africanist periodicals.

Bederman, Sanford H. *Africa: A Bibliography of Geography and Related Disciplines.* Atlanta, GA: Publishing Services Division, School of Business Administration, Georgia State University, 1974.

Blackhurst, Hector (ed) in assocation with the International African Institute. *Africa Bibliography.* Manchester, UK:

Manchester University Press. Published annually from 1984. From 1990, Edinburgh University Press.

Blake, David and Carole Travis. *Periodicals from Africa: a Bibliography and Union List, First Supplement.* New York and London: G.K. Hall, 1984.

Burt, Eugene C. *An Annotated Bibliography of the Visual Arts in East Africa.* Bloomington, IN: Indiana University Press, 1980.

Collison, Robert, revised John Roe. *The SCOLMA Directory of Libraries and Special Collections on Africa.* London: Crosby, Lockwood Staples, 1963, 3rd Edition 1973.

Conover, H. F. *Official Publications of British East Africa. Part I: The East Africa High Commission and other Regional Documents.* Washington, DC: Library of Congress, General Reference and Bibliography Division, 1960–1962.

Current Bibliography on African Affairs. Amityville, New York: Baywood Publishing Company. Published quarterly.

Darch, Colin and Alice Nkhoma-Wamunza (eds). *Africa Index to Continental Periodical Literature No. 6,* (covering 1981). New York and London: Hans Zell, 1985.

Delancey, M. W. *African International Relations: an Annotated Bibliography.* Boulder, CO: Westview Press, 1981.

Duignan, Peter (ed). *Guide to Research and Reference Works on Sub-Saharan Africa.* Hoover Institution Bibliographical Series XLVI. Stanford, CA: Hoover Institution Press, 1971.

Easterbrook, David L. *Africana Book Reviews 1885–1945.* Boston, MA: G. K. Hall, 1979.

Evalds, Victoria K. *Union List of African Censuses, Development Plans and Statistical Abstracts.* New York: Hans Zell, 1985.

Forde, Daryll. *Selected Annotated Bibliography of Tropical Africa.* New York: Kraus Reprint Company; International African Institute, 1969.

Gertzel, Cherry. *Bibliography: East and Central Africa for the Period 1940–1975.* Bedford Park, Australia: Flinders University Politics Discipline, 1978.

Griffiths, Ieuan Ll. *An Atlas of African Affairs.* London: Methuen, 1984.

Hannam, Harry (ed). *The SCOLMA Directory of Libraries and Special Collections on Africa in the United Kingdom and Western Europe, 4th edition.* Oxford: Hans Zell, 1983.

Howell, J. B. (compiler). *East African Community; Subject Guide to Official Publications.* Washington, DC: Library of Congress, 1976.

Krummes, D. C. *Transportation in East Africa: a Bibliography.* Monticello, IL: Vance Bibliographies, 1980.

Langlands, Bryan W. *Bibliography on the Distribution of Disease in East Africa.* Kampala: Makerere University College, Makerere Library Publications 3, 1965.

McIlwaine, J. H. St. J. *Theses on Africa 1963–75 Accepted by Universities in the United Kingdom and Ireland.* London: Mansell, 1978.

Matson, A. T. "Bibliography of the Works of Sir John Gray." *Uganda Journal,* 35, 2, 1971, 161–174.

Molnos, Angela. *Sources for the Study of East African Cultures and Development.* Nairobi: East African Research Information Centre, 1968.

————. *Development in Africa, Planning and Implementation, A Bibliography (1946–69) and Outline with Some Emphasis on*

Kenya, Tanzania and Uganda. Nairobi: East African Research Information Centre, 1970.

Ofcansky, Thomas P. *British East Africa 1856–1963. An Annotated Bibliography.* New York: Garland Publishing, 1985.

Ofori, P.E. *Islam in Africa: a Select Bibliographic Guide.* Nendeln, Liechtenstein: KTO Press, 1977.

Panofsky, Hans E. *A Bibliography of Africana.* Westport, CT, and London: Greenwood Press, 1975.

Pearson, J. D. (ed). *International African Bibliography 1973–78.* London: Mansell Publishing, 1982.

Pinfold, J. R. (ed). *African Population Census Reports: A Bibliography and Checklist.* New York: Hans Zell, 1985.

Scheven, Yvette. *Bibliographies for African Studies 1970–75.* Brandeis University, MA: Crossroads Press (African Studies Assocation), 1977.

―――. *Bibliographies for African Studies 1976–79.* Brandeis University, MA: Crossroads Press (African Studies Association), 1980.

―――. *Bibliographies for African Studies 1980–83.* Oxford: Hans Zell, 1984.

―――. *Bibliographies for African Studies 1979–1986.* Oxford: Hans Zell, 1988.

Shields, James A. *A Selected Bibliography on Education in East Africa 1941–1961.* Kampala: Makerere University College, Makerere Library Publications 2, 1962.

Tasfaye Keflu. *A Bibliography of the Economic and Social Aspects of Agriculture in Ethiopia, Kenya, Tanzania and Uganda, 1965– .* New York: Ithaca, 1972.

Thurston, Ann. *Guide to Archives and Manuscripts Relating to Kenya and East Africa in the United Kingdom, Vol. I: Official Records; Vol. II: Non-Official Archives and Manuscripts.* London: Hans Zell, 1991.

United States of America. Library of Congress. *National Program for Acquisition and Cataloguing. Accessions Lists, East Africa.* Washington, DC: bi-monthly

Vogel, H. *An Inventory of Geographic Research of the Humid Tropic Environment.* Dallas: Texas Instruments Inc., Sciences Services Division of US Army, Natick Laboratories, 1966.

Witherell, J. W. *The United States and Africa: Guide to U.S. Official Documents, 1785–1975.* Washington, DC: Library of Congress, 1978.

Zaretsky, Irving I. and Cynthia Shambaugh. *Spirit Possession and Spirit Mediumship in Africa and Afro-America, An Annotated Bibliography.* New York and London: Garland Publishing, 1978.

1.2 UGANDA: BIBLIOGRAPHIES

Afolabi, M. O. "President Idi Amin Dada of Uganda: A Bibliography." *Current Bibliography of African Affairs,* 10, 4, 1987, 309–327.

African Affairs contains regular bibliographies of new publications submitted for review and a listing of articles on Africa in non-Africanist periodicals.

Askgaard, Preben V. "A Bibliography on Amin's Uganda." *Ufahamu,* 5, 1, 1974, 104–124.

Augur, G. A. and O. Wonekhe. *Education in Uganda. A Bibliography, Progress Report.* Kampala: Makerere University, National Institute of Education, 1973.

Bell, C.R.V. *Education in Uganda before Independence.* University of Oxford Development Records Project, Report No. 11. Oxford: Rhodes House, 1985.

Bull, M. *The Medical Services of Uganda 1954–5.* University of Oxford Development Records Project, Report No. 20. Oxford: Rhodes House, 1986.

Collison, R. L. (ed). *Uganda. World Bibliographical Series, 11.* Oxford and Santa Barbara: ABC Clio Press, 1981.

Gertzel, Cherry. *Uganda: An Annotated Bibliography of Source Materials (with particular reference to the period since 1971 and up to 1988).* London, Melbourne, Munich, New York: Hans Zell, 1991.

Gray, Beverly Ann. *Uganda: Subject Guide to Official Publications.* Washington, DC: Library of Congress, 1977.

Hoben, Susan Y. *A Select Annotated Bibliography of Social Science Materials for Uganda Followed by an Expanded Bibliography.* Washington, DC: US Agency for International Development, 1979.

Hopkins, Terence K. with Perezi Kamunvire. *A Study Guide for Uganda.* Boston, MA: African Studies Center, Boston University, 1969.

Jamison, Martin. "Idi Amin of Uganda: A Selected Bibliography." *Bulletin of Bibliography and Magazine Notes,* 35, 3, 1978, 105–115, 131.

———. *Idi Amin and Uganda: An Annotated Bibliography.* Westport, CT, and London: Greenwood Press, 1992.

Kleinschmidt, Harald. *Amin Collection, Bibliographical Catalogue of Materials Relevant to the History of Uganda under the Military Government of Idi Amin Dada.* Heidelberg, Germany: P. Kivouvou Verlag—Editions Bantoues, 1983.

Kuria, Lucas, Iris Ragheb, and John Webster. *A Bibliography on Politics and Government in Uganda.* Syracuse, NY: Syracuse University, Maxwell School of Citizenship and Public Affairs, 1965.

Langlands, Bryan. "Uganda Bibliography" published regularly in *Uganda Journal,* Vol. 27, 1963 to Vol. 36, 1972.

McMaster, David N. "Occasional Papers of the Department of Geography, Makerere, Uganda, 1967— ." *African Research and Documentation,* 51, 1990, 8–18.

Matson, A.T. "H. B. Thomas: Bibliography of Published Works." *Uganda Journal,* 36, 1, 1972, 3–8.

Mittelman, James H. "The State of Research on African Politics: Contributions on Uganda." *Journal of African and Asian Studies,* XI, 3–4, 1976, 152–165.

Morris, H. F. *Government Publications Relating to Uganda 1900–1962.* Wakefield, UK: EP Microfilm Ltd, 1973.

Mutibwa, Olivia M. *Women in Uganda: A Bibliography.* Kampala: Uganda Association of University Women, 1986.

Oded, Arye. A Bibliographic Essay on the History of Islam in Uganda. *Current Bibliography on African Affairs,* 8, 1975, 54–63.

Peckham, R. et al. *A Bibliography of Anthropology and Sociology in Uganda.* New York: Syracuse University, Maxwell Graduate School of Citizenship and Public Affairs, Program of Eastern African Studies, 1966.

Thomas, H. B. *Catalogue of Books in the Secretariat Library.* Entebbe: Government Printer, 1940.

——— and R. Scott. *Uganda.* London: Oxford University Press, 1935, 485–582.

Uganda. Government. *Catalogue of Government Publications (Published Prior to 1 January 1965).* Entebbe: Government Printer, 1966.

Uganda. Ministry of Lands and Mineral Development. *Bibliography of Land Tenure.* Entebbe: Government Printer, 1957.

Walker, Audrey A. *Official Publications of British East Africa, Part 4, Uganda.* Washington DC, USA: Library of Congress, General Reference and Bibliography Division, 1960–1962, 1963.

1.3 AFRICA AND EAST AFRICA: REFERENCE WORKS, GENERAL HISTORIES AND STUDIES

Ade Ajayi, J. F. and M. Crowder (eds). *Historical Atlas of Africa.* Harlow, UK and Lagos, Nigeria: Longman, 1985.

Alpers, E. A. and C. Ehret. "Eastern Africa." In Richard Gray (ed). *The Cambridge History of Africa, Vol. 4, from c.1600-c.1790.* Cambridge, UK, and New York: Cambridge University Press, 1975, 469–536.

Arens, W. (ed). *A Century of Change in East Africa.* The Hague: Mouton, 1971.

Barkan, Joel. *An African Dilemma: University Students, Development and Politics in Ghana, Tanzania and Uganda.* Nairobi: Oxford University Press, 1975.

Barton, Frank. *The Press of Africa: Persecution and Perseverance.* London: Macmillan, 1979.

Beachey, R. W. *The Slave Trade of Eastern Africa.* London: Rex Collings, 1976.

Bohanan, P. (ed). *Homicide and Suicide in Africa.* Princeton, NJ: Princeton University Press, 1960.

Brownlie, I. *African Boundaries: A Legal and Diplomatic Encyclopaedia*, Berkeley, CA: University of California Press for the Royal Institute of International Affairs, 1979.

Cambridge History of Africa, Volumes I–VIII. Cambridge, UK: Cambridge University Press, 1975–1986.

Cartwright, John. *Political Leadership in Africa.* London: Croom Helm, 1983.

Davidson, Basil. *A History of East and Central Africa to the Late 19th Century.* Garden City, NY: Anchor Books, 1969.

Decalo, Samuel. *Coups and Army Rule in Africa: Studies in Military Style.* New Haven, CT, and London: Yale University Press, 1976.

Douglas, M. and P. M. Kaberry. *Man in Africa.* London: Tavistock, 1969.

Eken, S. "Breakup of the East African Community." *Finance and Development,* December, 1979, 36–40.

Fortes, M. and G. Dieterlen (eds). *African Systems of Thought.* London: Oxford University Press for the International African Institute, 1965.

Furley, Oliver and Tom Watson. *History of Education in East Africa.* New York and London: NOK, 1978

Gann, L. H. and Peter Duigan. *The Rulers of British Africa 1870–1914.* London: Hoover Educational Publications and Croom Helm, 1978.

———. *African Proconsuls: European Governors in Africa.* New York: Free Press, 1978.

Goldthorpe, J. E. and F. B. Wilson. *Tribal Maps of East Africa and Zanzibar.* Kampala: East African Institute of Social Research, East African Studies No. 13, 1960.

Green, Reginald Herbold. "The East African Community: The End of the Road." In Colin Legum (ed). *African Contemporary Record, 1976–77.* New York: Africana, 1977.

———. "The East African Community: Death, Funeral, Inheritance." In Colin Legum (ed). *African Contemporary Record.* New York: Africana of Holmes and Meier, 1979.

Greenberg, Joseph H. *The Languages of Africa.* 3rd Edition, Bloomington, IN: Indiana University Press, 1970.

Gulliver, P. H. (ed). *Tradition and Transition in East Africa.* London: Routledge and Kegan Paul, 1969.

Hailey, Lord. *Native Administration in the British African Territories: Part I, East Africa.* London: HMSO, 1950.

Hansen, H. B. and M. J. Twaddle (eds). *Religion and Politics in Eastern Africa Since Independence.* London: James Currey, 1994.

Harlow, Vincent and E. M. Chilver (eds). *History of East Africa, Vol. II.* Oxford: Clarendon Press, 1965.

Hunter, Guy. *The New Societies of Tropical Africa: A Selective Study.* London: Oxford University Press, 1962.

Ingham, Kenneth. *A History of East Africa.* London: Longman, 1962, 1963, 1965.

Jackson, R. H. and Carl Rosberg. *Personal Rule in Black Africa: Prince, Autocrat, Prophet, Tyrant.* Berkeley, CA: University of California Press, 1982.

Josephy, Alvin M. (ed) *The Horizon History of Africa.* New York: American Heritage Publishing, 1971.

Low, D. A. and Alison Smith (eds). *History of East Africa, Vol. III.* Oxford: Clarendon Press, 1976.

Marco Publishers (Africa) Ltd. *Who's Who in East Africa. 1965–1966.* Nairobi: Marco Publishers, 2nd Edition, 1966.

Mazrui, Ali. A. (ed). *Cultural Engineering and Nation Building in East Africa.* Evanston, IL: Northwestern University Press, 1972.

Middleton, J. and D. Tait (eds). *Tribes Without Rulers.* London: Routledge and Kegan Paul, 1958.

———— and John Beattie. *Spirit Mediumship and Society in Africa.* London: Routledge and Kegan Paul, 1969.

Moyse-Bartlett, H. *The King's African Rifles.* Aldershot, UK: Gale and Polden, 1956.

Nabudere, D. Wadada. *Imperialism in East Africa. Vol. I, Imperialism and Exploitation. Vol. 2, Imperialism and Integration.* London: Zed Press, 1982.

Nye, Joseph S. *Pan-Africanism and East African Integration.* Cambridge, MA: Harvard University Press, 1965.

Ogot, B. A. and J. A. Kieran (eds). *Zamani: A Survey of East African History.* 2nd Edition, Nairobi: East African Publishing House and Longman, 1974.

Oliver, Roland and Gervase Mathew (eds). *Oxford History of East Africa, Vol. 1.* Oxford: Clarendon Press, 1963.

Richards, Audrey I. (ed). *East African Chiefs: A Study of Political Development in Some Uganda and Tanganyika Tribes.* London: Faber and Faber, 1959.

Rigby, P. *Society and Change in Eastern Africa.* Kampala: Makerere Institute of Social Research (Nkanga 4), 1969.

Robinson, Ronald and John Gallagher with Alice Denny. *Africa and the Victorians: The Climax of Imperialism.* London: Macmillan and New York: St Martin's Press, 1961.

Salim, Ahmed Idha (ed). *State Formation in Eastern Africa.* Nairobi, London, Ibadan: Heinemann, 1984.

Schlosser, D. B. and R. Siegler. *Political Stability and Development: A Comparative Analysis of Kenya, Tanzania and Uganda.* Boulder, CO: Lynne Rienner, 1990.

Schnitzer, Eduard [Emin Pasha]. *Emin Pasha in Central Africa.* Ed. G. Schweinfurth et al. London: George Philip and Son, 1888.

Stemler, A.B.M., J. R. Harlan and J.M.J. Dewet. "Caudatum Sorghums and Speakers of Chari-Nile Languages in Africa." *Journal of African History,* 16, 2, 1975, 161–183.

UNESCO General History of Africa, Volumes I–VIII. Paris and Berkeley, CA: UNESCO and Heinemann, 1981–1992.

Unomah, A. C. and J. B. Webster. "East Africa: The Expansion of Commerce." In John E. Flint (ed). *The Cambridge History of Africa, Vol. 5, from c.1790–c.1870.* Cambridge, UK, and New York: Cambridge University Press, 1976, 270–318.

Webster, J. B. "Chronology, Migration and Drought." In J. B. Webster (ed). *Interlacustrine Africa.* London: Longman for Dalhousie University Press, 1979, 1–37.

Were, D. S. and D. A. Wilson. *East Africa Through a Thousand Years.* London: Macmillan, 1968.

Wilson, E. G. (ed). *Who's Who in East Africa, 1963–1964, 1965–66, 1967–1968,* Nairobi: Marco Publishers, 1964, 1966, 1968.

Wright, Marcia. "East Africa, 1870–1905." In Roland Oliver and G. N. Sanderson (eds). *The Cambridge History of Africa, Vol. 6, from 1870–1905.* Cambridge, UK, and New York: Cambridge University Press, 1985.

1.4 UGANDA: GENERAL WORKS (works covering both the pre- and post-independence periods)

Byrnes, Rita M. (ed). *Uganda, a Country Study.* Washington, DC: Federal Research Division, Library of Congress, 1992.

Campbell, Horace. *Four Essays on Neo-Colonialism in Uganda.* Toronto: Dumont Press, 1975.

Collins, R. O. *The Waters of the Nile: Hydropolitics and the Jonglei Canal 1900–1988.* New York: Oxford University Press, 1990.

Cunningham, J.F. *Uganda and Its Peoples.* London: Hutchinson, 1905.

Dahlberg, F. M. "The Emergence of a Dual Governing Elite in Uganda." *Journal of Modern African Studies,* 9, 4, 1971, 618–625.

Dinwiddy, Hugh. "Uganda: The Search for Unity, Early Days to 1966." *African Affairs,* 80, 321, 1981, 501–518.

Doornbos, Martin. "Ugandan Society and Politics: A Background." In G. N. Uzoigwe (ed). *Uganda: The Dilemma of Nationhood.* New York, London, Lagos: NOK Publishers International, 3–16.

[Fountain Publishers Ltd]. *Who's Who in Uganda 1988–1989.* Kampala: 1989

Government of Uganda, Department of Lands and Surveys. *Atlas of Uganda.* Entebbe: 1962.

Herrick, Allison Butler (ed). *Uganda, a Country Study.* Washington, DC: Federal Research Division, Library of Congress, 1969.

Ibingira, Grace. *The Forging of an African Nation.* Kampala:

Uganda Publishing House and New York: Viking Press, 1973.

Ingham, Kenneth. *The Making of Modern Uganda.* London: George Allen and Unwin, 1958.

Ingrams, H. *Uganda.* London: HMSO, Corona Library Series, 1960.

―――. *Uganda—A Crisis of Nationhood.* London: HMSO, 1969.

Jorgensen, J. J. *Uganda, A Modern History.* London: Croom Helm, 1981.

Kabwegyere, Tarsis B. *The Politics of State Formation: The Nature and Effects of Colonialism in Uganda.* Nairobi: East African Literature Bureau, 1974.

Karugire, S. R. *A Political History of Uganda.* Nairobi: Heinemann Books, 1980.

―――. *The Roots of Instability in Uganda.* Kampala: New Vision, 1988.

Kiwanuka, Semakula. "The Evolution of Chieftainship in Uganda." *Journal of Asian and African Studies,* IV, 3, 1969, 172–185.

―――. *From Colonialism to Independence.* Nairobi, Kampala, Dar es Salaam: East African Literature Bureau, 1973.

Langlands, B.W. *Notes on the Geography of Ethnicity in Uganda.* Kampala: Department of Geography, Makerere University, 1975.

Mamdani, Mahmood. *Politics and Class Formation in Uganda.* London: Heinemann, 1976.

————. *Imperialism and Fascism in Uganda.* London: Heinemann, 1983.

Mittelman, James H. *Ideology and Politics in Uganda: From Obote to Amin.* Ithaca, NY, and London: Cornell University Press, 1975.

Mukherjee, Ramakrishna. *Uganda: An Historical Accident? Class, Nation, State Formation.* Trenton, NJ: African World Press, 1986.

Nabudere, D. Wadada. *Imperialism and Revolution in Uganda.* Dar es Salaam: Onyx Press and Tanzania Publishing House, 1980.

Rowe, John A. "Historical Setting." In Rita M. Byrnes. *Uganda: A Country Study.* Washington, DC: Library of Congress, 1992, 4–38.

Sathyamurthy, T. V. *Central-Local Relations: The Case of Uganda.* Manchester: University of Manchester Department of Administration, 1982.

————. *The Political Development of Uganda: 1900–1986.* Brookfield, Vermont, USA: Gower Publishing Company, 1986.

Thomas H. B. and R. Scott. *Uganda.* London: Oxford University Press, 1935.

Uzoigwe, G.N. (ed). "The Peoples of Uganda in the Nineteenth Century." *Tarikh,* 3, 2, 1970.

————. (ed). *Uganda: The Dilemma of Nationhood.* New York, London, Lagos: NOK Publishers, 1982.

————. "Uganda and Parliamentary Government." *Journal of Modern African Studies,* 21, 2, 1983, 253–271.

2. Pre-Colonial History and Archaeology

(For most material published before 1963, see Sonia Cole, *The Prehistory of East Africa.*)

Atkinson, R. R. " 'State' Formation and Language Change in Westernmost Acholi in the Eighteenth Century." In A. I. Salim (ed). *State Formation in Eastern Africa.* Nairobi: Heinemann Educational, 1984, 91–125.

Chapman, S. "Kantsyore Island." *Azania,* 2, 1967, 165–191.

Cole, S. *The Prehistory of East Africa.* London: Weidenfeld and Nicolson, 1954; Penguin, 1963.

Connah, G. "Kibira Revisited: an Archaeological Reconnaissance in Southwestern Uganda." *Nyame Akuma,* 32, 1989, 46–54.

———, E. Kamuhangire and A. Piper. "Salt Production at Kibiro." *Azania,* 25, 1992,

Denoon, Donald. "The Historical Setting to 1900." In G. N. Uzoigwe (ed). *Uganda: the Dilemma of Nationhood.* New York, London, Lagos: NOK Publishers International, 17–56.

Gray, Sir J. M. "The Riddle of Biggo." *Uganda Journal,* 2, 1935, 226–233.

Hiernaux, J. and E. Maquet. *L'Age du fer à Kibiro, Uganda.* Tervuren, Belgium: 1968.

Lanning, E. C. "Ancient Earthworks in Western Uganda." *Uganda Journal,* 17, 1, 1953, 51–62.

———. "Masaka Hill." *Uganda Journal,* 18, 1, 1954, 24–29.

———. "The Munsa Earthworks." *Uganda Journal,* 19, 2, 1955, 177–182.

———. "Proto-Historic Pottery in Uganda." *Proceedings of the Third Pan-African Congress on Prehistory,* London: 1955, 313–318.

———. *Uganda's Past.* Nairobi: East African Literature Bureau, 1957.

———. "The Earthworks at Kibengo, Mubende District." *Uganda Journal,* 24, 2, 1960, 183–196.

Mathew, A. G. "Recent Discoveries in East African Archaeology." *Antiquity,* 27, 1953, 212–219.

O'Brien, T. P. *The Prehistory of the Uganda Protectorate.* Cambridge, UK: Cambridge University Press, 1939.

Oliver, Roland. "Ancient Capital Sites of Ankole." *Uganda Journal,* 23, 1, 1959, 51–63.

Oliver, R. and G. Mathew. *History of East Africa.* Vol. I, London: Oxford University Press, 1963.

——— and B. M. Fagan. *Africa in the Iron Age.* Cambridge, UK: Cambridge University Press, 1975.

Pearce, S. and M. Posnansky. "The Re-Excavation of Nsongezi Rockshelter, Ankole." *Uganda Journal,* 27, 1963, 85–94.

Posnansky, M. "Progress and Prospects in Historical Archaeology in Uganda." *Uganda Museum Occasional Papers,* 4, 1959, 31–40.

———. "Iron Age in East and Central Africa—Points of Comparison." *South African Archaeological Bulletin,* 16, 1961, 134–136.

———. "Dimple-based Pottery from Uganda." *Man,* 168, 1961

———. "Pottery Types from Archaeological Sites in East Africa." *Journal of African History,* 2, 2, 1961, 181–191.

————. "Towards an Historical Geography of Uganda." *East African Geographical Review,* 1, 1, 1963, 7–20.

————. "Kingship, Archaeology and Historical Myth." *Uganda Journal,* 30, 1, 1966, 1–12.

————. "The Iron Age in East Africa." in W. W. Bishop and J. D. Clark (eds). *Background to Evolution in Africa.* Chicago: University of Chicago Press, 1967.

————. "The Excavation of an Ankole Capital Site at Bweyorere." *Uganda Journal,* 32, 2, 1968, 165–182.

————. "Bantu Genesis: Archaeological Reflexions." *Journal of African History,* 9, 1968, 1–11.

————. "Bigo bya Mugenyi." *Uganda Journal,* 34, 2, 1970, 125–150 (includes a bibliography of the principal references to Bigo between 1909 and 1969).

————. "Terminology in the Early Iron Age of Eastern Africa, with special reference to the Dimple-based Wares of Lolui Island, Uganda." *Proceedings of the Panafrican Congress on Prehistory,* 6, 1973, 577–579.

———— and C. M. Nelson. "Rock Paintings and Excavations at Nyero, Uganda." *Azania,* 3, 1968, 147–166.

———— and J. W. Sekibengo. "Ground Stone Axes and Bored Stones from Uganda." *Uganda Journal,* 23, 2, 1959, 179–181.

Reid, A. "Ntusi and its Hinterland: Further Investigations of the Later Iron Age and Pastoral Ecology in Southern Uganda." *Nyame Akuma,* 33, 1990, 26–28.

Reid, A. and P. Robertshaw. "A New Look at Ankole Capital Sites." *Azania,* 22, 1987, 83–88.

Robertshaw, P. "The Interlacustrine Region: A Progress Report." *Nyame Akuma,* 30, 1988, 37–39.

Sassoon, H. "Kings, Cattle and Blacksmiths: Royal Insignia and Religious Symbolism in the Interlacustrine Area." *Azania,* 18, 1983, 93–106.

Shinnie, P. L. "Excavations at Bigo, Uganda." *Antiquity,* 33, 1959, 54–57.

———. "Excavations at Bigo 1957." *Uganda Journal,* 24, 1, 1960, 16–29.

———. *The African Iron Age.* Oxford: Clarendon Press, 1971.

Sinclair, Paul J. J. "Archaeology in Eastern Africa: An Overview of Current Chronological Issues." *Journal of African History,* 32, 2, 1991, 179–220.

Soper, R. C. "A General Review of the Early Iron Age in the Southern Half of Africa." *Azania,* 6, 1971, 15–17.

———. "Archaeological Sites in the Chobi Sector of Murchison Falls National Park, Uganda." *Azania,* 6, 1971, 53–87.

Steinhart, E. "The Emergence of Bunyoro: The Tributary Mode of Production and the Formation of the State, 1400–1900." In A. I. Salim (ed). *State Formation in Eastern Africa.* Nairobi: Heinemann Educational, 1984, 70–90.

Sundstrom, Lars. *The Exchange Economy of Pre-Colonial Tropical Africa.* London: C. Hurst, 1974.

Sutton, J. E. G. "The East African 'Neolithic'." *Proceedings of the Panafrican Congress on Prehistory,* 6, 1973, 88–90.

———. "The Interlacustrine Region: New Work on the Later Iron Age." *Nyame Akuma,* 29, 1987, 62–63.

———. "Ntusi and the Dams." *Azania,* 20, 1987, 172–175.

———. "Antecedents of the Interlacustrine Kingdoms." *Journal of African History,* 34, 1, 1993, 33–64.

Tshihiluka, T. "Ryamurari: Une ancienne capitale du royaume du Ndorwa au Bukire." *Etudes Rwandaises,* 14, 1981, 55–72. [Ndorwa lies partly in Kigezi, Uganda.]

———. "Ryamurari: Capitale de l'anciene royaume du Ndorwa (Mutara, Rwanda). Une interprétation culturelle préliminaire." *Africa-Tervuren,* 29, 1983, 19–26.

Wachsmann, K. P. "Ancient Earthworks in Western Uganda; Notes on Finds." *Uganda Journal,* 18, 2, 1954, 190–192.

Wayland, E. J. "Notes on the Biggo bya Mugenyi: Some Ancient Earthworks in Northern Buddu." *Uganda Journal,* 2, 1, 1934, 21–32.

Webster, J. B. *Chronology, Migration and Drought in Interlacustrine Africa.* New York: Africana Publishing and Dalhousie University Press, 1979.

———. "Through the Palace Gates, Chiefs and Chronology: Developing Reliable Dating Structures." *History in Africa,* 11, 1984, 811–830.

3. Local History, Sociology and Anthropology

An extensive literature in Ugandan languages is noted in the bibliographies of some of the major items listed here.

3.1 NORTH AND NORTHEASTERN UGANDA

Abrahams, R. G. "A Modern Witch Hunt among the Lango of Uganda." *Cambridge Anthropology,* 19, 1, 1985, 32–44.

———. "Dual Organisation in Labwor?" *Ethnos,* 51, I–II, 1986, 88–104.

Adefuye, Ade. "Palwo Economy, Society and Politics." *Transafrican Journal of History,* 5, 1, 1976, 1–20.

————. "The Kakwa of Uganda and the Sudan." In A. I. Asiwaju (ed). *Partitioned Africans*. Lagos: Lagos University Press, 1984, 51–69.

Adimola, A. B. "The Lamogi Rebellion." *Uganda Journal*, 18, 2, 1954, 166–177.

Allen, Tim. *Closed Minds, Open Systems: Affliction and Healers in West Nile, Uganda*. Papers in Development Studies, 9003. Manchester: Manchester University Press for the International Development Centre, 1990.

————. "The Quest for Therapy in Moyo District." In H. B. Hansen and M. J. Twaddle. *Changing Uganda: The Dilemmas of Structural Adjustment and Revolutionary Change*. London: James Currey and Athens, OH: Ohio University Press, 1991, 149–161.

Anywar, R. S. "The Life of Rwot Iburahim Awic." *Uganda Journal*, 12, 1, 1948, 71–81.

Apoko, Anna. "At Home in the Village." In Lorene K. Fox. *East African Childhood*. London and New York: Oxford University Press, 1976, 45–78.

Atkinson, R. R. " 'State' Formation and Language Change in Westernmost Acholi in the Eighteenth Century." In A. I. Salim (ed). *State Formation in Eastern Africa*. Nairobi: Heinemann Educational, 1984, 91–125.

Barber, James P. "The Karamoja District of Uganda: A Pastoral People under Colonial Administration." *Journal of African History*, 3, 1962, 111–124.

————. *Imperial Frontier: A Study of Relations Between the British and the Pastoral Tribes of North East Uganda*. Kampala: East African Publishing House, 1968.

Barnes-Dean, V.L. "Social Change and Lugbara Subsistence Agriculture in West Nile District." In C. P. Dodge and P. D.

Wiebe (eds). *Crisis in Uganda: The Breakdown of the Health Services.* Oxford: Pergamon, 1985, 201–207.

———. "Lugbara Illness Beliefs and Social Change." *Africa,* 56, 3, 1986, 334–351.

Bere, R. M. "Land and Chieftainship among the Acholi." *Uganda Journal,* 19, 1, 1945, 49–56.

———. "An Outline of Acholi History." *Uganda Journal,* 11, 1, 1947, 1–8.

Butt, A. J. *The Nilotes of the Anglo-Egyptian Sudan and Uganda.* London: Ethnographic Survey of Africa, 1952.

Casale, M. "Women, Power and Change in Lugbara (Uganda) Cosmology: A Reinterpretation." *Anthropos,* 77, 1982, 385–396.

Cox, T.R.F. "Lango Proverbs." *Uganda Journal,* 10, 2, 1946, 113–123.

Crazzolara, J. P. "The Lwoo People." *Uganda Journal,* 5, 1, 1937, 1–21.

———. *The Lwoo.* 3 Vols. Verona, Italy: Missionari Africane, 1950–4.

———. "Notes on the Lango-Omiru and on the Labwoor and Nyakwai." *Anthropos,* 55, 1960, 174–214.

Curley, R. T. "The Lango of North-Central Uganda." In A. Molnos. *Innovations and Communication.* Nairobi: East African Publishing House, 1972.

———. *Elders, Shades and Women: Ceremonial Change in Lango, Uganda.* Berkeley, CA: University of California Press, 1973.

————— and B. Blount. "The Origins of the Langi: A Lexicostatistical Analysis." *Journal of the Language Association of Eastern Africa,* 2, 1971, 153–167.

Dalfovo, A. T. "Logbara Riddles." *Anthropos,* 78, 1/2, 1983, 811–830.

Driberg, J. H. "The Lango District, Uganda Protectorate." *Geographical Journal,* 58, 1921, 119–133.

—————. *The Lango.* London: Fisher Unwin, 1923.

—————. *At Home With the Savage.* London: Fisher Unwin, 1932.

Dyson-Hudson, N. *Karimojong Politics.* Oxford: Clarendon Press, 1966.

Emwanu, G. "The Reception of Alien Rule in Teso, 1896–1927." *Uganda Journal,* 31, 2, 1967, 171–182.

Gartrell, B. "Prelude to Disaster: The Case of Karamoja." In D. H. Johnson and D. M. Anderson. *The Ecology of Survival: Case Studies from Northeast African History.* London: Lester Crook, 1988, 193–217.

Gertzel, Cherry. *Party and Locality in Northern Uganda, 1945–62.* London: Athlone Press for the Institute of Commonwealth Studies, 1974.

Girling, F. K. *The Acholi of Uganda.* London: HMSO, 1960.

Goldschmidt, Walter. *Sebei Law.* Berkeley, CA: University of California Press, 1967.

—————. *Kambuya's Cattle: the Legacy of an African Herdsman.* Berkeley, CA: University of California Press, 1969.

—————. *The Culture and Behavior of the Sebei.* Berkeley, CA: University of California Press, 1976.

————. *The Sebei: A Study in Adaptation.* New York: Holt, Rinehart and Winston, 1986.

Gray, Sir J. M. "Acholi History, 1860–1901." Part I. *Uganda Journal,* 15, 2, 1951, 121–143.

————. "Acholi History, 1860–1901." Parts II and III. *Uganda Journal,* 16, 1, 1952, 32–60; 16, 2, 1952, 132–144.

Gulliver, P. *The Family Herds: A Study of Two Pastoral Tribes in East Africa, the Jie and Turkana.* London: Routledge and Kegan Paul, 1953.

————. "The Age-Set Organization of the Jie Tribe." *Journal of the Royal Anthropological Institute,* 83, 1953, 147–168.

————. "The Jie of Uganda." In James L. Gibbs, Jr (ed). *Peoples of Africa.* New York: Holt, Rinehart and Winston, 1965, 157–196.

———— (ed). *Tradition and Transition in East Africa: Studies of the Tribal Element in the Modern Era.* London: Routledge and Kegan Paul, 1969.

———— and Pamela Gulliver. *The Central Nilo-Hamites.* Ethnographic Survey of Africa: East Central Africa, 7. London: International African Institute, 1953.

Hayley, T.T.S. *The Anatomy of Lango Religion and Groups.* Cambridge, UK: Cambridge University Press, 1947.

Heine, Bernd. "The Mountain People: Some Notes on the Ik of North-Eastern Uganda." *Africa,* 55, 1, 1983, 3–16.

Herring, R. S. "Centralization, Stratification and Incorporation: Case-Studies from North Eastern Uganda." *Canadian Journal of African Studies,* 7, 1973, 497–514.

———— et al. "The Construction of Dominance: The Strategies of

Selected Luo Groups in Uganda and Kenya.'' In A. I. Salim (ed). *State Formation in Eastern Africa*. Nairobi: Heinemann Educational, 1984, 126–161.

Huddle, J. G. "The Life of Yakobo Adoko of Lango District.'' *Uganda Journal*, 21, 2, 1957, 184–190.

Huntingford, G.W.B. *The Northern Nilo-Hamites*. Ethnographic Survey of Africa: East Central Africa, 6. London: International African Institute, 1953.

———. *The Northern Nilo-Hamites*. London: International African Institute, 1953.

Ingham, K. "British Administration in Lango District, 1907–1935.'' *Uganda Journal*, 21, 2, 1957, 156–168.

King, Anne. "The Yakan Cult and Lugbara Response to Colonial Rule.'' *Azania*, 5, 1970, 1–25.

Lamphear, J. *The Traditional History of the Jie of Uganda*. Oxford: Clarendon Press, 1976.

———. "Historical Dimensions of Dual Organization: The Generation-Class System of the Jie and the Turkana.'' In D. Maybury-Lewis and U. Alamagor (eds). *The Attraction of Opposites: Thought and Society in the Dualistic Mode*. Ann Arbor, MI: University of Michigan Press, 1989, 235–254.

——— and J. B. Webster. "The Jie-Acholi War: Oral Evidence from Two Sides of the Battle Front.'' *Uganda Journal*, 35, 1, 1971, 23–42.

Lawrance, J.C.D. "A History of Teso to 1937.'' *Uganda Journal*, 19, 1, 1955, 7–40.

———. *The Iteso. Fifty Years of Change in a Nilo-Hamitic Tribe of Uganda*. London: Oxford University Press, 1957.

Leys, Colin. *Politicians and Politics: An Essay on Politics in Acholi, Uganda, 1962–65.* Nairobi: East African Publishing House, 1967.

Mamdani, M. ''Forms of Labour and Accumulation of Capital: Analysis of a Village in Lango, Northern Uganda.'' *Mawazo,* 5, 4, 1984, 44–65.

Middleton, J. ''The Concept of Bewitching in Lugbara.'' *Africa,* 25, 1955, 151–160.

———. ''Notes on the Political Organization of the Madi of Uganda.'' *African Studies,* 14, 1955, 29–36.

———. *Lugbara Religion: Ritual and Authority Among an East African People.* London: Oxford University Press, 1960.

———. ''The Lugbara.'' In A. I. Richards (ed). *East African Chiefs.* London: Faber and Faber, 1960, 326–343.

———. ''Witchcraft and Sorcery in Lugbara.'' In J. Middleton and E. H. Winter (eds). *Witchcraft and Sorcery in East Africa.* London: Routledge and Kegan Paul, 1963, 257–275.

———. ''The Yakan or Allah Water Cult among the Lugbara.'' *Journal of the Royal Anthropological Institute,* 93, 1, 1963, 80–108.

———. *The Lugbara of Uganda.* New York: Holt, Rinehart and Winston, 1965. 2nd Edition (Case Studies in Cultural Anthropology), Fort Worth, TX: Harcourt Brace Jovanovich, 1992.

———. ''Political Incorporation among the Lugbara of Uganda.'' In Ronald Cohen and John Middleton (eds). *From Tribe to Nation in Africa.* Scranton, PA: Chandler, 1970, 55–70.

———. (ed). *Black Africa: Its Peoples and their Cultures Today.* London: Macmillan, 1970.

———. "Some Effects of Colonial Rule among the Lugbara." In V. Turner (ed). *Colonialism in Africa, Vol. III.* London, 1970, 6–48.

———. "Prophets and Rainmakers in Social Change amongst Lugbara." In T. O. Beidelman (ed). *The Translation of Culture.* London: Tavistock, 1971, 179–202.

———. "The Dance Among the Lugbara of Uganda." In P. Spencer (ed). *Society and Dance: The Social Anthropology of Process and Performance.* Cambridge, UK: Cambridge University Press, 1985, 165–182.

Ocitti, J. P. *African Indigenous Education as Practised by the Acholi of Uganda.* Nairobi: East African Literature Bureau, 1973.

Odada, M.A.E. "The Kumam: Langi or Iteso?" *Uganda Journal,* 35, 2, 1971, 139–152.

Ogot, B. A. *History of the Southern Luo, Volume 1, Migration and Settlement.* Nairobi: East African Publishing House, 1967.

Okot P'Bitek. *Religion of the Central Luo.* Nairobi, Kampala, Dar es Salaam: East African Literature Bureau, 1971.

Onyango-ku-Odongo, J. M. and J. B. Webster. *The Central Lwo During the Aconya.* Nairobi, Kampala, Dar es Salaam: East African Literature Bureau, 1976.

Sharman, A. " 'Joking' in Padhola: Categorical Relationships, Choice and Social Control." *Man,* 4, 1, 1969, 103–117,

Shiroya, O.J.E. "The Lugbara States in the Eighteenth and Nineteenth Centuries." In A. I. Salim (ed). *State Formation in Eastern Africa.* Nairobi: Heinemann Educational, 1984, 195–206.

Southall, Aidan. "Alur Tradition and its Historical Significance." *Uganda Journal,* 18, 2, 1954, 137–165.

———. *Alur Society, a Study in Processes and Types of Domination.* Cambridge, UK: W. Heffer and Sons, 1956.

———. "Rank Stratification among the Alur and other Nilotic Peoples." In A. Tuden and L. Plotnicov (eds). *Social Stratification in Africa.* New York: The Free Press, 1970.

———. "Incorporation among the Alur." In D. Cohen and J. Middleton (eds). *From Tribe to Nation in Africa.* Scranton, PA: Chandler, 1970.

———. "Partitioned Alur." In A. I. Asiwaju (ed). *Partitioned Africans: Ethnic Relations Across Africa's International Boundaries, 1884–1984.* London: Hurst, 1985, 87–103.

———. " 'The Rain Fell on Its Own': The Alur Theory of Development and its Western Counterparts." *African Studies Review,* 31, 2, 1988, 1–15.

Steinhart, E. "The Emergence of Bunyoro: The Tributary Mode of Production and the Formation of the State, 1400–1900." In A. I. Salim (ed). *State Formation in Eastern Africa.* Nairobi: Heinemann Educational, 1984, 70–90.

Tarantino, A. "The Origin of the Lango." *Uganda Journal,* 10, 1, 1946, 12–16.

———. "Lango Clans." *Uganda Journal,* 13, 1, 1949, 109–111.

———. "Notes on the Lango." *Uganda Journal,* 13, 1, 1949, 145–153.

———. "Lango Wars, Notes." *Uganda Journal,* 13, 2, 1949, 230–235.

Thomas, Elizabeth Marshall. *Warrior Herdsmen.* New York: Vintage Books, 1965.

Tosh, John. "The Langi in the Nineteenth Century." *Tarikh,* 3, 2, 1970, 59–68.

————. "Colonial Chiefs in a Stateless Society: A Case-Study from Northern Uganda." *Journal of African History,* 14, 1973, 473–490.

————. "Small-Scale Resistance in Uganda: The Lango Rising at Adwari in 1919." *Azania,* 9, 1974, 51–64.

————. *Clan Leaders and Colonial Chiefs in Lango, 1800–1939.* Oxford: Clarendon Press, 1978.

————. "Lango Agriculture during the Early Colonial Period: Land and Labour in a Cash-Crop Economy." *Journal of African History,* 19, 3, 1978, 415–439.

Turnbull, Colin. *The Mountain People.* London: Jonathan Cape, 1973; Picador, Pan Books, 1974.

Uchendu, Victor and K.R.M. Anthony. *Agricultural Change in Teso District.* Nairobi, Kampala, Dar es Salaam: East African Literature Bureau, 1975.

Uzoigwe, G. N. *Revolution and Revolt in Bunyoro-Kitara.* London: Longmans, 1970.

————. "The Kyanyangire, 1907: Passive Revolt Against British Overrule." In B. A. Ogot (ed). *War and Society in Africa.* London: Cass, 1972, 179–214.

————. "Precolonial Markets in Bunyoro-Kitara." In B. A. Ogot (ed). *Economic and Social History of East Africa.* Proceedings of the 1972 Conference of the Historical Association of Kenya. Nairobi: East African Literature Bureau, 1975, 24–65.

————. "The Agreement States and the Making of Uganda: I. Buganda." In G. N. Uzoigwe (ed). *Uganda: The Dilemma of Nationhood.* New York, London, Lagos: NOK Publishers International, 1982, 57–93.

————. "The Agreement States and the Making of Uganda: II.

Tooro, Ankole and Bunyoro Kitara.'' In G. N. Uzoigwe (ed). *Uganda: The Dilemma of Nationhood.* New York, London, Lagos: NOK Publishers International, 1982, 94–132.

Vincent, Joan. ''Colonial Chiefs and the Making of a Class: A Case Study from Teso.'' *Africa,* 47, 2, 1977, 140–158.

———. ''Teso in Transformation: Colonial Penetration in Teso Disctrict, Uganda, and its Contemporary Significance.'' In Lionel Cliffe et al. (eds). *Government and Rural Development in East Africa: Essays in Political Penetration.* The Hague: Mouton, 1978, 53–80.

———. *Teso in Transformation, Peasantry and Class in Colonial Uganda 1890–1927.* Berkeley, CA: University of California Press, 1982.

Weatherby, John. ''A Preliminary Note on the Sorat (Tepeth).'' *Uganda Journal,* 33, 1, 1969, 75–78, 124.

———. ''Raindrums of the Sor.'' In J. B. Webster. *Chronology Migrations and Drought in Interlacustrine Africa.* New York: Africana Publishing Company and Dalhousie University Press, 1979. 317–332.

———. ''The Secret Spirit Cult of the Sor in Karamoja.'' *Africa,* 58, 2, 1988, 229.

Webster, J. B., D. H. Okalany, C. P. Emudong and N. Egimu-Okuda. *The Iteso During the Asonya.* Nairobi: East African Publishing House, 1973.

Wilson, J. G. ''Preliminary Observation on the Oropom People of Karamoja, their Ethnic Status, Culture and Postulated Relation to the Peoples of the Late Stone Age.'' *Uganda Journal,* 34, 2, 1970, 125–146.

Wright, A.C.A. ''Notes on the Iteso Social Organization.'' *Uganda Journal,* 9, 1, 1942, 57–80.

Wright, M. J. "The Early Life of Rwot Isaya Ogwangguji, M.B.E." *Uganda Journal,* 22, 1, 1958, 131–138.

3.2 SOUTH AND SOUTHWESTERN UGANDA

Alnaes, Kirsten. "Songs of the Ruwenzururu Rebellion." In P. H. Gulliver (ed). *Tradition and Transition in East Africa.* London: Routledge and Kegan Paul, 1969, 243–273.

Atanda, J. A. "The Bakopi in the Kingdom of Buganda, 1900–1912." *Uganda Journal,* 33, 2, 1969, 151–162.

———. "British Rule in Buganda." *Tarikh,* 4, 4, 1969, 37–54.

Baitwababo, S. R. "Bashambo Rule in Rujumbura, 1780–1920." In B. G. McIntosh (ed). *Ngano* (Nairobi Historical Studies, No. 1). Nairobi: East African Publishing House, 1969, 1–25.

Bamunoba, J. K. and F. B. Welbourn. "Emandwa Initiation in Ankole." *Uganda Journal,* 29, 2, 1965, 13–25.

Bazaara, Nyangatyaki. "Famine in Bunyoro (Kitara) 1900–1939." *Mawazo,* 5, 3, 1983–4, 65–75.

Beattie, John. "Nyoro Kinship." *Africa,* xxvii, 4, 1957, 317–339.

———. "Nyoro Marriage and Affinity." *Africa,* xxviii, 1, 1957, 1–22.

———. "The Blood Pact in Bunyoro." *African Studies,* 17, 4, 1958, 198–203.

———. "Rituals of Nyoro Kingship." *Africa,* xxix, 2, 1959, 134–144.

———. *Bunyoro: An African Kingdom.* New York: Holt, 1960.

————. "On the Nyoro Concept of 'Mahano'." *African Studies,* 19, 3, 1960, 145–150.

————. "Group Aspects of the Nyoro Spirit Mediumship Cult." *Rhodes-Livingstone Journal,* 30, 1961, 11–38.

————. "Nyoro Mortuary Rites." *Uganda Journal,* 25, 2, 1961, 171–183.

————. "Sorcery in Bunyoro." in J. Middleton and E. H. Winter. *Witchcraft and Sorcery in East Africa.* London: Routledge and Kegan Paul, 1963, 27–55.

————. "Bunyoro: an African Feudality?" *Journal of African History,* 5, 1, 1964, 25–35.

————. "Rainmaking in Bunyoro." *Man,* 64, 179, 1964, 140–141.

————. *Understanding an African Kingdom: Bunyoro.* New York: Holt, Rinehart and Winston, 1965.

————. "Aspects of Nyoro Symbolism." *Africa,* xxxviii, 4, 1968, 413–442.

————. "Spirit Mediumship in Bunyoro." in J. Beattie and J. Middleton (eds). *Spirit Mediumship and Society in Africa.* London: Routledge and Kegan Paul, 1969, 159–170.

————. "Democratization in Bunyoro: The Impact of Democratic Institutions and Values on a Traditional African Kingdom." In J. Middleton (ed). *Black Africa.* New York: Collier-Macmillan, 1970, 101–110.

————. *The Nyoro State.* Oxford: Clarendon Press, 1971.

Benjamin, Ray. *Myth, Ritual and Kingship in Buganda.* New York: Oxford University Press, 1991.

Berger, Iris and Carole A. Buchanan. "The Cwezi Cults and the

History of Western Uganda.'' In Joseph T. Gallagher (ed). *East African Culture History.* Syracuse, NY: Maxwell School of Citizenship and Public Affairs, Syracuse University, 1976, 43–78.

Bessell, G. ''Nyabingi.'' *Uganda Journal,* 6, 2, 1938, 73–86.

Buchanan, Carole. ''Of Kings and Tradition: The Case of Bunyoro-Kitara.'' *International Journal of African Historical Studies,* 7, 3, 1975, 516–526.

————. ''Perceptions of Ethnic Interaction in the East African Interior: The Kitara Complex.'' *International Journal of African Historical Studies,* 11, 3, 1978, 410–428.

Bunker, Stephen G. ''Center-Local Struggles for Bureaucratic Control in Bugisu, Uganda.'' *American Ethnologist,* 10, 1982, 749–769.

————. ''Dependency, Inequality and Development Policy: A Case from Bugisu, Uganda.'' *The British Journal of Sociology,* 34, 2, 1983, 271–292.

————. ''Center-local Struggles for Bureaucratic Control in Bugisu, Uganda.'' *American Ethnologist,* 10, 4, 1983, 749–769.

————. *Double Dependency and Constraints on Class Formation in Bugisu, Uganda.* Urbana and Chicago: University of Illinois Press, 1983.

————. ''Peasant Responses to a Dependent State: Uganda 1983.'' *Canadian Journal of African Studies,* 19, 2, 1985, 371–386.

————. ''Property, Protest and Politics in Bugisu, Uganda.'' In D. Crummey. *Banditry, Rebellion and Social Protest in Africa.* London: James Currey; and Portsmouth, NH: Heinemann, 1986, 271–292.

————. *Peasants Against the State: The Politics of Market Control in Bugisu, Uganda.* Urbana and Chicago: University of Illinois Press, 1987.

Cohen, D. W. "The Cwezi Cult." *Journal of African History,* IX, 4, 1968, 651–657.

————. "A Survey of Interlacustrine Chronology." *Journal of African History,* XI, 2, 1970, 177–201.

————. *The Historical Tradition of Busoga: Mukama and Kintu.* Oxford: Clarendon Press, 1972.

————. *Towards a Reconstructed Past: Historical Texts from Busoga, Uganda.* London: The British Academy and Oxford University Press, 1986.

————. "The Cultural Topography of a 'Bantu Borderland': Busoga, 1500–1850." *Journal of African History,* 29, 1, 1988, 57–80.

Denoon, D. (ed). *A History of Kigezi.* Kampala: The National Trust Adult Education Centre, 1972.

Doornbos, Martin. "Kumanyana and Rwenzururu: Two Responses to Ethnic Inequality." In R. J. Rotberg and Ali A. Mazrui (eds). *Protest and Power in Black Africa.* New York and London: Oxford University Press, 1970, 1088–1136.

————. "Protest Movements in Western Uganda: Some Parallels and Contrasts." *Kroniek van Afrika,* 1970, 3.

————. "Some Structural Aspects of Regional Government in Uganda and Ghana." *Journal of Administration Overseas,* 12, 2, 1973.

————. "Images and Reality of Stratification in Pre-Colonial Nkore." *Canadian Journal of African Studies,* 3, 1973, 477–495.

————. "Land Tenure and Political Conflict in Ankole, Uganda." *Journal of Development Studies*, 12, 1, 1975.

————. *Regalia Galore: The Decline and Eclipse of Ankole Kingship.* Nairobi: East African Literature Bureau, 1975.

————. "Ethnicity, Christianity and the Development of Social Stratification in Colonial Ankole, Uganda." *International Journal of African Historical Studies*, 9, 4, 1976.

————. "Ankole." In R. LeMarchand (ed). *African Kingships in Perspective: Political Change and Modernization in Monarchical Settings.* London: Clark, Noble and Brendon, 1977.

Dunbar, A. R. *A History of Bunyoro-Kitara.* Nairobi: Oxford University Press for East African Institute of Social Research, 1965.

Edel, M. M. *The Chiga of Western Uganda.* New York: Oxford University Press, 1957.

————. "African Tribalism: Some Reflections on Uganda." *Political Science Quarterly*, 80, 3, 1965, 357–371.

Elam, Y. *The Social and Sexual Roles of Hima Women: A Study of Nomadic Cattle-Breeders in Nyabushozi County, Ankole, Uganda.* Manchester: Manchester University Press, 1973.

————. "Relationships between Hima and Iru in Ankole." *African Studies*, 33, 3, 1974, 159–172.

Elizabeth of Toro, Princess. *African Princess.* London: Hamish Hamilton, 1983.

Fallers, L. A. *The King's Men: Leaders and Status in Buganda on the Eve of Independence.* London: Oxford University Press, 1964.

————. *Bantu Bureaucracy—A Century of Political Evolution*

among the Basoga of Uganda. Cambridge, UK: W.H. Heffer and Sons, 1965.

Fallers, Margaret Chase. *The Eastern Lacustrine Bantu (Ganda and Soga).* (Ethnographic Survey of Africa: East Central Africa, Part 11). London: International African Institute, 1960.

Felkin, Robert W. "Notes on the Wanyoro Tribe of Central Africa." *Proceedings of the Royal Society of Edinburgh,* XIX, 1891, 136–192.

Fisher, A. B. *Twilight Tales of the Black Baganda.* London: Marshall, 1911.

Freedman, Jim. "Three Muraris, Three Gahayas and the Four Phases of Nyabingi." In J. B. Webster (ed). *Chronology, Migration and Drought in Interlacustrine Africa.* New York: Africana Publishing and Dalhousie University Press, 1979, 175–188.

———. *Nyabingi: The Social History of an African Divinity.* Butare, Rwanda, and Tervuren, Belgium: Institut National de Recherche Scientifique Butare—République Rwandaise, 1984.

Furley, Oliver. "The Reign of Kasagama." *Uganda Journal,* 25, 1, 1961.

Ghai, D. P. "The Buganda Trade Boycott: A Study in Tribal, Political and Economic Nationalism." In R. Rotberg and Ali A. Mazrui (eds). *Protest and Power in Black Africa.* London and New York: Oxford University Press, 1970, 755–770.

Gray, Sir J. M. "Mutesa's Caravan to Zanzibar, 1870–72." *Uganda Journal,* 11, 1, 1947, 96–97.

———. "A History of Ibanda, Saza of Mitoma, Ankole." *Uganda Journal* 24, 2, 1960, 166–182.

———. "Kakunguru in Bukedi." *Uganda Journal,* 27, 1, 1963, 31–59.

Gutkind, P. C. *The Royal Capital of Buganda.* The Hague: Mouton, 1963.

Hancock, I. R. "Patriotism and Neo-traditionalism in Buganda: the Kabaka Yekka ('The King Alone') Movement, 1961–62." *Journal of African History,* 11, 3, 1970, 419–434.

Hattersley, C. W. *The Baganda at Home.* London: Religious Tract Society, 1908. Reprinted London: Frank Cass, 1968.

Haydon, E. S. *Law and Justice in Buganda.* London: Butterworth, 1960.

Heald, Suzette. "The Ritual Use of Violence: Circumcision among the Gisu of Uganda." In D. Riches (ed). *The Anthropology of Violence.* Oxford and New York: Blackwell, 1986, 70–85.

———. *Controlling Anger: The Sociology of Gisu Violence.* Manchester: Manchester University Press; and New York: St Martin's Press for the International African Institute, 1989.

———. "Joking and Avoidance, Hostility, and Incest: An Essay on Gisu Moral Categories." *Man,* 25, 3, 1990, 377–392.

———. "Divinatory Failure: The Religious and Social Role of Gisu Diviners." *Africa,* 61, 3, 1991, 298–317.

Herring, Ralph S. "The Influence of Climate on the Migrations of the Central and Southern Luo." In B. A. Ogot (ed). *Ecology and History in East Africa.* Proceedings of the 1975 Conference of the Historical Association of Kenya. Nairobi: Kenya Literature Bureau, 1979, 77–107.

Hopkins, Elizabeth. "The Nyabingi Cult of Southwestern Uganda." In Robert I. Rotberg and Ali A. Mazrui (eds).

Protest and Power in Black Africa. London and New York: Oxford University Press, 1970, 258–336.

————. "Partition in Practice: African Politics and European Rivalry in Bufumbira." In S. Foster et al (eds). *Bismarck, Europe and Africa: The Berlin Africa Conference, 1884–1885, and the Onset of Partition.* London: Oxford University Press for the German Historical Institute, 1988, 415–440.

Hoyle, W. E. "Early Days in Kampala." *Uganda Journal,* 21, 1, 1957, 91–98.

Ingham, Kenneth. *The Kingdom of Toro in Uganda.* London: Methuen, 1975.

Kabuga, C.E.S. "The Genealogy of Kabaka Kintu and the Early Bakabaka of Buganda." *Uganda Journal,* 27, 2, 1963, 206–216.

Kagwa, Sir Apolo (trans. E. B. Kalibala and M. M. Edel). *The Customs of the Baganda.* New York: Columbia University Press, 1934.

————. *A Book of the Baganda Clans.* Kampala: Uganda Bookshop and Uganda Society, 1949.

Kagwa, Sir Apolo (trans. M.S.M. Kiwanuka). *The Kings of Buganda.* Nairobi: East African Publishing House, 1971.

Kahimbaara, J. A. and B. W. Langlands. *The Human Factor in the Changing Ecology of Mwenge.* Kampala: Makerere University, 1970.

Kanyamunyu, P. K. "The Tradition of the Coming of the Abalisa Clan to Buhwezu, Ankole." *Uganda Journal,* 15, 1951, 191–192.

Karugire, S. R. "Relations between Bahima and Bairu in 19th Century Nkore." *Tarikh,* 3, 1, 1970, 22–33.

————. *A History of the Kingdom of Nkore in Western Uganda to 1896.* Oxford: Clarendon Press, 1971.

Kasfir, Nelson. "Seizing Half a Loaf: Isaya Mukirane and Self-Recruitment for Secession." In W. H. Morris-Jones (ed). *The Making of Politicians.* London: Athlone Press, 1976, 66–77.

Kenny, M. G. "Mutesa's Crime: Hubris and the Control of African Kings." *Comparative Studies in Sociology and History,* 30, 4, 1988, 595–612.

Kiwanuka, M.S.M. "Sir Apolo Kagwa and the Pre-Colonial History of Buganda." *Uganda Journal,* 30, 2, 1966, 137–152.

————. *The Empire of Bunyoro Kitara: Myth or Reality?* Kampala: Longmans, 1968.

————. *A History of Buganda from the Foundation of the Kingdom to 1900,* London: Longmans, 1971.

Kreuer, Werner. *Ankole.* Wiesbaden, Germany: Steiner, 1979.

K. W. (Sir Tito Winyi). "The Kings of Bunyoro-Kitara. Part I." *Uganda Journal,* 3, 2, 1935, 155–160.

————. "The Kings of Bunyoro-Kitara. Part II." *Uganda Journal,* 4, 1, 1936, 75–83.

————. "The Kings of Bunyoro-Kitara. Part III." *Uganda Journal,* 5, 2, 1937, 53–69.

————. "The Procedure in Accession to the Throne of a Nominated King in the Kingdom of Bunyoro-Kitara." *Uganda Journal,* 4, 4, 1937, 289–299.

La Fontaine, J. *The Gisu of Uganda.* London: International African Institute, 1959.

————. ''Tribalism among the Gisu.'' In P.H. Gulliver (ed). *Tradition and Transition in East Africa: Studies of the Tribal Element in the Modern Era.* London: Routledge and Kegan Paul, 1969, 177–192.

Lanning, E. C. ''Notes on the History of Kooki.'' *Uganda Journal,* 23, 2, 1959, 162–172.

Lee, J. M. ''Buganda's Position in Federal Uganda.'' *Journal of Commonwealth Political Studies,* 3, 3, 1965, 165–181.

Low, D. A. *Buganda in Modern History.* London: Weidenfeld and Nicolson, 1971.

————. *The Mind of Buganda: Documents of the Modern History of an African Kingdom.* London: Heinemann, 1971.

———— and R. Cranford Pratt. *Buganda and British Overrule, 1900–1955.* London: Oxford University Press, 1960.

Lubogo, Y. K. *A History of Busoga.* Nairobi: East African Literature Bureau, 1960 (English Transl. Bantu Committee).

Luig, Ute. ''Sorcery Accusations among the Kiga of Mulago Village.'' *Uganda Journal,* 38, 1, 1976, 11–32.

Mafeje, Archie. ''The Legitimacy of the Uganda Government in Buganda.'' In L. Cliffe, J. S. Coleman and M. R. Doornbos (eds). *A Century of Change in Eastern Africa.* The Hague: Martinus Nijhoff, 1977, 99–118.

————. ''Agrarian Revolution and the Land Question in Buganda.'' In B. Berdichewsky (ed). *Anthropology and Social Change in Rural Areas,* The Hague: Mouton, 1979, 67–88.

Mair, Lucy. *An African People in the Twentieth Century.* London: G. Routledge, 1934.

————. ''Busoga Local Government.'' *Journal of Commonwealth Political Studies,* 5, 2, 1967, 91–108.

Mamdani, M. "Analyzing the Agrarian Question: The Case of a Buganda Village." *Mawazo,* 5, 3, 1984, 47–64.

Morris, H. F. "The Kingdom of Mpororo." *Uganda Journal,* 19, 1955, 204–207.

———. "The Making of Ankole." *Uganda Journal,* 21, 1, 1960, 1–15.

———. *A History of Ankole.* Nairobi, Kampala, Dar es Salaam: East African Literature Bureau. 1962.

———. *Heroic Recitations of the Bahiima of Ankole.* London: Oxford University Press, 1964.

———. "Buganda and Tribalism." In P. H. Gulliver (ed). *Tradition and Transition in East Africa.* Berkeley, CA: University of California Press, 1969, 328–338.

Mudoola, Dan. "Colonial Chief-Making: Busoga, A Case Study, 1900–1940." Universities Social Sciences Conference, Dar es Salaam, 1970.

———. "The Young Basoga and Abataka Association: A Case-Study in Chiefly Politics in Colonial Busoga." *Uganda Journal,* 38, 1, 1976, 33–57.

Mungonya, Z. K. "The Bacwezi in Ankole." *Uganda Journal,* 22, 1, 1958, 18–21.

Mushanga, M. Tibamanya and M. Louise Pirouet. "New Evidence from Mission Archives on the Death of Galt in Ankole, Uganda, 1905." *History in Africa,* 5, 1978, 121–130.

Nabwiso-Bulima, F. "The Evolution of the Kyabazingaship of Busoga." *Uganda Journal,* 30, 2, 1966, 89–100.

Nayenga, Peter. "Busoga in the Era of Catastrophes, 1898–1911." In B. A. Ogot (ed). *Ecology and History in East*

Africa. Proceedings of the 1975 Conference of the Historical Association of Kenya. Nairobi: Kenya Literature Bureau, 1979, 153–178.

―――. "Chiefs and the 'Land Question' in Busoga District, Uganda, 1895–1936." *International Journal of African Historical Studies,* 12, 2, 1979, 183–209.

Needham, R. "Right and Left in Nyoro Symbolic Classification." *Africa,* xxxvii, 3, 1967, 425–452.

Ngologoza, P. (ed) (trans. D. Denoon and B. J. Turyahikayo-Rugyema). *Kigezi and its People.* Kampala: East African Literature Bureau, 1970.

Ntare School History Society. "H. M. Stanley's Journey Through Ankole in 1889." *Uganda Journal,* 29, 2, 1965, 185–192.

Nyakatura, John (trans. and ed. Z. K. Rigby). *Aspects of Bunyoro Customs and Tradition.* Nairobi: East African Literature Bureau, 1970.

―――― (trans. and ed. G. N. Uzoigwe). *Anatomy of an African Kingdom: A History of Bunyoro-Kitara.* New York: Doubleday and NOK, 1973.

―――― (trans. and ed. G. N. Uzoigwe). "Succession and Civil War in Bunyoro Kitara." *International Journal of African Historical Studies,* VI, 1, 1973.

Oberg, K. "The Kingdom of Ankole." In M. Fortes and E. E. Evans-Pritchard. *African Political Systems.* London: International African Institute, 1966.

Oliver, R. "A Question about the Bacwezi." *Uganda Journal,* 17, 2, 1953, 135–137.

―――. "The Traditional Histories of Buganda, Bunyoro and Nkole." *Journal of the Royal Anthropological Institute,* 85, 1955, 111–117.

―――. "The Baganda and the Bakonjo." *Uganda Journal,* 18, 31–33, 1954.

Pawlikova-Vilhanova, Viera. *History of Anti-Colonial Resistance and Protest in the Kingdoms of Buganda and Bunyoro, 1862–1899.* Prague: Oriental Institute of the Czechoslovak Academy of Sciences, 1988.

Perlman, Melvin. "The Changing Status and Role of Women in Toro (W. Uganda)." *Cahiers d'Etudes Africaines,* 6, 4, 1966.

―――. "Children Born out of Wedlock and the Status of Women in Toro, Uganda." *Rural Africana,* 29, Winter, 1975.

―――. "Family Law and Social Change Among the Toro of Uganda." *Journal of African Law,* 29, 1, 1985, 82–93.

Robertson, A. F. *Community of Strangers. A Journal of Discovery in Uganda.* London: Scolar Press, 1978.

Roscoe, J. *The Bahima.* London: Macmillan, 1907.

―――. *The Baganda.* London: Macmillan, 1911.

―――. *The Northern Bantu. An Account of Some Central Tribes of the Uganda Protectorate.* Cambridge, UK: Cambridge University Press, 1915.

―――. *Twenty-Five Years in East Africa.* Cambridge, UK: Cambridge University Press, 1921.

―――. *The Soul of Central Africa.* Cambridge, UK: Cambridge University Press, 1922.

―――. *The Bakitara or Banyoro.* Cambridge, UK: Cambridge University Press, 1923.

―――. *The Banyankole.* Cambridge, UK: Cambridge University Press, 1923.

————. *The Bagesu.* Cambridge, UK: Cambridge University Press, 1924.

————. *Immigrants and Other Influences in the Lake Region of Central Africa.* Cambridge, UK: Cambridge University Press, 1924.

Rowe, John A. "Land and Politics in Buganda, 1875–1955." *Makerere Journal,* 10, 1, 1964, 1–13.

Sagan, Eli. *At the Dawn of Tyranny: The Origins of Individualism, Political Oppression and the State.* New York: Alfred A. Knopf; and Toronto: Random House, 1985; London: Faber and Faber, 1986.

Southall, R. J. *Parties and Politics in Bunyoro.* Kampala: Makerere Institute of Social Research, 1972.

Southwold, Martin. "The Ganda of Uganda." In James L. Gibbs Jr (ed). *Peoples of Africa.* New York: Holt, Rinehart and Winston, 1965, 81–118.

————. *Bureaucracy and Chiefship in Buganda: The Development of Appointive Office in the History of Buganda.* East African Studies, 14. Kampala: East African Institute of Social Research, n.d.

————. "Was the Kingdom Sacred?" *Mawazo,* I, 2, 1967, 17–23.

Stacey, T. *Summons to Ruwenzori.* London: Secker and Warburg, 1965.

Steinhart, Edward I. "Vassal and Fief in Three Lacustrine Kingdoms." *Cahiers d'Etudes Africaines,* 7, 1967, 606–623.

————. "The Nyangire Rebellion of 1907." In *Protest Movements in Colonial East Africa.* Eastern African Studies XII. Syracuse, NY: Program of Eastern African Studies, 1973.

―――. ''Royal Clientage and the Beginnings of Colonial Modernization in Toro.'' *International Journal of African Historical Studies,* 6, 1973, 265–285.

―――. *Conflict and Collaboration: The Kingdoms of Western Uganda, 1890–1907.* Princeton, NJ: Princeton University Press, 1977.

―――. ''The Kingdoms of the March: Speculations on Social and Political Change.'' In J. B. Webster (ed). *Chronology in African History.* Halifax, Canada: Longmans, 1977.

―――. ''The Politics of Intrigue in Ankole, 1905.'' *African Studies Review,* 20, 1977, 1–17.

―――. ''Ankole: Pastoral Hegemony.'' In H.J.M. Claessen and P. Skalnik (eds). *The Early State.* The Hague: Mouton, 1978

―――. ''Herders and Farmers: The Tributary Mode of Production in Western Uganda.'' In Donald Crummey and C. C. Steward (eds). *Modes of Production in Africa: The Precolonial Era.* Beverly Hills, CA, and London: Sage, 1981.

Stenning, Derrick J. ''Salvation in Ankole.'' In M. Fortes and G. Dieterlen (eds). *African Systems of Thought.* London: Oxford University Press for International African Institute, 1965, 258–275.

Syahuka-Muhindo, A. *The Rwenzururu Movement and the Democratic Struggle.* Kampala: Centre for Basic Research, 1991.

Taylor, B. K. *The Western Lacustrine Bantu.* London: International African Institute, 1962.

Thomas, H. B. ''Capax Imperii. The Story of Semei Kakunguru.'' *Uganda Journal,* 7, 2, 1939, 125–136.

―――. ''Kigezi Operations, 1914–1917.'' *Uganda Journal,* 30, 2, 1966, 165–173.

Tibenderana, P. K. "Supernatural Sanctions and Peace-Keeping among the Bakiga of Western Uganda during the Nineteenth Century." *Journal of African Studies,* 7, 3, 1980, 144–151.

Turyahikayo-Rugyema, B. "Markets in Pre-colonial East Africa: The Case of the Bakiga." *Current Anthropology,* June, 1976, 286–290.

———. "Bakiga Institutions of Government." *Uganda Journal,* 40, 1, 1982, 14–28.

Twaddle, M. J. "The *Bakungu* Chiefs of Buganda under British Colonial Rule, 1900–1930." *Journal of African History,* 10, 2, 1969, 309–322.

———. "Tribalism in Eastern Uganda." In P. H. Gulliver (ed). *Tradition and Transition in East Africa.* London: Routledge and Kegan Paul, 1969, 193–208.

———. "Ganda Receptivity to Change." *Journal of African History,* 15, 2, 1974, 303–315.

———. "The Nine Lives of Semei Kakungulu." *History in Africa.* 12, 1985, 325–333.

———. "Slaves and Peasants in Buganda." In L. J. Archer (ed). *Slavery and Other Forms of Unfree Labour.* London: Routledge, 1988, 118–129.

———. *Kakungulu and the Creation of Uganda 1969–1928.* London: James Currey, 1993.

Welbourn, F. B. "Some Aspects of Kiganda Religion." *Uganda Journal,* 26, 2, 1962, 171–182.

Were, Gideon. "Further Thoughts on the Early History of the Bagisu." *Journal of Eastern African Research and Development,* 1, 1, 1971, 99–100.

———. "The Economy of Pre-Colonial Bugisu." *Journal of African Studies,* 5, 2, 1978, 173–184.

White, R. G. "Blacksmiths of Kigezi." *Uganda Journal,* 33, 1, 1969, 65–73.

Whyte, M. A. "The Process of Survival in South-Eastern Uganda." In M. Bovin and L. Manger (eds). *Adaptive Strategies in African Arid Lands.* Uppsala, Sweden: Scandinavian Institute of African Studies, 1990, 121–145.

Whyte, S. R. "Uncertain Persons in Nyole Divination." *Journal of Religion in Africa,* XX, 1, 1990, 41–62.

Winter, E. H. *Bwamba: A Structural-Functional Analysis of a Patrilineal Society.* Cambridge, UK: W. Heffer and Sons, 1956.

————. *Beyond the Mountains of the Moon: The Lives of Four Africans.* London: Routledge and Kegan Paul, 1959.

Wrigley, C. C. "Some Thoughts about the Bacwezi." *Uganda Journal,* 22, 1, 1958, 11–17.

Yoder, J. "The Search for Kintu and the Search for Peace: Mythology and Normality in Nineteenth Century Buganda." *History in Africa,* 15, 1988, 363–376.

4. 1862–1962: History, Sociology and Anthropology

4.1 1862–1893: TOWARDS COLONIALISM (including general works which touch on Uganda, and some works which overlap the two periods)

Ashe, R. P. *Two Kings of Uganda.* London: Sampson Low, Marston, Searle and Rivington, 1889.

————. *Chronicles of Uganda.* London: Hodder and Stoughton, 1894.

Austin, Herbert H. *With MacDonald in Uganda.* London: Edward Arnold, 1903.

Baker, Sir Samuel W. *The Albert N'yanza*. London: Macmillan, 1866.

―――. *Ismailia*. London: Macmillan, 1874.

Barber, James P. "The MacDonald Expedition to the Nile 1887–99." *Uganda Journal*, 28, 1, 1–14.

Beachey, R. W. "The Arms Trade in East Africa in the Late Nineteenth Century." *Journal of African History*, III, 1962, 451–467.

―――. "MacDonald's Expedition and the Uganda Mutiny, 1887–1898." *Historical Journal*, 10, 1967, 237–254.

Bierman, John. *Dark Safari: The Life Behind the Legend of Henry Morton Stanley*. London: Hodder and Stoughton, 1990.

Colvile, H. E. *The Land of the Nile Springs*. London: Edward Arnold, 1895.

Cussac, J. *Evêque et Pionnier Monseigneur Streicher*. Paris: Editions de la Savane, 1955.

Dawson, James. *James Hannington, First Bishop of Eastern Equatorial Africa. A History of his Life and Work, 1847–1885*. London: Seeley, 1905.

Dunbar, A. R. *Omukama Chwa II Kabarega*. Uganda's Famous Men. Kampala, Nairobi, Dar es Salaam: East African Literature Bureau, 1965.

Faupel, J. F. *African Holocaust*. London: Geoffrey Chapman, 1962.

Fisher, R. B. *On the Borders of Pygmy Land*. London: Marshall, 1905.

―――. *Twilight Tales of the Black Baganda*. London: Marshall, 1912.

Galbraith, John S. *Mackinnon and East Africa, 1878–1895.* Cambridge, UK: Cambridge University Press, 1972

Gee, T. W. "A Century of Muhammedan Influence in Buganda. 1852–1951." *Uganda Journal,* 22, 2, 1958, 139–150.

Gorju, J. *Entre le Victoria, l'Albert et l'Edouard.* Rennes, France: Oberthur, 1920.

Grant, J. A. *A Walk Across Africa.* Edinburgh and London: Blackwood and Sons, 1864.

Hall, Richard. *Stanley: An Adventurer Explored.* London: Collins, 1974.

Hannington, James. *The Last Journals of James Hannington.* Ed. James Dawson. London: Seeley, 1888.

Harford-Battersby, C. F. *Pilkington of Uganda.* London: Marshall Brothers, 1898.

Harman, Nicholas. *Bwana Stokesi and his African Conquests.* London: Jonathan Cape, 1986.

Katumba, A. and F. B. Welbourn. "Muslim Martyrs of Buganda." *Uganda Journal,* 28, 2, 1964, 151–1 64.

Kiwanuka, M.S.M. *Muteesa of Uganda.* Kampala, Nairobi, Dar es Salaam: East African Literature Bureau, 1967.

———. "Kabaka Mwanga and His Political Parties." *Uganda Journal,* 33, 1, 1969, 1–16.

———. *The Empire of Bunyoro-Kitara: Myth or Reality?* Makerere History Papers, 1. Kampala: Longmans, 1969.

Leblond, G. *Le Père Auguste Achte.* Algiers: Maison-Carrée, 1928.

Low, D. A. *Religion and Society in Buganda 1875–1900.* Kampala: East African Institute of Social Research, n.d.

Luck, Anne. *Charles Stokes in Africa.* Nairobi: East African Publishing House, 1972.

Lugard, F.J.D. *The Rise of Our East African Empire.* Edinburgh and London: Blackwood, 1893.

————. *The Diaries of Lord Lugard* (eds M. Perham and M. Bull). London: Faber and Faber, 1959.

Mackay, J.W.H. (Mrs J. W. Harrison, sister of Alexander Mackay). *The Story of the Life of Mackay of Uganda; Pioneer Missionary.* London: Hodder and Stoughton, 1898. Cass Reprint, London: Frank Cass, 1970.

McLynn, Frank. *Stanley: The Making of an African Explorer.* London: Oxford University Press, 1991.

————. *Stanley: Sorcerer's Apprentice.* London: Oxford University Press, 1992.

Matson, T. "Baganda Merchant Venturers." *Uganda Journal,* 32, 1, 1968, 1–16.

Peters, Carl. *New Light on Dark Africa.* London: Ward Lock, 1891.

Portal, Gerald. *The British Mission to Uganda.* London: Edward Arnold, 1894.

Pringle, M. A. *A Journey in East Africa Towards the Mountains of the Moon.* Edinburgh and London: Blackwood, 1886.

Rowe, John A. "The Purge of Christians at Mwanga's Court." *Journal of African History,* V, 1, 1964, 55–72.

————. "Mika Sematimba." *Uganda Journal,* 28, 2, 1964, 179–200.

————. "The Western Impact and the African Reaction:

Buganda 1880–1900.'' *Journal of Developing Areas,* 1, October 1966, 55–65.

———. *Lugard at Kampala.* Makerere History Papers, 3. Kampala: Longmans, 1969.

———. "The Baganda Revolutionaries." *Tarikh,* 3, 2, 1970, 34–46.

Schweinfurth, G. et al. *Emin Pasha in Central Africa.* London: George Philip and Son, 1888.

Schweitzer, G. *Emin Pasha: His Life and Work.* London: Constable, 1898.

Speke, J. H. *Journal of the Discovery of the Sources of the Nile.* London: William Blackwood, 1963.

———. *What Led to the Discovery of the Source of the Nile.* London: 1864. London: Cass Reprint, 1967.

Stanley, Henry Morton. *Through the Dark Continent.* 2 Vols. London: George Newnes, 1878. Reprint, New York: Greenwood Press, 1969.

———. *In Darkest Africa.* London: Sampson, Low et al., 1878.

Stock, Eugene. *History of the Church Missionary Society.* Vol. III. London: Church Missionary Society, 1899.

Symons, A.J.A. *Emin: Governor of Equatoria.* London: Falcon Press, 1950.

Taylor, J. V. *The Growth of the Church in Buganda.* London: S.C.M. Press, 1961.

Thoonen, J. *Black Martyrs.* London: Sheed and Ward, 1942.

Thruston, A. B. *African Incidents.* London: John Murray, 1900.

Tucker, Alfred R. (Bishop). *Eighteen Years in Uganda and East Africa,* 2 Vols. London: Edward Arnold, 1908; 1 Vol. edition, 1911.

Twaddle, M. J. "The Muslim Revolution in Buganda." *African Affairs,* 71, 1972, 54–72.

————. "Decentralised Violence and Collaboration in Early Colonial Uganda." In A. Porter and R. Holland (eds). *Theory and Practice in the History of European Expansion Overseas.* London and Ottawa: Cass, 1988.

————. "The Emergence of Politico-Religious Groupings in Late Nineteenth Century Buganda." *Journal of African History,* 29, 1, 1988, 81–92.

Uzoigwe, G. N. "The Agreement States and the Making of Uganda: I. Buganda." In G. N. Uzoigwe (ed). *Uganda: The Dilemma of Nationhood.* New York, London, Lagos: NOK Publishers International, 1982, 57–93.

————. "The Agreement States and the Making of Uganda: II. Tooro, Ankole and Bunyoro Kitara." In G. N. Uzoigwe (ed). *Uganda: The Dilemma of Nationhood.* New York, London, Lagos: NOK Publishers International, 1982, 94–132.

Welbourn, F. B. "Speke and Stanley at the Court of Mutesa." *Uganda Journal,* 25, 2, 1961, 220–223.

Wilson, C. and R. Felkin. *Uganda and the Egyptian Soudan.* London: Sampson, Low, 2 Vols., 1882.

Winter, J. V. *The Sudanese Mutiny.* Nairobi: Eagle Press, 1950.

————. *The Uganda Mutiny.* London: Macmillan, 1954.

Wright, Michael. *Buganda in the Heroic Age.* Nairobi and London: Oxford University Press, 1971.

4.2: 1893–1962: THE PROTECTORATE ERA

Ansorge, W. J. *Under the African Sun.* London: Heinemann, 1899.

Apter, David. *The Political Kingdom in Uganda.* Princeton, NJ: Princeton University Press, 1961, 1967.

Austin, H. H. *With Macdonald in Uganda.* London: Edward Arnold, 1903.

Baker, S.J.K. "The Population Map of Uganda." *Uganda Journal,* 1, 2, 1934, 134–144.

Barber, James. *Imperial Frontier: A Study of Relations between the British and the Pastoral Tribes of North East Uganda.* Nairobi: East African Publishing House, 1968.

Bell, Hesketh. *Glimpses of a Governor's Life.* London: Sampson Low, Marston, 1946.

Bovill, M. and G. R. Askwith. *Roddy Owen.* London: John Murray, 1897.

Bowles, B. D. "Economic Anti-Colonialism and British Reaction in Uganda, 1936–1955." *Canadian Journal of African Studies,* 9, 1, 1975, 51–60.

[British Information Services]. *Uganda: the Making of a Nation.* New York: British Information Services, 1962.

Burke, Fred. "The New Role of the Chief in Uganda." *Journal of African Administration,* 10, 3, 1958, 153–160.

———. *Local Government and Politics in Uganda.* Syracuse, NY: Syracuse University Press, 1964.

Bustin, Edouard. "L'Africanisation des cadres administratifs de l'Ouganda." *Civilisations,* 9, 2, 1959, 133–150.

Byrd, Robert O. "Characteristics of Candidates for Election in a Country Approaching Independence: The Case of Uganda." *Midwest Journal of Political Science,* VII, 1, 1963, 1–26.

Churchill, Winston S. *My African Journey.* London: Hodder and Stoughton, 1908.

Cohen, Sir Andrew. *British Policy in Changing Africa.* London: Routledge and Kegan Paul, 1959.

Cook, Sir Albert. "Kampala During the Closing Years of the Last Century." *Uganda Journal,* 1, 2, 1934, 83–95.

———. "Further Memories of Uganda." *Uganda Journal,* 2, 2, 1935, 97–115.

———. *Uganda Memories.* Entebbe: Government Press, 1945.

Dundas, Sir Charles. *African Crossroads.* London: Macmillan, 1955.

———. "Decline of Immigrant Influence on the Uganda Administration, 1945–62." *Uganda Journal,* 31, 1, 1967, 73–88.

Fallers, L. A. "The Predicament of the Modern African Chief: An Instance from Uganda." *American Anthropologist,* 57, 2, 1955, 290–305.

Foster, Paul. *White to Move?* London: Eyre and Spottiswoode, 1961.

Gale, H. P. *Uganda and the Mill Hill Fathers.* London: Macmillan, 1959.

Gartrell, Beverly. "British Administrators, Colonial Chiefs and the Comfort of Tradition." *African Studies Review,* 26, 1, 1983, 1–24.

Gee, T. W. "A Century of Muhammedan Influence in Buganda. 1852–1951." *Uganda Journal,* 22, 2, 1958, 139–150.

————. "Uganda's Legislative Council Between the Wars." *Uganda Journal,* 25, 1, 1961, 54–63.

Gertzel, Cherry. *Party and Locality in Northern Uganda, 1945–1962.* London: University of London, Athlone Press, 1974.

————. "Kingdoms, Districts and the Unitary State, Uganda 1945–1962." Chapter I in D. A. Low and A. Smith (eds). *A History of East Africa III.* London: Oxford University Press, 1976, 65–106.

Ghai, D. P. "The Buganda Trade Boycott: A Study in Tribal, Political and Economic Nationalism." In R. Rotberg and Ali A. Mazrui (eds). *Protest and Power in Black Africa.* London and New York: Oxford University Press, 1970.

Gorju, J. *Entre le Victoria, l'Albert et l'Edouard.* Rennes, France: Imprimeries Oberthur, 1920.

Hall, Martin. *Through My Spectacles in Uganda.* London: Church Missionary Society, 1898.

Hayley, T.T.S. *An Anatomy of Lango Religion and Groups.* Cambridge, UK: Cambridge University Press, 1947.

Ibingira, Grace. *The Forging of an African Nation: The Political and Constitutional Evolution of Uganda from Colonial Rule to Independence.* Kampala: Uganda Publishing House; and New York: Viking Press, 1973.

Ingham, Kenneth. *The Making of Modern Uganda.* London: George Allen and Unwin, 1958.

Ingrams, H. *Uganda.* London: HMSO, 1960.

Irstam, Tor. *The King of Ganda: Studies in the Institutions of Sacral Kingship in Africa.* Westport, CT: Negro Universities Press, 1970.

Jackson, F. J. *Early Days in East Africa.* London: Arnold, 1930.

Johnston, Harry H. *The Uganda Protectorate.* 2 vols. London: Hutchinson, 1902.

Kabwegyere, Tarsis. "The Dynamics of Colonial Violence: The Inductive System in Uganda." *Journal of Peace Research,* 9, 4, 1972, 303–314.

———. *The Politics of State Formation: The Nature and Effects of Colonialism in Uganda.* Nairobi: East African Literature Bureau, 1974.

———. "Land and the Growth of Social Stratification." In B. A. Ogot (ed). *History and Social Change in East Africa.* Proceedings of the 1974 Conference of the Historical Association of Kenya. Nairobi, Kampala, Dar es Salaam: East African Literature Bureau, 1976, 111–133.

Kiwanuka, M.S.M. "The Diplomacy of the Lost Counties and its Impact on the Foreign Relations of Buganda, Bunyoro and the Rest of Uganda 1900–1964." *Mawazo,* 4, 2, 1974, 111–141.

Lawrance, J.C.D. "The Position of Chiefs in Local Government in Uganda." *Journal of African Administration,* 8, 4, 1956, 186–192.

Low, D. A. "The Composition of the Buganda Lukiko in 1902." *Uganda Journal,* 23, 1959, 64–68.

——— and R. Cranford Pratt. *Buganda and British Overrule, 1900–1955.* London: Oxford University Press, 1960.

———. *Political Parties in Uganda, 1949–62.* London: Athlone Press for the Institute of Commonwealth Studies, 1962.

———. "Uganda: The Establishment of the Protectorate, 1894–1919." Chapter I in V. Harlow and E. M. Chilver (eds). *A History of East Africa II.* London: Oxford University Press, 1965, 57–102.

Lowenkopf, M. ''Uganda: Prelude to Independence.'' *Parliamentary Affairs,* Winter 1961/2, 74–80.

Maxse, F. *Seymour Vandeleur.* London: Heinemann, 1906.

Molson, Lord. *Uganda. Report of a Commission of Privy Counsellors on a Dispute between Buganda and Bunyoro.* Cmd. 1017. London: HMSO, 1962.

Motani, Nizar A. *On His Majesty's Service in Uganda: The Origins of Uganda's African Civil Service, 1920–1940.* Syracuse, NY: Maxwell School of Citizenship and Public Affairs, Syracuse University, 1977.

Mukasa, Ham (trans and ed. Taban Lo Liyong). *Sir Apolo Kagwa Discovers Britain.* London: Heinemann, 1975.

Mukherjee, Ramakrishna. *The Problem of Uganda: A Study in Acculturation.* Berlin: Akademie-Verlag, 1956.

Mulira, E.M.K. *Troubled Uganda.* London: Fabian Society, Colonial Bureau Pamphlet, 1950.

Mulira, James. ''Nationalism and Communist Phobia in Colonial Uganda 1945–1960.'' *Mawazo,* 5, 1, 1983, 3–16.

Munster, the Earl of. *Report of the Uganda Relationships Commission.* Entebbe: Government Printer, 1961.

Mutibwa, Phares. ''Internal Self-Government, March 1961-October 1962.'' In G.N. Uzoigwe (ed). *Uganda: The Dilemma of Nationhood.* New York, London, Lagos: NOK Publishers International, 259–298.

Nyabongo, Akiiki. *Africa Answers Back.* London: George Routledge, 1936.

Oberg, K. ''The Kingdom of Ankole in Uganda.'' In M. Fortes and E. E. Evans-Pritchard (eds). *African Political Systems.*

London: Oxford University Press for the International Institute of African Languages and Cultures, 1940.

Oliver, Roland. *Sir Harry Johnston and the Scramble for Africa.* London: Chatto and Windus, 1957.

———. "Uganda, Colonial and Christian." *Journal of African History,* 1, 1960.

Portal, G. *The British Mission to Uganda.* London: Edward Arnold, 1894.

Postlethwaite, J.R.P. *I Look Back.* London: T.V. Boardman, 1947.

Pratt, R. Cornford. "Nationalism in Uganda." *Political Studies,* 9, 2, 1961, 157–178.

———. "Administration and Politics in Uganda, 1919–45." In V. Harlow, F. M. Chilver and Alison Smith (eds). *Oxford History of East Africa, Vol. II.* Oxford: Clarendon Press, 1963, 476–541.

Purvis, J. B. *Handbook to East Africa and Uganda.* London: Swan, Sonnenschein, 1900.

———. *Through Uganda to Mount Elgon.* New York: American Tract Society, 1909.

Roberts, Andrew. "The Sub-Imperialism of the Baganda." *Journal of African History,* 3, 3, 1962, 435–450.

———. "The 'Lost Counties' of Bunyoro." *Uganda Journal,* 26, 2, 1962, 194–199.

———. "Evolution of the Uganda Protectorate." *Uganda Journal,* 27, 1, 1963, 95–106.

Rowe, J. A. " 'Progress and a Sense of Identity': African Historiography in East Africa." *Kenya Historical Review,* 5, 1, 1977, 23–34.

Scotton, J. F. "The First African Press in East Africa." *International Journal of African Historical Studies,* 6, 2, 1974, 211–228.

Ternan, Trevor. *Some Experiences of an Old Bromsgrovian: Soldiering in Afganistan, Egypt and Uganda.* Birmingham, UK: Cornish Brothers, 1930.

Thomas H. B. "Capax Imperii: The Story of Semei Kakunguru." *Uganda Journal,* 6, 3, 1939, 125–136.

———. *The Story of Uganda.* London: Oxford University Press, 1955.

——— and R. Scott. *Uganda.* London: Oxford University Press, 1935.

——— and A. E. Spencer. *A History of the Uganda Land and Surveys and of the Uganda Land and Surveys Department.* Entebbe: Government Printer, 1938.

Thompson, Gardner. "Colonialism in Crisis: The Uganda Disturbances of 1945." *African Affairs,* 91, 365, 1992, 605–624.

Trowell, Margaret and K. P. Wachsmann. *Tribal Crafts of Uganda.* London: Oxford University Press, 1953.

Tucker, Alfred R. *Eighteen Years in Uganda and East Africa.* 2 Vols. London: Edward Arnold, 1908; 1 Vol. edition, 1911.

Turyahikayo-Rugyema, Benoni. "The Development of Mass Nationalism, 1952–1962." In G. N. Uzoigwe (ed). *Uganda: The Dilemma of Nationhood.* New York, London, Lagos: NOK Publishers International, 217–258.

Twaddle, M. J. "Was the Democratic Party of Uganda a Purely Confessional Party?" In E. Fasholé-Luke et al.(eds). *Christianity in Independent Africa.* London: Rex Collings, 1978, 255–266.

———. "Decentralised Violence and Collaboration in Early Colonial Uganda." *Journal of Imperial and Commonwealth History,* XVI, 3, 1988, 71–85.

Uzoizgwe, G. N. *Revolution and Revolt in Bunyoro-Kitara.* Makerere History Papers 5. Kampala: Longmans, 1970.

Wallis, H. R. *The Handbook of Uganda.* 2nd edn. London: Crown Agents for the Colonies, 1920.

Welbourn, F. B. *Religion and Politics in Uganda, 1952–62.* Nairobi: East African Publishing House, 1965.

Wild, J. V. *The Uganda Mutiny, 1897.* London: Macmillan, 1954.

———. *Early Travellers in Acholi.* Edinburgh and London: Nelson, 1954.

Wright, Michael. *Buganda in the Heroic Age.* Nairobi and London: Oxford University Press, 1971.

5. Post-Independence: History and Sociology

5.1 GENERAL WORKS

Doornbos, Martin. "Changing Perspectives on Conflict and Integration." In G. N. Uzoigwe (ed). *Uganda: The Dilemma of Nationhood.* New York, London, Lagos: NOK Publishers International, 1982, 313–332.

———. "The Uganda Crisis and the National Question." In H. B. Hansen and M. J. Twaddle (eds). *Uganda Now: Between Decay and Development.* London: James Currey and Athens, OH: Ohio University Press, 1988, 254–266.

East, Maurice. "Foreign Policy-Making in Small States: Some Theoretic Observations Based on a Study of the Uganda Ministry of Foreign Affairs." *Policy Sciences,* 4, 1973, 491–508.

Furley, O. W "Britain and Uganda from Amin to Museveni: Blind Eye Diplomacy." In K. Rupesinghe (ed). *Conflict Resolution in Uganda.* Oslo: International Peace Research Institute; London: James Currey; and Athens, OH: Ohio University Press, 1989, 275–294.

Hansen, H. B. and M. J. Twaddle (eds). *Uganda Now: Between Decay and Development.* London: James Currey and Athens, OH: Ohio University Press, 1988.

———— (eds). *Changing Uganda: The Dilemmas of Structural Adjustment and Revolutionary Change.* London: James Currey; and Athens, OH: Ohio University Press, 1991.

Ingham, Kenneth. "Uganda: The Kingdom and the Power." In K. Ingham. *Politics in Modern Africa: The Uneven Tribal Dimension.* London: Routledge, 1990, 11–40.

Jacobson, David. "Stratification and Nationalism in Uganda." *Journal of Asian and African Studies,* VI, 3–4, 1971, 217–225.

Kinanga, James Sabiti. *Uganda's New Clothes.* London: James Currey, 1994.

Kokole, Omari H. and Ali A. Mazrui. "Uganda: The Dual Policy and the Plural Society." In Larry Diamond (ed). *Democracy in Developing Countries, 2, Africa.* Boulder, CO: Lynne Rienner, 1988, 259–298.

Low, D. A. "The Dislocated Polity." In H. B. Hansen and M. J. Twaddle (eds). *Uganda Now: Between Decay and Development.* London: James Currey; and Athens, OH: Ohio University Press, 1988, 36–53.

Mazrui, Ali A. "The Social Origins of Uganda Presidents: From King to Peasant Warrior." *Canadian Journal of African Studies,* 8, 1, 1974, 3–23.

————. "Is Africa Decaying? The View from Uganda." In H. B.

Hansen and M. J. Twaddle (eds). *Uganda Now: Between Decay and Development.* London: James Currey; and Athens, OH: Ohio University Press, 1988, 336–358.

Mittelman, J. H. "The State of Research on African Politics: Contributions on Uganda." *Journal of Asian and African Studies,* XI, 3–4, 1976, 152–165.

Mugaju, J. B. "The Illusions of Democracy in Uganda." In W. O. Oyugi and A. S. Atieno Odhiambo (eds). *Democratic Theory and Practice in Africa.* London and Portsmouth NH: Heinemann, 1988, 86–98.

Mukama, Ruth. "Recent Developments in the Language Situation and Prospects for the Future." In H. B. Hansen and M. J. Twaddle (eds). *Changing Uganda: The Dilemmas of Structural Adjustment and Revolutionary Change.* London: James Currey; and Athens, OH: Ohio University Press, 1991, 334–350.

Muscat, Richard (ed). *A Short History of the Democratic Party.* Rome: Foundation for African Development, 1984.

Musoke, Mubiru. "Personality and Democracy in Ugandan Politics: A General Critique of Leadership and Civil Obedience since Independence." *Uganda Quarterly Review,* 1, 1, 1981, 6–42.

Mutibwa, Phares. *Uganda Since Independence: A Story of Unfulfilled Hopes.* London: Hurst, 1992.

Nabudere, Dan Wadada. "External and Internal Factors in Uganda's Continuing Crisis." In H. B. Hansen and M. J. Twaddle (eds). *Uganda Now: Between Decay and Development.* London: James Currey; and Athens, OH: Ohio University Press, 1988, 299–312.

Nye, J. Jr. "TANU and UPC: The Impact of Independence on two African Nationalist Parties." In J. Butler and A. A. Castagno (eds). *Boston Papers on Africa: Transition in African Politics.* New York: Frederick Praeger, 1967.

Obbo, Christine. "What Went Wrong in Uganda?" In H. B. Hansen and M. J. Twaddle (eds). *Uganda Now: Between Decay and Development*. London: James Currey; and Athens, OH: Ohio University Press, 1988, 205–223.

Omari, A. H. "Uganda-Tanzania Relations." *Journal of International Relations,* 3, 2, 1980, 41–66.

Rothchild, Donald and M. Rogin. "Uganda." In Gwendolen M. Carter (ed). *National Unity and Regionalism in Eight African States*. Ithaca, NY: Cornell University Press, 1966, 337–440.

Rupesinghe, Kumar (ed). *Conflict Resolution in Uganda*. Oslo and London: International Peace Research Institute in association with James Currey, 1989.

Southall, Aidan. "The Recent Political Economy of Uganda." In H. B. Hansen and M. J. Twaddle (eds). *Uganda Now: Between Decay and Development*. London: James Currey; and Athens, OH: Ohio University Press, 1988, 54–69.

Stonehouse, John. *Prohibited Immigrant*. London: The Bodley Head, 1960.

Tandon, Y. "An Analysis of the Foreign Policy of African States: A Case Study of Uganda." In K. Ingham (ed). *Foreign Relations of African States*. London: Butterworth, 1974, 191–211.

Toko, Gad W. *Intervention in Uganda: The Power Struggle and Soviet Involvement*. Pittsburgh: University of Pittsburgh Press, 1979.

Tumusiime, James (ed). *Uganda: Thirty Years 1962–1992*. Kampala: Fountain Press, 1992.

Twaddle, M. J. "Ethnic Politics and Support for Political Parties in Uganda." In P. Lyon and J. Manor (eds). *Transfer and Transformation: Political Institutions in the New Commonwealth*. Leicester, UK: Leicester University Press, 1983.

Woodward, Peter. "Uganda and the Southern Sudan: Peripheral Politics and Neighbour Relations." In H. B. Hansen and M. J. Twaddle (eds). *Uganda Now: Between Decay and Development.* London: James Currey; and Athens, OH: Ohio University Press, 1988, 224–238.

Wrigley, Christopher. "Four Steps Towards Disaster." In H. B. Hansen and M. J. Twaddle (eds). *Uganda Now: Between Decay and Development.* London: James Currey; and Athens, OH: Ohio University Press, 1988, 27–35.

Young, Crawford. "Tanzania and Uganda: Integration or Impasse?" In C. Young. *The Politics of Cultural Pluralism,* Madison, WI: Wisconsin University Press, 1976, 216–273.

5.2 OBOTE I AND II.

(See also 5.5 for immigrant communities.)

Aasland, Tertit. *On the Move-to-the-Left in Uganda, 1967–71.* Research Report No. 26, Uppsala: Scandinavian Institute of African Studies, 1974.

Adelson, J. "Ethnicity, the Military and Domination: The Case of Obote's Uganda 1962–1971." *Plural Societies,* Spring, 1978, 85–101.

Adoko, Akena. "On the Constitution of the Republic of Uganda." *Transition,* 33, 1967, 10–12.

———. *Uganda Crisis.* Kampala: African Publishers, n.d. [c. 1970].

———. "Speech to the Asian Conference, 8 December 1971. *East Africa Journal,* 9, 1972, 2–5.

———. *From Obote to Obote.* New Delhi: Vikas Publishing House, 1983.

————. *Coups and Corruption in Africa.* Kampala: African Publishers, 1984.

————. *Gold Crisis in Uganda.* New Delhi: Vikas Publishing House, n.d. [c. 1985].

————. *The Lea Affair: A British Diplomat's Scandal.* New Delhi: Vikas Publishing House, n.d. [c. 1985].

Agyeman, Opokee. "Kwame Nkrumah's Presence in A.M. Obote's Uganda: A Study in the Convergence of International and Comparative Politics." *Transition,* 9, 48, April/June, 1975, 13–24.

Amnesty International. *Human Rights Violations in Uganda: Extrajudicial Executions, Torture and Political Imprisonment* (AFR 59/12/82). London: Amnesty International, 1982.

————. *Memorandum to the Government of Uganda on an Amnesty International Mission to Uganda in January 1982 and Further Exchanges between the Government and Amnesty International.* London and New York: Amnesty International, 1983.

————. *Uganda Six Years After Amin: Torture, Killings, Disappearances* (AFR/59/06/85). London: Amnesty International, 1985.

Bradley, A. W. "Constitution Making in Uganda." *Transition,* 32, 7 (i), August/September, 1967, 25–31.

Chick, John. "Uganda: The Quest for Control." *The World Today,* January 1970, 18–28.

Cohen, D. L. "Ryan on Obote." *Mawazo,* III, 2, 1971, 46–50.

———— and J. Parson. "The Uganda People's Congress Branch and Constituency Elections of 1970." *Journal of Commonwealth Political Studies,* XI, 1, 1972, 46–66.

Commonwealth Observer Group. *Uganda Elections December 1980: The Report.* London: Commonwealth Secretariat, 1980.

Crisp, Jeff. "National Security, Human Rights and Population Displacements in Luwero District, Uganda, January to December 1982." *Review of African Political Economy,* 27, 8, 1983, 164–174.

———. "Ugandan Refugees in Sudan and Zaire: The Problem of Repatriation." *African Affairs,* 85, 339, 1986, 163–180.

Dahlberg, F. M. "The Emergence of a Dual Governing Elite in Uganda." *Journal of Modern African Studies,* 9, 4, 1971, 618–625.

Dinwiddy, Hugh. "The Ugandan Army and Makerere under Obote 1962–71." *African Affairs,* 82, 326, 1983, 43–60.

Dodge, C. P. and M. Raundalen (eds). *Crisis in Uganda: The Breakdown of Health Services.* Oxford: Pergamon Press, 1985.

———. *War, Violence and Children in Uganda.* Oslo: Norwegian University Press, 1987.

Engholm, Geoffrey and Ali A. Mazrui. "Violent Constitutionalism in Uganda." *Government and Opposition,* July/October, 1967, 585–599.

Gershenberg, Irving. "Slouching Towards Socialism: Obote's Uganda." *African Studies Review,* 15, 1, 1972, 69–85.

Gertzel, Cherry. "Report from Kampala," and "How Kabaka Yekka Came to Be." *Africa Report,* 9, 1964, 3–13.

———. "Uganda After Amin: The Continuing Search for Leadership and Control." *African Affairs,* 79, 317, 1980, 461–490.

Gingyera-Pinycwa, A.G.G. "Prospects for a One-Party System in Uganda." *East African Journal,* V, 10, 1968, 15–23.

———. "A. M. Obote, the Baganda and the Uganda Army." *Mawazo,* 3, 2, 1971, 32–43.

———. *Apolo Milton Obote and His Times.* New York and Lagos: NOK Publishers, 1978.

Hardwick, S. "Administrative Aspects of the Uganda Election—December 1980: A Comparison with Zimbabwe." *Public Administration and Development,* April–June, 1982, 105–112.

Herring, Ralph. "Centralization, Stratification and Incorporation: Case Studies from North Eastern Uganda." *Canadian Journal of African Studies,* 3, 1973, 497–514.

Hooper, Ed and Louise Pirouet. *Uganda. Minority Rights Group Report No. 66.* London: Minority Rights Group, 1989.

Hopkins, Terence K. "Politics in Uganda: The Buganda Question." In Jeffrey Butler and A. A. Castagno (eds). *Boston University Papers on Africa.* New York: Praeger, 1967, 251–290.

Ibingira, G. S. "The Impact of Ethnic Demands on British Decolonization in Africa—The Example of Uganda." In Prosser Gifford and W. R. Louis (eds). *The Transfer of Power in Africa, Decolonization 1940–1980.* New Haven, CT; and London: Yale University Press, 1982, 283–304.

Kabwegyere, Tarsis. "The Asian Question in Uganda." *East Africa Journal,* 9, 6, 1972, 10–13.

———. "The Dynamics of Colonial Violence: The Inductive System in Uganda." *Journal of Peace Research,* 9, 4, 1972, 303–314.

Karugire, S. R. *The Roots of Instability in Uganda.* Kampala: New Vision Printing and Publishing, 1988.

Kasfir, Nelson. "Cultural Sub-nationalism in Uganda." In Victor Olorunsola (ed). *The Politics of Cultural Sub-nationalism in Africa.* New York: Anchor Books, Doubleday, 1972, 51–148.

Kenny, Michael G. "Mutesa's Crime: Hubris and the Control of African Kings." *Comparative Study of History and Society,* 30, 4, 1988, 595–612.

Kuhlman, Tom. "Voluntary Repatriation by Force: The Case of Rwandan Refugees in Uganda." In Howard Adelman and John Sorenson. *African Refugees.* Boulder, CO; and Oxford, UK: Westview Press, 1994.

Langlands, Bryan. "Students and Politics in Uganda." *African Affairs,* 76, 302, 1977, 3–20.

Lee, J. M. "Buganda's Position in Federal Uganda." *Journal of Commonwealth Political Studies,* 3, 3, 1965, 165–181.

Leys, Colin. *Politicians and Policies: An Essay on Politics in Acholi, 1962–65.* Nairobi: East African Publishing House, 1967.

Mamdani, Mahmood. *Politics and Class Formation in Uganda.* New York: Monthly Review Press, 1976.

Mazrui, Ali A. "Leadership in Africa: Obote of Uganda." *International Journal,* Summer, 1970, 534–564.

———. *Engineering and Nation-Building in East Africa.* Evanston, IL: Northwestern University Press, 1972.

Mittleman, James H. *Ideology and Politics in Uganda: From Obote to Amin.* Ithaca, NY; and London: Cornell University Press, 1975.

Mpambara, S. M. *The Gold Allegation.* Kampala: Milton Obote Foundation, 1967.

Mudoola, Dan. "Political Transitions since Idi Amin: A Study in Political Pathology." In H. B. Hansen and M. J. Twaddle (eds). *Uganda Now: Between Decay and Development.* London: James Currey; and Athens, OH: Ohio University Press, 1988, 280–298.

Mujaju, Akiiki. "The Demise of UPCYL and the Rise of NUYO in Uganda." *African Review,* 3, 2, 1973, 291–307.

———. "The Political Crisis of Church Institutions in Uganda." *African Affairs,* 75, No. 298, 1976, 67–85.

———. "The Role of the UPC as a Party of Government in Uganda." *Canadian Journal of African Studies,* 10, 3, 1976, 443–467.

———. "The Gold Allegations Motion and Political Development in Uganda." *African Affairs,* 86, 345, 1987, 479–504.

Mutesa, Edward (Kabaka of Buganda). *Desecration of My Kingdom.* London: Constable, 1967.

Obote, Milton A. "The Footsteps of Uganda's Revolution." *East Africa Journal,* 5, 1968, 7–13.

———. *The Common Man's Charter with Appendices.* Entebbe: Uganda Government Press, 1970.

———. *Proposals for New Methods of Election of Representatives of the People to Parliament.* Kampala: Milton Obote Foundation, 1970.

Okello Oculi. "The Issue of Participation and the Common Man's Charter." *Mawazo,* 11, 2, 1969, 25–38.

Prunier, G. A. "Structures ethniques et système politique en Ouganda." *Culture et Développement,* 1982, 2–3, 1983, 365–391.

Robertson, A. F. (ed). *Uganda's First Republic: Chiefs, Administrators and Politicians, 1967–1971.* Cambridge, UK: African Studies Centre, 1982.

Rothchild, D. and J. W. Harbeson. "Rehabilitation in Uganda." *Current History,* March 1981, 115–119, 134–138.

Ryan, Selwyn. "Electoral Engineering in Uganda." *Mawazo,* 1, 4, 1970, 3–12.

————. "Uganda: A Balance Sheet of the Revolution." *Mawazo,* 3, 1, 1971, 37–64.

Saul, John. "The Unsteady State: Uganda, Obote and General Amin." *Review of African Political Economy,* 5, 1976, 12–38.

Tindigarukayo, J. K. "Uganda, 1979–1985: Leadership in Transition." *Journal of Modern African Studies,* 26, 4, 1988, 607–622.

Tribe, Michael. "Uganda 1971: An Economic Background." *Mawazo,* 3, 1, 15–26.

Twaddle, M. J. "Violence and Rumours of Violence in Uganda During the Early 1980s." *Cambridge Anthropology,* 13, 2, 1988/9, 28–44.

[Uganda Government]. *Uganda 1962–1963.* Entebbe: Government Printer, 1964.

Young, Crawford M. "The Obote Revolution." *Africa Report,* June 1966, 8–14.

5.3 IDI AMIN

(See especially Jamison, Martin. *Idi Amin and Uganda: An Annotated Bibliography.* Westport, CT; and London: Greenwood Press, 1978.)

(For Nubians and the expulsion of the Asians, see section 5.5.)
(For military rule and the Tanzania-Uganda war of 1979, see also section 10.)

Adams, Bert N. "Uganda Before, During and After Amin." *Rural Africana,* 11, Fall, 1981, 15–25.

Akinsanya, Adeoyo A. "The Entebbe Rescue Mission: A Case of Aggression?" *Pakistan Horizon,* 34, 3, 1981, 12–35.

Allen, Peter Jermyn. *Days of Judgment: A Judge in Idi Amin's Uganda.* London: William Kimber, 1987.

Amin, Idi. *Speeches by His Excellency the President General Idi Amin Dada.* Vol. 1, 1972; Vol. 2, 1973. Entebbe: Uganda Government Printers.

————. *Development on the Basis of Self-Reliance. 4 August, 1974.* Entebbe: Uganda Government Printers, 1974.

————. *The Shaping of Modern Uganda.* n.d. [1976], n.p.

Amnesty International. *Human Rights in Uganda* (AFR 59/05/78). London: Amnesty Interntional, 1978.

Andrews, Sally C. "The Legitimacy of the United States Embargo of Uganda." *Journal of International Law and Economics,* 13, 3, 1979, 651–673.

Atwoki, K. et al. *Amin.* London: Walton Press, 1979.

Bagaya, Elizabeth. See Elizabeth, Princess of Toro.

Barker, G. H. *A Circle of Trees.* Braunton, UK: Merlin Books, 1989.

Ben-Porat and Zeev Schiff. *Entebbe Rescue.* New York: Delacorte Press, 1977.

Bienen, Henry. "Military and Society in East Africa." *Comparative Politics,* April, 1974, 489–517.

Brett, E. A. "The Political Economy of General Amin." [Sussex] *Institute of Development Studies Bulletin,* 7, 1, 1973, 15–22.

Burrow, N. "Tanzania's Intervention in Uganda: Some Legal Aspects." *The World Today,* July, 1979, 306–310.

Campbell, Horace C. *Four Essays on Neo-Colonialism in Uganda: The Military Dictatorship of Idi Amin.* Toronto: Afro-Caribbean Publications, 1975.

Chick, John D. "Class Conflict and Military Intervention in Uganda." *Journal of Modern African Studies,* 10, 4, 1972, 634–637.

Dan, Uri. *Operation Uganda.* Jerusalem: Keter Publishing Company, 1976.

Day, Erin. "Uganda." In G. Ashworth (ed). *World Minorities: A Second Volume.* Sunbury, UK: Quartermaine House, 1978, 137–141.

Decalo, Samuel. "Idi Amin: The Brutal Reign of the Iron Marshal." In S. Decalo. *Psychoses of Power: African Personal Dictatorships.* Boulder, CO; and London: Westview Press, 1989, 77–128.

———. "Uganda: The Post Liberation Vacuum." In S. Decalo. *Coups and Army Rule in Africa.* New Haven and London: Yale University Press, 1990, 139–198.

Donald, Trevor. *Confessions of Idi Amin.* South Yarra: Gazelle Books, 1977.

Doornbos, Martin. "Faces and Phases of Ugandan Politics: Changing Perceptions of Social Structure and Political Conflict." *African Perspectives,* 2, 1978, 117–133.

Elizabeth, Princess of Toro (Elizabeth Bagaya). *Elizabeth of Toro: The Odyssey of an African Princess.* New York: Simon and Schuster, Touchstone, 1989.

Elliott, J.C.H. "The Uganda Budget, 1971–2." *Uganda Economic Journal,* 1, 1, 1971, 7–30.

Enahoro, Peter. "Whither Uganda?" *Africa: An International Business, Economic and Political Monthly,* 16, December 1972, 13–17.

Ford, Margaret. *Janani: The Making of a Martyr.* London: Marshall, Morgan and Scott, Lakeland, 1978.

Fredman, Steven J. "U.S. Trade Sanctions against Uganda: Legality under International Law." *Law and Policy in International Business,* 11, 3, 1979, 1149–1191.

Furley, Oliver. "Britain and Uganda from Amin to Museveni: Blind Eye Diplomacy." In K. Rupesinghe (ed). *Conflict Resolution in Uganda.* London: James Currey; and Athens, OH: Ohio University Press, 1989, 275–294.

Gershenberg, Irving. "A Further Comment on the 1971 Uganda Coup." *Journal of Modern African Studies,* 10, 4, 1972, 638–639.

Gittelson, Susan A. "Major Shifts in Recent Ugandan Foreign Policy." *African Affairs,* 76, No. 304, 1977, 359–380.

Glentworth, G. and I. Hancock. "Obote and Amin: Change and Continuity in Modern Ugandan Politics." *African Affairs,* 72, 3, 1973, 237–255.

Goldberg, Michel. *Namesake.* New Haven, CT: Yale University Press, 1982.

Grahame, Iain. "Uganda and Its President." *Army Quarterly and Defence Journal,* 104, 1974, 480–490.

———. *Amin and Uganda: A Personal Memoir.* London: Granada Publishing, 1980.

Gupta, Anirudha. "Amin's Fall: Would There be Other Dominoes?" *Africa Quarterly,* April/June, 1979, 4–13.

Gutteridge, William. "General Amin's Uganda." In W. Gutteridge. *Military Regimes in Africa.* London: Methuen, 1975, 157–165.

Gwyn, David. *Idi Amin: Death-Light of Africa.* Boston: Little, Brown, 1977.

Hansen, H. B. *Ethnicity and Military Rule in Uganda.* Uppsala: Scandinavian Institute of African Studies, Report No. 43, 1977.

Hastings, Max. *Yoni: The Lonely Road to Entebbe.* London: Weidenfeld and Nicolson, 1979. Also published as *Yoni: Hero of Entebbe.* New York: Dial Press/James Wade, 1979.

Helleiner, G. K. "Economic Collapse and Rehabilitation in Uganda." *Rural Africana,* 11, Fall 1981, 27–35.

Hills, Denis. *The White Pumpkin.* New York: Grove Press; and London: Allen and Unwin, 1975.

———. "The Jailer as Seen by his Ex-Prisoner." *New York Times Magazine,* 7 September 1975, 42–53.

———. *Rebel People.* London: George Allen and Unwin, 1978.

Ibingira, G. S. *Bitter Harvest.* Nairobi: East African Publishing House, 1980.

———. *African Upheavals Since Independence.* Boulder, CO: Westview Press, 1980.

Ingram, Derek and Andrew Walker. "Commonwealth Conference, 1977: Racial Conflict, Economic Challenges and the Problem of Uganda." *Round Table: The Commonwealth Journal of International Affairs,* 267, July 1977, 215–228.

International Commission of Jurists. *Uganda and Human Rights: Reports of the International Commission of Jurists to the United Nations.* Geneva: International Commission of Jurists, 1977.

Jacobs, B. L. "Uganda's Second Republic: The First Two Years." *Africa Today,* 20, 2, Spring 1973, 47–57.

———. "Autumn of Our Discontent: The Ugandan Scene." *Africa Today,* 21, 4, 1974, 73–82.

Jamal, Vali. "Asians in Uganda 1880–1972. Inequality and Expulsion." *Economic History Review,* Series 2, 29, 1976, 602–616.

Jones, Judge David Jeffrys. *Commission of Enquiry into the Missing Americans, Stroh and Siedle, Held at the Conference Room, Parliament House, Kampala.* Entebbe: Government Printer, 1972.

Kamau, Joseph and Andrew Cameron (pseudonyms). *Lust to Kill: The Rise and Fall of Idi Amin.* London: Corgi, 1979.

Kambites, J. and S. "A Return to Uganda." *National Geographic,* July 1980, 73–88.

Karaza-Karumaya. "Burning Books with Idi Amin. A Personal Reminiscence of Censorship in Uganda." *Zambia Library Association Journal,* 10, 2, 1978, 48–57.

Kasfir, Nelson. *The Shrinking Political Arena: Participation and Ethnicity in African Politics with a Case-Study of Uganda.* Berkeley: University of California Press, 1976.

———. "Explaining Ethnic Participation." *World Politics,* 31, III, 1979, 356–388.

———. "State, Magendo and Class Formation in Uganda." *Journal of Commonwealth and Comparative Politics,* XXI, November 1983, 1–20.

Kasozi, Abdu B. K. "The Uganda Muslim Supreme Council: An Experiment in Muslim Administrative Centralisation and Institutionalisation 1972–82." *Journal of the Institute of Muslim Minority Affairs,* 6, 1, 1985, 34–52.

Kato, Wycliffe. "An Escape from Kampala." *Granta*, 22, Autumn 1987, 79–128.

―――. *Escape from Idi Amin's Slaughterhouse*. London and New York: Quartet Books, 1989.

Kayiira, L. A. and E. Kannyo. "Politics and Violence in Uganda." *Africa Report*, 23, 1, 1979, 39–43.

Kiggundu, S. I. and I.K.K. Lukwago. "The Status of the Muslim Community in Uganda." *Journal of the Institute of Muslim Minority Affairs*, 1, 2, 1982, 120–132.

Kivengere, Festo, with Dorothy Smoker. *I Love Idi Amin: The Story of Triumph Under Fire in the Midst of Suffering and Persecution in Uganda*. London: Marshall, Morgan and Scott, New Life Ventures; and Old Tappan, NJ: Fleming H. Revell, 1977.

Kiwanuka, Semakula. *Amin and the Tragedy of Uganda*. Munich and London: Weltforum Verlag, 1979.

Kyemba, Henry. *State of Blood: The Inside Story of Idi Amin*. New York: Grossett and Dunlap, Ace Books, 1977; London: Transworld Publishers, Corgi Books, 1977.

Langlands, Bryan. "Students and Politics in Uganda." *African Affairs*, 76, No. 302, 1977, 3–20.

Lhoest, B. *L'Ouganda sous Idi Amin Dada (1971–1979)*. Brussels: Section des Sciences Politiques, Faculté des Sciences Sociales, Politiques et Économiques, Université Libre de Bruxelles, 1984/5.

Listowel, Judith. *Amin*. Dublin: Irish University Press, 1973.

Lloyd, Richard. *Beyond the CIA: The Frank Terpil Story*. New York: Seaver Books, 1983.

Lockhard, Kathleen G. "Religion and Politics in Independent Uganda: Movement Towards Secularization?" In James R. Scarritt (ed). *Analyzing Political Change in Africa: Applications of a New Multi-Dimensional Framework.* Boulder, CO: Westview Press, 1980.

Lofchie, Michael. "The Uganda Coup—Class Action by the Military." *Journal of Modern African Studies,* X, 1, 1972, 464–490.

———. "The Political Origins of the Ugandan Coup." *Journal of African Studies,* 1, 4, 1972, 19–35.

Low, D. A. "Uganda Unhinged." *International Affairs,* 49, 2, 1973, 219–228.

Mamdani, Mahmood. *Imperialism and Fascism in Uganda.* London: Heinemann, 1983.

Martin, David. *General Amin.* London: Faber and Faber, 1974.

Martin, Michel L. "The Uganda Military Coup of 1971: A Study of Protest." *Ufahamu,* 3, 3, 1972, 81–121.

Mathews, K. and A. H. Omari. "Uganda-Tanzania Relations, 1971–1980." *Journal of International Relations* (Dar es Salaam), 3, 2, 1980, 41–68.

Mazrui, Ali A. "The Lumpen Proletariat and the Lumpen Militariat: African Soldiers as a New Political Class." *Political Studies,* 21, 1, 1973, 1–12.

———. "Racial Self-Reliance and Cultural Dependency: Nyerere and Amin in Comparative Perspective." *Journal of International Affairs,* 27, 1, 1973, 105–121.

———. "Piety and Puritanism under a Military Theocracy: Uganda Soldiers as Apostolic Successors." In C. M. Kelleher. *Political Military Systems: Comparative Perspectives.*

Sage Research Progress Series on War, Revolution and Peacekeeping. Vol. 4. Beverly Hills, CA: Sage, 1974.

———. "The Militarization of Charisma: An African Case-Study." *SSIP Mitteilungen Bulletin,* 38–9, 1974, 76–106.

———. "The Resurrection of the Warrior Tradition in African Political Culture." *Journal of Modern African Studies,* 13, 1, 1975, 67–84.

———. *Soldiers and Kinsmen in Uganda.* Beverly Hills, CA: Sage, 1975.

———. "Religious Strangers in Uganda: From Emin Pasha to Amin Dada." *African Affairs,* 76, 302, 1977, 21–38.

———. "Between Development and Decay: Anarchy, Tyranny and Progress Under Amin." *Third World Quarterly,* II, 1980, 44–58.

Melady, Thomas and Margaret. *Idi Amin Dada: Hitler of Africa.* Kansas City, KA: Andrew and McMeel, 1977.

Miller, Judith. "When Sanctions Worked." *Foreign Policy,* 39, Summer 1980, 118–129.

Miller, Norman N. "Military Coup in Uganda." American Universities Field Staff, *Field Staff Reports,* East Africa Series, 10, 3, 1971, 1–18.

Mittelman, James Howard. "The Uganda Coup and the Internalisation of Political Violence." *Munger Africana Library Notes,* 14, September 1972, 1–36.

———. *Ideology and Politics in Uganda. From Obote to Amin.* Ithaca, NY; and London: Cornell University Press, 1975.

Mmbando, S. I. *The Tanzania-Uganda War in Pictures.* Dar es Salaam: Longmans, 1980.

Msabaha, I.S.R. "War on Idi Amin: Towards a Synthetic Theory of Intervention." *African Review* (Dar es Salaam), 12, 1, 1985, 24–43.

Mujaju, Akiiki B. "The Political Crisis of Church Institutions in Uganda." *African Affairs,* 75, 1, 1976, 67–85.

Mulira, J. "Soviet Prop to Idi Amin's Regime: An Assessment." *African Review,* 13, 1, 1986, 105–122.

Naudin, Pierre. "The Violation of Human Rights in Uganda." In William A. Veenhover (ed.-in-chief). *Case Studies on Human Rights and Fundamental Freedoms. A World Survey, Vol. V.* The Hague: Martinus Nijhoff for the Foundation for the Study of Plural Societies, 1976, 415–432.

Nayenga, Peter F. B. "Myths and Realities of Idi Amin Dada's Uganda." *African Studies Review,* 22, 2, 1979, 127–140.

Nurnberger, R. D. "The United States and Idi Amin: Congress to the Rescue." *African Studies Review,* 25, 1, 1982, 49–65.

Ofer, Yehuda. *Operation Thunder: The Entebbe Raid. The Israelis' Own Story.* London: Penguin Books, 1976.

Okoth, Godfrey P. "The OAU and the Uganda-Tanzania War, 1978–79." *Journal of African Studies,* 14, 3, 1987, 152–162.

Parson, Jack D. "Africanising Trade in Uganda: The Final Solution." *Africa Today,* 20, 1, 1973, 59–72.

Pirouet, M. Louise. "Religion in Uganda under Amin." *Journal of Religion in Africa,* XI, 1, 1980, 13–29.

Plender, Richard. "The Expulsion of Asians from Uganda: Legal Aspects." *New Community,* 1, 1972, 420–427.

Posnett, R. "Uganda After Amin." *World Today,* April, 1980, 147–153.

Prunier, G. A. "Kuanguka kwa fashisti Idi Amin. Tanzania's Ambiguous Ugandan Victory." *Culture et Développement,* 3–4, 1984, 735–756.

Ramchandani, R. R. *Uganda Asians: The End of an Enterprise.* Bombay: United Asia Publications, 1976.

Ravenhill, F. J. "Military Rule in Uganda: The Politics of Survival." *African Studies Review,* 17, 1, 1974, 229–260.

Rowe, J. A. "Islam under Idi Amin: A Case of Déja Vu?" In H.B. Hansen and M.J. Twaddle (eds). *Uganda Now: Between Decay and Development.* London: James Currey; and Athens, OH: Ohio University Press, 1988, 267–279.

Ryan, S. D. "Civil Conflict and External Involvement in Eastern Africa." *International Journal,* Summer 1973, 465–510.

St Jorre, John de. "The Ugandan Connection." *New York Times Magazine,* 9 April 1978, 26–28, 82–88.

Saul, John S. "The Unsteady State: Uganda, Obote and General Amin." *Review of African Political Economy,* 5, 1, 1976, 12–38.

Schultheis, Michael J. "The Economy and General Amin, 1971–4." *Studies in Comparative International Development,* 10, 3, 1975, 3–34.

Sempangi, Kefa. "Uganda's Reign of Terror." *Worldview,* 18, 5, 1975, 16–21.

———. *Reign of Terror, Reign of Love.* Tring, UK: Lion Publishing, 1979. Also published as *A Distant Grief.* Glendale, CA: G/L Publications, Regal Books, 1979.

Shaw, Timothy M. "Uganda Under Amin: The Costs of Confronting Dependence." *Africa Today,* 20, 2, 1973, 32–45.

Short, Philip. "Amin: An African Experiment with 'Bludgeon Diplomacy'." *International Perspectives,* January/February 1973, 43–46.

Smith, George Ivan. *Ghosts of Kampala: The Rise and Fall of Idi Amin.* London: Weidenfeld and Nicolson, 1980.

Sookdeo, Anil. "Understanding the Violence in Uganda." *Transafrica Forum,* 5, 3, 1988, 17–30.

Southall, Aidan. "General Amin and the Coup: Great Man or Historical Inevitability?" *Journal of Modern African Studies,* 13, 1, 1975, 85–105.

———. "The Current State of National Integration in Uganda." In D. R. Smock and K. Bentsi-Enchill (eds). *The Search for National Integration in Africa.* New York and London: Free Press, 1975, 307–331.

———. "The Bankruptcy of the Warrior Tradition." *Journal of African and Asian Studies,* 12, 1977, 166–176.

———. "Social Disorganisation in Uganda: Before, During and After Amin." *Journal of Modern African Studies,* 18, 4, 1980, 627–656.

Ssempebwa, E. "Recent Land Reforms in Uganda." *Makerere Law Journal,* 7, 1, 1977.

Steiner, Rolf, with Yves-Guy Berges (trans. Steve Cox). *The Last Adventurer.* London: Weidenfeld and Nicolson, 1978.

Stevenson, William. *90 Minutes at Entebbe: The First Full Story of Operation Thunderbolt, the Spectacular Israeli Strike Against Terrorism.* New York: Bantam Books, 1976.

Stone, Elaine Murray. *Uganda, Fire and Blood.* Plainfield, NJ: Logos International, 1977.

Stranex, Ruth. *Amudat Sister.* London: Patmos Press, 1977.

Strate, Jeffrey T. *Post-Military Coup Strategy in Uganda.* Athens, OH: Ohio University Center for International Studies, 1973.

Taban, Alfred Logune. "The Ugandan Exodus." *Sudanow,* 4, 7, 1979, 9–17.

Tandon, Yash. "The Expulsions from Uganda: the Asians' Role in East Africa." *Patterns of Prejudice,* 6, 6, 1972.

Tanzania, Government of. "Tanzania and the War Against Amin's Uganda. Tanzania Blue Book on the War Against Amin's Uganda released in Monrovia, Liberia on 17 July 1979." In K. Mathews and S. S. Mushi (eds). *Foreign Policy on Tanzania 1961–1981: A Reader.* Dar es Salaam: Tanzania Publishing House, 1981, 305–314.

Thomas, Caroline. "Concepts in Competition: Illustrations from the Tanzanian Intervention in Uganda." In C. Thomas. *New States, Sovereignty and Intervention.* London: Gower, 1985, 90–121.

———. "Challenges of Nation-Building: Uganda—A Case-Study." *India Quarterly,* 41, 3–4, 1985, 320–349.

Toko, Gad W. *Intervention in Uganda: The Power Struggle and Soviet Involvement: Reflections of a Ugandan Exile.* Pittsburgh: University Center for International Studies, University of Pittsburgh, UCIS Occasional Working Paper Series, no. 1, 1979.

Toro, Princess Elizabeth of (Elizabeth Bagaya). *African Princess.* London: Hamish Hamilton, 1983.

Twaddle, M. J. "The Amin Coup." *Journal of Commonwealth Political Studies,* 10, 2, 1972.

———. "Order and Disorder in Uganda." *World Today,* October 1973, 449–454.

————. "The Ousting of Idi Amin." *The Round Table,* No. 275, 1979, 216–221.

Uganda Government. *Achievements of the Government of Uganda During the First Year of the Second Republic.* Entebbe: Government Printer, 1972.

————. *The First 366 Days.* Entebbe: Government Printer for the Ministry of Information and Broadcasting, 1972.

————. *Uganda, The Second Year of the Second Republic.* Entebbe: Government Printer for the Ministry of Information and Broadcasting, 1973.

Ullman, Richard H. "Human Rights and Economic Power: The United States versus Idi Amin." *Foreign Affairs,* 56, 3, 1978, 529–543.

Ventner, A. J. "Amin's Chamber of Horrors." *South African Journal of African Affairs,* 9, 2, 1979, 104–110.

Wani, Ibrahim J. "Humanitarian Intervention and the Tanzania-Uganda War." *Horn of Africa,* 3, 2, [n.d.] 18–27.

Williamson, T. *Counterstrike Entebbe.* London: Collins, 976.

Wooding, D. and R. Barnett. *Uganda Holocaust.* London and Glasgow: Pickering and Inglis, 1980.

Woodward, Peter. "Ambiguous Amin." *African Affairs,* 77, 307, 1978, 153–164.

5.4 MUSEVENI

Allen, Tim. "Understanding Alice: Uganda's Holy Spirit Movement in Context." *Africa,* 61, 3, 1991, 37–39.

Amnesty International. *Uganda: The Human Rights Record 1986–1989.* AFR 59/01/89. London: Amnesty International, 1989.

————. *Uganda: The Failure to Safeguard Human Rights.* AFR 59/05/92. London: Amnesty International, 1992.

Baker, Delbert W. *From Exile to Prime Minister* [Life of Dr Samson Kisekka]. Washington, DC: Review and Herald Publishing Association, 1988.

Behrend, Heike. "Is Alice Lakwena a Witch?" In H. B. Hansen and M. J. Twaddle (eds). *Changing Uganda: The Dilemmas of Structural Adjustment and Evolutionary Change.* London: James Currey; and Athens, OH: Ohio University Press, 1991, 162–177.

Brett, E. A. "Rebuilding Survival Structures for the Poor: Organizational Options for Reconstruction in the 1990s." In H. B. Hansen and M. J. Twaddle (eds). *Changing Uganda: The Dilemmas of Structural Adjustment and Revolutionary Change.* London: James Currey; and Athens, OH: Ohio University Press, 1991, 297–310.

Ddungu, Expedit and A. A. Wabwire. *Electoral Mechanisms and the Democratic Process: The 1989 Resistance Council and National Resistance Council Elections.* Kampala: Centre for Basic Research, 1991.

[Fountain Publishers]. *Who's Who in Uganda 1988–9.* Kampala: Fountain Publishers, n.d. [1989].

Furley, O. "Uganda's Retreat from Turmoil?" *Conflict Studies,* 196, 1987, 1–32.

Kasfir, Nelson. "Uganda's Uncertain Quest for Recovery." *Current History,* April, 1985, 169–173.

————. "The Ugandan Elections of 1989: Power, Populism and Democratization." In H.B. Hansen and M.J. Twaddle (eds). *Changing Uganda: The Dilemmas of Structural Adjustment and Revolutionary Change.* London: James Currey; and Athens, OH: Ohio University Press, 1991, 247–278.

Kisekka, Samson. *Challenges to Leadership in the Developing World. Speeches of Dr Samson Kisekka, Vice-President of the Republic of Uganda.* Kampala: Kisekka Foundation, 1992

Mamdani, Mahmood. "Uganda in Transition: Two Years of the NRA/NRM." *Third World Quarterly.* 10, 3, 1988, 1155–1181.

Museveni, Yoweri (President). *Selected Articles on the Uganda Resistance War.* Nairobi: National Resistance Movement, 1985.

———. *An Address by His Excellency the President Yoweri Kaguta Museveni.* Entebbe: Government Printer, 7 April 1987.

———. *An Address to the Nation by His Excellency the President Yoweri K. Museveni.* Entebbe: Government Printer, 15 May 1987.

Nsibambi, Apolo R. "Resistance Councils and Committees." In H. B. Hansen and M. J. Twaddle (eds). *Changing Uganda: The Dilemmas of Structural Adjustment and Revolutionary Change.* London: James Currey; and Athens, OH: Ohio University Press, 1991, 279–296.

Pirouet, M. Louise. "Human Rights Issues in Museveni's Uganda." In H. B. Hansen and M. J. Twaddle (eds). *Changing Uganda: The Dilemmas of Structural Adjustment and Revolutionary Change.* London: James Currey; and Athens, OH: Ohio University Press, 1991, 197–209.

Rusk, John D. "Uganda Breaking out of the Mold." *Africa Today,* 33, 2–3, 1986, 91–102.

———. "On the Way to Recovery: Museveni's Uganda in 1988." *Canadian Journal of Development Studies,* 11, 2, 1990, 347–357.

Throup, David. "Kenya's Relations with Museveni's Uganda." In H. B. Hansen and M. J. Twaddle (eds). *Changing Uganda: The Dilemmas of Structural Adjustment and Revolutionary Change*. London: James Currey; and Athens, OH: Ohio University Press, 1991, 187–196.

Twaddle, M. J. "Museveni's Uganda: Notes Towards an Analysis." In H. B. Hansen and M. J. Twaddle (eds). *Uganda Now: Between Decay and Development*. London: James Currey; and Athens, OH: Ohio University Press, 1988. 313–335.

[Uganda]. *Constitution of the Republic of Uganda, Revised Edition, 1986*. Kampala: Law Development Centre, 1986.

[Uganda] *Twelve Months of the NRM Government*. Kampala: Government Printer, 1987.

Waliggo, John M. "The Role of the Christian Churches in the Democratization Process in Uganda." In Paul Gifford. *The Churches and Africa's Democratization*. London: James Currey, 1994.

Woodward, Peter. "Uganda and Southern Sudan 1986–9: New Regimes and Peripheral Politics." In H.B. Hansen and M.J. Twaddle (eds). *Changing Uganda: The Dilemmas of Structural Adjustment and Revolutionary Change*. London: James Currey; and Athens, OH: Ohio University Press, 1991, 178–186.

5.5 IMMIGRANT COMMUNITIES: KENYAN LUO, BANYARWANDA (v. also 5.2, Obote I and II), ASIANS, NUBIANS (v. also 5.3, Idi Amin), EUROPEANS.

Adams, Bert N. "A Look at Uganda and Expulsion through ex-Ugandan Asian Eyes." *Kroniek van Afrika*, 3, 6, 1975, 237–249.

———— and Mike Bristow. "The Politico-Economic Position of Ugandan Asians in the Colonial and Independent Eras."

Journal of Asian and African Studies, 13, 3–4, 1978, 151–166.

————. "Ugandan Asian Expulsion Experiences: Rumour and Reality." *Journal of Asian and African Studies,* 14, 3–4, 1979, 191–203.

Bharati, Agehananda. *The Asians in East Africa: Jayhind and Uhuru.* Chicago: Nelson Hall, 1972.

Clay, Jason W. *The Eviction of Banyaruanda: The Story Behind the Refugee Crisis in Southwest Uganda.* Cambridge, MA: Cultural Survival Inc., 1984.

Crisp, Jeff. "Ugandan Refugees in Sudan and Zaire: The Problem of Repatriation." *African Affairs,* 85, 339, 1986, 163–180.

Don Nanjira, D.D.C. *The Status of Aliens in East Africa: Asians and Europeans in Tanzania and Uganda.* New York: Praeger, 1976.

Engholm, Geoffrey. "The Decline of the Immigrant Influence on the Uganda Administration 1845–52." *Uganda Journal,* 31, 1, 1967, 73–88.

Foster, B. E. "The Rwandan Refugees in Uganda." In Hjort af Ornas and M.A.H. Salih (eds). *Ecology and Politics: Environmental Stress and Security in Africa.* Uppsala: Scandinavian Institute of African Studies, 1989, 145–155.

Ghai, Dharam G. and Yash P. Ghai. *Portrait of a Minority: Asians in East Africa.* London and Nairobi: Oxford University Press, 1971.

————. *The Asian Minorities of East and Central Africa.* London: Minority Rights Group, 1971.

Gregory, Robert G. *India and East Africa: A History of Race Relations Within the British Empire, 1890–1939.* Oxford: Clarendon Press, 1971.

———. ''Cooperation and Collaboration in Colonial East Africa: The Asians' Political Role.'' *African Affairs,* 80, 319, 1981, 259–274.

Gupta, A. ''Ugandan Asians, Britain, India and the Commonwealth. *African Affairs,* 73, 292, 1974, 312–324.

Hansen, H. B. ''Pre-colonial Immigrants and Colonial Servants. The Nubians in Uganda Revisited.'' *African Affairs,* 90, 361, 1991, 559–580.

Harrison, Charles. ''Uganda: The Expulsion of the Asians.'' In W. A. Veenhoven et al. (eds). *Case Studies on Human Rights and Fundamental Freedoms: A World Survey,* Vol. 4. The Hague: Foundation for the Study of Plural Societies by Martinus Nijhoff, 1976, 287–315.

Hollingsworth, L. W. *The Asians of East Africa.* London: Macmillan, 1960.

Humphrey, Derek and Michael Ward. *Passports and Politics.* London: Penguin, 1974.

——— and Mike Bristow. ''Ugandan Asian Expulsion Experiences: Rumour and Reality.'' *Journal of Asian and African Studies,* 14, 3–4, 1979, 191–203.

Jamal, Vali. ''Asians in Uganda 1880–1972. Inequality and Expulsion.'' *Economic History Review,* Series 2, 29, 1976, 602–616.

Kabwegyere, Tarsis. ''The Asian Question in Uganda.'' *Kenya Historical Review,* 2, 2, 1974, 175–188.

Kasfir, Nelson. ''Explaining Ethnic Political Participation.'' [Nubians in Uganda]. *World Politics,* XXXI, 3, 1979, 365–388.

Kokole. Omari H. ''The 'Nubians' of East Africa: Muslim Club or African 'Tribe'? The View from Within.'' *Journal of the Institute of Muslim Minority Affairs,* 6, 2, 1985, 420–448.

Kotecha, Ken C. "The Shortchanged: Uganda Citizenship Laws and How They Were Applied to its Asian Minority." *International Lawyer,* 9, 1, 1975, 1–29.

Kuper, Hilda. " 'Strangers' in Plural Societies: Asians in South Africa and Uganda." In L. Kuper and M. G. Smith (eds), *Pluralism in Africa,* Berkeley, CA: University of California Press, 1969.

Langley, Winston E. and Julius E. Okola. "Uganda: Expulsion of Aliens and Human Rights." *Current Bibliography on African Affairs,* 7, 4, 1974, 345–359.

Mamdani, Mahmood. *From Citizen to Refugee: Uganda Asians Come to Britain.* London: Frances Pinter, 1973.

Mangat, J. S. *A History of the Asians in East Africa, c. 1886–1945.* Oxford: Clarendon Press, 1969.

———. "The Immigrant Communities (2): the Asians." *History of East Africa, III.* Oxford: Clarendon Press, 1976, 467–488.

Mazrui, Ali A. "The De-Indianization of Uganda: Who Is A Citizen?" In D.R. Smock and K. Bentsi-Enchill (eds). *The Search for National Integration in Africa.* New York: 1975, 77–90.

———. "Religious Strangers in Uganda: From Emin Pasha to Amin Dada." *African Affairs,* 76, 302, 1977, 21–38.

———. "Casualties of an Underdeveloped Class Structure: The Expulsion of Luo Workers and Asian Bourgeoisie from Uganda." In W. A. Shack and E. P. Skinner. *Strangers in African Societies.* Berkeley, CA: University of California Press, 1979, 261–278.

Melady, T. and M. *Uganda: The Asian Exiles.* Maryknoll, NY: Orbis Books, 1976.

Milewski, M. "Indian Immigrants and the Development of the Cotton Industry." *South Asia Bulletin,* Fall, 1982, 29–34.

Mittelman, James and O. S. Marwal. "Asian Alien Pariahs: A Cross-Regional Perspective." *Studies in Race and Nations,* 6, 1, 1975, 1–17.

Morris, H. S. "Indians in East Africa: A Study in a Plural Society." *British Journal of Sociology,* 8, 4, 1957, 194–211.

————. "Communal Rivalry among Indians in Uganda." *British Journal of Sociology,* 8, 4, 1957, 306–317.

————. "The Indian Family in Uganda." *American Anthropologist,* 61, 5, 1959, 779–789.

————. *The Indians in Uganda.* Chicago: University of Chicago Press, 1968.

Mwamba, Zuberi I. "Uganda and the Asian Expulsion." *Black World,* 22, 5, 1973, 40–47.

O'Brien, Justin [Yashpal Tandon]. *Brown Britons.* London: Runnymede Trust, 1972.

Pain, Dennis. "The Nubians: Their Perceived Stratification System and its Relation to the Asian issue." In M. J. Twaddle (ed). *Expulsion of a Minority: Essays on Ugandan Asians.* London: Athlone Press, 1975.

Parkin, D. *Neighbours and Nationals in an African City.* London: Routledge and Kegan Paul, 1969.

Parson, Jack. "Africanizing Trade in Uganda: The Final Solution." *Africa Today,* 20, 1, 1973, 59–72.

Patel, Hasu H. "General Amin and the Indian Exodus from Uganda." *Issue: A Quarterly Journal of Africanist Opinion,* 2, 4, 1972, 12–22.

Pirouet, M. Louise. "Refugees In and From Uganda in the Post-Colonial Period." In H. B. Hansen and M. J. Twaddle (eds). *Uganda Now: Between Decay and Development.*

London: James Currey; and Athens, OH: Ohio University Press, 1988, 239–254.

Plender, Richard. "The Uganda Crisis and the Right of Expulsion Under International Law." *Bulletin of the International Commission of Jurists,* 9, December 1972, 19–32.

Rai, K. *Indians and British Colonialism in East Africa 1883– 1939.* Patna, India: Associated Book Agency, 1979.

Ramchandani, R. R. *Uganda Asians: The End of an Enterprise.* Bombay: United Asia Publications, 1976.

Richards, Audrey I. (ed). *Economic Development and Tribal Change: A Study of Immigrant Labour in Buganda.* Cambridge, UK: W. Heffer and Sons for East African Institute of Social Research, 1954.

Shack, W. A. and E. P. Skinner. *Strangers in African Societies.* Berkeley: University of California Press, 1979.

Sofer, C. and C. Ross. "Some Characteristics of an East African European Population." *The British Journal of Sociology,* 2, 4, 1951, 315–331.

Soghayroun, Ibrahim el-Zein. *The Sudanese Muslim Factor in Uganda.* Khartoum: Khartoum University Press, 1981.

Tandon, Yashpal. "General Amin and the Uganda Asians: Doing the Unthinkable." *Round Table: The Commonwealth Journal of International Affairs,* January 1973, 91–104.

Thomas, H. B. and R. Scott. "The European and Asiatic Communities." In H.B. Thomas and R. Scott. *Uganda.* Oxford: Clarendon Press, 1935, 358–370.

Tilbe, Douglas. *The Ugandan Asian Crisis.* London: British Council of Churches, Community and Race Relations Unit, 1972.

Trappe, Paul. *Social Change and Development Institutions in a Refugee Population.* Geneva: UNRISD and Office of the UNHCR, 1971.

———. *Development from Below as an Alternative: A Case Study from Uganda.* Basel, Switzerland: Social Strategies, Monographs on Sociology and Social Policy, 6, 1978.

Twaddle, M.J. (ed). *Expulsion of a Minority: Essays on Uganda Asians.* London: Athlone Press 1986.

6. History of Christianity and Islam in Uganda (including general works which have sections on Uganda)

Allen, John. "Muslims in East Africa." *African Ecclesiastical Review,* 7, 3, 1965, 255–262.

Anderson, W. B. *The Church in East Africa 1840–1974.* Dodoma, Tanzania: Central Tanganyika Press, 1977.

Ashe, R. P. *Two Kings of Uganda.* London: Sampson Low, Marston, Searle and Rivington, 1889.

———. *Chronicles of Uganda.* London: Hodder and Stoughton, 1894.

Asili, C. *Christian Development in Lango, Uganda, 1912–1972.* Gulu, Uganda: Catholic Press, 1972.

Auclair, Elie J. *Vie de Mgr Forbes.* Quebec: Imprimerie Ernest Tremblay, 1928.

Behrend, Heike. "The Holy Spirit Movement and the Forces of Nature in Northern Uganda, 1985–1987." In H.B. Hansen and M.J. Twaddle (eds). *Religion and Politics in Eastern Africa Since Independence.* London: James Currey, 1994, Ch. 5.

Biermans, John. *A Short History of the Vicariate of the Upper Nile, Uganda.* London: Mill Hill Fathers, 1920.

Bouniol, J. *The White Fathers and Their Missions.* London: Sands, 1928.

Brierly, Jean and T. Spear. "Mutesa, the Missionaries and Christian Conversion in Buganda." *International Journal of African Historical Studies,* 21, 4, 1986, 601–618.

Brown, Leslie C., Rt Revd. *Three Worlds, One Word.* London: Rex Collings, 1981.

Burridge, William. *Destiny Africa.* London: Geoffrey Chapman, 1966.

Byabazaire, D. M. *The Contribution of the Christian Churches to the Development of Western Uganda 1894–1974.* Frankfurt: Peter Lang, 1979.

Byaruhanga-Akiiki, A.B.T. *Religion in Bunyoro.* Nairobi: Kenya Literature Bureau, 1982.

Casada, J. A. "James A. Grant and the Introduction of Christianity in Uganda." *Journal of Church and State,* 15, 3, 1983, 507–522.

[Catholic Union of Great Britain]. *Memorandum on the War in Uganda.* London: Catholic Union, 1892.

Charsley, Simon. "Dreams and Purposes: An Analysis of Dream Narrative in an Independent African Church." *Africa: Journal of the International African Institute,* 57, 3, 1987, 281–296.

Church Missionary Society. *Register of Missionaries and Native Clergy, 1804–1894.* Printed for Private Circulation. London: Church Missionary Society, 1895.

Church, J. E. *Awake, Uganda! The Story of Blasio Kigozi and His Vision of Revival.* n.p., 1957. [First edition published in Luganda in 1937.]

―――. *Quest for the Highest: An Autobiographical Account of the East African Revival.* Exeter, UK: Paternoster Press, 1981.

Constantin, François. "Muslims and Politics: The Attempts to Create Muslim National Organizations in Tanzania, Uganda and Kenya." In H. B. Hansen and M. J. Twaddle (eds). *Religion and Politics in Eastern Africa Since Independence.* London: James Currey, 1994, Ch. 2.

Cook, H. Bickersteth (Mrs). *A Doctor and His Dog in Uganda.* London: 1903.

Cook, Sir Albert. "Kampala During the Closing Years of the Last Century." *Uganda Journal,* 1, 2, 1934, 83–95.

―――. "Further Memories of Uganda." *Uganda Journal,* 2, 2, 1935, 97–115.

―――. *Uganda Memories.* Entebbe: Government Press, 1945.

Coomes, Anne. *Festo Kivengere: A Biography.* Eastbourne, UK: Monarch, 1990.

Cussac, J. *Evêque et Pionnier Monseigneur Streicher.* Paris: Éditions de la Savane, 1955.

Dawson, E. C. *The Last Journals of James Hannington.* London: Seeley, 1888.

―――. *James Hannington, First Bishop of Eastern Equatorial Africa. A History of his Life and Work, 1847–1885.* London: Seeley, 1905.

De l'Éprevier, Colonel. *La Révérende Mère Salomé.* Paris: Gabriel Beauchesne, 1935.

Dobson, J. H. *Daybreak in West Nile.* London: Africa Inland Mission, 1964.

Doornbos, Martin. "Church and State in Eastern Africa: Some Unresolved Questions." In H. B. Hansen and M. J. Twaddle (eds). *Religion and Politics in Eastern Africa Since Independence.* London: James Currey, 1994, Ch. 15.

Duchêne, L. *Les Pères Blancs—1868–1892* (3 Vols). Algiers: Maison-Carrée, 1902.

Faupel, J. F. *African Holocaust.* London: Geoffrey Chapman, 1962.

Fisher, Ruth. *On the Borders of Pygmy Land.* London: Marshall Brothers, 1905.

———. *Twilight Tales of the Black Baganda.* London: Marshall Brothers, 1911.

Forbes, F. A. *Planting the Faith in Darkest Africa.* London: Sands, 1927.

Ford, Margaret. *Janani: The Making of a Martyr.* London: Lakeland, 1978.

Foster, W. D. *Sir Albert Cook: A Missionary Doctor in Uganda.* Privately printed for the author by Newhaven Press, East Sussex, UK, 1978.

Gale, H. P. *Uganda and the Mill Hill Fathers.* London: Macmillan, 1959.

Gallina, Ernesto. *Africa Present—A Catholic Survey of Facts and Figures.* London: Geoffrey Chapman, 1970.

Garlick, P. L. *Uganda Contrasts.* London: Church Missionary Society, 1927.

———. *The Wholeness of Man.* London: Highway Press, 1943.

Gee, T. W. "A Century of Muhammedan Influence in Buganda. 1852–1951." *Uganda Journal,* 22, 2, 1958, 139–150.

Gingyera-Pinycwa, A.G.G. *Issues in Pre-Independence Politics in Uganda: A Case Study on the Contribution of Religion to Political Debate in Uganda in the Decade 1952–62.* Nairobi: East African Literature Bureau, 1976.

Glenday, David. "Acholi Birth Ceremonies and Infant Baptism: A Pastoral Paper." *Missiology,* 8, 2, 1980, 167–176.

Gorju, J. *Entre le Victoria, l'Albert et l'Edouard.* Rennes, France: Oberthur, 1920.

Goulet, A. *Sur les Rives du Victoria.* Paris: Librairie Missionaire, 1948.

Gray, J. M. "Correspondence Relating to the Death of Bishop Hannington." *Uganda Journal,* XIII, 1, 1949, 1–22.

Gresford Jones, H. *Uganda in Transformation.* London: Church Missionary Society, 1926.

Groves, C. P. *The Planting of Christianity in Africa. Vol. II, 1840–1878; Vol. III, 1878–1914; Vol. IV, 1914–1954.* London: Lutterworth Press, 1954, 1955, 1958.

Guillebaud, Lindsay. *A Grain of Mustard Seed: The Growth of the Ruanda Mission of C.M.S.* London: Ruanda Mission and Church Army Press, 1959.

Hall, Martin J. *Through My Spectacles in Uganda.* London: Church Missionary Society, 1898.

Hannington, James. *The Last Journals of James Hannington.* Ed. James Dawson. London: Seeley, 1888.

Hansen, H. B. "European Ideas, Colonial Attitudes and African Realities: The Introduction of a Church Constitution in

Uganda, 1898–1908.'' *The International Journal of African Historical Studies,* 13, 2, 1980, 140–180.

———. ''Missions and Colonialism in Uganda: A Case Study on Forced Labour.'' In T. Christensen and W.R. Hutchison. *Missionary Ideologies in the Imperialist Era, 1880–1920.* Aarhus, Denmark: Forlaget Aros, 1982, 104–116.

———. *Mission, Church and State in a Colonial Setting. Uganda 1890–1925.* London: Heinemann, 1984.

———. ''Church and State in Early Colonial Uganda.'' *African Affairs,* 85, 338, 1986, 55–74.

———. ''Dilemmas and Challenges in the Study of Religion and Politics.'' In H. B. Hansen and M. J. Twaddle (eds). *Religion and Politics in Eastern Africa Since Independence.* London: James Currey, 1994, Ch. 16.

——— and M. J. Twaddle. *Religion and Politics in Eastern Africa Since Independence.* London: James Currey, 1994.

Harford-Battersby, C. F. *Pilkington of Uganda.* London: Marshall Brothers, 1898.

Harman, Nicholas. *Bwana Stokesi and his African Conquests.* London: Jonathan Cape, 1986.

Hastings, Adrian. *Church and Mission in Modern Africa.* London: Burns and Oates, 1967.

———. ''From Mission to Church in Buganda.'' *Zeitschrift für Missionswissenschaft und Religionswissenschaft,* 53, 1969, 206–228.

———. ''The Catholic Church in Uganda.'' *African Ecclesiastical Review (AFER),* XI, 3, 1969, 239–244.

———. *A History of African Christianity, 1950–1975.* Cambridge, UK: Cambridge University Press, 1979.

Hellberg, C. J. *Missions on a Colonial Frontier West of Lake Victoria.* Lund, Sweden: Gleerups, Studia Missionalia Upsaliensia, VI, 1965.

Hewitt, Gordon. *The Problems of Success. A History of the Church Missionary Society, 1910–1942. Vol. I, Tropical Africa, the Middle East and At Home.* London: SCM Press, 1971, 205–260.

Holway, James D. "CMS Contact with Islam in East Africa before 1914." *Journal of Religion in Africa,* 4, 3, 1972, 200–212.

Hooton, W. S. and J. Stafford Wright. *The First Twenty-Five Years of the Bible Churchmen's Missionary Society.* London: Bible Churchmen's Missionary Society, 1947.

Ineichen, Bernard. "The Strange Story of the Bishop's Head: Or how the Sleeping Sickness came to South Busoga (and Won't Go Away Again)." *Kenya Historical Review,* 2, 2, 1974, 273–278.

Johnson, T. B. *Tramps Round the Mountains of the Moon.* London: T. Fisher Unwin, 1912.

"J. M.": see Mercui, J.

Jones, H. Gresford. *Uganda in Transformation.* London: Church Missionary Society, 1926.

Kabale [Roman Catholic] Diocese. *Beginnings of Kabale Diocese, 1923–1973.* Kisubi, Uganda: Marianum Press, 1973.

Kasozi, Abdu B. "Why did the Baganda Adopt Foreign Religions in the 19th Century?" *Mawazo,* 4, 3, 1975, 129–153.

————. *The Spread of Islam in Uganda.* Nairobi: Oxford University Press in association with the Islamic African Centre, 1986.

———. "Christian-Muslim Inputs into Public Policy Formation in Kenya, Tanzania and Uganda." In H. B. Hansen and M. J. Twaddle (eds). *Religion and Politics in Eastern Africa Since Independence*. London: James Currey, 1994, Ch. 12.

Kassimir, Ronald. "Complex Martyrs: Symbols of Catholic Church Formation and Political Differentiation in Uganda." *African Affairs*, 90, 360, 1991, 357–382.

———. "Catholics and Political Identity in Toro." In H. B. Hansen and M. J. Twaddle (eds). *Religion and Politics in Eastern Africa Since Independence*. London: James Currey, 1994, Ch. 8.

Katumba, A. and F. B. Welbourn. "Muslim Martyrs of Buganda." *Uganda Journal*, 28, 2, 1964, 151–164.

Kavulu, David. *The Uganda Martyrs*. Makerere History Papers, 2. Kampala: Longmans, 1969.

Kettani, M. A. "Muslim East Africa: An Overview." *Journal of the Institute of Muslim Minority Affairs*, 1982, 1–2, 104–119.

Kiggundu, S. I. and I.K.K. Lukwago. "The Status of the Muslim Community in Uganda." *Journal of the Institute of Muslim Minority Affairs*, 1982, 1–2, 120–132.

King, Noel Q. *Christian and Muslim in Africa*. New York: Harper and Row, 1971.

———, Abdu Kasozi and Arye Oded. *Islam and the Confluence of Religions in Uganda, 1840–1966*. Tallahassee, FL: American Academy of Religion, 1973.

Kitching, A. L. *On the Backwaters of the Nile*. London: Fisher Unwin, 1912.

———. *From Darkness to Light. Study of Pioneer Missionary Work in the Diocese of the Upper Nile*. London: Society for Promoting Christian Knowledge, 1935.

Kivengere, Bishop Festo, with Dorothy Smoker. *Revolutionary Love.* Fort Washington, PA: Christian Literature Crusade, 1983.

Kokole, Omari H. " 'The Nubi' and Islam in Ugandan Politics, 1971–1979." In H. B. Hansen and M. J. Twaddle (eds). *Religion and Politics in Eastern Africa Since Independence.* London: James Currey, 1994. Ch. 4.

Kupalo, Ancilla. "African Sisters' Congregations: Realities of the Present Situation." In E. Fasholé-Luke et al. (eds). *Christianity in Independent Africa.* London: Rex Collings, 1978, 122–135.

Langlands, B. W. and G. Namirembe. *Studies in the Geography of Religion in Uganda.* Kampala: Makerere University, Occasional Paper No. 4, Department of Geography, 1967.

Lavigerie, Cardinal Charles A. *Instructions aux Missionaires.* Namur: Editions Grands Lacs, 1950.

Le Gall, J. P. *Le Voyage du Pape Paul VI en Ouganda.* Vatican: 1969.

Leblond, G. *Le Père Auguste Achte.* Algiers: Maison-Carrée, 1928.

Lefebvre, R. *Kizito: The Story of a Black Boy Martyr.* Rome: St Peter Claver, 1936.

Lewis, I. M. (ed). *Islam in Tropical Africa.* Oxford: Clarendon Press, 1966.

Lloyd, A. B. *In Dwarf Land and Cannibal Country.* London: Fisher Unwin, 1899.

———. *Uganda to Khartoum.* London: Fisher Unwin, 1906.

Lockhard, Kathleen G. "Religion and Politics in Independent Uganda: Movement Towards Secularization?" In James R.

Scarritt (ed). *Analyzing Political Change in Africa: Applications of a New Multi-Dimensional Framework.* Boulder, CO: Westview Press, 1980.

Louis, Sister M. *Love Is the Answer: The Story of Mother Kevin.* Dublin: Fallons, 1964.

Low, D. A. *Religion and Society in Buganda 1875–1900.* Kampala: East African Institute of Social Research, n.d.

———. "Converts and Martyrs in Uganda." In C. G. Baeta (ed). *Christianity in Tropical Africa.* London: International African Institute and Oxford University Press, 1968, 150–164.

Luck, Anne. *African Saint: The Story of Apolo Kivebulaya.* London: S.C.M. Press, 1963.

———. *Charles Stokes in Africa.* Nairobi: East African Publishing House, 1972.

[Mackay's Sister]. *A. M. Mackay: Pioneer Missionary of the Church Missionary Society to Uganda.* London: Hodder and Stoughton, 1890. Reprint, London: Frank Cass, 1970.

———. *The Story of Mackay of Uganda, Pioneer Missionary.* London: Hodder and Stoughton, 1898.

Marchetti, Mario. *E l'Uganda una Missione?* Gulu, Uganda: Catholic Press. 1971.

Marie-André du Sacré-Coeur, Soeur. *Uganda terre de martyrs.* Tournai, Belgium: Casterman, 1963.

Matheson, Elizabeth. *An Enterprise So Perilous.* London and Dublin: Mellifont, n.d.

Matson, A. T. "The Instructions Issued in 1876 and 1878 to the Pioneer C.M.S. Parties to Karagwe and Uganda." Part I, *Journal of Religion in Africa,* XII, 3, 1981, 192–237; Part II, *JRA,* XII, 1, 1982, 26–46.

Medeghini, A. *Storia d'Uganda.* Bologna, Italy: Editrice Nigrizia, 1973.

Mercui, J. ('J.M.'). *L'Ouganda et les agissements de la Compagnie 'East Africa'.* Algiers: Procure des Missions d'Afrique, 1892. This was expanded into *La mission catholique at les agissements de la Compagnie anglaise.* Algiers: Maison-Carrée, 1894.

Mujaju, Akiiki B. "The Political Crisis of Church Institutions in Uganda." *African Affairs,* 75, 1, 1976, 67–85.

Mullins, J. D. *The Wonderful Story of Uganda.* London: Church Missionary Society, 1904.

Negri, A. *Il Vicariato del Nilo Equatoriale—1937.* Verona, Italy: Istituto Missioni Africane, 1937.

Nicolet, J. *Yohana Kitagana.* Namur, Belgium: Grands Lacs, 1947.

Nicq, A. *Le Père Simeon Lourdel.* Algiers: White Fathers, 1906.

Oded, Arye. *Islam in Uganda: Islamization in a Centralized State in Pre-Colonial Africa.* Jerusalem: Israel Universities Press, 1974.

Oliver, Roland. *The Missionary Factor in East Africa.* London: Longmans Green, 1952.

Pirouet, M. Louise. *Strong in the Faith: The Witness of the Uganda Martyrs.* Mukono, Uganda: Church of Uganda Literature Bureau, 1969.

———. *Black Evangelists.* London: Rex Collings, 1978.

———. "East African Christians and World War I." *Journal of African History,* XIX, 1, 1978, 117–130.

———. "Religion in Uganda Under Amin." *Journal of Religion in Africa,* 11, 1, 1980, 12–29.

————. "Women Missionaries in Uganda." In T. Christensen and W. R. Hutchison (eds). *Missionary Ideologies in the Imperialist Era, 1890–1920.* Aarhus, Denmark: Forlaget Aros, 1982.

————. "Traditional Religion and the Response to Christianity: Environmental Considerations. A Case Study from Uganda." *Geographia Religionum,* Band 6, *Beiträge zur Religion/Umwelt Forschung I,* Berlin: 1989, 191–200.

————. "The Churches and Human Rights in Kenya and Uganda." In H. B. Hansen and M. J. Twaddle (eds). *Religion and Politics in Eastern Africa Since Independence.* London: James Currey, 1994, Ch. 14.

Purcell, Mary. *Simeon Lourdel—Apostle of Uganda.* London: Fallons, 1942.

Rathe, Gerard. *Mud and Mosaics. An African Journey from the Niger to the Copperbelt.* Hinckley, UK: Samuel Walker, 1960.

Richardson, Kenneth. *Garden of Miracles. A History of the Africa Inland Mission.* London and Eastbourne: Victory Press, 1968.

Rowe, J. A. "The Purge of Christians at Mwanga's Court." *Journal of African History,* V, 1, 1964, 55–72.

————. "Islam under Idi Amin: A Case of Déja Vu?" In H. B. Hansen and M. J. Twaddle (eds). *Uganda Now: Between Decay and Development.* London: James Currey; and Athens, OH: Ohio University Press, 1988, 267–279.

Russell, J. K. *Men Without God? A Study of the Impact of the Christian Message in the North of Uganda.* London: Highway Press, 1964.

Sempangi, F. Kefa. "Uganda's Reign of Terror." *Worldview,* 18, 5, 1975, 16–21.

Sharp, Leonard E. S. *Island of Miracles: The Story of the Lake Bunyonyi Leprosy Settlement, Uganda.* London: Ruanda Mission, n.d.

Shorter, Aylward and Eugene Kataza (eds). *Missionaries to Yourselves. African Catechists Today.* London: Geoffrey Chapman, 1972.

Ssemakula, Paul. *A Brief Story of the Uganda Martyrs.* Gulu, Uganda: Catholic Press, 1964.

Stock, Eugene. *History of the Church Missionary Society. Vol. III.* London: Church Missionary Society, 1899, *Vol. IV,* 1916.

Stuart, Mary. *Land of Promise: A Story of the Church in Uganda.* London: Highway Press, 1958.

Taylor, J. V. *The Growth of the Church in Buganda.* London: S.C.M. Press, 1961.

Thomas, H. B. and R. Scott. "Christian Missions and other Native Religious Organizations." In H. B. Thomas and R. Scott. *Uganda.* Oxford: Clarendon Press, 1935, 326–339.

Thoonen, J. *Black Martyrs.* London: Sheed and Ward, 1942.

Tiberondwa, A. K. *Missionary Teachers as Agents of Colonialism: Uganda 1877–1925.* Lusaka: Neczam, 1978.

Tourigny, Yves. *Facts and Comments—The Catholic Church in Uganda.* Kisubi, Uganda: Kisubi Press, 1948.

———. "In Memoriam—Archbishop Henri Streicher, CBE." *Uganda Journal,* XVII, 1, 1953, 63–67.

———. *So Abundant a Harvest. The Catholic Church in Uganda 1879–1979.* London: Darton, Longman and Todd, 1979.

Trimingham, J. S. *Islam in East Africa.* Oxford: Clarendon Press, 1964.

Tucker, Alfred R. *Visits to Ruwenzori*. London: Church Missionary Society, 1899.

———. *Eighteen Years in Uganda and East Africa*, 2 Vols. London: Edward Arnold, 1908; 1-volume edition, 1911.

Tuma, Tom. "African Chiefs and Church Work in Busoga Province of Uganda, 1900–1940." Part I, *Kenya Historical Review*, 4, 2, 1976, 283–295; Part II, *Kenya Historical Review*, 5, 1, 1977, 93–106.

———. "Major Changes and Developments in Christian Leadership in Busoga Province, Uganda, 1960–1974." In E. Fasholé-Luke et al. (eds). *Christianity in Independent Africa*. London: Rex Collings, 1978, 60–78.

———. *Building a Ugandan Church. African Participation in Church Growth and Expansion in Busoga 1891–1940*. Nairobi: Kenya Literature Bureau, 1980.

——— and Phares Mutibwa (eds). *A Century of Christianity in Uganda 1877–1977*. Nairobi: Uzima Press, 1978.

Waliggo, J. M. "Ganda Traditional Religion and Catholicism in Buganda, 1948–1975." In E. Fasholé-Luke et al. (eds). *Christianity in Independent Africa*. London: Rex Collings, 1978, 413–425.

———. "The Religio-Political Context of the Uganda Martyrs and its Significance." *African Christian Studies*, 2, 1, 1986, 3–40.

———. *A History of African Priests. Katigondo Major Seminary 1911–1986*. Nairobi: Marianum Press Consultants, 1989.

———. "The Catholic Church and the Root Cause of Political Instability in Uganda." In H. B. Hansen and M. J. Twaddle (eds). *Religion and Politics in Eastern Africa Since Independence*. London: James Currey, 1994, Ch. 7.

————. ''The Role of the Christian Churches in the Democratization Process in Uganda.'' In Paul Gifford (ed). *The Churches and Africa's Democratization.* London: James Currey, 1994.

Ward, Kevin. *Called to Serve. Bishop Tucker Theological College, Mukono. A History 1913–1989.* Mukono, Uganda: Bishop Tucker Theological College, 1989.

————. ''Obedient Rebels: the Relationship Between the Early 'Balokole' and the Church of Uganda. The Mukono Crisis of 1941.'' *Journal of Religion in Africa,* XIX, 3, 1989, 194–227.

————. ''The Church of Uganda Amidst Conflict: The Interplay between Church and Politics in Uganda Since 1962.'' In H. B. Hansen and M. J. Twaddle (eds). *Religion and Politics in Eastern Africa Since Independence.* London: James Currey, 1994, Ch. 6.

Warren, Sheelagh. *Come Back at Two.* London: Excalibur, 1993.

Welbourn, F. B. *East African Rebels.* London: SCM Press, 1961.

————. *Religion and Politics in Uganda, 1952–1965.* Nairobi: East African Publishing House, 1965.

————. *East African Christian.* London: Oxford University Press, 1965.

Wilson, C. and R. Felkin. *Uganda and the Egyptian Soudan.* London: Sampson, Low, 1882.

Winter, Mark. ''The Balokole and the Protestant Ethic—A Critique.'' *Journal of Religion in Africa,* XIV, 1, 1983, 59–73.

Wooding, D. and R. Barnett. *Uganda Holocaust.* London: Pickering and Inglis, 1980.

7 Economics and Economic History

7.1 GENERAL WORKS ON AFRICA AND EAST AFRICA

Amin, Mohamed, D. Willetts and A. Matheson. *Railway Across the Equator. The Story of the East African Line.* London: Bodley Head, 1986.

Anderson, David. "Dust Bowl, Demography and Drought: The Colonial State and Soil Conservation in East Africa During the 1930s." *African Affairs,* 83, 332, 1984, 321–344.

Beckenham, Arthur F. *Wagon of Smoke: An Informal History of the East African Railways and Harbours Administration 1948–1961.* London: Cadogan Publications, 1987.

Brett, E. A. *Colonialism and Underdevelopment in East Africa: The Politics of Economic Change, 1919–39.* London: Heinemann, 1973.

Clark, P. G. *Development Planning in East Africa.* Nairobi: East African Publishing House, 1965.

Clayton, E. S. "Mechanisation and Employment in East African Agriculture." *International Labour Review,* April 1972, 309–334.

Cliffe, L., J. S. Coleman and M. R. Doornbos (eds). *Government and Rural Development in East Africa: Essays on Political Penetration.* The Hague: Martinus Nijhoff, 1977.

Coles, Diana M. S. *The Vegetable Oil Crushing Industry in East Africa.* Nairobi: Oxford University Press for Makerere Institute of Social Research, 1968.

Gitelson, Susan A. *Multilateral Aid for National Development and Self-Reliance: A Case-Study of the UNDP in Uganda and Tanzania.* Nairobi: East African Literature Bureau, 1975.

Good, C. M. *Rural Markets and Trade in East Africa: A Study of the Functions and Development of Exchange Institutions in Ankole, Uganda.* Chicago: University of Chicago Department of Geography, Research Paper 128, 1970.

Gray, Richard and David Birmingham (eds). *Pre-colonial African Trade: Essays on Trade in Central and Eastern Africa Before 1900.* London: Oxford University Press, 1970.

Hazelwood, A. "The End of the East African Community: What Are the Lessons for Regional Integration Schemes?" *Journal of Common Market Studies,* September, 1979, 40–58.

Hill, M. F. *Permanent Way. Vol. I. The Story of the Kenya and Uganda Railway.* Nairobi: East African Railways and Harbours, 1950.

Hutton, John (ed). *Urban Challenge in East Africa.* Nairobi: East African Publishing House, 1972.

Kennedy, T. J. "Study of Economic Motivation Involved in Peasant Cultivation of Cotton." *East African Economics Review,* 10, 2, 1963, 88–95.

Killick, Tony. *The Economies of East Africa.* Boston, MA: Hall, 1976.

Mead, D. C. "Economic Cooperation in East Africa." *Journal of Modern African Studies,* 7, 2, 1969, 277–287.

Miller, Charles. *The Lunatic Express.* New York: Macmillan, 1971.

Mugomba, A. T. "Regional Organisations and African Underdevelopment: The Collapse of the East African Community." *Journal of Modern African Studies,* 16, 2, 1978, 261–272.

Njala, A. S. and A. A. Obura. "Evolution of the East African Currencies." *Bank of Uganda Quarterly Bulletin,* 3, 2, 1971, 51–54.

O'Conner, Anthony M. *An Economic Geography of East Africa.* London: A. Bell and Sons, 1966.

Oloya, J. J. *Coffee, Cotton, Sisal and Tea in East African Economies.* Nairobi: East African Literature Bureau, 1969.

Patience, K. *Steam in East Africa: A Pictorial History of the Railways in East Africa 1893–1976.* Nairobi: Heinemann, 1976.

Patterson, J. H. *The Man-Eaters of Tsavo.* London: Macmillan 1907.

Robson, P. "The Shiftability of Industry and the Measurement of Gains and Losses in the East African Common Market: Some Further Considerations." *Bulletin of the Oxford University Institute of Economics and Statistics,* 30, 2, 1968, 153–155.

Rothchild, D. "A Hope Deferred: East African Federation, 1963–1964." In G. Carter (ed). *Politics in Africa: Seven Cases.* New York: Harcourt Brace and World, 1966, 42–46.

Safier, M. "Towards the Definition of Economic Development over East Africa." *East African Geographical Review,* 7, April 1969, 1–13.

Thomas, P. A. (ed). *Private Enterprise and the East African Company.* Dar es Salaam: Tanzania Publishing House, 1969.

Van Zwanenberg, R.M.A. and Anne King. *An Economic History of Kenya and Uganda, 1800–1970.* Atlantic Highlands, NJ: Humanities Press, 1975.

Wood, L. J. and Christopher Ehret. "The Origins and Diffusion of the Market Institution in East Africa." *Journal of African Studies,* 5, 1, 1978, 1–17.

Zajadacz, Paul. *Studies in Production and Trade in East Africa.* Munich, Germany: Weltforum Verlag, 1970.

7.2 Economic History of Uganda

7.2.1 GENERAL

Baffoe, F. "The Political Economy of Population Policies: the Uganda Experience." In U. U. Uche (ed). *Law and Population Change in Africa.* Nairobi: East African Publishing House, 1986.

Baird, Mark et al. *Uganda: Country Economic Memorandum.* Washington, DC: World Bank, Eastern Africa Regional Office, 1982.

Banugire, Firimooni R. "Class Struggle, Class Politics and the 'Magendo' Economy, Uganda." *Mawazo,* 6, 2, 1985, 52–66.

———. "Uneven and Unbalanced Development: Development Strategies and Conflict." In K. Rupesinghe (ed). *Conflict Resolution in Uganda.* Oslo: International Peace Research Institute; London: James Currey; and Athens, OH: Ohio University Press, 1989, 207–222.

———. "Employment, Incomes, Basic Needs and Structural Adjustment Policy in Uganda 1980–1987." In B. Onimode (ed). *The IMF, the World Bank and the African Debt. Vol. 2: The Social and Political Impact.* London: Zed Books and the Institute for African Alternatives, 1989, 95–110.

Belshaw, D.G.R. "Public Investment in Agriculture and the Economic Development of Uganda." *The East African Economics Review,* 2, 1962, 69–94.

———. "Price and Marketing Policy for Uganda's Export Crops." *East African Journal of Rural Development,* 1, 2, 1968.

———. "Agriculture-led Recovery in Post-Amin Uganda: The Causes of Failure and the Bases for Success." In H. B. Hansen and M. J. Twaddle (eds). *Uganda Now: Between*

Decay and Development. London: James Currey; and Athens, OH: Ohio University Press, 1988, 111–125.

Bowles, B. O. "Economic Anti-Colonialism and British Reaction in Uganda, 1936–1955." *Canadian Journal of African Studies,* 9, 1, 1975, 51–59.

Boyd, R. E. "Empowerment of Women in Contemporary Uganda: Real or Symbolic?" *Labour, Capital and Society,* 22, 1, 1989, 19–40.

Brett, E. A. "Problems of Cooperative Development in Uganda." In R. Apthorpe (ed). *Rural Cooperatives and Planned Change in Africa, Vol. 4.* Geneva: 1970.

————. *Colonialism and Underdevelopment in East Africa: The Politics of Economic Change, 1919–1939.* London: Heinemann, 1973.

————. "Relations of Production, the State and the Ugandan Crisis." *West African Journal of Sociology and Political Science,* 1, 3, 1978, 249–284.

Byabazaire, D. M. *The Contribution of the Christian Churches to the Development of Western Uganda 1894–1974.* Frankfurt: Peter Lang, 1979.

Clark, Nancy. "The Economy." In Rita M. Byrnes. *Uganda: A Country Study.* Washington: Library of Congress, 1992, 98–144.

Clark, P. G. "Development Strategy in an Early State Economy: Uganda." *Journal of Modern African Studies,* 4, 1, 1966, 47–64.

Clark, Ralph. *Aid in Uganda: Programmes and Policies.* London: Overseas Development Institute, 1966.

Cleave, J. H. "Food Consumption in Uganda." *East African Journal of Rural Development,* 1, 1, 1968, 70–87.

Due, J. F. "The Uganda Sales Tax on Importation and Manufacture." *East African Economic Review,* 5, 1, 1969, 1–16.

Economist Intelligence Unit. *Country Profile: Uganda, 1989–90.* London: *The Economist,* 1989.

———. *Country Report: Uganda, Ethiopia, Somalia, Djibouti.* Nos 1–3. London: *The Economist,* 1991.

Edmunds, Keith. "Crisis Management: The Lessons for Africa from Obote's Second Term." In H. B. Hansen and M. J. Twaddle (eds). *Uganda Now: Between Decay and Development.* London: James Currey; and Athens, OH: Ohio University Press, 1988, 95–110.

Elkan, Walter. *An African Labour Force: Two Case Studies in East African Employment.* Kampala: East African Institute of Social Research, 1956.

———. "Central and Local Taxes on Africans in Uganda." *Public Finance,* 13, 4, 1958, 312–320.

———. "Regional Disparities in the Incidence of Taxation in Uganda." *Review of Economic Studies,* 26, 2, 1959, 135–147.

———. *The Economic Development of Uganda.* London: Oxford University Press, 1961.

——— and L. A. Fallers, "The Mobility of Labour." In W.E. Moore and A.S. Feldman (eds). *Labour Commitment and Social Change in Developing Areas.* New York: Social Science Research Council, 1960.

Ewusi, K. "Changes of Distribution of Earnings of Africans in Recorded Employment in Uganda." *Economic Bulletin* (Ghana), 3, 1, 1973, 39–49.

Fair, Denis. "Uganda: Faltering Footsteps Towards Economic Recovery." *Africa Insight,* 16, 3, 1986, 157–162.

Frederick, Kenneth D. "The Role of Market Forces and Planning in Uganda's Economic Development, 1900–1938." *Eastern African Economic Review* (n.s.), 1, 1969, 47–62.

Fredman, Steven J. "U.S. Trade Sanctions against Uganda: Legality under International Law." *Law and Policy in International Business,* 11, 3, 1979, 77–95.

Furley, O. W. "The Origins of Economic Paternalism in a British Territory: Western Uganda." *Social and Economic Studies,* 11, 1, 1962, 57–72.

Ghai, Dharam P. "Concepts and Strategies of Economic Independence." *Journal of Modern African Studies,* 11, 1, 1973, 21–42.

Gittelson, Susan A. "How Are Development Projects Selected? The Case of the UNDP in Uganda and Tanzania." *African Review,* 2, 1972, 365–379.

Green, R. H. "Ugandans Prepare to Work for Progress." *East African Journal,* August 1966, 9–21.

Hall, Sir John. "Some Aspects of Economic Development in Uganda." *African Affairs,* 21, 202, 1952, 124–134.

Hansen, H. B. and M. J. Twaddle (eds). *Uganda Now: Between Decay and Development.* London: James Currey; and Athens, OH: Ohio University Press, 1988.

————. *Changing Uganda: The Dilemmas of Structural Adjustment and Revolutionary Change.* London: James Currey; and Athens, OH: Ohio University Press, 1991.

Harris, Douglas. *Development in Uganda, 1947 to 1955–6.* Wisbech, England: Balding and Mansell for the Government of Uganda, n.d. [1956?]

Helleiner, G. K. "Economic Collapse and Rehabilitation in Uganda." *Rural Africana,* 11, Fall 1981, 27–35.

International Bank for Reconstruction and Development (World Bank) Mission to Uganda. *The Economic Development of Uganda.* Baltimore: Johns Hopkins University Press, 1962.

Jamal, Valimohamed. "Coping under Crisis in Uganda." *International Labour Review,* 127, 6, 1988, 679–701.

———— and John Weekes. "The Vanishing Rural-Urban Gap in Sub-Saharan Africa." *International Labour Review,* 127, 3, 1988, 271–292.

Kaberuka, Will. *The Political Economy of Uganda, 1890–1979: A Case-Study of Colonialism and Underdevelopment.* New York and Los Angeles: Vantage Press, 1990.

Kabwegyere, T. B. "Family Life and Economic Change in Uganda." In M. B. Sussman and B. E. Cogwell (eds). *Cross-National Family Research.* Leiden: E. J. Brill, 1972, 147–157.

Kayizzi-Mugerwa, S. and A. Bigsten. "On Structural Adjustment in Uganda." *Canadian Journal of Development Studies,* 13, 1, 1992, 57–76.

Kennedy, T. A. "An Estimate of Uganda's Balance of Payments, 1949–1957." *The East African Economic Review,* 6, 1, 1959, 1–13.

Knight, J. B. "The Determination of Wages and Salaries in Uganda." *Bulletin, Institute of Economics and Statistics, Oxford University,* 29, 3, 1967, 233–264.

————. "Earnings, Employment, Education and Income Distribution in Uganda." *Bulletin, Institute of Economics and Statistics, Oxford University,* 30, 4, 1968, 267–297.

Lateef, K. Sarwar. "Structural Adjustment in Uganda: The Initial Experience." In H. B. Hansen and M. J. Twaddle (eds).

Changing Uganda: The Dilemmas of Structural Adjustment and Revolutionary Change. London: James Currey; and Athens, OH: Ohio University Press, 1991, 20–42.

Laumer, H. "Channels of Distribution in Uganda." In Paul Zajadacz (ed). *Studies in Production and Trade in East Africa.* Munich: Weltforum Verlag, 1970.

Loxley, J. "The IMF, the World Bank and Reconstruction in Uganda." In B.K. Campbell and J. Loxley. *Structural Adjustment in Africa.* Basingstoke, UK: Macmillan, 1989, 67–91.

Lury, D. A. "Dayspring Mishandled? The Uganda Economy, 1945–60." In D. A. Low and Alison Smith (eds). *[Oxford] History of East Africa,* Vol. III, Oxford: Clarendon Press, 1976, 212–250.

Mamdani, M. "Forms of Labour and Accumulation of Capital: Analysis of a Village in Lango, Northern Uganda." *Mawazo,* 5, 4, 1984, 44–65.

Mugaju, J. B. "Development Planning versus Economic Performance in Uganda, 1961–1971." *Transafrican Journal of History,* 19, 1990, 99–116.

Mugyenyi, Joshua B. "IMF Conditionality and Structural Adjustment under the National Resistance Movement." In H. B. Hansen and M. J. Twaddle (eds). *Changing Uganda: The Dilemmas of Structural Adjustment and Revolutionary Change.* London: James Currey; and Athens, OH: Ohio University Press, 1991, 61–77.

Nabudere, Dan Wadada. *The IMF-World Bank's Stabilisation and Structural Adjustment Policies and the Uganda Economy, 1981–1989.* Leiden: African Studies Centre, 1990.

Obbo, Christine. "Catalysts of Urbanism in the Countryside— Mukono, Uganda." *African Studies Review,* 31, 4, 1988, 39–47.

O'Conner, A. M. "Regional Contrasts in Economic Development in Uganda." *East African Geographical Review*, 1, 1963, 33–43.

Orde Brown, G. St. J. *Labour Conditions in East Africa.* London: Colonial Office, 1946.

Ouma, S.O.A. "Corruption in Public Policy and its Impact on Development: The Case of Uganda since 1979." *Public Administration and Development*, 11, 5, 1991, 473–490.

Parson, Jack. "Africanizing Trade in Uganda: The Final Solution." *Africa Today*, 20, 1, 1973, 59–72.

Powesland, P. G. *Economic Policy and Labour: A Study in Uganda's Economic History.* East African Studies, No. 10, Kampala: East African Institute of Social Research, 1957.

Prunier, G. "L'Ouganda: une économie malade de la politique." *Tiers-Monde,* April–June, 1986, 319–330.

Ravenhill, J. "Regional Integration and Development in Africa: Lessons from the East African Community." *Journal of Commonwealth and Comparative Politics,* November 1979, 227–246.

Richards, Audrey I. (ed). *Economic Development and Tribal Change: A Study of Immigrant Labour in Buganda.* Cambridge, UK: W. Heffer and Sons for East African Institute of Social Research, 1954.

Saben, G. P. *Saben's Commercial Directory and Handbook of Uganda.* Kampala: Uganda Argus, 1947–48, 1950–51, 1953–54, 1955–56, 1960–61.

St Jorre, John de. "The Ugandan Connection." *New York Times Magazine,* 9 April 1978, 26–28, 82–88.

Schultheis, Michael J. "The Uganda Economy and General Amin, 1971–4." *Studies in Comparative International Development,* 10, 3, 1975, 3–34.

Seers, Dudley et al. *The Rehabilitation of the Economy of Uganda.* 2 Vols. London: Commonwealth Secretariat, 1979.

Stamper, B. M. "Uganda 1971/2–1975/6." In B.M. Stamper (ed). *Population and Planning in Developing Nations: A Review of Sixty Development Plans for the 1970s.* New York: New York Population Council, 1977.

Taber, S. R. "The 1969 Uganda Census: Provisional Results." In S. Ominde and C.J. Ejiogu (eds). *Population Growth and Economic Development in Africa.* London: Heinemann, 1972.

Tandon, Yash. "Technical Assistance Administration and High Level Manpower Requirements in Uganda." In Y. Tandon (ed). *Technical Assistance Administration in Africa.* Stockholm: Almquist and Wicksell, 1973.

Taylor, T. F. "The Struggle for Economic Control of Uganda 1919–1922." *International Journal of African Historical Studies,* 11, 1, 1978, 1–31.

Tibazarawa, C. M. "The East African Community—A Tragedy in Regional Cooperation." *The Courier,* 112, 1988, 48–50.

Tindigarukayo, J. "On the Way to Recovery: Museveni's Uganda in 1988." *Canadian Journal of Development Studies,* 11, 2, 1990, 347–357.

Tribe, Michael. "Uganda 1971: An Economic Background." *Mawazo,* 3, 1, 15–26.

Wiebe, Paul D. and Cole P. Dodge. *Beyond Crisis: Development Issues in Uganda.* Hillsboro, KS: Multibusiness Press, 1987.

7.2.2 AGRICULTURE, CASH CROPS AND PASTORALISM

Baker, Randall. "The Distribution of Cattle in Uganda." *East African Geographical Review,* 6, 1968, 63–73.

————. "Problems of the Cattle Trade in Karamoja, Uganda." *Nurnberger Wirtschafts und Sozialgeographische Arbeiten,* 8, 1968, 211–226.

————. "Stages in the Development of a Dairy Industry in Bunyoro, Western Uganda." *Transactions of the Institute of British Geographers,* 53, 1971, 43–54.

————. " 'Development' and Pastoral People of Karamoja, North-Eastern Uganda." In T. Monod (ed). *Pastoralism in Tropical Africa/Les Sociétés Pastorales en Afrique Tropicale.* London: Oxford University Press, 1975, 187–229.

Bazaaraa, Nyangabyaki. "Famine in Bunyoro (Kitara) 1900–1939." *Mawazo,* 5, 3, 1984, 65–75.

Bowden, Edgar and Jon Moris. "Social Characteristics of Progressive Buganda Farmers." *East African Journal of Rural Development,* 11, 1969, 56–62.

Brown, E. and H. H. Hunter. *Planting in Uganda.* London: Longman, 1913.

Bunker, Stephen G. "Class, Status and the Small Farmer: Rural Development Programs and the Advance of Capitalism in Uganda and Brazil." *Latin American Perspectives,* 8, 1, 1981, 89–107.

————. "Dependency, Inequality and Development Policy: A Case Study from Bugisu, Uganda." *British Journal of Sociology,* June 1983, 182–207.

————. *Peasants Against the State: The Politics of Market Control in Bugisu, Uganda, 1990–1983.* Urbana and Chicago: University of Illinois Press, 1987.

Charsley, S. R. "Population Growth and Development in Northeast Bunyoro." *East African Geographical Review,* 6, April 1968, 13–22.

Doornbos, Martin and Michael Lofchie. "Ranching and Scheming: A Case Study of the Ankole Ranching Scheme." In Michael Lofchie (ed). *The State of the Nations: Constraints on Development in Independent Africa.* Berkeley and Los Angeles: University of California Press, 1971.

Dyson-Hudson, Rada and Neville. "Subsistence Herding in Uganda." *Scientific American,* 20, 2, 1969, 76–89.

Ehrlich, Cyril. "The Economy of Buganda, 1893–1903." *Uganda Journal,* 20, 1, 1956, 17–26.

———. "Cotton and the Uganda Economy, 1903–1909." *Uganda Journal,* 21, 2, 1957, 169–172.

Fleuret, P. "Farmers, Cooperatives and Development Assistance in Uganda: An Anthropological Perspective." In D. W. Brokensha and P. Little (eds). *Anthropology of Development and Change in East Africa.* Boulder, CO: Westview Press, 1988, 59–76.

Hamilton, A. C. *Deforestation in Uganda.* Nairobi: Oxford University Press, 1984.

Holdcroft, Lane E. *Agriculture and Development in Africa: The Case of Uganda.* Indianapolis, IN: Universities Field Staff International, UFSI Reports, Africa, No. 12, 1989.

Hunt, D. M. *Credit for Agricultural Development: A Case Study of Uganda.* Nairobi: East African Publishing House, 1975.

Jamal, Vali. "The Agrarian Context of the Ugandan Crisis." In H. B. Hansen and M. J. Twaddle (eds). *Changing Uganda: The Dilemmas of Structural Adjustment and Revolutionary Change.* London: James Currey; and Athens, OH: Ohio University Press, 1991, 78–97.

Jameson, J. D. *Agriculture in Uganda.* London: Oxford University Press for Uganda Government Ministry of Agriculture and Forestry, 1970.

Janhke, H. E. *Conservation and Utilization of Wildlife in Uganda: A Study in Environmental Economics.* Munich: Weltforum, for Ifo-Institut für Wirtschaftsforschung, 1975.

Jones, E. *Agriculture in Eastern Province, Uganda.* Entebbe: Government Printer, 1960.

Kajubi, W. Senteza. "Coffee and Prosperity in Uganda: Some Aspects of Social and Economic Change." *Uganda Journal,* 29, 2, 1965, 135–147.

Kasfir, Nelson. "Land and Peasants in Western Uganda: Bushenyi and Mbarara Districts." In H. B. Hansen and M. J. Twaddle (eds). *Uganda Now: Between Decay and Development.* London: James Currey; and Athens, OH: Ohio University Press, 1988, 158–174.

Kibukamusoke, D.E.B. "Competitive Effects of Coffee on Cotton Production in Buganda." *Empire Cotton Growing Review,* 39, 2, 1962, 106–113.

Langlands, B. W. "The Banana in Uganda, 1860–1920." *Uganda Journal,* 30, 1, 1966, 39–62.

Lury, D. A. "Cotton and Coffee Growers and Government Development Finance in Uganda 1945–1960." *East African Economic Review,* 10, 1, 1962, 47–53.

McMaster, David. *A Subsistence Crop Geography of Uganda.* World Land Use Survey Occasional Papers No. 2. Bude, UK: Geographical Publications Ltd., 1962.

Mafeje, Archie. "Agrarian Revolution and the Land Question in Buganda." In W. Arens (ed). *A Century of Change in Eastern Africa.* The Hague: Mouton, 1976, 23–46.

Mamdani, M. "Analyzing the Agrarian Question: The Case of a Buganda Village." *Mawazo,* 5, 3, 1984, 47–64.

Martin, A. *The Marketing of Minor Crops in Uganda.* London: HMSO, 1963.

Masefield, G. B. *The Uganda Farmer.* London and New York: Longmans Green, 1949.

———. "Agricultural Change in Uganda, 1945–1960." *Stanford University Food Research Institute Studies,* 3, 2, 1962, 87–124.

Mettrick, Hal. *Aid in Uganda: Agriculture.* London: Overseas Development Institute, 1967.

Narasimban, P. S. *Uganda: Conditions of Work and Life in Plantations.* Geneva: International Labour Office, 1969.

Nsereko, Joseph. *Selected Causes of Agricultural Problems in a Peasant Society with Examples from Uganda.* Nairobi: Kenya Literature Bureau, 1979.

Nsibambi, Apolo. "Solving Uganda's Food Problem." In H. B. Hansen and M. J. Twaddle (eds). *Uganda Now: Between Decay and Development.* London: James Currey; and Athens, OH: Ohio University Press, 1988, 135–157.

Okereke, Okoro. *The Economic Impact of the Uganda Co-operatives.* Nairobi, Kampala, Dar es Salaam: East African Literaure Bureau, 1974.

Opio-Odongo, J.M.A. "Use of an Experimental Smallholding in Extension Education: The Case of Makerere University." *Agricultural Administration and Extension,* 26, 3, 1987, 125–136.

Parsons, D. J. *The Systems of Agriculture Pràctised in Uganda.* Entebbe: Department of Agriculture, Memoirs of the Research Division, Series 6, 1960.

———. *Farming Systems in Northern Uganda.* Entebbe: Department of Agriculture, 1960.

Purseglove, J. W. "Resettlement in Kigezi." *Journal of African Administration,* 3, 1, 1951, 13–21.

Richards, Audrey. "Some Effects of the Introduction of Freehold Land into Buganda." In D. Biebuyck (ed), *African Agrarian Systems.* London: Oxford University Press for the International African Institute, 1963, 267–280.

———, G. Sturrock, and J. Fortt (eds). *Subsistence to Commercial Farming in Present-Day Buganda.* Cambridge, UK: Cambridge University Press, 1973.

Steinhart, Edward I. "Herders and Farmers: The Tributary Mode of Production in Western Uganda." In Donald Crummey and C. C. Steward (eds). *Modes of Production in Africa: The Precolonial Era.* Beverly Hills, CA, and London: Sage, 1981.

Taylor, Thomas. "The Establishment of a European Plantation Sector Within the Emerging Colonial Economy of Uganda." *International Journal of African Historical Studies,* 19, 1, 1986, 35–58.

Thomas, H. B. and R. Scott. "Native Agriculture and Food Supply." In H.B. Thomas and R. Scott. *Uganda.* Oxford: Clarendon Press, 1935, 112–124.

———. "Cotton and the Cotton Industry." In H. B. Thomas and R. Scott. *Uganda.* Oxford: Clarendon Press, 1935, 125–140.

———. "The Extension of Economic Agriculture." In H. B. Thomas and R. Scott. *Uganda.* Oxford: Clarendon Press, 1935, 141–156.

———. "Forests." In H. B. Thomas and R. Scott. *Uganda.* Oxford: Clarendon Press, 1935, 157–169.

———. "The Native and His Livestock." In H. B. Thomas and R. Scott. *Uganda.* Oxford: Clarendon Press, 1935, 195–211.

Tosh, John. "Lango Agriculture During the Early Colonial Period: Land and Labour in a Cash-Crop Economy." *Journal of African History,* 19, 3, 1978, 415–439.

Tothill, J. D. (ed). *A Report on Nineteen Surveys Done in Small Agricultural Areas in Uganda.* Entebbe: Government Printer, 1938.

——— and Staff of the Department of Agriculture, Uganda. *Agriculture in Uganda.* London: Oxford University Press, 1940.

Uchendu, Victor and K.R.M. Anthony. *Agricultural Change in Teso District.* Nairobi, Kampala, Dar es Salaam: East African Literature Bureau, 1975.

Vail, David J. *A History of Agricultural Innovation and Development in Teso District, Uganda.* Syracuse, NY: Maxwell School of Citizenship and Public Affairs, Syracuse University, 1972.

Vincent, Joan. "Rural Competition and the Cooperative Monopoly: A Ugandan Case Study." In June Nash, J. Dandler and N. Hopkins (eds). *Popular Participation in Social Change: Cooperatives, Collectives and Nationalised Industry.* The Hague: Mouton, 1976.

Watson, J. M. "Some Aspects of Teso Agriculture." *East African Agricultural Journal,* 6, 4, 1941, 209–212.

——— (ed). *The Transformation of Land Policy in Buganda Since 1896.* Leiden: Afrika Studiecentrum, 1971.

Whyte, Michael. "Nyole Transformation in Eastern Uganda." In H. B. Hansen and M. J. Twaddle (eds). *Uganda Now: Between Decay and Development.* London: James Currey; and Athens, OH: Ohio University Press, 1988, 126–134.

Widstrand, Carl G. (ed). *Cooperatives and Rural Development in East Africa.* New York: Africana Publishing, 1970.

Winter, Edward H. *Bwamba Economy.* Kampala: East African Institute of Social Research, 1955.

Wrigley, Christopher C. *Crops and Wealth in Uganda: A Short Agrarian History.* East African Studies No. 12. Kampala: East African Institute of Social Research, 1959.

Youé, Christopher P. "Peasants, Planters and Cotton Capitalists: The 'Dual Economy' in Colonial Uganda." *Canadian Journal of African Studies,* 12, 2, 1978, 163–184.

Young, C. et al. *Cooperatives and Development: Agriculture Politics in Ghana and Uganda.* London: University of Wisconsin Press, 1982.

Young, M. Crawford. "Agricultural Policy in Uganda: Capability and Choice." In Michael Lofchie (ed), *The State of the Nations,* Berkeley and Los Angeles: University of California Press, 1971.

———, N. P. Sherman and Tim Rose. *Cooperatives and Development: Agricultural Politics in Ghana and Uganda.* Madison, WI: Wisconsin University Press, 1981.

7.2.3 MODERN SECTOR, INDUSTRIAL DEVELOPMENT, MARKETING AND URBANIZATION

Aldworth, William R. *Report on the Marketing Program of the Uganda Cooperative Central Union Ltd.* Washington, DC: Agricultural Cooperative Development International, 1984.

Aluma, J.R.W. and J. Kamugisha-Ruhombe. "Manual Workers in Uganda. Research Report." *Labour, Capital and Society.* 20, 1, 1987, 66–84.

Badenoch, A. C. "Graduated Taxation in the Teso District of Uganda." *Journal of Local Administration Overseas,* 1, 1, 1962, 15–22.

Bakwesegha, Christopher J. "Patterns, Causes and Consequences of Polarized Development in Uganda." In S. El-Shakho and R. A. Obudho (eds). *Urbanization, National Development and Regional Planning in Africa.* Washington, DC; and London: Praeger, 1975, 47–66.

————. *Profiles of Urban Prostitution: A Case Study from Uganda.* Nairobi: Kenya Literature Bureau, 1982.

Barnes, J. W. (ed). *The Mineral Resources of Uganda.* Entebbe: Government Printer, 1961.

Barongo, Y. R. "The De-Embourgeoisement of Ugandan Society: The First Stage in the Break with International Capitalism." *Journal of African Studies,* 11, 3, 1984, 100–109.

Baryaruha, Azarias. *Factors Affecting Industrial Employment: A Study of the Ugandan Experience 1954–1964.* Nairobi: Oxford University Press for East African Institute of Social Research, 1967.

Bigstein, A. and S. K. Mugerwa. "Adaptation and Distress in the Urban Economy: A Study of Kampala Households." *World Development,* 20, 10, 1992, 1423–1441.

Cohen, D. L. and M. A. Tribe. "Suppliers' Credits in Ghana and Uganda: An Aspect of the Imperialist System." *The Journal of Modern African Studies,* 10, 4, 1972, 525–541.

Coles, D.M.S. *The Vegetable Oil Crushing Industry in East Africa.* Nairobi: Oxford University Press for the Makerere Institute of Social Research, 1969.

Commonwealth Team of Experts. *The Rehabilitation of the Economy of Uganda.* 2 Vols. London: Commonwealth Secretariat, 1979.

Dahlberg, F. M. "New Men: Entrepreneurs in Lira." *Sociologus,* 23, 2, 1973, 116–126.

———. "The Provincial Town." *Urban Anthropology,* 3, 2, 1974, 171–183.

Due, J. F. "The Uganda Sales Tax on Importation and Manufacture." *East African Economic Review,* 5, 1, 1969, 1–16.

Economist Intelligence Unit. *Country Profile: Uganda, 1989–90.* London: *The Economist,* 1989.

———. *Country Report: Uganda, Ethiopia, Somalia, Djibouti.* Nos 1–3. London: *The Economist,* 1991.

Edmunds, Keith. "Crisis Management: The Lessons for Africa from Obote's Second Term." In H. B. Hansen and M. J. Twaddle (eds). *Uganda Now: Between Decay and Development.* London: James Currey; and Athens, OH: Ohio University Press, 1988, 95–110.

Ehrlich, Cyril. *The Uganda Company Limited: The First Fifty Years.* Entebbe: Government Printer, 1953.

———. "Some Social and Economic Implications of Paternalism in Uganda." *Journal of African History,* 4, 2, 1963, 275–285.

———. "The Uganda Economy, 1903–1945." In V. Harlow and E. M. Chilver (eds). *A History of East Africa 2.* London: Oxford University Press, 1965, 395–475.

Elkan, Walter. "A Half Century of Cotton Marketing in Uganda." *Indian Journal of Economics,* 38, 4, 1958, 365–374.

———. "Criteria for Industrial Development in Uganda." *East African Economic Review,* 5, 2, 1959, 50–57.

———. *Migrants and Proletarians: Urban Labour in the Economic Development of Uganda.* Kampala: East African Institute of Social Research, 1960.

———. "The Impact of the Owen Falls Hydro-Electric Project on the Economy of Uganda." In W. M. Warren and N. Rubin (eds). *Dams in Africa: an Inter-Disciplinary Study of Man-Made Lakes in Africa.* London: Cass, 1968, 90–105.

——— and G. G. Wilson. "The Impact of the Owen Falls Hydroelectric Project on the Economy of Uganda." *Journal of Development Studies,* July 1967, 387–404.

Farrant, M. R. "Market Boys of Kampala." *East African Journal,* 7, 9, 1970, 13–19.

Fawcett, A. H. "Katwe Salt Deposits." *Uganda Journal,* 37, 1973, 63–80.

Ford, V.C.R. *The Trade of Lake Victoria.* Kampala: East African Institute of Social Research, 1955.

Frank, Charles S. *The Sugar Industry in East Africa.* Nairobi: East African Publishing House for East African Institute of Social Research, 1965.

Fredman, Steven J. "U.S. Trade Sanctions against Uganda: Legality under International Law." *Law and Policy in International Business,* 11, 3, 1979, 1149–1191.

Fuller, Thomas. "African Labor and Training in the Uganda Colonial Economy." *International Journal of African Historical Studies,* 10, 1, 1977, 77–95.

Gerken, E. et al. *The Industrial Town as a Factor of Economic and Social Development: The Example of Jinja, Uganda.* Munich: Weltforum Verlag, 1972.

Gershenberg, Irving. "Banking in Uganda Since Independence." *Economic Development and Cultural Change,* 20, 3, 1972, 504–523.

———. *Commercial Banking in Uganda.* Kampala: Makerere Institute of Social Research, 1973.

————. "Does Parentage Matter? An Analysis of Transnational and Other Firms: An East African Case." *Journal of Developing Areas,* October, 1978, 3–10.

Glentworth, Garth and Muloni Wozei. "The Role of Public Corporations in National Development in Uganda." *African Review,* 1, 3, 1972, 54–90.

Good, C. M. *Rural Markets and Trade in East Africa: A Study of the Functions and Development of Exchange Institutions in Ankole, Uganda.* Chicago: University of Chicago, Department of Geography Research Paper No. 128, 1970.

————. "Salt, Trade and Disease: Aspects of Development in Africa's Northern Great Lakes Region." *International Journal of African Historical Studies,* 5, 4, 1972, 543–586.

————. "Periodic Markets and Travelling Traders in Uganda." *Geographical Review,* 65, 1, 1975, 49–72.

Griffiths, I. L. "The Motor Industry in Uganda." *East African Economic Review,* 5, 1, 1969, 79–85.

Grillo, Ralph. "Anthropology, Industrial Development and Labour Migration in Uganda." In David Brokensha and M. Pearsell (eds). *The Anthropology of Development in Sub-Saharan Africa.* Lexington, KY: University of Kentucky Press, 1969, 77–84.

————. "The Tribal Factor in an African Trade Union." In P. H. Gulliver (ed). *Tradition and Transition in East Africa.* Berkeley: University of California Press, 1969.

Hawkins, E. J. *Roads and Road Transport in an Underdeveloped Country: A Case Study of Uganda.* Colonial Research Studies No. 32. London: HMSO, 1962.

Hill, M. *Permanent Way. Vol. I. The Story of the Kenya and Uganda Railway.* Nairobi: East African Railways and Harbours, 1950.

Hoyle, B. S. "The Economic Expansion of Jinja, Uganda." *Geographical Review,* 53, 3, 1963, 377–388.

———. "Industrial Developments at Jinja, Uganda." *Geography,* 52, 1, 1967, 64–67.

Isoba, John C. G. "The Rise and Fall of Uganda's Newspaper Industry, 1900–1976." *Journalism Quarterly,* 57, 2, 1980, 224–233.

Jacobson, David. *Itinerant Townsmen: Friendship and Social Order in Urban Uganda.* Menlo Park, CA: Cummings, 1973.

Jamal, Valimohamed. "An Analysis of Social Facility Provision in Uganda." *East African Geographical Review,* 10, 1972, 75–88.

———. "The Role of Cotton in Uganda's Economic Development." In S. R. Pearson and John Cownie (eds). *Commodity Exports and African Economic Development.* Lexington, MA: Lexington Books, 1974, 135–154.

Job, A. L. "Mining in Uganda." *Uganda Journal,* 31, 1, 1967, 43–61.

Joy, J. L. "Mechanical Cultivation in Acholi." In J.L. Joy (ed). *Symposium on Mechanical Cultivation in Uganda.* Kampala: 1960.

Katwire-Igufa, H. and J. R. Bibangambah. "Roadside Marketing: A Case Study of Kampala/Entebbe Road in Uganda." *East African Journal of Rural Development,* 14, 1–2, 1981, 144–162.

Kendall, H. *Town Planning in Uganda.* London: Crown Agents, 1955.

Kumalo, C. "African Elites in Industrial Bureaucracy [in Kampala]." In P. C. Lloyd (ed). *The New Elites of Tropical Africa.* London: 1966.

Langlands, Bryan. "Teso District: A Study in Regional Economic Development." In H. Berger (ed). *Ostafrikanische Studien.* Nürnberg, Germany: Friedrich-Alexander Universität, 1968, 199–210.

Madhvani Group. *Enterprise in East Africa.* Nairobi: United Africa Press, 1971.

Martin, A. *The Marketing of Minor Crops in Uganda.* London: HMSO, 1963.

Matson, A. T. "Baganda Merchant Venturers." *Uganda Journal,* 32, 1, 1968, 1–15.

Mazrui, Ali A. "The Baganda and the Japanese." *Kenya Historical Review,* 4, 2, 1976, 167–186.

————. "Privatization versus the Market: Cultural Contradictions in Structural Adjustment." In H. B. Hansen and M. J. Twaddle (eds). *Changing Uganda: the Dilemmas of Structural Adjustment and Revolutionary Change.* London: James Currey; and Athens, OH: Ohio University Press, 1991, 351–378.

Meagher, K. "The Hidden Economy: informal and parallel trade in north western Uganda." *Review of African Political Economy,* 47, 1990, 64–83.

Miller, Judith. "When Sanctions Worked." *Foreign Policy,* 39, Summer 1980, 118–129.

Milton Obote Foundation. *Labour Problems in Uganda.* Kampala: Milton Obote Foundation, 1966.

Mukwaya, A. B. "The Marketing of Staple Foods in Kampala, Uganda." In P. Bohannan and G. Dalton (eds). *Markets in Africa.* Evanston, IL: Northwestern University Press, 1962, 643–666.

Mulira, James. "Soviet Bloc: Trade, Economic, Technical and Military Involvement in Independent Africa. A Case Study of Uganda, 1962–1979." *Genève-Afrique,* 19, 1, 1981, 39–79.

Mulumba, S. S. *Urbanization in Developing Countries, A Case-Study: Kampala, an Elementary Survey of Land and Dwelling Environments.* Cambridge, MA: Massachusetts Institute of Technology, Education Resource Programs, 1974.

Munger, E. S. *Relational Patterns of Kampala, Uganda.* Chicago: University of Chicago, Department of Geography Research Paper No. 21, 1951.

Nyanzi, Semei. *The Role of State Enterprises in African Development.* The Hague: Institute of Social Studies, Occasional Paper No. 94, 1982.

Obbo, Christine. "Catalysts of Urbanism in the Countryside—Mukono, Uganda." *African Studies Review,* 31, 3, 1988, 39–47.

O'Conner, A. M. *Railways and Development in Uganda.* Nairobi: Oxford University Press for East African Institute for Social Research, 1965.

———. "Uganda: The Spatial Dimension." In H. B. Hansen and M. J. Twaddle (eds). *Uganda Now: Between Decay and Development.* London: James Currey; and Athens, OH: Ohio University Press, 1988, 83–94.

Olivier, Henry. "Some Aspects of the Owen Falls Scheme." *Uganda Journal,* 17, 1, 1953, 28–37.

Oloka-Onyango, Joe. "Development Financing: The Case of the Uganda Development Bank." *Ufahamu,* 15, 3, 1986–7, 137–155.

Parkin, David J. "Tribe as Fact and Fiction in an East African City." P.H. Gulliver (ed). *Tradition and Transition in East Africa.* Berkeley: University of California Press, 1969, 273–296.

Scott, R. D. "Trade Unions and Labour Relations in Uganda." *Bulletin of the Inter-African Labour Institute* (CCTA, Brazzaville, Congo Republic), II, 2, 1964.

———. "Agitators or Educators? A Critical Review of the African Labour College." *Makerere Journal,* 10, November, 1964, 15–22.

———. "Labour Legislation and the Federation Issue." *East Africa Journal,* I, 7, 1964.

———. *The Development of Trade Unions in Uganda.* Nairobi: East African Publishing House, 1966.

———. "Trade Unions and Ethnicity in Uganda." *Mawazo,* I, 3, 1968, 42–52.

Smith, J. *Road Transport in Uganda.* Kampala: Makerere University, 1970.

Sofer, C. and R. "Recent Population Growth in Jinja." *Uganda Journal,* 17, 1, 1953, 38–50.

———. *Jinja Transformed.* Kampala: East African Institute of Social Research, 1955.

Southall, Aidan. "Determinants of the Social Structure of African Urban Populations, with Special Reference to Kampala, Uganda." In I. Wallerstein (ed). *Social Change: The Colonial Situation.* New York: Wiley, 1966, 321–339.

———. "Small Urban Centres in Rural Development: What Else Is Development Other than Helping Your Own Home Town?" *African Studies Review,* 31, 3, 1988, 1–15.

———— and P.C.W. Gutkind. *Townsmen in the Making: Kampala and Its Suburbs.* Kampala: East African Institute of Social Research, 1957.

Splansky, J. B. "Some Geographic Characteristics of Permanent Retail Institutions in Ankole." *East African Geographical Review,* 7, April, 1969, 61–78.

Stoutjesdijk, E. J. *Uganda's Manufacturing Sector.* Nairobi: East African Publishing House, 1967.

Thomas, H. B. and R. Scott. "Minerals and Mining." In H. B. Thomas and R. Scott. *Uganda.* Oxford: Clarendon Press, 1935, 212–221.

————. "Communications." In H. B. Thomas and R. Scott. *Uganda.* Oxford: Clarendon Press, 1935, 234–243.

————. "Trade and Commerce." In H. B. Thomas and R. Scott. *Uganda.* Oxford: Clarendon Press, 1935, 340–357

Vincent, J. *African Elite: Big Men of a Small Town.* New York: Columbia University Press, 1971.

————. *Teso in Transition: The Political Economy and Peasant and Class in Eastern Africa.* Berkeley: University of California Press, 1982.

Walker, D. "Criteria for Industrial Development: A Comment." *The East African Economics Review,* 6, 1, 1959, 58–66.

———— and C. Ehrlich. "Stabilization and Development Policy in Uganda: An Appraisal." *Kyklos,* 12, 3, 1959, 58–66.

Wilson, Gail. *Owen Falls: Electricity in a Developing Country.* Nairobi: East African Publishing House, 1967.

Witthuhn, Burton O. "An Imposed Urban Structure: A Case Study from Uganda." In S. El-Shakho and R.A. Obudho (eds). *Urbanization, National Development and Planning in Africa.* New York: Praeger, 1974, 67–74.

Wrigley, Christopher C. "Buganda: An Outline Economic History." *Economic History Review,* 2nd Series, 10, 1, 1957, 69–80.

8. Education

Abidi, S.A.H. *Who's Who in Uganda Libraries, Including Who Was Who.* Kampala: Council for Library Training, Makerere University, 1986.

Adams, B. N. et al. "Socio-Economic Status and Educational Aspirations in Uganda." *Canadian Journal of African Studies,* 21, 2, 1987, 222–230.

Anderson, C. A. "University Planning in an Underdeveloped Country: A Commentary on the University of East Africa Plan, 1967–1970." *Minerva,* 7, 1, 1968, 36–51.

Apoko, Anna. "At Home in the Village: Growing up in Acholi." In Lorene K. Fox (ed). *East African Childhood.* London and New York: Oxford University Press, 1967, 45–78.

Bagunywa, A.M.K. *Critical Issues in African Education: A Case Study of Uganda.* Nairobi: East African Publishing House, 1986.

Barkan, J. D. "What Makes the East African Student Run?" *Transition,* VII, 3, 1968.

Carter, Felice. "The Education of African Muslims in Uganda." *Uganda Journal,* 29, 2, 1965, 193–200.

Castle, E. B. *Growing up in East Africa.* London: Oxford University Press, 1966.

Court, D. "The Idea of Social Science in East Africa: An Aspect of the Development of Higher Education." *Minerva,* Summer 1979, 144–182.

Currey, Janice. "Family Background, Academic Achievement and Occupational Status in Uganda." *Comparative Education Review,* 21, February 1977, 14–28.

Denoon, Donald. "The Education of Southern Sudanese Refugees." In Dunstan Wai (ed). *The Southern Sudan and the Problem of National Integration,* London: Frank Cass, 1973, 137–145.

Dinwiddy, Hugh and M. J. Twaddle. "The Crisis at Makerere." In H. B. Hansen and M. J. Twaddle (eds). *Uganda Now: Between Decay and Development.* London: James Currey; and Athens, OH: Ohio University Press, 1988, 195–204.

Evans, D. R. *Teachers as Agents of National Development: A Case-Study of Uganda.* New York: Praeger, 1971.

———. "Image and Reality: Careers of Educated Ugandan Women." *Canadian Journal of African Studies,* 6, 2, 1972, 213–232.

Furley, Oliver. *Uganda's Retreat from Turmoil?* London: Centre for Security and Conflict Studies, 1987.

———. "Education in Post-Independence Uganda: Change Amidst Strife." In H. B. Hansen and M. J. Twaddle (eds). *Uganda Now: Between Decay and Development.* London: James Currey; and Athens, OH: Ohio University Press, 1988, 175–194.

——— and Tom Watson. *A History of Education in East Africa.* New York: NOK Publishers, 1978.

Goldthorpe, J. E. *An African Elite: Makerere College Students, 1922–65.* Nairobi: Oxford University Press, 1965.

Harris, G. "Political Instability and the Information World in Uganda." *African Research and Documentation,* 37, 1985, 42–46.

Hartwell, Ash and Gerard Benaars (eds). *School and Community in East Africa.* Kampala: Nkanga Editions, Makerere Institute of Social Research, No. 9, 1975.

Hawes, H. "The Primary School Curriculum in Uganda." *Uganda Journal,* 34, 2, 1970, 179–194.

——— and S. Bwanswa-Sekandi. "Unaided Primary Schools in Uganda." *Teacher Education in New Countries,* 10, 1, 1969, 26–34.

Heyneman, S. P. "Influences on Academic Achievement: A Comparison of Results from Uganda and More Industrialized Societies." *Sociology of Education,* 49, 3, 1976, 200–211.

———. "Why Impoverished Children Do Well in Ugandan Schools." *Comparative Education,* June, 1979, 175–185.

———. "Education During a Period of Austerity: Uganda, 1971–1981." *Comparative Education Review,* 27, 3, 1983, 403–413.

Hindmarsh, Roland. "Uganda." In David G. Scanlon (ed). *Church, State and Education in East Africa.* New York: Teachers' College Press, Columbia University, 1966, 137–163.

Jones, T. J. *Education in East Africa* (Report of the Phelps-Stokes Commission). New York: Phelps-Stokes Fund, 1924.

Kabera, J. B. "Education of Refugees and their Expectations in Africa: The Case of Returnees, With Special Reference to Uganda." *African Studies Review,* 32, 1, 1989, 31–39.

Kajubi, W. Senteza. "Integration and National Development from the Viewpoint of Education in Uganda." In C. P. Dodge and P. D. Wiebe. *Crisis in Uganda: The Breakdown of the Health Services.* Oxford: Pergamon, 1985, 15–24.

———. "Educational Reform during Socio-Economic Crisis." In H. B. Hansen and M. J. Twaddle (eds). *Changing Uganda: The Dilemmas of Structural Adjustment and Revolutionary Change.* London: James Currey, and Athens, OH: Ohio University Press, 1991, 322–333.

Kasozi, Abdu B. K. *The Crisis of Secondary School Education in Uganda.* Kampala: Longmans, 1979.

Katorobo, J. *Education for Public Service in Uganda.* New York: Vantage Press, 1987.

Kiwanuka-Tondo, J. "Educational Broadcasting in Africa: The Case of Uganda." *African Media Review,* 4, 2, 1990, 48–63.

Livingston, Thomas W. "Paradox in Early Mission Education in Buganda." *Journal of African Studies,* 2, 2, 1975, 161–176.

Lucas, Eric. *English Traditions in East African Education.* London: Oxford University Press, 1959.

McGregor, G. P. *King's College Budo: The First Sixty Years.* London: Oxford University Press, 1967.

MacPherson, Margaret. *They Built for the Future.* Cambridge, UK: Cambridge University Press, 1964.

Marshall, James. *A School in Uganda.* London: Victor Gollancz, 1976.

Mora, Colleen Lowe. "The Revitalization of Makerere." *Africa Report,* 34, 2, 1989, 48–51.

Moris, Jon R. *Agriculture in the Schools: The East African Experience.* Kampala: Government Printer, 1975.

Namuddu, C. "Educational Research Capacity and Environment in Uganda 1970–1981." In S. Shaeffer and J. A. Nkinyangi (eds). *Educational Research Environments in the Developing World.* Ottawa: International Development Research Centre, 1983, 215–234.

Nsibambi, A. R. "The Politics of Education in Uganda, 1964–70." *Uganda Journal,* 38, 1, 1976, 58–82.

Obote, Apolo Milton. "Policy Proposals for Uganda's Educational Needs." *Mawazo,* 2, 2, 1969, 3–9.

———. "Policy Proposals for Uganda's Educational Needs." *Ugasto,* 4, 1969, 4–10.

———. "On Student Power." *East African Journal,* 6, 8, 1969, 11–13.

Ocaya-Lakidi, Dent. "Modernisation of Education in Uganda: From Initiation Rites to Graduation Ceremonies." *Mawazo,* 4, 2, 1974, 87–110.

Passi, F. O. "Planning for the Supply and Demand of Qualified Teachers in Uganda." *International Review of Education,* 36, 4, 1990, 441–452.

Prewitt, Kenneth. *Education and Political Values: An East African Case Study.* Nairobi: East African Publishing House, 1971.

———. "University Students in Uganda: Political Consequences of Selection Patterns." In W. J. Hanna et al. (eds). *University Students and African Politics.* New York: African Publishing Company, 1975, 167–186.

Rothchild, D. "The University of East Africa as a Political Institute." In R. J. Olembo (ed). *Human Adaptation in*

Tropical Africa, Nairobi: East African Publishing House, 1968, 132–140.

Rukare, Enoka. *African Institutes of Education.* Kampala: Department of Education, Makerere University, 1975.

Scanlon, D. G. *Education in Uganda.* Washington, DC: United States Office of Education, 1964.

Sekamwa, J. C. and S.M.E. Lugumba. *Educational Development and Administration in Uganda 1900–1970: Selected Topics.* Kampala: Longmans Uganda, 1973.

Southall, R. J. *Federalism and Higher Education in East Africa.* Nairobi: East African Publishing House, 1974.

——— and J. M. Kaufert. "Converging Modes of University Development: Ghana and East Africa." *Canadian Journal of African Studies,* 8, 3, 1974, 607–628.

Tembo, L. et al. *The Development of Higher Education in Eastern and Southern Africa.* Nairobi: Hedaya, 1985.

Thomas, H. B. and R. Scott. "Education." In H. B. Thomas and R. Scott. *Uganda.* Oxford: Clarendon Press, 1935, 312–325.

Trowell, Margaret. "The Uganda Museum" and "The School of Art." In M. Trowell, *African Tapestry.* London: Faber and Faber, 1957, 71–79, 103–128.

Visocchi, A. M. *Non-Formal Education for Rural Development in Western Uganda.* Manchester: Manchester University Press, 1978.

Weeks, S. G. *Divergence in Educational Development: The Case of Kenya and Uganda.* New York: Teachers College Press, 1967.

Williams, Peter. *Aid in Uganda—Education.* London: Overseas Development Institute, 1966.

9. Medicine

Abaru, D. E. "Sleeping Sickness in Busoga, Uganda, 1976–1983." *Tropical Medicine and Parasitology,* 36, 2, 1985, 72–76.

Achtar, Rais (ed). *Health and Disease in Tropical Africa: Geographical and Medical Viewpoints.* New York: Harwood Academic, 1987.

Barnett, T. and P. Blaikie. *Aids in Africa: its Present and Future Impact.* New York and London: Guildford Press, 1992.

Bond, George C. and Joan Vincent. "Living on the Edge: Changing Social Structures in the Context of AIDS." In H. B. Hansen and M. J. Twaddle (eds). *Changing Uganda: The Dilemmas of Structural Adjustment and Revolutionary Change.* London: James Currey; and Athens, OH: Ohio University Press, 1991, 113–129.

Cliff, A. D. and M. R. Smallman-Raynor. "The AIDS Pandemic: Global Geographical Patterns and Local Spatial Processes." [Uganda] *Geographical Journal,* 158, 2, 1992, 182–198.

Cook, Sir Albert. *Uganda Memories.* Entebbe: Government Press, 1945.

Davies, J.N.P. "The Cause of Sleeping Sickness, Entebbe, 1902–3." *East African Medical Journal,* 39, 1962, 81–89, 148–161.

Dodge, Cole P. "Health Implications of War in Uganda and Sudan." *Social Science and Medicine,* 31, 6, 1990, 691–698.

———— and Magne Raundalen. *War, Violence and Children in Uganda.* Oslo: Norwegian University Press, 1989.

———— and Paul D. Wiebe. *Crisis in Uganda: The Breakdown of Health Services.* Oxford: Pergamon Press, 1985.

Ford, John. *The Rise of Trypanosomiases in African Ecology.* London: Oxford University Press, 1971.

Foster, W. D. *The Early History of Scientific Medicine in Uganda.* Nairobi: East African Literature Bureau, 1970.

————. *Sir Albert Cook: A Missionary Doctor in Uganda.* Hove, UK: printed for the author by Newhaven Press, 1978.

Fredland, Richard A. *AIDS in Africa: A Political Overview.* Universities Field Staff International, UFTS Reports, Africa, 8. Indianapolis, IN: January 1989.

Garlick, P. L. *The Wholeness of Man.* London: Highway Press, 1943.

Good, C. M. "Salt, Trade and Disease: Aspects of Development in Africa's Great Lakes Region." *International Journal of African Historical Studies,* 5, 1972, 543–586.

Goodgame, R. W. "AIDS in Uganda: Clinical and Social Features." *New England Journal of Medicine,* 323, 6, 1990, 383–389.

Hall, S. A. and B. W. Langlands (eds). *Uganda Atlas of Disease Distribution.* Nairobi: East African Publishing House, 1975.

Haq, C. "Management of AIDS Patients: Case Report from Uganda." In N. Miller and R. C. Rockwell (eds). *AIDS in Africa: The Social and Policy Impact.* Lewiston, NY: Edwin Mellen Press, 1988, 87–95.

Hecklau, H. K. "Disasters and Diseases as They Affect the Growth and Distribution of the Population of Uganda." In J. I. Clarke et al. (eds). *Population and Disaster,* Oxford: Blackwell in association with the International Geographical Union, Commission on Population Geography, 180–192.

Holden, P. "Colonial Sisters: Nurses in Uganda." In J. M. Morse (ed). *Issues in Cross-Cultural Nursing.* Edinburgh: Churchill Livingstone, 1988, 11–26.

Hooper, Ed. "AIDS in Uganda." *African Affairs,* 86, 345, 1987, 469–478.

———. *Slim.* London: Bodley Head, 1990.

Hunter, S. S. "Orphans as a Window on the AIDS Epidemic in Sub-Saharan Africa: Initial Results and Implications of a Study in Uganda." *Social Science and Medicine,* 31, 6, 1990, 681–690.

Kalibala, S. and N. Kaleeba. "AIDS and Community-Based Care in Uganda: The AIDS Support Organization, TASO." *AIDS Care,* 1, 2, 1989, 173–175.

Kawuma, H. J. "Buluba Leprosy Hospital, Uganda: A Review of Admissions, 1981–1984." *Leprosy Review,* 58, 3, 1987, 257–262.

Langlands, B. W. *Sleeping Sickness in Uganda, 1900–1920.* Kampala: Makerere University, Department of Geography, Occasional Paper 1, 1967.

Larson, A. "Social Control of Human Immunodeficiency Virus Transmission in Africa: Historical and Cultural Bases of East and Central African Sexual Relations." *Review of Infectious Diseases,* 11, 5, 1989, 716–731.

Louis, Sister M. *Love Is the Answer: The Story of Mother Kevin.* Dublin: Fallons, 1964.

[Mengo Hospital]. *The Jubilee Report of the C.M.S. Medical Mission, Kampala, 1927.* London: [C.M.S., 1927].

Odonga, Alexander mwa. *Makerere University Medical School 1924–1974.* Kisubi, Uganda: Marianum Press, 1989.

Okware, S. I. "Planning AIDS Education for the Public in Uganda." In World Health Organization. *AIDS: prevention and control. Invited Presentations and Papers from the World Summit of Ministers of Health on Programmes for*

AIDS Prevention . . . London . . . 1988. Geneva: World Health Organization, 1988.

Orley, John. *Culture and Mental Illness.* Nairobi: East African Publishing House for Makerere Institute of Social Research, 1970.

Scheyer, Stanley and David Dunlop. "Health Services and Development in Uganda." *Rural Africana,* n.s., 11, Fall, 1981, 37–57.

Sekimpi, D. K. "Acquired Immunodeficiency Syndrome (AIDS) and Occupational Health in Uganda." In A. F. Fleming et al. (eds). *The Global Impact of AIDS. Proceedings of the First International Conference on the Global Impact of AIDS.* New York: Alan Liss, 1988,

Sharp, L.E.S. and Janet Metcalf. *Island of Miracles.* London: Ruanda Mission, n.d.

Thomas, H. B. and R. Scott. "Public Health." In H. B. Thomas and R. Scott. *Uganda.* Oxford: Clarendon Press, 1935, 298–311.

Watson, Catherine. "An Approach to AIDS." *Africa Report,* 33, 6, 1988, 32–38.

Whyte, Susan Reynolds. "Medicine and Self-Help: The Privatization of Health Care in Eastern Uganda." In H. B. Hansen and M. J. Twaddle (eds). *Changing Uganda: The Dilemmas of Structural Adjustment and Revolutionary Change.* London: James Currey; and Athens, OH: Ohio University Press, 1991, 130–148.

Williams, E. H. "Admission to a Rural Hospital in the West Nile District of Uganda Over a 27 Year Period." *Journal of Tropical Medicine,* 89, 4, 1986, 193–211.

Yeager, R. "Historical and Ecological Ramifications for AIDS in Eastern and Central Africa." In N. Miller and R.C. Rockwell (eds). *AIDS in Africa: The Social and Policy Impact.* Lewiston, NY: Edwin Mellen Press, 1988, 71–83.

10. Military History and the Security Forces

(For the Amin coup of 1971 and the Entebbe Raid of 1976, see section 5.3.)
(For pre-colonial warfare, see section 2)

Austin, Herbert H. *With MacDonald in Uganda.* London: Edward Arnold, 1903.

Avirgan, Tony and Martha Honey. *War in Uganda: The Legacy of Idi Amin.* Dar es Salaam: Tanzania Publishing House, 1983.

Bienen, Henry. "Public Order and the Military in Africa." In H. Bienen (ed). *The Military Intervenes.* New York: Russell Sage Foundation, 1986.

Brittain, V. "The Liberation of Kampala." *New Left Review,* 156, 1986, 51–61.

Burrow, N. "Tanzania's Intervention in Uganda: Some Legal Aspects." *The World Today,* July, 1979, 306–310.

Cholmeley, Captain R. S. *Uganda Volunteers and the War.* Kampala: A.D. Cameron, 1917.

Clayton, Anthony and David Killingray. *Khaki and Blue: Military and Police in British Colonial Africa.* Athens, OH: Ohio University Center for International Studies, 1989.

Collins, Robert O. "The Turkana Patrol, 1918." *Uganda Journal,* 25, 1, 1961, 16–33.

Colvile, H. E. *The Land of the Nile Springs.* London: Edward Arnold, 1895.

Cooper, Carol. "Nyerere and Territorial Integrity: A Janus-Faced Approach to a Cardinal Tenet." *Horn of Africa,* 2, 1979, 55–60.

Decalo, Samuel. *Coups and Army Rule in Africa: Studies in Military Style.* New Haven, CT: Yale University Press, 1976.

Dinwiddy, Hugh. "The Uganda Army and Makerere under Obote, 1962–71." *African Affairs,* 82, 326, 1983, 43–59.

Dodge, Cole P. and Magne Raundalen (eds). *War, Violence and Children in Uganda.* Oslo: Norwegian University Press, 1987.

Furley, O. W. "The Sudanese Troops in Uganda." *African Affairs,* 58, no. 233, 1959, 311–328.

Gingyera-Pinycwa A.G.G. and Ali A. Mazrui. "Regional Development and Regional Disarmament: Some African Perspectives." In Frederick S. Arklunt (ed). *Arms and African Development.* New York: Proceedings of the First Pan-African Citizens' Conference, 115–132.

Gutteridge, William. *The Military in African Politics.* London: Methuen, 1969.

Harwich, Christopher. *Red Dust: Memories of the Uganda Police, 1935–1955.* London: Stuart, 1961.

Hodges, Geoffrey. *The Carrier Corps: Military Labor in the East African Campaign, 1914–1918.* New York: Greenwood Press, 1986.

Hordern, Charles. *History of the Great War: Military Operations, East Africa.* London: HMSO, 1941.

Hore, H. R. "The History of the Uganda Volunteer Reserve." *Uganda Journal,* 8, 2, 1940, 65–75.

Jenkins, E. V. *A History of the King's African Rifles, Formerly Known as the Uganda Rifles.* Entebbe: Government Press, 1912.

Kakembo, Robert H. *An African Soldier Speaks.* London: Edinburgh House Press, 1946.

Kanyeihamba, George. "Power that Rode Naked Through Uganda under the Muzzle of a Gun." In H. B. Hansen and M. J. Twaddle (eds). *Uganda Now: Between Decay and Development.* London: James Currey; Nairobi: Heinemann; and Athens, OH: Ohio University Press, 1988, 70–82.

Kasfir, Nelson. "Civilian Participation Under Military Rule in Uganda and Sudan." *Armed Forces and Society,* 1, 3, 1975, 344–363.

Lardner, E.G.D. *Soldiering and Sport in Uganda, 1909–10.* London: Walter Scott Publishing, 1912.

Lee, J. M. *African Armies and Civil Order.* London: Institute for Strategic Studies, 1969.

Lloyd-Jones, W. *King's African Rifles, Being an Unofficial Account of the Origin and Activities of the King's African Rifles.* London and Bristol: Arrowsmith, 1926.

Lwanga-Lunyiigo, S. "Uganda and World War I." *Makerere Historical Journal,* 3, 1, 1977, 27–42.

Macdonald, J.R.L. *Soldiering and Surveying in East Africa.* London: Edward Arnold, 1897.

Matthews, Lloyd. "Uganda." In J. Keegan (ed). *World Armies.* 2nd Edn. Detroit: Gale Research, 1983, 598–600.

Mazrui, Ali A. "Piety and Puritanism under a Military Theocracy: Uganda Soldiers as Apostolic Successors." In C. M. Kelleher (ed). *Political-Military Systems: Comparative Perspec-*

tives. Beverly Hills, CA, and London: Sage Publications, 1974, 105–124.

————. *Soldiers and Kinsmen in Uganda: The Making of a Military Ethnocracy.* Beverly Hills, CA: Sage Publications, 1975.

————. "Ethnic Stratification and the Military-Agrarian Complex: The Uganda Case." In N. Glazer and D. P. Moynihan (eds). *Ethnicity: Theory and Experience.* Cambridge, MA: Harvard University Press, 1975, 420–449.

————. (ed). *The Warrior Tradition in Modern Africa.* Leiden: E. J. Brill, 1977. Previously published as *Journal of Asian and African Studies,* XII, 1 and 2, 1977.

———— and D. Rothchild. "The Soldier and State in East Africa: Some Theoretical Conclusions on the Army Mutinies of 1964." *Western Political Quarterly,* 20, 1967, 82–96.

Miller, Charles. *Battle for the Bundu: The First World War in East Africa.* London and New York: Macmillan, 1974.

Mmbando, S. I. *The Tanzania-Uganda War in Pictures.* Dar es Salaam: Longmans, 1980.

Moyse-Bartlett, H. *The King's African Rifles: A Short History.* Nairobi: Regal Press, n.d.

————. *The King's African Rifles. A Study in the Military History of East and Central Africa.* Aldershot, UK: Gale and Polden, 1956.

Msabaha, I.S.R. "War on Idi Amin: Towards a Synthetic Theory of Intervention." *African Review* (Dar es Salaam) 12, 1, 1985, 24–43.

Mudoola, Dan. "Communal Conflict in the Military and Its Political Consequences." In K. Rupesinghe (ed). *Conflict*

Resolution in Uganda. London: James Currey; and Athens, OH: Ohio University Press, 1989, 116–40.

———. "Institution Building: The Case of the NRM and the Military 1986–1989." In H. B. Hansen and M. J. Twaddle (eds). *Changing Uganda: The Dilemmas of Structural Adjustment and Revolutionary Change.* London: James Currey; Athens, OH: Ohio University Press, 1991, 230–246.

Museveni, Yoweri (President). *Selected Articles on the Uganda Resistance War.* Kampala: National Resistance Movement, 1985.

———. *Three Essays on Military Strategy in Uganda.* Kampala: National Resistance Army, n.d.

Ofcansky, Thomas P. "National Security." In Rita M. Byrnes. *Uganda: A Country Study.* Washington, DC: Library of Congress, 1992, 193–236.

Okoth, P. Godfrey. "The OAU and the Uganda-Tanzania War, 1978–79." *Journal of African Studies,* 14, 3, 1987, 152–162.

Omara-Otunnu, Amii. *Politics and the Military in Uganda 1890–1985.* London: Macmillan in association with St Antony's College, Oxford, 1987.

Pain, Dennis. "Acholi and Nubians: Economic Forces and Military Employment." In P. Wiebe and Cole P. Dodge (eds). *Beyond Crisis: Development Issues in Uganda.* Kampala: Makerere Institute of Social Research and the African Studies Association, 1987, 41–54.

Prunier, G. A. "*Kyanguka Kwa Fashisti Idi Amin:* Tanzania's Ambiguous Ugandan Victory." *Cultures et Développement,* 16, 3–4, 1984, 735–756.

Ravenhill, F. J. "Military Rule in Uganda: The Politics of Survival." *African Studies Review,* 17, 1, 1974, 229–260.

————. "The Military and Politics in Uganda." *Africa Quarterly,* 19, 2, 1979, 122–147.

Strate, Jeffrey T. *Post-Military Coup Strategy in Uganda.* Athens, OH: Ohio University Center for International Studies, 1973.

[Tanzania]. *Tanzania and the War Against Amin's Uganda.* Dar es Salaam: Government Printer, 1979.

Ternan, Trevor. *Some Experiences of an Old Bromsgrovian: Soldiering in Afghanistan, Egypt and Uganda.* Birmingham, UK: Cornish Brothers, 1930.

Thomas, C. "Concepts in Competition: Illustration from the Tanzanian Intervention in Uganda." In C. Thomas. *New States, Sovereignty and Intervention.* Aldershot, UK: Gower, 1985, 90–121.

Thomas, H. B. "Kigezi Operations, 1914–1917." *Uganda Journal,* 30, 2, 1966, 165–73.

———— and R. Scott. "The Armed Forces." In H. B. Thomas and R. Scott. *Uganda.* Oxford: Clarendon Press, 1935, 263–271.

Thruston, A. B. *African Incidents.* London: John Murray, 1900.

Twining, E. F. "Uganda Medals and Decorations." *Uganda Journal,* 2, 3, 1935, 209–225.

Wallis, H. R. "The War in Uganda." *National Review* (London), 74, 1919, 556–561.

Wani, Ibrahim J. "Humanitarian Intervention and the Tanzania-Uganda War." *Horn of Africa* 3, 2, 1980, 18–27.

Whitehead, E. F. "A Short History of Uganda Military Units Formed During World War II." *Uganda Journal,* 14, 1, 1950, 1–14.

Winter, J. V. *The Sudanese Mutiny*. Nairobi: Eagle Press, 1950.

———. *The Uganda Mutiny*. London: Macmillan, 1954.

Winter, Roger P. "The Armies of Uganda and Human Rights: A Personal Observation." *Cultural Survival,* 11, 4, 1987, 46–48.

Worker, J. C. "With the 4th (Uganda) K.A.R. in Abyssinia and Burma." *Uganda Journal,* 12, 1, 1948, 52–56.

11. Law

11.1 LAND TENURE

Beattie, John. "The Kibanja System of Land Tenure in Bunyoro." *Journal of African Administration,* 6, 1, 1954, 18–28.

Brock, Beverley. "Customary Land Tenure, Individualisation and Agricultural Development in Uganda." *East African Journal of Rural Development,* 2, 2, 1969.

Kiapi, Abraham. "Legal Obstacles to Rural Development in Colonial Uganda." *Mawazo,* 4, 3, 1975, 101–112.

Kisamba-Mugerwa, W. "Institutional Dimensions of Land Tenure Reform." In H. B. Hansen and M. J. Twaddle (eds). *Changing Uganda: The Dilemmas of Structural Adjustment and Evolutionary Change.* London: James Currey; and Athens, OH: Ohio University Press, 1991, 311–321.

Mafeje, Archie. "Agrarian Revolution and the Land Question in Buganda." In B. Berdichewsky (ed). *Anthropology and Social Change in Rural Areas,* The Hague: Mouton, 1979, 67–88.

Mukwaya, A. B. *Land Tenure in Buganda: Present Day Tendencies.* Kampala: East African Institute of Social Research, 1953.

Obol-Ochola, James. *Land Law Reform in East Africa.* Kampala: The National Trust, n.d.

Ocheng, D. O. "Land Tenure in Acholi." *Uganda Journal,* 19, 1, 1955, 57–61.

Robertson, D. W. *The Historical Considerations Contributing to the Soga System of Land Tenure.* Entebbe: Government Printer, 1940.

Segal, Aaron. "The Politics of Land in East Africa." *Economic Development and Culture Change,* XVI, 2, 1968, 275–296.

Ssempebwa, E. F. "Recent Land Reforms in Uganda." *Makerere Law Journal,* 1, 1, 1977, 1–28.

Thomas, H. B. and R. Scott. "Land, Survey, and Maps." In H. B. Thomas and R. Scott. *Uganda.* Oxford: Clarendon Press, 1935, 98–111.

West, Henry W. *The Mailo System in Buganda: A Preliminary Case Study in African Land Tenure.* Entebbe: Government Printer, 1964.

———. *The Transformation of Land Tenure in Buganda since 1896.* African Society Documents, Vol. 2. Leiden: Afrika-Studiecentrum, 1969.

———. *Land Policy in Buganda.* Cambridge, UK: Cambridge University Press, 1972.

11.2 LAW AND HUMAN RIGHTS

(See also Sections 5.2, 5.3, 5.4, especially Amnesty International and International Commission of Jurists.)

Allen, Sir Peter Jermyn. *Days of Judgment.* London: William Kimber, 1987.

Andrews, Sally C. "The Legitimacy of the United States Embargo of Uganda." *Journal of International Law and Economics,* 13, 3, 1979, 651–673.

Baldwin, Fletcher N. "Constitutional Limitations on Government in Mexico, the United States and Uganda." In Richard P. Claude (ed). *Comparative Human Rights.* Baltimore, MD, and London: Johns Hopkins University Press, 1976, 76–98.

Beattie, John. "Informal Judicial Activity in Bunyoro." *Journal of African Administration,* ix, 4, 1957, 188–195.

Brown, D. and P.A.P.J. Allen. *An Introduction to the Laws of Uganda.* London: 1968.

Brown, Winifred. *Marriage, Divorce and Inheritance: The Uganda Council of Women's Movement for Legislative Reform.* Cambridge African Monographs 10. Cambridge, UK: African Studies Centre, 1988.

Cohen, David W. " 'A Case for the Basoga': Lloyd Fallers and the Construction of an African Legal System." In Kristin Mann, Allen Isaacman and Luise White (eds). *Law in Colonial Africa.* Portsmouth, NH: Heinemann; and London: James Currey, 1991, 239–254.

Crisp, J. "National Security, Human Rights and Population Displacements in Luwero District, Uganda, January to December 1982." *Review of African Political Economy,* 27–8, 1984, 164–174.

Fallers, Lloyd A. *Law Without Precedent: Legal Ideas in Action in the Courts of Colonial Busoga.* Chicago: University of Chicago Press, 1973.

Haydon, E. S. *Law and Justice in Buganda.* London: Butterworth, 1960.

Hone, H. R. (compiler). *Handbook on Native Courts for the Guidance of Administrative Officers.* Entebbe: Government Printer, 1941.

Kayonga, Anna Mary Mukamwezi. *Searching for Social Justice: A Challenge to Church and State in Uganda.* Rome: Pontificia Studiorum Universitas A S. Thoma Aq. in Urbe, 1989.

Khiddu-Makubuya, E. "The Rule of Law and Human Rights in Uganda: The Missing Link." In H. B. Hansen and M. J. Twaddle (eds). *Changing Uganda: The Dilemmas of Structural Adjustment and Revolutionary Change.* London: James Currey; and Athens, OH: Ohio University Press, 1991, 217–223.

Kotecha, Ken C. "The Shortchanged: Uganda Citizenship Laws and How They Were Applied to its Asian Minority." *International Lawyer,* 9, 1, 1975, 1–29.

Langley, Winston E. and Julius E. Okola. "Uganda: Expulsion of Aliens and Human Rights." *Current Bibliography on African Affairs,* 7, 4, 1974, 345–359.

Mahalu, C. R. "The Legal Regime for Refugees in Eastern African States." *Archiv des Völkerrechts,* 26, 1, 1988, 23–48.

Maitum, Mary I. D. "Women, the Law and Convention: A Ugandan Perspective." *Journal of Eastern African Research and Development,* 15, 1985, 151–164.

Morris, H. F. "Jurisdiction of the Buganda Courts and the Scope of Customary Law in Uganda." *Journal of African Law,* 9, 3, 1965, 154–161.

———. "Two Early Surveys of Native Courts in Uganda." *Journal of African Law,* 11, 3, 1967, 159–174.

————. *Evidence in East Africa.* London: Sweet and Maxwell; and Lagos: African Universities Press, 1968.

————. *Some Perspectives on East African Legal History.* Uppsala: Scandinavian Institute of African Studies, 1970.

————. *Indirect Rule and the Search for Justice: Essays in East African Legal History.* Oxford: Clarendon Press, 1972.

———— and J. S. Read. *Uganda.* Volume 13 in *The British Commonwealth: The Development of its Laws and Institutions.* London: Stevens, 1966.

Njuba, Sam K. "Legal Adjustment to Revolutionary Change." In H. B. Hansen and M. J. Twaddle (eds). *Changing Uganda: The Dilemmas of Structural Adjustment and Revolutionary Change.* London: James Currey; and Athens, OH: Ohio University Press, 1991, 210–216.

Nkamuhayo, P. and G. Seidel. "The Context of Human Rights in Uganda Today." *Review of African Political Economy,* 45/6, 1989, 174–179.

Pirouet, M. Louise. "Human Rights Issues in Museveni's Uganda." In H. B. Hansen and M. J. Twaddle (eds). *Changing Uganda: The Dilemmas of Structural Adjustment and Revolutionary Change.* London: James Currey; and Athens, OH: Ohio University Press, 1991, 197–210.

Rupesinghe, Kumar. *Conflict Resolution in Uganda.* Oslo: International Peace Research Institute; London: James Currey; and Athens, OH: Ohio University Press, 1989.

Sawyer, G.F.A. *East African Law and Social Change.* Nairobi: East African Publishing House, 1967.

Sookdeo, A. "Understanding the Violence in Uganda." *Transafrica Forum,* 5, 3, 1988, 17–30.

Thomas H. B. "Imperatrix v. Juma and Urzee." *Uganda Journal,* 7, 2, 1939, 70–84.

—— and R. Scott. "Justice." In H. B. Thomas and R. Scott. *Uganda.* Oxford: Clarendon Press, 1935, 244–262.

Tibamanya mwene Mushanga. *Criminal Homicide in Uganda.* Kampala: East African Literature Bureau, 1974.

11.3 LEGISLATION, ADMINISTRATION AND GOVERNMENT

Anyang-Nyongo, Peter. "The Civil Servant in Uganda." *East African Journal,* 8, 4, 1971, 9–19.

Apter, D. E. "Some Problems of Local Government in Uganda." *Journal of African Administration,* 9, 1, 1959, 27–37.

Barkan, Joel D. et al. *Uganda District Government and Politics, 1947–1967.* Madison, WI: African Studies Program; and Kampala: Institute of Public Administration, 1977.

Burke, Fred. *Local Government and Politics in Uganda.* Syracuse, NY: Syracuse University Press, 1964.

Chew, D.C.E. "Internal Adjustments to Falling Civil Service Salaries: Insights from Uganda." *World Development,* 18, 7, 1990, 1003–1014.

Dundas, Sir Charles. *Native Administration in Uganda.* Entebbe: Government Printer, 1940.

Engholm, G. F. *The Development of Procedure in Uganda's Legislative Council.* London: Chiswick Press, 1956.

Furley, Oliver. "The Legislative Council, 1921–1945: The Formative Years." In G. N. Uzoigwe (ed). *Uganda: The Dilemma of Nationhood.* New York, London, Lagos: NOK Publishers International, 1982, 133–166.

―――. "The Legislative Council, 1945–1961: The Wind of Change." In G. N. Uzoigwe (ed). *Uganda: The Dilemma of Nationhood.* New York, London, Lagos: NOK Publishers International, 1982, 167–216.

Gartrell, Beverly. "British Administrators, Colonial Chiefs and the Comfort of Tradition." *African Studies Review,* 26, 1, 1983, 1–24.

Gee, W. T. "Uganda's Legislative Council between the Wars." *Uganda Journal,* 25, 1, 1961, 54–64.

Gingyera-Pinycwa, A.G.G. "Towards Constitutional Renovation: Some Political Considerations." In H. B. Hansen and M. J. Twaddle (eds). *Changing Uganda: The Dilemmas of Structural Adjustment and Revolutionary Change.* London: James Currey; and Athens, OH: Ohio University Press, 1991, 224–229.

Gukiina, Peter M. *Uganda: A Case Study in African Political Development.* Notre Dame, IN: University of Notre Dame Press, 1972.

Ingham, Kenneth. "British Administration in Lango District, 1907–1935." *Uganda Journal,* 19, 2, 1955, 156–168.

Kanyeihamba, G. W. *Constitutional Law and Government in Uganda.* Nairobi: East African Literature Bureau, 1975.

Kasfir, Nelson. "Government and Politics." In Rita M. Byrnes. *Uganda: A Country Study.* Washington: Library of Congress, 1992, 149–192.

Khiddu-Makubuya, E. "The Legal Framework for Democracy in Uganda." *Mawazo,* 6, 1, 1985, 10–26.

Kokole, O. H. and Ali A. Mazrui. "Uganda: The Dual Polity and the Plural Society." In L. Diamond et al. (eds). *Democracy in Developing Countries,* Volume 2, Africa. Boulder, CO: Lynne Rienner, 1988, 259–298.

Mair, Lucy. "Busoga Local Government." *Journal of Commonwealth Political Studies,* 5, 2, 1967, 91–108.

Mugaju, J. B. "The Illusions of Democracy in Uganda." In W.O. Oyugi et al. (eds). *Democratic Theory and Practice in Africa.* London: James Currey, 1988, 85–98.

Mugambwa, J. A. "A 'Protected State' in the Uganda Protectorate. A Reexamination of Buganda's Colonial Legal Status." *African Journal of International and Comparative Law,* 1, 3, 1989, 446–465.

Njuba, Sam K. and James S. Read. *Uganda: The Development of its Laws and Constitution.* London: Steven and Sons, 1966.

Ocaya-Lakidi, Dent. "From Local Governments to Mere Local Administrations, 1949–1973." In G. N. Uzoigwe (ed). *Uganda: The Dilemma of Nationhood.* New York, London, Lagos: NOK Publishers International, 299–312.

Oloka-Onyango, J. "Law, 'Grass-Roots Democracy' and the National Resistance Movement in Uganda." *International Journal of the Sociology of Law,* 17, 4, 1989, 465–480.

Pratt, R. C. "Administration and Politics in Uganda, 1919–1945." In V. Harlow, E. M. Chilver and A. Smith (eds). *History of East Africa.* II, Oxford: Clarendon Press, 1956, 476–542.

Robertson, A. F. *Uganda's First Republic: Chiefs, Administrators and Politicians, 1967–1971.* Cambridge, UK: African Studies Centre, 1982.

Sathyamurthy, T. V. "Central Government-District Administration Relations: the Case of Uganda." *Africa Quarterly,* 22, 2, 1984, 5–44.

Thomas, H. B. and R. Scott. "The Constitution and Machinery of Government." In H. B. Thomas and R. Scott. *Uganda.* Oxford: Clarendon Press, 1935, 65–84.

Uzoigwe, G. N. (ed). *Uganda: The Dilemma of Nationhood.* New York, London, Lagos: NOK Publishers, 1982.

12. Women

Boyd, R. E. "Empowerment of Women in Uganda: Real or Symbolic?" *Review of African Political Economy,* 45/6, 1989, 106–117.

Brown, Winifred. *Marriage, Divorce and Inheritance: The Uganda Council of Women's Movement for Legislative Reform.* Cambridge African Monographs 10. Cambridge, UK: African Studies Centre, 1988.

Byrnes, Rita M. "The Society and its Environment." In Rita M. Byrnes. *Uganda: A Country Study.* Washington, DC: Library of Congress, 1992, 43–92, sub-section "Women in Society."

Elkan, Walter. "The Employment of Women in Uganda." *Bulletin d'Institut Inter-Africain de Travail* (Brazzaville), 4, 4, 1957, 8–23.

Evans, David R. "Image and Reality: Career Goals of Educated Ugandan Women." *Canadian Journal of African Studies,* 4, 3, 1970, 213–232.

Lubega, Florence. "Women of Uganda." *Journal of the Ministry of Community Development,* 1963.

Mair, Lucy. *Native Marriage in Uganda.* London: Oxford University Press for the International Institute of African Languages and Cultures, 1940.

Maitum, Mary I. D. "Women, the Law and Convention: A Ugandan Perspective." *Journal of Eastern African Research and Development,* 15, 1985, 151–164.

Perlman, Melvin. "The Changing Status and Role of Women in Toro (W. Uganda)." *Cahiers d'Etudes Africaines,* 6, 4, 1966.

————. "Children Born out of Wedlock and the Status of Women in Toro, Uganda." *Rural Africana,* 29, Winter, 1975.

Obbo, Christine. *African Women: Their Struggle for Economic Independence.* London: Zed Press, 1980.

————. "Stratification and the Lives of Women in Uganda." In Claire Robertson and Iris Berger (eds). *Women and Class in Africa.* New York: Africana, 1986, 178–194.

————. "The Contribution of Women in Agricultural Production in Uganda." In Association of African Women for Research and Development. *Seminar on Research on African Women: What Type of Methodology? 1983.* Dakar: AAWORD, 1986, 54–61.

————. "Women, Children and a 'Living Wage'." In H. B. Hansen and M. J. Twaddle (eds). *Changing Uganda: The Dilemmas of Structural Adjustment and Revolutionary Change.* London: James Currey; and Athens, OH: Ohio University Press, 1991, 98–112.

Tadria, Hilda M. K. "Changes and Continuities in the Position of Women in Uganda." In P. D. Wiebe and C. P. Dodge (eds). *Beyond Crisis: Development Issues in Uganda.* Kampala: Makerere Institute of Social Research, 1987, 79–90.

Uganda Council of Women. *Law About Marriage in Uganda.* Kampala: Uganda Bookshop, 1961.

Watson, Catherine. "Uganda's Women: A Ray of Hope." *Africa Report,* 33, 4, 1988, 29–32.

ABOUT THE AUTHOR

M. Louise Pirouet (B.A., London; P.G.C.E., London; Ph.D., East Africa) taught for some years in Britain and Kenya, before being appointed a research assistant and then lecturer at Makerere University, Kampala, Uganda where she worked from 1963–1972. As well as teaching and researching she administered a scheme for the conservation of church and mission archives throughout East Africa. From 1975–1978 she lectured at Nairobi University, Kenya. On her return to Britain in 1978 she was appointed Senior Lecturer in Religious Studies at Homerton College, University of Cambridge. She retired from teaching in 1989 but remains a member of Homerton College, the Institute of Commonwealth Studies, University of London, and the University of Cambridge African Studies Centre. From 1978–1989 she was a member of the Uganda Coordinating Group of Amnesty International (British Section). Among her publications are *Black Evangelists* (London: Rex Collings, 1978); the Minority Rights Group's Report No. 66, *Uganda* (1989) (together with Ed Hooper); the sections on Africa in *Christianity Worldwide: Church History 4: AD 1800 Onwards* (London, SPCK 1989, of which she was also the editor); contributions to *Uganda Now: Between Decay and Development* (H. B. Hansen and M. J. Twaddle, eds. London: James Currey, 1989) and to *Changing Uganda: The Dilemmas of Structural Adjustment and Revolutionary Change* (H. B. Hansen and M. J. Twaddle, eds. London: James Currey, 1991), as well as numerous articles.